Heroes of Invention

Technology, Liberalism and British Identity, 1750–1914

Christine MacLeod

CAMBRIDGE
UNIVERSITY PRESS

CAMBRIDGE UNIVERSITY PRESS
Cambridge, New York, Melbourne, Madrid, Cape Town, Singapore, São Paulo

Cambridge University Press
The Edinburgh Building, Cambridge CB2 8RU, UK

Published in the United States of America by Cambridge University Press,
New York

www.cambridge.org
Information on this title: www.cambridge.org/9780521873703

First published 2007

Printed in the United Kingdom at the University Press, Cambridge

A Catalogue record for this publication is available from the British Library

ISBN 978-0-521-87370-3 hardback

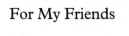

For My Friends

Contents

Acknowledgements

I can claim to share only one feature with the 'heroes of invention' who are the subject of this book: the illusion of sole attribution. Like them, I am indebted to a large cast of friends, colleagues and institutions. Not least among the pleasures of reaching the final full stop is the opportunity to record my gratitude for their invaluable help and support.

Few things can be more heartening than an unprompted offer to read early drafts of one's chapters. I am immensely grateful to Patricia Fara, Will Hardy, Alessandro Nuvolari, Kirsty Reid, Lindsay Sharp and A. P. (Tony) Woolrich for their critical engagement with my ideas. Their sound advice, inspired suggestions and unfailing encouragement have manifestly improved this book, as have the comments of the Press's two anonymous referees. While they have collectively saved me from a multitude of errors, I claim the IPR over any that may remain. It is a great pleasure to recall conversations with friends and colleagues who have shared their ideas and challenged me to rethink my own, in particular, Marco Belfanti, Maxine Berg, Janet Browne, Kristine Bruland, Gill Cookson, Carolyn Cooper, Luisa Dolza, Madge Dresser, Robert Fox, Anna Guagnini, Mark Goldie, Graeme Gooday, Daryl Hafter, Liliane Hilaire-Pérez, Ian Inkster, David Jeremy, Ludmilla Jordanova, Pamela Long, Ben Marsden, Christopher May, Joseph Melling, David Miller, Simon Naylor, Claire O'Mahony, Wilf Prest, Philip Richardson, Jennifer Ridden, Jutta Schwarzkopf, Pam Sharpe, Kenneth Sokoloff, Jennifer Tann and Bryan Williams. I have also learned much from participants in seminars and conferences to which I have presented aspects of this work, in Britain, France, Italy, the Netherlands and the USA, especially from members of the British Academy 'Patents in History' European network, who are equally adept at debating the history of technology and promoting cosmopolitan sociability. James Andrew, David Bryden, Richard Hills, Thomas Jackson, Melanie Kelly, Richard Sheldon and Jeremy Stein have been generous in supplying me with references. Caroline Williams, Tim Cole, Dorothy Livingston and Patricia Fara went out of their way to photograph monuments for me; Amanda Howe magnanimously took me statue-hunting in Barnsley; Eileen Power tacitly improved my grammar, while Charmaine Storer has kept my desk-bound frame from seizing up.

The generosity of the research leave schemes offered by the Leverhulme Trust, the Arts and Humanities Research Council and the University of Bristol has allowed me the time necessary to research, think and write that is not normally available in the midst of a busy teaching and administrative schedule.

I am acutely aware that many technical innovations have facilitated my work to a degree unimaginable when I tentatively began this project in the late 1980s. In particular, I have benefited from the increasing avail-ability of electronic and on-line resources. Without the machine-readable version of *Palmer's Index to The Times*, it would have been impossible to discover the extent to which inventors and engineers were commemo-rated and celebrated in Victorian Britain. I am equally grateful to every-one who participated in the production of the magnificent *Oxford Dictionary of National Biography* (2004), which has saved me innumerable hours of research. The directors of the 'Science in the Nineteenth-Century Periodical' project, at the Universities of Leeds and Sheffield, Geoffrey Cantor and Sally Shuttleworth, kindly allowed me access to this invaluable database prior to its publication; associate director, Graeme Gooday, first brought it to my attention, and Jon Topham gave gener-ously of his time to demonstrate its use. In recent months, my task of collecting illustrations has been lightened by access to the web-sites maintained by many museums, libraries and galleries and the help pro-vided by their staff. Closer to home, Ann Pethers' skills have ensured superb photographs of items in the University of Bristol Library and Bristol Central Library.

None of this is to underrate the importance of access to more tradi-tional sources. In addition to the insights and excitement to be had from seeing original documents, books and works of art, I have benefited enormously from the knowledge and advice of many archivists, librarians and curators. I have been especially fortunate to enjoy the efficiency and good humour with which Sheena Carter oversees the historical collec-tions in the University of Bristol Library. At the Courtauld Institute, Philip Ward-Jackson not only guided my expeditions into the photo-graphic collections of the Conway Library, but also shared with me his unrivalled knowledge of Victorian statuary. John Liffen, of the Science Museum, was especially helpful in directing me to archival materials and his own findings on the Patent Office Museum. Thanks are also due to the staff of the Birmingham City Archives, Bodleian Library, Bolton District Archives, Bristol University Library, Bristol Central Library,

British Library, Cambridge University Library, Glasgow University Archives, Institution of Mechanical Engineers, Mitchell Library, National Archives, Kew, National Library of Scotland, Science Museum Library and University College London Archives, of whose collections and services I have made extensive use.

Together with my mother, Jean MacLeod, and my late father, Roderick MacLeod, close friends have given me the love, support, and encouragement, not to mention the welcome distractions, without which I would never have completed this book. In particular, I should like to thank: Sally Brown, Patrick Chabal and Farzana Shaikh, Marie-Ange Danthois, Rosie Davies, Phoebe Emond, Jane Fowles, Nancy Frankel, Liliane Hilaire-Pérez, Sally-Ann Kitts, Jean Marr-Wilkins, Heather Milne, Alison Parry, Hazel Pennington, Chris Rainger, Kirsty Reid, Dee Reynolds, Margaret Sampson, Ron and Margo Santoni, Julia Sheppard, Penny Starns, Sarah Street, Kate Sullivan, Hugh Tulloch, Ian Wei, Caroline and Richard Williams and Nuala Zahedieh. I look forward to having more time to enjoy their company.

Abbreviations

BJHS	*British Journal for the History of Science*
BPP	British Parliamentary Papers
EHR	*Economic History Review*
HJ	*Historical Journal*
HT	*History of Technology*
ILN	*The Illustrated London News*
JHI	*Journal of the History of Ideas*
JSA	*Journal of the Society of Arts*
NPG	National Portrait Gallery
PD	*Parliamentary Debates*
P&P	*Past and Present*
T&C	*Technology and Culture*
TNS	*Transactions of the Newcomen Society*

Illustrations

1   Introduction: inventors and other heroes

The inventor was an improbable hero. Neither his conceptual pedigree nor his personal attributes marked him out as a transparently heroic figure. Long distrusted as a monopolist and 'projector', he toiled in an anonymous workshop, far from the glorious field of battle, or the terrors of the ice floes, the desert, or the jungle. Yet, in a century remarkable for its celebration of heroes, the inventor too had his pedestal and his laurel wreath. Notoriously, in the essays of Samuel Smiles, he took centre stage, the epitome of 'self help', but this was only one facet of a cult whose origins preceded Smiles' worthy gospel by several decades and whose significance ran much deeper. The intrusion of inventors amidst the warriors, monarchs and statesmen who dominated the pantheon of early nineteenth-century Britain represented a challenge to aristocratic society. As astute observers recognized, the 'colossal' statue of James Watt, installed in Westminster Abbey in 1834, was the harbinger of a new age; it was the cultural counterpart of the Reform Act of 1832.[1]

The politics of invention

James Watt was posthumously fashioned into the standard-bearer of the rising industrial classes. He personified their claim that it was not military prowess that made Great Britain great, but the ingenuity and enterprise of its 'industrious' citizens: the country's strength and global influence rested on the prosperity generated by manufacturing and trade; peaceful competition was a more secure route than war to individual happiness and national supremacy. Never was this claim in greater jeopardy than during the Napoleonic wars and their aftermath: Nelson's victory at Trafalgar in 1805 and Wellington's at Waterloo, ten years later, appeared

---

[1] Christine MacLeod, 'James Watt, heroic invention, and the idea of the industrial revolution', in Maxine Berg and Kristine Bruland (eds.), *Technological revolutions in Europe: historical perspectives* (Cheltenham and Northampton, MA: Edward Elgar, 1998), pp. 96–7; James Fentress and Chris Wickham, *Social memory* (Oxford: Blackwell, 1992), p. 127.

to confirm the fitness of an aristocratic military caste for government. It fed a swelling tide of nationalism and triggered a cult of hero worship, which found its most visible expression in the erection of large-scale public monuments to the victors of the battlefield.[2] It threatened to suppress the demands for political representation and fiscal justice that the excluded classes had been advancing for over half a century – with mounting confidence since the American and French revolutions. In this bellicose climate, it became necessary to advance that campaign by redefining the nation and the nation's heroes: they would be men of peaceful conquest. The death of James Watt in 1819 provided the reformers' first opportunity to subvert the dominant heroic image.

Eulogistic obituaries lauded Watt's inventive genius and exaggerated the role of his improved steam engine in creating Britain's wealth and defeating Napoleon. The efforts of influential friends to commemorate his memory culminated in a grandiose public meeting at Westminster in 1824, chaired by the prime minister, Lord Liverpool, which launched the national appeal for his monument. There, a glittering array of leading politicians, men of science, literary figures and manufacturers promoted Watt's reputation as a saviour of his country and a benefactor of humanity: thanks to him, they proclaimed, steam power promised a future of peace and prosperity, British naval supremacy, and the extension of Christian civilization around the globe. In effect, a significant element of the governing class was endorsing the growth of industry and opening a dialogue with the men whose business ventures had promoted it. Across the country, manufacturers and their workers responded enthusiastically to the opportunity to install 'one of their own' in the national pantheon. Alarmed by this new alliance, however, radical politicians sought to reclaim Watt for their own cause; simultaneously they opened a debate about the nature of invention. The press started to show a new respect for inventors, and cartoonists lampooned the prospect of a steam-powered future, paying tribute thereby to the new-found significance of technology.

Gradually, during the 1830s and 40s, this new regard for technical achievements expanded, fuelled by the daring feats of the civil engineers, as they propelled railways across the landscape, bridged estuaries and gorges, and tunnelled (not without terrifying mishaps) beneath the River Thames. In a highly visible way they were taming nature. The leading

---

[2] Linda Colley, *Britons: forging the nation, 1707–1837* (New Haven and London: Yale University Press, 1992); Alison W. Yarrington, *The commemoration of the hero, 1800–1864: monuments to the British victors of the Napoleonic wars* (New York and London: Garland, 1988).

civil engineers – George and Robert Stephenson, Marc and Isambard Kingdom Brunel, in particular – became celebrities in their lifetimes. Explanations of Britain's extraordinary growth in prosperity since the eignteenth century were increasingly couched in terms of technological change, often by reference to particular inventors. Historians and social commentators began to chronicle the rise of manufacturing industry (not always favourably): authors as disparate as Lord Macaulay and Friedrich Engels credited the importance of Watt, Richard Arkwright and other industrial pioneers. Inventors received sympathetic treatment from Charles Dickens and Mrs Gaskell, not to mention the mixed attentions of a bevy of minor novelists, poetasters and *Mr Punch*; their lives were sanctioned by obituaries in *The Times*.

The popular celebration of inventors reached its zenith in the third quarter of the nineteenth century. The Great Exhibition of 1851 played a pivotal role, orchestrating a sense of national pride in British manufacturing supremacy and an ethos of peaceful international competitiveness. From the revolutionary design of the Crystal Palace, to the power and ingenuity on display in the machinery hall, everything put new technology in a positive light and excited curiosity about its creators. Less ostentatiously, the Patent Law Amendment Act of 1852, the first major reform of the patent system in over 200 years, stirred up a ferment of controversy. Not only did its passage through Parliament stimulate debate over the inventor's role in the creation of national wealth, but it also sparked the 'patent controversy', which threatened the patent system with abolition and kept the issue in the public eye for another three decades. Prompted perhaps by this threat, Bennet Woodcroft, at the head of the new Patent Office, made enormous efforts to preserve and publicize the achievements of inventive men, both living and dead. He supplied Samuel Smiles and other biographers with information, and began to rescue machinery that marked 'the great steps in every invention' for the new Patent Office Museum at South Kensington.

Controversy of a different kind was provoked in 1854 by the outbreak of war in the Crimea and, a few years later, in India. Pacifists and others who had believed that war was an anachronism, doomed to extinction as modern nations engaged in mutually beneficial free trade, were shocked to find inventors supplying the state with new technologies of destruction. In more conservative eyes, however, this was further cause to celebrate the contribution that inventors and manufacturing industry made to Britain's international predominance: the heroes of the battlefield were impotent without the support of ingenious men on the home front, both directly in the production of weapons and indirectly in filling the nation's coffers, thanks to its booming industries. Few were prouder of their place in 'the workshop of the world' than the skilled men whose trades were at the forefront of industrialization, and many of them identified with the inventors who had been instrumental in their success. In the heavy industries and mechanized textile trades, in particular, they drank toasts to the memory of their heroes and celebrated them on their trade-union insignia. Just as in 1832 the manufacturers had staked their claim to enfranchisement under the banner of Watt and steam-powered industry, so at mid-century skilled working man campaigned for equal political rights by reference to the ingenious artisans' role in the nation's greatness.

As hero-worshipping Britain went 'statue mad' during Victoria's reign and embellished the country's squares, parks and buildings with the images of great men (only rarely women), inventors too were ostentatiously commemorated.[3] Towns and cities, universities and professional bodies paid public tribute to men with whose inventive achievements they wished to be identified. They launched public subscriptions in order to honour, in bronze or marble, both those recently deceased and others long dead. While the contributors of guineas headed the lists of subscribers, often the most striking feature was the preponderance of working men who donated their shillings and pence. Occasionally, it was skilled workers who took the initiative, as they did in Bolton (Lancs.) and Penzance (Cornwall), where the statues of Samuel Crompton and Sir Humphry Davy, respectively, still bear testimony to their campaigns. These were bold, symbolic, statements about the contribution of working people to Britain's industrial supremacy. Soon, the most prominent inventors could expect official recognition in their lifetimes, as the state became more liberal in its award of honours to professional men and industrialists. A few inventors were even elevated to the peerage: by 1900, engineering, physics and surgery were all represented in the House of Lords, as was the textile industry.[4]

It was a dizzy ascent, from 'projector' to peer, in scarcely a century. But it proved to be a brief interlude of glory: the inventor would soon return to the obscurity from which he had emerged. The twentieth century's energies were turned inevitably to honouring the dead of the Great War,

---

[3] Benedict Read, *Victorian sculpture* (New York and London: Yale University Press, 1982), pp. 3–24, 67; Ludmilla Jordanova, *Defining features: scientific and medical portraits, 1660–2000* (London: Reaktion Books, with the National Portrait Gallery, 2000), pp. 86–137.

[4] F. M. L. Thompson, *Gentrification and the enterprise culture, Britain 1780–1980* (Oxford: Oxford University Press, 2001), pp. 45–74; R. Angus Buchanan, *The engineers: a history of the engineering profession in Britain, 1750–1914* (London: Jessica Kingsley, 1989), pp. 192–3.

and simultaneously public art ceased to favour the individual statue.[5] Already, however, the independent inventor's star was dimming, as more powerful groups became attuned to the value of commemorative activity and laid claim to his glory. Professional scientists, campaigning for the public funding of research, were redefining invention as 'applied science': the hard intellectual work, they often implied, lay in the discovery of natural phenomena; the application of such new knowledge to practical ends was a straightforward, virtually automatic procedure that scarcely merited notice, let alone reward. Better organized, in the Royal Society, new university laboratories, and specialist institutions, they reclaimed the space around the monument to Sir Isaac Newton in Westminster Abbey, establishing there a 'scientists' corner' – its most triumphant (and ironic) moment being the burial in 1882 of that ultimate threat to Christianity, Charles Darwin.[6] At considerable expense, the engineers' equally assertive professional bodies maintained their presence close to the same site, with a series of commemorative windows. Devoid of such support in death as in life, the heterogeneous ranks of 'mere' inventors faded from public view.[7] Simultaneously, the publishing industry was redirecting its focus from the biographies of inventors towards the technologies themselves, while academics in the new social sciences elaborated deterministic theories of invention at the expense of the heroic inventor.[8] In a grand final flourish, the showmanship of Thomas Edison and Gulielmo Marconi and the daring feats of the Wright Brothers made them transatlantic household names, the epitome of inventive modernism at the dawn of the twentieth century – none of them available, however, to become British heroes. The inventor, increasingly taken for granted by the British public, came to be seen as an eccentric individualist: he reverted into a benign version of the 'projector', not least in the cartoons of William Heath Robinson and films such as *The Man in the White Suit* (1951).[9]

---

[5] Thomas W. Laqueur, 'Memory and naming in the Great War', in John R. Gillis (ed.), *Commemorations: the politics of national identity* (Princeton, NJ: Princeton University Press, 1994), pp. 150–67; Rosalind Krauss, 'Sculpture in the expanded field', in Hal Foster (ed.), *Postmodern culture* (London: Pluto Press, 1985), pp. 33–4; Read, *Victorian sculpture*, pp. 3–4.

[6] James Moore, 'Charles Darwin lies in Westminster Abbey', *Biological Journal of the Linnean Society* 17 (1982), 97–113.

[7] Buchanan, *Engineers*, pp. 194–5.

[8] David McGee, 'Making up mind: the early sociology of invention', *T&C* 36 (1995), 773–801.

[9] Simon Heneage, 'Robinson, William Heath (1872–1944)', *Oxford Dictionary of National Biography*, Oxford University Press, 2004, www.oxforddnb.com/view/article/ 35803, accessed 12 September 2006; Jon Agar, 'Technology and British cartoonists in the twentieth century', *TNS* 74 (2004), 191–3; www.screenonline.org.uk/film/id/441408/ index.html, accessed 12 September 2006.

As the tide of celebration ebbed, it stranded the reputations of a famous few above the high-water mark. Watt, Stephenson, Trevithick, Arkwright, Crompton and Davy headed the list of names secured in the grand narrative of Britain's Industrial Revolution (Brunel's is a later revival); those of Lords Armstrong, Kelvin and Lister remain familiar to people with a specialist interest in the history of engineering, science and medicine. They all lived at the right time to be swept up into the Victorian hero-worshippers' net and preserved for posterity. If we recognize the names of their inventive predecessors (Thomas Newcomen, William Lee, John Kay, for example), it is also largely thanks to the historical and commemorative efforts of the Victorians. Their twentieth-century successors, lacking such champions, have fared relatively badly. Securing a place in another grand narrative – that of British victory in the Second World War – appears to provide their strongest suit. The names, for example, of Sir Barnes Wallis and Sir Frank Whittle are remembered (and celebrated on film) thanks to the former's invention of the dambusting 'bouncing bomb' and the latter's struggle to convince the Air Ministry of the strategic value of his jet engine. Belatedly, Alan Turing's vital contribution to wartime code breaking is receiving public recognition. Other twentieth-century inventors, such as Laszlo Biro, Henry Ford and Sir James Dyson have succeeded in branding their names on the consumer goods that they invented or redesigned, because they became manufacturers.[10] Name recognition, however, is not the same as popular celebration: the hero-worship of inventors is one nineteenth-century 'tradition' that has not survived.[11]

Inventing culture

This book explores the inventor's rise and fall, from several perspectives. At one level, it can be read as a study in 'the social history of remembering'.[12] Peter Burke recommends close scrutiny of 'the process by which the remembered past turns into myth', here using the term 'myth' to mean 'a story with a symbolic meaning, made up of stereotyped incidents

---

[10] See Sir James Dyson's profile on his company's web site: www.dyson.co.uk/jd/profile/default.asp?sinavtype=pagelink, accessed 12 September 2006.

[11] Eric Hobsbawm, 'Introduction: inventing traditions', in Eric Hobsbawm and Terence Ranger (eds.), *The invention of tradition* (Cambridge: Cambridge University Press, 1983), pp. 1–14.

[12] Peter Burke, 'History as social memory', in Thomas Butler (ed.), *Memory: history, culture and the mind* (Oxford: Basil Blackwell, 1989), p. 100. For an extended study of heroic myth-making, see Graeme Morton, *William Wallace, man and myth* (Stroud: Sutton Publishing, 2001).

and involving characters who are larger than life, whether they are heroes or villains'. Why, he ponders, do only a few monarchs 'become heroes in popular memory', only a few pious individuals become saints?[13] Similarly, I wish to know why so few British inventors are famous today, and why those particular ones (mostly males, born in the eighteenth and early nineteenth centuries)? This is not, however, a systematic analysis of the myths or stories that are woven around many inventors, though such an undertaking could prove very fruitful: as Carolyn Cooper has suggested, they 'may be able to tell us truths about basic human experience, such as "how inventive minds work".'[14] Nonetheless, as Cooper and others appreciate, historians of technology put considerable effort into exposing the inaccuracies in popular myths surrounding inventors – often to little avail.[15] If the mythologizing of inventors has hitherto attracted little attention, scientists have fared better.[16] Not only have historians of science problematized the notion of the scientific hero and offered valuable insights into the making of individual and collective reputations, but they have pursued the philosophical implications of celebrity and myth for the way that scientists see themselves and science itself is understood.[17] In particular, the strategic process by which the credit for scientific 'discoveries' is attributed to particular individuals has become an

---

[13] Burke, 'History as social memory', pp. 103–104; Fentress and Wickham, *Social memory*, pp. x–xii, 73–4, 88.

[14] Carolyn C. Cooper, 'Myth, rumor, and history: the Yankee whittling boy as hero and villain', *T&C* 44 (2003), 85; also 94–6.

[15] Ibid., 82–4, 90–4. See also Eric Robinson, 'James Watt and the tea kettle: a myth justified', *History Today* (April 1956), 261–5; David Philip Miller, 'True myths: James Watt's kettle, his condenser, and his chemistry', *History of Science* 42 (2004), 333–60; D. A. Farnie, 'Kay, John (1704–1780/81)', *ODNB*, www.oxforddnb.com/view/article/15194, accessed 27 October 2006.

[16] See, however, Patrick O'Brien, 'The micro foundations of macro invention: the case of the Reverend Edmund Cartwright', *Textile History* 28 (1997), 201–33; MacLeod, 'James Watt'; Christine MacLeod and Alessandro Nuvolari, 'The pitfalls of prosopography: inventors in the *Dictionary of National Biography*', *T&C* 48 (2006), 757–76; Christine MacLeod and Jennifer Tann, 'From engineer to scientist: re-inventing invention in the Watt and Faraday centenaries, 1919–1931', *BJHS* 40 (2007), 389–411.

[17] Pnina G. Abir-Am, 'Essay review: how scientists view their heroes: some remarks on the mechanism of myth construction', *Journal of the History of Biology* 15 (1982), 281–315; Pnina G. Abir-Am, 'Introduction', in Pnina G. Abir-Am and C. A. Eliot (eds.), *Commemorative practices in science*, *Osiris* 14 (2000), 1–14; Alan J. Friedman and Carol C. Donley, *Einstein as myth and muse* (Cambridge: Cambridge University Press, 1985); Ludmilla Jordanova, 'Presidential address: remembrance of science past', *BJHS* 33 (2000), 387–406; Patricia Fara, 'Isaac Newton lived here: sites of memory and scientific heritage', ibid., 407–26; Patricia Fara, *Newton: The making of genius* (Basingstoke: Macmillan, 2002); Steven Shapin, 'The image of the man of science', in Roy Porter (ed.), *The Cambridge history of science, Volume 4: eighteenth century science* (Cambridge: Cambridge University Press, 2003), pp. 159–83; Janet Browne 'Presidential address: commemorating Darwin', *BJHS* 38 (2005), 251–74.

important field of study and prompted debate about the very concept of 'discovery' itself.[18]

My interest in the popular memory of the inventor was sparked by astonishment at the turn-round in his reputation. Having begun my research in the seventeenth century, when the 'patentee' was frequently viewed as the comrade-in-arms of the pickpocket and fraudster, it intrigued me that his descendants should be offered to Victorian working men as models of good character. Even more startling was the discovery that, not only had Westminster Abbey opened its doors to Watt's monument, but the king, at the instigation of his prime minister, had headed the list of subscribers. In parallel, the research of Harry Dutton was revealing a growing regard for patentees during the second quarter of the nineteenth century: judges and juries were becoming more sympathetic and finding more often in their favour; Parliament held its first enquiry into the operation of the patent system and, in 1852, finally legislated to make it more transparent and accessible to inventors.[19] Given that it is generally much easier to lose a good reputation than to overcome a bad one, how, against the odds, had the nineteenth-century inventor become a reformed character, even a hero?

Furthermore, what part had this cultural development played in the history of the patent system – in its modernization in 1852 and its subsequent survival through three decades of sustained campaigning for its abolition? How did it affect the conception of invention and technological change? Did those who wished to abolish the patent system conceive of

---

[18] Augustine Brannigan, *The social basis of scientific discoveries* (Cambridge: Cambridge University Press, 1981); Barry Barnes, *T. S. Kuhn and social science* (London: Macmillan, 1982); Simon Schaffer, 'Scientific discoveries and the end of natural philosophy', *Social Studies of Science* 16 (1986), 387–420; Robert Bud, 'Penicillin and the new Elizabethans', *BJHS* 31 (1998), 305–33; Thomas Nickles, 'Discovery', in R. C. Olby *et al.* (eds.), *Companion to the history of modern science* (London: Routledge, 1990), pp. 148–65; Richard Yeo, *Defining science: William Whewell, natural knowledge, and public debate in early Victorian Britain* (Cambridge: Cambridge University Press, 1993); Simon Schaffer, 'Making up discovery', in Margaret A. Boden (ed.), *Dimensions of creativity* (Cambridge, MA, and London: MIT Press, 1994), pp. 13–51; Michael Shortland and Richard Yeo, 'Introduction' to Michael Shortland and Richard Yeo (eds.), *Telling lives in science: essays on scientific biography* (Cambridge: Cambridge University Press, 1996), pp. 1–44; Geoffrey Cantor, 'The scientist as hero: public images of Michael Faraday', in ibid., pp. 171–94; Thomas F. Gieryn, *Cultural boundaries of science: credibility on the line* (Chicago: Chicago University Press, 1999); David Philip Miller, *Discovering Water: James Watt, Henry Cavendish and the nineteenth-century 'water controversy'* (Aldershot: Ashgate, 2004), esp. pp. 11–26; Marsha L. Richmond, 'The 1909 Darwin celebration: re-examining evolution in the light of Mendel, mutation, and meiosis', *Isis* 97 (2006), 447–84.

[19] H. I. Dutton, *The patent system and inventive activity during the industrial revolution, 1750–1852* (Manchester: Manchester University Press, 1984), pp. 42–6, 59–64, 76–81.

invention and the role played by the individual inventor differently from its supporters? Clearly, the providential theory of invention current before 1800 offered neither scope for heroic action, nor justification for the rewarding of individuals with patents, so what had replaced it?[20] How invention was understood had important ramifications for the nascent 'invention industry' and its clients, prompting both the elaboration of heroic notions of 'genius' and also a reaction against them, which elicited more deterministic and democratic explanations. These competing accounts of invention provide a theoretical framework to the politics of reputation.

The significance of the inventor's construction as a hero extends much further than the development of the patent system and nineteenth-century philosophies of invention. It offers a novel perspective on nineteenth-century British culture more generally, one that chimes with recent challenges by historians to the discourses of 'decline' and aristocratic hegemony. Quantitative demonstrations of Britain's economic robustness in the twentieth century tend to be vitiated by a national myth that its industry, in tandem with its science and technology, has been in decline for over a century. As one of this myth's most cogent critics, David Edgerton, remarks, 'this declinist historiography of British science and technology has been primarily cultural'.[21] In the late nineteenth century, profound anxieties about the loss of international leadership, as other countries began to industrialize energetically, coalesced with the opportunistic propaganda of scientists and engineers campaigning for state sponsorship. Together they launched an influential discourse of 'decline'. This has obscured the evidence of positive attitudes towards innovation and the burgeoning provision of scientific and technical education in late-Victorian and Edwardian Britain.[22]

As for inventors, the discourse of 'decline' has ignored the Victorians' fervent celebration of them as heroes. Instead, it has privileged the complaints of campaigners for reform of the patent system, who portrayed inventors as the pitiable victims of ruthless capitalists unrestrained by a negligent state, and later of scientists, who argued that only well-funded

---

[20] Christine MacLeod, *Inventing the industrial revolution: the English patent system, 1660–1800* (Cambridge: Cambridge University Press, 1988), pp. 202–4.

[21] David Edgerton, *Science, technology and the British industrial 'decline', 1870–1970* (Cambridge: Cambridge University Press for the Economic History Society, 1996), p. 68.

[22] Ibid., pp. 5–29, and passim; David Edgerton, 'The prophet militant and industrial: the peculiarities of Correlli Barnett', *Twentieth Century British History* 2 (1991), 360–79; Frank Turner, 'Public science in Britain', *Isis* 71 (1980), 360–79; David Cannadine, 'Engineering history, or the history of engineering? Re-writing the technological past', *TNS* 74 (2004), 174–5.

laboratory research could save the nation from foreign competition. It is such cultural shifts, rather than an actual change in the nature of invention and innovation, that accounts for the inventor's eclipse at the start of the twentieth century. Present-day ignorance of the names and achievements of the successors of the industrial revolution's 'heroes' should not be excused – as it regularly is – by reference to their absorption into the anonymous routine of corporate research laboratories, which, in any case, remained scarce before 1914.[23] We have been culturally programmed simultaneously to underrate the one and overrate the other, and seem unable to strike an accurate balance that values creativity without putting it on a false pedestal.[24]

This study is also intended, therefore, as a corrective to the common misconception that, beyond Samuel Smiles' now unfashionable pages, British inventors and engineers have always suffered from opprobrium or neglect – the victims of Luddite mobs, grasping capitalists, cynical politicians and high-minded critics of industrial society. Their nineteenth-century interlude of glory casts a relatively unfamiliar gleam on the cultural history of the period. Although the precise term 'the Industrial Revolution' was not in common usage until the 1880s, the preceding century witnessed a growing awareness and analysis of the revolutionary developments that were transforming the British economy. We are more familiar with the voices of those who deplored industrialization's harmful effects than of those who welcomed its benefits and hymned its achievements. By no means is it my intention to silence the former, but lack of attention to the latter has produced an unbalanced picture of nineteenth-century popular culture, which is only starting to be remedied. This is especially true of the century's second half, as the visible excitement of early railway construction and the triumphalism of the Great Exhibition in 1851 appear to fade, submerged beneath the anxieties generated by Britain's supposedly faltering international competitiveness.

In part, this simply reflects the focus of much historical literature. As its title indicates, *Iron Bridge to Crystal Palace*, Asa Briggs' anthology of visual sources – many of them celebrating heroic technical achievements – terminates in 1851; Klingender's *Art and the industrial revolution* covers a similar period.[25] The familiar names of the early canal and railway engineers present publishers and television producers with easier options than

[23] Edgerton, *Science*, pp. 31–2.
[24] For a critique of today's 'ideology of creativity', see Thomas Osborne, 'Against "creativity": a philistine rant', *Economy and Society* 32 (2003), 507–25.
[25] Asa Briggs, *Iron Bridge to Crystal Palace: impact and images of the industrial revolution* (London: Thames & Hudson, 1979); Francis D. Klingender, *Art and the industrial revolution*, ed. Arthur Elton (London: Evelyn, Adams & Mackay, 1968).

their less well-known successors.[26] To a certain degree, it also results from reading a late twentieth-century preoccupation with decline back into the second half of the nineteenth. To suggest, for example, that the deaths, in 1859, of Robert Stephenson and Isambard Kingdom Brunel marked the end of an era, such that 'the public began to lose confidence in the engineer so that he began to lose confidence in himself', is to ignore the evidence of advancing status to which the engineering professions laid claim during the subsequent half century.[27] Loss of confidence was not on the agenda of men who, as we shall see, adorned Westminster Abbey with monuments to eminent colleagues and increasingly expected high honours to reward their successful completion of a major project.

Stefan Collini contends that our very concept of 'culture' has been shaped, as a distinct and separate phenomenon, through the critique of industrial society advanced by literary historians, such as Raymond Williams, who adopted the 'catastrophist' view of the industrial revolution that the Hammonds and other first-generation economic historians popularized.[28] From 1882, when Arnold Toynbee vilified what he was the first to term (in English) 'the Industrial Revolution', to study British industrialization was normally to study the evils of capitalism and the degradation of working people.[29] 'Culture' represented the humane, ethical alternative to one-dimensional economic rationality, the bulwark against a new, debased civilization founded solely on the profit motive.[30] Williams explained that his book, *Culture and society*, rested on 'the discovery that the idea of culture, and the word itself in its general modern uses, came into English thinking in the period … of the Industrial Revolution'.[31] He structured it around the responses to 'the new

---

[26] R. A. Buchanan, 'The Rolt Memorial Lecture 1987: the lives of the engineers', *Industrial Archaeology Review* 11 (1988–9), 5.

[27] L. T. C. Rolt, *Victorian engineering* (Harmondsworth: Penguin Books, 1974), p. 163. Cf. Buchanan, *Engineers*, and W. J. Reader, '"At the head of all the new professions": the engineer in Victorian society', in Neil McKendrick and R. B. Outhwaite (eds.), *Business life and public policy: essays in honour of D. C. Coleman* (Cambridge: Cambridge University Press, 1986), pp. 173–84.

[28] Stefan Collini, 'The literary critic and the village labourer: "culture" in twentieth-century Britain', *Transactions of the Royal Historical Society*, 6th series, 14 (2004), 93–116.

[29] D. C. Coleman, *Myth, history and the industrial revolution* (London and Rio Grande: Hambledon Press, 1992), pp. 16–30; David Cannadine, 'The present and the past in the English industrial revolution', *P&P* 103 (1984), 133–8; Timothy Boon, 'Industrialisation and catastrophe: the Victorian economy in British film documentary, 1930–50', in Miles Taylor and Michael Wolff (eds.), *The Victorians since 1901: histories, representations and revisions* (Manchester: Manchester University Press, 2004), pp. 111–14.

[30] Collini, 'Literary critic', passim.

[31] Raymond Williams, *Culture and society, 1780–1950* (London: Chatto & Windus, 1958), p. vii.

industrial system' of major literary and philosophical figures, who lived
through its first century. Thomas Carlyle, that arch-critic of 'industrialism' (a word he coined), looms large. 'It is here', says Williams of Carlyle's
thought, 'that the idea of culture as the body of arts and learning, and the
idea of culture as a body of values superior to the ordinary progress of
society, meet and combine'.[32] Nothing celebratory of 'the new industrial
society' emerges from beneath this condemnatory weight: it is crushed
out of the record.[33]

So entrenched is this critical stance that it led one influential analyst of
British twentieth-century economic decline and his disciples to locate the
source of all our woes in the 'anti-industrial spirit' of Victorian opinion
formers. In a book that chimed with the excoriation of contemporary
anti-business values by the first Thatcher government (1979–83), Martin
Wiener argued that, for over a century, the effectiveness of British industrialists had been hobbled by the aristocratic subversion of bourgeois
culture. 'The rentier aristocracy succeeded to a large extent in maintaining a cultural hegemony, and consequently in reshaping the industrial
bourgeoisie in its own image.'[34] This elite culture was allegedly characterized by its suspicion of 'progress' and 'material and technological
development'; it stressed 'non-industrial, non-innovative and nonmate-
rial qualities, best encapsulated in rustic imagery'. While conceding that,
with the Great Exhibition of 1851, 'industry was taking on a heroic aura',
Wiener contended that 1851 marks 'an end not a beginning ... the high-
water mark of educated opinion's enthusiasm for industrial capitalism'.[35]
By 1900, he believed, the backward-looking 'Southern' metaphor of
Englishness had triumphed: a putative 'Northern' metaphor that celebrated the values of industrial enterprise was devalued and derogated as
'provincial'. Wiener cited not only the literary tradition that Raymond
Williams charted but also the later Victorians' fascination with history
and antiquities, their idealization of the countryside, and the fashion for
Gothic architecture.[36]

[32] Ibid., p. 84.
[33] For a similar emphasis, see the anthology of literary extracts compiled by Williams'
contemporary, Humphrey Jennings, who commented 'that he found a theme emerging
from the collection almost spontaneously – that the coming of the Machine was destroying something in our life': *Pandaemonium: the coming of the machine as seen by contemporary
observers* (London: Deutsch, 1985), p. xvi.
[34] Martin J. Wiener, *English culture and the decline of the industrial spirit, 1850–1950* (Cambridge:
Cambridge University Press, 1981), p. 8. There are, of course, echoes here of C. P. Snow's
classic diatribe, *The two cultures and the scientific revolution* (Cambridge: Cambridge
University Press, 1961); see also Correlli Barnett, *The audit of war: the illusion and reality of
Britain as a great nation* (London: Macmillan, 1986).
[35] Wiener, *English culture*, p. 28.   [36] Ibid., pp. 41–67.

Wiener's argument has provoked debate at many points. Most pertinent here is the challenge, by a number of historians, to the idea of aristocratic cultural hegemony.[37] It was in the industrial cities, they argue, that a dynamic, distinctively bourgeois culture asserted and symbolized the authority of industrial and commercial wealth. Far from kowtowing to aristocratic prejudice, urban elites established a collective identity that proudly proclaimed their own achievements. 'Culture itself was a crucial domain for the articulation of class in the nineteenth-century industrial city.'[38] It was in this urban public sphere, as Simon Gunn argues, that new wealth established its power base. Fiercely resisting any involvement in urban life by the landed aristocracy, it secured its dominance over the city's other inhabitants through a network of voluntary associations, which from the late eighteenth century fostered the institutions of sociability and cultural improvement.[39] On the one hand, philosophical and choral societies, sporting and social clubs offered the middle classes leisure and educational facilities; on the other, voluntary societies (usually founded by a public meeting) raised subscriptions to fund hospitals, schools and assembly rooms, or campaigned for improvements in the urban environment.[40] Victoria's reign saw these older sites of select conviviality increasingly eclipsed by an 'expanded public sphere' of public exhibitions and concerts, department stores and restaurants, accessible to all those in possession of sufficient cash, the correct appearance and passable etiquette. Designed to impress, it was a culture that emphasized visibility and display; intimidating in its rituals and formal requirements, it constructed an appropriate stage for their performance.[41]

City centres were radically transformed to accommodate the new institutions of municipal government and facilities for public entertainment and instruction: urban elites seized the opportunity to remodel

---

[37] Thompson, *Gentrification* (Thompson anticipates my argument here in an expostulation on p. 150); Neil McKendrick, '"Gentlemen and players revisited": the gentlemanly ideal, the business ideal and the professional ideal in English literary culture', in McKendrick and Outhwaite (eds.), *Business life and public policy*, pp. 98–136; James Raven, 'British history and the enterprise culture', *P&P* 123 (1989), 178–204; the essays in Bruce Collins and Keith Robbins (eds.), *British culture and economic decline* (London: Weidenfeld and Nicolson, 1990); W. D. Rubinstein, *Capitalism, culture, and economic decline in Britain, 1750–1990* (London: Routledge, 1993).

[38] Simon Gunn, *The public culture of the Victorian middle class: ritual and authority in the English industrial city, 1840–1914* (Manchester: Manchester University Press, 2000), p. 4.

[39] Ibid., pp. 13–30.

[40] R. J. Morris, *Class, sect and party: the making of the British middle class, Leeds 1820–1850* (Manchester: Manchester University Press, 1990), pp. 161–203; R. J. Morris, 'Voluntary societies and British urban elites, 1780–1870', *HJ* 26 (1983), 95–118.

[41] Gunn, *Public culture*, pp. 26–30.

them in their own image. Monumental in scale, this 'architecture of rhetoric' dignified the city, demanded respect for its governors, and addressed the inhabitants explicitly through a profusion of symbols and morally uplifting inscriptions.[42] In the reconstructed centres of Manchester, Leeds, Birmingham, Liverpool, Glasgow and other great cities, grandiose town halls and assize courts, surrounded by magnificent public art galleries, libraries and museums defied those critics of 'industrialism' who perceived it as the road to moral and cultural perdition. In the proud words of the foundation stone of the Birmingham Museum and Art Gallery, 'By the gains of industry we promote art.'[43] It might equally have boasted, 'By the gains of industry we make Great Britain great.' While the power base of the bourgeoisie was in the cities, its ambitions were played out on a national stage and anchored in its sense of self-importance.

In a close engagement with Wiener's interpretation of the Victorians' 'historical turn', Charles Dellheim contends that their relationship with the past was not reactionary, but ambivalent and complex. While a 'cult of the past' might suggest bourgeois deference to an aristocracy whose claims to status and power were rooted in history, it may alternatively represent an attempt by the liberal middle-class to subvert aristocratic pretensions: the bourgeoisie sought to legitimate its own claims by 'fabricating traditions'.[44] 'There was no intrinsic contradiction', maintains Dellheim, 'between the pursuit of technological progress and the rehabilitation of historic forms: the medievalized façade and the modern interior of St Pancras [railway station] are two faces of the same model.'[45] It was the very confidence of the industrial middle class that allowed it, by the 1870s, to adapt the Gothic form for its own secular purposes. The iconography of Manchester Town Hall and the Bradford Wool Exchange, with their combination of civic and national, religious and commercial, scientific and historical themes, celebrated 'the romance of industry and the heroism of exchange'.[46] Among the chosen champions of 'industrialism', in the contest for social recognition and political power that was waged by the middle and working classes, was a small band of iconic inventors.

---

[42] Ibid., pp. 39–43; Nicholas Taylor, 'The awful sublimity of the Victorian city', in H. J. Dyos and Michael Wolff (eds.), *The Victorian city: images and reality*, 2 vols. (London: Routledge & Kegan Paul, 1973), vol. II, pp. 431–48; K. Hill, 'Thoroughly imbued with the spirit of Ancient Greece: symbolism and space in Victorian civic culture', in Alan Kidd and David Nicholls (eds.), *Gender, civic culture and consumerism: middle-class identity in Britain, 1800–1940* (Manchester: Manchester University Press, 1999), pp. 99–100.

[43] Cited in Hill, 'Thoroughly imbued', p. 102.

[44] Charles Dellheim, *The face of the past: the preservation of the medieval inheritance in Victorian England* (Cambridge: Cambridge University Press, 1982), pp. 1–29.

[45] Ibid., p. 1.   [46] Ibid., p. 173, and pp. 133–81.

Heroes and their commemoration

The title of this book contains two nouns whose meaning exercised nineteenth-century intellectuals to an unprecedented degree. Since their debates about the nature of invention are discussed at some length in Chapters 5, 6 and 9, I shall limit my conceptual clarifications here to the 'hero'. What is the status I am claiming for inventors? Obviously, inventors were not nineteenth-century Britain's only heroes. Who occupied its pantheon? How did contemporaries conceive of the hero? How did they glorify and commemorate him?

In eighteenth-century Britain, the archetypal hero belonged to ancient mythology. A human of unusual abilities and extreme traits of character, usually a warrior, the hero was god-like in everything except his mortality.[47] Through the ages, new layers of symbolic meaning had been added to and recast the classical heroes' legendary reputations.[48] The quintessential heroes of English medieval romance, however, King Arthur and his knights, had to await the positive reassessment of the Middle Ages that came with the Gothic revival and the novels of Sir Walter Scott in the next century. Their chivalric ideals, so inspiring to Victorian artists and poets, failed to stir Enlightened hearts, for whom the Middle Ages spelled barbarity and Catholic superstition.[49] Deprived also of the panoply of saints and martyrs – previously the objects of a quasi-heroic devotion and imbued with similar symbolic significance – Protestant Englishmen were encouraged to make the same kind of emotional investment in their monarch and 'defender of the faith' by a Church calendar that commemorated such 'providential' events as the nation's deliverance from the Spanish Armada and the Gunpowder Plot, the restoration of Charles II and the victories of William III. It seems a fairly thin cultural gruel, though, by the late seventeenth century, one contested by 'rival ideologies and faiths'.[50] Ironically, Stuart-Georgian England, suggests James Johnson,

---

[47] John Hope Mason, *The value of creativity: the origins and emergence of a modern belief* (Aldershot: Ashgate, 2003), pp. 15–16; Robert Folkenflik, 'Introduction', in Robert Folkenflik (ed.), *The English hero, 1660–1800* (Newark, NJ: University of Delaware Press, 1982), pp. 10–13. For Prometheus, ancient mythology's heroic inventor, see below, pp. 47–8.

[48] Willem P. Geritsen and Anthony G. van Mellen (eds.), *A dictionary of medieval heroes* (Woodbridge: Boydell Press, 1998), pp. 1–7, and I. J. Engels, 'Hector', in ibid., pp. 139–45.

[49] Frank Brandsma, 'Arthur', 'Galahad', 'Lancelot'; Bart Besamusca, 'Gawain'; M.-J. Heijkant, 'Tristram'; all in Geritsen and van Mellen (eds.), *Dictionary of medieval heroes*, pp. 39, 111–12, 118–20, 167–9, 280.

[50] David Cressy, 'National memory in early modern England', in John R. Gillis (ed.), *Commemorations: the politics of identity* (Princeton, NJ: Princeton University Press, 1994), p. 71.

may have suffered from a surfeit of heroes – both historical and literary, ancient and modern, biblical and secular, military and civilian – to the point of confusion and uncertainty 'as to the attributes of the hero, the constituent elements of heroism, or even as to whether the heroic concept had any validity'.[51] In particular, various authors queried the traditional emphasis on military courage and conquest, preferring construction to destruction and restating the Christian virtues, such as piety, humility and charity: Jesus and St Paul were the true heroes, contended Richard Steele in 1701.[52]

The mid-eighteenth century witnessed, however, 'a remarkable cluster of cultural manifestations of British nationalism', which included the British Museum (1753), Johnson's *Dictionary* (1755), the Royal Academy (1768), the *Encyclopaedia Britannica* (1768) and the *Biographia Britannica* (1747–66).[53] The latter professed itself 'a British Temple of Honour, sacred to the piety, learning, valour, public spirit, loyalty and every other glorious virtue of our ancestors'. In company with other biographical compilations of the time, its aim was to set 'worthy examples before the eyes of posterity' and encourage others to emulate their achievements.[54] These exemplars of virtue or 'worthies' were distinct from the heroes, whose exceptional gifts made them necessarily inimitable and whose momentous actions typically transgressed norms of behaviour to the point of insubordination, even treachery; tragedy always hovered in the wings.[55] The thoroughly rational Enlightenment had little time for such mavericks. It allowed that the heroic life could be lived by low-born men and (even) women in domestic situations and countenanced the creation of England's 'own special hero, John Bull the Common Man' – while refusing to worship him.[56] In France, the new republic followed the tenets of the *Encyclopédistes* in dedicating the Panthéon not to the nation's 'heroes' but to its *grands hommes* ('great men'), preferring to honour an assembly of citizens who contributed their 'greatness of mind', in intellectual, political, artistic and military pursuits. It sought in their collective

---

[51] James William Johnson, 'England, 1660–1800: an age without a hero?', in Folkenflik (ed.), *English hero*, p. 25.

[52] Ibid., p. 32; Robert Folkenflik, 'Johnson's heroes', in Folkenflik (ed.), *English hero*, pp. 143–6.

[53] Keith Thomas, *Changing conceptions of national biography: the Oxford DNB in historical perspective* (Cambridge: Cambridge University Press, 2005), p. 13.

[54] Quoted in ibid., pp. 12, 17.

[55] Geoffrey Cubitt, 'Introduction: heroic reputations and exemplary lives', in Geoffrey Cubitt and Allen Warren (eds.), *Heroic reputations and exemplary lives* (Manchester: Manchester University Press, 2000), pp. 1–15; Lucy Hughes-Hallett, *Heroes: saviours, traitors, and supermen* (London: Harper Perennial, 2005), pp. 1–14.

[56] Johnson, 'An age without a hero?', pp. 33–4.

achievements a 'counterweight to despotic power, a bulwark against arbitrary government'; a warrior who defended the nation might be included, but not a king.[57] This was paralleled in Britain, where an informal cult of great minds emerged, promoted most ostentatiously by supporters of the Glorious Revolution of 1688 and the Hanoverian succession as the nation's bulwarks against tyranny and the Papacy. Whig grandees followed the example of Queen Caroline, wife of George II, in landscaping their gardens around monuments to such towering intellects as Locke, Newton, Boyle, Bacon, Milton, Pope and Shakespeare; a thriving trade in busts, statuettes, engravings and medallions carried their images wider and further down the social scale.[58] Whether such men were leading 'worthies', whose example could be emulated, or geniuses, different in kind and more akin to the heroes in their superhuman abilities, became a subject for debate.[59]

Until the 1790s, the hero's commemoration was normally a private matter. While monuments might be open to public view, they were privately financed acts of homage, which occupied privately owned sites. Charles II had begun the tradition of political statuary at the Restoration, when he installed an equestrian statue of his father in Whitehall (on the site of the Regicides' execution).[60] In the 1730s, the city fathers of Bristol and Hull paid similar tributes to William III from their own coffers; both monuments depicted him as the Roman emperor, Marcus Aurelius. And William's great general, the duke of Marlborough, owed his monument – a statue atop a 134-foot column on his Blenheim estate – to his adoring widow, Sarah.[61] Some colleges and hospitals commemorated their founders on the exterior of their buildings but, in general, monuments to private citizens in outdoor, public spaces were rare; most were situated either in places of worship or in the gardens of country houses.[62] When the Whigs

---

[57]   Mona Ozouf, 'The Panthéon: the Ecole Normale of the dead', in Pierre Nora (ed.), *Realms of memory: the construction of the French past*, ed. Lawrence D. Kritzman, trans. Arthur Goldhammer, 3 vols. (New York: Columbia University Press, 1996–98), vol. III, pp. 326–30. See also Dominique Poulot, 'Pantheons in eighteenth-century France: temple, museum, pyramid', in Richard Wrigley and Matthew Craske (eds.), *Pantheons: transformations of a monumental idea* (Aldershot: Ashgate, 2004), pp. 123–45.

[58]   Fara, *Newton*, pp. 43–5; Patricia Fara, 'Faces of genius: images of Isaac Newton in eighteenth-century England', in Cubitt and Warren (eds.), *Heroic reputations*, pp. 73–6; N. B. Penny, 'The Whig cult of Fox in early nineteenth-century sculpture', *P&P* 70 (1976), 96–9.

[59]   Richard Yeo, 'Genius, method, and morality: images of Newton in Britain, 1760–1860', *Science in Context* 2 (1988), 257–84. See also below, pp. 21–3 and 51–3.

[60]   Jo Darke, *The monument guide to England and Wales: a national portrait in bronze and stone* (London: Macdonald Illustrated, 1991), pp. 12, 29.

[61]   Ibid., pp. 80, 100, 153–4, 215. Blenheim was the gift of Queen Anne.

[62]   Yarrington, *Commemoration of the hero*, pp. vi–vii, 1–60.

erected an august bronze statue to their lost leader, Charles James Fox, in London's Bloomsbury Square, in 1814, it was only a minor break with convention, since Bloomsbury, owned by the duke of Bedford, was effectively 'Whig territory'; the fifth duke's statue already presided over nearby Russell Square. Simultaneously, however, statues to Admiral Nelson, paid for by public subscription, were under construction in the thoroughfares of several provincial cities.[63]

Thanks to private acts of homage, Sir Isaac Newton was to be found at three posthumous sites (to which the public had limited access): the nave of Westminster Abbey; Trinity College, Cambridge (in both the chapel and the library); and the Temple of British Worthies – an allegorical tribute in marble to Whig ideals, designed for Lord Cobham's beautifully landscaped garden at Stowe.[64] The imposing monument erected to Newton's memory in Westminster Abbey by his heir elect (and niece's husband), John Conduit, was both typical of its time and highly unusual. During the mid-eighteenth century, the Abbey, according to Matthew Craske, 'is more accurately described as a gallery in which benefactors received the public acclaim of their inheritors than as a "pantheon" of public heroes'; the majority of their subjects, like Newton, had died without direct male heirs.[65] Yet, while Newton's eminence demanded his presence in any such pantheon, most of his sepulchral contemporaries owed their place to fortune rather than fame, including not a few whose epitaphs sought to restore reputations tarnished by scandal and intrigue. Mounting protests against mediocrity's 'jobbing' of the Abbey, which threatened to deprive future greatness of sufficient commemorative space, led to its reclamation, from the 1760s, as a place of public recognition; monuments would increasingly be sponsored by 'Parliament, patriotic bodies and committees'.[66]

It was St Paul's Cathedral, however, that was to house Britain's first national pantheon, as an aristocratic Parliament voted large sums of public money to commemorate military and political leaders of the French wars. Between 1794 and 1823, it commissioned thirty-six monuments, for a symmetrical and hierarchical scheme around the cathedral's north and

---

[63] Penny, 'The Whig cult of Fox', 100. For Nelson, see below, p. 19.

[64] Fara, *Newton*, pp. 39–49.

[65] Matthew Craske, 'Westminster Abbey 1720–1770: a public pantheon built upon private interest', in Wrigley and Craske (eds.), *Pantheons*, pp. 62, 67.

[66] Ibid., 67–9, 75–7. See also Stuart Burch, 'Shaping symbolic space: Parliament Square, London as a sacred site', in Angela Phelps (ed.), *The construction of built heritage* (Aldershot: Ashgate, 2002), p. 225. I am grateful to Madge Dresser for this reference.

south transepts.[67] This elaborate, public tribute to militaristic ideals was not without its critics, from humanist and radical, as well as religious, standpoints, but it commanded general public approval. But how far were its subjects meant to be seen as heroes, or was St Paul's, despite its military focus, more akin to France's Panthéon? According to Holger Hoock, such an extended series of monuments indicates 'an emphasis on creating a "shrine" to service as a patriotic value (if not to the State itself), as much as to individual heroism'.[68] At the centre of the scheme, however, was the grave of one whose celebrity in life was posthumously inflated into an enduring fame as Britain's greatest naval hero, Lord Nelson. And when Nelson's body was finally joined there by the duke of Wellington's, in 1852, St Paul's contained a second national hero of even greater stature.

The popularity of Nelson and, later, Wellington knew no bounds. To a considerable degree spontaneous, it was also ideologically constructed and manipulated in the government's favour to curry support for an expensive and contentious war. The nation's grateful adulation of the Royal Navy came increasingly to focus on Admiral Nelson. The victor of Cape St Vincent, Copenhagen, and the Nile became 'a popular cult figure' several years before his final (and fatal) triumph at Trafalgar, thanks to his personal bravery and daring tactics in battle, embellished by a reputation for being a just, generous and compassionate leader of men.[69] He could stand comparison with any of Homer's heroes, not least in his 'telescopic' subversion of orders.[70] Although a political outsider, cold-shouldered by high society for his scandalous affair with Emma Hamilton, Nelson drew rapturous crowds wherever he went; he played unselfconsciously to the gallery. While the state was niggardly in its rewards, many a city conferred its freedom on him.[71] His death in 1805 signalled the launch of public subscriptions to memorialize him in seven British towns and cities. The most ambitious and complex of them – in

---

[67] Holger Hoock, 'The British military pantheon in St Paul's Cathedral: the state, cultural patriotism, and the politics of national monuments, c. 1790–1820', in Wrigley and Craske (eds.), *Pantheons*, pp. 83–6. A few of the monuments, principally of politicians, were sited instead in Westminster Abbey.

[68] Ibid., p. 97.

[69] Gerald Jordan and Nicholas Rogers, 'Admirals as heroes: patriotism and liberty in Hanoverian England', *Journal of British Studies* 28 (1989), 201–24.

[70] Hughes-Hallett, *Heroes*, p. 5; Hoock, 'British military pantheon', p. 95.

[71] Jordan and Rogers, 'Admirals as heroes', 213–22; Colley, *Britons*, pp. 180–3. The chief beneficiary of the nation's largesse was Admiral Nelson's brother, a Norfolk clergyman, who in 1805 was awarded 'an earldom, £100,000, and a perpetual annuity of £5,000 per annum': W. D. Rubinstein, 'The end of "Old Corruption" in Britain, 1780–1860', *P&P* 101 (1983), 67.

Liverpool, by Richard Westmacott – cost £9,000 and was as flamboyant as the admiral it commemorated.[72] The City of London commissioned an imposing memorial for the Guildhall, while Flaxman's monument to him in St Paul's offered 'a lesson in patriotic inspiration ... expressive of decorous manly sentiment'.[73]

Following the euphoria of Wellington's victory at Waterloo, many designs for major commemorative works were produced, in the expectation that he might be rewarded with a triumphal arch or even a palace (following the precedent of Marlborough's Blenheim).[74] It was the 1840s, however, before the most ambitious schemes came to fruition and the capital had a truly national monument; meanwhile, Wellington's representation as the naked Achilles, in a statue commissioned from Westmacott by 'the ladies of England' and unveiled near Hyde Park Corner in 1822, was the source of both controversy and ribald humour.[75] Nothing, however, could diminish the Iron Duke's heroic status. The jubilant British people momentarily forgot their hereditary fear of standing armies to glorify the successful general who had finally secured both peace and British supremacy in Europe. Yet, despite his towering military reputation, Wellington did not fit the classical stereotype of a hero and regularly suffered by comparison with his defeated foe. Unlike Napoleon (or Nelson), he was not charismatic, did not inspire undying devotion, did not seem touched by 'destiny'; instead, he was loyal, dutiful, hardworking, methodical – and unromantically long-lived![76] Eventually, his biographers constructed Wellington as the model English gentleman, making virtues out of his deficiencies: 'Wellington was recast in such a way that he became both the epitome of hierarchy and an example of the new meritocracy.'[77] To British eyes in 1815, however, he was simply

---

[72] Yarrington, *Commemoration of the hero*, pp. 102–66, 327–8; Terry Cavanagh, *Public sculpture of Liverpool* (Liverpool: Liverpool University Press, 1996), pp. 51–4; Yvonne Whelan, *Reinventing modern Dublin: streetscape, iconography and the politics of identity* (Dublin: University College Dublin Press, 2003), pp. 44–52.

[73] Hoock, 'British military pantheon', pp. 93–4; Yarrington, *Commemoration of the hero*, pp. 63–7, 77–9; Philip Ward-Jackson, *Public sculpture of the City of London* (Liverpool: Liverpool University Press, 2003), pp. 170–3.

[74] Alison Yarrington, *His Achilles' heel? Wellington and public art* (Southampton: University of Southampton, 1998), pp. 4–7.

[75] Ibid., pp. 10–14; Darke, *Monument guide*, p. 62. This remained the sole, outdoor national monument in London until the 1840s: Yarrington, *Commemoration of the hero*, pp. 167–216, 327–8.

[76] Iain Pears, 'The gentleman and the hero: Wellington and Napoleon in the nineteenth century', in Roy Porter (ed.), *Myths of the English* (Cambridge: Polity Press, 1992), pp. 216–36.

[77] Ibid., p. 231. Wellington's conservatism was to make him a highly controversial figure, especially following his diehard resistance to the Reform Bill in 1831–2.

the saviour of his country, the greatest military commander since Marlborough – perhaps ever. Three years later he was to bring this martial glamour into the heart of power, when he joined Lord Liverpool's Tory administration. For the next three decades, the British people would have a living hero to worship and British politics a heroic reputation to conjure with.

Wellington's enduring prominence bore no little responsibility for the peculiarly nineteenth-century, quasi-religious phenomenon of hero worship, which expressed itself in 'statumania', historical painting, the introduction of centenary festivals and the rise of biography as a literary genre.[78] Deep-rooted in social anxieties and emergent cultural values, in Britain its bible was indisputably Thomas Carlyle's On heroes and hero-worship (1841).[79] Walter Houghton identifies Carlyle's primary spur as the 'need for a Messiah', an agent of the divine plan, a strong and virtuous hero sent by God to lead a new crusade for a morally superior civilization at a period of great social and religious uncertainty. Carlyle's idea of the hero expanded to include (and helped to rehabilitate) even unpopular men of action, such as Mohammed and Oliver Cromwell, as well as the great writers who formed a 'perpetual priesthood' that carried 'the prophetic torch' during such dispiriting times as his own.[80] His faith in heroic action as the mainspring of history contested the 'scientific' view associated, in particular, with Hegel, which believed the individual was conditioned by his environment and mankind was subject to the interplay of impersonal forces, able to do no more than speed up or temporarily delay the inevitable.[81] Through superior abilities and force of personality, Carlyle's elite intuited the will of God, inspired the masses and changed

---

[78] The study of political commemoration and 'statumania' was pioneered in France, where repeated changes of regime during the century after 1789 produced a richly symbolic streetscape: Maurice Agulhon, 'Politics, images, and symbols in post-Revolutionary France', in Sean Wilentz (ed.), Rites of power: symbolism, ritual and politics since the Middle Ages (Philadelphia: University of Pennsylvania Press, 1985), pp. 184–5; Paul A. Pickering and Alex Tyrrell, 'The public memorial of reform: commemoration and contestation', in Paul A. Pickering and Alex Tyrrell (eds.), Contested sites: commemoration, memorial and popular politics in nineteenth-century Britain (Aldershot: Ashgate, 2004), pp. 10–11.

[79] Walter E. Houghton, The Victorian frame of mind, 1830–1870 (New Haven, Yale University Press, 1957), pp. 305–40.

[80] Samuel Johnson anticipated Carlyle's heroic perception of writers and intellectuals, and was himself to be Carlyle's prime example of the hero as man of letters: Folkenflik, 'Johnson's heroes', pp. 143, 153–65.

[81] Houghton, Victorian frame of mind, pp. 197–215, 310–16. For the paradox inherent in Carlyle's idea of the heroic man of destiny, see Michael K. Goldberg's introduction to Thomas Carlyle, On heroes, hero-worship, and the heroic in history (Berkeley: University of California Press, 1993), pp. lii–lxi.

history; like ancient heroes, they were to be 'worshipped and followed', but not emulated.[82]

Emulation belonged to a different, incommensurable type of heroic discourse, that of 'exemplarity', where the individual life had a didactic purpose with 'no necessary relationship to historical narrative'.[83] It assumed a democratic similarity between the subject and the reader, who could be inspired to follow closely in the hero's footsteps, especially since its primary goal was a good character and moral worth, rather than great achievements.[84] Although most familiar to us in the writings of Samuel Smiles, which celebrated the lives and works of many inventors, engineers and other men of humble origins, it was a genre with a pedigree that stretched back to the previous century's collections of 'worthies'.

Further encouragement to revere great historical individuals came from the surrogate religion proposed by the French social theorist, Auguste Comte. Comte elaborated his system of 'positive' philosophy as a new, scientific foundation for social regeneration. To fellow agnostics he offered the Religion of Humanity, which would honour those men and women throughout the ages who had 'promoted the progress of mankind'.[85] In 1849, Comte published his *Positivist calendar*, in which he arranged the names of 559 eminent individuals, 'beginning with Moses and ending with the poets and thinkers of the first generation of the nineteenth century'.[86] They were categorized into months, with each month named after the greatest man (sic) in each sphere, each week named after the fifty-two next greatest, and so on down to the individual days (with substitutes for leap years). While Shakespeare presided over the tenth month (modern drama), to Gutenberg was given the honour of heading the ninth (modern industry). Here, Columbus led the first week (explorers), the French inventor, Vaucanson led the second (inventors of machines and instruments, including Harrison, Dollond and Arkwright), Watt led the third (pioneers of steam power), and Montgolfier the fourth (inventors and engineers). According to Comte's most loyal British disciple,

---

[82] Ibid., pp. xli–li; Cubitt, 'Introduction', p. 17. For inventors' eligibility for Carlyle's pantheon, see below, pp. 121–2.

[83] Cubitt, 'Introduction', pp. 9–16.

[84] As Smiles discovered, it was advisable to select subjects who were safely dead: Anne Secord, '"Be what you would seem to be": Samuel Smiles, Thomas Edward, and the making of a working-class scientific hero', in *Science in Context* 16 (2003), 164–70.

[85] Cubitt, 'Introduction', p. 17; Christopher Kent, *Brains and numbers: elitism, Comtism, and democracy in mid-Victorian England* (Toronto: University of Toronto Press, 1978), pp. 59–62.

[86] Frederic Harrison, S. H. Swinney and F. S. Marvin (eds.), *The new calendar of great men: biographies of the 559 worthies of all ages and nations in the positivist calendar of Auguste Comte* (new edn, London: Macmillan and Co., 1920), p. v.

Frederic Harrison, 'The names are chosen not as being those of Saints or Heroes; but as men to be remembered for effective work in the development of human society.' Eminence that was 'merely negative and destructive' was omitted, even if that meant excluding Napoleon.[87] Unlike Carlyle's heroes, sent by God to alter single-handedly the course of history, Comte's 'worthies' were to be admired for simply having made a greater than normal contribution – a matter of degree, not kind – in the tradition of the *Encyclopédie* and the Panthéon.

By contrast with Comte's cosmopolitan calendar, however, most nineteenth-century European pantheons served a nationalist cause. With the British mainland secure in its national identity at this time, there yet remained much scope for a patriotism that gradually transmuted into imperialism.[88] Britain was still mourning Wellington when the Crimea produced a new generation of military heroes, soon to be outshone by General Henry Havelock and others who suppressed the Indian 'mutiny' in 1857.[89] The chauvinistic fever was stoked by a ransacking of history to recreate the unscrupulous privateers of Elizabeth I's reign as virtuous patriots in Victoria's. Charles Kingsley, for example, conceived his *Westward Ho!* (1855) as 'a prose epic of England's seadogs ... "their voyages and their battles ... their heroic lives and no less heroic deaths."'[90] It was an odyssey that climaxed in 1888, when the tercentenary of the Spanish Armada's defeat coincided with the bicentenary of the Glorious Revolution. Devon, in particular, seized this occasion to indulge in pageants of Protestant patriotism. Tavistock, the birthplace of Sir Francis Drake, erected a bronze statue of this 'swaggeringly handsome ... buccaneer' in 1884; Plymouth, the port from which Drake had sailed after insouciantly completing his legendary game of bowls, followed suit the following year and, in 1888, also began to erect the Armada column, with its panoply of patriotic symbols.[91]

By this time, Britain was extremely well versed in celebrating its heroes with public statues and centenary festivals.[92] There was scarcely

---

[87] Ibid., p. vi; Houghton, *Victorian frame of mind*, pp. 322–4.

[88] Cf. Whelan, *Reinventing modern Dublin*, pp. 14–20, 33–8, 53–93; John R. Gillis, 'Memory and identity: the history of a relationship', in Gillis (ed.), *Commemorations*, pp. 3–11.

[89] Graham Dawson, *Soldier heroes: British adventure, empire, and the imagining of masculinities* (London and New York: Routledge, 1994), pp. 79–116, and passim.

[90] Houghton, *Victorian frame of mind*, p. 324; Hughes-Hallett, *Heroes*, pp. 227–325, esp. pp. 323–4, and pp. 590–1.

[91] Darke, *Monument guide*, pp. 104–6; *ILN* 93 (14 July 1888), 41–50; ibid. (21 July 1888), 76.

[92] Roland Quinault, 'The cult of the centenary, c. 1784–1914', *Historical Research* 71 (1998), 303–23; Paul Connerton, *How societies remember* (Cambridge: Cambridge University Press, 1989), pp. 63–4.

a town of any size that had not graced its main square, town hall, or railway station with a monument to a famous son, be he a 'sea-dog', an explorer, a philanthropist, a poet, an industrialist, or indeed an inventor. Grantham had staked in bronze its claim to Newton, and Stratford, its to Shakespeare; Winchester would open the new century with its millennium tribute to King Alfred, another historical figure venerated by the Victorians.[93] Political campaigners strove to memorialize their martyrs or mark their collective achievements in similar fashion, with a keen eye to the symbolism of place.[94] At an official level, the redesigned Parliament Square and the newly rebuilt Palace of Westminster offered prestigious 'sacred sites' for the commemoration of political figures; the National Portrait Gallery spread its net a little more widely.[95] Amidst this diversity, there were a few men and one woman who attracted nationwide devotion, evinced by a host of statues – Sir Robert Peel, the duke of Wellington, Prince Albert and Queen Victoria.[96] 'Statumania' was effectively launched by the death of Peel in 1850 and exhausted by that of Victoria (who amassed over thirty posthumous statues) in 1901. Measured by monuments, the monarchy, its statesmen and its armed forces undoubtedly continued to provide Britain's greatest heroes, while the tragic figures of Antarctic exploration, led by Captain Scott, inspired Edwardian Britain to an orgy of grief and a late flourish of memorials to a relatively novel type of hero.[97] Yet, as in Comte's *Calendar*, there remained many niches to which the next rank could aspire – among them, inventors.

[93] Darke, *Monument guide*, pp. 158–9, 191, and passim; Fara, 'Isaac Newton lived here', 413–20; Joanne M. Parker, 'The day of a thousand years: Winchester's 1901 commemoration of Alfred the Great', *Studies in Medievalism* 12 (2002), 113–36.

[94] Madge Dresser, 'Set in stone? Statues and slavery in London', *History Workshop Journal* 64 (2007, in press); Pickering and Tyrrell, 'The public memorial of reform', p. 5; Morton, *William Wallace*, pp. 112–33.

[95] Burch, 'Shaping symbolic space', pp. 228–31; Paul Barlow, 'Facing the past and present: the National Portrait Gallery and the search for "authentic" portraiture', in Joanna Woodall (ed.), *Portraiture: facing the subject* (Manchester: Manchester University Press, 1997), pp. 219–38.

[96] Read, *Victorian sculpture*, pp. 95–7; Tori Smith, '"A grand work of noble conception"; the Victoria Memorial and imperial London', in Felix Driver and David Gilbert (eds.), *Imperial cities: landscape, display and identity* (Manchester: Manchester University Press, 1999), pp. 22–3; Darke, *Monument guide*, pp. 13–14, and passim.

[97] Max Jones, *The last great quest: Captain Scott's Antarctic sacrifice* (Oxford: Oxford University Press, 2003), pp. 132–59, 295–6, and passim; Max Jones, ' "Our king upon his knees": the public commemoration of Captain Scott's last Antarctic expedition', in Cubitt and Warren (eds.), *Heroic reputations*, pp. 105–22. For an important precedent, see John MacKenzie, 'The iconography of the exemplary life: the case of David Livingstone', in ibid., pp. 84–104.

Synopsis: the contingency of reputation

Inventors today are as unheroic as public statuary is unfashionable. We have lost the medium as well as the message. The Victorian age was exceptional. The second half of the nineteenth century witnessed a brief interlude in British history when inventors enjoyed widespread popular acclaim and the nature of invention was subjected to intense public debate. This book explores the reasons for the inventor's sudden rise to heroic stature and equally sudden fall. At its heart is the premise that heroes are made, not born. Reputation is contingent on specific cultural values. However magnificent an individual's achievements may be, fame and honour hinge on a particular society's estimation of them and how it chooses to interpret them. In Chapters 2 and 3, I suggest why it was unlikely that British inventors would be perceived in heroic terms before the mid-eighteenth century, and why that began to change. Not only was invention believed to be a divine attribute, which mortals emulated at their peril, but the dubious activities of seventeenth-century 'patentees' and 'projectors' engendered a deep distrust of inventors that could only be overcome by manifest success. Without the ostentatious growth of manufacturing industries and other marvels, such as balloon flight and smallpox vaccination, it seems unlikely that this distrust would have evaporated. Nor, without the Enlightenment's philosophical re-evaluations of humanity's place in the universe could society have allowed human 'creators' to infringe the divine monopoly with impunity, let alone to take all the credit.

Yet, the early nineteenth century was still far from perceiving inventors as heroes. It took the vested interests of a political faction – with a middle-class wind in its sails – to attempt that unexpected, even shocking leap into the national pantheon on behalf of James Watt in 1824. This is the subject of Chapter 4. In the following chapter, we explore the cultural shift in the perception of inventors, invention and manufacturing industry that was accelerated by Watt's glorification, and the way it affected both society's treatment of inventors and the narration of the industrial revolution by contemporary historians. Chapter 6 demonstrates that this bourgeois challenge to aristocratic cultural dominance did not go uncontested among radical activists. Angry at the prospect of Watt's reputation being pressed into the service of industrial capitalism, radicals immediately sought to recapture it for the cause of working men.

The following four chapters move the analysis forward, examining the factors that, from the mid-nineteenth century, promoted the pantheon's expansion beyond Watt to celebrate a new generation of inventors and innovative engineers. Chapter 7 acts as a bridge between the century's two halves, allowing us to trace the emergence of an heroic elite among the civil engineers, led by the Brunel and Stephenson father-and-son partnerships. In the next chapter, we investigate the impact of the Great Exhibition of 1851 and the idolizing of inventors as heroes of peace and free trade, which was severely tried by the outbreak of war in 1854. Simultaneously, as we see in Chapter 9, heroic concepts of invention were being interrogated under the spotlight of the 'patent controversy', which erupted in 1852. Competing theories of technological change, which were elaborated to attack the patent system, threatened to undermine the inventor's status. Chapter 10 picks up the theme of Chapter 6, to examine how and why skilled workers celebrated particular inventors as representatives of their own contribution to Britain's industrial preeminence. I suggest that in the 1860s this took on an added political dimension as they campaigned for the extension of the parliamentary franchise.

If the inventor was a national hero for the Victorians, how could he so quickly return to obscurity and a reputation for eccentricity in the twentieth century? Chapters 11 and 12 explore the reasons for his demise, which was foreshadowed even before the First World War set a new commemorative agenda, and an epilogue briefly pursues his fortunes into the twenty-first century. By 1914, an elite few had been ensconced in the national pantheon: their achievements had been written into the grand narrative of the industrial revolution, and their names would thereby enter the historical record and lay claim to posthumous fame.[98] It is principally these men who, at the start of the twenty-first century, continue to form the British people's idea of 'the inventor' – who he is, how he works, what he achieves and that he is indeed a 'he'.[99] Consequently, it is important to understand how this archetype was born and to ask whether it matters that it is now so badly out of date.

---

[98] Coleman, *Myth, history and the industrial revolution*, pp. 36–42.

[99] Judith McGaw, 'Inventors and other great women: toward a feminist history of technological luminaries', *T&C* 38 (1997), 214–31; Autumn Stanley, 'Once and future power: women as inventors', *Women's Studies International Forum* 15 (1992), 193–202; Susan McDaniel, Helene Cummins, and Rachelle Spender Beauchamp, 'Mothers of invention? Meshing the roles of inventor, mother and worker', *Women's Studies International Forum* 11 (1988), 1–12.

2   The new Prometheus

'For upon every invention of value we erect a statue to the inventor, and give him a liberal and honourable reward.'[1] Anyone who has read this proposal in Sir Francis Bacon's utopian fable, *New Atlantis*, might not be surprised to find monuments to James Watt and other inventors adorning the squares and public buildings of British cities. Surprise, nonetheless, would be appropriate because, during most of the two centuries between Bacon's paean to inventors and Watt's apotheosis in 1824, British inventors were generally perceived in anything but a heroic light. They struggled to emerge from a web of ideas and prejudice which, at best, regarded them as the passive instruments of God's providence and, at worst, mistrusted them as dangerous visionaries, or charlatans and fraudsters. While Protestant theologians might interpret inventions as one of the mysterious ways in which an omnipotent Deity intervened in human affairs, another scholarly tradition took the mythical rebel, Prometheus, as its model of individual creativity. Ominously, Prometheus had incurred a dreadful punishment for stealing fire from the gods – a transgression that allowed mankind to challenge the divine monopoly of knowledge and assert its independence. These myths were an expression of the anxiety and ambivalence with which innovation was generally regarded in early modern Europe.

In Britain, such fears were exacerbated by the monarchy's abuse of patents for invention, at a time when society was wrestling with the novel risks associated with investment in speculative business ventures or 'projects'. Indeed, there was little awareness of the inventor, much more of the 'projector' and 'patentee' (whose project carried the specious warrant of a royal patent). Implicated in the controversy over monopolies

---

[1] Francis Bacon, *The advancement of learning and New Atlantis*, ed. Thomas Case (London: Oxford University Press, 1951), pp. 297–8. It is unknown when Bacon wrote the *New Atlantis*, though his diaries indicate the conception of such a utopia by 1608: Julian Martin, *Francis Bacon, the state and the reform of natural philosophy* (Cambridge: Cambridge University Press, 1992), p. 213, n. 66.

that had helped to destabilize the early Stuart monarchy in the prelude to civil war, and subsequently in the stock-market boom of the early 1690s, their credit plummeted again in the infamous South Sea Bubble of 1717–20.[2] Only gradually would the technically adept inventor succeed in dispelling the image of the quack patentee and the mendacious projector. Meanwhile, his reputation was endangered from another direction: mechanical devices, which might delight and amuse the elite, threatened to impoverish working people. Machine-breaking riots acted as a customary deterrent to their introduction but, as the eighteenth-century state withdrew from regulation of the labour market, the spectres of technological unemployment and loss of skilled status returned.[3] Inventors who produced new labour-saving devices risked incurring the wrath, even the violence, of marginalized workers.

The heroes of *New Atlantis*

In 1592, Francis Bacon, then a young lawyer in the service of the earl of Essex, announced his aspiration to harness knowledge to the advantage of the Crown.[4] In a learned entertainment, which he devised for Elizabeth I's court, Bacon asserted that the goal of intellectual inquiry went beyond the 'delight' and 'contentment' conventionally associated with contemplation: it should be 'to produce worthy effects and to endow the life of man with infinite commodities'.[5] With his audience probably still reeling from his extraordinary redefinition of the philosopher's role, Bacon advocated a wholesale reform in the methods of enquiry: nothing could be learned from the books of the 'great reputed authors'; his 'philosopher of nature' would cogitate instead a host of new observations and the results of fresh experimentation. Not that Bacon proposed an unseemly descent into the ranks of the 'empirics'; rather, he would loftily extract new knowledge from the 'industrious observations, grounded conclusions, and profitable inventions and discoveries' gathered by his subordinates.[6] He aimed to accelerate the discovery of useful knowledge by

[2] Christine MacLeod, 'The 1690s patents boom: invention or stock-jobbing?', *EHR* 39 (1986), 549–71.

[3] Joan Thirsk and J. P. Cooper (eds.), *17th century economic documents* (Oxford: Clarendon Press, 1972), pp. 294–5; C. R. Dobson, *Masters and journeymen: a prehistory of industrial relations, 1717–1800* (London: Croom Helm, 1980), pp. 27, 160–8.

[4] Martin, *Francis Bacon*, pp. 60–71; Pamela O. Long, 'Power, patronage, and the authorship of *Ars*: from mechanical know-how to mechanical knowledge in the last scribal age', *Isis* 88 (1997), 4.

[5] Francis Bacon, 'Of tribute, or giving what is due' (1592), quoted in Martin, *Francis Bacon*, p. 66.

[6] Martin, *Francis Bacon*, pp. 66–7.

endowing the methods of craftsmen with more intelligent and systematic procedures. While he acknowledged the 'change ... in the world' produced by the Renaissance triad of inventions (printing, artillery and the compass), he belittled their novelty and scorned them as 'stumbled upon and lighted on by chance': a well-ordered system of inquiry, he declared, would produce many similar 'worthy effects', and ultimately the 'command' of nature herself.[7] Not only, however, did Bacon's programme endorse artisanal goals and methods, but he also insisted that the 'mechanical or experimental arts' were themselves an essential subject for study. His was no linear model of technological change derived from the application of 'science', but a reciprocal exchange of knowledge, in which an investigation of 'artificial' techniques and processes led to new understandings of nature.[8]

In the *New Atlantis*, Bacon envisaged 'an imperial monarchy sustained by natural philosophy'.[9] He imagined a major state institution whose goal was 'the knowledge of causes, and secret motions of things; and the enlarging of the bounds of human empire, to the effecting of all things possible.'[10] In the magnificent research facilities of 'Solomon's House', two integrated hierarchies of thirty-six 'brethren' (an elite of state employees) collected and processed information according to Bacon's prescription for the inductive production of natural knowledge. At the apex of the first hierarchy, three 'dowry-men or benefactors' devoted their time to 'looking into the experiments of their fellows, and cast about how to draw out of them things of use and practice for man's life and knowledge'.[11] The

---

[7] Ibid., pp. 67–8; Charles Webster, *The great instauration: science, medicine and reform, 1626–1660* (London: Duckworth, 1975), pp. 335–42. For the Renaissance's celebration of 'modern' inventions, see Alex Keller, 'Mathematical technologies and the growth of the idea of technical progress in the sixteenth century', in Allen G. Debus (ed.), *Science, medicine and society in the Renaissance: essays to honor Walter Pagel*, 2 vols. (London: Heinemann, 1972), vol. I, pp. 18–22; Roy S. Wolper, 'The rhetoric of gunpowder and the idea of progress', *JHI* 31 (1970), 589–91; George Basalla, *The evolution of technology* (Cambridge: Cambridge University Press, 1988), p. 130.

[8] Martin, *Francis Bacon*, pp. 152–4. See also M. E. Prior, 'Bacon's man of science', *JHI* 15 (1954), 348–55; Rexmond C. Cochrane, 'Francis Bacon and the rise of the mechanical arts in eighteenth-century England', *Annals of Science* 12 (1956), 137–56; Paolo Rossi, *Philosophy, technology and the arts in the early modern era*, trans. Salvator Attanasio, ed. Benjamin Nelson (New York and London: Harper & Row, 1970), pp. 117–21; Webster, *Great instauration*, pp. 326–33.

[9] Martin, *Francis Bacon*, pp. 134–40, quotation on p. 135.

[10] Bacon, *Advancement of learning*, p. 288.

[11] Ibid., pp. 296–7. Martin's description of the hierarchy is misleading, in placing the 'dowry-men' as the final link in the entire structure and thereby wrongly implying a model in which theoretical science is applied to technology: Martin, *Francis Bacon*, pp. 137–8.

whole group would then decide how to advance their research by subjecting this new knowledge to 'more penetrating' experiments, which would in turn permit 'greater' inferences. It would also debate which of their discoveries should be published 'and which not': perhaps surprisingly, they did not reveal everything even to the state – some they saw 'fit to keep secret'.[12]

In a discordant sequel to this carefully developed model of collective discovery and invention, Bacon endorsed the elevation of individual 'inventors' to heroic status. He describes 'two very long and fair galleries' in Solomon's House, one of which is a museum of all 'the more rare and excellent inventions', the other a pantheon where 'we place the statues of all principal inventors'.

> There we have the statue of your Columbus, that discovered the West Indies; also the inventor of ships; your monk [Roger Bacon] that was the inventor of ordnance and gunpowder; the inventor of music; the inventor of letters; the inventor of printing; the inventor of observations of astronomy; the inventor of works in metal; the inventor of glass; the inventor of silk of the worm; the inventor of wine; the inventor of corn and bread; the inventor of sugars; and all these by more certain tradition than you have... For upon every invention of value we erect a statue to the inventor, and give him a liberal and honourable reward.[13]

Bacon thus slips from radical philosopher of knowledge, aware of the incremental development of techniques (characteristic of the skilled crafts), to his role as the Crown's law officer, responsible for the administration of letters patent, which enshrined the notion of a single inventor.[14] In his list of great inventors – all anonymous except for Columbus – Bacon jumbles the usual totems of 'modern' ingenuity with arts known in the ancient world and even in prehistory, where the notion of an individual inventor is even less plausible.[15] He may have pondered the

---

[12] Bacon, *Advancement of learning*, p. 297. Bacon, the state servant who was acutely aware that 'knowledge is power', did not expand on what sort of knowledge he believed too dangerous to be in the possession of either state or public: Martin, *Francis Bacon*, pp. 138–9.

[13] Bacon, *Advancement of learning*, pp. 297–8.

[14] Bacon became Solicitor General in 1607 and Attorney General in 1613. For the law officers' role in the administration of patents, see MacLeod, *Inventing the industrial revolution*, pp. 40–1.

[15] For Ancient Greek and Roman ideas about inventors and 'intellectual property', see Pamela O. Long, 'Invention, authorship, "intellectual property," and the origins of patents: notes toward a conceptual history', *T&C* 32 (1991), 846–70; Agnès Bérenger, 'Le statut de l'invention dans la Rome impériale: entre méfiance et valorisation', in Marie-Sophy Corcy, Christiane Douyère-Demeulenaere, and Liliane Hilaire-Pérez (eds.), *Les archives de l'invention: Ecrits, objets et images de l'activité inventive, de l'Antiquité à nos jours* (Toulouse: CNRS-Université Toulouse-Le Mirail, Collections Méridiennes, 2007), 513–25.

example of Filippo Brunelleschi, the architect of the stupendous dome of Florence's cathedral, whose claim to 'the glory that rightly belongs to the inventor' had been recognized by the city, not only in the highly advantageous patent it granted him, but also in its posthumous tribute in 1444.[16] On his tomb in the cathedral (adorned with a portrait bust), Brunelleschi's epitaph reads: 'Not only this celebrated temple with its marvellous shell but also the many machines his divine genius invented can document how Filippo the architect excelled in the Daedalian art.'[17] Renaissance Italy created the concept of the inventive genius, but it was to be nearly four centuries before western Europe began to take it seriously and to celebrate inventors in the way that Florence commemorated Brunelleschi.

Bacon's concern for the glorification and encouragement of inventors found echoes in several other (fruitless) schemes for social and political reform published in mid-seventeenth-century England.[18] A direct and immediate reward, financial or honorary, was proposed by several natural philosophers in the circle of Samuel Hartlib, as well as by Gerrard Winstanley, the Digger.[19] The author, 'RH' (possibly Robert Hooke), of a self-professed continuation of *New Atlantis*, which was dedicated to the newly restored Charles II in 1660, devoted seventeen pages to the marvellous discoveries and inventions made on 'Salomon's Island'; thirteen of

[16] Frank D. Prager, 'A manuscript of Taccola, quoting Brunelleschi, on problems of inventors and builder', *Proceedings of the American Philosophical Society* 112 (1968), 138–42; Frank D. Prager and Gustina Scaglia, *Mariano Taccola and his book 'De Ingeniis'* (Cambridge, MA: MIT Press, 1972), pp. 11–13, both cited in Pamela O. Long, *Openness, secrecy, authorship: technical arts and the culture of knowledge from antiquity to the renaissance* (Baltimore and London: Johns Hopkins University Press, 2001), pp. 98–9. For Brunelleschi's patent, see Long, *Openness, secrecy, authorship*, pp. 96–7; Christopher May, 'Antecedents to intellectual property: the European prehistory of the ownership of knowledge', *HT* 24 (2002), 13–14.
[17] Isabelle Hyman (ed.), *Brunelleschi in perspective* (Englewood Cliffs, NJ: Prentice-Hall, 1974), p. 24, cited (and 'translation slightly altered') in Long, *Openness, secrecy, authorship*, p. 99. See also Christine Smith, *Architecture in the culture of early humanism: ethics, aesthetics, and eloquence, 1400–1470* (New York: Oxford University Press, 1992), pp. 27–8, and Long, 'Invention, authorship', 878–84. For early Italian patents more generally, also see P. J. Federico, 'Origin and early history of patents', *Journal of the Patent Office Society* 11 (1929), 293; Marcus Popplow, 'Protection and promotion: privileges for inventions and books of machines in the early modern period', *HT* 20 (1998), 103–24; Carlo Marco Belfanti, 'Guilds, patents, and the circulation of technical knowledge: northern Italy during the early modern age', *T&C* 45 (2004), 569–89.
[18] For contrasting views on Bacon's influence in the seventeenth century, see Michael Hunter, *Science and society in Restoration England* (Cambridge: Cambridge University Press, 1981), pp. 14–21, and Webster, *Great instauration*, pp. 25, 96–7, 491–505, and passim. For his subsequent influence, see Herbert Weisinger, 'English treatment of the relationship between the rise of science and the Renaissance, 1740–1840', *Annals of Science* 7 (1951), 260–6.
[19] Gerrard Winstanley, *The law of freedom*, ed. Christopher Hill (Harmondsworth, 1973), pp. 355–6, 365; Webster, *Great instauration*, pp. 370–5.

these described the elaborate ceremonies which rewarded 'the ingenious Verdugo', with all the honour and glory normally reserved for the victors of war. The individual's role in invention is underlined by the importance which 'RH' attached to recording the invention for posterity, so that it 'should not perish with the author'.[20] Neither was it overlooked in Thomas Sprat's *History of the Royal Society* (1667), despite the Society's endorsement of 'Baconian' collective and craft-based methods in its projected histories of trades. Sprat announced that 'Invention is an heroic thing', which required boldness, courage and impetuosity – 'a large, and an unbounded mind' – to overcome the many difficulties 'with which a mean heart would be broken'.[21] Heroic and collective concepts of invention both co-existed with more pious, providential explanations that attributed inventions to a divine master-plan, generally with little thought given to resolving the tensions among them.[22]

Yet, in these circles, acutely aware of the chaos and bloodshed of the recent civil war, a radical challenge was issued to the traditional heroes of the battlefield.[23] Just as 'the ingenious Verdugo' usurped the warriors' honours on 'Salomon's Island', so some early fellows of the Royal Society counter-posed the humanitarian benefits of investigating the natural world to the catastrophic effects of waging war. Henry Power spoke admiringly of 'the winged souls of our modern heroes', who had bestowed useful inventions on the world.[24] John Evelyn was more specific, naming his heroes of discovery and invention, and raising them above the warriors whom the Ancients had worshipped:

I had rather be the author of one good and beneficial invention, than to have been Julius Caesar, or the great Alexander himself; and do range the names of a Gilbert, a Bacon, a Harvey, a Gutenberge [sic], Columbus, Goia, Metius, Janellius, Thyco [sic], Galileo … who gave us the use of the load-stone, taught us the art of printing; found out the circulation of the blood, detected new worlds, invented the telescope, and other opticall glasses, engines and automates, amongst the heroes, whom they deifi'd, and placed above the stars; because they were the authors of ten thousand

---

[20] *New Atlantis, begun by the Lord Verulam, Viscount St Albans: and continued by R. H. Esquire* (London, 1660), pp. 53–70. See also Adrian Johns, *The nature of the book: print and knowledge in the making* (Chicago and London: University of Chicago Press, 1998), pp. 480–91.

[21] Thomas Sprat, *History of the Royal Society* (London, 1667), p. 392 and passim, quoted in Hope Mason, *Value of creativity*, pp. 66–7. By 'invention', Sprat may, of course, have intended what we understand by 'discovery'.

[22] MacLeod, *Inventing the industrial revolution*, pp. 201–4.

[23] Johnson, 'An age without a hero?', 26–31; Folkenflik, 'Johnson's heroes', 144–5.

[24] Henry Power, *Experimental philosophy* (London, 1664), pp. 190–1, quoted in Richard Foster Jones, *Ancients and moderns: a study of the rise of the scientific movement in seventeenth century England* (2nd edn, Berkeley and Los Angeles: University of California Press, 1965), p. 327 n. 38.

more worthy things, than those who had never been named but for their bloodshed and cruelty, pride and prodigious lusts ... but for the pens of such great genius's and learned men, of whom some of them did the least deserve.[25]

It was to be the 1790s before such opinions surfaced again in any number, and a renewed challenge was issued to the celebration of military heroism that had dominated Great Britain's bellicose eighteenth century.[26] In the interim, the inventor's aspirations to glory suffered from a long hiatus of neglect and distrust.

Projectors and patentees

Ironically, scarcely had his *New Atlantis* proposed that inventors be treated as heroes than Bacon was implicated in a political controversy that tarnished their collective reputation. The Crown's abuse of letters patent to reward courtiers and their clients with monopoly licences provoked popular outrage.[27] Bacon was impeached for taking bribes and briefly imprisoned in the Tower – the scapegoat sacrificed to protect James I and VI and the duke of Buckingham from Parliament's fury.[28] The more lasting outcome was the Statute of Monopolies (21 Jac. I. c. 3), which in 1624 recognized the value of new inventions by exempting them from its general proscription of letters patent, and thereby established the idiosyncratic statutory foundation of England's patent system. Unfortunately, there remained loopholes elsewhere in the act, which the Crown continued to exploit until, amidst a deafening outcry in 1640, the Long Parliament suppressed the whole system.[29]

'Monopoly' had become a bugbear and the word retained its deeply pejorative force for at least two centuries.[30] The inventor almost disappeared in this cacophony of protest: a patentee was equated with a monopolist, who extorted high prices from the consumer and condemned honest tradesmen to financial ruin. A mid-seventeenth-century engraving, attributed to Wenceslaus Hollar, conveys unambiguously his negative image (figure 2.1).[31] It depicts the 'Patenty' as a wolf-faced pedlar: his clothes are studded with patents (monopolies) for everyday items, from salt and

---

[25] Gabriel Naudé, *Instructions concerning erecting of a library, interpreted by J. Evelyn* (London, 1661), Dedication, quoted in Jones, *Ancients and moderns*, p. 328 n. 38.

[26] See below, pp. 69–74.   [27] Webster, *Great instauration*, pp. 343–6.

[28] Markku Peltonen, 'Bacon, Francis, Viscount St Alban (1561–1626)', *ODNB* online edn, May 2006, www.oxforddnb.com/view/article/990, accessed 18 October 2006.

[29] MacLeod, *Inventing the industrial revolution*, pp. 14–15, 17–19. The patent system was restored, with Charles II, in 1660.

[30] Ibid., pp. 15–17.

[31] R. Pennington, *A descriptive catalogue of the etched work of Wenceslaus Hollar, 1607–1677* (Cambridge: Cambridge University Press, 1982), pp. 72–3.

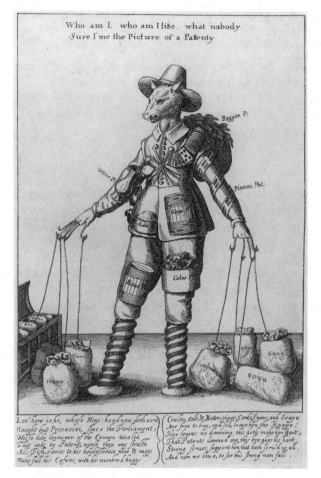

2.1 *The Patenty*, a mid-seventeenth-century engraving attributed to Wenceslaus Hollar (1607–77), encapsulates contemporary hostility towards monopolists, who controlled the sale of everyday items by royal letters patent.

soap to pipes and playing cards; his pack contains patent rags; his fingers are metal hooks that grasp the bulging moneybags in his coffers; his screw-like legs have 'screw'd us all'. The accompanying verse calls the patentee:

> Wolfe like devourer of the Common wealth
> That robs by Patent, worse than any stealth.

By implication, 'patentee' was synonymous with fraudster, cheat or swindler, effectively a criminal.

While the later Stuarts preserved the patent system from further taint of royal malpractice,[32] it suffered by implication in the excesses of London's burgeoning stock market, especially during the 'bubbles' of the early 1690s and 1717–20.[33] Consequently, it was less as 'monopolists', more as 'projectors' that eighteenth-century inventors tended to be distrusted by the public.[34] The 1690s speculative mania, which for the first time seriously exposed the naïve ebullience of English commercial society, made a deep impression on Daniel Defoe, then a young trader in London. Badly duped by a 'patent-monger' and bankrupted, Defoe returned to the fray, determined this time to keep his wits about him. In *An essay upon projects* (1697), he proposed various ingenious schemes, designed not to make money but to reform key sectors of England's economy and society. The *Essay* encapsulates Defoe's 'vision of what a progressive England could be, or what the projecting spirit could achieve'.[35] As an essential first step, however, he had to convince his readers not to reject all projectors and their schemes out of hand. Like Defoe himself, the public needed to learn how to discriminate between the deceitful type of projector who 'turn their thoughts to private methods of trick and cheat, a modern way of thieving ... by which honest men are gull'd with fair pretences to part from their money' and the genuine variety who 'urg'd by the same necessity, turn their thoughts to honest invention, founded upon the platform of ingenuity and integrity'.[36] It was far from an easy lesson: the examples which Defoe gave of stock-jobbed inventions – a diving bell, saltpetre production and 'windmills to draw water' – were ostensibly as plausible as those he gave of successful projects that had proved their initial detractors wrong, starting with Noah's Ark and continuing through to William Lee's knitting frame, London's water supply and Dockwra's Penny Post.[37] Neither

---

[32] MacLeod, *Inventing the industrial revolution*, pp. 20–39.

[33] D. C. Coleman, *The economy of England, 1450–1750* (Oxford: Oxford University Press, 1977), pp. 169–70; W. R. Scott, *The constitution and finance of English, Scottish and Irish joint-stock companies to 1720*, 3 vols. (Cambridge: Cambridge University Press, 1912), vol. II, ch. 17; vol. III, passim.

[34] MacLeod, '1690s patents boom', 557–69.

[35] Daniel Defoe, *An essay upon projects*, ed. Joyce D. Kennedy, Michael Siedel, Maximilian E. Novak (New York: AMS Press, c. 1999), pp. xxvii–xlii, quotation on p. xliii. See Paula R. Backscheider, 'Defoe, Daniel (1660?–1731)', *ODNB*, www.oxforddnb.com/view/article/7421, accessed 15 September 2006.

[36] Defoe, *Essay upon projects*, p. 17; see also ibid., pp. xxiii–xxvi. For the positive contribution of projectors to the early modern economy, see Joan Thirsk, *Economic policy and projects: the development of a consumer society in early modern England* (Oxford: Oxford University Press, 1978).

[37] Defoe, *Essay upon projects*, pp. 10–15, 18.

did Defoe's use of the term 'projector' for both categories lessen the confusion: although he employs it neutrally at this point, his connotations are generally negative.[38] If it was Defoe's intention to demonstrate that discrimination was indeed very difficult so that investors should scrutinize every project with extreme care, this did little to extricate the reputation of the inventor from the 'contempt ... [which] bespatters the other, who like cuckolds bear the reproach of other people's crimes'.[39]

When Defoe resumed his analysis of the credibility of projectors and new inventions around 1720, the investing public had recently demonstrated again that its fear of projectors could be lulled and its scepticism suspended by the prospect of spectacular gains.[40] While conservative critics condemned the moral weakness, both personal and national, that led to disaster on the Exchange, Defoe was among those who insisted that the phoenix of economic growth and individual fortune would continue to rise from the financial ashes – the Bubble might be diabolical but, through God's providence, right understanding would lead to ultimate success.[41] To thrive in the commercial world meant not withdrawing but playing the game more expertly – acquiring the knowledge by which to assess the schemes and inventions for which projectors sought one's capital. As Larry Stewart has argued, this demand for greater understanding of innovations boosted the careers of natural philosophers, who demonstrated mechanics and hydraulics in the coffee houses of London and advised opportunistic landowners and entrepreneurs on the feasibility of their own and others' projects.[42] Unlike thirty years before, in the 1720s the demand for patents for invention did not falter,

---

[38] Ibid., p. xliv, n. 7.   [39] Ibid., p. 17.

[40] For an authoritative account of the South Sea Bubble, see John Carswell, *The South Sea Bubble* (rev. edn, Stroud: Alan Sutton, 1993); Peter M. Garber, *Famous first bubbles: the fundamentals of early manias* (London and Cambridge, MA: MIT Press, 2000).

[41] Simon Schaffer, 'Defoe's natural philosophy and the worlds of credit', in John Christie and Sally Shuttleworth (eds.), *Nature transfigured: science and literature, 1700–1900* (Manchester and New York: Manchester University Press, 1989), pp. 25–7, 30–7. As Schaffer emphasizes, Defoe's faith in commerce and credit was far from a commonplace in Augustan society: ibid., p. 37.

[42] Larry R. Stewart, *The rise of public science: rhetoric, technology, and natural philosophy in Newtonian Britain, 1660–1750* (Cambridge: Cambridge University Press, 1992), pp. 285–6, 333–5, 388–90; see also Larry Stewart, 'Public lectures and private patronage in Newtonian England', *Isis* 77 (1986), 47–58; A. J. G. Cummings and Larry Stewart, 'The case of the eighteenth-century projector: entrepreneurs, engineers, and legitimacy at the Hanoverian court in Britain', in Bruce T. Moran (ed.), *Patronage and institutions: science, technology, and medicine at the European court, 1500–1750* (Rochester, NY and Woodbridge: Boydell, 1991), pp. 235–61; Simon Schaffer, 'The show that never ends: perpetual motion in the early eighteenth century', *BJHS* 28 (1995), 185–7.

and throughout the century short-term surges of speculation on financial markets were to be reflected in patenting peaks.[43]

In sharp contrast with Defoe's policy of informed engagement, Jonathan Swift believed no honest projector existed. Only recently has the third part of Swift's *Gulliver's Travels*, the 'Voyage to Laputa', begun to attract the same scholarly interest as the other three elements of this great satire. Challenging the common identification of the 'Academy of Projectors of Lagado' with the early Royal Society, Pat Rogers suggests a more contemporary target for Swift's parody in the welter of projects and patents floated in Exchange Alley during the South Sea Bubble.[44] Just like the jobbers whom Defoe excoriated, Swift's projectors lured the gullible into fantastic engineering schemes, then when 'the work miscarried, the projectors went off' to draw other dupes into 'the same experiment'.[45] John Christie advises, however, against distinguishing too sharply between the Royal Society and the Exchange: 'they are in truth the same place, identified as one in their fanatically based creation of illusory goals.'[46] The flying island of Laputa ('the whore' in Italian) is Swift's dystopian inversion of Bacon's scientific and political utopia in *New Atlantis*, a demonstration of the hegemonic political power that is implied by Bacon's hierarchical system for the interrogation of nature in Solomon's House. This philosophical tyranny, Swift suggests, was tragically futile, for their experiments – to extract sunbeams from cucumbers, food from excrement – were all 'fruitless reversals of productive natural processes' which had reduced the land to infertility and the people to abject misery.[47] The Laputans were fanatics and mute quantifiers, whose language lacked any word for 'imagination, fancy and invention'; Swift dubs their fanatical scheme a 'project'.[48] Under this heading, Swift, the Tory radical, subsumes all the innovations he considers a threat to society, politics and salvation: the marriage between the new science and the stock exchange is one truly made in Hell.

---

[43] MacLeod, *Inventing the industrial revolution*, pp. 150–7.

[44] Pat Rogers, 'Gulliver and the engineers', *Modern Language Review* 70 (1975), 260–70; see also Arthur E. Case, *Four essays on Gulliver's Travels* (Princeton, NJ: Princeton University Press, 1950), pp. 97–107.

[45] *The prose works of Jonathan Swift*, ed. Herbert Davis, 14 vols. (rev. edn, Oxford: Basil Blackwell, 1959), vol. XI, pp. 177–8, quoted in Rogers, 'Gulliver and the engineers', p. 261.

[46] John R. R. Christie, 'Laputa revisited', in Christie and Shuttleworth (eds.), *Nature transfigured*, pp. 45–60, quotation on p. 60.

[47] Ibid., pp. 54–6.

[48] Ibid., pp. 56–9. The theme of the threat of science to religion (and Swift's disparagement of *Robinson Crusoe* in the 'Voyage to Laputa') is convincingly demonstrated in Dennis Todd, 'Laputa, the Whore of Babylon, and the Idols of Science', *Studies in Philology* 75 (1978), 93–120.

If the inventor still struggled to throw off the slur of 'projector', 'patentee' was little better. There were good reasons for this. In part, many inventors were over-sanguine, had a poor grasp of scientific principles and underestimated the difficulties of reducing a good technical idea to commercial practice. Moreover, the patent system suffered from the government's benign neglect: loosely administered, with its regulation left largely to the hazards of litigation, its users exploited it in a variety of heterodox ways (as well as to protect technically and legally sound inventions).[49] The Patent, a poem (1776), which attacked corruption in high places, equated the minimal competence of George III's government with the value of the king's patents for invention, mocking their frequently exaggerated claims:

> Hail to the Patent! Which enables Man
> To vend a Folio ... or a Warming-pan,
> This makes the Windlass work with double force,
> And Smoke-jacks whirl more rapid in their course;
> Confers a sanction on the Doctor's pill,
> Oft known to cure, but oft'ner known to kill,
> What man would scruple to resign his breath,
> Provided he could die a Patent death.[50]

In a revealing comment, James Watt advised Matthew Boulton against their joining an association of patentees, which was being established for mutual defence following the annulment of Richard Arkwright's patent. Apart from good strategic and possibly legal reasons against such an alliance, Watt remarked, 'the greater number of patentees are such as we could not associate with, and if we did it would do us more harm than good.'[51] Their friend, Erasmus Darwin, similarly fought shy of gaining a reputation as an inventor for fear that it might damage his medical practice.[52]

Gradually, under the guidance of journalists and itinerant lecturers, the British public began to take the 'projecting age' in its stride.[53] Risk came

[49] MacLeod, Inventing the industrial revolution, pp. 75–96.

[50] The patent, a poem, by the author of The Graces (London, 1776). For a similarly sardonic popular song, The patent coffin, by Mr Dibdin (broadsheet, 1818), see Ruth Richardson, Death, dissection and the destitute (new edn, London: Phoenix, 2001), p. 82.

[51] James Watt to Matthew Boulton, 21 July 1785, quoted in Samuel Smiles, The lives of Boulton and Watt (London: John Murray, 1865), p. 347. See also Eric Robinson, 'James Watt and the law of patents', T&C 13 (1972), 115–39; and Jennifer Tann, 'Richard Arkwright and technology', History 58 (1973), 36–41.

[52] D. G. King-Hele, Doctor of revolution: the life and genius of Erasmus Darwin (London: Faber, 1977), p. 81.

[53] Simon Schaffer, 'A social history of plausibility: country, city and calculation in Augustan Britain', in Adrian Wilson (ed.), Rethinking social history: English society 1570–1920 and its

to be accepted as the concomitant of success, and in commercial, if not clerical, circles the mathematical calculation of probabilities began to oust faith in providence.[54] The mid-eighteenth century witnessed a rash of private initiatives to encourage and reward ingenuity, most famously the Society of Arts, founded in London in 1753. Within a decade, the Society's 2,000 members were subscribing over £3,000 a year, to be distributed in premiums and medals to inventors willing to forego a patent; they also invested in the diffusion of best practice through publication and the Society's Repository of Inventions, which was open to public inspection.[55] Not only were such initiatives indicative of a growing respect for inventors, especially among 'the middling sort', but they also helped to raise their prestige by providing them with a new forum at a respectable distance from Exchange Alley.[56] The suspicion of dishonest projectors and monopolists was being redirected away from inventors, most visibly in the work of Adam Smith. Smith equated the 'projector', whose rapacity and chicanery threatened to distort the free-market economy not with the inventor but with the rogue entrepreneur, and commended patents for invention as a rare beneficial monopoly, which allowed the market to reward ingenuity in proportion to its merit.[57]

To the extent that inventors were still seen as 'projectors', it was increasingly as over-ambitious and unrealistic visionaries than as calculating swindlers and cheats. That trusty barometer of social change, Samuel Johnson, opined in 1753 that,

Those who find themselves inclined to censure new undertakings, only because they are new, should consider that the folly of Projection is seldom the folly of a

interpretation (Manchester and New York: Manchester University Press, 1993), pp. 135–44; James Raven, *Judging new wealth: popular publishing and responses to commerce in England, 1750–1800* (Oxford: Clarendon Press, 1992), pp. 9–13, 249–58.

[54] Julian Hoppit, *Risk and failure in English business* (Cambridge: Cambridge University Press, 1987); Julian Hoppit, 'Financial crises in eighteenth-century England', *EHR* 39 (1986), 39–58; Ian Hacking, *The emergence of probability: a philosophical study of early ideas about probability, induction and statistical inference* (Cambridge: Cambridge University Press, 1975), pp. 166–75.

[55] D. G. C. Allan, *William Shipley, founder of the Royal Society of Arts* (London: Hutchinson, 1968), pp. 32–4, 42–57, 67; Sir Henry Trueman Wood, *A history of the Royal Society of Arts* (London: John Murray, 1913), pp. 20–1, 28–46, 243–4; D. Hudson and K. W. Luckhurst, *The Royal Society of Arts, 1754–1954* (London: John Murray, 1956), p. 102; MacLeod, *Inventing the industrial revolution*, pp. 194–6.

[56] Liliane Hilaire-Pérez, *L'invention technique au siècle des Lumières* (Paris: Albin Michel, 2000), pp. 143, 191–209, 321–2; Cochrane, 'Francis Bacon', 144–53; Witt Bowden, *Industrial society in England towards the end of the eighteenth century* (2nd edn, London: Frank Cass & Co., 1965), pp. 24–38.

[57] D. C. Coleman, 'Adam Smith, businessmen, and the mercantile system in England', *History of European Ideas* 9 (1988), 161–70; MacLeod, *Inventing the industrial revolution*, pp. 197, 216–17; Hope Mason, *Value of creativity*, pp. 88–94; Arnold Plant, 'The economic theory concerning patents for invention', *Economica* 1 (1934), 30–51.

fool; it is commonly the ebullition of a capricious mind, crowded with a variety of knowledge, and heated with an intenseness of thought; it proceeds often from the consciousness of uncommon powers, from the confidence of those who, having already done much, are easily persuaded that they can do more.[58]

A similarly tolerant perspective, expressed anonymously three decades later, attested to the deeply ingrained distrust of new inventions, which led to the ill treatment 'of some of the most useful members of society, under the name of *projectors*'. Inventors, it had to be acknowledged, 'are often chimerical and extravagant in their expectations; but whose *warm brains* generate those prolific seeds, those new ideas, and combinations of ideas, which *persevering industry* broods upon, and brings to perfection'.[59] Society, suggested the author, might have to condone eccentricity and some technical and financial catastrophes as the necessary price of brilliant leaps of imagination. Such was the reputation, for example, of Henry Bell, who successfully introduced steam navigation on the Clyde and was described as 'a hero of a thousand blunders and one success'; 'his mind was a chaos of extraordinary projects, the most of which, from his want of accurate scientific calculation, he never could carry into practice.'[60] An early memoir of Richard Arkwright implied that he was no different in kind, only in luck, from the majority of those who sought to enrich themselves through innovation, since the problems of raising capital forced inventors into risky alliances and turned the whole process into a 'lottery'.[61] Even James Watt, when in a more relaxed mood, could describe himself ironically as a 'projector'. Referring to his fellow patentee, Henry Cort, the inventor of important new techniques in the iron industry, Watt told Boulton: 'He seems a simple good-natured man, but not very knowing ... I think him a *brother projector*.'[62]

---

[58] *The Advertiser* 99 (16 October 1753), quoted in Stewart, *Rise of public science*, p. 255.

[59] [T.], *Letters on the utility and policy of employing machines to shorten labour* (London: T. Becket, 1780), pp. 17–18.

[60] 'Henry Bell (1767–1830)', in Robert Chambers (ed.), *A biographical dictionary of eminent Scotsmen*, 4 vols. (Glasgow: Blackie & Son, 1835), vol. I, pp. 194–5 (citing oral information).

[61] 'Arkwright, Sir Richard', in John Aikin MD and Rev. William Enfield LLD (eds.), *General biography; or lives, critical and historical, of the most eminent persons of all ages, countries, conditions, and professions*, 10 vols. (London: G. G. and J. Robinson and Edinburgh: Bell and Badfute, 1799–1815), vol. I, pp. 389–90. 'Railroads and locomotive steam carriages', *Quarterly Review* 42 (1830), 404. See also Edward Morris, *The life of Henry Bell, the practical introducer of the steam-boat into Great Britain and Ireland* (Glasgow: Blackie & Son, 1844) p. 49, where 'projectors' is used non-pejoratively to refer to entrepreneurs who lost money by extending the route of the *Charlotte Dundas* to Inverness.

[62] James Watt to Matthew Boulton, 14 December 1782, quoted in Smiles, *Lives of Boulton and Watt*, p. 327n; my emphasis. Similarly, Thomas Telford referred to William Hazeldine, millwright, ironfounder and inventor, as 'the Arch conjuror himself, Merlin

The machinery question

Some inventors encountered enmity generated by the threat to employment of new labour-saving devices. To many working people, their livelihoods jeopardized by mechanization, inventors must have seemed
traitors to their kind. Arkwright was surely no hero to those (principally
women and their dependents) who saw their income from spinning wool
or cotton disappearing, as production was transferred into the factories.
Parish ratepayers would have shared their anxieties. In October 1779,
with trade depressed, a crowd of 4,000 converged on Arkwright's mill at
Birkacre (Lancs.) and destroyed all the machinery and much of the
building.[63] Eleven years earlier, James Hargreaves reportedly had had
to make a rapid escape, when his house was attacked by Blackburn
weavers, fearful, perhaps, of the impact of his spinning jenny on their
wives' and daughters' incomes from spinning.[64] The inventor of a
machine to spin worsted yarn, Joseph Brookhouse, was burnt in effigy
by a Leicestershire crowd in 1787 and permanently forced out of the area.
There is some suggestion that he and his partners, being Presbyterians,
were treated less than sympathetically by the high Tory corporation,
which contained some rival manufacturers: the rioters chanted 'No
Presbyterians, no machines'.[65]

When hostility to machinery found verbal expression, it was usually
focused on the machines themselves, but sometimes it vilified or mocked
inventors. The wool-combers, for example, formed a powerful body of
male workers, who struggled for half a century to maintain the status and
high wages that their scarce skills brought them; in response, their
employers, the worsted spinners looked to inventors to remove the combers' control over their trade. Although a celebration in song of the
Reverend Edmund Cartwright's invention of a wool-combing machine
('Big Ben') proved to be premature, it was indicative of the way in which
inventors could be drawn into industrial disputes, and illustrates the
process whereby the workers' relationship to new technology might

Hazeldine': Thomas Telford to M. Davidson, 19 February 1796, quoted in Alastair
E. Penfold (ed.) *Thomas Telford: engineer* (London: Thomas Telford Ltd, 1980), p. 17.
See also Lord Dundonald, in 1799, quoted in Dutton, *Patent system*, p. 154.

[63] Andrew Charlesworth et al., *An atlas of industrial protest in Britain, 1750–1990* (London:
Macmillan, 1996), pp. 19–21.

[64] Ibid., p. 18. See also Adrian Randall, *Before the Luddites: custom, community and machinery
in the English woollen industry, 1776–1809* (Cambridge: Cambridge University Press,
1991), pp. 72–5, 234–6.

[65] David L. Wykes, 'The Leicester riots of 1773 and 1787: a study of the victims of popular
protest', *Transactions of the Leicestershire Archaeological and Historical Society* 54 (1978–9),
41–2.

divide them into 'winners' and 'losers'. The song, composed by one of his workers, opened with a hubristic call to 'all ye master combers' to come hear how 'Big Ben' would 'comb more wool in one day than fifty of your men, with their hand-combs and comb-pots'.[66] Shortly afterwards, Cartwright withdrew from business, after an arson attack, in 1792, destroyed the Manchester mill where his patent power-looms were being installed (threatening the jobs of weavers, another group of skilled workers).[67] From the other side of this long-running conflict, a verse heard in Bradford (Yorks.) in 1820 expressed the combers' undisguised delight at the failure of inventors to devise a viable wool-combing machine:

> The comber next employs his ancient art
> Which no machinery can supersede
> In vain the ingenious stretch their utmost skill
> As oft as tried, the expensive schemes of art
> Abortive prove; the comber still employ'd
> Sings at his work and triumphs o'er them all.[68]

A strike by the wool-combers in 1825 drew the threat from a resident of Bradford that combing machinery would soon be 'brought to succeed'; worsted-spinners in Leeds enjoined solidarity among themselves and taunted the strikers with notices that warned, 'No advance – take combers at old prices ... The combers had better turn in and do the work than let it be done by Big Ben.'[69] This strike was credited with having prompted the invention of the Platt and Collier machine (patented in 1827), 'the first really practical device', and a further strike in 1834, with having stimulated its diffusion, although the mechanization of the trade took another twenty years to complete.[70] The monument, which the city of Bradford raised in 1875, to Samuel Cunliffe Lister, who had built his great fortune partly on the invention and patenting of wool-combing

---

[66] Song attributed to Matthew Charlton and quoted in Kenneth G. Ponting (ed.), *A memoir of the life, writings, and mechanical inventions, of Edmund Cartwright, D. D., F. R. S., inventor of the power loom* (London: Adams & Dart, 1971), pp. 105–7.

[67] Ibid., pp. 107–10. See O'Brien, 'Micro foundations of macro invention', 216–18.

[68] J. Nicholson, *The commerce of Bradford* (1820), quoted in Gary Firth, 'The genesis of the industrial revolution in Bradford, 1760–1830', unpublished Ph.D. thesis, University of Bradford (1974), p. 428. See also Kevin Binfield (ed.), *Writings of the Luddites* (Baltimore and London: Johns Hopkins University Press, 2004), pp. 54–5.

[69] James Burnley, *The history of wool and wool-combing* (London: Low, Marston, Searle & Rivington, 1889), pp. 170, 174.

[70] Kristine Bruland, 'Industrial conflict as a source of technical innovation: three cases', *Economy and Society* 11 (1982), 114–17. A further example of this phenomenon was William Fairbairn's invention of a riveting machine: *The life of Sir William Fairbairn, Bart, partly written by himself*, ed. and completed by William Pole [1877], repr. with introduction by A. E. Musson (Newton Abbot: David & Charles, 1970), p. 420.

2.2 Bas-relief on the monument to Samuel Cunliffe Lister, in Lister Park, Bradford, by Matthew Noble (1875), showing the wool-combing machine that Lister claimed to have invented (photograph by the author).

machinery, illustrated on its bas-reliefs both the trade of the wool-combers and the machinery which eventually broke their power and displaced them (figure 2.2).[71]

An example of right action in the eyes of threatened workers was provided by the probably apocryphal story of Laurence Earnshaw, as recounted by John Aikin. Earnshaw, a highly skilled mechanic, 'about 1753, invented a machine to spin and reel cotton at one operation, which he showed to his neighbours and then destroyed, through the generous, though mistaken, apprehension, that it might take bread from the mouths of the poor.' His birthplace was said to be venerated locally almost to the degree that was Isaac Newton's in Woolsthorpe (Lincs.).[72] By contrast, a patentee of spinning machinery, James Taylor of Ashton-under-Lyne

---

[71] For the bas-relief that illustrates hand combing, see Ian Beesley, *Through the mill: the story of Yorkshire wool in photographs* (Clapham: Dalesman Books and National Museum for Photography, Film and Television, 1987), plate 11. Bradford celebrated the inventions and enterprise of Samuel Cunliffe Lister, with only a brief lament for 'the old hand combers who were, so to speak, overwhelmed with the invention', and much rejoicing over the improved working and living conditions that mechanization had brought: *The Times*, 17 May 1875, 12 d–e; see below, pp. 330–2.

[72] John Aikin, *A description of the country from thirty to forty miles around Manchester* (London, 1795, repr. Newton Abbot: David & Charles, 1968), pp. 466–7. Aikin's source was the *Gentleman's Magazine* 57, pt 2 (1787), 665, 1165–6, 1200. For Aikin, see below, p. 71.

(Lancs.), was reputedly 'compelled to relinquish it, by the ill-treatment he received from the prejudice of the working classes against the improvement'.[73] Wadsworth and Mann comment sceptically that it was probably through lack of capital that Earnshaw and Taylor failed to develop their inventions; the story of the former's altruism and the latter's persecution arose in the wake of the anti-machinery riots of 1779.[74]

Aikin's remark that Earnshaw's concern for the livelihood of the poor was 'mistaken' is indicative of the diminishing fear of technological unemployment among many who acquired a rudimentary understanding of economics. Since the early eighteenth century, a growing faith in the elasticity of markets endorsed the expectation that any innovation that reduced the producer's costs would increase the demand for his goods and thereby expand employment. It was a faith that informed Parliament's increasing willingness to repeal the Tudor legislation that had regulated the labour market and it encouraged the Crown's law officers to accept petitions for patents which announced their intention to save 'the labour of many hands'.[75] In 1797, Sir Frederick Eden was in no doubt that Britain's prosperity was largely the result of the 'unexampled extension and excellency' of its manufactures, and placed much weight on 'the introduction of machines for facilitating labour'.[76] Yet, as Josiah Tucker confessed, 'the majority of mankind, and *even some persons of great name and character* ... [regard it as] a monstrous paradox ... [that] the abridgement of labour ... [would lead to] a much greater number of hands [being employed].'[77] Indeed, there were good reasons for individuals to reject this reliance on the benign workings of the market, for the people who enjoyed the new employment opportunities were rarely those made redundant by the machinery; old skills became obsolete, cheaper 'hands' were found, and the transition was usually painful. As for inventors, it is unclear how exactly their reputations were affected – though, given the

[73] *Gentleman's Magazine* 83, pt 1 (1813), 662; English patent 693 (1754).

[74] A. P. Wadsworth and Julia de Lacy Mann, *The cotton trade and industrial Lancashire, 1600–1870* (Manchester: Manchester University Press, 1965), pp. 474–5.

[75] MacLeod, *Inventing the industrial revolution*, pp. 159–73; Adrian J. Randall, 'The philosophy of Luddism: the case of the west of England woollen workers, ca. 1790–1809', *T&C* 27 (1986), 1–17. For the debate as a whole, see Maxine Berg, *The machinery question and the making of political economy, 1815–1848* (Cambridge: Cambridge University Press, 1980).

[76] Sir Frederick Morton Eden, *The state of the poor*, 3 vols. (London: B. and J. White, 1797), vol. I, pp. 441–2.

[77] Josiah Tucker, *Instructions for travellers* (Dublin, 1758), repr. in Robert L. Schuyler (ed.), *Josiah Tucker: a selection from his economic and political writings* (New York: Columbia University Press, 1931), pp. 241–2; my emphasis.

eighteenth-century crowd's capacity for discriminatory actions, it seems unlikely that all were tarred with the same brush.

Prometheus ancient and modern

Irrespective of his ambivalent status in the workshop and market-place, in the libraries and salons of Europe the stock of the inventor was indubitably rising. The Enlightenment discourse of 'genius', while focusing primarily on literature and natural philosophy, was to have important implications for all aspects of human creativity, including mechanical invention.[78] Not only was it to give philosophical sanction to the concept of the proactive inventor whose ideas were his own and independent of any divine scheme, but it would also provide the grounds for seeing him in a more positive light, as a benefactor not a threat to society. There remained, nonetheless, a strong current of thought which identified any human attempt to imitate the godly Creator with rebellion, disharmony and disaster, and which notoriously found fictional expression in Mary Shelley's *Frankenstein; or the modern Prometheus* (1818).

Christian thought had allowed little credit to the human inventor: major inventions constituted a means whereby an omniscient God influenced human affairs and individuals were, at most, His obedient instruments.[79] Concomitantly, the natural world was the product of providential design, in which 'the uniformity and simplicity of nature provided evidence of a divine blueprint and of God as a causal agent'.[80] In a society where innovation remained generally more a source of anxiety than excitement, a providential explanation reassured believers that the all-wise Creator dispensed only salutary inventions: although something novel might appear harmful, His benevolent intent would ultimately be revealed.[81] This explanatory framework was informed by neo-Platonist philosophy, which professed that whatever new knowledge humanity

---

[78] See below, pp. 51–4.

[79] For valuable surveys of ancient myths of invention and their influence on medieval and Renaissance thought, see Hope Mason, *Value of creativity*, pp. 12–23; Olga Raggio, 'The myth of Prometheus: its survival and metamorphoses up to the eighteenth century', *Journal of the Warburg and Courtauld Institutes* 21 (1958), 44–62.

[80] Patricia Fara, *Sympathetic attractions: magnetic practices, beliefs, and symbolism in eighteenth-century England* (Princeton, NJ: Princeton University Press, 1996), p. 100.

[81] Hope Mason, *Value of creativity*, p. 161; MacLeod, *Inventing the industrial revolution*, pp. 203–4; David Spadafora, *The idea of progress in eighteenth-century Britain* (New Haven and London: Yale University Press, 1990), pp. 104, 110–14, 123–7, 369; Stewart, *Rise of public science*, pp. 42–59; Margaret C. Jacob, *The Newtonians and the English revolution* (Hassocks: Harvester Press, 1976), pp. 180–1; Paul J. Korshin, 'The intellectual context of Swift's flying island', *Philological Quarterly* 50 (1971), 636.

discovered had been present, throughout time, in the Ideas that existed in the mind of God. 'All reality, visible and invisible, was an emanation from a supreme One, in a vast descending chain of being.'[82] During the Renaissance the extreme form of this belief, which permitted humanity no theoretical scope whatever for creativity, was reinterpreted (in particular, by Marsilio Ficino) to accept that human spirituality and goodness might be expressed through a replication of the divine capacity for invention.[83] Symptomatic of this neo-Platonic philosophy was the continued use of the word 'invention' in a way which was close to its root in the Latin verb 'invenire' – to discover – and little distinction was drawn between the actions of inventing and discovering. Just as a new planet, new lands, or laws of nature were presumed to have existed prior to their discovery (or 'invention'), so the perfect idea of a new technique or product had always been extant, awaiting human invention (or 'discovery').[84]

Protestants had been quick to represent the invention of printing as a divine intervention to advance the Reformation, 'a pivotal moment in a vast, predestined scheme of doom and salvation'.[85] In the influential words of John Foxe, 'notwithstanding "whatever man soever was the instrument, without all doubt God himself was the ordainer and disposer thereof, no otherwise, than he was the gift of tongues".'[86] Overseas trade and exploration were similarly given divine sanction by the invention of the compass. British writers tended to interpret the loadstone's mysterious, magnetic powers as God's particular gift to their own commercial nation.[87] When, in 1794, Ralph Walker employed a providential argument to promote his new longitude compass, he was

---

[82] Hope Mason, *Value of creativity*, pp. 25–6.   [83] Ibid., pp. 30, 43–9.

[84] W. C. Kneale, 'The idea of invention', *Proceedings of the British Academy* 41 (1955), 85–108; Samuel Johnson, *A dictionary of the English language*, 2 vols. (London, 1755), vol. I, sub 'Invention'. The earliest explicit (and philosophical) distinction between the two terms that I have found is by Joseph Bramah in his critique of Watt's patent for the separate condenser: *A letter to the Rt Hon. Sir James Eyre, Lord Chief Justice of the Common Pleas; on the subject of the cause, Boulton & Watt v. Hornblower & Maberly: for infringement of Mr Watt's patent for an improvement on the steam engine* (London: John Stockdale, 1797), pp. 83–4. See also J. F. Lake Williams, *An historical account of inventions and discoveries in those arts and sciences which are of utility or ornament to man, lend assistance to human comfort, a polish to life, and render the civilized state, beyond comparison, preferable to a state of nature; traced from their origin; with every subsequent improvement*, 2 vols. (London: T. & J. Allman, 1820), vol. I, pp. 4–5.

[85] Johns, *Nature of the book*, p. 329. For the long-running debate over the origins of the printing press, see ibid., pp. 329–37; by 1700, there were reputedly thirty European towns claiming primacy.

[86] John Foxe, *Acts and monuments*, vol. I, pp. 926–8, quoted in Johns, *Nature of the book*, p. 329. For other examples, see MacLeod, *Inventing the industrial revolution*, pp. 202–4.

[87] Fara, *Sympathetic attractions*, p. 146.

drawing on a well-established discourse among theologians and natural philosophers:

Nothing shows the Supreme Architect in a more exalted point of view... By it he enables us to behold his works, and our fellow creatures, in all the different corners of the world ... to colonize and carry on commerce for our benefit and happiness, stirring up our minds to activity and industry; above all, expanding our ideas, and giving us a just sense of his greatness and government of this world.[88]

Naturally, the argument from providence was a common stratagem, available to anyone who wished to justify an unpopular invention. One of Cartwright's workmen, crowing over the success of his wool-combing machine and the impending ruin of the master combers with their 'old-fashion'd ways', described the inventor as 'our British Archimedes, [who] ... by Providence was sent for the good of all mankind'.[89]

In Judaeo-Christian theology there was only one Creator, and a strong tradition of 'active hostility to human creativity'. According to the Book of Genesis, this monotheistic creation of the universe had produced order, stability and harmony; evil entered the world at the Fall, when man was tempted by Satan to eat from the tree of knowledge, which would make humans dangerously 'like Gods'. From this first rebellion stemmed every threat to that original harmonious order.[90] The story of the Fall had much in common with pagan creation myths. Neither tradition looked favourably on human ingenuity: infringements of the jealously guarded, divine monopoly of creation were subject to severe, sometimes gruesome, punishment. Daring, ambitious, sexually amoral and vain, mythical inventors also had a reputation for cunning and trickery; often identified with the smith, the maker of both tools and weapons, their activities were perceived as deeply ambiguous – as much destructive as creative.[91]

The most notorious of these mythical heroes was Prometheus, whose theft of fire from the gods the Greeks transmitted in two contrasting versions. According to the poet Hesiod, this treacherous theft terminated the original golden age, depriving man of the gods' benevolence and

---

[88] Ralph Walker, *A treatise on magnetism, with a description and explanation of a meridional and azimuth compass, for ascertaining the quantity of variation, without any calculation whatever, at any time of the day* (London: G. Adams, 1794), pp. 42–3, quoted in Fara, *Sympathetic attractions*, pp. 146–7.

[89] Quoted in Ponting (ed.), *Memoir of the life ... of Edmund Cartwright*, pp. 106–7. Although the verse did not name Cartwright, there is no doubt that he was 'our British Archimedes': see above, pp. 41–2. Cf. L. T. C. Rolt, *The aeronauts: a history of ballooning, 1783–1903* (2nd edn, Gloucester: Sutton, 1985), p. 72.

[90] Hope Mason, *Value of creativity*, pp. 23–30, quotations on p. 28.

[91] Ibid., pp. 12–35.

forcing him to become self-reliant. By contrast, in the play, *Prometheus Bound* (usually attributed to Aeschylus), Prometheus is the cunning but courageous benefactor of humanity, who with the fire brings also reason and intelligence, from which all arts and sciences have their origin – but not the sense of justice, which would allow mankind to live in harmony. Common to both versions, however, is the dreadful punishment inflicted on Prometheus for his bold challenge to the authority of Zeus, and both suggest that the price of material progress is discord.[92] In Roman mythology, Prometheus becomes the sculptor, who shapes mankind and all other living creatures from clay in the image of the gods, a scene often depicted on sarcophagi. More surprisingly, in medieval Christian iconography he is to be found 'animating' Adam and the rest of creation with his fire.[93] Tamed in this heterodox manner, the myth of Prometheus persisted – his torture was a popular subject for Renaissance artists – and was reworked by fifteenth-century humanists as an allegory of the mental suffering integral to the achievement of wisdom. His fate was also promulgated by Catholic theologians as a warning to Protestant heretics of the dire effects of 'sinful arrogance of spirit'.[94]

This largely negative set of beliefs about creativity constituted, in Hope Mason's words, 'a lost tradition', which shadowed the dominant, positive currents of Judaeo-Christian theology and neo-Platonic philosophy.[95] The hubristic, heroic image advanced by Bacon (and Brunelleschi) was a deeply problematic one. Restoration England was reminded of these ambiguities by John Milton's characterization of Satan, in *Paradise Lost* (1667), as the bold and determined opponent of God's absolute rule, who recruits the human race to his sinful rebellion. Writing in the aftermath of England's 'great rebellion', Milton repeatedly presents human 'inventions' and independence in a bad light. While Adam contentedly trusts that God will provide for all humanity's needs, the sons of Cain (his name meaning 'smith' or 'worker in metal') are 'inventors rare, unmindful of their maker', who proudly fail to acknowledge God's gifts and ally themselves with Satan.[96] It is, however, a common complaint that Milton gave the devil all the best tunes: his 'superbly heroic' Satan overshadowed a vapid Christ, and won for Milton the admiration of such radicals as the poets, William Blake and Percy Bysshe Shelley. The similarities between Milton's Satan and Prometheus are evident, and *Paradise Lost* endorses the idea of the fortunate Fall – that out of the need for self-reliance (the consequence of Adam and Eve's ejection from Paradise) sprang all

---

[92] Ibid., pp. 16–17; Raggio, 'Myth of Prometheus', 44–5.
[93] Raggio, 'Myth of Prometheus', 46–50.   [94] Ibid., 50–8.
[95] Hope Mason, *Value of creativity*, p. 20.   [96] Ibid., pp. 28–9, 64–6.

humanity's subsequent achievements.[97] For Milton's contemporary, John Locke, human inventiveness likewise resulted from the Fall: the necessity to labour, in tandem with the sins of pride and greed, had led man to employ his reason and to produce 'arts and inventions, engines and utensils' that improved humanity's material condition.[98]

It was the next century, however, before British writers mounted an explicit challenge to Platonist and providentialist accounts of innovation. According to Bernard Mandeville there had never been a golden age from which mankind had fallen, nor was there any natural goodness in man, but, as his *Fable of the Bees* (1723) explained, the vices which characterized humanity unintentionally produced beneficial outcomes. One such consequence – the product of sins such as vanity, envy and greed – was the drive to accumulation and improvement. It was at the heart of commercial society, stimulating a constant demand for novelty, which in turn acted as a spur to ingenuity and industry. Responding to that stimulus was the inventive individual, in both economic and artistic spheres; innovators, argued Mandeville, possessed an abundance of sinful desires, which urged them on to attempt ever-higher goals.[99] Although in Mandeville's account still tinged with evil, the demythologized inventor was now a totally free agent, and invention was entirely the outcome of human activity, the contingent result of necessity and wants – not the unfolding of a divine plan.[100] For David Hume also, invention was integral to human nature but, divesting it of Mandeville's sardonic gloss, Hume saw the exercise of ingenuity as subject to the promptings not only of necessity but also of the pleasure to be gained from meeting an intellectual challenge.[101] Difficulty was the grit in the oyster: it inspired the individual to productive activity and sharpened his wits to discover improvements and seize opportunities – their number multiplying in commercial society. Dismissive of the notion that God had designed the universe for man's benefit, Hume was confident that humanity could rise to all the challenges that an unregulated natural world might concoct, for, as he grandly announced, 'mankind is an inventive species'.[102]

---

[97] Ibid., pp. 65–6; Arthur O. Lovejoy, *Essays in the history of ideas* (New York: George Braziller, 1955), pp. 277–9.; Paul A. Cantor, *Creature and creator: myth-making and English Romanticism* (Cambridge: Cambridge University Press, 1984), pp. 103–9.

[98] Hope Mason, *Value of creativity*, pp. 70–1.

[99] Bernard Mandeville, *The fable of the bees*, ed. F. B. Kaye, 2 vols. (Oxford: Clarendon Press, 1924), vol. II, pp. 144–5; Hope Mason, *Value of creativity*, pp. 75–9.

[100] Hope Mason stresses, however, that 'the doctrine of the Fortunate Fall and the idea of Providence' continued to provide the principal justifications for commerce, since Mandeville's ideas were too morally 'troubling': *Value of creativity*, p. 161.

[101] Hope Mason, *Value of creativity*, pp. 79–85.

[102] David Hume, *A treatise of human nature*, ed. P. Nidditch (Oxford, 1978), bk II, pt ii, sect. 1, p. 484, quoted in Hope Mason, *Value of creativity*, p. 81.

Half a century later, the engineer, Joseph Bramah, sought to define the extent of human inventiveness. Himself a prolific inventor and patentee, called to testify in the case of *Boulton and Watt* v. *Hornblower and Maberly*, Bramah expressed his fury at the patentees' successful prosecution of their Cornish rivals. He accused them of failing in their responsibility to specify unambiguously the boundaries of their intellectual property (by analogy with the encloser's duty to mark out the land he appropriated from the commons). In Bramah's view, God had furnished humanity with a 'universal storehouse', stocked with eternally unchanging 'natural principles and properties of elements'. This was mankind's 'common property', which was available for each individual to rearrange and vary in 'quantity and proportion', thereby producing an infinite set of new combinations or inventions.[103] In effect, Bramah reduced God to the supplier of raw materials to human inventors. While not intended to belittle the Deity's role, it was a far cry from the providential conception of divine creativity that pious Christians still enunciated.

[A]t what point of creation do the works of men begin? The answer is, just where the independent works of God end, who by his own secret *principles* and *methods* (that surely none will have the hardihood to claim) established the elements and their properties; and stocked the universal storehouse ... out of which the same creating will directs every man to go and take materials fit in kind and quality, for the execution of his design. Thus far is the wondrous work performed by the Deity alone; what succeeds is done through the agency of man.[104]

Bramah's implicit charge was that, by specifying nothing more than a set of principles (for the application of steam), Watt had indeed had 'the hardihood to claim' what belonged to God alone and thereby had trespassed on the commons. Yet, in this demarcation of the human sphere from the divine, Bramah envisaged for mankind a much expanded field of action, allowing that the human mind was capable of formulating 'new effects from the varied applications of the same cause, and the endless changes producible by different combinations and proportions'.[105] Although, as an inventor, Bramah might be accused of having a particular interest in

---

[103] Bramah, *Letter to the Rt Hon. Sir James Eyre*, pp. 77–9. See Jennifer Tann, 'Mr Hornblower and his crew: Watt engine pirates at the end of the 18th century', *TNS* 51 (1979–80), 95–105. In his presidential address to the Institution of Civil Engineers in 1839, James Walker departed from his prepared text to remind his colleagues how small and dependent were mankind's capacities in comparison to 'the Mind which gave to them [i.e. the raw materials] the properties they have ... and impressed upon matter those beautiful and uniform laws which govern it': 'Address of the President to the Annual General Meeting', 15 January 1839, *Proceedings of the Institution of Civil Engineers* (1839), 17–18.

[104] Bramah, *Letter to the Rt Hon. Sir James Eyre*, p. 83.

[105] Ibid., p. 77. See also B. Merriman, in *Gentleman's Magazine*, September 1785, 684.

enlarging the individual's role in invention, his humanistic definition is symptomatic of wider currents of Enlightenment thought. James Watt himself had already ventured much further, as he drafted reforms intended to strengthen the position of embattled patentees:

How it can be considered as conferring a Monopoly to grant a man the exclusive privilege of using a thing, which had perhaps never existed if his ingenuity or industry had not been exerted in discovering it and bringing it to perfection.[106]

Watt's query, which echoed Adam Smith's justification of patents, vested the entire merit in the individual inventor, without whom a particular invention would 'perhaps never [have] existed' – 'perhaps' being his nominal concession to a more deterministic or Platonic concept of invention.

Although inventiveness was gaining acceptance as a positive, human attribute, there remained a wide gulf between such apologies as these and the heroic status accorded to inventors in Bacon's *New Atlantis*. Meanwhile, the celebration of individual originality rehearsed in the eighteenth-century's emergent discourse of genius offered them yet no place. While 'invention' was recognized to be a defining characteristic of genius, this was the inventiveness of great poets, whose capacity for originality rested in imagery, plots and word-play, and of other authors of unusually original ideas. For British commentators the chief exemplars of genius were Homer and Shakespeare, accompanied sometimes by Milton, Pope, Bacon and Locke.[107] With considerable difficulty, the concept was expanded to accommodate the scientific genius of Sir Isaac Newton. This proved problematic, not because anyone doubted the brilliance of Newton's mind, but because Newton was 'the supreme icon of rationality': in Britain it was imagination – not rationality or sagacity – that was conceived to be the hallmark of literary genius, and initially imagination was not considered to be an attribute of natural philosophers.[108] Moreover, in several discussions of genius, imagination ran dangerously close to insanity and religious enthusiasm. Many of

---

[106] James Watt, 'Thoughts on patents', quoted in Robinson, 'James Watt and the law of patents', 137. For Smith, see above, p. 39.

[107] Alexander Gerard, *An essay on genius* (London and Edinburgh: W. Strahan, T. Cadell & W. Creech, 1774), pp. 10–19; Fara, *Newton*, pp. 21, 158, 174–5; Jonathan Bate, *The genius of Shakespeare* (London: Picador, 1997), pp. 165–72, 184–5; Penelope Murray, 'Introduction', in Penelope Murray (ed.), *Genius: the history of an idea* (Oxford: Basil Blackwell, 1989), pp. 1–8.

[108] French writers, by contrast, emphasized rationality, with the noted exceptions of Diderot and Rousseau: Hope Mason, *Value of creativity*, pp. 115–27; Fara, *Newton*, pp. 128–31, 181–91. See also Simon Schaffer, 'Genius in Romantic natural philosophy', in Andrew Cunningham and Nicholas Jardine (eds.), *Romanticism and the sciences* (Cambridge: Cambridge University Press, 1990), pp. 82–98.

Newton's admirers insisted that it was hard, methodical thought that had produced his incomparable insights into the workings of the cosmos.[109] Neither were flashes of inspiration or the equation of imagination with a deranged mind qualities that would have benefited the reputation of inventors – already too closely associated, as we have seen, with the dubious activities of 'wild projectors'.

Only in the later eighteenth century did the discussion of genius and originality – itself fuelled by the growing demand for copyright protection of authors' intellectual property – expand to encompass scientific 'invention'.[110] In an influential essay, published anonymously in 1759, the English poet, Edward Young, anticipated leading figures of the European Romantic movement in his emphasis on the inspirational or irrational traits of an active imagination, by which genius was distinguished from ordinary learning. Young interpreted genius as a spontaneous form of creativity that dispensed with all rules of composition; originality grew organically 'from the vital root of genius'. By implication, the original work was necessarily its author's inalienable property, unlike an imitation, which was 'often a sort of manufacture wrought up by those mechanics, art, and labour, out of pre-existent materials not their own'.[111] Furthermore, genius consisted in 'the power of accomplishing great things without the means generally reputed necessary to that end. A genius differs from a good understanding, as a magician from a good architect; that raises his structure by means invisible; this by the skilful use of common tools.'[112]

This near-occult insistence on the untrammelled imagination was contested by two contemporary Scottish theologians, Alexander Gerard and William Duff, who re-stated the necessary role of judgement in moderating

---

[109] Fara, *Newton*, pp. 155–64, 170–2, 182–3, quotation on p. 172; Yeo, 'Genius, method, and morality', 259, 261–5; Neil Kessel, 'Genius and mental disorder: a history of ideas concerning their conjunction', in Murray (ed.), *Genius*, pp. 196–9.

[110] Mark Rose, *Authors and owners: the invention of copyright* (Cambridge, MA and London: Harvard University Press, 1993), pp. 6–8, 104–29, 135–8; M. H. Abrams, *The mirror and the lamp: romantic theory and the critical tradition* (New York: Oxford University Press, 1953), pp. 159–67.

[111] Edward Young, *Conjectures on original composition*, ed. Edith J. Morley (London, 1918), p. 7, quoted in Clare Pettitt, *Patent inventions: intellectual property and the Victorian novel* (Oxford: Oxford University Press, 2004), p. 13. See also Yeo, 'Genius, method, and morality', 261–2.

[112] [Edward Young], *Conjectures on original composition* (London: A. Millar, 1759), p. 26, quoted in Fara, *Newton*, p. 170; Giorgio Tonelli, 'Genius from the Renaissance to 1770', in Philip P. Wiener (ed.), *Dictionary of the history of ideas*, 4 vols. (New York: Charles Scribner's Sons, 1973), vol. II, p. 294; Rudolf Wittkower, 'Genius: individualism in art and artists', in Wiener (ed.), *Dictionary*, vol. II, p. 306; Hope Mason, *Value of creativity*, pp. 108–9.

the excesses of the imagination.[113] Both these Enlightenment theorists sought to establish scientific discovery as a product of genius that was explicable in the same terms as literary and artistic creativity. They both regarded Newton as 'an original Genius of the first rank' (though Gerard remarked that Newton 'had the direction and example of Bacon who, without any assistance, sketched out the whole design').[114] While, on the one hand, denying that imagination was sufficient, on the other, they rebutted the views of those, such as James Ogilvie, who conceived of it as the function solely of the judgement or understanding, which owed nothing to imagination and so was completely unlike poetic genius.[115] Judgement, said Gerard, was 'necessary for perfecting the operations of genius of every kind ... but it cannot be reckoned properly the inventive power'.[116] Gerard wished to demonstrate that imagination was essential in the case of scientific genius, where 'the necessity of judgement is obvious', and, by contrast, that poor judgement detracted from perfection in the case of literary or artistic genius, where imagination was uncontroversial.[117]

While both types of genius required the same qualities of mind, Gerard allowed that they were directed at different goals:

> The ends, to which genius may be adapted, are reducible to two; the discovery of truth, and the production of beauty. The former belongs to the sciences, the latter to the arts. Genius is, then, the power of invention, either in science or in the arts, either of truth or of beauty.[118]

This allowed him to fine-tune the differences in the way these two types of genius employed their similar mental faculties: the 'discovery of truth' generally required a closer and steadier concentration than did the 'production of beauty'; it must also eliminate 'the passions', which, while essential to the arts, would 'infect our conclusions, and obstruct our discoveries'.[119]

In 1774, the writer, translator and would-be patentee, William Kenrick, pursued the comparison further, to make an unusually strong case for the superior merits of scientific and mechanical invention. Kenrick was writing

---

[113] Gerard says in the 'Advertisement' that he began his *Essay on genius* in 1758, although it was not published until 1774.

[114] William Duff, *An essay on original genius and its various modes of exertion in philosophy and the fine arts particularly in poetry*, ed. John L. Mahoney (Gainesville, FL: Scholars' Facsimiles and Reprints, 1964), p. 119; Gerard, *Essay on genius*, pp. 15–19, quotation on p. 18. See Yeo, 'Genius, method, and morality', 262–4.

[115] Tonelli, 'Genius', p. 294.

[116] Gerard, *Essay on genius*, p. 32; Duff, *Essay on original genius*, pp. 8–9, 19. While Gerard still used 'invention', Duff used the new terminology of 'creative imagination', which was to become a Romantic catchword: Wittkower, 'Genius', p. 307.

[117] Gerard, *Essay on genius*, pp. 35–6, 72, 78, 388; Duff, *Essay on original genius*, p. 89.

[118] Gerard, *Essay on genius*, p. 318.   [119] Ibid., pp. 324–6, 352.

in response both to a major legal ruling on the nature of (literary) intellectual property, which exposed the disadvantages of the inventor's dependence on the patent system, and to his own failure to obtain a patent for a perpetual motion machine (because he refused to reveal the details to the Attorney General).[120] It was, he argued, as 'the mathematician, the experimentalist, the mechanic, and not the writer' that Newton's name was venerated. Yet, it was only as an author that he would be automatically rewarded (by the free protection of his copyright); by contrast, 'the artist or artificer' enjoyed no such entitlement to 'a property in ... ingenuity', being required to purchase a patent at 'prodigious expense'.[121] On this Kenrick took a utilitarian stance: it was especially unjust because 'the industry of the inventor provides for the convenience of hundreds, the subsistence of thousands, and the support of the State.'[122]

By the late eighteenth century, Newton rivalled Shakespeare for the accolade of Britain's greatest cultural hero.[123] His fame was widespread, the praise he attracted was extravagant, and his personal prestige reflected its glow on the reputation of British natural philosophy. Yet the Newtonian worldview was not without its critics: they came from a wide spectrum of society – high-church Anglicans to political radicals – and disputed Newton's theological and philosophical views as well as points of science.[124]

Far more menacing to the 'man of science's' reputation, however, was the fictional invention of Mary Shelley – *Frankenstein, or the modern Prometheus*, first published in 1818 and an instant success. Interpretations of Shelley's novel are as varied as they are numerous, but recent scholarship is insistent that Shelley intended no blanket condemnation of scientific activity and advocates locating her bizarre tale in its historical and literary contexts.[125] The character of Frankenstein is 'an "extraordinary"

[120] C. S. Rogers and Betty Rizzo, 'Kenrick, William (1729/30–1779)', *ODNB*, www.oxforddnb.com/view/article/15416, accessed 18 October 2006.

[121] W. Kenrick, LL D, *An address to the artists and manufacturers of Great Britain* (London, 1774), p. 9; MacLeod, *Inventing the industrial revolution*, pp. 198–9.

[122] Kenrick, *Address*, p. 13.

[123] Fara, *Newton*, pp. 20–1, 47–58; Maureen McNeil, 'Newton as national hero', in John Fauvel, Raymond Flood, Michael Shortland and Robin Wilson (eds.), *Let Newton be!* (Oxford: Oxford University Press, 1988), pp. 222–40; Derek Gjertson, 'Newton's success', in ibid., pp. 28–30.

[124] Geoffrey Cantor, 'Anti-Newton', in Fauvel *et al.* (eds.), *Let Newton be!*, pp. 202–21; Simon Schaffer, 'Priestley and the politics of spirit', in R. G. W. Anderson and Christopher Lawrence (eds.), *Science, medicine and dissent: Joseph Priestley, 1733–1804* (London: Wellcome Institute, 1987), p. 45; Yeo, 'Genius, method, and morality', pp. 264–5.

[125] Among the most insightful are Crosbie Smith, 'Frankenstein and natural magic', in Stephen Bann (ed.), *Frankenstein, creation and monstrosity* (London: Reaktion Books, 1994), pp. 39–59; Ludmilla Jordanova, 'Melancholy reflection: constructing an identity

rather than conventional man of science', who has dabbled in the works of medieval alchemists.[126] However, the usual scholarly description of Frankenstein as a 'scientist' rather than an 'inventor' is perhaps indicative of our own cultural assumptions about the division of inventive labour.[127] Although Shelley recounts his study of various branches of natural philosophy, Frankenstein's achievement was in fact *to invent* the creature.[128] Not only does her subtitle refer explicitly to the great mythological inventor, but the plot, simply told, is a modern reworking of the myth: Frankenstein, like Prometheus, usurps the divine right of creation – 'infusing life into an inanimate body' – and is eternally punished for his transgression (with mental and emotional, if not physical, torture).[129] It is not the understanding of the natural world which is dangerous, Shelley implies, but the uses to which that knowledge might be put; even an initially benign invention could have disastrous, unintended consequences.

The 'creature' which Victor Frankenstein brings to life, although hideously botched and ugly, is as innocent as Adam was in the Garden of Eden ('I am thy creature: I ought to be thy Adam: but I am rather the fallen angel, whom thou drivest from joy for no misdeed . . . I was benevolent').[130] Rejected by his creator, this innocent creature suffers great emotional anguish (and attack at the hands of terrified villagers, whom we might equate with Luddites) but is still harmless, indeed virtuous: while hiding in the cottage of the De Lacey family, he performs many anonymous acts of kindness.[131] It is only when rejected a second time, by this

for unveilers of nature', in ibid., pp. 60–76; Hope Mason, *Value of creativity*, pp. 1–4; Pettitt, *Patent inventions*, pp. 13–20; also, for a fuller (and slightly different) version of the latter, Clare Pettitt, 'Representations of creativity, progress and social change in the work of Elizabeth Gaskell, Charles Dickens and George Eliot', unpublished D.Phil. thesis, University of Oxford (1997), pp. 93–142. For a survey of interpretations, see Fred Botting, *Making monstrous: Frankenstein, criticism, theory* (Manchester: Manchester University Press, 1991).

[126] Smith, 'Frankenstein and natural magic', p. 41.   [127] See below, pp. 358–65.

[128] Pettitt draws attention to this 'concurrent but contradictory narrative' of the orthodox 'fully enrolled student' of natural philosophy: *Patent inventions*, p. 18; see also Jordanova, 'Melancholy reflection', pp. 63–6.

[129] Simultaneously, of course, he usurps the female role in reproduction. Among many valuable feminist perspectives on *Frankenstein*, see Sandra M. Gilbert and Susan Gubar, 'Horror's twin: Mary Shelley's monstrous Eve', *The madwoman in the attic: the woman writer and the nineteenth-century literary imagination* (New Haven: Yale University Press, 1979), pp. 213–47; Margaret Homans, *Bearing the word: language and female experience in nineteenth-century women's writing* (Chicago and London: Chicago University Press, 1986), pp. 100–19; Mary Poovey, *The proper lady and the woman writer: ideology as style in the works of Mary Wollstonecraft, Mary Shelley and Jane Austen* (Chicago: Chicago University Press, 1984).

[130] Mary Shelley, *Frankenstein or the modern Prometheus, the 1818 text*, ed. Marilyn Butler (Oxford: Oxford University Press, 1993), pp. 77–8.

[131] Ibid., pp. 83, 88.

family which he has come to love, that he turns into 'the monster', who vows to wreak vengeance on his creator.[132] Beyond the control of its inventor, the benign invention is mishandled by its potential users (the De Laceys), who fail to understand – even to ask – what benefits it might bring them; in their ignorant panic, they too lose control and trigger the catastrophes that ensue. At first, the damage is specific and local: in his fury, the abandoned creature turns arsonist, destroying the empty cottage with (Promethean) fire. The situation is not yet irredeemable but, yet again, uncomprehending humanity explicitly rewards his benevolence with ungrateful violence and injustice: having rescued a girl from drowning, he is shot by her male companion who seemingly misinterprets his actions. The die is now cast. 'Inflamed by pain, I vowed eternal hatred and vengeance to all mankind.'[133] Soon afterwards, he chances on the first opportunity to revenge himself on Frankenstein, proceeding mercilessly to destroy everyone his creator most values – along with his peace of mind, self-respect and hope of salvation.

In a sophisticated interpretation of the novel, Clare Pettitt argues that *Frankenstein* articulates Mary Shelley's anxieties about the ownership of intellectual property. Just as the creature 'remains so emphatically Frankenstein's intellectual property' that neither can escape the bond, so the author is forcibly identified with the work; once published and put into the readers' hands, the text (and thereby its author) becomes subject to misinterpretation, vilification and attack.[134] Pettitt rightly situates her interpretation in the eighteenth-century debate on genius, and insists on the still minimal disciplinary boundaries between discussions of literary and technical invention at this period. The 'inspiration' narrative of invention, which Shelley interweaves with the counterpoised narrative of orthodox scientific method, is one of 'almost supernatural enthusiasm', compulsive obsession, 'dizzy' ambition. As Pettitt says, 'all the referents of Romantic inspiration are here'.[135] Frankenstein is displaying the spontaneous imagination of Edward Young's poetic genius, his fancy unfettered by the 'judgement' that Gerard and Duff each warned was vital for 'perfecting' his operations, and at times he is on the verge of madness; he transgresses, as Ludmilla Jordanova argues, through

---

[132] Ibid., pp. 110–13.   [133] Ibid., pp. 113, 115–16.

[134] Pettitt, *Patent inventions*, pp. 14–16.

[135] Ibid., 12–14, 17–18, quoting Shelley, *Frankenstein*, pp. 33–5; also Pettitt, 'Representations', pp. 85–92. Hope Mason likewise emphasizes that Frankenstein is 'not simply a scientist, he is a man of vision' and could equally well have been a poet, entrepreneur, or statesman – he is 'creative', an adjective unavailable to Shelley: *Value of creativity*, pp. 1–2, 4–5.

'absence of balance'.[136] That loss of balance finally reaches the point where 'a real insanity possessed me'.[137] Ironically, although Frankenstein's psychological state and social isolation may be of the kind associated with 'genius', his method of invention betrays him – by Young's criterion – as a mere imitator, and a disgustingly poor one at that. By contrast with God's effortless creation of the perfect man, Frankenstein's 'hideous' creature is laboriously constructed from cadavers, unearthed from graveyards and stolen from slaughterhouses: it parodied, in Young's dismissive words, 'a sort of manufacture wrought ... out of pre-existent materials not their own'.[138]

Shelley tapped the myth of Prometheus, more completely than is generally recognized, to employ the concept of the 'fortunate Fall' and to contrast the Romantics' 'heroic' inventor unfavourably with older ideologies of invention, which are partly providentialist, partly Baconian. Not only does Victor Frankenstein exemplify the hubris and dreadful punishment of the legendary Prometheus, but his creature re-enacts the fate of humanity, cast off by Zeus (or cast out of the Garden of Eden by God) to fend for itself because of Prometheus' (or Satan's) crime. During his initial wanderings, the creature is forced by necessity to become self-reliant. Significantly, he first discovers fire (a campfire left alight by itinerant beggars – a Promethean windfall) and learns by hard experience – truly a case of 'trial and error' – that fire produces pain as well as pleasurable warmth. By conducting experiments with the fire he discovers the different properties of wet and dry wood; next morning, he observes how a gentle breeze fans the fire back into life and, by analogy, makes his first invention ('a fan of branches') to reproduce the natural effect.[139] That night, he deduces how to cook food and compares the effect of heat on berries, nuts and roots.[140] For all his native wit, however,

---

[136] Jordanova, 'Melancholy reflection', p. 66; similarly, Smith, 'Frankenstein and natural magic', pp. 41–7, 51–4; Schaffer, 'Genius in Romantic natural philosophy', pp. 82–3; for Young, Gerard and Duff, see above, pp. 52–3.

[137] Shelley, *Frankenstein*, p. 166; Smith, 'Frankenstein and natural magic', pp. 57–9.

[138] Shelley, *Frankenstein*, pp. 36–7, 38–40; Smith, 'Frankenstein and natural magic', pp. 53–4.

[139] This capacity to use instruments is itself a demonstration that the creature is human, since this was regarded as a major feature that distinguished man from other animals. See, for example, Mrs Barbauld and Dr Aikin, *Evenings at home: or, The juvenile budget opened* (Dublin: H. Colbert, 1794), pp. 165, 169, 196–7.

[140] We perceive a primitive 'hunter-gatherer' society. Eventually, Shelley teasingly moves the hunter-gatherers, who have already turned to pasturage (the De Lacey family keeps a pig), on to the next stage of society: '[m]en who before this change seemed to have been hid in their caves, dispersed themselves, and were employed in various arts of cultivation': Shelley, *Frankenstein*, p. 92. For the stage theory of history developed by Scottish Enlightenment thinkers, see Spadafora, *Idea of progress*, pp. 270–4.

he cannot reproduce the fire, because he had 'obtained it through accident'.[141] It is a good Baconian lesson, about the need to understand nature in order to command her. A more methodical approach will be needed: intelligent observation and experimentation take the isolated individual only part way to a full understanding, and accidental invention, as Bacon said, is a slow and haphazard way to proceed.[142] Subsequently, while hiding in the cottage, the creature not only learns how to use other tools, but also those more advanced inventions of human societies, language and the skills of sociability.[143] By contrast with the inspirational invention of the solitary and independent Frankenstein, this is a providential account, in which the creature's basic needs are met by a series of happy accidents; to progress further, necessity combined with curiosity excite him to uncover the secrets of nature and put them to use. Although cast out 'a poor, helpless, miserable wretch', he wants for nothing; subsequently, in the society of others, he learns a great deal – easily and quickly, just as Bacon had predicted.[144]

Victor Frankenstein is not a 'projector', he is neither a mercenary schemer nor an unrealistic dreamer (though he is tinged with alchemy); he is technically adept and idealistic, a university-educated 'man of science'. Superficially, he is a highly successful inventor: he brings to life a 'creature', who will possess not only human emotions, intelligence and sensibilities, but also superhuman strength and agility. Unlike the Creator, however, Frankenstein feels no love for his creation: he cannot accept its flaw, its 'monstrous' appearance, which is the consequence of his own faulty methods of invention. That Shelley builds her story around the subject of invention and its consequences is itself indicative of the growing awareness of technology's importance, but it is ultimately a conservative account, which endorses providentialist and Platonic explanations. By contrast, if the individual inventor is a heroic figure, for Shelley he is a hero in the worst of Greek traditions.[145] Fortunately for British men of science, the half century before *Frankenstein*'s publication had seen the emergence of more positive currents of thought, not only in the widespread regard for Sir Isaac Newton, but also thanks to appreciation of the country's growing industrial strength and a number of highly visible technological achievements.

---

[141] Shelley, *Frankenstein*, pp. 81–2.   [142] See above, pp. 28–30.
[143] Shelley, *Frankenstein*, pp. 87–92.   [144] Ibid., p. 80.
[145] See Hope Mason, *Value of creativity*, pp. 15–16.

3   The inventor's progress

Inventors rose in public esteem during the eighteenth century. Not only did the inventor emerge as a distinct persona, but he appeared in a positive light – as a national benefactor, in some quarters, more valuable to his country than those who risked their lives on the battlefield. A few individuals became famous, locally and even nationally. It was a remarkable ascent, given the obscurity and even hostility that had previously surrounded them.

The strongest case for revising the inventor's reputation as an untrustworthy and incompetent 'projector' stemmed from the country's growing awareness of major technological achievements.[1] Fundamental changes were occurring in the economy, and British society gradually came to terms with the risks and opportunities presented by commercialization. An increasing proportion of Britain's growing population was earning its living outside agriculture, and migrating into the towns and cities: by 1800 approximately two-thirds were employed in manufacturing, mining or the service sector – just under half of them in an urban context.[2] Most of these new jobs involved little technological change, in handicraft occupations pursued in small workshops or cottages, open-cast mining that used picks and shovels, road haulage and carting (dependent on the time-honoured power of horses), and domestic service.[3] A minority were

---

[1] Men of science were also coming to be generally more highly regarded, as the government looked to them to provide expert advice and conduct investigations, especially during Sir Joseph Banks' long presidency of the Royal Society: John Gascoigne, 'The Royal Society and the emergence of science as an instrument of state policy', *BJHS* 32 (1999), 171–84; Shapin, 'Image of the man of science', p. 182 .

[2] Robert C. Allen, 'Britain's economic ascendancy in a European context', in Leandro Prados de la Escosura (ed.), *Exceptionalism and industrialisation: Britain and its European rivals, 1688–1815* (Cambridge: Cambridge University Press, 2004), pp. 16–17.

[3] Pat Hudson, 'Industrial organisation and structure', in Roderick Floud and Paul Johnson (eds.), *The Cambridge economic history of modern Britain, Volume 1: 1700–1860* (Cambridge: Cambridge University Press, 2004), pp. 28–57; C. Sabel and J. Zeitlin, 'Historical alternatives to mass production', *P&P* 108 (1985), 133–76; Raphael Samuel, 'Workshop of the world: steam power and hand technology in mid Victorian Britain', *History Workshop* 3 (1977), 6–72.

being created in very different industries, which used new technologies and innovative forms of organization. From the early eighteenth century, miners worked deeper and deeper underground, their operations facilitated by steam-powered pumps; the silk industry pioneered the concentration of workers in mechanized factories; the iron industry's transition to the use of coal demanded new skills and involved reorganization on larger, integrated sites; various skilled crafts were being broken down into a multiplicity of single tasks, while simultaneously new skills were being demanded in the manufacture and maintenance of machinery.[4]

Perceptive commentators called attention to these developments, marvelling at the ingenuity of their countrymen and speculating on the implications for Britain's economic and political future. After centuries of technological indebtedness to the European continent, Josiah Tucker could boast in 1758 that, 'few countries are equal, perhaps none excel the English in the numbers and contrivance of their machines to abridge labour'.[5] Since 1719 Parliament had been enacting legislation to prevent the emigration of artisans in trades, such as clock-making, in which the British now excelled, and subsequently it extended the ban to cover the export of specific instruments and machines.[6] Out of this consciousness of a turn-round in Britain's technical capacity was to emerge a new respect for its inventors. Successful inventions, such as the steam engine, cotton-spinning machinery, and vaccination against smallpox, would publicly demonstrate both the technical facility and the personal credibility of their creators. Whatever one's doubts about the immediate safety or the long-term consequences of such inventions, it was hard to dismiss them as the unworkable gimcracks of charlatans. For the most part, they were a source of wonder, curiosity and burgeoning national pride. The most amazing of them all, however, came from France.

---

[4] Maxine Berg, *The age of manufactures, 1700–1820: industry, innovation and work in Britain* (2nd edn, London and New York: Routledge, 1994), pp. 169–279; Kristine Bruland, 'Industrialisation and technological change', in Floud and Johnson (eds.), *Cambridge economic history*, pp. 117–46; Roger Burt, 'The extractive industries', in ibid., pp. 417–50; J. R. Harris, 'Skills, coal, and British industry in the eighteenth century', *History* 61 (1976), 167–82; A. E. Musson and Eric Robinson, *Science and technology in the industrial revolution* (Manchester: Manchester University Press, 1969), pp. 393–509; Jennifer Tann, *The development of the factory* (London: Cornmarket Press, 1970).
[5] Tucker, *Instructions for travellers*, p. 240.
[6] J. R. Harris, *Industrial espionage and technology transfer: Britain and France in the eighteenth century* (Aldershot: Ashgate, 1998), pp. 7–27, 453–77; David J. Jeremy, 'Damming the flood: British government efforts to check the outflow of technicians and machinery, 1780–1843', in D. J. Jeremy (ed.), *Technology transfer and business enterprise* (Aldershot: Ashgate, 1994), pp. 1–34; Christine MacLeod, 'The European origins of British technological predominance', in Prados de la Escosura (ed.), *Exceptionalism and industrialisation*, pp. 111–26.

The romance of invention

Nothing can have matched the sense of wonder and achievement generated by the first manned balloon flight on 21 November 1783. It was the eighteenth-century equivalent of the moon landing by Apollo XI in 1969, an atavistic dream come true. The mythical Icarus and his many successors who donned wings or projected other contraptions had been vindicated by the Montgolfier brothers, papermakers from the south of France, who launched their hot-air balloon before the dauphin and the royal court, and watched it drift for eight kilometres across Paris. It was the culmination of nearly six months' test flights, which had been supervised by the Académie des Sciences, encouraged by the king, and marvelled at by ecstatic crowds. Within a fortnight, J.-A.-C. Charles' hydrogen balloon also flew across Paris. In France, *aerostation* continued to absorb scientists and government alike, in the expectation of extensive practical applications.[7] While British patriots smarted at this French *coup d'invention* and the Royal Society churlishly declined to engage in a scientific competition, the public was entranced. A series of unmanned ascents attracted large crowds of cheering spectators and, when a young Italian, Victor Lunardi, finally took off from British soil in September 1784, his heroism was widely acclaimed.[8] Early balloon flights were reported enthusiastically in the newspapers and periodical press, and ballooning caught the imagination of poets, novelists and artists. Although the satirists were never far behind and *The Times* condemned it as an idle and dangerous folly, ballooning continued to provoke wonder, terror and other strong emotions.[9] It was the most visible and awe-inspiring symbol of humanity's increasing ability to master the natural world by means of technology: the land, the sea and now the air were all part of man's domain, the planet was becoming manageable – in hindsight, a profoundly mistaken and tragic belief but no less powerful for that. In France, the hot-air balloon was called a *montgolfière* and the hydrogen balloon a *charlière*, after their respective inventors.[10] As figure 3.1 suggests, the Montgolfiers' fame readily crossed the Channel but, with no British claimant to the honour, the invention trumped the inventor in English nomenclature, and in both countries

---

[7] Richard Gillespie, 'Ballooning in France and Britain, 1783–1786: aerostation and adventurism', *Isis* 75 (1984), 248–61.

[8] Ibid., 261–4.

[9] Ibid., 264–7; Maurice J. Quinlan, 'Balloons and the awareness of a new age', *Studies in Burke and His Time* 14 (1973), 224–38.

[10] Gillespie, 'Ballooning in France and Britain', 252.

3.1 *Montgolfier in the Clouds, Constructing of Air Balloons for the Grand Monarque*, caricature print, published by S. Fores, London, 2 March 1784. Less than four months after the first manned balloon flight, this English print tries to salvage national pride by mocking the militaristic, aerial ambitions of the French inventors and their king.

the derring-do of the aeronauts soon tended to steal the show.[11] The early excitement of ballooning is preserved in a host of place names that commemorate sites of ascent, descent or simple enthusiasm.[12] By

---

[11] In Britain, unlike France, showmanship predominated in the absence of serious scientific interest: ibid., 261–7.

[12] For example, 'Air Balloon Hill', near Bristol, and 'Balloon Court', newly built cottages at Trowbridge (Wilts.), named after landings there in 1784: John Penny, *Up, up, and away! An account of ballooning in and around Bristol and Bath 1784 to 1999* (Bristol: Bristol Branch of the Historical Association, 1999), pp. 2, 4.

1800, for example, Manchester had a Balloon Street, and by 1824, two pubs called 'The Balloon'.[13]

Terrestrial technological tourism had entertained the upper classes throughout the eighteenth century. Increasingly, the diet of country houses and landscaped parks could be spiced with visits to observe the mechanical intricacies of water-pumping schemes and textile mills, the architectural wonders of iron bridges and aqueducts that carried a canal high above a valley, even the sublime thrills of a descent by ladder or rope-basket into a working mine – perhaps to the clanking accompaniment of a steam engine.[14] Inspired by the grandeur or the sheer novelty of these sights, tourists responded in poetry and prose, watercolours and charcoal; they bought souvenirs (engravings, jugs, plates, handkerchiefs) that depicted a bridge or a blast furnace – usually in an idyllic rural scene.[15] They were joined by visitors of more serious intent: professional writers, such as Defoe and Arthur Young, whose respective *Tours* discussed these technological wonders in their wider economic and social context, and journalists who penned more ephemeral reports; poets, who set descriptions of coal mining and steel making amidst grand mountain scenery; artists, such as Joseph Wright of Derby or Philippe Jacques de Loutherbourg, commissioned to paint Arkwright's Cromford mills or the Darbys' ironworks at Coalbrookdale; and no doubt a host of industrial spies, both British and foreign.[16] Their discourse was overwhelmingly

---

[13] Musson and Robinson, *Science and technology*, p. 442; [Edward Baines], *Baines's Lancashire: a new printing of the two volumes of history, directory and gazetteer of the County Palatine of Lancaster by Edward Baines* [1824]], ed. Owen Ashmore, 2 vols. (Newton Abbot: David & Charles, 1968), vol. II, p. 321.

[14] Esther Moir, 'The industrial revolution: a romantic view', *History Today* 9 (1959), 589–97.

[15] Such souvenirs are on display, for example, in the Ironbridge Gorge Museums, Coalbrookdale, and the Wellcome Gallery of the Science Museum, London.

[16] Klingender, *Art and the industrial revolution*, pp. 37–56; Briggs, *Iron Bridge to Crystal Palace*, pp. 7–103; Ivanka Kovacevich, 'The mechanical muse: the impact of technical inventions on eighteenth-century neoclassical poetry', *Huntington Library Quarterly* 28 (1964–5), 263–81; Katherine Turner, 'Defoe's *Tour*: the changing "face of things"', *British Journal for Eighteenth-Century Studies* 24 (2001), 196–7; Stephen Daniels, *Fields of vision: landscape, imagery and national identity in England and the United States* (Princeton, NJ: Princeton University Press, 1993), pp. 43–79; Stephen Daniels, 'Loutherbourg's chemical theatre: *Coalbrookdale by Night*', in John Barrell (ed.), *Painting and the politics of culture: new essays on British art, 1700–1850* (Oxford: Oxford University Press, 1992), pp. 195–230; David Fraser, 'Fields of radiance: the scientific and industrial scenes of Joseph Wright', in Denis Cosgrove and Stephen Daniels (eds.), *The iconography of landscape: essays on the symbolic representation, design and use of past environments* (Cambridge: Cambridge University Press, 1988), pp. 119–41; D. Fraser, 'Joseph Wright and the Lunar Society: painter of light', in Judy Egerton (ed.), *Wright of Derby* (London: Tate Gallery, 1990), pp. 15–24; William Powell Jones, *The rhetoric of science: a study of scientific ideas and imagery in eighteenth-century English poetry* (London: Routledge & Kegan Paul, 1966), pp. 202–4.

one of 'progress'. The settings were rural and picturesque – occasionally sublime – and the warm glow of technical achievement combined with gainful employment had not yet been sullied by the urban squalor and scandalous working conditions that dimmed the nineteenth century's perspective.[17] Only the most perspicacious glimpsed and denounced the negative aspects of industrialization – Cassandras, ignored by a reading public eager to hear about 'the discovery of every new invention and the improvements in every useful art', as reported by the *Gentleman's Magazine* and similar publications.[18]

The increasing importance of manufactures was dawning also on serious students of the British economy. Of particular note was the cotton industry's sudden prominence: it was no less visible in official statistics than it was on the Lancashire landscape. Imports of raw cotton soared in value from £160,000 in 1772 to £917,000 in 1789, and from £1,129,000 in 1792 to £8,964,000 in 1827; by 1801, the industry accounted for two-fifths of Great Britain's manufactured exports.[19] Cotton manufacturers, campaigning for tariff protection against Indian competition, emphasized its economic significance by pointing both to its rapid ascent and its technological innovativeness. Especially influential was Patrick Colquhoun's well-informed but partisan tract of 1788, which conveyed cotton's importance to a generation of commentators. Rarely was the industry discussed thereafter without enthusiastic reference to its novel technology.[20] Will Hardy persuasively suggests that it was cotton's close association with overseas trade or 'commerce' which gave it especial resonance in eighteenth-century Britain, where commerce was perceived as the bedrock of national prosperity and security: on it was built the towering edifice of the Royal Navy, the national debt and ultimately the Protestant monarchy.[21] It was an auspicious time to be identified as an inventor of cotton machinery.

---

[17] Spadafora, *Idea of progress*, pp. 53–62; Turner, 'Defoe's *Tour*', 196–7.

[18] Bowden, *Industrial society*, pp. 15–16.

[19] The import figures are for England and Wales and for Great Britain respectively: B. R. Mitchell and Phyllis Deane, *Abstract of British historical statistics* (Cambridge: Cambridge University Press, 1962), pp. 286, 289; Pat Hudson, *The industrial revolution* (London and New York: Edward Arnold, 1992), pp. 182–5.

[20] [Patrick Colquhoun], *An important crisis, in the callico and muslin manufactory in Great Britain, explained* (London, 1788); William Hardy, *The origins of the idea of the Industrial Revolution* (Oxford: Trafford Publishing, 2006), pp. 30–3, 68–71. I am very grateful to Will Hardy for allowing me to see an earlier draft of this important revisionist work, on which I have drawn extensively here.

[21] Hardy, *Origins of the idea*, pp. 37–60. See also Colley, *Britons*, pp. 64–6; Fara, *Sympathetic attractions*, pp. 3–4; John Brewer, *The sinews of power: war, money and the English state, 1688–1783* (London: Unwin Hyman, 1989).

By the time of his death in 1792, Sir Richard Arkwright was acclaimed as the founding father of the British cotton industry.[22] Ironically, it may have been the fierce litigation of his patent for the water-frame (spinning machine), in 1781–5, that first brought Arkwright to public attention, while simultaneously casting doubt on his role in its invention.[23] Neatly sidestepping this controversial issue, William Combe began the tradition of ascribing the rise of the cotton industry (and more besides) to Arkwright:

> Some years previous to this period, an event happened which portended a considerable revolution in the manufactures of Great Britain. This was the invention of Mr Arkwright's celebrated machine.[24]

Commentators continued to associate Arkwright with the new inventions, usually choosing their words carefully to avoid a direct ascription, but there was equal emphasis on his promotion of the factory system and the cotton industry more generally.[25] They also began to praise the example of his meteoric social ascent, from obscurity to enormous wealth, a country seat, and a knighthood.[26]

Arkwright was one of a small number of inventors whose names began to be cited sporadically during the final decade of the eighteenth century, in both press and Parliament, as men who deserved the nation's gratitude. The others were James Watt and Matthew Boulton, Josiah Wedgwood, and James Brindley. None of the five was simply an inventor: four of them were highly successful entrepreneurs, who had established manufacturing firms that commercialized their inventions and designs, while Brindley was renowned as the engineer responsible for the duke of Bridgewater's famous canal. Manufacturing success, however, scarcely provided a sure route to national recognition. The fame of Wedgwood is

---

[22] *The Times*, 7 August 1792, 3c; 14 August 1792, 2b.

[23] John Hewish, *Prejudicial and inconvenient? A study of the Arkwright patent trials, 1781 and 1785* (London: British Library, 1985); John Hewish, 'From Cromford to Chancery Lane: new light on the Arkwright patent trials', *T&C* 28 (1987), 80–6.

[24] Adam Anderson, *An historical and chronological deduction of the origins of commerce*, 4 vols. (London: J. Walter, 1789), vol. IV, rev. William Combe, pp. 705–6, quoted in Hardy, *Origins of the idea*, p. 70. See also François Crouzet, *Britain ascendant: comparative studies in Franco-British economic history* (Cambridge: Cambridge University Press, 1985), pp. 127–48.

[25] David MacPherson, *Annals of commerce, manufactures, fisheries, and navigation*, 4 vols. (London: Nichols, 1805), vol. IV, pp. 79–80. See also Aikin, *Description of the country*, p. 170.

[26] Barbauld and Aikin, *Evenings at home*, p. 166. This may have been the source of the mistaken assumption that Arkwright's knighthood was awarded for his inventions or enterprise; rather, it was for his having presented Derbyshire's 'loyal address' to George III after an attempt on the king's life: R. A. Davenport, *Lives of individuals who raised themselves from poverty to eminence or fortune* (London: SDUK, 1841), p. 437.

explicable through identification with his ceramics, which graced the dinner tables of fashionable society. But why should the public recognize the names of steam-engine makers in Birmingham or a cotton manufacturer in deepest Derbyshire, however profitable their enterprises (and however notorious the litigation of their respective patents)?

The key to their initial fame was probably their celebration in the literary sensation of 1791, Erasmus Darwin's poem, *The botanic garden*. Physician, polymath, inventor and paternal grandfather of Charles Darwin, Erasmus Darwin had already published one part of this epic poem, *The loves of the plants*, in 1789. His witty and fanciful (sometimes ridiculous) account of the sexual exploits of the vegetable kingdom was received with critical acclaim – and no little parody. Two years later he reissued it, together with a second part, *The economy of vegetation*, which was essentially an encyclopaedia of science and technology in rhyming couplets of neoclassical and mythological imagery.[27] With great ingenuity and enthusiasm, Darwin expounded complex scientific ideas, explained how machinery worked, and speculated optimistically on future inventions. Not only did he praise contemporary men of science by name as inventors and discoverers – several of whom, including Wedgwood, Boulton and Watt, were his friends and fellow members of the Lunar Society – but he addressed them in heroic terms, glorifying them further through their juxtaposition with mythological gods and heroes, and lending enchantment with references to nymphs, gnomes, giants and mysterious places.[28]

The hard labour of canal construction Darwin idealized in the persona of the 'immortal Brindley' (whose arm normally wielded surveying instruments, not a pick):[29]

---

[27] Maureen McNeil, *Under the banner of science: Erasmus Darwin and his age* (Manchester: Manchester University Press, 1987), pp. 8–30; Janet Browne, 'Botany for gentlemen: Erasmus Darwin and *The Loves of the Plants*', *Isis* 80 (1989), 593–620; Londa Schiebinger, 'The private life of plants: sexual politics in Carl Linnaeus and Erasmus Darwin', in Marina Benjamin (ed.), *Science and sensibility: gender and scientific enquiry, 1780–1945* (Oxford: Blackwell, 1991), pp. 121–43; Jones, *Rhetoric of science*, pp. 209–12; King-Hele, *Doctor of revolution*, pp. 190–7, 209–21; Kovacevich, 'Mechanical muse', 274–7.

[28] For the Lunar Society, see: McNeil, *Under the banner of science*, pp. 10–19 and passim; Robert E. Schofield, *The Lunar Society of Birmingham: a social history of provincial science and industry in eighteenth-century England* (Oxford: Clarendon Press, 1963); Jennifer S. Uglow, *The lunar men: the friends who made the future, 1730–1810* (London: Faber & Faber, 2002). Darwin checked with his immediate friends how they wished him to represent their achievements: McNeil, *Under the banner of science*, pp. 21, 28.

[29] When Brindley died in 1772, Darwin told Wedgwood the canal companies should erect a monument to him in Westminster Abbey: King-Hele, *Doctor of revolution*, p. 92. He reiterated this view (though now proposed Lichfield cathedral for its site) in *The economy of vegetation*, footnote to canto III, line 341.

> So with strong arm immortal BRINDLEY leads
> His long canals, and parts the velvet meads;
> Winding in lucid lines, the watery mass
> Mines the firm rock, or loads the deep morass,
> With rising locks a thousand hills alarms,
> Flings o'er a thousand streams its silver arms,
> Feeds the long vale, the nodding woodland laves,
> And Plenty, Arts, and Commerce freight the waves.
>
> (*Economy of vegetation*, canto III, lines 329–32)

Wedgwood and his new factory in the Staffordshire potteries – named 'Etruria' at Darwin's suggestion – received glowing tribute, as did his famous Portland vase (illustrated in engravings by William Blake).[30] The steam engine inspired fifty witty lines, full of classical references and dramatic imagery, in which Darwin described how it worked, charted its many uses (including the provision of power to Boulton's coining machinery), and famously imagined a glorious future for it in the realms of transport:

> Soon shall thy arm, UNCONQUER'D STEAM! Afar
> Drag the slow barge, or drive the rapid car;
> Or on wide-waving wings expanded bear
> The flying-chariot through the fields of air.
>
> (*Economy of vegetation*, canto I, lines 289–92)

In a footnote, Darwin explained, 'A few years ago Mr Watt of Glasgow much improved this machine, and Mr Boulton of Birmingham has applied it to a variety of purposes, such as raising water from mines'; he appended, at some length, a history of the steam engine up to Watt's invention of the separate condenser.[31] When told of Darwin's poetic intentions, Watt had quipped: 'I know not how steam-engines come among the plants: I cannot find them in the *Systema Naturae*, by which I should conclude that they are neither plants, animals, nor fossils.'[32]

Gossypia, the cotton plant, secured Arkwright's system of mechanical spinning a place in *The loves of the plants*:

> First with nice eye emerging Naiads cull
> From leathery pods the vegetable wool;
> With wiry teeth *revolving cards* release

---

[30] King-Hele, *Doctor of revolution*, pp. 74, 201–2, 209.

[31] Erasmus Darwin, *Botanic garden* [1791] (4th edn, London: J. Johnson, 1799) pt I (*Economy of vegetation*), p. 31; additional note XI.

[32] King-Hele, *Doctor of revolution*, p. 203. Boulton and Watt's steam engine and their works at Soho, in Birmingham, drew heroic couplets also from Anna Seward and James Bisset: Kovacevich, 'Mechanical muse', 273–4, 278–80.

The tangled knots, and smoothe the ravell'd fleece;
Next moves the *iron-hand* with fingers fine,
Combs the wide card, and forms the eternal line;
Slow, with soft lips, the *whirling Can* acquires
The tender skeins, and wraps in rising spires;
With quicken'd pace *successive rollers* move,
And these retain, and those extend their *rove*,
Then fly the spoles, the rapid axles glow;
And slowly circumvolves the labouring wheel below.

(*Loves of the plants*, canto II, lines 93–104)

'On the river Derwent, near Matlock, in Derbyshire', added Darwin, 'Sir Richard Arkwright has erected his curious and magnificent machinery for spinning cotton, which had in vain been attempted by many ingenious artists before him.'[33] In his posthumously published poem, *The temple of nature* (1803), Darwin elevated Arkwright's name to the text and his role to one of apparently single-handed achievement:

So ARKWRIGHT taught from Cotton-pods to cull,
And stretch in lines the vegetable wool;
With teeth of steel its fibre-knots unfurl'd
And with the silver tissue clothed the world.

(*The temple of nature*, canto IV, lines 261–4)

'Whom', asks McNeil, 'did Arkwright teach?'[34] This stanza is a stark example of Darwin's preoccupation with the niceties of technology and the achievement of its putative creators, to the complete exclusion of the workers and the labour process.

This disregard, which Darwin seems to have shared with his fellow 'Lunaticks', had much in common with the admiration for disembodied technology evident among contemporary tourists. If the inventor was rising in popular estimation, it was partly with the assistance of the same psychological mechanism that made generals, not common soldiers, into national heroes.[35] A further feature of Darwin's poetry, which helped to portray men of science in a heroic light, was his graphic commemoration of those who died in the course of conducting experiments – with lightning conductors, balloons and diving bells.[36] The

---

[33] Darwin, *Botanic garden*, pt II (*Loves of the plants*), footnote to canto II, line 87.
[34] McNeil, *Under the banner of science*, pp. 17–19.
[35] Dawson, *Soldier heroes*, pp. 79–83; Stephen Pumfrey, 'Who did the work? Experimental philosophers and public demonstrators in Augustan England' *BJHS* 28 (1995), 131–56.
[36] Darwin, *Botanic garden*, pt I (*Economy of nature*), canto I, lines 371–82; canto IV, lines 148–62, 229–33.

physical risks which such men were prepared to take as they grappled with the forces of nature suggested that scholars and men of peace could be no less courageous than those who risked their lives in warfare. This perspective was entirely compatible with Darwin's political views. Like many British reformers and radicals, Darwin and other members of the Lunar Society welcomed the French Revolution and deplored the British government's armed response.[37] Joseph Priestley sought sanctuary in the United States, following the attack by a 'Church and King' mob on his and other Dissenters' houses (including those of two other 'Lunaticks') in Birmingham in 1791, and James Watt's reputation was temporarily compromised by his son's minor but direct participation in the French revolution.[38]

National benefactors

An undercurrent of protest against the neglect of inventors and discoverers, in comparison with the honours heaped upon military heroes, persisted through the bellicose eighteenth century. For some critics, it was simply a plea to reward inventive talent; for others, primarily a concern to condemn the horrors of war. A minority desired to create new, pacific heroes who would not merely stand beside the old 'feudal' champions but oust them completely.[39] In the 1790s, opponents of the war against revolutionary France developed an argument that the source of Britain's strength lay not in its armed forces (recently humiliated in America) but in its robust economy, especially its manufacturing industry, which was clearly superior to anything across the Channel. James Currie, for example, a physician and fellow of the Royal Society who wrote under the pseudonym of 'Jaspar Wilson', argued that Britain had prospered 'in spite of the wretched politics of her rulers'. 'The security of property and the liberty of spirit diffused through the nation', said Currie, 'have called forth the talents of our people ... The genius of Watt, Wedgewood [sic], and Arkwright, has counteracted the expense and

[37] McNeil, *Under the banner of science*, pp. 64–9; King-Hele, *Doctor of revolution*, pp. 211–12, 230–2, 243–5; N. Garfinkle, 'Science and religion in England, 1790–1800: the critical response to the work of Erasmus Darwin', *JHI* 14 (1955), 376–88; Alan Bewell, '"Jacobin plants": botany as social theory in the 1790s', *The Wordsworth Circle* 20 (1989), 132–9.

[38] McNeil, *Under the banner of science*, pp. 79–85; R. B. Rose, 'The Priestley riots of 1791', *P&P* 18 (1960), 68–88; Dorothy A. Stanfield, *Thomas Beddoes M. D. 1760–1808: chemist, physician, democrat* (Dordrecht, Boston, Lancaster: D. Reidel Pub. Co., 1984), pp. 2–4; Peter M. Jones, 'Living the enlightenment and the French revolution: James Watt, Matthew Boulton, and their sons', *HJ* 42 (1999), 157–82.

[39] See above, pp. 32–3.

folly of the American war.'[40] In a friendly admonition, his colleague in the Royal Society, the antiquary George Chalmers, disputed whether 'a chemist in Birmingham, a potter in Stafford, and a millwright in Manchester' could be responsible for such great effects 'if the million be not already enlightened and active' and hence responsive to their ideas. Britain's unprecedented export boom of 1786–92, thought Chalmers, should be credited more widely: it was 'owing to our having a greater number of people, who are better instructed, and more industrious, who employ greater capitals, to more profitable purposes, who derive an energy from the constitution, and place a confidence in their rulers.'[41]

Their scale of values was shared by others who were generally less radical in politics. Sir Frederick Eden, for example, who espoused Adam Smith's economic ideas and defended labour-saving machinery as an indispensable means of improving the welfare of Britain's growing population, suggested that men whose inventions benefited the people should be raised to equal standing with military heroes – if not higher.

The Dutch, who erected a statue to the man who taught them to cure herrings, acted upon just principles: he who opens a new channel of commerce, and discovers a new means of subsistence, merits no less estimation than the philosophers, and defenders of their country. The inventor of a machine appears to me to rank equally among the benefactors of mankind: he supplies society with additional hands (for machinery is nothing more) and, consequently, provides additional means of raising subsistence.[42]

This view was echoed by the Scottish historian, David Macpherson, an authority on British overseas trade. The benefits which Arkwright had conferred upon the nation, said Macpherson, were 'infinitely greater than those he acquired for himself, and far more solid and durable than a hundred conquests … his name ought to be transmitted to future ages along with those of the most distinguished real benefactors of mankind.'[43]

---

[40] Jaspar Wilson [*pseud.* James Currie], *A letter, commercial and political, addressed to the Rt Honble William Pitt* (3rd edn, London, 1793), p. 7.

[41] George Chalmers, *An estimate of the comparative strength of Great Britain during the present and four preceding reigns* (new edn, London: John Stockdale, 1794), pp. xxiii–xxiv; Alexander Du Toit, 'Chalmers, George (*bap.* 1742, *d.* 1825)', *ODNB*, www.oxforddnb.com/view/article/5028, accessed 18 October 2006.

[42] Eden, *State of the poor*, vol. I, p. 443; Donald Winch, 'Eden, Sir Frederick Morton, second baronet (1766–1809)', *ODNB*, www.oxforddnb.com/view/article/8450, accessed 18 October 2006. See also Arthur Young, *Northern tour* (1770), vol. I, quoted in G. E. Mingay, *Arthur Young and his times* (London: Macmillan, 1975), p. 92; G. E. Mingay, 'Young, Arthur (1741–1820)', *ODNB*, online edn, October 2005, www.oxforddnb.com/view/article/30256, accessed 18 October 2006.

[43] Macpherson, *Annals of commerce*, vol. IV, pp. 79–80; M. J. Mercer, 'Macpherson, David (1746–1816)', *ODNB*, www.oxforddnb.com/view/article/17722, accessed 12 September 2007. For Arkwright's later reputation as an inventor and entrepreneur, see below, pp. 193–8.

It was primarily thanks to radical editors that inventors and engineers began to be memorialized in biographical dictionaries (themselves a recent innovation).[44] John Aikin was a dissenting physician and friend of Erasmus Darwin who, with William Enfield, a Unitarian minister, produced a highly regarded biographical dictionary of men 'engaged in public affairs'.[45] They selected the subjects of their *General biography* on the principles of 'invention and improvement', chiefly in the fields of 'art, science or literature'. Aikin asserted that it was the exercise of 'an inventive talent' that distinguished the superior individual from 'the common mass' in any sphere, but cited as his particular examples James Brindley and Sir Isaac Newton. 'How much higher, as an intellectual being,' he exclaimed, 'does a Brindley rank, directing the complex machinery of a canal, which he himself has invented, than an Alexander at the head of his army!'[46] Aikin's model of invention and discovery was essentially an incremental one: it was the exceptionally large steps, therefore, that merited proper acknowledgement.

When the addition made has been something considerable, the improver seems to have a just title to have his name perpetuated; and accordingly we have been careful not to omit recording every person, of whom it may be said, that any of the nobler pursuits of the human mind received from his labours a conspicuous advancement.[47]

There were entries for Richard Arkwright, James Brindley, John Smeaton, John Harrison and Josiah Wedgwood. The most surprising omissions were James Watt, Matthew Boulton and Edward Jenner.

Arkwright's entry was unusually frank in its discussion of his claim to the water-frame's invention: the evidence was inconclusive. His merit was to have established 'a great national manufacture', succeeding where others had failed, thanks to his 'perseverance, skill and activity'.[48] Brindley's contained a long paragraph in praise of a new 'order of men, at present distinguished by the name of civil engineers', which had been called into existence by 'the improved state of our "manufactories", and the increase of our trade' during the past half century.[49] Undoubtedly,

---

[44] Richard Yeo, 'Alphabetical lives: scientific biography in historical dictionaries and encyclopaedias', in Shortland and Yeo (eds.), *Telling lives in science*, pp. 143–54.

[45] Aikin and Enfield (eds.), *General biography*, vol. I, p. 3. See Marilyn L. Brooks, 'Aikin, John (1747–1822)', *ODNB*, www.oxforddnb.com/view/article/230, accessed 18 October 2006; R. K. Webb, 'Enfield, William (1741–1797)', *ODNB*, www.oxforddnb.com/view/article/8804, accessed 18 October 2006. Since Enfield died two years before the first volume's publication, Aikin alone was probably responsible for writing the preface, though not for the principles of selection.

[46] Aikin and Enfield (eds.), *General biography*, vol. I, p. 4.   [47] Ibid.

[48] 'Arkwright, Sir Richard', by 'N', in ibid., vol. I, pp. 389–90.

[49] 'Brindley, James', in ibid., vol. II, pp. 300–1.

the highly visible development of the waterway network, especially during the height of the canal 'mania' of 1791–6, had ignited a particular interest in Brindley, who thirty years before had surveyed the route for the duke of Bridgewater's pioneering canal to take coal into Manchester. His lifelong illiteracy and reputedly unconventional methods of work helped to embellish the story: he appeared in an early history of the waterways as 'one of those geniuses which nature sometimes brings to maturity without the necessity of cultivation' – a reputation that has endured.[50]

A contemporary work, British public characters, which was published annually between 1798 and 1806, cast its net more widely than the General biography, but limited itself to men (and a few women) who were currently in the public eye and 'who acquire and demand public confidence'.[51] Its anonymous editors' political stance was announced by the inclusion in its first volume of not only Admiral Nelson but also Darwin and his fellow radical, Joseph Priestley; Priestley's entry pointedly proclaimed that, 'his chemical labours do honour to the nation that produced and exiled him'.[52] Subsequent volumes included Edmund Cartwright ('so well known as a skilful mechanic, and an agreeable poet, is the younger brother of John Cartwright, Esq'), Watt, Boulton, Jenner and Henry Greathead (reputed inventor of the lifeboat). The inclusion of Cartwright and Greathead was unusual, the former explicable through his fraternal connection to radicalism, the latter because of the humanitarian nature of his invention, for which he had been rewarded by Parliament and other bodies.[53]

The healing arts always provided an easy contrast with the battlefield's destructiveness: Jenner's discovery of vaccination was 'a victory of man, – not over men, – but over a cruel and unrelenting disease'; it was 'beyond all comparison, the most valuable, and the most important discovery, ever made'. The author envisaged 'a more enlightened' society where inventors and discoverers, such as Jenner, were honoured in the ways presently reserved for military heroes, responsible 'for the desolation of

---

[50] John Phillips, A general history of inland navigation, foreign and domestic (5th edn, London, 1805), repr. as Charles Hadfield (ed.), Phillips' inland navigation (Newton Abbot: David & Charles, 1970), pp. 100–1, 104, 105. See also Aikin, Description of the country, pp. 139–45. For the excitement generated by the Bridgewater canal, see Spadafora, Idea of progress, pp. 57–9; Hugh Malet, Bridgewater: the canal duke, 1736–1803 (Manchester: Manchester University Press, 1977), pp. 66–8. Also see C. T. G. Boucher, James Brindley, engineer, 1716–1772 (Norwich: Goose, 1968).

[51] British public characters of 1798 (London: Richard Phillips, 1798), p. iv. According to LeFanu, Richard Phillips was both its editor and its publisher: W. R. LeFanu, A bio-bibliography of Edward Jenner, 1749–1823 (London: Harvey & Blythe Ltd, 1951), p. 145.

[52] 'Joseph Priestley', in British public characters of 1798, p. 435.

[53] For other claimants to the laurels, see James Burnley, 'Greathead, Henry (1757–1816?)', rev. Arthur G. Credland, ODNB, www.oxforddnb.com/view/article/11362, accessed 20 October 2006, and below, pp. 342–3.

provinces, and the destruction of human kind'.[54] Several pages later, however, he speculated that the protection against smallpox that vaccination afforded to British troops in the Egyptian campaign might have played a valuable part in deciding the war.[55] This concession signals the tension that was to characterize not only several accolades to Watt in 1824 but many mid-nineteenth-century tributes to other inventors. Unless the writer were a determined pacifist or anti-militarist, there was always a temptation to argue the inventor's case, not on the basis of the moral superiority of the arts of peace over the resort to arms, but on the pragmatic point that scientific and technical ingenuity underpinned the military state to at least the same extent as did its army and navy. The latter perspective dates from the fifteenth century when, according to Pamela Long, 'the *praxis* of military leadership came to be closely associated with armaments and techniques – in contrast to most ancient models, in which generalship was perceived to rest on character and qualities of leadership rather than on technology'.[56]

One revolutionary innovation, in particular, was to make this case very forcefully when the Napoleonic wars resumed in 1803. This was the integrated series of steam-powered, block-cutting machines that the French refugee, Marc Isambard Brunel, designed for the Royal Dockyard at Portsmouth. Under Samuel Bentham's dynamic leadership, the dockyard was already undergoing extensive modernization and mechanization when Brunel proposed to mass-produce the wooden pulley blocks, needed in enormous quantities on sailing ships. In 1803, the first set of machinery was dispatched from Henry Maudslay's engineering workshop in London to be installed in the dockyard.[57] By September 1805, when Lord Nelson called to inspect the highly ingenious production lines, the block mills were already attracting an influx of equally curious, if less distinguished, visitors to the point where they were becoming a nuisance. It was a problem exacerbated by the machinery's appearance in various encyclopaedias, not to mention the visit in 1814 of the Prince Regent, accompanied by the emperor of Russia, the king of Prussia, and other allied dignitaries, reported extensively in *The Times*.[58] Although attention

---

[54] *British public characters of 1802–1803*, p. 18.   [55] Ibid., p. 37.

[56] Long, 'Power, patronage and the authorship of *ars*', p. 5. See also Pamela O. Long and Alex Roland, 'Military secrecy in antiquity and early medieval Europe: a critical reassessment', *History and Technology* 11 (1994), 259–90, and below, pp. 95, 220–36.

[57] Carolyn C. Cooper, 'The Portsmouth system of manufacture', *T&C* 25 (1984), 182–225; Jonathan Coad, *The Portsmouth block mills: Bentham, Brunel and the start of the Royal Navy's industrial revolution* (Swindon: English Heritage, 2005), pp. 49–65. I am grateful to Tony Woolrich for drawing to my attention both Coad's splendid book and the significance of encyclopaedia entries.

[58] Coad, *Portsmouth block mills*, pp. 10–13, 101–3.

focused principally on the machinery not its makers, it would be hard to imagine that the reputations of Brunel, Bentham and Maudslay, in particular, and of inventors collectively were not enhanced by its fame. A similar process was quietly advancing the public's regard for a range of inventors, whose devices were described and illustrated in the rapidly expanding genre of technical encyclopaedias.[59]

There is also evidence of individual inventors, relatively unknown today, enjoying a high local or even national reputation, which may have helped to counteract the residual distrust of projectors and patentees. Cuthbert Clarke, for example, a tenant farmer of Belford (Northumbria) was said by Arthur Young to be 'very famous in the north for his knowledge of mechanics'. Young listed several of Clarke's inventions, including a machine for draining swamps, which had won an award from the Society of Arts, and 'the grand machine on which he builds his reputation ... for the threshing of corn'.[60] Another prolific northern inventor, Adam Walker, acquired renown through his popular scientific lectures in the north and midlands during the 1770s, which led into a successful career in London.[61] Perhaps best known today for his role in the foundation of the British Association for the Advancement of Science, the Scottish physicist, Sir David Brewster was propelled to fame in 1816 by his invention of the kaleidoscope (an offshoot of his research in optics). His daughter recalled that,

[it] spread his name far and near, from schoolboy to statesman, from peasant to philosopher, more surely and lastingly than his many noble and useful inventions [i.e. scientific discoveries]. This beautiful little toy, with its marvellous witcheries of light and colour, spread over Europe and America with a *furor* which is now scarcely credible.[62]

An associated group of ingenious men, who enjoyed lasting esteem and advanced the credibility of inventors, belonged to London's instrument-making and clock-making trades. Highly innovative, they worked closely with natural philosophers; many were themselves elected to the Royal Society. Moreover, they signed their products, their shops lined the best streets in London and Bath, and they courted the patronage of royalty and aristocracy. Two of the eighteenth-century's most prominent clock-makers, George Graham and Thomas Tompion, were buried in Westminster Abbey; the inscription to Graham stating that his

[59] See the bibliography of Yeo, 'Alphabetical lives', 164–9.
[60] Young, *Northern tour*, vol. III, pp. 44–52, quoted in Bowden, *Industrial society*, p. 20.
[61] *European Magazine*, XXI, 411–13; Langford, *Century of Birmingham life*, vol. I, p. 252; both cited in Bowden, *Industrial society*, pp. 20–1.
[62] Mrs Gordon, *The home life of Sir David Brewster, by his daughter* (Edinburgh: Edmonston & Douglas, 1869), p. 95.

'inventions do honour … the British genius … [and his] accurate performances, are the standard of mechanical skill'.[63]

It also seems indicative of the growing respect which society accorded inventors that the most successful among them wished to be remembered as such and be identified with their inventions. From the mid-eighteenth century, it was not unusual for an inventor or engineer who commissioned a portrait of himself to be depicted with an accoutrement that referred to his greatest technical achievement. Not only was this an expression of pride in his work, but it was also an assertion of ownership of his intellectual property, at a time when that might easily be jeopardized by a priority dispute, an adverse decision at law, or another man's pre-emptive patent.[64] The well-known portrait of Richard Arkwright, by Joseph Wright of Derby (figure 3.2), which displays at his side a set of the rollers that formed the crucial part of his water-frame, was painted in 1789 – four years after his patent was revoked.[65] Similarly, John Harrison sits proudly surrounded by his greatest horological inventions, in the portrait painted by Thomas King in 1765–6. Having reached the standard of precision required by the Longitude Act, with the marine chronometer (the size of a large pocket watch) indicated by his right hand, he was then engaging the government in a prolonged tussle to receive the reward due to him.[66] The portrait was soon reproduced (figure 3.3), and Harrison enjoyed the distinction of being the only living person memorialized in the *Biographia Britannica* (1766).[67] James Watt was portrayed by von Breda, in 1792, with a diagram of his steam engine on

[63] R. Sorrenson, 'George Graham, visible technician', *BJHS* 32 (1999), 206; Fara, *Sympathetic attractions*, pp. 84–6; J. Bennett *et al.*, *Science and profit in 18th-century London* (Cambridge: the Whipple Museum, 1985), passim; Maurice Daumas, *Scientific instruments of the seventeenth and eighteenth centuries and their makers*, trans. M. Holbrook (London: B. T. Batsford, 1972), pp. 93, 159–66, 173–6, 228–9, 231–4. For a measure of their continuing fame in the late nineteenth century, see MacLeod and Nuvolari, 'Pitfalls of prosopography', 767–8.

[64] MacLeod, *Inventing the industrial revolution*, pp. 60–74; Dutton, *Patent system*, pp. 69–85.

[65] J. J. Mason, 'Arkwright, Sir Richard (1732–1792)', *ODNB*, www.oxforddnb.com/view/article/645, accessed 27 October 2006; also R. S. Fitton, *The Arkwrights, spinners of fortune* (Manchester: Manchester University Press, 1989), pp. 200–3; R. B. Prosser, *Birmingham inventors and inventions* [Birmingham: privately published, 1881], with a new foreword by Asa Briggs (Wakefield: S. R. Publishers, 1970), p. 10; Tann, 'Richard Arkwright and technology', 29–44.

[66] Mezzotint by Philippe Talsaert (1768), after a portrait in oils by T. King, 1765–6; Andrew King, 'Harrison, John (*bap.* 1693, *d.* 1776)', *ODNB*, www.oxforddnb.com/view/article/12438, accessed 18 October 2006; Anthony G. Randall, 'The timekeeper that won the longitude prize', in William J. H. Andrewes (ed.), *The quest for longitude* (Cambridge, MA: Collection of Scientific Instruments, Harvard University, 1996), pp. 236–54.

[67] Harrison's obituary in the *Gentleman's Magazine* (1776) describes him as 'a most ingenious mechanic': Benedict Anderson, *Imagined communities: reflections on the origin and spread of nationalism* (rev. edn, London: Verso, 1991), p. 188; B. Reading, engr., repr. in *European*

3.2 In this portrait, after Joseph Wright of Derby, Richard Arkwright proudly displays the rollers from his water-frame, patented in 1769.

the desk beside him: prepared finally to prosecute infringements of his patent, Watt claims the honour of invention while maintaining the dignity of the 'philosopher', seated in his study (figure 3.4).[68]

Magazine (October 1789); W. Hollar, stipple (NPG); repr. in *The gallery of portraits: with memoirs,* 7 vols. (London: Charles Knight for SDUK, 1833), vol. V, pp. 153–5.

[68] Tann, 'Mr Hornblower and his crew', 95–105. For the numerous reproductions of von Breda's and other portraits and busts of Watt, see Library of Congress, *A. L. A. portrait*

3.3 *John Harrison*, mezzotint engraving by P. L. Tassaert, after an oil painting by Thomas King, 1768. The final version of Harrison's marine chronometer (H4) rests beside his right hand; behind him are two earlier inventions, the gridiron pendulum of 1726, and the H3 version of the chronometer.

His friend, Captain Joseph Huddart, sitting beside a globe, places the points of his compass to a diagram of his rope-making machinery (the subject of both piracy and workers' hostility).[69] Less genteelly, Walter Taylor of Southampton holds the circular saw that he claimed to have

index: index to portraits contained in printed books and periodicals, ed. W. C. Lane and N. E. Browne (Washington, DC: American Library Association, 1906), pp. 1531–2. See also 'James Watt' folder, NPG Archives, London.

[69] 'Captn. Joseph Huddart, F. R. S. from a picture in the possession of Chas Turner, Esqr', engr. by James Stow, after John Hoppner, RA (London, 1801), 'Joseph Huddart' folder, NPG Archives; [William Cotton], *A brief memoir of the late Capt'n Joseph Huddart, FRS* (London, School-Press, 1855), pp. iv–v, 21–22.

3.4 *James Watt* by Carl Fredrik von Breda, 1792. While indistinct, the engineering drawing on the table allows a fashionably dressed Watt to assert his claim over the invention without sacrificing his status as a philosopher.

invented.[70] Marc Brunel, fashionably dressed, rests his hands on a sheaf of engineering drawings, in front of a prominently displayed mortizing machine, used at Portsmouth.[71] Sir Humphry Davy, newly elected president of the Royal Society, is presented as a 'glamorous man' by

[70] Portrait in oils, of Walter Taylor (1734–1803), c. 1784, by Gainsborough Dupont, in J. P. M. Pannell, 'The Taylors of Southampton: pioneers in mechanical engineering', *Proceedings of the Institution of Mechanical Engineers* 169 (1955), 927, fig. 7.

[71] Portrait in oils by James Northcote, c. 1812, NPG 978, in Coad, *Portsmouth block mills*, p. 51. See also Brunel's later portrait by Samuel Drummond (1835), in front of the entrance to the Thames Tunnel, NPG 89, in Adam Hart-Davis, *Chain reactions: pioneers of British science and technology and the stories that link them* (London: National Portrait Gallery, 2000), p. 109.

3.5 *Edward Jenner* by James Northcote, 1803, completed 1823. A manuscript of *The origin of the vaccine inoculation*, its title page illustrated with a watercolour of a cow, rests against a cow's hoof, on the author's desk.

Sir Thomas Lawrence in 1821; this portrait effectively closed Davy's priority dispute with George Stephenson over the invention of the miners' safety lamp, depicting it prominently on the table beside Davy's right hand.[72] The lamp also stands at Davy's side in a more contemplative portrait of the same year by Thomas Phillips.[73] Edward Jenner repeatedly appears with cows and dairymaids (symbols of his discovery of vaccination), although in James Northcote's second portrait of him (figure 3.5)

---

[72] Jordanova, *Defining features*, p. 101; G. R. Newton after Sir Thomas Lawrence, *Sir Humphry Davy*, 1830, line engraving: NPG, also in David Knight, 'Davy, Sir Humphry, baronet (1778–1829)', *ODNB*, www.oxforddnb.com/view/article/7314, accessed 18 October 2006. For the priority dispute over the safety lamp, see Michael W. Flinn, *The history of the British coal industry, volume 2, 1700–1830: the industrial revolution* (Oxford: Clarendon Press, 1984), pp. 138–45.

[73] NPG 2546, in Hart-Davis, *Chain reactions*, p. 167.

the cow is elevated to the frontispiece of the treatise on vaccination at his elbow, as Jenner is redefined from rustic amateur in the fields to intellectual in the study.[74] John Smeaton is pictured with the Eddystone lighthouse, while James Brindley and Thomas Telford pose in front of landscapes that feature their aqueducts and bridges.[75]

However, we should not be over-sanguine. If, by the late eighteenth century, British public opinion was becoming more sympathetic to inventors, it was still a far cry from the status they enjoyed elsewhere, especially in France and the United States. The Royal Society had long cast envious glances at the generous royal patronage enjoyed by the Académie des Sciences; one of its more inventive fellows had recommended to Queen Anne that she introduce measures to promote and protect inventions 'as in France'.[76] There, as Liliane Hilaire-Pérez has shown, inventors were at the heart of the Enlightenment project and their prestige benefited from the state's pursuit of economic development: invention became *une affaire d'État* ('an affair of state'), especially from the mid-century. *On peut même dire que le seul fait d'inventer est déjà considéré comme un acte de civisme, tant l'invention porte les espoirs réformateurs de l'État.* ('It might even be said that simply inventing was regarded as an act of good citizenship, so much did invention bear the reforming hopes of the state.')[77] With most of their rewards coming directly from the state, French inventors were forced less often into the company of 'projectors' and so were hardly besmirched by the excesses of the stock market. Moreover, the thorough examination of inventions by the Académie des Sciences and other official bodies meant that a French *privilège* carried a relatively reliable royal guarantee of its technical feasibility, which contrasted sharply with the lack of scrutiny bestowed on English patents.[78] The status of French inventors rose with the increasing respect for craft skills, endorsed by the publication of the *Encyclopédie*, and was enhanced further by the discourse of 'genius' and 'talent' that grew up in Enlightened circles,

[74] NPG 62; Jordanova, *Defining features*, pp. 23–5, 87–95, 107, 116–21; Jordanova, 'Remembrance of science past', 391–403.

[75] A. W. Skempton, 'Smeaton, John (1724–1792)', *ODNB*, online edn, October 2005, www.oxforddnb.com/view/article/25746, accessed 27 October 2006; Roland Paxton, 'Telford, Thomas (1757–1834)', *ODNB*, www.oxforddnb.com/view/article/27107, accessed 27 October 2006; Metius Chappell, *British engineers* (London: William Collins, 1942), pp. 11, 13, 17.

[76] Stewart, *Rise of public science*, p. 51; MacLeod, *Inventing the industrial revolution*, p. 195.

[77] Hilaire-Pérez, *L'Invention technique*, p. 52; also ibid., pp. 65–75, 131–2, 315–17. Cf. Margaret C. Jacob, *Scientific culture and the making of the industrial west* (New York and Oxford: Oxford University Press, 1997), pp. 165–74, 185.

[78] Hilaire-Pérez, *L'Invention technique*, pp. 83–4, 114–24, 313–17; Robin Briggs, 'The *Académie royale des sciences* and the pursuit of utility', *P&P* 131 (1991), 38–87.

especially in the works of Diderot. Although most inventors found their integration into elite scientific circles barred by the status anxieties of the academicians, they discovered alternative routes to *la gloire*.[79] Thus, as well as enjoying access to financial support for trials, models and publication from various government bodies, they also received the lucrative patronage of royal and aristocratic clientèles, enthusiastic for novelty; Hilaire-Pérez describes Versailles as *un véritable chantier expérimental* ('a veritable site for experiments').[80] Nor was their eminence a casualty of the Revolution: the patent law of 1791 uniquely recognized the inventor's 'natural right' in his intellectual property – the latter concept itself newly minted to garner popular support.[81]

The previous year had seen the newly independent United States enact its first patent law, its speed of action itself a testimony to the importance which this new republic also placed on innovation. An even stronger signal was Congress's allocation of the scrutiny of patent applications to a tribunal of three cabinet members – an unrealistic addition to ministerial workloads, which was revised by the act of 1793.[82] Congress also designed its patent system to facilitate the American inventor's registration and exploitation of his intellectual property, not least by requiring only a small fee.[83] It was indicative of a trust in the average inventor's probity and diligence that, by contrast, the United Kingdom's legislators failed to endorse for most of the nineteenth century.[84]

---

[79] Hilaire-Pérez, *L'Invention technique*, pp. 143–68. For Diderot's views on inventive genius, see Hope Mason, *Value of creativity*, pp. 115–20; Liliane Hilaire-Pérez, 'Diderot's views on artists' and inventors' rights: invention, imitation, and reputation', *BJHS* 35 (2002), 129–50.

[80] Hilaire-Pérez, *L'Invention technique*, pp. 169–73; quotation on p. 172.

[81] F. Machlup and Edith Penrose, 'The patent controversy in the nineteenth century', *Journal of Economic History* 10 (1950), 15–17; Hilaire-Pérez, *L'Invention technique*, pp. 173, 183–5; Jacob, *Scientific culture*, pp. 178–85.

[82] Steven Lubar, 'The transformation of antebellum patent law', *T&C* 32 (1991), 934–5.

[83] B. Zorina Khan and Kenneth L. Sokoloff, 'Patent institutions, industrial organization and early technological change: Britain and the United States, 1790–1850', in Berg and Bruland (eds.), *Technological revolutions in Europe*, pp. 297–8. Nonetheless, many American inventors 'complained bitterly' about their patent system, and Lubar suggests the American public's admiration for inventors at this time is a myth that needs to be scrutinized: Lubar, 'Transformation of antebellum patent law', 936–8. For the traditional interpretation see, e.g. Jennifer Clark, 'The American image of technology from the Revolution to 1840', *American Quarterly* 39 (1987), 431–49.

[84] Christine MacLeod, Jennifer Tann, James Andrew and Jeremy Stein, 'Evaluating inventive activity: the cost of nineteenth-century UK patents and the fallibility of renewal data', *EHR* 56 (2003), 542.

Contests of fame

We will conclude this chapter by comparing the reputations of James
Watt, Edward Jenner and Henry Greathead, as they stood at the beginning of the nineteenth century. All three were of sufficient distinction to
be noticed by *British public characters*, but subsequently the histories of
their respective reputations diverged. Greathead is now virtually
unknown, despite the persistent regard for his invention among the
British public (attested by the high level of legacies and donations
received by the Royal National Lifeboat Service), while Watt and
Jenner both remain internationally famous. However, as the next chapter
will demonstrate, it was Watt, rather than Jenner, whose reputation was
posthumously constructed to epitomize 'the great inventor' and a British
national hero – an outcome that was by no means evident in 1800.

Neither Greathead nor Jenner sought a patent for their respective inventions. Both were awarded large parliamentary grants, during a short interlude when such sums were regularly considered to be a suitable reward for
inventors who, for various reasons, the patent system had failed. This
upsurge in grants is itself testimony to the growing regard for inventors in
British society. The precedent for such alternative rewards is sometimes
said to have been the Longitude Act of 1713, which promised up to
£20,000 for a method of accurately determining the longitude at sea, but,
strictly speaking, the act offered an incentive, a prize with a specific goal in
view. The first large premium awarded by Parliament to compensate an
inventor *after the event* was that made to Sir Thomas Lombe in 1732: rather
than renew his patent, as he requested, Parliament granted him £14,000.[85]
In 1815, Patrick Colquhoun listed fourteen major, and miscellaneous
minor, grants made since 1760, which totalled over £77,000: four before
1788 of £2,000 to £5,000; ten since 1788 of £500 to £20,000.[86]

Jenner received the unprecedented sum of £10,000 in 1802 and a
further £20,000 in 1807. Parliament lauded both his 'discovery' – 'perhaps the most important made since the creation', according to the
Chancellor of the Exchequer – and his disinterested communication of
it to the public.[87] The same day, it awarded £1,200 to Greathead in
consideration of the lives saved by his invention.[88] Speakers in both men's
causes emphasized their contribution to the upholding of Britain's international position, praising the role of vaccination in preserving her armed

---

[85] MacLeod, *Inventing the industrial revolution*, pp. 49, 193.
[86] P. Colquhoun, LL D, *A treatise on the wealth, power, and resources, of the British empire* (2nd
edn, London: Joseph Mawman, 1815), pp. 231–2.
[87] *The Times*, 3 June 1802, 2c.
[88] Ibid. Colquhoun gives £1,500 as the sum awarded: *Treatise*, p. 232.

forces from the ravages of smallpox and the particular importance of the lifeboat to a 'maritime country'. One MP, however, struck a radical chord when recommending Greathead's invention: 'considering the immense sums voted to destroy the human race, he was sorry there should be any hesitation in voting a liberal reward for its preservation.'[89]

Both men received awards and honours from other institutions. Two bodies with strong maritime connections, Trinity House and Lloyds of London, each awarded Greathead one hundred guineas; the Society of Arts gave him fifty guineas and a gold medallion.[90] The emperor of Russia sent him a diamond ring.[91] In 1804, the *European Magazine* published his portrait (figure 3.6). Jenner was first honoured by his professional colleagues: in 1801, medical officers of the Royal Navy presented him with a gold medal engraved with a scene in which Britannia acclaims his invention's healing powers, and supporters in Plymouth commissioned his first portrait by James Northcote. The following year, the nobility and gentry of his native Gloucestershire subscribed over £300 to present him with a 'handsome and valuable' service of plate.[92] Among a host of national and international tributes, Jenner received the freedom of the City of London (a rare accolade) and of Dublin, Edinburgh and Glasgow; honorary doctorates from Oxford and Harvard; and appointment as physician-extraordinary to George IV. Medals were struck in his honour by rulers (including Napoleon) and societies across Europe and the Americas.[93] At his death in 1823, medical men in Gloucestershire launched a subscription to erect a marble statue to him, which was installed in the nave of Gloucester cathedral two years later.[94] It represents Jenner standing, in his Oxford doctoral gown, and holding a scroll and academic cap; it is inscribed only with his name and vital

---

[89] *The Times*, 3 June 1802, 2c.
[90] 'Mr Henry Greathead, the inventor of the life-boat', in *British public characters of 1806* (London: Richard Phillips, 1806), pp. 200–1. See James Burnley, 'Greathead, Henry (1757–1816?)', rev. Arthur G. Credland, *ODNB*, www.oxforddnb.com/view/article/11362, accessed 20 October 2006.
[91] *The Times*, 24 February 1804, 3b.
[92] Jordanova, 'Remembrance of science past', 402–3; [John Ring], 'Dr Jenner', *British public characters of 1802–1803* (London: Richard Phillips, 1803), 18–49, p. 41; *The Times*, 8 January 1802, 2b. Subscriptions were of one to five guineas: Lord Berkeley to Lord Liverpool, 7 December 1801, Add. MS 38235, fo. 331, British Library.
[93] *The Times*, 12 August 1803, 3b; Derrick Baxby, 'Jenner, Edward (1749–1823)', *ODNB*, www.oxforddnb.com/view/article/14749, accessed 18 October 2006; also exhibits at, and literature published by, the Jenner Museum, Berkeley, Glos. For a full list of Jenner's honours, see John Baron, *The life of Edward Jenner, M. D., LL.D., F. R. S., Physician Extraordinary to the King, etc. etc.* 2 vols. (London: Henry Colborn, 1827), vol. II, pp. 449–56.
[94] Baron, *Life of Edward Jenner*, vol. II, pp. 318–23; John Empson, 'Little honoured in his own country: statues in recognition of Edward Jenner MD FRS', *Journal of the Royal Society of Medicine*, 89 (1996), 514. I am grateful to David Mullin, Director of the Jenner Museum, for these references.

European Magazine.

Mʳ HENRY GREATHEAD
of South Shields,
the Inventor of the Life Boat.

3.6 *Mr Henry Greathead of South Shields, the inventor of the Life Boat*. In this engraving by Ridley, from the *European Magazine*, 1804, Greathead wears a medallion inscribed with 'Life boat', reinforcing his claim to this much contested invention.

dates. According to *The Times*, it conveyed 'an idea of that spirit of philanthropy, which ever activated the illustrious discoverer of vaccination'.[95]

By comparison, James Watt received little public acclaim during his lifetime: his sole public mark of distinction was an honorary doctorate of laws, conferred by the University of Glasgow in 1806 (though, late in life, he reputedly declined the offer of a baronetcy).[96] Having profited from his patented invention (extended by a private act of Parliament in 1775 to a total of thirty-one years), he did not look to Parliament for monetary

---

[95] *The Times*, 23 November 1825, 2c. See below, p. 88.

[96] Rt Hon Lord Kelvin GCVO, *James Watt: An oration delivered at the University of Glasgow on the commemoration of its ninth jubilee* (Glasgow: James Maclehose & Sons, 1901), pp. 20–2.; Jennifer Tann, 'Watt, James (1736–1819)', *ODNB*, www.oxforddnb.com/view/article/28880, accessed 18 October 2006. Watt was a fellow of the Royal Societies of

reward. Watt's memoir in *British public characters of 1802–1803* is highly complimentary but much less effusive than either Jenner's or Greathead's. It begins with the significant comment that, 'the character and talents of this excellent man are not known so extensively as they merit.' By contrast, it continues, 'among mechanics and men of science, indeed, the celebrity of the name of Watt yields to that of no living character.'[97] Watt's invention of the separate condenser is set in the context of the steam engine's long-term development and more immediately in the shadow of Black's 'discovery of latent heat'. It describes Watt conducting experiments in order to remedy the inefficient use of fuel in the Newcomen engine, until his 'fertile genius immediately suggested the solution', and refers to the 'considerable difficulties and embarrassment [mainly financial]' he still had to overcome.[98] In this it differs markedly from Jenner's entry, which acknowledges neither predecessors nor inventive process (the mark of a true Romantic genius): 'but this, like Minerva, sprang to light, not in a state of infancy and imbecility, but mature and perfect, and clad in impenetrable armour.'[99] Similarly, while Watt's invention is credited with producing great national advantages in mining and manufactures – his steam engines saving the country £75,000 a day – Jenner attracts superlatives that raise him far beyond the crowd.

The discovery we celebrate, is the pride of Britain, – the boast of science, – and the glory of the healing art. The victory we commemorate, is a victory of man, – not over men, – but over a cruel and unrelenting disease. Vaccine inoculation is, beyond all comparison, the most valuable, and the most important discovery, ever made. It is a discovery, to which even that of [William] Harvey must yield the palm.[100]

Greathead also was hymned far more effusively than Watt, his memoir presenting him in heroic terms, as though he were a great adventurer or conqueror: 'a man arose, who taught us how to buffet the storm, contend victoriously with the waves, protract the period of human existence, and rescue the industrious mariner from the watery grave.'[101]

A feature that Watt and Jenner shared was the controversy they each attracted. Boulton and Watt ruthlessly prosecuted infringements of Watt's extended patent in the 1790s and their monopoly was deeply resented by competitors and many customers; in retirement, after 1800, Watt devoted much effort to preserving a similarly strong hold over the historical

Edinburgh (1784) and London (1785), and the Batavian Society (1787); he was elected, as a foreign associate, to the Académie des Sciences, in 1814: F. Arago, *Life of James Watt* (3rd edn, Edinburgh, 1839), p. 171.
[97] 'Mr James Watt', in *British public characters of 1802–1803*, p. 501.
[98] Ibid., pp. 505–10, 513. See above, pp. 38, 40.
[99] 'Dr Jenner', in *British public characters of 1802–1803*, p. 29.
[100] Ibid., p. 18.   [101] 'Mr Henry Greathead', *British public characters of 1806*, p. 183.

The Cow-Pock _ or _ the Wonderful Effects of the New Inoculation !_ Vide, the Publications of y Anti Vaccine Society.

3.7 *The Cow Pock – or – The Wonderful Effects of the New Inoculation*, by James Gillray, 1802. In this scurrilous cartoon, Gillray depicts Jenner using an udder-shaped instrument to inoculate a patient with 'vaccine pock hot from ye cow', from his scruffy assistant's tub. While miniature cows burst out of inoculated patients, the picture on the wall shows worshippers prostrated before a monument to a cow.

record.[102] As yet, however, steam failed to attract the same degree of attention from the cartoonists as the fantastic allegations of some of Jenner's detractors. The bucolic origins of the country doctor and his miraculous prophylactic presented opponents and caricaturists with an easy target. James Gillray's print, *The Cow Pock – or – The Wonderful Effects of the New Inoculation* (1802), depicted 'vaccination as a wild orgy of transformation', with patients sprouting horns and other bovine features from various parts of their bodies (figure 3.7).[103] Gillray was playing on the threat posed by vaccination to deep-seated social and cultural taboos: by introducing matter derived from cows directly into a patient's body, the technique violated the

---

[102] Hugh Torrens, 'Jonathan Hornblower (1753–1815) and the steam engine: a historiographic analysis', in Denis Smith (ed.), *Perceptions of great engineers, fact and fantasy* (London: Science Museum for the Newcomen Society, National Museums and Galleries on Merseyside and the University of Liverpool, 1994), pp. 25–7. See also Hardy, *Origins of the idea*, pp. 73–5.

[103] Tim Fulford, Debbie Lee and Peter J. Kitson, *Literature, science and exploration in the romantic era* (Cambridge: Cambridge University Press, 2004), pp. 204–5.

sharp boundary between humans and other animals. The anxieties that this provoked fuelled a virulent pamphlet campaign against Jenner, led by surgeons who practised the old method of inoculation against smallpox, and wielded verbal imagery not far removed from Gillray's.[104]

To counteract these and other allegations, Jenner assiduously cultivated powerful patrons – including George III and the president of the Royal Society – and favourable publicity. In particular, he encouraged the popular poet of rural life, Robert Bloomfield, to write in praise of vaccination: *Good Tidings; Or, News from the Farm*, published in 1804, was well received. Southey and Coleridge, both enthusiasts for vaccination, also helped Jenner to promote it in popular journals and reviews.[105] Among Jenner's loudest supporters, however, were leaders of Britain's armed forces. Vaccination having been introduced in the army and navy as early as 1800, smallpox ceased to incapacitate Britain's fighting men, causing Jenner to be hailed as a hero in the war against Napoleon. Admiral Berkeley justified his call for Parliament to reward Jenner by reference to 'the number of valuable men it [i.e. vaccination] had been the means of preserving in the army and navy', while General Tarleton predicted that 'in future ages, the glory of Dr Jenner's fame will be superior to the trophied urn of the most renowned of warriors.'[106] The military also carried vaccination to the colonies, where it was recruited to empire's rhetorical cause as the atonement for sins past and the 'enlightened' promise of imperial benevolence in the future. While this was by no means a view universally shared by Britain's colonial subjects, it helped to consolidate the metropolitan image of Jenner as a national and imperial hero of the first order.[107]

Jenner failed, however, to become a popular hero. His support, initially so noticeable among Britain's military and civilian elite, remained socially superficial. Lower down the social scale, especially in the towns, the case for vaccination went unread and unheard; even the Royal Jennerian Society, established specifically to disseminate vaccination among London's poor, was unable to reach more than a tiny minority.[108] Worse, it became associated with compulsion, an assault simultaneously on the body and the civil liberties of those who were required to receive it, under duress, whether in the army, a workhouse or a prison.[109] Probably

---

[104] Ibid., pp. 203, 208–10.   [105] Ibid., pp. 211–18.
[106] *The Times*, 3 June 1802, 2c; Charles Murray, *Debates in Parliament respecting the Jennerian discovery* (London: W. Phillips, 1808), pp. 5, 78, quoted in Fulford *et al.*, *Literature, science and exploration*, p. 307, n. 54; see also ibid., pp. 218–22.
[107] Fulford *et al.*, *Literature, science and exploration*, pp. 222–7.   [108] Ibid., p. 221.
[109] Hostility grew in the wake of the 1853 Act, which made vaccination compulsory, under threat of fines and imprisonment: Nadja Durbach, '"They might as well brand us": working-class resistance to compulsory vaccination in Victorian England', *Social History of Medicine* 13 (2000), 45–62; Dorothy Porter and Roy Porter, 'The politics of

88   Heroes of Invention

even most of those who enjoyed the protection conveyed by voluntary vaccination quickly came to take it for granted – the inventor of a prophylactic technique was less likely to attract the healthy person's persistent gratitude than the inventor of a specific cure or the doctor who personally saved a patient's endangered life. Furthermore, in contrast with major industrial inventions, vaccination created no centres of employment, no workforce that identified with the inventor or recognized him as the creator of their particular trade – and correspondingly no large interested constituency to which politicians could appeal.[110]

The narrow base of Jenner's active support was revealed in 1823, when Gloucestershire's subscription to raise a monument to his memory struggled to raise sufficient funds. His friend and biographer, John Baron, recounted the disappointing outcome of their appeal to the British medical profession: neither individuals nor learned bodies responded in the numbers expected, and only after 'considerable difficulty' was £700 collected to commission the statue by Robert William Sievier.[111] As part of this campaign, local MPs had tried to obtain funding from Parliament but, despite their proposal being 'met with very considerable cordiality' in the Commons, it was not put to the vote. In particular, the Chancellor of the Exchequer, Frederick Robinson, and the Home Secretary, Robert Peel, both expressed admiration for Jenner but refused to support the proposal.[112]

It was not to be Jenner but Watt, who only a year later was launched on the career of British national hero by a segment of the country's political and scientific elite, with the eager support of its manufacturing classes. It was the steam engine, not vaccination, which came to be seen as the quintessence of British ingenuity and replaced the Renaissance's triad of printing, compass and gunpowder as the acme of modern inventiveness.[113] The frontispiece of the first issue of the *Mechanic's Magazine*, in 1823, paid tribute to Bacon's programme of scientific reform at the same time as it symbolized the new supremacy of steam (figure 3.8).

prevention: anti-vaccinationism and public health in nineteenth-century England', *Medical History* 32 (1988), 231–52; R. M. MacLeod, 'Law, medicine and public opinion: the resistance to compulsory health legislation, 1870–1907', *Public Law* (1967), 107–28, 189–211; R. L. Lambert, 'A Victorian National Health Service: state vaccination, 1855–1871', *HJ* 5 (1962), 1–18.

[110] See below, pp. 110–19, 281–312.
[111] Baron, *Life of Edward Jenner*, vol. II, pp. 318–20.
[112] Ibid., vol. II, pp. 320–2. Cf. their response to the proposal to celebrate Watt: below, pp. 97–106. The Government's offer of a public funeral and burial in Westminster Abbey had been declined by Jenner's family: ibid., pp. 317–18; *The Times*, 18 February 1823, 2c. Thirty years later, the subscription which was launched to erect a statue of Jenner in Trafalgar Square, London, was also poorly supported in Britain: see below, pp. 231–4.
[113] Richard Guest, *A compendious history of the cotton manufacture* [Manchester, 1823] (facsimile edn, London: Frank Cass & Co. Ltd, 1968), pp. 3–4. See also Andrew Ure, in *Glasgow Mechanics' Magazine* 2 (1824), 382–3.

3.8 The frontispiece to the first volume of the *Mechanic's Magazine*,1823, celebrates the steam engine, on land and sea, and ten men of science whose names are inscribed on classical columns (photograph by Ann Pethers).

Instead of the sailing ship passing through the mythical pillars of Hercules, in the engraving which formed the frontispiece to Bacon's *Instauratio magna* (1620), a paddle steamer battles the waves beneath a cliff, on which stands a beam engine, pumping water from a mine.[114] Above,

[114] Martin, *Francis Bacon*, pp. 134–5.

the winged figure of Mercury stands over the Baconian motto, 'knowledge is power', and between two rows of classical columns, inscribed with the surnames of ten men of science from the past two centuries. One column is headed by Watt, the other by the marquis of Worcester – two major figures in the history of the steam engine. These are neither mythical inventors, nor are they represented in a way that suggests they are merely the instruments of a benign Providence. On the contrary, with their names inscribed on triumphal columns in the Roman manner, these men are undoubtedly honoured as heroes.

4   The apotheosis of James Watt

The year 1824 witnessed a turning point in the status of inventors and inventions. For the first time, an inventor was celebrated as a national benefactor by the political nation, and in a style unprecedented for any commoner and civilian. At an extraordinary meeting held in the Freemasons' Hall, Westminster, in June 1824, Lord Liverpool, the prime minister, and senior members of his cabinet joined with other politicians and distinguished men of science, letters and commerce to commemorate the achievements of James Watt. Their high-flown rhetoric in praise of Watt and his steam engine launched a public subscription to erect a monument to his memory in Westminster Abbey. Even more remarkably, the subscription list was headed by a gift of £500 from George IV. Lord Liverpool had proposed this donation to the king 'as an additional proof of the encouragement Your Majesty is always ready to afford, to the important interests of science and literature'.[1] This was sophistry on the prime minister's part (it would have provoked hollow laughter among impecunious men of science and letters), but it was an astute political move, which would allow the government to share in the reflected glory of a new kind of hero.[2] And if Liverpool's advice was sophistic, his endorsement of the meeting was by no means hypocritical: his high regard for inventors such as Watt and Arkwright is well documented.[3]

---

[1] Add MSS 38,576, fo. 141.
[2] Cf. *Morning Chronicle*, 19 June 1824, 4d. For George IV's (revised) reputation as a patron of the arts and, in the 1820s, his improved relationship with Liverpool, see Christopher Hibbert, 'George IV (1762–1830)', *ODNB*, online edn, October 2005, www.oxforddnb.com/view/article/10541, accessed 18 October 2006. For his patronage of Congreve's rocketry inventions, see Roger T. Stearn, 'Congreve, Sir William, second baronet (1772–1828)', *ODNB*, www.oxforddnb.com/view/article/6070, accessed 3 November 2006.
[3] See below, p. 102.

Challenging the military nation

Although scarcely remembered now, the meeting was widely reported at the time.[4] Not only was the occasion remarkable for the distinction and diversity of its attendance but it was also a cultural anomaly. It represented a subtle challenge to the aristocratic and militaristic hold on British culture recently consolidated by over twenty years of successful warfare. Nearly a decade after Waterloo, British politics were still dominated by the reverberations of the long and hard-fought campaign to defeat Napoleon. The glamour of a victorious war, as Linda Colley contends, had played a major role in reconfirming the landed elite's hold on power: members of the post-Waterloo nobility gained kudos through their 'association with red-blooded heroism: a splendid tableau of immaculately cut uniforms, glorious wounds, [and] heroic mutilations'.[5] The gloss of military heroism completed the re-invention of Britain's aristocratic caste into a self-consciously patriotic 'service elite', whose retention of power could be legitimized equally by its distinguished performance of duty as by birth and property.[6] It was at odds, however, with the mounting pressures for social and political reform that accompanied Britain's development into Europe's leading industrial and commercial power; gradual industrialization gathered pace simultaneously with the wars against France. For reformers, it was essential that the popular lionizing of military heroes, such as Nelson and Wellington, should cease to colour politics in peacetime. Indeed, they struggled to counter Tory jibes that the war had been successfully concluded despite Whig protest and pessimism; ineffectively, they denounced the continuing expense and threat to liberty of a standing army.[7]

The entry of Wellington, trailing clouds of glory, into Liverpool's cabinet in 1818 heightened the danger: the duke's chief asset for the government was his prestige (his conservative views aligned him with the ultra-Tories rather than the prime minister's liberal Tory faction).[8]

---

[4] *The Times*, 19 June 1824, 6c; *Morning Chronicle*, 19 June 1824, 4a–d; *The Scotsman*, 23 June 1824, 395; *Mechanic's Magazine*, 26 June 1824; *The Birmingham Chronicle*, 15 July 1824, 230 (in Boulton & Watt MSS, MI/8/16, Birmingham City Archives); Robert Stuart, *Historical and descriptive anecdotes of steam engines, and of their inventors and improvers* (London: Wightman & Co., 1829), pp. 567–76. See also below, p. 123.

[5] Colley, *Britons*, pp. 148–92, esp. pp. 177–8.

[6] Ibid., pp. 185–92.

[7] William Anthony Hay, *The Whig revival, 1808–1830* (Basingstoke and New York: Palgrave Macmillan, 2005), pp. 92, 97–8; Houghton, *Victorian frame of mind*, pp. 308–9, 324. See above, pp. 19–20.

[8] Norman Gash, 'The duke of Wellington and the prime ministership, 1824–30', in Norman Gash (ed.), *Wellington: studies in the military and political career of the first duke of Wellington* (Manchester: Manchester University Press, 1990), pp. 117–38. See also above, pp. 20–1.

Generally perceived as the saviour of his country, even Wellington's parliamentary opponents had to admire him; whatever his political ambitions, they would not be easy to countervail. It would be necessary to challenge the military occupation of the national pantheon as much as the aristocratic control of Parliament. None of their existing icons was sufficient to this task, least of all Charles James Fox, whose partisan memory disconsolate Whigs had been venerating for over a decade. With Fox, however, they had recognized the value of erecting memorials in full public view, rather than on their country estates: Westmacott's bronze statue, which since 1814 had turned Bloomsbury Square into a Whig shrine, was succeeded by his marble monument for Westminster Abbey in 1822, emphasizing Fox's dedication to the causes of peace and anti-slavery.[9] A new, less factional icon was required to counteract triumphant militarism.

Liberal Whigs and their allies found a challenger to the Iron Duke's heroic supremacy in the unlikely person of James Watt, who died opportunely in 1819. Out of Watt, the urbane inventor, they sought to construct a rival figurehead, an embodiment of a different vision of Britain – one founded on commercial rather than landed wealth, which would dominate the world through peaceful trade, not force of arms. In glorifying Watt, they could simultaneously recognize the growing economic importance and political significance of British manufacturers and traders.[10] This was an appealing strategy especially for Scottish Whigs, such as Francis Jeffrey, editor of the *Edinburgh Review*, and his close friend, Henry Brougham MP, who sought to integrate North Britain more firmly into the Union without compromising their liberal principles: Watt was proof that Scotland had more to offer the United Kingdom than mere hordes of recruits for the army.[11] Together with other Scots intellectuals, Jeffrey and Brougham had founded the *Edinburgh Review* in 1802, and developed it into a dominant, national source of liberal opinion. Moreover, since his election to Parliament in 1810, Brougham had been pioneering new tactics to build the Whigs' support in the provinces and ultimately to transform an aristocratic, metropolitan faction into an effective, reforming party – which was to be rarely out of government for the half century after 1832. Campaigning on liberal issues that appealed

---

[9] Penny, 'The Whig cult of Fox', 100–2.
[10] Donald Read, *The English provinces, c. 1760–1960: a study in influence* (London: Edward Arnold, 1964), pp. 79–81.
[11] J. E. Cookson, 'The Napoleonic wars, military Scotland, and Tory Highlandism in the early nineteenth century', *Scottish Historical Review* 78 (1999), 60–75; J. E. Cookson, 'The Edinburgh and Glasgow Duke of Wellington statues: early nineteenth-century unionist nationalism as a Tory project', *Scottish Historical Review* 83 (2004), 24–40.

to provincial merchants and manufacturers, he educated and harnessed public opinion through an astute combination of local meetings, articles in the press, and debates in the House of Commons, where his oratorical and strategic skills secured significant victories over a previously unassailable government.[12] There was political capital to be gained in provincial constituencies by a campaign to celebrate a successful inventor and entrepreneur, and advantage to be had from erecting a symbol of peaceful progress in opposition to the aristocratic, militaristic triumphalism that they deplored (on both sides of the House).[13] They joined forces with leading men of science, who realized that Watt's steam engine represented a wonderful demonstration of the utility of scientific knowledge, which could bolster their campaign for financial support from the public purse.

Whether Liverpool identified potential allies here who would help him resist the ultra-Tories in his own government (including, of course, Wellington) or his aim was rather to attenuate the advantage of the Whigs' ingenious ploy, he caught the mood and stepped in to associate both his liberal Tory faction and the monarchy with this alternative version of British national identity. The radicals, however, were outraged: William Cobbett, in particular, recognized this co-option of Watt's reputation by economically liberal Whigs and Tories for the propaganda coup that it was – he knew he had missed a trick.[14]

It was Francis Jeffrey who publicly suggested that the honours for defeating the French should be extended to Watt and his steam engine.[15] His eulogy, published first in *The Scotsman* (edited by the political economist, J. R. McCulloch), staked Watt's claim:

It is our improved steam-engine that has fought the battles of Europe, and exalted and sustained, through the late tremendous contest, the political greatness of our

---

[12] Hay, *Whig revival*, pp. 1–9, 183–4, and passim.

[13] Brougham and Jeffrey both belonged to the 'Watt camp' in the 'water controversy', in which the rival claims of Watt and Henry Cavendish to having 'discovered' the chemical composition of water were fiercely disputed: Miller, *Discovering water*, pp. 22–4, 169–77, 186–91. Brougham wrote the epitaph for both the Westminster Abbey and the Glasgow monuments in close collaboration with Jeffrey, exchanging drafts with him, and consulting the ever-exacting James Watt Jnr: ibid., pp. 97–8. He published it in his *Lives of men of letters and science who flourished in the time of George III*, 2 vols. (London: Charles Knight, 1845–6), vol. I, p. 387. Jeffrey took responsibility for the inscription on the Greenock statue: Sir Francis Chantrey to James Watt Jnr, 3 May 1839, James Watt MSS, W/10/9, Birmingham City Archives; *The Times*, 18 October 1838, 5f.

[14] See below, pp. 157–8.

[15] Patrick Colquhoun had argued that Britain's new wealth was crucial in successfully resisting the French 'tyrant', but he attributed it neither to the steam engine nor to Watt (by implication, he credited it to foreign trade and commerce): *Treatise on the wealth, power, and resources*, p. 72; also pp. 68, 116.

land. It is the same great power which now enables us to pay the interest of our debt, and to maintain the arduous struggle in which we are still engaged, with the skill and capital of countries less oppressed with taxation . . . It is to the genius of one man, too, that all this is mainly owing; and certainly no man ever before bestowed such a gift on his kind.[16]

In this cleverly crafted passage, without even an oblique reference to the duke of Wellington, Jeffrey questioned his reputation as the nation's saviour. First, he maintained that there was a more profound explanation for British military might than individual heroism or inspired leadership in battle, locating it instead in the country's underlying economic strength; this he attributed (with gross exaggeration) to the impact of steam power.[17] Secondly, Jeffrey reminded his readers that the French wars had been enormously expensive: the burden of the national debt would require that taxation remain high for many years, retarding any progress towards free trade. Without the additional resources generated by steam, he implied, Britain would be sinking under the weight of the Tories' reckless (and misguided) expenditure. Thirdly, Jeffrey suggested that, if there was a hero of this story, it was not the victor of Waterloo, but the man of genius who was the sole 'inventor' of the steam engine; no individual achievement in the history of mankind could compare with that of James Watt!

Not content with this brazen attempt to steal the general's battle honours, Jeffrey then contrived to replace him as the nation's 'model civilian'.[18] In his paean to Watt, as the engineer-turned-renaissance man, Jeffrey created an idealized gentleman who graced the libraries and drawing rooms of high society – swiftly expunging any trace of the instrument-maker's workshop or the steam-engine manufactory.

Independently of his great attainments in mechanics, Mr Watt was an extraordinary, and in many respects a wonderful man. Perhaps no individual in his age possessed so much and such varied and exact information, – had read so much, or

---

[16] Francis Jeffrey, 'Character of Mr Watt', *The Scotsman*, 4 September 1819; repr. in *Edinburgh Magazine*, September 1819, 203. Michael Fry, 'Jeffrey, Francis, Lord Jeffrey (1773–1850)', *ODNB*, online edn, May 2006, www.oxforddnb.com/view/article/14698, accessed 19 October 2006; Phyllis Deane, 'McCulloch, John Ramsay (1789–1864)', *ODNB*, www.oxforddnb.com/view/article/17413, accessed 18 October 2006.

[17] For a generally accepted, revisionist assessment of the economic role of Watt's steam engine, see G. N. von Tunzelmann, *Steam power and British industrialization to 1860* (Oxford: Oxford University Press, 1978); also, A. E. Musson, 'Industrial motive power in the United Kingdom, 1800–70', *EHR* 29 (1976), 415–39. For attempts to measure the natural resources available for the war effort, see J. E. Cookson, 'Political arithemetic and war in Britain, 1793–1815', *War and Society* I (1983), 37–60. Jeffrey may also have had in mind the deployment of steam power in Portsmouth Royal Dockyard: see above, pp. 73–4.

[18] See above, p. 20.

remembered what he had read so accurately and well . . . he was curiously learned in many branches of antiquity, metaphysics, medicine, and etymology, and perfectly at home in all the details of architecture, music, and law. He was well acquainted, too, with most of the modern languages – and familiar with the most recent literature.[19]

Moreover, said Jeffrey, Watt wore his learning lightly, he was unassuming, kind, and responsive to the needs of others, his conversation 'full of colloquial spirit and pleasantry'. 'There was nothing of effort, indeed, or impatience, any more than of pride or levity in his demeanour'; but, abhorring all ignorant and pretentious bluster, he 'never failed to put all such impostors out of countenance, by the manly plainness and honest intrepidity of his language and deportment'. Masculinity evidently did not need the battlefield for its demonstration. Unstinting in his praise, Jeffrey admitted no hint of the melancholy moods that troubled Watt through much of his life, no reference to the determined enforcement of his patent that provoked bitter resentment among rival engineers (he 'died, we verily believe, without a single enemy').[20] Any mention of 'melancholy' might have suggested that mental instability which was often associated with the imaginative excesses of 'genius'.[21] Jeffrey avoided the word 'genius' (except in its older usage, 'the genius of one man'), preferring instead to depict Watt as an encyclopaedic sage, a model of enlightened sociability. Jeffrey's Watt epitomized the Scottish Enlightenment in the service of the United Kingdom: cerebral, liberal, humane, he brought peace, wisdom and prosperity without ever leaving the salon.

Rarely can an obituary have been so influential.[22] Jeffrey's elegant prose was immediately reprinted in newspapers and journals, and quoted throughout the century.[23] Invited to contribute a 'character' of his father to the latest *Supplement* to that other great organ of the Scottish

---

[19] Jeffrey, 'Character of Mr Watt'.

[20] Ibid. For a different perspective, see below, p. 107.

[21] Hope Mason, *Value of creativity*, pp. 110–11, 116–18, 138–40; Jordanova, 'Melancholy reflection', pp. 70–3; Murray (ed.), *Genius*, pp. 2–5; Kessel, 'Genius and mental disorder', pp. 196–9; Yeo, 'Genius, method, and morality', 270–8; Schaffer, 'Genius in Romantic natural philosophy', pp. 82–98; Simon Schaffer, 'Natural philosophy and public spectacle', *History of Science* 21 (1983), 27–31. In the terminology of William Cullen, 'melancholia' was a disease 'characterised by erroneous judgement': Robert Morris, James Kendrick *et al.*, *Edinburgh medical and physical dictionary* (Edinburgh, 1807), vol. II, unpaginated, quoted in Jordanova, 'Melancholy reflection', p. 60. Any mention of Watt's 'melancholy' might have endangered the ascription to him of 'genius' in the more balanced definitions of Duff or Gerard: see above, pp. 52–3.

[22] For other obituary notices, see: Boulton & Watt MSS (Muirhead), MI/5/14; James Watt MSS, 4/84/23.

[23] For example, *Monthly Magazine, or British Register* 48 (1 October 1819), 238–9; *The Birmingham Chronicle*, 15 July 1824, 230; [George L. Craik], *The pursuit of knowledge under difficulties*, 2 vols. (London: Charles Knight, 1830–1), vol. II, p. 321; Arago, *Life of*

Enlightenment, the *Encyclopaedia Britannica*, James Watt Jnr naturally appended Jeffrey's eulogy.[24] (So hackneyed was it by 1835 that the editor of a volume of Scottish biographies preferred to quote Sir Walter Scott's equally flattering (if less presumptive) character of Watt, from the introduction to *The monastery*.)[25] Jeffrey's impact on the speakers at the Westminster meeting in June 1824 is apparent. In particular, although none quite endorsed his exclusion of Wellington from the honours of Napoleon's defeat, their near-universal, nuanced attempts to redistribute the glory demonstrated how sensitive a political issue it had become.

Watt in Westminster Abbey

By 1824, the economic depression and social tensions of the immediate postwar period had dissipated, confidence in the permanence of industrial growth had revived, and the return to prosperity briefly left the Whigs with little extra-parliamentary discontent on which to fasten. Where economic policy was concerned, the two front benches were finding they had more in common with one another than with their own back benches.[26] In May 1824, Edward Littleton MP wrote to the prime minister on behalf of 'several of the principal manufacturers of the kingdom' to seek the government's sanction for a public monument in Watt's memory. Littleton had ascertained that 'several of the most influential' members of the Commons would 'warmly' endorse the proposal and was

James Watt, p. 171; [Sir David Brewster], Review of *Éloge Historique de James Watt. Par M. Arago* [etc], in *Edinburgh Review* 142 (January 1840), 466–502; Dionysius Lardner, *The steam engine explained and illustrated* (7th edn, London: Taylor & Walton, 1840), pp. 315–18; John Bourne, *A treatise on the steam engine* (London: Longman, Brown, Green & Longman, 1853), pp. 21, 22; James Patrick Muirhead, *The life of James Watt* (2nd edn, London: James Murray, 1859), p. 508; [Anon.], *The story of Watt and Stephenson, illustrated* (London and Edinburgh: W. & R. Chambers Ltd, 1892), pp. 56–9; T. Edgar Pemberton, *James Watt of Soho and Heathfield: annals of industry and genius* (Birmingham: Cornish Brothers Ltd, 1905), pp. 35–44.

24 *Memoir of James Watt, FRSL & FRSE: from the Supplement to the Encyclopaedia Britannica* (London: Hodgson, 1824); M. Napier (ed.), *Supplement to the Fourth, Fifth, and Sixth Editions of the Encyclopaedia Britannica*, 6 vols. (Edinburgh: A. Constable, 1815–24). For James Watt Jnr's authorship, see Miller, *Discovering water*, pp. 94–6. Watt Jnr told Macvey Napier, 30 October 1823, 'I fully agree with you that it should comprehend, or conclude with, the eloquent eulogium of Mr Jeffrey': Add MSS 34,613 fo. 204.

25 Robert Chambers, *A biographical dictionary of eminent Scotsmen*, 4 vols. (Glasgow: Blackie & Sons, 1835), vol. IV, p. 409. See below, p. 131.

26 Hay, *Whig revival*, pp. 122–3; Norman Gash, *Lord Liverpool: the life and political career of Robert Banks Jenkinson, Second Earl of Liverpool, 1770–1828* (London: Weidenfeld & Nicolson, 1984), pp. 157–8; Austin Mitchell, *The Whigs in opposition, 1815–1830* (Oxford: Clarendon Press, 1967), p. 183; Chester W. New, *The life of Henry Brougham* (Oxford: Clarendon Press, 1961), pp. 266–8. For Wellington's emergence in 1824 'as the unofficial head of an anti-Canningite, anti-Catholic group' in the cabinet, see Gash, 'Duke of Wellington', p. 122.

confident that it would be 'a most popular act with the manufacturing body of the kingdom, who justly regard Mr Watt as the greatest promoter of the manufacturing skill and pre-eminence of the country that has ever lived'.[27] Liverpool, wary of setting an expensive precedent, declined to support an official monument financed by a parliamentary vote, but agreed to ministers attending a public meeting in a private capacity; he took the chair and donated £100.[28] Moreover, he solicited the king's endorsement. Why Littleton became involved in the project is unclear. Subsequently, he simply referred to having taken 'a leading part, I selected the speakers and engaged Sir James Mackintosh to write the resolutions'.[29] Whatever Littleton's motives, his principled position on the parliamentary fence – wavering between Liverpool's Tories (he was allied by marriage to George Canning, the Foreign Secretary) and Brougham's Whigs – made him the perfect go-between.[30]

It seems undeniable that, 'a meeting more distinguished by rank, station, and talent, was never before assembled to do honour to genius, and to modest and retiring worth'.[31] It brought together leading politicians, the presidents of the Royal Society of London, the Royal Academy, and the Society of Antiquaries, other distinguished men of science and letters, and a host of MPs, merchants, financiers and manufacturers. Before it closed, over £1,600 (including the royal £500) had already been donated and a resolution passed to erect a monument in either St Paul's Cathedral or Westminster Abbey.[32] Within a few months, the appeal raised £6,000 and, in 1834, the 'colossal' statue commissioned from Sir Francis Chantrey was erected in the Abbey.[33] Especially

---

[27] Add MSS 38,298, fo. 316.

[28] C. H. Turner (ed.), *Proceedings of the public meeting held at the Freemasons' Hall on the 18th June, 1824, for erecting a monument to … James Watt* (London: John Murray, 1824), pp. iii-ix; Add MSS 38,299, fo. 13. Jenner's case had recently been rejected: see above, p. 88.

[29] 'Memorandum', October 1824, Hatherton MSS, D260/M/F/5/26/2, fo. 53, Staffordshire County Record Office.

[30] G. F. R. Barker, 'Littleton, Edward John, first Baron Hatherton (1791–1863)', rev. H. C. G. Matthew, *ODNB*, online edn, May 2005, www.oxforddnb.com/view/article/16784, accessed 18 October 2006.

[31] Turner, *Proceedings*, p. ix.

[32] Turner, *Proceedings*, pp. 93–6; *The Times*, 19 June 1824, 6c; *Morning Chronicle*, 19 June, 1824, 8a–d.

[33] James Watt Jnr spent £4,000 of his own fortune in employing Chantrey to commemorate his father with statues and busts that he donated to Watt's friends, Handsworth parish church, the town of Greenock, and the University of Glasgow's Hunterian Museum: R. Gunnis, *Dictionary of British sculptors, 1660 –1851* (new edn, London: the Abbey Library, n.d.), p. 33; Alison Yarrington, Ilene D. Lieberman, Alex Potts and Malcolm Baker (eds.), *An edition of the ledger of Sir Francis Chantrey, R. A., at the Royal Academy, 1809–1841* (London: Walpole Society, 1994), pp. 52–4, 143–4, 159, 213, 217.

obtrusive among the delicate Tudor and Stuart monuments, it could scarcely escape comment, some of it extremely hostile.[34] It resembled Chantrey's design of the statue for Watt's tomb in Handsworth parish church, near Birmingham, but instead of his everyday clothes, this time Chantrey dressed the great 'philosopher' in academic robes (figure 4.1).[35]

It was Watt's son, James Watt Jnr, and some of his closest friends who galvanized the appeal. When his father died on 25 August 1819, Watt Jnr compiled a list of his friends.[36] They numbered 130 men and several women, mostly resident in Birmingham, London, Glasgow and Edinburgh. Many were distinguished in science, the arts and business; among them, some of the most active members of the monument committee, such as Charles Hampden Turner, Sir Humphry Davy, Henry Brougham, Matthew Robinson Boulton (the son of Watt's late business partner) and Thomas Murdock;[37] others attended the Westminster meeting and subscribed generously to the fund. Further afield, other friends, such as Francis Jeffrey, Sir Walter Scott, Kirkman Finlay and G. A. Lee, took leading roles in the Scottish and Manchester memorial campaigns.[38] Several intersecting circles of friendship and interest are visible. The most influential was centred on the Athenaeum, the London club founded in 1823 especially to cater for literary and scientific men; it introduced them to senior politicians of both parties, including Liverpool and Robert Peel. Nine of the meeting's twelve speakers were members of the Athenaeum. It provided nearly half (thirty-six) of the committee's membership and at least fifty-two subscribers, who contributed over £1,300 (almost a quarter of the total donated).[39] As well as Scott, Jeffrey, Davy and Boulton, it included other friends, such as the engineers Thomas Telford and George Rennie, and a tight-knit group of Whig

---

[34] See below, pp. 120–1.

[35] The University of Glasgow had awarded Watt an honorary LL D in 1806. Watt is also represented in his academic gown in George Square, Glasgow, but returns to his everyday clothes for the Hunterian Museum: Yarrington et al., Chantrey's ledger, pp. 143–4, 213, 215–16, 217; Ray McKenzie, Public sculpture of Glasgow (Liverpool: Liverpool University Press, 2002), pp. 123, 393.

[36] 'List of my father's friends, 25–31 Aug. 1819', Boulton & Watt MSS (Muirhead), MI/5/14(1)a; my thanks to Richard Hills for this reference. Charles Hampden Turner wrote to the Mechanic's Magazine to insist that it was Watt's 'personal friends' who instigated the meeting and applied to the government initially for 'a parliamentary grant': no. 48 (24 July 1824), 306; my thanks to Jim Andrew for this reference.

[37] 'Minutes of the Committee for the Erection of a Monument to the late James Watt', Boulton & Watt MSS (Muirhead), MI/5/6; my thanks to Jennifer Tann for drawing my attention to these papers.

[38] For a more detailed analysis of the committee's membership, see MacLeod, 'James Watt', pp. 101–5, 116.

[39] An alphabetical list of the members, with the rules and regulations, of the Athenaeum (London, 1826); Monument to the late James Watt, Boulton and Watt MSS, Timmins vol. 2, fo. 44.

4.1 The marble monument to James Watt by Sir Francis Chantrey, 1834, incongruously sited among the aristocratic tombs in St Paul's Chapel, Westminster Abbey.

merchants who had interests in the Limehouse Rope Manufactory (established by Watt's close friend and fellow inventor, the late Joseph Huddart).[40] This last group included Charles Hampden Turner, who,

[40] [Joseph Huddart the younger], *Memoir of the Late Captain Joseph Huddart, F. R. S.* (London: W. Phillips, 1821) was dedicated to Charles Hampden Turner, in recognition of Huddart Snr's 'esteem and regard for you, cherished by him for many years'.

in collaboration with Littleton, edited the published *Proceedings* of the meeting.[41]

There was a considerable overlap between the Athenaeum and the Royal Society of London, which was represented on the committee by its president, Sir Humphry Davy, both secretaries (W. T. Brande and John Herschel) and nearly a dozen other fellows. Davy took a prominent role in the meeting, speaking immediately after the prime minister, and seized the opportunity to promote the cause of science. More than any other speaker, Davy took his cue from Jeffrey's eulogy. Emphasizing Watt's role in Britain's victory over the French – while avoiding any implication that he was *solely* responsible – Davy delineated Watt as a man of science: it was scientific research ('a new species of intellectual and experimental labour') that had raised Britain to economic and military preeminence. Watt, declared Davy, was 'one of the most illustrious fellows' of the Royal Society; he was not only 'a great practical mechanic', but 'equally distinguished as a natural philosopher and a chemist, and his inventions demonstrate his profound knowledge of those sciences, and that peculiar characteristic of genius, the union of them for practical application.'[42] Then, echoing Jeffrey, Davy proceeded,

our modern Archimedes ... has permanently elevated the strength and wealth of this great empire; and during the last long war, his inventions and their applications were amongst the great means which enabled Britain to display power and resources so infinitely above what might have been expected from the numerical strength of her population.[43]

Davy's point would not have been lost on his audience, since men of science regularly drew unfavourable comparisons between the French government's financial assistance for research and their own enforced self-reliance: if natural philosophy could offer such economic and strategic benefits as these, it was obviously in the state's interest to support it.

---

[41] Littleton noted that 'I afterwards sent to each speaker the short-hand writers' notes of the speeches and procured their corrections of them by their own hands ... Brougham's correction was excessive, Huskisson's considerable, Peel's less, Liverpool's none at all beyond care of punctuation': Hatherton MSS, D260/M/F/5/26/2, fo. 53. Compare the report in the *Morning Chronicle*, 19 June 1824, 4a–d, with Turner (ed.), *Proceedings*.

[42] Turner, *Proceedings*, p. 8. For Davy's anti-reformist discourse, which regularly assured middle-class audiences that science posed no threat to the status quo, see Jan Golinski, *Science as public culture: chemistry and enlightenment in Britain, 1760–1820* (Cambridge: Cambridge University Press, 1992), pp. 242–5. For his earlier support for Cavendish in the water controversy, see Miller, *Discovering water*, pp. 66, 102.

[43] Turner, *Proceedings*, p. 13.

Next to speak was Boulton, who insisted on the fundamental role of steam power in the advance of manufacturing – the cotton and iron industries, in particular – and the importance of that advance in raising the British economy to its current strength. He paid tribute to Watt's 'eminent scientific attainments', and to '[t]he cotemporary [sic] improvements of an Arkwright, a Wedgwood, and of many other distinguished manufacturers'. According to his calculation, the steam engines produced by Boulton, Watt & Co. alone, when substituted for animal power, saved the economy £2.5 million per annum. Replicated on a national scale, it would provide 'a clear indication of one of the sources of power and wealth which have supported this nation through its late arduous struggle, and which have accelerated the renovation of its impaired energies with a celerity exciting surprise in every reflecting mind'.[44]

The politicians rivalled one another in expressing sympathy for the scientific and industrial perspectives of Davy and Boulton. Not that they were insincere: whatever anxieties they harboured about the social consequences of mechanization, Liverpool, Huskisson and Peel had put on record their appreciation of the economic importance of manufactures, especially the export-orientated and increasingly steam-powered cotton industry.[45] Liverpool had recently told Parliament that Britain's agriculture could not survive independently of its industry:

he would ask their Lordships to consider what it was that formed the power and strength of this country: what it was that enabled us to conduct so many wars, and especially the last, as we had done? What but the extent and prosperity of our manufactures. Even the agricultural interest themselves were supported by it.[46]

Already in 1812, while still firmly convinced of the prime importance of agriculture, he had singled out 'the machinery and mechanical inventions of this country, which more than any other cause, had raised this kingdom to its high rank among the commercial nations of the world'.[47]

These Tory ministers variously met the 'Napoleonic' challenge set them by Jeffrey and the Whigs. Opening the meeting, Liverpool had

---

[44] Ibid., pp. 16–20.
[45] Hardy, *Origins of the idea*, pp. 37–49; Boyd Hilton, *Corn, cash, commerce: the economic policies of the Tory government, 1815–1830* (Oxford: Oxford University Press, 1977), pp. 303–7. For the Tories' social concerns, see Berg, *Machinery question*, pp. 253–68.
[46] Hansard, *P. D.*, 2nd ser., IX (1823), 1532, quoted in William Hardy, 'Conceptions of manufacturing advance in British politics, c. 1800–1847', unpublished DPhil thesis, University of Oxford (1994), p. 196.
[47] *Statesman*, 25 July 1812, p. 1, quoted in Iorwerth Prothero, *Artisans and politics in early nineteenth-century London: John Gast and his times* (London: Methuen & Co., 1981), p. 56.

anticipated both the principal themes, recognizing the scientific foundations of Watt's invention as well as the economic and strategic benefits of
steam power. He avoided the issue of the Napoleonic Wars, preferring to
predict the advantages that steam-powered warships would bring to the
Navy, while ranking Watt 'amongst the benefactors of mankind ...
because there are none who deserve more of their country than those
who add to [its] productive powers and industry'.[48] By contrast, William
Huskisson, president of the Board of Trade and the cabinet's leading
proponent of free trade, took the bull by the horns, acknowledging the
case for steam power's role in the defeat of Napoleon but adroitly restoring the military heroes to centre-stage.

[B]ut for those important mechanical and scientific improvements, making as
they did a gradual, silent, but certain accession to the wealth and industry of the
country, we might have been obliged to sue for a humiliating peace before all
the energies of Nelson were called forth at the Battle of Trafalgar, or before the
military sway of the Continent was broken down by the Duke of Wellington, and
the seal set for the peace of Europe by the victory of Waterloo [cheers]. I therefore
feel, that when we are met to erect a monument to Mr Watt, we shall agree to place
it by the side of some of those heroes who fell in the hour of victory [applause].
And let no man think that there is not a connection between his modest but
permanent and invaluable services, and those more brilliant acts which have
called for and received the gratitude of their country.[49]

If Huskisson's artful rhetoric undercut the Whigs' hyperbole, he also
seized the opportunity to flatter the president of the Royal Society: he
both endorsed Davy's view that Watt's invention was the product of
scientific endeavour ('no mere accident') and praised Davy's own invention of the miners' safety lamp as 'an incalculable benefit to society'.[50]

Huskisson's primary concern, however, was free trade.[51] Its economic
and political benefits, systematically expounded by Adam Smith in
1776, became an article of faith in nineteenth-century Britain, the ideological underpinning of foreign, as well as fiscal, policy. Warfare was
supposedly obsolescent; liberals confidently expected that the mutual
interdependence of trading nations would guarantee an international

[48] Turner, *Proceedings*, pp. 1–7.
[49] *Morning Chronicle*, 19 June 1824, 4b. Cf. Gash, *Lord Liverpool*, p. 221: Huskisson was
currently at odds with Wellington over foreign policy.
[50] *Morning Chronicle*, 19 June 1824, 4b.
[51] For the liberal Tories' commitment to free trade and an economy based on manufactures
and commerce as much as on agriculture, see William Hardy, *The Liberal Tories and the
growth of manufactures* (Shepperton: the Aidan Press, 2001), pp. 17–35; Barry Gordon,
Economic doctrine and Tory liberalism, 1824–1830 (London and Basingstoke: Macmillan,
1979), pp. 2–4, 14–25.

system of peaceful harmony and British predominance. Pursuing this dogma, Huskisson credited the steam engine with improving the material conditions of 'mankind generally', and envisaged for it a complementary moral and religious role.[52] Steam power, he enthused, was central to their civilizing mission in every corner of the globe: it would prove a 'great moral lever', since the acquisitiveness that would be stimulated by an array of cheap manufactured goods would drive even 'savage nations' to greater efforts, more industrious habits, and 'an improvement of their condition'.[53] (Christian missionaries, he added – to applause – also played a major part in this 'improvement'.) The Janus-face of capitalism and evangelical imperialism was unashamedly on display.

The home secretary, Robert Peel, was loudly applauded when, acknowledging his origins in the Lancashire cotton industry, he expressed his personal sense of obligation to Watt's ingenuity and expounded the cotton industry's and Manchester's particular debts to steam.[54] Subsequently, he added, 'I feel the class of society from which I derive my origin exalted and honoured, by possessing such a man [as Watt] among its ranks.'[55] In different ways, each of these senior Tories exploited the opportunity to improve the government's relations with the manufacturing sector, which often felt beleaguered by Tory concern for working conditions in factories, oppressed by Tory fiscal protection of agriculture, and angered by Tory resistance to electoral reform. They signalled their willingness 'to do business' with it, in so far as the need to fund the war-inflated national debt (at the expense of lower tariffs) and the political weight of their Ultra colleagues would allow.[56] As for the weightiest Ultra of all, despite their differences over policy, Peel fought a conciliatory rearguard action in support of his absent colleague's heroic

---

[52] Gareth Stedman Jones cites Huskisson's speech as 'a striking example' of 'evangelical cosmology', which sanctified the market 'as an impersonal agent of moral law': *An end to poverty? A historical debate* (London: Profile, 2004), pp. 178–9. My thanks to Richard Sheldon for this reference.

[53] *Morning Chronicle*, 19 June 1824, 4b. Huskisson revised this passage considerably, adding 'a thirst for instruction' among the benefits he envisaged, and extending them more explicitly to 'the humblest classes of the community' at home: Turner, *Proceedings*, pp. 28–9.

[54] *Morning Chronicle*, 19 June 1824, 4d. For Peel's generally positive views on technological change and industrialization, see Hardy, *Liberal Tories*, pp. 40–55.

[55] Turner, *Proceedings*, p. 70.

[56] Rising revenues from taxation, as the economy recovered, were allowing Liverpool's government to start to dismantle the web of protective tariffs that had been erected to fund the national debt – beginning with the budget of February 1824: Gash, *Lord Liverpool*, pp. 217–19; Hardy, *Liberal Tories*, pp. 29–35; Hilton, *Corn, cash, commerce*, pp. 303–7.

status. Implicitly rebutting renewed Whig assertions of Watt's superiority over Wellington, Peel contended that an isolated monument to Watt would be invidious. The great inventor's fame would shine more brightly, he suggested, if 'his monument [were] placed under that dome which contains the reliques of the poet, the warrior, and the statesman, whom I cannot but consider as *in concordia anima*'.[57]

Two leading Scottish Whigs had indeed echoed Jeffrey's eulogy, in returning Watt to a pinnacle of unrivalled national importance. First, Sir James Mackintosh disingenuously summarized the preceeding speeches and pushed them to unlooked-for conclusions, with which neither Davy nor Huskisson could have been happy. 'It has been well described to you', professed Mackintosh, 'that the inventions of Mr Watt have been mainly conducive to the preservation of the State'. He then cited Francis Bacon's high opinion of inventors and suggested that, if Bacon were alive, 'he would undoubtedly have placed [Watt] at the head of all inventors of all ages'. Moreover, said Mackintosh, '[t]hat great philosopher goes on to state, that whereas lawgivers, extirpators of tyrants, fathers of their country, and the like, are honoured as demi-gods, inventors are honoured with the title of Gods'.[58] Next to speak, Henry Brougham paraphrased Jeffrey's tribute to Watt's intellectual versatility and moral worth, before slipping in a sly comparison with Sir Isaac Newton and launching a bold claim for the commemoration of this superior hero of peace in either St Paul's Cathedral or Westminster Abbey. Brougham implied that military heroes, by contrast, had no place in a Christian church or cathedral:

Where can the monument of this great man be more appropriately placed than in the temple of that religion which teaches peace to all and instruction to the poor? The temples of the pagans had been adorned by statues of warriors, who had dealt desolation on their race; but ours shall be graced with the statues of those who have contributed to the triumph of humanity and science, and amongst others, to him who, without giving sorrow to any man, has achieved what has been an honour and a benefit to the human race [applause].[59]

---

[57] *Morning Chronicle*, 19 June 1824, 4d. Peel elaborated this point in the published *Proceedings*, where he was supported by the Tory peer, Lord Aberdeen: Turner (ed.), *Proceedings*, pp. 71–2. Sir James Mackintosh, for the Whigs, used Turner's volume to try to counteract Peel's direct appeal to the manufacturers, expressing delight at the presence of 'many of that enlightened, ingenious, independent, and upright class of men, the manufacturers of England', and said they should regard the occasion as a tribute also to them and 'the useful arts': ibid., pp. 51–2.

[58] *Morning Chronicle*, 19 June 1824, 4c.

[59] Ibid., 4d. Brougham subsequently moderated this stark denigration of military heroism, judging perhaps that it might obstruct his rapprochement with the liberal Tories: Turner (ed.), *Proceedings*, pp. 59–60. Indeed, as Littleton commented, Brougham's alteration of his text was 'excessive'. He also used the published proceedings to promote the Mechanics' Institutes, which he was then helping to establish: ibid., pp. 53–4.

Despite such skirmishes of interpretation, Scottish Whigs and liberal Tories occupied sufficient common ground to pursue the same goal. Together they breached the aristocratic and military command of Westminster Abbey's unofficial pantheon with a monument to a new kind of hero.

Littleton's belief that a tribute to Watt would find favour among the manufacturers was confirmed both by their support for the Westminster memorial and by the enthusiastic response generated in the provinces, especially in Manchester and Glasgow, the two hubs of the British cotton industry. Trade and manufacturing were well represented on the monument committee, in particular by the cotton industry with ten members, including an Arkwright and a Strutt. Wool and pottery each provided a famous name – Benjamin Gott of Leeds and Josiah Wedgwood II; there were two ironmasters, six partners in the Limehouse Rope Manufactory, and the Bristol merchant who supplied Watt with brandy. Many had known Watt personally, some as friends, some as customers for his steam engines, and they were among the most generous subscribers (the Limehouse partners, for example, donated almost £250). A printed list names 200 subscribers, mostly from London, who (excluding the king) gave nearly £3,300.[60] Apart from a sprinkling of knights and baronets, it comprises men who signed their names with no adornment grander than 'Esq.' or 'MP'; at least twenty could have added 'FRS'. It was probably a direct business link with Boulton, Watt & Co. that prompted at least four London brewers, thirteen London merchant houses, three steam-ferry companies, nine Welsh ironmasters, a Cornish mines developer (Lord de Dunstanville) and the West India Dock Company.[61] Many Birmingham subscribers had been personal friends and business associates of Watt, including M. R. Boulton and his sister, William Murdoch and his sons, and William Creighton, who all made generous donations. The Birmingham Canal Navigation proprietors voted £100 in gratitude for Watt's services as a member of their committee.[62] Nearly £100 came from the shillings and pence of the workmen and clerks at Soho.[63] By February 1825, Turner could report that London's subscription had

[60] Boulton & Watt MSS, Timmins, vol. 2, fo. 44.

[61] West Indian sugar plantations provided the second largest group of customers for Watt engines after the cotton industry, many of them exported through London: Jennifer Tann, 'Steam and sugar: the diffusion of the stationary steam engine to the Caribbean sugar industry, 1770–1840', *HT* 19 (1997), 63–84.

[62] Boulton and Watt MSS, Timmins, vol. 2, fo. 44; *The Times*, 1 October 1824, 2d.

[63] *The Birmingham Chronicle*, vol. II, no. 81 (15 July 1824), 228; 'Soho Foundry Subscriptions towards the Fund, for erecting a Monument, to the Memory of the late James Watt, Esq', Boulton & Watt (Muirhead) MSS, MI/5/9. My thanks to Jennifer Tann for this reference and to Jeremy Stein for transcribing and calculating this list.

grown to £4,000; Manchester's separate appeal had reached £1,100, and Birmingham's, £900.[64]

There is one occupational group – the engineers – and one English region – Cornwall – which were noticeable by their virtual absence from both the monument committee and the printed subscription list. Three prominent civil engineers, Thomas Telford, George Rennie and James Walker were on the committee, and at least three further 'civils' subscribed. This represented a tiny proportion of the profession, but it overwhelmed the machine builders' contribution. Although London was a major centre of mechanical engineering, there were no 'mechanicals' on the committee, and only Henry Maudslay's name appears on the subscription list (it is possible that more subscribed later). Boulton, Watt & Co.'s other competitors in London may have been disinclined to burnish the Birmingham firm's reflected glory, or perhaps they resented the government's recent decision to maintain the ban on machinery exports, which favoured the Manchester cotton interests that were prominent in commemorating Watt.[65] Alternatively, their absence may be indicative of a persistent hostility towards Watt, owing to the tight control over steam-engineering that he exercised through his extended patent (1769–1800), exacerbated by his jealous re-writing of history to exclude his rivals from the credit they deserved, and possibly by Boulton, Watt & Co's harassment of their competitors (notoriously Murray, Fenton & Wood, of Leeds).[66] As Watt himself had commented in 1783, men of business 'hate me more as a monopolist than they admire me as a mechanic'.[67] It is unclear whether he was referring to his competitors among the engine-builders or his customers, who grumbled about paying royalties to use his engines. Certainly, in Cornwall both these groups were especially critical of Watt. The Cornish mining industry, which had bought many early Boulton & Watt's engines, resented the firm's patents: until 1800 these prevented them from buying cheaper, more technically advanced engines

---

[64] 'Minutes', 16 February 1825, Boulton & Watt (Muirhead) MSS, MI/5/6.

[65] A. E. Musson, 'The "Manchester School" and exportation of machinery', *Business History* 14 (1972), 28–9. In 1826 James Watt Jnr offered his help to the Manchester Chamber of Commerce in its continuing resistance to the repeal of this legislation: ibid., 34n.

[66] For this aspect of Watt, which is totally at odds with Jeffrey's portrayal of him, see Torrens, 'Jonathan Hornblower', pp. 23–34. See also the comments of David Brewster, in Gordon, *Home life of Sir David Brewster*, pp. 123–4; and for a parallel case with some helpful thoughts on 'the social construction of invention', Carolyn C. Cooper, *Shaping invention: Thomas Blanchard's machinery and patent management in nineteenth-century America* (New York and Oxford: Columbia University Press, 1991), pp. 29–56. For Soho's rivalry with Leeds, see G. Tyas, 'Matthew Murray: a centenary appreciation', *TNS* 6 (1925), 113–15, 133–43; my thanks to Alessandro Nuvolari for this suggestion.

[67] Quoted in Jacob, *Scientific culture*, p. 116.

locally. So strong was this feeling that it fuelled an anti-patent prejudice among Cornish engineers and mining companies that persisted through at least the first half of the nineteenth century.[68] It may even have reverberated into the twentieth. In 1920, the engineers who (at a meeting to honour Watt's centenary) decided to established the Newcomen Society chose to name it after Thomas Newcomen, because 'Watt's name might not be entirely free from notes of discord inherited from the past'.[69]

The hero of North Britain

It was in Scotland that Watt's memory burned brightest. Throughout the nineteenth and early twentieth centuries, both Greenock, his birthplace, and Glasgow, where he had invented the separate condenser, regularly celebrated their connection with him. In 1824, each decided to erect its own memorial, as did Edinburgh. Scotland's capital city, however, had no direct connection with Watt, and its decision stemmed less from a sense of civic pride than from the Whigs' political interests on the grander British stage. The Whig intellectuals who congregated around Jeffrey's *Edinburgh Review* debated whether their commemorative efforts would be better spent at Westminster or in Edinburgh – in the United Kingdom's capital city or in Scotland's. However much their interests and loyalty lay with the Union, they regretted losing a powerful symbol of Scottish 'genius' to London at a point when they needed it in Edinburgh. Indeed, some calculated that both goals might be achieved simultaneously: irrespective of their own financial contribution, the aristocracy's hold on Westminster Abbey would certainly be breached; by redirecting it, they could open a second front to challenge the Tories' commemorative monopoly of Edinburgh. For, it was in Scotland's capital that the fiercest battle for control of the national memory was being fought. In the 1820s, Edinburgh Whigs found it hard to avoid the triumphalism of their political enemies. '[B]y means of statues and street names (there are interlocking Pitt and Dundas Streets in the New Town)', writes Alex Tyrrell, 'the Edinburgh Tories were making the city "a pedagogical

[68] Alessandro Nuvolari, *The making of steam power technology: a study of technical change during the British industrial revolution* (Eindhoven: Eindhoven University Press, 2004), pp. 101–3, 115–18.

[69] A. Titley, 'Beginnings of the Society', *TNS* 22 (1942), 38, quoted in H. S. Torrens, 'Some thoughts on the history of technology and its current condition in Britain', *HT* 22 (2000), 225; I am grateful to Tony Woolrich for drawing this reference to my attention.

space" for the propagation of their own "civic virtues".[70] In particular,
the Tories intended Calton Hill with its Nelson monument, at the south
end of the New Town, to be the acropolis on which Scotland's contribution to British military prowess would be celebrated. Only their fall from
power in the late 1820s was to frustrate the completion of these plans.
The incoming Whig and radical councillors made it a priority to seize
control of the National Monument project and to transform it 'from
a Pantheon of conservative military virtues into a Parthenon where
"Scotland's civil as well as military achievement" would be celebrated'.[71]
In 1824, however, some Scottish Whigs made a valiant attempt to intrude
a monument to Watt into Edinburgh's Tory cityscape.

   Francis Jeffrey and Sir Walter Scott (no Whig but a friend and admirer
of Watt's) lost no time calling a meeting in Edinburgh, to organize a
subscription to the Westminster Abbey project.[72] From their close circle
of friends, however, Professor James Pillans rose to object. According to
The Scotsman, 'he wished that a Scottish monument were erected, – not a
monument hid in a church, but one which every mechanic could see in
full day, and might benefit by'.[73] With this appeal to a wider social
purpose, Pillans, a 'lifelong Whig' and fervent educational reformer,
struck a chord.[74] Another intimate of Jeffrey's, Henry Cockburn, while
not opposing Scott and Jeffrey's resolution, urged the 'mechanics'
present to call another meeting to pursue Pillans' suggestion. Whether
the dissident proposal was stage-managed or spontaneous, the meeting
resolved to pursue both goals, before ending on a note of good humour –
Scott minimized the problems of going to Westminster Abbey (and raised
a laugh) by observing 'that no man had done so much as Mr Watt to bring
London near Edinburgh'.[75] The *Glasgow Chronicle*'s report reveals more

---

[70] Alex Tyrrell with Michael T. Davis, 'Bearding the Tories: the commemoration of the
Scottish Political Martyrs of 1793–94', in Paul A. Pickering and Alex Tyrrell (eds.),
Contested sites: commemoration, memorial and popular politics in nineteenth-century Britain
(Aldershot: Ashgate, 2004), p. 28.

[71] Ibid., p. 29, citing Cookson, 'The Napoleonic wars', 74. For the Whigs' concern with the
historical record and membership of the modern 'pantheon', see J. W. Burrow, *A liberal
descent: Victorian historians and the English past* (Cambridge: Cambridge University Press,
1981).

[72] Colin Kidd suggests that, although Scott's politics were Pittite, his ideas 'were deeply
indebted to the sociological Whig ideology of the Scottish Enlightenment': *Subverting
Scotland's past: Scottish Whig historians and the creation of an Anglo-British identity,
1689–c.1830* (Cambridge: Cambridge University Press, 1993), pp. 9–10.

[73] *The Scotsman*, 10 July 1824, 529b.

[74] Elizabeth J. Morse, 'Pillans, James (1778–1864)', *ODNB*, online edn, October 2006,
www.oxforddnb.com/view/article/22282, accessed 18 October 2006.

[75] *The Scotsman*, 10 July 1824, 529b. Since the meeting predated passenger railways, Scott
was presumably referring to the steam packets that had recently begun to carry passengers on coastal and river journeys.

explicitly the tensions between the unionist and nationalist agendas. It gave a more nationalistic gloss to Pillans' speech: 'it would redound more to the credit of Scotland, to open a subscription of our own, for a monument in the country of Mr Watt's birth; in the place where his inventions were first conceived and brought to light.'[76] Scott and Jeffrey replied, with their eyes on the British stage, that 'the monument was to be a great national one ... in the metropolis of the empire.' Jeffrey was about to close the meeting, when Cockburn (arriving from another, about the National Monument on Calton Hill) entered the room 'and began protesting about so precipitate a vote on so important a measure'. The *Chronicle* believed the dissidents had won the day, since most of the sixty to seventy participants left without subscribing to the Westminster appeal.[77] Its forecast was correct.

The subsequent meeting drew 500 men 'of all classes and parties', the majority of them probably artisans.[78] Cockburn made the opening speech, in which he emphasized Watt's Scottish origins and his civilian virtues. 'It seemed as if he had been cast by Providence among a highly manufacturing and commercial nation,' said Cockburn, 'as a model of what a liberal and useful citizen in such a country ought to be.' While sensible of the honour paid to Watt by the Westminster Abbey proposal, he believed the two projects were by no means incompatible: there should also be a Scottish monument. His first reason appealed to nationalist feelings: 'because this was his own country, and it was their duty to encourage similar exertions, by shewing to Scotchmen the ultimate rewards which genius and industry would meet with'. His second (though perhaps, he suggested, the more important) played the populist card: 'no exclusive monument should be placed in a situation inaccessible to the great body of the people'. To 'great applause', Cockburn argued that even the trivial sum which the Abbey charged to view 'the genius, science, and virtue of the nation' was too much; Watt's monument should be in the open air, visible to even 'the poorest mechanic', to stir his heart and awaken his genius. Moreover, it would 'adorn the metropolis of Scotland', boosting the city's claim to be 'the most magnificent and beautiful in the empire'.[79] Throughout this grandiloquent speech, Cockburn played fast and loose with the idea of 'the nation', slipping seamlessly between the Scottish and the British. It was indicative of the

[76] *Glasgow Chronicle*, 10 July 1824, 2e. James Watt Jnr, who was anxious lest the ambition for separate monuments in Scotland should undermine London's, nonetheless felt 'proud of the additional honour ... by his own countrymen, in the more confined use of the term': James Watt Jnr to Edward John Littleton, 20 August 1824, Hatherton MSS, D260/M/F/5/26/2, fo. 55.
[77] *Glasgow Chronicle*, 10 July 1824, 2e.   [78] *The Scotsman*, 24 July 1824, 557.   [79] Ibid.

twin identities that many contemporary Scots enjoyed: while they recognized the benefits of the Union, they held fast to their Scottish nationhood.[80]

Cockburn's resolution was seconded by the Solicitor-General for Scotland, John Hope. As an appointee of Liverpool's government (but one who moved easily in Whig legal circles), Hope's participation implied that liberal Tories acquiesced in the Whigs' commemorative plans north of the border as much as at Westminster. Again, however, it was on the basis that Watt should be honoured not in splendid isolation but through admission to the company of 'the great and powerful of the land'. Hope repeated the deflating formula that, 'It was peculiarly fit and proper that the statue of the philosopher should be placed beside those of the states-man, the warrior and the poet.'[81] This alliance was not the only innova-tion. Since the first meeting, negotiations had taken place with the directors of the School of Arts, founded in 1821 to educate 'mechanics in such branches of physical science as are of practical application in their several trades'.[82] As a result, the project had taken a utilitarian turn. Cockburn concluded with the proposal that they combine 'an architec-tural edifice worthy of Watt, and calculated to adorn the city' with the School's plans for permanent accommodation. Leonard Horner, the sec-retary to the directors of the School (and a member of the Westminster committee), confirmed that the directors would contribute £500 to the project. Objections were raised: first, that Glasgow, with its much higher population of mechanics, would reap greater benefit from such a school and donate more generously towards it; secondly, that it would prove an ineffective memorial to Watt, whose name would soon be overlooked – the new School was really a monument to Horner! Cockburn, however, assured the meeting that Glasgow already had its own plans to commem-orate Watt, and carried the resolutions with ease.[83] A week later, *The Scotsman* tried to rebut the second objection: Watt's name and allusions to his invention would be inscribed on the building's exterior and a statue or bust would grace the vestibule; it was hoped to obtain a 'commanding situation' – depending on the amount of money raised.[84]

---

[80] Graeme Morton, *Unionist nationalism: governing urban Scotland, 1830–1860* (Phantasie, E. Linton: Tuckwell Press, 1999), pp. 16–17.

[81] *The Scotsman*, 24 July 1824, 557; Gordon F. Millar, 'Hope, John (1794–1858)', *ODNB*, www.oxforddnb.com/view/article/13733, accessed 18 October 2006.

[82] W. L. Bride, *James Watt – his inventions and his connections with Heriot-Watt University* (Edinburgh: Heriot-Watt University, 1969), p. 25.

[83] *The Scotsman* fully endorsed the project, predicting that Edinburgh would soon become a major centre of manufacturing: 24 July 1824, 559b–c. The objections were raised by Mr Craig, who may have been the same man as seconded Pillans' resolution on 9 July.

[84] *The Scotsman*, 31 July 1824, 577.

There indeed was the rub: the ambitious project stalled for lack of money. In Edinburgh's largely service economy, a committee dominated by city officials and professional men raised approximately £765 in three weeks, from individuals in a broad range of professional and manufacturing occupations (plus £500 donated, as promised, by the School of Arts). There were over 160 subscriptions, but few were larger than ten guineas.[85] In 1840 an attempt was made by frustrated subscribers to liberate the funds for a cut-price statue by Chantrey.[86] Only in 1851 did the (renamed) Watt Institution and School of Arts find sufficient additional funding to purchase its building in Adam Square and to commission a statue of Watt, by Peter Slater, to adorn its exterior.[87]

The west of Scotland proved to be a surer heartland. Along the River Clyde, where industry and shipping dominated the local economy and the links with Watt were clearer, wealthy manufacturers and merchants donated in greater numbers and more generously. Although there was some pressure for a combined memorial on the Clyde, sufficient enthusiasm was generated to carry forward two separate schemes.[88] Glasgow felt it had a special claim to celebrate Watt. At a meeting in the Town Hall, in November 1824, the Lord Provost announced that, while several citizens were contributing to London's appeal, he was confident that all would support 'a monument, which would at once perpetuate Mr Watt's memory, and adorn the city which gave birth to those mighty efforts of his genius'.[89] The speakers echoed many of the sentiments already expressed in London and Edinburgh, but with more civic, less nationalist, rhetoric than in the latter. The professor of chemistry at Glasgow University reiterated Davy's linkage between natural philosophy, the steam engine, and 'the prosperity and aggrandizement of Great Britain'; a leading cotton spinner considered Watt's contribution 'to this empire' far more productive than 'all the tribe of politicians put together'.[90] In six months,

---

[85] *The Scotsman*, 24 July 1824, 559; 14 August 1824, 606. I am grateful to David Bryden, who kindly gave me copies of some of the Glasgow and Edinburgh subscription lists. Subscribers have been identified through *Glasgow Post Office directory*, 1828, and *Pigot & Co.'s new commercial directory of Scotland*, 1825–6.

[86] *The Scotsman*, 16 December 1840, 3f.

[87] Bride, *James Watt*, p. 26; H. W. Dickinson and Rhys Jenkins, *James Watt and the steam engine: the memorial volume prepared for the committee of the Watt centenary commemoration at Birmingham 1919*, intro. Jennifer Tann (Ashbourne: Moorland, 1981), p. 87. The embryonic Scottish nationalist movement was soon to evoke William Wallace and Robert the Bruce as Scottish heroes: Morton, *William Wallace*, pp. 114–17.

[88] *Glasgow Chronicle*, 28 October 1824, 3a; 30 October 1824, 1d; 2 November 1824, 3a.

[89] James Cleland, *Historical account of the steam engine* (Glasgow: Khull, Blackie & Co., 1825), p. 30; Stana Nenadic, 'Cleland, James (1770–1840)', *ODNB*, www.oxforddnb.com/view/article/5594, accessed 18 October 2006.

[90] Cleland, *Historical account*, pp. 33–4.

under the aegis of a large committee, which was dominated by a broad swathe of commercial occupations but also included city officials, university professors and other professional men, Glasgow raised over £3,000. The city commissioned another 'colossal' statue from Chantrey; erected in George Square in 1832, it is a close copy of the monument in Westminster Abbey (figure 4.2).[91]

Glasgow's cotton trade was conspicuously generous and, unlike in London, the engineers and metalworkers were well represented. Two features are particularly striking: first, the great variety of trades whose members subscribed, including many that had no contact with steam engines, such as bakers, grocers, tailors and dealers in spirits and china; secondly, the substantial sums collected in over a dozen workplaces – mainly engineering shops and foundries but also two printers' and a bricklayer's.[92] They imply a popular admiration for Watt that extended well beyond those most immediately affected by his inventions. The tenor of the speeches in Glasgow was more populist than elsewhere: several men spoke warmly of their friendship with Watt and his personal qualities. One of them, James Ewing, expanded the range of Watt's 'gifts' to the city to include its water supply, gas lighting and steam boats. He also emphasized Watt's – and some of the speakers' – lowly origins, as an inspiration to other mechanics, before ending with a Nelsonian quip – 'Glasgow expects every man to do his duty' – which drew loud cheers.[93]

Much more than in Edinburgh, there was a deliberate involvement of skilled workers in the campaign. The *Glasgow Mechanics' Magazine*, launched in 1824, had taken Watt as its figurehead (his engraved portrait formed the frontispiece to its first issue, and a three-page biography followed in July), and it provided extensive coverage of both the London and the local monument campaigns.[94] It also reported the mechanics' class at Anderson's Institution, which opened its own subscription. The students had been impressed by their tutor's opinion, that

it was not long since the term Mechanic, even in this very country, enlightened as it now pretends to be, was used as a term of reproach ... To Mr Watt, however, we are indebted for rescuing that name from opprobrium, and for rendering it as honourable a title as any man could possess.[95]

[91] Yarrington *et al.*, *Ledger of Sir Francis Chantrey*, pp. 215–16; McKenzie, *Public sculpture of Glasgow*, pp. 122–4.
[92] *Glasgow Chronicle*, 25 November 1824, 3b; 11 December 1824, 3a; 30 December 1824, 3b; 5 February 1825, 3d; 2 April 1825, 3c; *Glasgow Mechanics' Magazine* 2 (27 November 1824), 303–4.
[93] *Glasgow Mechanics' Magazine* 2 (27 November 1824), 300–2.
[94] See above, pp. 88–90, and below, pp. 153–4.
[95] *Glasgow Mechanics' Magazine* 2 (4 December 1824), 318–19.

4.2 Bronze statue to James Watt by Sir Francis Chantrey, in George Square, Glasgow, 1832 (photograph by the author).

A month later, the *Magazine* quoted extensively from Andrew Ure's lecture on steam, which attracted 'a very brilliant and most respectable company' to the Institution, and raised £54 for the campaign. Ure had not stinted his superlatives, as he swept through the history of the steam engine and dazzled his audience with the statistics of its present importance; his rhetoric had soared ever higher as he advanced to the victories of Nelson and Wellington – impossible 'without the boundless resources furnished by Watt'! – and paired his hero with Newton ('[Watt] has done for the earth what Newton did for the Heavens').[96] Testifying to the involvement of artisans, the *Magazine* published a raucous letter from a subscriber to Glasgow's campaign – to which 'we, in common with other mechanics, are a *mity* [sic] contributor'. Its author, 'L. M'L.', protested that Watt's monument should be a new building for the Mechanics' Institute, where 'to be still training his *hobby*, the steam engine, to new feats, new exploits, new achievements'.[97] At a time when Mechanics' Institutes were being established throughout Britain, it is not surprising that many people shared this man's opinion. In Dundee, this preference prevailed. Requested by the Edinburgh committee to subscribe to its monument, the 'principal inhabitants' of Dundee rebelled: by November 1824, they had raised sufficient funds to inaugurate their own Watt Institution.[98]

The town of Greenock endorsed its belief that Scotland should have its own monument, there in Watt's birthplace, with an impressively large subscription. It had reached £1,703 by October 1826, when James Watt Jnr presented the town with £2,000 for a new library suitable to house the marble statue, which was again commissioned from Chantrey.[99] The laying of the foundation stone, in 1835, elicited a procession of masonic lodges from the west of Scotland, resplendent in their regalia as they gathered to honour Watt, despite the driving rain which muted the occasion.[100]

Manchester, the bastion of free trade

Initially, Manchester resisted a minority call to raise its own statue to Watt. Its citizens contributed £1,100 to the monument in Westminster Abbey, although Manchester was neither Watt's birthplace, nor ever his home.[101] It was, however, the centre of the English cotton industry, and its lack of fast-flowing rivers necessitated a high degree of dependence on the steam engine.[102] 'It was in Manchester, as Boulton reported to Watt in 1781, that manufacturers went "Steam Mill Mad", with the

[96] Ibid., 2 (1 January 1825), 381–4.   [97] Ibid., 3 (21 May 1825), 254.
[98] James V. Smith, *The Watt Institution Dundee, 1824–49*, The Abertay Historical Society publication, 19 (Dundee, 1978), p. 6; I am grateful to David Bryden for this reference.
[99] Cleland, *Historical account*, pp. 65–6; *The Times*, 6 October 1826, 3c; George Williamson, *Memorials of the lineage, early life, education, and development of the genius of James Watt* (Edinburgh: the Watt Club, 1856), p. v.
[100] Yarrington *et al.*, *Ledger of Sir Francis Chantrey*, p. 217; *The Times*, 24 August 1835, 2f; 4 September 1835, 3a; 18 October 1838, 5f.
[101] 'Minutes', 16 February 1825, Boulton & Watt (Muirhead) MSS, MI/5/6. See also *Manchester Guardian*, 31 July 1824, 2a.
[102] *Manchester Guardian*, 10 July 1824, 3e.

introduction of Watt's rotative engine', and the Lancashire cotton indus-try temporarily became the firm's largest market.[103] Mancunians appa-rently felt genuine admiration and gratitude to Watt for his contribution to their prosperity. Not only were many leading citizens actively engaged in the city's scientific culture through membership of the 'Lit and Phil' and similar societies, but their tendency to liberal economic views allied them with Watt's political admirers at Westminster and in Edinburgh.[104] To liberal Mancunians, Watt's steam engine symbolized both the power of scientific knowledge and the wider benefits of unfettered, worldwide trade.

At the signed request of thirty-four manufacturers and merchants, a 'numerous and highly respectable' public meeting was called, and the Manchester members of the national monument committee drove their resolutions through to the desired conclusion.[105] Their rhetoric lost nothing in its journey north. Opening the proceedings, George Philips emulated the liberal bombast he had heard at the Westminster meeting – and initiated other claims which he had subsequent cause to regret.[106] An enterprising and successful cotton spinner with interests in the West India trade, Philips was active both in Manchester's cultural life and in metro-politan Whig circles; MP for Wootten Bassett, he was known as the 'unofficial member for Manchester' (the city was only enfranchised in 1832).[107] Through 'the genius of Mr Watt,' said Philips, '[Britain] had acquired a mastery over the winds and waves; the space which separated nations was contracted, and they were brought into closer contact with each other.' He elucidated the free-trader's faith in the pacific impli-cations of commercial self-interest, based on 'mutual wants, and ... mutual dependance'. And if peace failed? 'The steam engine would aid the triumphs of our navy, as it had promoted the increase of our

---

[103] Musson, 'Industrial motive power', 429.
[104] All ten of the Manchester men on the national monument committee were members of the 'Lit and Phil', including its president, John Dalton: A. Thackray, 'Natural knowl-edge in a cultural context: the Manchester model', *American Historical Review* 79 (1974), 672–709; Robert Kargon, *Science in Victorian Manchester: enterprise and expertise* (Manchester: Manchester University Press, 1977), pp. 5–14. For further analysis of the committee members and the Manchester subscribers, see MacLeod, 'James Watt', pp. 104–6.
[105] *Manchester Guardian*, 26 June 1824, 3b, 2e; 10 July 1824, 1a.
[106] See below, p. 157.
[107] A. C. Howe, 'Philips, Sir George, first baronet (1766–1847)', *ODNB*, www.oxforddnb. com/view/article/38689, accessed 18 October 2006. Philips' partners in the West India trade were Samuel Boddington and Richard Sharp, who were both on the national committee and partners in the Limehouse Ropery. Since 1807 Philips had been a member of Sir James Mackintosh's dining club, the King of Clubs: ibid.

manufactures and commerce.'[108] Philips' pragmatic case was succeeded
by a history of the steam engine from H. H. Birley, the cotton manufacturer notorious for leading the Yeomanry's lethal charge into the crowd at
Peterloo. Curiously for a Tory, Birley concluded by quoting the paragraph in Jeffrey's eulogy that consecrated Watt as the hero of the Napoleonic
wars – exemplifying perhaps Gatrell's argument that Manchester's Tory
manufacturers, lacking firm institutional or intellectual foundations, often
adhered to Liberal causes.[109]

The Reform Act (1832) and the Municipal Corporations Act (1835)
granted Manchester a political status more commensurate with its economic strength. In this context of rising civic pride (and prosperity), in
January 1836, the centenary of Watt's birth, several Mancunians who had
subscribed to the Westminster Abbey monument revived the proposal to
raise a local statue in his memory. Again, a well-attended public meeting
credited Watt's 'bold and original inventions' with Manchester's rapid
rise to affluence.[110] Again, it selected a committee that was dominated by
the overlapping interests of the cotton industry and the 'Lit and Phil'. The
choice of appropriate sites for Watt's statue and a second, to the duke of
Bridgewater (who had projected Manchester's first canal to bring cheap
coal into the city), was central to the call by the engineer, William Fairbairn,
for Manchester to improve its built environment. Fairbairn proposed a third
statue, to Sir Richard Arkwright, thereby identifying Manchester with all
the technological roots of its aggrandizement – steam, cotton, canals and
coal.[111] That none of these initiatives succeeded may be ascribed to the
competing financial demands of two other projects dear to the hearts of
Manchester liberals – the Manchester Athenaeum and the Anti-Corn-Law
League – and to the subsequent downturn in trade.

Finally in 1857, during a prolonged period of prosperity, Manchester
got its own statue of Watt. The initiative came specifically from the
'Lit and Phil', under William Fairbairn's leadership, and the statue's
unveiling was timed to take advantage of the Institution of Mechanical
Engineers' meeting there, thus involving the profession in a belated
tribute to its greatest luminary.[112] Veterans of the 1824 and 1836

---

[108] *Manchester Guardian*, 10 July 1824, 3c.
[109] V. A. C. Gatrell, 'Incorporation and the pursuit of Liberal hegemony in Manchester,
1790–1839', in Derek Fraser (ed.), *Municipal reform and the industrial city* (Leicester:
Leicester University Press, 1982), pp. 29–32.
[110] *Manchester Guardian*, 16 January 1836, 1a, 2e, 3a–d.
[111] William Fairbairn, *Observations on improvements of the town of Manchester, particularly as
regards the importance of blending in those improvements, the chaste and beautiful, with the
ornamental and useful* (Manchester: Robert Robinson, 1836).
[112] *Manchester Guardian*, 11 December 1855, 3a; 27 June 1857, 4e; *Proceedings of the
Institution of Mechanical Engineers* (1857), 85.

committees rallied to the call, and the *Manchester Guardian* reiterated the usual tributes to Watt as the supreme originator of Manchester's wealth – supplemented by a reference to his inventions' role in Britain's having withstood 'the shock of arms' in the Crimea.[113] The target was modest – £1,000 for a copy by Theed of Chantrey's statue in Westminster Abbey and its casting in bronze by Messrs Robinson and Cottam of Pimlico. The actual cost was £750 and the surplus funds purchased two new wall pedestals.[114]

Cottonopolis, secure in its victory over the corn laws, gave Watt's statue the fourth and final plinth on the new square created outside the Infirmary, beside the other heroes it celebrated in the 1850s. He was preceded by Dalton, the local scientist of international renown;[115] Peel, the reluctant champion of the Anti-Corn-Law League;[116] and (more controversially among pacifists) Wellington, the great military hero and Peel's equally reluctant lieutenant in the repeal of the corn laws.[117] In the 1860s, the city added Richard Cobden, free trade's greatest exponent and most loyal campaigner.[118] It did not commemorate the famous inventors of cotton machinery – Hargreaves, Arkwright or Crompton – whose patents it had fought or whose unpatented inventions it had used gratis, although there was some talk in 1855 of showing appreciation to 'the Duke of Bridgewater, Brindley, and Crompton' or to 'Robert Fulton and the elder Stephenson'.[119] Nor did it give Watt the prominence that the rhetoric seemed to promise: his statue is modest by comparison with the grand compositions that commemorate Peel and Wellington. Between 1824 and 1857 Watt's cause had been overtaken by the deaths of men to whom Manchester felt more immediate gratitude or, in the case of Dalton, a more neighbourly affection. Fairbairn was completing unfinished business on behalf of both his city and his profession. Nonetheless, the statue represented a remarkable tribute to Watt's reputation as the

---

[113] *Manchester Guardian*, 12 December 1855, 3e–f.   [114] Ibid., 26 June 1857, 2f.
[115] The subscription raised £5,312, of which £1,175 was spent on a bronze statue; £4,125 on scholarships and prizes: ibid., 25 March 1854, 7b, 8b.
[116] £5,105 was subscribed: ibid., 15 October 1853, 8b–f.
[117] F. C. Mather, 'Achilles or Nestor? The duke of Wellington in British politics, 1832–1846', in Norman Gash (ed.), *Wellington: studies in the military and political career of the first duke of Wellington* (Manchester: Manchester University Press, 1990), p. 189. For Quaker and radical opposition to Wellington's statue, see Anthony Howe, *The cotton masters, 1830–1860* (Oxford: Clarendon Press, 1984), p. 232; Rhodes Boyson, *The Ashworth cotton enterprise: the rise and fall of a family firm* (Oxford: Clarendon Press, 1970), p. 229.
[118] *The Times*, 19 April 1865, 12c; 23 April 1867, 6d.
[119] In 1890, Ford Madox Brown depicted John Kay in one of his murals for Manchester Town Hall – fleeing angry weavers who feared for their livelihoods: Dellheim, *Face of the past*, p. 173.

progenitor of industrialization and global trade – especially since it was 1868 before Birmingham, Watt's home for almost fifty years, memorialized him.[120]

In 1824, the citizens of Birmingham had scarcely considered the possibility of a local monument. Proudly they welcomed the honour paid by the nation, through Watt, to 'the mechanical arts', and contributed nearly £1,200 to its success.[121] Two speakers at the public meeting, held in Birmingham in July 1824, echoed Peel's sentiments. George Simcox, in particular, expressed his pleasure at the inclusion of Watt's monument among 'those of poets, statesmen, warriors, and philosophers'.

For, sir, if I mistake not, it is the first niche in this Temple of Fame, which has been devoted to the commemoration of mechanical genius, united with the discoveries of science. These honours have more frequently been reserved for successful warriors – but surely he is the greatest benefactor of his country and of mankind at large, whose achievements are of that nature which will remain as long as the world itself shall exist … And I cannot but think it a matter of peculiar congratulation to a commercial body like ourselves, that the nation, with the Sovereign at its head, has thus honoured the mechanical arts.[122]

The challenge repulsed

By the time that Chantrey's three statues of Watt were inaugurated in Westminster Abbey, Glasgow and Greenock, the Whigs had returned to power and begun to refashion the political landscape. The Reform Act (1832) extended the parliamentary franchise to middle-class men, who had lately paraded their claim under the banner of Watt, the great philosopher and model citizen.[123] In singing their hero's praises, as the progenitor of Britain's manufacturing strength and international predominance – even as the true victor of the Napoleonic wars – these men had been presenting their own case for recognition: the British state had to be remodelled to reflect their economic weight. Of course, Watt's adoption as a figurehead was only a minor ploy, towards the end of a long campaign for political reform, but his admittance into the national pantheon (with the blessing of the king and his ministers) was symbolically a triumph for the bourgeoisie. It was also a feather in the cap of the men of science.

---

[120] See below, pp. 291–2.
[121] Boulton & Watt MSS, MI/8/16; *Birmingham Chronicle*, 15 July 1824, 228.
[122] *Birmingham Chronicle*, 15 July 1824, 229.
[123] For a revisionist assessment of the Reform Act, see Philip Salmon, *Electoral reform at work: local politics and national parties, 1832–1841* (Woodbridge: Royal Historical Society and Boydell Press, 2002).

Many disapproved – both of the statue in Westminster Abbey and of what it represented. On the one hand, its huge size and its inappropriate site offended some aesthetic sensibilities, while its significance alarmed conservative critics. There was much pressure on St Paul's Cathedral and Westminster Abbey both above ground for memorials and below ground for burials. Increasing concern was expressed that these great churches were losing their primary purpose as places of worship to their secondary function as sites of national remembrance. Moreover, the clutter of statuary was aesthetically displeasing, detracting from the beauty of the building and even preventing appreciation of the memorials themselves. *The Times* consequently welcomed proposals in 1843 to remove some to the new Houses of Parliament.[124] Watt's statue was regularly singled out for criticism: A. W. N. Pugin, for example, 'was disgusted beyond measure at perceiving that the chapel of St Paul had been half filled up with a huge figure of James Watt, sitting in an armchair on an enormous pedestal, with some tasteless ornaments', and thought Chantrey deserved to be crushed beneath it.[125]

Dean Stanley's critique, however, demonstrates that such aesthetic protests often concealed deeper anxieties. 'Of all the monuments in the Abbey', he remarked, 'perhaps this is the one which provokes the loudest execrations from those who look for uniformity of design, or congeniality with the ancient architecture.' It was the 'colossal champion of a new plebian art', 'an enormous monster', which had cracked open the ancient pavement as it was manoeuvred into place, and towered above the delicate traceries of noble tombs, 'regardless of all proportion, or style, in the surrounding objects'. Yet in this 'very incongruity' Dean Stanley identified its significance: 'when we consider what this vast figure represents, what class of interests before unknown, what revolutions in the whole framework of modern society, equal to any that the Abbey walls have yet commemorated'.[126] Watt's monument was disconcerting to those who

[124] *The Times*, 20 September 1843, 4a–b; 23 August 1844, 5f; 24 August 1844, 4d; 26 August 1844, 3d; see also *The Builder* 45 (1883), 308.

[125] A. W. N. Pugin, *Contrasts: or a parallel between the noble edifices of the Middle Ages, and corresponding buildings of the present day; shewing the present decay of taste* (2nd edn, London: Charles Dolman, 1841; repr. with an introduction by H. R. Hitchcock, Leicester University Press, 1969), p. 40. When Watt's monument was evicted from the Abbey in 1961 and despatched to the British Transport Commission's museum in Clapham, the then Dean explained, it was 'wholly out of place, by reason of its very great size': *Sunday Times*, 17 June 1962, 16. It is now in the Scottish National Portrait Gallery, Edinburgh.

[126] Arthur Penrhyn Stanley, *Historical memorials of Westminster Abbey* (3rd edn, London: John Murray, 1869), pp. 349–50; P. C. Hammond, 'Stanley, Arthur Penrhyn (1815–1881)', *ODNB*, online edn, May 2006, www.oxforddnb.com/view/article/26259, accessed 18 October 2006.

found in its size, its style and its celebration of a man who rose from lowly origins to wealth, fame and social recognition, the epitome of a new, philistine Britain dedicated to the ethos of utility and the pursuit of meritocratic success.[127]

Harriet Martineau, who, while scarcely a conservative in politics, was concerned to keep 'the material interests of society' in their proper place, also appreciated its significance. Her wry comment resists the admission of science and technology to the realms of culture as much as it celebrates the symbolic breach in the aristocratic bastion of state:

> His statue now graces Westminster Abbey, where he may, by some, be thought to hold a middle rank between the Edwards and the Henries who lie there glorious in their regality, and the higher sovereigns, – the kings of mind whose memorials sanctify the Poets' Corner.[128]

A friend of Thomas Carlyle, Martineau apparently shared his ranking of heroic figures. While Carlyle might perceive steam as the malign but magnificent force that was transforming modern society and reluctantly admire Watt (his fellow Scot) for his ingenuity and hard work, he found no place for 'the Scottish Brassmith' in On heroes, hero-worship, and the heroic in history (1841). Carlyle's true heroes were the great political and military leaders, the prophets, the poets and other men of letters; the activities of scientists and engineers, however impressive, posed a threat to civilized values – and were duly placed in Chartism (1839).[129] Sussman argues that Carlyle was able to accommodate the great inventors in his pantheon by elevating them above the mundane mechanical world and conceiving of them 'as holy men who can fathom mysterious spiritual forces. They are wizards, magicians.'[130] Indeed, in his essay on Chartism, Carlyle describes Watt as a Faustian figure, 'searching out, in his workshop, the Fire-secret'.[131] But, pace Sussman, Carlyle was unwilling to admit even the greatest inventors to his inner sanctum. Like Martineau, he places them in a separate category, to be honoured but culturally not

---

[127] Houghton, *Victorian frame of mind*, pp. 2–9, 183–92.

[128] Harriet Martineau, *The history of England during the thirty years' peace: 1816–1846*, 2 vols. (London: Charles Knight, 1849–50), vol. I, p. 413. R. K. Webb, 'Martineau, Harriet (1802–1876)', *ODNB*, online edn, October 2006, www.oxforddnb.com/view/article/18228, accessed 18 October 2006. Martineau was by no means alone in her scale of values: Hope Mason, *Value of creativity*, pp. vi, 228–9.

[129] Carlyle, *On heroes*, p. 124, where Watt is mentioned as one of the Scots whose achievements stemmed from the Reformation inspired by John Knox. For Carlyle's concept of the hero, see above, p. 21.

[130] Herbert L. Sussman, *Victorians and the machine* (Cambridge, MA: Harvard University Press, 1968), p. 28.

[131] Thomas Carlyle, *Chartism*, in *The works of Thomas Carlyle, centenary edition*, 30 vols. (London: Chapman and Hall, 1896–9), vol. XXIX, p. 183.

integrated: 'England was not only to have her Shakespeares, Bacons, Sydneys, but her Watts, Arkwrights, Brindleys! We will honour greatness in all kinds.'[132]

Indicative of the prevalence of this hierarchy of values was Edinburgh's erection of a grandiose monument to Sir Walter Scott at a time when Watt's memorial still languished for lack of funds.[133] A public meeting in October 1832, two months after Scott's death, attracted approximately 1,200 people of all political colours; by the following May, over £5,700 had been subscribed, most of it by Edinburgh's citizens (and grateful bankers). This was similar to the amount donated for Watt's monument in Westminster Abbey, but Edinburgh's sculptural ambitions for its literary hero were much grander yet. The subscription had to be reopened in 1840 and a further £3,000 raised by holding 'Waverley Balls' in London and Edinburgh, before the Gothic fantasy to which they aspired could be inaugurated in 1846.[134] Evidently, Edinburgh society cherished Scott far more dearly than Watt. Not only had Scott lived locally and been active in Edinburgh circles, but his pen had brought Scotland's past alive and reinvigorated its national identity.[135] Watt represented a new type of national hero, at odds with the militaristic values of William Wallace and Robert the Bruce that Scott's novels celebrated. Watt's natural constituency was not among the capital's professional groups but on the Clyde, where manufacturers and traders admired his ingenuity and appreciated his contribution to their economic power – the symbol of a forward-looking, commercial and harmonious Scotland. Only later in the century did Scots develop a self-identity as an ingenious nation.[136] Meanwhile, although the commemoration of Watt testifies to a new-found respect for inventors and engineers, it is evident that, particularly outside the heartlands of commerce (in both England and Scotland), the upper and middle classes were yet hesitant in their admiration for utility. Watt attracted gratitude and respect; Scott stirred deeper emotions.[137]

François Arago, the secretary to the Académie des Sciences, ended his *Éloge* of Watt with a twenty-page tirade against the ingratitude

---

[132] Ibid., p. 181.

[133] N. M. McQ. Holmes, *The Scott Monument: a history and architectural guide* (Edinburgh: Edinburgh Museums and Art Galleries, 1979), pp. 3–13. This is not to say that Scott was one of Carlyle's heroes: Carlyle, *On heroes*, p. li.

[134] Morton, *Unionist nationalism*, pp. 163–70. £500 was donated by the Bank of Scotland and other Scottish banks in respect for Scott's valiant attempts to pay off his publishers' debts: ibid., p. 167.

[135] Ibid., pp. 156–62.   [136] See below, pp. 345–9.

[137] Houghton, *Victorian frame of mind*, pp. 308–9, 334.

and snobbery of the British who failed to honour the new heroes in their midst.[138] He decried 'the disapprobation of some narrow-minded beings ... [who consider that] warriors, magistrates, and statesmen ... have alone a right to statues', and questioned whether such conservative critics would approve even of 'a simple bust' to Homer, Aristotle, Descartes or Newton. Likewise, they had begrudged Watt a peerage – as they had Newton, but after 150 years of 'progress in science and philosophy' one might have expected more.[139] Arago contrasted such 'haughty pretensions' with the widespread appreciation of Watt's achievement that he had found on his travels throughout Britain. He claimed to have asked over a hundred people from 'all classes of society' and from 'all shades of political opinion' about Watt's impact on 'the wealth, the power, the prosperity of England', and they had consistently placed Watt's 'services ... above all comparison'.[140] Nearly all, he maintained, quoted from the speeches made at the Westminster meeting in 1824. Arago's harsh judgement incited a succession of complaints, in the 1840s, about the government's poor treatment of Watt, which chimed with the scientific community's long-running campaign for public funding and mounting demands for the patent system's reform. Most virulent in his criticism was Sir David Brewster, who resurrected Watt's 'claim' to the defeat of Napoleon. Quoting from Huskisson's and others' speeches, he denounced not only the ingratitude but also the anti-intellectualism of Britain's governing class, which 'is startled at noon, and haunted at midnight, with the spectres of knowledge and reform'.[141]

Just as the middle classes did not overthrow the aristocracy but were absorbed into the political nation, neither did James Watt oust the warriors and statesmen (let alone the poets!) from the national pantheon.[142] The exaggerated claims made for Watt's role in the Napoleonic Wars eventually faded from sight; they never posed a serious threat to the heroic status of Nelson and Wellington, nor to a narrative history of Britain in which battles overshadow blast furnaces. It is the admiral who presides over the square in central London that was named for his greatest victory; it is the general whose statue rides high at Marble Arch – and, despite no direct Scottish association (not even a visit), also outside General Register

---

[138] For the *Éloge* and its role in the water controversy, see Miller, *Discovering water*, pp. 105–27.

[139] Arago, *Life of James Watt*, pp. 149, 165.   [140] Ibid., p. 160.

[141] [Brewster], Review of *Éloge Historique de James Watt*, p. 502; Miller, *Discovering water*, pp. 152–66. See also, for example, Lardner, *Steam engine*, pp. 318–19.

[142] Harold Mah, 'Phantasies of the public sphere: rethinking the Habermas of the historians', *Journal of Modern History* 72 (2000), 168–9.

House in Edinburgh.[143] By mid-century, both were celebrated by monuments on the streets of London (a feat that Watt failed to achieve) and with statues and street names in far more provincial cities. When Wellington died in 1852, his funeral was a state occasion of unparalleled magnificence: nearly forty years after Waterloo, the nation mourned its saviour as if it had been yesterday. Thomas Cooper, the Chartist, remembered all the reasons that radicals had to hate him, yet commented:

> But all this had passed away, and Wellington had become not only the great pillar of state and most valued counsellor of the Queen; but next to her, the most deeply respected and most heartily honoured person in the realm ... We all felt as if we lived, now *he* was dead, in a different England.[144]

Yet, if Watt had not reached the pantheon's highest plinths, he had achieved entry to its halls. It was, as Peel had implied, not only a mark of individual distinction but also a sign of social upheaval for a man of science and a manufacturer to be commemorated in the glorious company of the warrior, the statesman and the poet. With Watt's apotheosis, the inventor was ceasing to be a 'projector', the patentee was abrogating the reproach of 'monopolist', and the economic history of the reign of George III (1760–1820) was coming to be celebrated as 'the Industrial Revolution' that was making Britain the wealthiest country in the world. These are themes that we shall pursue in the next chapter.

---

[143] Neither's memorial, however, was without its problems: Yarrington, *Commemoration of the hero*, pp. 277–325; Yarrington, *His Achilles heel?* For the Scottish monuments, see Cookson, 'The Edinburgh and Glasgow Duke of Wellington statues', 26–33.

[144] *The life of Thomas Cooper, written by himself*, ed. John Savile (New York: Leicester University Press, 1971), pp. 329–30, 332.

James Watt had staked a posthumous claim for the recognition of inventors as national benefactors and heroes of civil society. As William Fairbairn said, Watt had 'given a freedom and impetus to the inventive genius of his country'.[1] A marked improvement in the status of inventors is immediately discernible. It stimulated demands for a more efficient patent system and brought inventors more immediate benefits, especially in litigation. In tandem, Watt's reputation influenced Whig historians, some of whom pressed home the rhetorical advances made in 1824, as they sought an explanation for Britain's extraordinary growth in prosperity since the eighteenth century. Other authors began to explore the nature of inventiveness, focusing primarily on Watt: in 1824, several speakers had tentatively probed the nature of his special talents – if his invention was no mere 'accident', then what was his peculiar 'genius'? In this and the following chapter, we will examine the ways in which Watt's growing reputation was both exploited and contested in the subsequent quarter century.

The age of steam

Watt's elevation to heroic status re-invigorated public interest and confidence in the steam engine. Promoters of steam-powered transport seized the opportunity to advance their case. The *Morning Chronicle*, which had reported the Westminster meeting and contributed £25 towards Watt's monument, trumpeted the cause of steam-driven railways: following that ringing endorsement of steam by the political nation, surely Parliament could not bow to the canal lobby and prevent Britain from reaping 'the full benefit of his discovery'.[2] According to an article in

---

[1] Fairbairn, *Observations*, p. 17.
[2] *Morning Chronicle*, 19 June 1824, 8; 18 August 1824, 4a; Boulton & Watt MSS, Timmins vol. 2, fo. 44. The new editor of the *Morning Chronicle*, John Black, was in sympathy with the views of the Utilitarian radicals, led by Jeremy Bentham and James Mill: John Stuart Mill, *Autobiography* (London: Longman, Green, Reader and Dyer, 1873), p. 55.

the *Quarterly Review*, the current vogue for railway speculations had been stoked by 'the great encouragement held out by the first Minister of the crown and his colleagues (at a meeting for considering the proposal of a monument to the late James Watt) to those who should effect a further improvement of this mighty engine, and to the promoters and discoverers of other useful inventions'.[3]

Authors and publishers responded with a rush of new books on the steam engine – at least nine, including two in French, between 1824 and 1830.[4] Information, previously confined to periodical articles and encyclopaedia entries, exploded to fill hundreds of pages. The late eighteenth century's focus on the cotton industry was now directed to its emergent prime mover.[5] In the most impressive example of this phenomenon, the engineer and draughtsman John Farey expanded his earlier (and already substantial) entry on steam in Rees's *Cyclopaedia* (1816) to over 700 pages.[6] Farey, who had known Watt personally, detailed the technology and history of the steam engine, with credit for improvements carefully ascribed and brief biographies included.[7] Readers were left in no doubt of either Watt's achievement or the epoch-making powers of steam. All other inventions, said Farey, appeared 'insignificant' in comparison with the steam engine: without it, 'that amazing increase of productive industry' during the preceding thirty years would have been impossible; indeed Britain 'would have retrograded greatly'.[8] In the following decades, books about steam poured from the presses – the excitement fuelled to new heights by the railways. Dionysius Lardner's popular work, for example, ran to eleven British editions and was translated into several European languages.[9]

---

[3] [John Barrow], 'Canals and railroads', *Quarterly Review* 31 (March 1825), 349–78.

[4] Jennifer Tann, 'Introduction', in Dickinson and Jenkins, *James Watt and the steam engine*, pp. xix–xx.

[5] See above, pp. 64, 67–8.

[6] Abraham Rees (ed), *The cyclopaedia; or, universal dictionary of arts, sciences, and literature*, 45 vols. (London: Longman, Hurst, Rees, Orme and Brown, 1802–20); A. P. Woolrich, 'John Farey, jr, technical author and draughtsman: his contribution to Rees's *Cyclopaedia*', *Industrial Archaeology Review* 20 (1998), 49–67; A. P. Woolrich, 'John Farey and his *Treatise on the Steam Engine* of 1827', *HT* 22 (2000), 63–106.

[7] A. P. Woolrich, 'John Farey Jr (1791–1851): engineer and polymath', *HT* 19 (1997), 114–15. Farey had begun writing the text of the *Treatise* in 1820: ibid., 118.

[8] John Farey, *A treatise on the steam engine, historical, practical, and descriptive* (London: Longman, Rees, Orme, Brown and Greene, 1827; repr. Newton Abbot: David & Charles, 1971), vol. I, pp. 3–4; see also ibid., vol. I, p. 406, and below, pp. 129–36.

[9] Dionysius Lardner, *The steam engine familiarly explained and illustrated* (London: Taylor & Walton, 1836); J. N. Hays, 'Lardner, Dionysius (1793–1859)', *ODNB*, www.oxforddnb.com/view/article/16068, accessed 17 October 2006.

Not that every author was uncritical. Elijah Galloway, for instance, tempered his opinion of Watt as 'a truly wonderful man... [who] has done more for art and commerce than any single individual ever known' with the unusual criticism that 'few have put upon record so many absurd and impracticable schemes'.[10] In a nationalistic account, Thomas Tredgold revived Jonathan Hornblower's complaint of having been unjustly prevented by Watt's patent from introducing a superior engine, and departed from the heroic model to suggest that, without Watt, the idea of the separate condenser would soon have occurred to someone else; indeed, in the absence of his patent, mines might have been drained more cheaply.[11] Given the hostility that Watt's patent had generated, it is perhaps surprising that the criticisms were so mild and few; a quarter century after the patent's expiry, with Watt's reputation riding so high, there was presumably no market for squabbles over priority.

Although no full-length biography of Watt was published in English until 1839 – when two translations of Arago's *Éloge* appeared – there was a profusion of shorter pieces.[12] This lack was no reflection on his standing, since biography was still an emergent literary genre: even Newton had to wait until 1831 for a full-length biography in English.[13] Biographical sketches in the steam-engine literature and in 'improving' texts, such as the Society for the Diffusion of Useful Knowledge's (SDUK) volume, *The pursuit of knowledge under difficulties* (1830–1), as well as numerous entries in biographical dictionaries and encyclopaedias, maintained Watt's presence.[14] His inclusion among the forty or so new lives in the *Supplement* to the *Encyclopaedia Britannica* (1815–24) had itself been a mark of distinction. The editor, Macvey Napier, justified the biographical entries 'on account of their eminence in Science or Literature' – fifty-eight of the *Encyclopaedia's* 165 were men of science.[15] Appropriately for an *Éloge*, Arago was unstinting in his praise of Watt and his work.[16] A few years later, Lord Brougham drew heavily on Arago's text (while toning down his high-flown prose), when he hymned Watt in the select company celebrated in his *Lives of men of letters and science, who flourished in the time of George III.*[17] Only Watt's steam engine was deemed of sufficient

[10] Elijah Galloway, *History and progress of the steam engine* (2nd edn, London: Thomas Kelly, 1830), p. 94.
[11] Thomas Tredgold, *The steam engine: comprising an account of its invention and progressive improvement* (London: J. Taylor, 1827), pp. 25–9.
[12] Dickinson and Jenkins, *James Watt and the steam engine*, pp. xix, 367.
[13] Shortland and Yeo, 'Introduction', in Shortland and Yeo (eds.), *Telling lives in science*, pp. 14–22.
[14] [Craik], *Pursuit of knowledge*, vol. II, pp. 295–323.
[15] Yeo, 'Alphabetical lives', p. 155. See also above, p. 96.   [16] See above, p. 123.
[17] Brougham, *Lives of men of letters and science*, vol. I, pp. 372–89.

significance to make the editors of the fourth English edition of Beckmann's *History of inventions* (1846) break their resolution merely to update the subjects that had appeared in earlier editions. They believed it was 'imperative to make an exception in favour of the *steam-engine*, the most important of all modern inventions', and reinforced this judgement by reproducing an engraved portrait of Watt as the frontispiece to their second volume.[18]

Two major biographies appeared in the 1850s, one authored by Watt's cousin, James Patrick Muirhead, the other by George Williamson, on behalf of the Watt Club of Greenock.[19] In his review, Smiles bewailed the lack of biographies of the 'heroes of mechanical science': there was yet no 'respectable memoir' of Arkwright, Crompton, Brindley or Rennie, let alone of those of previous centuries, such as Savery and Newcomen. It was fortunate, therefore, that 'the greatest name in the roll of English inventors' had left a large archive to assist his biographers – a boon that Smiles himself exploited a few years later.[20] Muirhead commented on Watt's fame: great as it had been during his lifetime, it had grown 'since his death in a degree that may, perhaps, be termed unprecedented'.[21] The historian, Henry Thomas Buckle, indignantly agreed: Watt's reputation was being inflated out of all proportion. He was outraged when Muirhead quoted the botanist, William Withering, to the effect that Watt was equal, even superior, in ability to Newton. Buckle evidently felt he had to tread carefully – he 'would not wish to diminish one jot the veneration in which the great name of Watt is justly held' – but this was going too far: 'I cannot but protest against such indiscriminate eulogy, which would rank Watt in the same class as one of those godlike intellects of which the world has not produced a score.'[22] While Watt's engine merited recognition as a new invention (not merely an improvement) 'under its scientific aspect, it was merely a skilful adaptation of laws previously known; and one of its most important points, namely, the economy of heat, was a practical application of ideas promulgated by Black'.[23] In Buckle's scheme of history,

---

[18] John Beckmann, *A history of inventions, discoveries, and origins*, trans. William Johnston, 4th edn, ed. William Francis and J. W. Griffith, 2 vols. (London: Henry G. Bohn, 1846), vol. II, p. v.

[19] Muirhead, *Life of James Watt*; Williamson, *Memorials*.

[20] [Samuel Smiles], 'James Watt', *Quarterly Review* 104 (October 1858), 411.

[21] Muirhead, *Life of James Watt*, p. 1.

[22] Henry Thomas Buckle, *History of civilization in England* [1857–61], The World's Classics, ed. Henry Froude, 3 vols. (London: Oxford University Press, 1903–4), vol. III, pp. 405–6, n. 708.

[23] Ibid., vol. III, pp. 404–5. Cf. D. S. L. Cardwell, *The Fontana history of technology* (London: Fontana, 1994), pp. 160–1.

technological progress had deeper roots than mere individual genius: it arose from the inexorable pressure of economic forces on human ingenuity.[24]

Whether the subject was the steam engine or its 'inventor', readers were left in no doubt of its importance. The Board of Trade statistician, George Porter, was still emulating Jeffrey's hyperbole, nearly two decades later: the steam engine together with cotton machinery had produced 'almost magical effects upon the productive energies of this kingdom', without which British economic resources would have been insufficient to keep Napoleon at bay.[25] In 1836, William Fitton, a leading Lancashire radical, paid such claims an unintended tribute when, speaking in favour of the Ten-Hours Movement, he 'proceeded to deny strenuously that "England owes its greatness to the modern discoveries of steam and machinery"'.[26] More in tune with the mainstream, the radical journalist, John Wade, perceived Watt's steam engine as 'the foundation ... for the prodigious advance in wealth and population which marked the reign of George III', a development he considered to be more influential in the period's history than any war or other political event.[27] Significantly, Wade, a notorious scourge of elite parasitism and abuses of power, departed from fellow radicals, such as William Cobbett and Henry Hunt, in his broad sympathies for the 'industrious orders', combined with a faith in political economy, free trade and Malthusianism.[28] Ebenezer Elliott, the 'Corn Law Rhymer', similarly broke from the Chartists, criticizing their campaign for playing into the hands of the aristocracy while the people starved.[29] Sympathetic to industry, Elliott

---

[24] Peter J. Bowler, *The invention of progress: the Victorians and the past* (Oxford: Basil Blackwell, 1989), pp. 27–31. For similar views, see below, pp. 161–70 and 276–9.

[25] G. R. Porter, FRS, *The progress of the nation, in its various social and economical relations, from the beginning of the nineteenth century*, 3 vols. (London: John Murray, 1836–43), vol. I, pp. 187–8, vol. II, p. 285. See Henry Parris, 'Porter, George Richardson (1792–1852)', *ODNB*, www.oxforddnb.com/view/article/22567, accessed 17 October 2006.

[26] D. S. Gadian, 'Class and class-consciousness in Oldham and other north-western industrial towns, 1830–50', *HJ* 21 (1978), 166.

[27] [John Wade], *History of the middle and working classes; with a popular exposition of the economical and political principles which have influenced the past and present conditions of the industrious orders* (London: Effringham Wilson, 1833), pp. 82–3.

[28] Philip Harling, 'Wade, John (1788–1875)', *ODNB*, www.oxforddnb.com/view/article/28378, accessed 17 October 2006.

[29] Paul A. Pickering and Alex Tyrrell, *The people's bread: a history of the Anti-Corn Law League* (London and New York: Leicester University Press, 2000), pp. 146–8; Angela M. Leonard, 'Elliott, Ebenezer (1781–1849)', *ODNB*, www.oxforddnb.com/view/article/8673, accessed 17 October 2006.

proclaimed that Watt's invention could undermine the landlords' control and improve the people's lives:

> Watt! and his million-feeding enginery!
> Steam miracles of demi-deity!
> From John o' Groat's to Cornwall's farthest bay!
> Engine of Watt! unrivall'd is thy sway.
> Compared with thine, what is the tyrant's power?
> His might destroys, while thine creates and saves.
> Thy triumphs live and grow, like fruit and flower;
> But his are writ in blood, and read on graves![30]

Some of the most powerful imagery came from the pens (and paintbrushes) of those who greeted the growth of steam power with dismay. In a famous passage, Carlyle envisaged steam-driven revolutionary change hurtling around the globe, unstoppable and profound in its effects:

Cannot the dullest hear the Steam-Engines clanking around him? Has he not seen the Scottish Brassmith's IDEA (and this but a mechanical one) travelling on firewings round the Cape, and across two Oceans; and stronger than any other Enchanter's Familiar, on all hands unwearyingly fetching and carrying: at home, not only weaving Cloth; but rapidly enough overturning the whole old system of Society; and, for Feudalism and Preservation of the Game, preparing us, by indirect but sure methods, Industrialism and the Government of the Wisest?[31]

Through such images the steam engine's epochal role entered the wider consciousness. Carlyle, a radical Tory, may have dreaded its consequences, but he caught the emotional charge, the almost sexual urgency, of steam-powered industry's 'Titanic energy and … essential anonymity'.[32] Under its pressure, the medieval world was crumbling, the feudal hierarchy and its institutions were yielding to democracy and social fluidity. Elsewhere, his personification of Watt as the still germinating seed of the machine age, lying beneath the medieval green sward, lends a terrible inevitability to this apocryphal transformation: 'Saint Mungo rules in Glasgow; James Watt still slumbering in the deep of Time … The

---

[30] Ebenezer Elliott, *The poetical works* (1876), vol. I, *Juvenile poems: Steam at Sheffield*, lines 66–7, 164–9; see also lines 194–8 ('Literature Online': http://lion.chadwyck.co.uk/). Elsewhere, sometimes in footnotes to his verses, Elliott elaborated on his reasons for celebrating Watt: *The Giaour, a satire, addressed to Lord Byron* (1823), fn. line 673; *More verses and prose* (1850), vol. II, *Miscellanies: Hymn [Men! Ye who sow the earth with good!]*, fn. line 14; *Lines written for the Sheffield Mechanics' first exhibition*, lines 14–15 ('Literature Online': lion.chadwyck.co.uk/).

[31] Thomas Carlyle, *Sartor resartus* (1832), cited in Houghton, *Victorian frame of mind*, pp. 4–5. The 'Scottish Brassmith' refers, of course, to Watt. See also Berg, *Machinery question*, pp. 12–15, 261–3.

[32] Burrow, *Liberal descent*, p. 66. See also Sussman, *Victorians and the machine*, pp. 19–39.

centuries are big; and the birth hour is coming, not yet come.'[33] Carlyle was not unique in the portentousness of his image of Watt. Already in 1820, in a much-reproduced passage, Sir Walter Scott had described him as '[t]his potent commander of the elements – this abridger of time and space – this magician, whose cloudy machinery has produced a change in the world'.[34]

No longer simply a source of motive power, by the early 1830s steam was hailed or condemned as an agent of social and political transformation. Peter Gaskell, for example, a ferocious critic of the factory system, attributed revolutionary social changes to steam-powered manufacturing. Gaskell, who was drawing on his observations as a doctor in Stockport, at the heart of the cotton-spinning industry, blamed steam for converting Britain in scarcely twenty years from an agricultural nation to an industrial one – with devastating effects on families and their ways of life.[35] Steam, protested Gaskell, was transforming the very fabric of society:

A complete revolution has been affected [sic] in the distribution of property, the very face of a great country has been re-modelled, various classes of its inhabitants utterly swept away, the habits of all have undergone such vast alterations, that they resemble a people of a different age and generation.[36]

Notoriously, this was a conception of recent English history shared by Friedrich Engels, who, in the 1840s, told his German readership that the inventions of the steam engine and cotton machinery had given rise to 'an industrial revolution', which had transformed England between 1760 and 1844, at least as much as the political revolution had transformed France.[37] In Engels' view, it was essentially a technological revolution: beginning with Watt, Hargreaves and Arkwright, a succession of inventors had extended innovative changes throughout the manufacturing and transport sectors. Its effects, however, were reverberating across the entire society, principally through the proletarianization of the working

---

[33] *Past and present*, in *Works*, X, p. 66, cited in Sussman, *Victorians and the machine*, pp. 31–2.

[34] [Walter Scott], *The Monastery: a romance, by the author of 'Waverley'* (Edinburgh: Constable, 1820), preface.

[35] P. Gaskell, *The manufacturing population of England, its moral, social, and physical conditions, and the changes which have arisen from the use of steam machinery; with an examination of infant labour* (London: Baldwin & Cradock, 1833), pp. 6, 9–10, 52. See Hardy, *Origins of the idea*, p. 93.

[36] Gaskell, *Manufacturing population*, p. 33. For Tory fears of the social effects of industrialization more generally and their calls for a tax on machinery, see Berg, *Machinery question*, pp. 263–8.

[37] Friedrich Engels, *The condition of the working class in England*, ed. David McLellan (Oxford and New York: Oxford University Press, 1993), p. 15.

class: deprived of any property in land or security of employment, the members of the proletariat were demanding 'with daily increasing urgency, their share of the advantages of society'. The industrial revolution, Engels believed, was leading inexorably to a political revolution.[38]

Liberal commentators, on the other hand, invested equally high expectations in the capacity of steam power to bring about peaceful social change. George Craik ended his chapter on Watt with an excited description of the steam engine's 'conquests'; most recently, 'the great experiment of the Liverpool and Manchester Railway ... [was permitting] undreamt-of rapidity' of travel. Once railways became universal, prophesied Craik, 'in what a new state of society shall we find ourselves! ... A nation will then be indeed a community; and all the benefits of the highest civilization, instead of being confined to one central spot, will be diffused equally over the land, like the light of heaven.'[39] With supreme confidence, through to the outbreak of the Crimean War (and even beyond), many invested their hopes for peaceful international relations in the stimulus to trade and communication provided by steam-powered manufacturing and steam-driven transport; 'a higher state of civilization' would ensue, both at home and wherever British merchants ventured overseas.[40] In his presidential address to the Institution of Civil Engineers in 1846, Sir John Rennie celebrated steam as the 'grand improver and civiliser of the age' in both peace and war.[41] According to his colleague, William Fairbairn, it had 'altered the conditions of man, and revolutionized the world'.[42]

Among the most sanguine in their prophecies were the authors of technical treatises on the steam engine and its history. One of the most popular, Dionysius Lardner envisioned a nirvana of ease and material comforts, to be enjoyed in the assurance of international peace: the global commerce, which steam transport had stimulated, 'has knit together remote countries by bonds of amity not likely to be broken'.[43] At the same time, said Lardner, steam-driven presses were reducing the costs of print and promoting international communication: 'it is thus that reason

[38] Ibid., pp. 15–31.   [39] Craik, *Pursuit of knowledge*, vol. II, pp. 320–1.
[40] See, for example, Farey, *Treatise on the steam engine*, vol. I, p. v, and above, pp. 103–4.
[41] Sir John Rennie, 'Presidential address', *Proceedings of the Institution of Civil Engineers*, 7 (1847), 81–2.
[42] William Fairbairn, 'The rise and progress of manufacture and commerce and of civil and mechanical engineering in Lancashire and Cheshire', in Thomas Baines, *Lancashire and Cheshire, past and present*, 2 vols. (London: W. Mackenzie, 1868–9), vol. II, p. iv. See also Frederick C. Branwell, *Great facts: a popular history and description of the most remarkable inventions during the present century* (London: Houltson & Wright, 1859), p. 302.
[43] Lardner, *Steam engine* (7th edn, London, 1840), p. 5.

has taken the place of force, and the pen has superseded the sword; it is thus that war has almost ceased upon the earth.'[44] The opening of the Glasgow and Greenock Railway in 1841 called forth a set of mock-heroic verses from Alexander Rodger, which announced its theme by way of an explicit rejection of past heroes, 'Who marched off to fame – to their knees up in gore', in favour of 'The genius of Watt, and the triumphs of Steam'.[45] Many steam-filled verses later, he concluded by proposing a toast to the memory of Watt,

> Who, wisely directing the Steam's latent powers,
> Has given a new face to this planet of ours –
> May his name float along on Time's mighty stream,
> Till sun, moon, and stars, be enveloped in Steam.[46]

High expectations of the pacifying powers of steam were not only the pipe dreams of engineers and popularizers of science. The political benefits of international commerce constituted an article of faith among proponents of free trade. As we have seen, several speakers in 1824 implied that improved (steam) transport, in partnership with reduced tariffs on trade, would inevitably lower the barriers of suspicion and antipathy between nations; Huskisson hymned the benefits of commerce advancing peacefully, hand-in-hand with Christianity.[47] When such utopian prophecies were subjected to the pragmatic scrutiny of policy, however, only the Cobdenites held firmly to these idealistic extremes. From the mid-1830s, Richard Cobden, a pacifist and manufacturer from Manchester, promulgated a benign, quasi-religious vision of free trade as the bedrock of global peace: everyone would benefit from the international division of labour it entailed.[48]

Other proponents of free trade (including radicals, such as Joseph Hume and Robert Torrens) were more concerned, however, with maintaining Britain's current position as 'the workshop of the world'. They raised the mercantilist spectre of manufacturing being lost to countries where food (and consequently, labour) was cheaper; repeal of the corn laws, they argued, would stifle imminent foreign competition.[49] For Thomas Babington Macaulay, speaking in 1842, their repeal promised

---

[44] Ibid., p. 5. See also Hugo Reid, *The steam engine* (Edinburgh: William Tait, 1838), pp. 154–6.

[45] Alexander Rodger, 'Verses written upon the opening of the Glasgow and Greenock Railway, 30 March, 1841', *Stray Leaves* (Glasgow: Charles Rattray, 1842), lines 1–6.

[46] Ibid., lines 43–8.   [47] See above, pp. 103–4.

[48] Bernard Semmel, *The rise of free trade imperialism: classical political economy and the empire of free trade and imperialism, 1750–1850* (Cambridge: Cambridge University Press, 1970), pp. 155–63. See below, p. 216.

[49] Ibid., pp. 146–54, 163–9.

Britain 'almost a monopoly' of global trade in manufactures; Britons could be confident that other countries would supply them, in return, with an abundance of food.[50] Six years later, in the wake of repeal, he praised the benefits of steam transport as moral and intellectual, as well as material: it would tend 'to bind together all the branches of the great human family'. It also promised to speed the passage of troops and artillery across continents and navies against wind and tide – a paradox Macaulay did not stay to comment on.[51] Others were even more candid in their assumption that what the steam engine had secured was less the free and equal intercourse of nations than the 'pax Britannica', which could slide all too easily into colonialism. A hubristic example of this may be found in an expeditionary account, written in 1837:

We have the power in our hands, moral, physical, and mechanical; the first, based upon the Bible; the second, upon the wonderful adaptation of the Anglo-Saxon race to all climates, situations, and circumstances ... the third, bequeathed to us by the immortal Watt. By his invention every river is laid open to us, time and distance are shortened.[52]

By implication, the invention of 'the immortal Watt' was part of the divine plan, the technological component of Britain's civilizing mission. It was an extension of the providential cosmology espoused by evangelicals and expressed by Huskisson, when he had lauded Watt's steam engine in 1824.[53]

Such modes of thought were casting British and indeed global history into a technologically determined form: human agency yielded to the agency of steam power. Such thinking was by no means novel, earlier historians had attributed grand effects to the three Renaissance inventions of printing, gunpowder and the compass. In the case of steam, however, there was no similar mystery concerning the inventor's identity: attributions were clear (if controversial in some quarters), and there were

[50] Hansard, *P.D.*, 3rd ser., LX (21 February 1842), 754, cited in Semmel, *Rise of free trade*, p. 149.

[51] Lord Macaulay, *The history of England from the accession of James the Second* [new edn 1857], ed. Charles Harding Firth, 6 vols. (London: Macmillan & Co., 1913), vol. I, p. 364. See William Thomas, 'Macaulay, Thomas Babington, Baron Macaulay (1800–1859)', *ODNB*, online edn, October 2005, www.oxforddnb.com/view/article/17349, accessed 17 October 2006.

[52] Macgregor Laird and R. A. K. Oldfield, *Narrative of an expedition into the interior of Africa* (London: Laird and Oldfield, 1837), vol. II, pp. 397–8, quoted in Daniel R. Headrick, *The tools of empire: technology and European imperialism in the nineteenth century* (New York and Oxford: Oxford University Press, 1981), p. 17. See also, Sir Archibald Alison, 1st Bart., *History of Europe during the French Revolution*, 10 vols. (Edinburgh: William Blackwood; London: T. Cadell, 1833–42), vol. VIII, p. 5.

[53] See above, p. 104.

some discussions of the socio-economic context that had stimulated it.[54] Nonetheless, while Watt was generally regarded as the steam engine's undoubted human creator, it was often spoken of as having (like Frankenstein's monster) an existence independent of its inventor and the society in which it was developed. The steam engine (or sometimes the disembodied 'mind' of Watt) was presented as the significant historical agent, independently capable of transforming the world. Usually, this was the impression conveyed by unthinking hyperbole (and bad poetry), which was all the more influential in literature written for children. One author offered his young readers a paean to the qualities of 'the mind which gave to the world its greatest physical transformer – the instrument which is changing the entire civilization of the world'.[55] For R. B. Prosser of the Patent Office, the inclusion in his history of Birmingham inventors of 'the most philosophical inventor that the world ever saw' was axiomatic, although he considered that 'Watt's inventions have exercised so vast an influence upon the world that it has been customary to regard them as belonging rather to mankind in general than as associated with any particular place'.[56] Another popularizer of science and technology raised 'Watt's invention of the steam engine' above the French revolution in historical importance: it had 'exercised the deepest, as well as widest and most permanent influence over the whole civilised world'.[57]

Less often, one finds more considered accounts, in which specific social and political events are explained as the outcomes of technological change. The steam engine offered contemporaries a tangible, technological explanation for the rapid, otherwise often bewildering, changes that were affecting their lives so profoundly. Indicative of its hold on common ways of thought is this piece, which was published in 1860 as an uncontroversial account of recent British history:

The passage of the Reform Bill was the consummation of social and political changes that had long since been effected in the condition of the community. Previous to the manufacturing era, the soil, its minerals, and its agricultural produce were the great elements of national wealth; and, as a consequence, political power was entirely in the hands of its possessors: when, however, steam came as an agent of manufacture, a rival element of national wealth was produced,

---

[54] For example, see below, pp. 164–70, 175–9. Also note Buckle's protest, above, pp. 128–9.

[55] [Thomas Cooper, the Chartist], *The triumphs of perseverance and enterprise: recorded as examples for the young* (London: Darton & Co., 1856), p. 97. For an incisive discussion of the concept of technological determinism, see Donald MacKenzie, 'Marx and the machine', *T&C* 25 (1984), 473–502.

[56] Prosser, *Birmingham inventors*, p. 37.

[57] J. Hamilton Fyfe, *The triumphs of invention and discovery* (London: T. Nelson & Co., 1861), pp. 43–4.

and from it grew up a wealthy and powerful commercial interest ... nothing could check the growth of this interest, fed by the expansive power of the steam engine. It grew, attained independence, and set the seal to that independence in the Reform Bill ... The *steam-engine* then, first, gave birth to a commercial community; secondly, gave it wealth and power; and thirdly, gave it a political recognition.[58]

Whig history and the Industrial Revolution

This fascination with the steam engine and its 'inventor' began to influence the analysis of British economic growth, which in the eighteenth century had become a subject of pressing interest for both British and French intellectuals and politicians.[59] By the 1820s, commentators generally attributed British manufacturing competitiveness to a combination of superior machinery, abundant resources of capital, credit and fuel, and the people's skill and ingenuity or enterprise.[60] Whigs tended to emphasize a distinctive feature that chimed with their political ideology – liberty, protected by the Bill of Rights (1689). J. R. McCulloch, for example, in pursuing the case for freer trade throughout the 1820s and 30s, maintained a twofold explanation of Britain's 'commercial superiority' – in part constitutional (which never varied), in part economic and geographic (where his emphasis changed over time). It was fundamental to McCulloch's faith in both political and economic liberty, as the sine qua non of economic development, that he gave pride of place to 'the comparative freedom of our constitution – the absence of all oppressive feudal privileges, and our perfect security of property'. This untrammelled market-place, he argued in 1820, would permit the exploitation of Britain's comparative advantage 'in those branches in which our insular situation, our inexhaustible supplies of coal, and our improved machinery, give us a natural and real advantage'.[61] (The growing importance of steam power was bestowing additional value on Britain's large and accessible coalfields.) In 1827, two recent books on the cotton industry (by Guest and Baines respectively) prompted McCulloch to renew his emphasis on that industry and simultaneously to highlight the role of its

---

[58] John Giles, 'Social science and the steam engine', *The Builder* 18 (1860), 613. See also, for example, W. A. Mackinnon, *On the rise, progress, and present state of public opinion* (1828), p. 10, cited in Hardy, *Origins of the idea*, p. 113; C. J. Lever, *Tale of the trains* (1845), quoted in Ian Carter, *Railways and culture in Britain: the epitome of modernity* (Manchester: Manchester University Press, 2001), p. 3.

[59] See above, pp. 60, 64, 69–70.

[60] Hardy, 'Conceptions of manufacturing advance', pp. 134–9, 191–206; Hardy, *Origins of the idea*, pp. 51–6.

[61] 'Restrictions on foreign commerce', *Edinburgh Review* 33 (May 1820), 338, 346.

principal inventors. After describing the achievement of each in turn, he excoriated Guest for denying Hargreaves and Arkwright the credit of their inventions.[62] McCulloch attributed the awe-inspiring rise of cotton 'partly and principally ... to the extraordinary genius and talent of a few individuals' – cultivated, of course, by 'the confidence and energy' that stemmed from political guarantees of property and free enterprise, in tandem with the resourcefulness which was kindled by 'the universal diffusion of intelligence'.[63]

By 1835, McCulloch's socio-economic analysis had shifted again, though he still gave priority among multiple economic factors to 'our superiority in machines' and, in consequence, to machine making as the most important branch of industry. But this, he reasoned, could scarcely have been achieved if Britain had had to depend on imported metals, still less if it had lacked abundant coal supplies to process them. Consequently, he now revised the period's usual ranking of inventors, idiosyncratically downgrading Watt and the textile inventors, and under-lining the substitution of coal for wood in the smelting and refining of iron, with which he credited 'Lord Dudley'. 'We do not know,' he commented, 'that it is surpassed even by the steam-engine or the spinning-frame. At all events, we are sure that *we* owe as much to it as to either of these great inventions.'[64]

A similar account of recent British economic history, in which economic and political liberty provided the springboard for technological progress, was regularly propounded by other Whig politicians and writers during the second quarter of the nineteenth century. Such assumptions underpinned, for instance, Lord Brougham's speech against the corn law in 1839, where he confidently deployed this image of British industrial-ization as evidence for his case:

The [export] bounty was taken off in 1774, and the same period was the most remarkable, the most brilliant, and I will say the proudest in the history of the English nation ... The whole face of nature was changed; the whole aspect of the earth in this country became ... one large, wealthy, industrious, expert and skilful

---

[62] See below, pp. 193–8.

[63] [J. R. McCulloch], 'Rise, progress, present state, and prospects of the British cotton manufacture', *Edinburgh Review* 46 (June 1827), 22.

[64] [J. R. McCulloch], 'Philosophy of manufacture', *Edinburgh Review* 61 (July 1835), 456. Dudley's patent had recently been cited in the appendix to *Report from the select committee appointed to inquire into the present state of the law and practice relative to the granting of patents for invention*, BPP 1829, III, p. 582. For Dudley, see P. W. King, 'Dudley, Dud (1600?–1684)', *ODNB*, www.oxforddnb.com/view/article/8146, accessed 17 October 2006.

workshop. These were the miracles of manufacturing industry. This was the period of manufactories.[65]

At its heart, said Brougham, was the development of mining and machinery, especially 'the new power of steam ... enlarging the sphere of human potency and giving man a new existence and a new dominion on the earth'. There was virtually a consensus concerning Brougham's characterization of recent economic history, if not its causation. His protectionist opponents disputed neither his chronology of 'the period of manufactures' nor his emphasis on steam and other new technologies; instead they strove to redefine it as a period not of relative free trade but of effective protection – manufacturing had blossomed, they argued, under the shelter of import tariffs.[66]

Despite its focus on the seventeenth century, that influential epitome of Whig history, Macaulay's *History of England* (1848–55), sought to integrate the industrial revolution into the grand narrative of constitutional progress. Hitherto, English historians, unperturbed by the innovations of Scottish 'sociological history', had scarcely deviated from the narrow path of political narrative; their recognition of technological change rarely extended beyond the Renaissance's triad of printing, gunpowder and the compass.[67] Macaulay, however, had already testified to his faith in the social benefits of economic growth, and demonstrated an unusually heightened awareness of the history of invention – both medieval and modern. In 1830, he attacked the poet, Robert Southey, for his negative assessment of Britain's present condition: despite four decades of Tory 'misgovernment', Macaulay alleged, since 1790 'the industry of individuals' (much of it innovative) had made the country 'richer and richer'.[68] His essay on Francis Bacon lauded James I & VI's chancellor as a Utilitarian before his time. Bacon's philosophy of science, said Macaulay, revolved around the concepts of 'utility and progress' – calculated, with its emphasis on 'fruit', to promote 'the multiplying of human enjoyments and the

---

[65] Hansard, *P.D.*, 3rd ser., XLV (18 February 1839), 542–3; my thanks to Will Hardy for drawing this speech to my attention.

[66] [Sir Archibald Alison], 'Free trade and protection', *Blackwood's* 55 (1844), 399; also the duke of Wellington, in Hansard, *P.D.*, 3rd ser., XXII (1830), 974.

[67] Rosemary Mitchell, *Picturing the past: English history in text and image, 1830–1870* (Oxford: Clarendon Press, 2000), pp. 112–13.

[68] Lord Macaulay, 'Southey's Colloquies on Society' (1830), in *Literary and historical essays contributed to the Edinburgh Review* (London: Humphrey Milford, Oxford University Press, 1934), pt I, pp. 129–33. He expected Britain to be as different from 1830 a century later, as it was a century earlier, principally because of technological changes: ibid., p. 133.

mitigating of human sufferings'.[69] By contrast, Macaulay deplored the 'barrenness' of ancient natural science, which had no concern to ameliorate daily life; while Plato had striven in vain to make man perfect, Bacon succeeded in showing the way 'to make imperfect man comfortable'.[70] In an extended, hubristic passage, he listed 'the first fruits' of the new natural philosophy, beginning with 'It has lengthened life; it has mitigated pain' and ending,

it has enabled man to descend to the depths of the sea, to soar into the air, to penetrate securely into the noxious recesses of the earth, to traverse the land in cars which whirl along without horses, and the ocean in ships which run at ten knots an hour against the wind.[71]

Consequently, it is unsurprising that, in charting the history of English liberties, Macaulay should have widened his gaze to encompass social, economic and technological developments. In the famous third chapter of his *History*, he identified an acceleration in Britain's economic growth since the mid-eighteenth century, and naturally attributed it to the security provided by the political settlement of 1689. As for new technology, the constitutional guarantees secured through the Glorious Revolution had provided ideal conditions for the pursuit of invention and enterprise, not least for the application of steam power.

Under the benignant influence of peace and liberty, science has flourished, and has been applied to practical purposes on a scale never before known. The consequence is that a change to which the history of the world furnishes no parallel has taken place in our country.[72]

Although Macaulay's economic and social interludes are often said to detract from the dramatic force of his political narrative, they had a strategic role to play. As John Burrow argues, it was Macaulay's objective 'to extend the Whig glorification of the growth of English liberty to include the consequent and no less glorious growth of British prosperity'.[73] By the same token, his comparative descriptions of the material advances made between 1688 and the 1840s were intended to refute those who mourned for a supposed golden age and doubted the Whigs' faith in progress. More immediately, Macaulay was addressing 'the condition of England question'. As social investigators revealed the wretched conditions of working people in many factories and industrial towns, the

---

[69] Lord Macaulay, 'Lord Bacon' (1837), in *Literary and historical essays*, pt I, pp. 289–410, quotation on pp. 364–5. For 'Macaulay's adulation of Bacon' in its wider historical context, see Weisinger, 'English treatment', 265.

[70] Macaulay, 'Lord Bacon', p. 379.   [71] Ibid., p. 385.

[72] Macaulay, *History of England*, vol. I, pp. 272, 364.   [73] Burrow, *Liberal descent*, p. 63.

'evils of industrialization' offered nostalgic radicals and Tories a powerful new weapon with which to attack Whig governments. Macaulay attempted to counter this outcry with the long-term improvements in living standards – these new comforts, pleasures and benefits to health were the everyday advantages of scientific researches and industrial expansion, the tangible evidence of progress.[74] He condemned as 'fools' those who opposed the introduction of vaccination and railways, denied that the benefits of technical progress were enjoyed only by an elite, and with considerable prescience forecast that, 'we too shall, in our turn, be outstripped, and in our turn be envied [for a lost simplicity of life]'.[75]

Less august works of history also began to incorporate accounts of Britain's industrial development, especially the popular histories published by Charles Knight. From 1827, Knight was closely associated with Brougham and the Whigs, and played a major role in the publishing ventures of the SDUK.[76] In the early 1840s, he published a multi-volume work of history, which not only gave 'the national industry' an unusual degree of attention but also conceived of it in overwhelmingly technological terms. Craik and MacFarlane's *Pictorial history of England during the reign of George the Third* began conventionally enough, with 500 pages devoted to political and military history, but then allowed 'the national industry' a substantial fifty pages. It dated the start of 'our modern system both of manufactures and trade' to the early years of George III's reign, and offered a broad survey of trade, agriculture, transport, mining and manufacturing, which concentrated on technological change. Transport improvements and the steam engine were particularly emphasized for their 'stimulating effect' on other branches of industry. Watt received pride of place – the steam engine represented 'a series of improvements perhaps unequalled as the produce of a single mind' – but a range of other inventors received due mention.[77]

Commissioned by Knight to produce a history of her own times, Harriet Martineau allowed technological change a similar rank in her historical scheme – as worthy of notice but only once the main business

[74] Ibid., pp. 62–9. For the influence of 'the condition of England question' and associated social concerns on the concept of the 'industrial revolution', see Hardy, *Origins of the idea*, pp. 88–129.

[75] Macaulay, *History of England*, vol. I, pp. 420–1.

[76] Rosemary Mitchell, 'Knight, Charles (1791–1873)', *ODNB*, www.oxforddnb.com/view/article/15716, accessed 17 October 2006; Mitchell, *Picturing the past*, pp. 111–39; Valerie Gray, 'Charles Knight and the Society for the Diffusion of Useful Knowledge: a special relationship', *Publishing History* 53 (2003), 23–74.

[77] George L. Craik and Charles MacFarlane, *The pictorial history of England during the reign of George the Third: being a history of the people, as well as a history of the kingdom*, 7 vols. (London: Charles Knight & Co., 1841–44), vol. II, pp. 574–5, 579–82, 600–3.

had been dealt with. For Martineau, it is evident that politicians made history, inventors merely improved the comforts of everyday life. Her overview of the period 1815–46 began with 'the lowest class of improvements – the Arts of Life': she cited the electric telegraph ('a marvel of the time'), 'sun-painting' (i.e. photography), lucifer matches, waterproof clothing (which was especially important for the working class), the Thames Tunnel ('the first object of curiosity to foreigners visiting London'), steam and railways. Of the latter, she tartly remarked, 'enough has been said. Everybody knows ... what they do in superseding toil, in setting human hands free for skilled labour, in bringing men face to face with each other and with nature and novelty' – impressive in their way, but not, she implied, on a par with advances in scientific knowledge, let alone such vital political achievements as the abolition of slavery.[78] When discussing 'living benefactors', Martineau began (was first again lowest?) with George Stephenson, 'the greatest of our engineers', who was primarily responsible for the introduction of railways, but all other members of this category, except the chemist, Michael Faraday, and the astronomer, William Herschel, won their place for literary or artistic merit.[79] Critical of the ethos of utility, the radical and non-conformist Martineau paid tribute to William Hyde Wollaston, with a rebuke to those who would remember him principally as the discoverer of a method to make platinum ductile and malleable:

[I]t is an injury to great chemical discoverers to specify as the result of their labours those discoveries which take the form of inventions ... It is a good thing to invent a useful instrument, for the service or the safety of society and men: but it is a much greater thing to evolve a new element, to discover a new substance, to exhibit a new combination of matter, and to add confirmation to a general law. Wollaston did much in both ways to serve the world.[80]

She admired Thomas Telford (like Stephenson, a civil engineer) for the 'poetry' of his stupendous constructions, 'for where are lofty ideas and a stimulus to the imagination to be found, if not in such spectacles as the Menai Bridge, and the Caledonian Canal?'[81] But Martineau clearly found no poetry in the steam engine: as we have seen, she assessed Watt as superior to mere monarchs but inferior to 'the kings of mind whose memorials sanctify the Poets' Corner'.[82]

---

[78] Martineau, *History of England*, vol. II, pp. 707–8.
[79] Ibid., vol. II, p. 702.   [80] Ibid., vol. I, pp. 592–3.
[81] Ibid., vol. II, p. 193. 'These are our poems', said Carlyle of a locomotive, in 1842: Berg, *Machinery question*, p. 15.
[82] Martineau, *History of England*, vol. I, p. 413.

Finally, Knight himself authored *A popular history of England*, in eight volumes, with which he intended to break new ground: it should be both 'for and about the people'.[83] A great admirer of Macaulay, Knight wished to emulate his achievement in demonstrating 'the connection between the progress of good government' and that of 'industry, art, and letters', but to integrate the two more closely, with the improvement of the social conditions of 'the People' much to the fore: there would be no separate rag-bag of a third chapter.[84] Knight struggled to achieve his goals, hampered by the shortage of sources and techniques for their analysis, but produced, nonetheless, four consecutive chapters on the origins of the industrial revolution. The developments in commerce and manufacturing that occurred during the eighteenth century, he declared, '[constituted] the most important feature of her advancing political condition', and were fundamental to 'our present place among the nations'.[85]

A contemporary work intended for schools, Ince and Gilbert's *Outlines of English history* made a point of remarking major inventions and discoveries, throughout its chronological chapters, as either 'memorable events' or 'names of note'. True to their Whiggish colours, the authors cited Newton, Locke and Bacon as 'three of the greatest geniuses who ever arose to adorn and instruct mankind'.[86] When they reached the reign of George III, inventions and manufactures took over the narrative, for these had 'tended very materially to enable the nation to bear up against the enormous expense of foreign wars and the extravagances of the government', and their inventors should be more 'honoured as benefactors of mankind ... than all the naval and military heroes of the past or present century'.[87] Similarly, among the most 'memorable events' (to date) of Victoria's reign were the introduction of the Penny Post and the telegraph, the construction of the Thames Tunnel, the Great Exhibition, and the launch of Brunel's *Great Eastern*. The volume ended with a page-long encomium to the railways and telegraphs as creators of prosperity and transmitters of knowledge – all of them the product of 'the perseverance of George Stephenson and his illustrious son', with the aid of Marc

---

[83] Mitchell, *Picturing the past*, p. 123. Its cost alone was likely to defeat Knight's goal of its being 'for' the people: ibid., p. 139.

[84] Charles Knight, *Passages of a working life during half a century*, 3 vols. (London: Bradbury & Evans, 1864–5), vol. III, pp. 283–4, cited in Mitchell, *Picturing the past*, p. 123.

[85] Charles Knight, *The popular history of England*, 8 vols. (London: Bradbury & Evans, 1855–63), vol. V, p. 1; cited in Mitchell, *Picturing the past*, p. 125.

[86] Henry Ince and James Gilbert, *Outlines of English history* (rev. edn, London: W. Kent & Co., 1864), p. 124; they claimed that earlier editions had sold a quarter of a million copies.

[87] Ibid., p. 134.

and Isambard Brunel and Joseph Locke. 'Had the world before this period exhibited, in any branch of renown, such a quintuple alliance?'[88]

A new history of Britain had been sanctioned. The notion of the industrial revolution (if not the precise term) was firmly established during the middle decades of the nineteenth century. It was generally understood as a structural transformation – from an economy based on agriculture to one driven by manufacturing and trade. Most visibly, it was a technological revolution in which Watt and his steam engine played the leading role, in partnership principally with the inventors of cotton machinery and the early railway engineers. This vision had been promoted by 'the bursts of enthusiastic admiration which, after [Watt's] death ... seemed to exhaust the powers of language in eulogizing the man and his imperishable inventions'.[89] It is encapsulated in a mid-century engraving, which shows Watt sitting beside his hearth, apparently dozing or deep in thought; at his feet is a drawing of the steam engine, his kettle boils furiously on the hob. The steam billowing from the kettle's spout frames an industrial scene, of factories, railways, mines and steam ships. We are asked to believe that, from one man's imagination, inspired by the mundane circumstance of observing a kettle boil, has emerged the brave new world of industrial Britain.[90]

When, however, 'the Industrial Revolution' became the subject of academic study, in the late nineteenth century, much of this early celebration of new technology and the growth of manufactures disappeared beneath a pessimistic focus on the detrimental social consequences of industrialization and rapid urbanization. The social concerns that dominated the works of mid-century critics such as Gaskell, Engels and Marx resonated with those of the first generation of professional economic historians, such as Arnold Toynbee, J. L. and Barbara Hammond, and Sidney and Beatrice Webb, and came thereby to dominate school textbooks and other popular histories.[91] Yet, although the ideology of catastrophe largely subsumed celebration for half a century, the technological changes of the period continued to provide the basic structure of all narratives of the industrial revolution – to re-emerge in T. S. Ashton's

---

[88] Ibid., p. 145.   [89] Craik and Macfarlane, *Pictorial history*, vol. III, p. 674.

[90] Basalla, *Evolution of technology*, p. 38. For the legend of the kettle, see Robinson, 'James Watt and the tea kettle', 261–5; and Miller, 'True myths', 333–60.

[91] Hardy, *Origins of the idea*, pp. 101–29; Cannadine, 'The present and the past', 133–8; Coleman, *Myth, history and the industrial revolution*, pp. 22–8. Alternatively, it may have helped to produce the neglect of technological change and engineering achievement in twentieth-century general histories of which Buchanan complains: R. Angus Buchanan, *Brunel: the life and times of Isambard Kingdom Brunel* (London: Hambledon and London, 2002), pp. 209–10. See also above, pp. 9–13.

famous 'wave of gadgets', which in 1948 initiated a new, more positive phase in the scholarly literature.[92]

The first use of the term 'the Industrial Revolution' (in English), which is usually attributed to Toynbee in 1882, merely provided a convenient tag for a concept that had been current for over fifty years. Toynbee drew together the strands of understanding into an explicit and influential synthesis.[93] Although his account rested on the belief that 'the essence of the Industrial Revolution' was the establishment of a free market economy, he credited two individuals with particular responsibility for this revolutionary (and, in his view, disastrous) development.[94] One was Adam Smith, who, in his *Wealth of nations* (1776), had distilled the doctrine of free trade; the other was James Watt, whose contemporaneous invention had facilitated that doctrine's worldwide implementation. Together, their works had 'destroyed the old world and built a new one'. Toynbee was fascinated by the notion that the two men had met one another, in Glasgow, 'when one was dreaming of the book, and the other of the invention, which were to introduce a new industrial age'.[95] Writing in the same year, the positivist author, Frederic Harrison expressed a similar sense of the complete disjuncture effected by the technology of the industrial revolution:

Take it all in all, the merely material, physical, mechanical change in human life in the hundred years, from the days of Watt and Arkwright to our own, is greater than occurred in the thousand years that preceded, perhaps even in the two thousand years or twenty thousand years.[96]

[92] Coleman, *Myth, history and the industrial revolution*, p. 30; Cannadine, 'The present and the past', 139–58; T. S. Ashton, *The industrial revolution, 1760–1830* (Oxford: Oxford University Press, 1948). Among professional economic historians, this emphasis on technological change has diminished only in the last three decades with the emergence of the 'new economic history' and its focus on historical growth accounting; so far, popular histories remain immune (or oblivious) to this. There are signs, however, of its resurgence: see, for example, Joel Mokyr, *The gifts of Athena: historical origins of the knowledge economy* (Princeton and Oxford: Princeton University Press, 2002).

[93] Hardy, *Origins of the idea*, pp. 139–60.

[94] Arnold Toynbee, *Lectures on the industrial revolution in England* (London, 1884); repr. as *Toynbee's Industrial Revolution*, with an introduction by T. S. Ashton (Newton Abbot: David & Charles, 1969), p. 85.

[95] Toynbee, *Lectures on the industrial revolution*, pp. 14, 189. G. N. Clark suggested that Toynbee, one of John Ruskin's 'warmest admirers and ablest pupils', had been influenced by his tutor's condemnation of industrialization: *The idea of the industrial revolution* (Glasgow: Jackson, Son & Co, 1953), p. 19.

[96] Frederic Harrison, 'A few words about the nineteenth century', *Fortnightly Review*, April 1882; Martha S. Vogeler, 'Harrison, Frederic (1831–1923)', *ODNB*, online edn, May 2006, www.oxforddnb.com/view/article/33732, accessed 17 October 2006.

Watt and inventive genius

The glorification of Watt also led to a heightened interest in the nature of invention and the psychology of the inventor. At a period when attempts were rarely made to explain technical change, 1827 was a remarkable year, for it saw the publication of two extended and carefully argued discussions of the nature of invention. Both gave prominence to Watt; there were other common elements in their accounts of invention, but ultimately they adopted very different positions. In concluding his comprehensive treatise on the steam engine, John Farey offered an explanation of Watt's exceptional abilities as an inventor, which was couched in the Romantic discourse of 'the genius'. In contrast, the radical journalist Thomas Hodgskin sought to forestall the elevation of Watt into a heroic figure superior to other workmen, and to maintain a more democratic notion of invention as an incremental process that stemmed from the daily exercise of working men's skills.[97] Since Hodgskin's discussion of inventiveness was part of a broader radical critique of political economy, it will be reserved until the next chapter. The focus here will be on Farey and those who followed him in the mainstream project of elevating Watt to the status of a 'genius'.

Early in his treatise, Farey sought to distinguish the steam engine from all other inventions. He acknowledged that the ship, together with the art of navigation, might precede the steam engine in a ranking based on utility and as an instance of humanity's 'persevering ingenuity' in providing for its material needs; 'as a production of genius', however, the steam engine unquestionably took precedence.[98] The art of navigation, said Farey, had evolved throughout human history, improving gradually through 'the combined ingenuity and experience of all nations'; it was the collective effort of many lesser minds proceeding haphazardly and building slowly on previous experience.[99] It was also probably through chance events that most other important inventions – the telescope, gunpowder and the compass – had been made. The steam engine, however, was different: it was 'the result of philosophical inquiry, and the production of very ingenious minds ... an application of scientific knowledge'. A British invention, it evinced the superior qualities of mind possessed by those few men, who had invented it over a relatively short space of time and had endowed their country with a 'new power' of enormous economic value.[100]

---

[97] See below, pp. 161–9.   [98] Farey, *Treatise on the steam engine*, vol. I, p. 3.
[99] Ibid., pp. 3–4. Farey revisits this model of incremental invention on pp. 651–2.
[100] Ibid., p. 4.

Given this emphasis on individual mental abilities, it was not inappropriate that Farey should attempt a psychological investigation of the nature of inventive 'genius'; it was, however, a brave and novel step. In exploring 'Mr Watt's character as an inventor', Farey took his cue from the writings of eighteenth-century literary theorists and philosophers, whose primary interest had been to understand the nature of artistic and poetic invention or originality.[101] Mechanical invention had been largely foreign to the concerns of all but a few, although the colossal reputation of Sir Isaac Newton had forced the question of scientific discovery onto their attention. It was consequently a bold stroke by Farey to adapt the conceptual apparatus that had been developed to describe the loftiest intellects of the arts and sciences to the hitherto dubious category of the mechanical inventor. Indeed, it is hard to imagine his attempting it with any subject other than Watt, who in the eight years since his death had been regularly described as a man of genius.[102] Nor is it likely that he could have done so without the prior establishment of Watt as both a towering intellect and a national benefactor – purged of all taint of the dangerous 'projector' – by Jeffrey and his Scottish supporters.[103] It was by analogy with Newton, rather than the poets, that Farey made his bid for Watt's admission to the ranks of genius, beginning with the claim that Watt occupied 'the same super-eminent station' among mechanical inventors 'as the illustrious Newton held among philosophers of a higher order'.[104]

'Mr.Watt', said Farey, 'was not less remarkable for that fertility of genius which produces new ideas and combinations, than for the sound judgment which he exercised in the arrangement of his plans before putting them into execution.'[105] The combination of both qualities in a single person was extremely rare, and it was this, argued Farey, which marked out Watt. It differentiated him, on the one hand, from sound but unoriginal engineers, such as Smeaton, who possessed judgement but little 'inventive faculty' and, on the other, from most inventors, who generated original ideas but lacked the judgement necessary to apply

---

[101] See above, pp. 51–3.

[102] Farey was not the first to conceive of Watt's qualities of mind in these terms, although he was apparently alone in publishing a considered analysis. See for example the obituary in the *Birmingham Gazette*, 30 August 1819, and Andrew Ure's and Professor Jardine's remarks reprinted in the *Glasgow Mechanics' Magazine* 2 (1824–5), 298–9, 301, 303, 384.

[103] *The Scotsman*, 24 July 1824. See also Fairbairn, *Observations*, p. 16.

[104] Farey, *Treatise on the steam engine*, vol. I, p. 650. For the contemporary debate over Newton's status as a genius see Yeo, 'Genius, method, and morality', 257–84.

[105] Farey, *Treatise on the steam engine*, vol. I, p. 650.

them in practice.[106] Farey believed that the essence of invention was the spontaneous production of novel ideas and combinations of ideas, which arose in the mind when it was allowed to roam uncontrolled by 'the will': the 'stronger and less controlled' this capacity for spontaneity, the more original would be the individual's thoughts; the stronger the will, the more closely he would abide by existing rules.[107] Judgement, however, was a completely distinct mental faculty, requiring the exercise of rational analysis in the assessment of one's own or others' ideas: it comprised the capacity to analyse complex ideas into simpler elements, to classify and compare them, to perceive their positive and negative qualities, to foresee how they would operate in practice, and to discard those which were unsuited to the task.[108] Whether Farey had read the work of authors such as Gerard and Duff, who placed a similar emphasis on the necessary balance between imagination and judgement, is unknown.[109]

Most men of genius, thought Farey, were too fond of their own ideas to exercise sufficient impartiality in their assessment; they experienced 'a sort of parental affection', which led them to ignore the stock of existing knowledge even when it was more appropriate. Arrogantly reliant on their own capacity to generate ideas at pleasure, they were 'rarely studious' and forfeited the possibility of learning from others. They also tended to be inconsistent, distracted by the rush of new ideas, and incapable of producing a rounded design that met all the specified criteria.[110] By implication, they were 'projectors' who disappointed the public by over-ambitious schemes – as much a danger to themselves as to those who unwisely trusted them. By contrast,

[Watt] had a most methodical imagination, which could be directed by the will to produce a number of ideas, answering so far to description, that amongst them it was not difficult to select that which would answer the intended purpose. He had also the habit of incorporating his new ideas with those which he acquired by communication or observation, and of arranging the whole into one uniform series, from which he could choose those which were suitable for his combinations; and he appears to have been very free from undue partiality to his own ideas in such selections.[111]

---

[106] Ibid., p. 651. For a positive re-evaluation of Smeaton's historical significance, see Walter G. Vincenti, *What engineers know and how they know it: analytical studies from aeronautical history* (Baltimore: Johns Hopkins University Press, 1991), p. 138; my thanks to Alessandro Nuvolari for this reference.

[107] Farey, *Treatise on the steam engine*, vol. I, p. 651.   [108] Ibid., p. 651.

[109] See above, pp. 52–3. See also the characterization of Henry Bell in similar terms, above, p. 40.

[110] Farey, *Treatise on the steam engine*, vol. I, pp. 652–3.   [111] Ibid., p. 652.

The final virtue mentioned was more a trait of character than a faculty of mind. This was in line with the high estimation of Watt's personal qualities, which were regularly recited in tandem with his technical brilliance, through all the biographical accounts from Jeffrey's eulogy onwards. Farey's Watt exemplified 'the admirable balance of all the faculties', which Charles Lamb had recently protested to be the true characteristic of genius.[112] Ideally situated between, on the one side, the wild projector and, on the other, the professionally competent engineer, Watt was the sane genius, the responsible inventor, the creative hero.[113]

Essentially, Farey's delineation of Watt's 'genius' was an elaboration of the personal and professional qualities that Jeffrey had praised. For the next two decades, biographers and historians of steam remained largely content to quote Jeffrey's text rather than to attempt their own analysis of Watt's powers of invention. It fell to John Bourne, the author of another *Treatise on the steam engine*, first published in 1846, to revivify the case for Watt's supreme intellectual powers, and to Alexander Bain, the Scottish psychologist, to re-analyse them.

As was customary, Bourne began his *Treatise* (reluctantly!) with a historical sketch of the development of the steam engine, which at first seems to be collective and deterministic:

It appears to us to be a vice of many commentators that they have attached too much importance to the deeds of individual projectors, and have estimated at far too low a rate the current intelligence of the time, of which indeed the proficiency of those exalted persons is to be regarded as merely the exponent.[114]

Moreover, the fact that – *pace* Arago's 'pitiful' claims for Denis Papin and France – the engine was 'from first to last' a British invention was the result, not of any superior inventive capability among the British, but rather of 'the force of circumstances', which made a power source, such as the steam engine, especially valuable on this side of the Channel. With the same coal resources and the same incentives to drain deep mines, the French would have been just as likely to pioneer the steam engine.[115] It is all the more surprising, therefore, when Bourne reaches Watt's contribution to this collective, national effort that he breaks into a rapturous

---

[112] Yeo, 'Genius, method, and morality', 270–1; Wittkower, 'Genius', pp. 308–9.
[113] This was a contrast later echoed in praise of George Stephenson. While Richard Trevithick was described as 'wild, brave, adventurous, passionate, original, shock-headed', with 'a more daring genius', Stephenson was 'the healthiest minded inventor who ever arose. Sagacious, patient, persevering, and modest': *The Working Man* 2 (1866), 27.
[114] Bourne, *Treatise on the steam engine*, p. 1.   [115] Ibid., p. 1.

eulogy. Farey's comparison of Watt with Newton is 'just', says Bourne, but it would be more instructive to see him 'as the Shakespeare of mechanical science, for he owes his greatness to the same high gifts which distinguished the prince of poetry'.[116] Like Shakespeare, Watt's supremacy lay in 'an inexhaustible fertility of invention, and invention is the poetry of science, for it springs out of an action of mind more nearly akin to poetic ideality [sic] than logical demonstration'.[117] As Bourne lyrically hymns the flights of this 'untaught mechanist' to 'the giddiest heights of fancy ... wilder visions and more fantastic combinations', we seem to be more in the spirited company of Edward Young than treading the carefully balanced path of Duff and Gerard.[118] But not for long: having emphasized the exceptional fertility of Watt's creative imagination, Bourne reminds us that Shakespeare was equally master of 'the most vulgar details of ordinary life'. Both men were capable of being 'practical and worldly', and certainly Watt had no shortage of the necessary 'steadiness or circumspection' wherever those qualities were required. As in Farey's account, Watt's imagination was perfectly tempered by judgement. Again, John Smeaton suffers unjustly by comparison: 'Smeaton was able to *improve*, but Watt was able also to *create*'.[119] It is an early use of the word 'create' in this sense of a positive human attribute, and an extremely unusual application of the concept to the technical, rather than the artistic or literary, sphere.[120]

Eventually, we reach Bourne's main agenda: his concern that the introduction of a more formal and scientific education for engineers will quench their creativity.

The hot-beds of a college may produce abundant crops of mediocre engineers; but such men as Brindley, Rennie, Telford, and Watt, are not forced into greatness by fictitious heats, but gather strength from the vicissitudes of that rugged region where genius spontaneously unfolds its robust glories.[121]

This is the chief value to Bourne of Watt's example: Watt is 'the untaught mechanist', his imagination untrammelled by the straitjacket of correct procedures and scientific formulae, but fed by his free-ranging intellectual curiosity, which (quoting Jeffrey) spanned a notoriously wide variety of disciplines. A scientific understanding of nature was important but must not be allowed to dominate. Bourne counselled the aspiring artisan 'not to suffer his mind to become technical ... not [to] coop up his

---

[116] Ibid., p. 21.   [117] Ibid., p. 21   [118] See above, p. 52.
[119] Bourne, *Treatise on the steam engine*, p. 21; original emphases.
[120] Hope Mason, *Value of creativity*, pp. 4–5.
[121] Bourne, *Treatise on the steam engine*, p. 21. For the nineteenth-century debate on engineering education and training, see Buchanan, *The engineers*, ch. 9.

imagination within the narrow limits of a craft, but suffer it to roam over creation in its endless fields of beauty'. Like William Morris or John Ruskin, Bourne's faith in the future of industrial society was grounded in (and conditional upon) that society's preservation of humane values and respect for the craftsman's intuitive ways of working. Thus, despite his encomium to the Shakespearean genius of Watt, Bourne's emphasis on the collective inventiveness of artisans resonates, as we shall see, with Thomas Hodgskin's anti-heroic model.[122]

By contrast, a rare contribution to the debate on the nature of invention from beyond its normal constituencies focused exclusively on the psychology of the exceptionally gifted inventor. In his influential text, *The senses and the intellect* (1855), the Scots psychologist, Alexander Bain, offered physiological explanations of mental and physical processes. Perhaps it was his own early experiences in a weaving mill, or the mounting controversy over patent reform that led him to include the unusual subject of mechanical invention at several places in his wide-ranging academic analysis.[123] While standing outside the hagiographic tradition, he was drawn by Watt's reputation to use him as his case study.[124] He pondered what distinguished the minds of great inventors; how one might explain their 'superiority' above the mass of humanity. Surely many people had shared certain necessary intellectual characteristics with Watt – an intensive knowledge of mechanics, familiarity with machines, perceptiveness – so what further, uncommon ability did Watt enjoy?[125]

For Bain the power of reasoning was significantly more important than any fertility of imagination and, in the tradition of associationist psychology, he explained reasoning as proceeding by analogy: the good reasoner identifies similarities and recognizes exactly 'how far the analogy holds'; he is able to pierce the superficial appearances of things to perceive their

---

[122] See below, pp. 162–9.

[123] Graham Richards, 'Bain, Alexander (1818–1903)', *ODNB*, www.oxforddnb.com/view/article/30533, accessed 17 October 2006; David Hotherstall, *History of Psychology* (3rd edn, New York and London: McGraw-Hill Inc. 1984), pp. 73–5. For the mid-nineteenth-century patent controversy, see below, pp. 249–51.

[124] It may only be coincidental that, in his biography of Watt published the following year, George Williamson suggested – as if to raise Watt above the crowd – that we should turn to 'the mental analyst' and 'the psychologist', rather than the biographer or the political economist, in order to understand Watt's life, 'during which INVENTION, like a second nature, seemed to rule and sway his intellectual being': Williamson, *Memorials*, p. 245.

[125] Alexander Bain, *The senses and the intellect* (London, John W. Parker & Son, 1855), p. 493.

essential similarities.[126] It is in these terms that he explains Watt's identification of the centrifugal governor as the device necessary to accomplish the opening and closing of a valve as the engine speed varied. No existing mechanism would answer Watt's purpose, 'He had therefore to venture out into the region of mechanical possibility, to seek among mechanical laws in general, or among very remote natural phenomena, for a parallel situation ... bringing together the like out of the unlike.'[127] This 'identifying power' – which others might well describe, *pace* Bain, as 'imagination' – constituted the principal feature of the inventive person's intellect; a single discovery did not prove someone an inventor, 'but a career of invention implies a large reach of the identifying faculty'.[128]

Elsewhere in his text, Bain set out in more general terms the mental characteristics which he believed to be indispensable for both invention and scientific discovery. Although there remains scope for imagination in 'the powerful action of the associating forces', Bain's emphasis is far more on the powers of reasoning and disciplined thought than had been common in British discussion of originality and invention since the eighteenth century. According to Bain, the inventor's essential mental resources were:

the intellectual store of ideas applicable to the special department; the powerful action of the associating forces; a very clear perception of the end, in other words, sound judgment; and, lastly, that patient thought, which is properly an entranced devotion of the energies to the subject in hand, rendering application to it spontaneous and easy.[129]

To these mental qualities Bain adds a further 'point of character', which he considered to be of particular importance in the spheres of practical invention and business enterprise, and which led him subsequently to suggest that originality in both science and practice might take two forms: 'I mean an active turn, or a profuseness of energy, put forth in trials of all kinds on the chance of making lucky hits.' It was only through such 'a fanaticism of experimentation' that, for example, Daguerre could have stumbled upon photography: the succession of processes involved had not been deducible from previous knowledge; it could only have arisen from 'an innumerable series of fruitless trials'.[130] Bain was consequently prepared to give accident a place in his inventive methodology, though only on the usual, meritorious premise that accidents mean nothing to those not already engaged in the search. It was the probable

---

[126] Ibid., p. 524. For the associationist tradition in British philosophy of mind, which developed from the seventeenth-century mechanistic paradigm, see Abrams, *The mirror and the lamp*, pp. 156–66.
[127] Bain, *Senses*, p. 525.   [128] Ibid., p. 526.   [129] Ibid., p. 595.   [130] Ibid., p. 595.

route, he thought, by which the 'ancient' inventions of glass, gunpowder, soap or scarlet dye were made – 'intense application – "days of watching, nights of waking"'. As he developed this 'Daguerrean' model of invention via observation and experimentation, Bain must have decided that it was not easily assimilated with his 'Wattean' model of invention, achieved through 'the identifying processes of abstraction, induction, and deduction'. He reasoned, consequently, that there must be two forms of originality, one bodily and sensual, the other purely intellectual: the former demanded energy, inquisitiveness, perseverance; the latter was achievable, however, without these 'active qualities'.[131]

It is hardly surprising that a psychologist should have developed a model of invention that rested on the analysis of individual mental abilities and personality traits, nor, given his cultural prominence, that Watt should be his principal subject. Yet, there remained a significant body of opinion that looked to more impersonal forces to explain invention. For some, it was still unthinkable not to see the hand of God or Providence in technological change as in other things, but there was also a current of secular thought, which regarded invention as the necessary and progressive outcome of humanity's interaction with its natural environment. As we shall see in the following chapter, during the late 1820s the role of the individual in technological change was subjected to intense scrutiny, in a highly political context. Although such views proved to have little impact on the overwhelmingly hagiographic treatment of Watt, they were to resurface in the 1850s to underpin the abolitionists' attack on the patent system.[132]

---

[131] Ibid., pp. 595–7.   [132] See below, pp. 267–71.

6   'What's Watt?' The radical critique

If the Whigs hoped that their celebration of Watt would find universal favour among the working classes, they were to be disappointed. As was the case with most aspects of 'the machinery question', the reactions of working people and their leaders were varied and sometimes complex. Most supportive among the popular press was the *Mechanic's Magazine*, under its proprietor and editor, Joseph Clinton Robertson. The previous year he had launched the journal with a front page that carried a (rather poor) likeness of Watt and the start of a six-page laudatory sketch of his career, in which he highlighted Watt's origins in the skilled trade of mathematical instrument-making.[1] The *Mechanic's Magazine* now reported in full the Westminster meeting, prefacing it with a lengthy expression of pride in the mere presence there of the king's ministers and 'some of the most illustrious members of the senate – a Wilberforce, a Mackintosh, a Brougham'.[2] This great honour was enhanced when Sir Humphry Davy, gave 'the sanction of science to the popular opinion, which places James Watt foremost on the list of those who have conferred benefits on their country and on mankind'. The *Mechanic's Magazine* encouraged its working-class readers to bask in Watt's reflected glory and to be inspired to greater efforts by his example: it assured them 'how justly the merits of humble industry were appreciated, and how frankly acknowledged by almost everyone who spoke', and on their behalf it subscribed five guineas.[3] A month later, its front page carried a drawing of the statue that Watt Jnr had commissioned for his father's tomb in Handsworth church, but which was currently on exhibition at Somerset House, in London. In this first statue, Chantrey represents Watt as the working engineer, wearing his everyday dress of breeches, waistcoat, neck-tie and top-coat, and concentrating on the plans on his knees, to which he holds a pair of compasses. To the masthead above, Robertson

---

[1] Patricia Anderson, *The printed image and the transformation of popular culture, 1790–1860* (Oxford: Clarendon Press, 1991), pp. 46–9.
[2] *Mechanic's Magazine* 1 (26 June 1824), 242.   [3] Ibid., 243, 249.

added a few lines from Thomson's *Seasons*, which presumably he intended as an inspirational commentary on the beneficence and glory of the great inventor:

> Rough Industry; Activity untir'd,
> With copious life inform'd, and all awake:
> While in the radiant front, superior shines
> That first paternal virtue – Public Zeal;
> Which throws o'er all an equal wide survey,
> And, ever musing on the common weal,
> Still labours glorious with some great design.[4]

This devotion to Watt's memory, as promoted by the *Mechanic's Magazine*, long provided a cultural point of reference and source of pride among a section of working-class men, in particular those who belonged to the skilled trades that arose on the back of mechanization, such as engineering and mule-spinning.[5]

To others, however, the issue was less straightforward. Deeply suspicious of the politicians who were elevating Watt into a hero of science and manufacturing, radical journalists such as William Cobbett and Thomas Hodgskin accused them of hypocrisy and encouraged scepticism in their readers. Subsequently, Hodgskin, having realized that the glorification of Watt threatened to undermine his considered challenge to political economy, elaborated a theory of invention which reduced the heroic inventor to simply a particularly able worker – *primus inter pares*. Although little noticed at the time (or sadly since), it was the first coherent rebuttal of T. R Malthus' 'population principle' to be grounded on the expectation of persistent technological progress. Hodgskin outlined the most remarkable feature of modern economic growth – the coexistence of an increasing population with an improving standard of living – and made a causal link between the two phenomena.

Radical reactions

In 1824, the popular radicals sniped at the celebration of Watt: they distrusted it as an attempt to distract attention from working people's current grievances and to sanitize the industrial history of the last fifty years. Their quarrel was not with Watt, whom they generally admired for his ingenuity and skill, but with their usual political opponents, who appeared to be manipulating his reputation for their own ends. Many

---

[4] James Thomson, 'Summer', *The Seasons*, quoted in *Mechanic's Magazine* 1 (24 July, 1824), 305; my thanks to Jim Andrew for this reference.
[5] See below, pp. 285–9, 291–2.

popular radicals were sceptical about all commemorations, even those of their own most admired predecessors; determinedly rational, they tended to honour an individual primarily through the close study of his writings and speeches, dismissing statues, portraits and other 'relics' as 'a species of idolatry'.[6] Their heroes were mostly Enlightenment philosophers, such as Voltaire, foreign republicans and revolutionaries, such as Bolivar and, of course, Tom Paine.[7] Neither could they afford the expense: in the early 1820s, their priority was to support imprisoned 'friends of reform' or to pay their fines. Few at this time 'were alert to the oppositional potential of public monuments', even allowing the memorialization of the veteran reformer, Major John Cartwright, to fall to the Whigs and some of his worst political enemies.[8] (This began to change in the 1830s, with the campaign to commemorate the Scottish political martyrs of 1793–4.)[9] Nonetheless, the faith of radicals, such as Richard Carlile, in natural philosophy as 'the ultimate expression of reason' and 'an unrestricted field of knowledge', beyond the boundaries of class, predisposed them to admire Watt's achievements, and to elevate a representative of the peaceful arts over the exemplars of military heroism.[10]

The Westminster meeting was reported sardonically by *The Chemist*, which, under the editorship of Thomas Hodgskin, was aggressively critical of the 'establishment', both political and scientific. (Its first volume had attacked Davy for having a proud and disdainful attitude toward working-class practitioners of natural philosophy.)[11] Hodgskin's three-page report strove to separate the subject of the commemoration from his celebrants, whose efforts on Watt's behalf he applauded as an implicit criticism of their normal behaviour and values. Hodgskin evinced great pride in the honouring of Watt, who was 'not only a mechanic, he was also a chemist' and an experimentalist, whose 'first important discoveries were

---

[6] Paul. A. Pickering, 'A "grand ossification": William Cobbett and the commemoration of Tom Paine', in Pickering and Tyrrell (eds.), *Contested sites*, p. 69.

[7] James A. Epstein, *Radical expression: political language, ritual, and symbol in England, 1790–1850* (New York and Oxford: Oxford University Press, 1994), p. 119.

[8] Pickering, '"Grand ossification"', pp. 68–9. For the monument to Cartwright, see John W. Osborne, *John Cartwright* (Cambridge: Cambridge University Press, 1972), pp. 152–3.

[9] Tyrrell and Davis, 'Bearding the Tories', pp. 30–41. Joseph Hume explained that he intended 'to upset the convention that public memorials were for "conquerors and statesmen, who have been successful in *their* career, though often of questionable utility to humanity and good government"': ibid., p. 31.

[10] Epstein, *Radical expression*, pp. 123–9.

[11] David Stack, *Nature and artifice: the life and thought of Thomas Hodgskin (1787–1869)* (London: The Boydell Press, for the Royal Historical Society, 1998), p. 81.

made in chemistry'.[12] Watt's virtuous character merited the highest admiration; through his singular combination of moral strength and powerful intellect he, above all others, deserved national honours. They could rejoice that

[Watt] was not a warrior, over whose victories a nation may mourn, doubtful whether they have added to its security, and certain they have diminished enjoyment and abridged freedom. His were the conquests of mind over matter ... [which have] abridged our toils, and added to our comforts and our power.

With gleeful irony, Hodgskin applauded the 'consecration' of this new set of values by the presence of 'statesmen ... who unfortunately have in general only taken the lead when restrictions were to be imposed, industry depressed, or wars encouraged'.[13] True to his radical philosophy, which blamed the people's misery on interference from an unjust political system, he enjoyed the sight of senior politicians honouring one who had made no pretension to public service but cared only for his own fortune.[14] Watt's example, crowed Hodgskin, proved that 'he is the best citizen who pays the closest attention to his own interest', and his apotheosis represented a blow against the 'political quack' and the 'moral charlatan' who 'claim a right to make laws for the rest of the world'. The editor and proprietors of *The Chemist* donated two guineas to the 'monument to the humble mechanic, the working chemist, the self-interested James Watt'.[15]

Hodgskin was careful not to endorse Jeffrey's hyperbolic elevation of Watt's mental abilities. Superlatives were absent from his sober judgement on Watt's discoveries, inventions and improvements: 'his peculiar merit appears to have consisted in a steady application of the discoveries of science to the purposes of life'.[16] Hodgskin's depreciation of Watt's talents was to be essential to the forceful challenge that he subsequently mounted to classical political economy. In *Popular political economy* (1827), he explicitly resisted the delineation of individual inventors as heroic figures and disputed the notion that Watt was worthy of particular credit for his role in improving the steam engine. The inventive skill inherent in *all* working men, he believed, should be recognized as the source of material progress.[17]

---

[12] *The Chemist* 1 (1824), 250–2. Hodgskin had been closely involved with the establishment of the *Mechanic's Magazine* in 1823, and presumably endorsed its celebration of Watt in the first issue: see above, p. 153. For Watt's chemical interests, see Miller, *Discovering water*, passim.
[13] *The Chemist* 1 (1824), 251.   [14] Stack, *Nature and artifice*, pp. 8–22, 206–7.
[15] *The Chemist* 1 (1824), 252; Boulton & Watt MSS, Timmins, vol. 2, fo. 44.
[16] *The Chemist* 1 (1824), 250–1.   [17] See below, pp. 164–70.

More boisterous in his criticism was William Cobbett – spurred on perhaps by frustration in his persistent attempts to rally fellow radicals to commemorate Thomas Paine.[18] Cobbett demanded to know '"WHAT'S WATT"? I, of late, hear a great deal about IT; but, for the life of me, I cannot make out *what* this *Watt* IS.' Feigning ignorance of the subject of the recent brouhaha, Cobbett targeted the royal donation of £500 and reprinted a letter from 'Timotheus' to the *Manchester Gazette*, which allowed him a swipe at the radicals' prime bête noire, Malthus. 'Timotheus' mocked the Malthusian threat of over-population via the unfortunate George Philips MP, who had told the Manchester meeting in 1824 that,

WATT made '*hundreds of thousands* of human beings *start into life*'. The devil he did! ... Here is *redundant population* with a vengeance. Why, this Watt, if such were his exploits, ought to be scratched out of his grave by Malthus ... and to have his bones and hair and nails stewed out of his steamers.[19]

Cobbett resumed the attack by reprinting a second letter from 'Timotheus', which berated the hypocrisy of the cotton lords for failing to back their fine words with money, and (with another jibe at 'Mr Population Philips') condemned the factory system for its inhumanity, its unequal rewards and its shoddy products. 'Timotheus' proposed a cut-rate, cast-iron statue of 'the great mechanic' on a five-sided plinth. Its panels would depict wretched poverty, child workers exhausted by long hours and mutilated by machinery, 'a negro wench' dismayed at her flimsy calico dress disintegrating before its first wash, and '"the greatest cotton-spinner in England"' [Richard Arkwright] driving home to his mansion in a carriage which bear his arms – 'a pair of decaying human lungs, and ... an overflowing bag of gold'; his road is 'macadamized' by ruined paupers – his ex-workmen who had 'spun their strength away'. Such was Watt's true legacy – the 'effects of the system which Mr Watt's inventions have established amongst us'.[20] When a Manchester steam-engine boiler exploded, killing or injuring seven workers, Cobbett reported it under the headline 'Cotton-Lords and Watt's What'. He demanded that the owners of these 'infernal machine[s]' should be legally answerable for the sufferings caused by their 'avarice or carelessness'. The *Manchester Guardian* taunted Cobbett that he could not distinguish safe, low-pressure Watt engines from the new generation of exploding, high-pressure ones.[21]

---

[18] Pickering, '"Grand ossification"', pp. 57–80.
[19] *Cobbett's Political Register* 51 (7 August 1824), 325–7, 371–4. For Philips' speech, see *Manchester Guardian*, 10 July 1824, 3c.
[20] *Cobbett's Political Register* 52 (30 October 1824), 297–305.
[21] Ibid., 52 (25 December 1824), 803–7; *Manchester Guardian*, 1 January 1825, 3b.

Both Cobbett and Hodgskin belonged to the radical wing which rejected anti-machinery prejudice, believing that, under the right political system, machinery could be of great benefit to working people.[22] They could admire Watt the inventor and skilled worker, while deploring the perversion of not only his greatest invention but also his posthumous reputation: Watt's adoption by elite circles and as a 'philosopher', exiled from his workshop, diminished the value to them of his reputation – indeed it might prove a threat.[23] They were far from alone in believing that the working man's problems stemmed, not from the machinery itself, but from its abuse under capitalist ownership. In the workers' hands, by contrast, labour-saving machinery would liberate, not enslave; it would alleviate their burden, not add to it through long hours in the factory solely for the employers' benefit.[24] The Owenites, for example, envisaged a co-operative society, in which all the heavy jobs (in the home and fields, as well as the industrial workplace) would be mechanized: 'and the more machinery they might invent the more time they would have to spend in amusements, or to devote to literary and scientific acquirements'.[25] In line with these expectations, Owenite communities installed or planned to install new technical devices, including steam pumps.[26]

Consequently, many radical thinkers and trade unionists anticipated Karl Marx in advising working men to concentrate on capturing the political system rather than on destroying or taxing machinery, thereby guaranteeing their fair share of the benefits of technological progress (and the righting of injustices and redistribution of property in general).[27] Among them, Samuel Smiles, expounding 'the right to leisure' in 1845, expressed this common faith in the 'neutrality' of technology:

the true, the benevolent, the humane, the Christian application of James Watt's stupendous discovery of the steam-engine would be – to abridge, instead of increasing, the toil of the labouring classes, and enable them to employ the time, thus set free, in the cultivation and enjoyment of the highest faculties of their nature. This would be the true improvement of James Watt's splendid gift to man.[28]

Although Smiles' name would later become a byword for the type of improvement literature in which a man's inventiveness and character

[22] Berg, *Machinery question*, pp. 269–90; Binfield (ed.), *Writings of the Luddites*, pp. 184–5. For further consideration of 'the machinery question' as it affected popular perceptions of inventors, see above, pp. 41–5.
[23] See below, p. 162.   [24] MacKenzie, 'Marx and the machine', 498–502.
[25] *The New Moral World* 4 (21 July 1838), quoted in Berg, *Machinery question*, p. 279.
[26] Berg, *Machinery question*, pp. 276–82.
[27] Berg, *Machinery question*, pp. 269–91; MacKenzie, 'Marx and the machine', 473–502.
[28] *The autobiography of Samuel Smiles*, ed. Thomas Mackay (London: John Murray, 1905), p. 133.

provided his passport out of the working class, at this point he was clearly in tune with this strand of radical thought.[29] (Another leading radical, William Lovett, was to reflect on his youthful naivety: 'I was one who accepted this grand idea of machinery working for the benefits of all, without considering that those powers and inventions have been chiefly called forth, and industriously and efficiently applied by the stimulus our industrial system has afforded.'[30])

Smiles' faith was echoed by a contemporary inventor, living in fear of the machine-breakers' wrath. As a mechanic employed at Hornby's cotton-weaving firm in Blackburn (Lancs.), William Kenworthy developed devices to increase the speed of power looms, and rose to become a partner.[31] The automatic features that he jointly patented with James Bullough, in 1841, led Blackburn power-loom overlookers to condemn the new loom as a 'local evil'.[32] Whether it was this specific protest or the widespread strikes and Chartist meetings, sparked by deepening depression in the cotton industry, something prompted Kenworthy in 1842 to issue a pamphlet in self-justification. Adding his voice to the agitation for a ten-hour day, Kenworthy advocated reducing the hours of labour to solve the dual predicament of technological unemployment and arduous working conditions.[33] In an impassioned riposte to demands for inventions to be 'peremptorily prohibited', Kenworthy took a providentialist line: 'Any attempt to arrest "the march of intellect" would not only be preposterous but sinful, in the eyes of Heaven and Earth.'[34] The problem, he believed, was the abuse of inventions through the excessively long hours demanded of machine operators, but only continuous innovation (fairly employed) would bring shorter hours without damaging Britain's competitiveness.[35]

There can be no doubt that inventions were designed to do away with manual drudgery, and thus to prove blessings to mankind; but by their abuse we have

---

[29] Smiles believed he had never deviated from this vision and had been misinterpreted by those who saw him as an apostle of 'getting on': Kenneth Fielden, 'Samuel Smiles and self-help', *Victorian Studies* 12 (1968–9), 164–6; Adrian Jarvis, *Samuel Smiles and the construction of Victorian values* (Stroud: Sutton Publishing Ltd, 1997), pp. 22–50.

[30] Quoted in Berg, *Machinery question*, p. 289. For a modern critique of the neutrality of technology, see Langdon Winner, 'Do artifacts have politics?' *Daedalus* 109 (1980), 121–36.

[31] *Textile Recorder* 11 (1884), 248.

[32] *Great industries of Great Britain*, 3 vols. (London: Cassells [1877–80]), vol. II, p. 169.

[33] Charlesworth *et al.*, *Atlas of industrial protest*, pp. 51–8.

[34] William Kenworthy, *Inventions and hours of labour. A letter to master cotton spinners, manufacturers, and mill-owners in general* (Blackburn, 1842), repr. in *The battle for the ten hour day continues: four pamphlets, 1837–43*, ed. Kenneth E. Carpenter (New York: Arno Press, 1972), p. 7.

[35] Ibid., pp. 8–15.

rendered them curses rather than blessings; and the reaction of such a system has been, that the lives of inventors have been endangered in many instances.[36]

Kenworthy had cause for apprehension. Irrespective of the radicals' reasoned arguments, hostility to machinery and its inventors regularly resurfaced during the first half of the nineteenth century.[37] The opening of the railway between Liverpool and Manchester, in 1830, for example, occasioned a demonstration by the 'lowest orders of mechanics and artisans'. Their hisses were directed principally at the duke of Wellington (then standing firm against parliamentary reform), but their grievances were both political and economic. The mechanization of weaving, in particular, was causing great distress among Lancashire's handloom weavers. Fanny Kemble interrupted her breathless excitement to remark that,

high among the grim and grimy crowd of scowling faces a loom had been erected, at which sat a tattered, starved-looking weaver, evidently set there as a *representative man*, to protest against [the] triumph of machinery.[38]

A decade later, anti-machinery and anti-factory sentiments were expressed by Chartist protestors and pamphleteers, especially those – such as the handloom weavers – whose trades were being undermined by mechanization; the dreadful conditions suffered by striking factory workers in 1842 provoked a temporary sharing of this perspective.[39] Among the Chartists' leaders, Feargus O'Connor regarded machinery as having 'the same effect on operatives as the railway had on horses sold to the knackers for their flesh'.[40] Writing in similar vein, Engels reinforced his case with a poem, 'The steam king', written by Edward P. Mead of Birmingham, as representative of the views of workers about the factory system. Here, steam is anything but the potential bringer of peace and harmony, envisaged by many liberals and radicals; it is rather 'a ruthless King' and 'a tyrant', who destroys both mind and body, devours children, turns 'blood to gold', and produces 'hells upon earth'.[41] A Chartist lampoon of Bunyan's *Pilgrim's progress*, published in 1839, harked back to an older, 'Swiftian' critique of inventors as naïve fools – now in the service of capital. The pilgrim, 'Radical', arriving in the 'City

[36] Ibid., p. 15.   [37] See above, pp. 41–5.
[38] Quoted in Michael Freeman, *Railways and the Victorian imagination* (New Haven and London: Yale University Press, 1999), p. 31. For the long, painful decline of hand weaving, see Geoffrey Timmins, *The last shift: the decline of hand-loom weaving in nineteenth-century Lancashire* (Manchester: Manchester University Press, 1993); Berg, *Machinery question*, pp. 226–52.
[39] Berg, *Machinery question*, pp. 288–9.
[40] J. T. Ward, *Chartism* (London: Batsford, 1973), p. 170, quoted in Berg, *Machinery question*, p. 287.
[41] Quoted in Engels, *Condition of the working class*, pp. 194–5.

of Plunder', discovers that in 'Quack Quadrant', a group of projectors is experimenting with a mechanical scheme to regenerate humanity. 'They intended to set carriages to run on the level plains, to carry the rich at thirty miles per hour and to gratify and "ameliorate" the poor by allowing them to look at the wonderful exhibition.'[42] It was an eloquent comment on the disparate impact of technical changes which were indiscriminately hymned by the mainstream press as 'progress'.

The industrial inventor's invidious position was further exposed when employers turned to him specifically to provide the weapons with which to discipline and break the power of skilled workers. It was in these terms that Richard Roberts described having been cajoled to invent the self-acting mule. In the mid-1820s, he remembered, a group of Lancashire cotton factory owners, frustrated by the growing militancy of their unionized mule spinners, implored him to invent a mule that would not require their skilled men's attendance.[43] Roberts' initial reluctance to comply with the employers' request owed nothing to any concern for their workers' livelihoods; rather, as a professional machine maker, he recognized the enormous technical challenge and commercial risk it involved. The diffusion of the self-actor was to proceed slowly at first, in part because the mere threat of its introduction often sufficed to deter the pursuit of a wage claim; with factory owners hesitant to invest in the patented new machinery, it was ten years before Roberts started to profit by his invention. As he testified (with some exaggeration) in 1851, the self-actor strengthened the employers' hand so much that 'the turn-outs have almost entirely ceased in the spinning department'.[44]

Redefining invention

We have seen John Farey attempting to explain the 'genius' of James Watt by reference to individual qualities that made him extraordinarily inventive. As Thomas Hodgskin recognized, this was potentially at odds with

---

[42] *The political pilgrim's progress* (Newcastle upon Tyne, 1839), originally published in the *Northern Liberator*, and quoted in Berg, *Machinery question*, p. 288.

[43] Bruland, 'Industrial conflict', 100–4; Richard L. Hills, *Life and inventions of Richard Roberts, 1789–1864* (Ashbourne: Landmark, 2002), pp. 142–54.

[44] *Report from the select committee of the House of Lords to consider the bill intituled 'An act further to amend the law touching letters patent for inventions'; and the bill, intituled, 'An act for the further amendment of the law touching letters patent for invention'*, BPP 1851, XVIII, pp. 426–9. The extent to which the new technology gave employers the upper hand has been questioned by W. H. Lazonick, 'Industrial relations and technical change: the case of the self-acting mule', *Cambridge Journal of Economics* 3 (1979), 231–62. See also Per Bolin Hort, *Work, family and the state: child labour and the organization of production in the British cotton industry, 1780–1920* (Lund: Lund University Press, 1989), pp. 107–16.

elements of the radicals' case for political rights and economic justice, in so far as this was based on the workers' 'property of skill'.[45] By the time that he published *Popular political economy* in 1827, the increasing vehemence of Hodgskin's critique of orthodox political economy had estranged him from the philosophical radicals led by Brougham and James Mill.[46] Elaborating his subversive case that the nation's true capital lay in the skills of its working men, Hodgskin gave a carefully crafted and distinctive account of invention which was completely different from Farey's.

Hodgskin appreciated that, if Watt was no ordinary workman whose inventiveness went beyond simply exercising the skills of his trade, not only was his exemplar unavailable to the radicals, but his exceptionality might jeopardize their case for financial and political recognition of the workers' major contribution to national prosperity.[47] He elaborated a collective theory of invention, which was consistent with his radical challenge to orthodox political economy; it reduced Watt to the status of a representative skilled worker. We may ground his ideas in the traditional pride in workmanship and the ethos of mutual responsibility that had informed the culture and consciousness of Europe's skilled trades since the Middle Ages. Despite the declining power of the guilds in eighteenth-century Britain and the legislative assault on their regulations early in the next century (in particular, the repeal of the Elizabethan Statute of Artificers in 1814), artisans attempted to uphold their claims to the status and privileges that an apprenticeship traditionally conferred. They articulated 'a specific rhetoric of property', based on their entitlement both to society's proper respect and the law's protection of their investment in the acquisition of skill.[48] Not only did this imply the fair remuneration of their economic value, but it also underpinned their case for the suffrage and political representation.[49] Moreover, despite the individual intellectual property to which a few were able to lay claim through their purchase of a patent, many probably still conceived of

---

[45] John Rule, 'The property of skill in the period of manufacture', in Patrick Joyce (ed.), *The historical meanings of work* (Cambridge: Cambridge University Press, 1987), pp. 104–13.

[46] Stack, *Nature and artifice*, pp. 137–9; Gareth Stedman Jones, 'Rethinking Chartism', in his *Languages of class: studies in English working class history, 1832–1982* (Cambridge: Cambridge University Press, 1983), pp. 133–9.

[47] An article in the *Saturday Magazine* (1837), contesting radical ideas about the labour theory of value, asserted that 'James Watt and Robert Fulton were worth more to society than 500,000 ordinary men': quoted in Pettitt, *Patent inventions*, p. 67.

[48] Rule, 'Property of skill', p. 105.

[49] Jones, 'Rethinking Chartism', pp. 109–10, 126–7, 138n. There was an unarticulated tension between the artisans' exclusive claim to 'property of skill' and the universal property in labour (both skilled and unskilled) to which many radicals and Chartists appealed.

technological change as comprising collective progress in their practice of skills. The latter position had been taken by several guilds in the late seventeenth and early eighteenth centuries, which had contested the Crown's intrusion on their control through its grant of letters patent to individual craftsmen.[50]

It was a concept, for example, that unselfconsciously informed John Blackner's history of the Nottingham hosiery trade, in which he celebrated the knitting frame as both a locally developed invention and the principal agent of the region's prosperity. Apprenticed as a stocking-maker, Blackner had been editor successively of the *Statesman* (the London radical news-paper), and the *Nottingham Review*.[51] In his *History of Nottingham* (1815), he gave to William Lee and Jedediah Strutt the joint credit for inventing the basic machines from which all others had 'progressively emanated'; other-wise, in those rare instances where the claim to an invention was uncon-tested, he promised that 'the name of the inventor shall be duly honoured'.[52] Yet, this was by no means a heroic account of individual genius: knowing the trade from the inside, Blackner offered a pragmatic assessment of its development, giving credit wherever he thought it was due. He characterized Strutt simply as 'an industrious and ingenious work-man (for I understand [he] was a wheelwright)',[53] and described the steps taken by other workmen to develop his invention further: 'the frame ... has been brought to its present high state of perfection by the united talents of many.'[54] In particular, the 'mechanical judgement and dexterity in workmanship' of the frame-smiths and the 'inventive skill and ... nicety in adjustment' of the setters-up were responsible for the frame's perfec-tion.[55] As the market prompted, so these skilled workers responded with new ideas: 'Trade engenders new desires ... [These] beget refined wants, which propel the hand to industry and foster in the brain the germs of invention.'[56] Blackner's pride in his fellow workers' achievements was evident, and he was happy to emphasize their skills and manual dexterity; there were no false claims to 'philosophy' or 'science', nor indeed any sense that such a gloss was necessary for their ingenuity to be applauded. Neither was Blackner ostensibly making any political case.

---

[50] MacLeod, *Inventing the industrial revolution*, pp. 82–4, 112–13.
[51] Mark Pottle, 'Blackner, John (1770?–1816)', *ODNB*, www.oxforddnb.com/view/article/2532, accessed 18 October 2006.
[52] John Blackner, *The history of Nottingham* (Nottingham: Sutton and Son, 1815), pp. 219–20.
[53] Ibid., p. 220; Blackner praised the Strutts, his fellow radicals, 'as patriots [who] stand second to none in the kingdom'.
[54] Ibid., pp. 218–19.   [55] Ibid., p. 245. See also, ibid., pp. 223, 228, 231, 234.
[56] Ibid., p. 195.

By contrast, Hodgskin's account of invention, a decade later, was highly political. Indeed, David Stack's argument, that Hodgskin's political philosophy was rooted in his deist theology, requires us to look beyond the defence of 'property in skill' as a sufficient explanation for Hodgskin's unusual concern to explicate invention. Stack contends that Hodgskin based his critique of political economy on 'his defence of a beneficent, self-sufficient, and progressive Nature'. Contrary to Malthus' and Ricardo's pessimistic predictions of a stationary state with economic growth necessarily restricted by demographic pressure, Hodgskin believed that the persistent accumulation of knowledge would lift such constraints on growth.[57] His notion of collective invention, which was founded on the mundane development of skill, was at heart a deist version of providentialism. It provided a major plank of his refutation of Malthus' attack on the ideological foundations of radicalism, and it may even have occurred to Hodgskin through the contemporary fascination with Watt's inventiveness. However, individual 'genius', of the type advanced by Jeffrey or Farey, would introduce a cause exogenous to Hodgskin's model of cumulative, collective invention. His response to the commemoration of Watt in 1824 had been both complex and pointed, combining a muted admiration for the man with irony for the manner of his glorification. He now had to counteract more forcefully the notion that Watt was an exceptional genius and philosopher. To maintain his anti-Malthusian argument for a benevolent Nature, invention had to be the necessary outcome of population growth, not the fortuitous product of one individual's brilliance.

If Farey considered the development of the ship and navigation to exemplify an alternative, perhaps lesser, type of invention to the productions of genius, Hodgskin believed it represented the *only* type there was and applied it explicitly to the steam engine.[58] But his basic dispute was not with Farey and others who saw Watt as an exceptional figure: it was with the mainstream political economists, whose concept of capital he challenged in the name of labouring men. (Stack considers that it was in Hodgskin's work that 'radicalism's critique of capital reached its highest theoretical attainment'.[59]) Hodgskin's model of invention was an outgrowth from his redefinition of capital as the product exclusively of working people's labour and, above all, their skill. His concept was collective and historical: every invention constituted only the latest stage in the accumulation of improvements made by countless generations of skilled workers responding to the needs of their own time and circumstance. Skill, for Hodgskin, comprised a complex bundle of both mental and

---

[57] Stack, *Nature and artifice*, pp. 18, 23–33, 108.   [58] See above, p. 145.
[59] Stack, *Nature and artifice*, p. 112.

physical capacities: no manual art could be learned without the exercise of both; invention required both mental agility, based on a sound body of transmitted knowledge, and manual dexterity to put ideas into practice.[60] In particular, he emphasized the intellectual components of skilled work, which tended to be underrated. In *Labour defended against the claims of capital* (1825), he refers to the draughtsman, shipwright or engineer 'who "in his mind's eye" sees the effect of every contrivance, and who adapts the parts of a complicated machine to each other'.[61] By implication, every novel task undertaken by the skilled worker led, in its solution, to an invention.

The more complex the machinery, the more it was dependent on the knowledge derived from centuries of experience. The steam engine, for example, 'in its present admirable, but not yet perfect form', said Hodgskin, '[represented] an immense reach of intellect, numberless observations, a prodigious quantity of knowledge, *gathered in all the ages of the world*, and a vast variety of experiments'.[62] This conception of the icon of British industrial and military supremacy as a great collaborative effort progressing through history posed a direct challenge to the emergent heroic account, in which the mind of Watt had transcended time and place to invent the perfect engine. Even the steam engine, Hodgskin implied, belonged rightly to the people, through their ancestral (and continuing) contribution to its invention, not to the moneyed classes who merely purchased it – nor, indeed, to its most recent 'inventor'.

It followed that Watt the incomparable genius had to be reconfigured as Watt the exemplar of working-class inventive ability – just another cog in the wheel of nature's unfolding plan. Hodgskin denounced the 'vanity' of the heroic ideology's assumptions, before inserting 'even James Watt' into his historical context: the individual was more dependent on both nature and society than he might like to think.[63] In this rare rearguard action against the heroic ideology, Hodgskin demonstrated his faith in a beneficent nature gradually revealing its laws to inquisitive men.

---

[60] Thomas Hodgskin, *Popular political economy: four lectures delivered at the London Mechanics' Institution* (London: Charles Tait, and Edinburgh: William Tait, 1827), pp. 46–8.

[61] [Thomas Hodgskin], *Labour defended against the claims of capital* [1825], 3rd edn, ed. G. D. H. Cole (London: Cass, 1963), pp. 86–7. See the admiring description of the visualizing powers of a highly skilled fellow stonemason, by Hugh Miller in *My school and schoolmasters: or the story of my education*, ed. W. M. Mackenzie (Edinburgh: George A. Morton; London: Simpkin, Marshall & Co. 1905), pp. 270–1.

[62] [Hodgskin], *Labour defended*, p. 68; my emphasis.

[63] There are parallels here with Joseph Priestley's scepticism concerning Newton's 'genius' and anxiety that Newton's inflated reputation would intimidate and therefore deter other seekers after truth: Schaffer, 'Priestley', p. 45.

The endeavour to trace the discoveries and inventions of individuals to general natural laws is not flattering, I am aware, to that vanity which loves to think itself, by the possession of some peculiar genius, distinguished from the common herd of mankind. But let us not injure society and vilify nature, that we may set up some palpable objects for reverence. It is plain that every individual, be his singularities and his intellectual powers what they may, has his character, his sentiments, his thoughts, his passions, – yea, even his intellect itself – fashioned by the time at which he lives, and by the society of which he is a member; so that any thing which is peculiar to himself forms but the smallest part of the whole man. Whatever may be his natural endowments ... every man is indebted for whatever he possesses of knowledge, of skill, of inventive power, to the knowledge and skill of every other man, either living or dead.[64]

Like Columbus, Bacon, Newton, Luther or the inventor of printing, Watt should be regarded 'as one of those master-spirits who gather and concentrate within themselves some great and scattered truths, the consequences of numberless previous discoveries which, fortunately for them, are just dawning on society as they arrive at the age of reflection'. It only took 'some little additional discovery of their own' for such people to connect together the whole and produce the discovery, theory or invention with which the age was pregnant.[65] Placing the final piece in the jigsaw ought not to be mistaken for the invention or discovery of the whole.

From this collaborative and incremental conception of technological change, there followed two crucial aspects of Hodgskin's thesis. One allowed him to dispute Adam Smith's view of the relationship between invention and the division of labour (and hence between knowledge and economic growth); the other, to deny Malthusian fears of overpopulation as fundamentally misconceived – a rebuttal which radicals recognized as essential to their case that evil inhered in government, not in the 'inevitable laws of our nature'.[66] Hodgskin's primary faith was in a providential conception of nature, wherein the Deity had harmoniously ordered the world for the benefit of humanity.[67] He consequently rejected Malthus' pessimism and regarded the supposed 'positive' and 'prudential' checks to overpopulation (that arose through only misery or abstinence) as a

[64] [Hodgskin], *Labour defended*, p. 87.
[65] Ibid., pp. 88–90. Cf. how Condillac and Condorcet accommodated Newton's singular 'genius' to their egalitarian ideology: Fara, *Newton*, pp. 186–7.
[66] T. R. Malthus, *An essay on the principle of population as it affects the future improvement of society, with remarks on the speculations of Mr Godwin, Mr Condorcet, and other writers* (London: J. Johnson, 1798), p. 204, quoted in Stack, *Nature and artifice*, p. 23. '"Malthusian" first became an abusive epithet, both among trade unionists and radicals in the 1820s': Jones, 'Rethinking Chartism', p. 115.
[67] Stack, *Nature and artifice*, pp. 6–7, 94–8. Cf. Andrew Ure, in *Glasgow Mechanics' Magazine* 2 (1824), 382.

denial of this natural harmony. Contradicting Malthus' exculpation of political institutions, which were regularly overwhelmed by the human urge to procreate, Hodgskin celebrated the creative impulse of population growth and turned the blame for social degradation back onto oppressive and rapacious governments.[68] He espoused instead the overarching faith in progress expressed by French political economists, in particular Turgot and Say. For them, economic growth stemmed principally from the progress of knowledge, which in turn was a product of population increase: statistically, the larger the population, the higher the incidence of 'genius' was likely to be. By implication, the British classical economists were mistaken to predict that economic growth was finite, because the human mind knew no limits.[69]

Hodgskin found in population increase both a heightened stimulus to invention and a raised probability of its occurrence. Just as every individual inventor was stimulated to invent by 'the natural but insatiable desire of providing for his wants or bettering his condition', so humanity as a whole had progressed from savagery to civilization under the promptings of hunger. Once population pressure had exhausted the earth's wild fruits, 'man' had been roused to discover the means of hunting and fishing, thence agriculture and rude manufactures; the requirements of an expanding population were still operating to bring about agricultural improvements and 'the wonderful inventions of our own times'. In the tradition of eighteenth-century theorists who emphasized the creative stimulus that arose from contending with difficulty, Hodgskin rejoiced that, 'Necessity is the mother of invention; and the continual existence of necessity can only be explained by the continual increase of people.'[70]

Hodgskin took this insight a stage further: the needs of the time, in tandem with the state of knowledge and skill that a particular society had reached, helped to *shape* invention. Watt, he contended, had made significant improvements to the steam engine, because it was only in eighteenth-century Britain that all the conditions were present: the necessity for a new source of power, arising from 'the commercial demand' for labour-saving machinery, had been matched by the availability of both the requisite fuel and the mechanical skills to effect the invention among millwrights, founders, smiths and other metalworkers. In another country or a previous century, both the incentive and the knowledge that enabled Watt to make his great inventions would have been lacking.

---

[68] Stack, *Nature and artifice*, pp. 23–33, 99–103.   [69] Ibid., pp. 103–4.
[70] Hodgskin, *Popular political economy*, p. 86; see above, pp. 48–9. Cf. Toynbee, *Lectures on the industrial revolution*, p. 113.

No possible motive could there have existed for the invention; it being of no utility except in crowded countries, in which fuel is plentiful and manufactures established; or having invented it, if it were possible, there would be no body to make or use it, no purpose to which it could be applied.[71]

The corollary was that the circumstances were more powerful than any individual: if not Watt, then some other Briton would have soon made the same inventions, since '[s]uch minds and such men arise naturally and necessarily from the general progress in knowledge'.[72]

Although Hodgskin made population pressure central to technological progress, he suggested other, supplementary factors that made some societies more inventive than others, and he criticized the political economists for not exploring this crucial question – an early and long-unheeded call to 'open the black box' of technology. In particular, it should be investigated whether any forms of 'social regulation' were especially conducive to the production of new knowledge. True to his radical colours, Hodgskin predicted that the degree of freedom that governments allowed their citizens would prove to be crucial. In comparison with the rest of Europe, the British people had been 'the freest to inquire' and consequently the chief progenitors of 'wealth-creating knowledge'; any restriction on the press, on freedom of worship or freedom of speech was harmful in deterring inquiry throughout every branch of knowledge, not just those immediately affected.[73] Whatever its accuracy, it was a useful correlation to brandish at a government whose commitment to liberalism was, to say the least, suspect. There are obvious similarities here with the ideas of Whig historians and political economists, such as Macaulay, who identified the source of national prosperity in Britain's constitutional freedoms. But Hodgskin, with his concern for working people, neither shared Macaulay's faith in the unidirectional progress of liberty, nor assumed that its benefits extended throughout society.

Having countered Malthus, Hodgskin turned to refute Adam Smith. He did not deny Smith's premise that the division of labour promoted the growth of productivity and thereby augmented national wealth, nor, perhaps surprisingly, did he doubt that it generated an increase in skill by allowing the worker to concentrate on a single operation.[74] Instead, he challenged Smith's argument that the invention of machines to abridge and

---

[71] Hodgskin, *Popular political economy*, p. 88.   [72] Ibid., p. 90.

[73] Ibid., pp. 97–9.

[74] Ibid., pp. 100–8. For a careful exploration of this controversial question, see Charles More, *Skill and the English working class, 1870–1914* (London: Croom Helm, 1980), esp. pp. 181–97.

save labour always arose from the division of labour, and reversed the causal direction between the two phenomena. 'Inventions', contended Hodgskin, 'always precede division of labour, and extend it, both by introducing new arts and by making commodities at a less cost.'[75] He illustrated this point by reference to the creation of new trades, such as engineering and power-loom weaving: they were the outcome of inventions that demanded new specializations of occupation; steam engines and textile machinery, for example, existed before there were specialists to produce them.[76] Hodgskin thereby bolstered his case that, by right, all the benefits of the division of labour '*naturally* centre in the labourer; belong to him, and contribute to his ease or add to his opulence'.[77] This was crucial to his argument that there was no capital except in skill and labour. If one accepted Smith's causal ordering, the moneyed man, who claimed the credit for organizing the division of labour, might thereby establish an entitlement to the fruits of technological progress. The capitalist's case would collapse if that division arose initially from the inventions proceeding unassisted from the workers' knowledge, skill and powers of observation. Consequently, although the division of labour might facilitate the making of subsequent improvements, Hodgskin insisted that it was secondary to, and derivative of, the skill inherent in the workers' mind and hands. Moreover, as Stack argues, his reversal of Smith's causal direction, 'removed those limitations on the division of labour that Smith had thought would ultimately produce a stationary state'.[78]

Among radicals, Hodgskin's intense concern to explain invention (and capture it for the cause) seems to have been unique. Perhaps his emphasis on skills and knowledge, rather than simply on labour, was perceived as elitist and potentially divisive: the labour of every worker, not the inventiveness of the skilled, provided a broader basis for their political rights.[79] William Thompson also identified the foundation of national wealth with the skills possessed by working men and the consequent necessity, in the words of his

---

[75] Hodgskin, *Popular political economy*, p. 80. See also MacLeod, *Inventing the industrial revolution*, pp. 216–17.

[76] Whether Hodgskin appreciated the degree to which Smith would divide labour is unclear: rather than the simplification of a manufacturing process into minute tasks, Hodgskin appears to have had in mind the division of work into specialized trades.

[77] Hodgskin, *Popular political economy*, p. 108; original emphasis.

[78] Stack, *Nature and artifice*, p. 120.

[79] For Hodgskin's limited influence on radical thought, see Stack, *Nature and artifice*, pp. 135–6, 140–7. For artisans' continuing insistence on recognition for their role, see Brian Maidment, 'Entrepreneurship and the artisan: John Cassell, the Great Exhibition and the periodical idea', in Louise Purbrick (ed.), *The Great Exhibition of 1851: new interdisciplinary essays* (Manchester and New York: Manchester University Press, 2001), pp. 80, 107.

title, 'to secure to labour the whole products of its exertions'.[80] Although Thompson said relatively little about invention, he shared Hodgskin's assumption that inventions stemmed chiefly from working people. As an Owenite, however, he virulently attacked Hodgskin as neither a 'labourer' nor true friend of the labourers since, by failing to endorse co-operative socialism, Hodgskin offered no means whereby the labourer could receive the full value of his product.[81] Thompson believed it was a mistake to encourage the formation of a skilled elite through the unequal remuneration of work, because, by lessening the skills of the majority, it would reduce the pool of inventive people. By contrast, 'where the skill of all was improved and nearly equal, the chances of invention would be increased as a hundred or a thousand to one'.[82] Implicitly attacking both the patent system and the exaggerated rewarding of a select few, whether with fame or money, Thompson suggested that invention flourished best where pursued for its own sake (for the enjoyment of mental exercise and the popular approbation accorded those who identified the public interest with their own) in conditions of free co-operation and mutual assistance. He feared, however, that, 'the pleasures of skill and invention are not now sought for their own sakes, but as the means of gratifying antipathy by rising above others, and becoming to them objects of envy and false admiration.'[83]

Democratic invention

Shorn of both its faith in a deistic providence and its extreme radicalism, Hodgskin's incremental model of invention found numerous echoes in the mid-nineteenth century, particularly among authors concerned to promote working-class education. It was not incompatible with a democratic, biographical approach, where inventors succeeded through the practice of virtues imitable by all – perseverance, hard work, attentiveness, the study of science – rather than through the superior qualities of mind associated with the natural 'genius' of a few, especially talented individuals, or which were bestowed through divine inspiration.[84] It was

---

80 For Thompson's ideas more generally, see Jones, 'Rethinking Chartism', pp. 120–5; Berg, *Machinery question*, pp. 281–3; Noel Thompson, 'Thompson, William (1775–1833)', *ODNB*, www.oxforddnb.com/view/article/27284, accessed 18 October 2006.

81 Stack, *Nature and artifice*, pp. 150–2.

82 [William Thompson], *Labor rewarded. The claims of labor and capital conciliated: or, how to secure to labor the whole products of its exertions, by one of the idle classes* (London: Hunt & Clarke, 1827), p. 26.

83 Ibid., p. 27.

84 Among many possible examples: John G. Edgar, *Footprints of famous men, designed as incitements to intellectual industry* (London: David Bogue, 1854), pp. 344–52; [Cooper], *Triumphs of perseverance*, pp. 91–7.

difficult, however, to walk this ideological tightrope and, where Hodgskin emphasized the quotidian skills of working men as part of a grand collective project, few authors could resist the urge to praise the individual talents and characteristics of their subjects – whether for the sake of a good story, a moral lesson, or a political motive. On the other hand, because it implied that no *particular* inventor was needed, Hodgskin's model leant itself to a deterministic explanation of invention, which virtually removed human agency and was deployed from mid-century to attack the rationale for a patent system.[85] Many working-class inventors – encouraged not least by the *Mechanic's Magazine* – wanted a reformed patent system that would protect their individual intellectual property against the depredation of employers and other capitalists: Hodgskin's collective model threatened to undermine such protection.

Already in 1825, in a popular science book written for children, Maria Edgeworth had presented inventors in a very positive light. Although she mentioned only a select few by name, her approach was more democratic than heroic.[86] The daughter of Richard Edgeworth, an inventor and member of the Lunar Society, Edgeworth's aim was to capture young people's interest in science and technology through the unusually experiential (first-hand) lessons offered to two fictional children. The eponymous Harry and Lucy learn about spinning by visiting a Lancashire cotton factory, where their father explains the inventions of Hargreaves, Arkwright and Crompton. Harry is 'glad papa always remembers and tells the name of the inventors'.[87] ('Papa', a man ahead of his time in this regard, is not in fact entirely reliable: gas lighting, for example, remains an anonymous invention.) They also learn how Arkwright, who 'like Hargrave [sic], was originally a poor and illiterate man', rose to immense wealth and a knighthood. '"And all the consequence of one man's invention,"' said Harry of the Arkwright family's material success. '"And industry and perseverance,"' said his father', not losing the opportunity to impart a moral lesson.[88] Josiah Wedgwood was another of Edgeworth's exemplars who, through his improvements in the pottery trade, 'made a large fortune ... [but] with a character, a reputation, above all fortune'.[89] A steamboat excursion provokes a friendly, and mockingly nationalistic, dispute over who invented it, while the family's purchase of 'one of the

---

[85] See below, pp. 267–71.
[86] Maria Edgeworth, *Harry and Lucy concluded; being the last part of Early lessons*, 4 vols. (London: R. Hunter and Baldwin, Cradock and Joy, 1825). For an anticipation of Edgeworth's approach, which mentioned Arkwright and Wedgwood, see Barbauld and Aikin, *Evenings at home*, pp. 166, 170.
[87] Edgeworth, *Harry and Lucy*, vol. I, p. 228.   [88] Ibid., pp. 229–30.
[89] Ibid., vol. II, p. 19.

Scotch novels' allows Edgeworth to reprint Scott's encomium of Watt.[90] Harry announces that he would like to meet 'great mechanics ... [and] great chemists ... and all sorts of sensible and *inventing* people'.[91] By the end, he earnestly wishes to become one himself: '"I have long had, deep down in my mind ... a great ambition to make, some time or other in my life, some great discovery or invention."'[92] Invention, Edgeworth suggests, might now be deemed a respectable and realistic ambition for a middle-class boy – as well as for his working-class counterparts (if not for his sister).[93]

Edgeworth was keen to demystify the process of invention, in particular to explode the myths that relied on chance or luck.[94] Several times, Harry and Lucy were firmly told that inventions were never made by accident. At most, an accident might hint at a solution to 'an observing mind' which was already engrossed in a problem. Many people, for example, had seen a spinning wheel overturned onto its side, without it prompting the idea of a spinning jenny, as it reputedly had to James Hargreaves. Without emphasizing the role of skill, Edgeworth, nonetheless, implied that invention was within the grasp of the superior working man who kept his wits about him. As she explained, '[t]o invent is to combine, or put things together for a particular purpose. This, which requires thought, cannot be done by mere chance.'[95] To eliminate entirely the taint of serendipity – of even 'casual observation' – required, she seems to imply, the removal of the inventive process from the workshop to the laboratory and the application of the scientific method (which working men were currently being urged to learn in the new Mechanics' Institutes). For Edgeworth, the epitome of a good invention was Davy's safety lamp, both in its life-saving effect and in the method of its invention:

[it] was the consequence of a settled good purpose working in the mind of a man of science, genius [i.e. ingenuity], knowledge, and humane views ... by his observing and reasoning on all appearances before him, and employing alternately theory and experiment.[96]

[90] Ibid., pp. 311–12, 335–6.   [91] Ibid., p. 338.   [92] Ibid., vol. IV, p. 329.
[93] Despite the author's own gender, Lucy remains in her brother's shadow, her femininity not threatened by too close an engagement with scientific experiments or new technologies. Perhaps, like Maria, she would become a popularizer of his achievements!
[94] The 'mythology' of accidental inventions was not only the stuff of popular legends but also was sanctioned by providentialist views, which downplayed the role of human agency: Bowden, *Industrial society in England*, p. 55; Schaffer, 'Priestley', p. 50.
[95] Edgeworth, *Harry and Lucy*, vol. I, p. 222. See also ibid., vol. II, pp. 15–16; vol. IV, p. 325. For a similar account of invention as a methodical combination of elements (by a working man), see Charles Babbage, *On the economy of machinery and manufactures* (London: Charles Knight, 1832), p. 136.
[96] Edgeworth, *Harry and Lucy*, vol. IV, p. 325.

Davy himself had recently praised Watt for a similar methodical approach.[97]

Because inventive success, according to Edgeworth, was grounded in good practice rather than exclusive inspiration, it followed that two or more people might achieve it simultaneously. She accepted as axiomatic that the same invention might be made independently in different countries, 'simply because the same wants are felt, and because the same progress has been made in knowledge'.[98] This interaction of a demand-side prompt with a supply of new knowledge aligned Edgeworth quite closely with Hodgskin's explanation, without entangling her in the anti-Malthusian, providential argument from population increase. Instead, she suggested that invention had become more prevalent 'because knowledge is more generally diffused. More people try experiments.'[99] It was not more people but better educated people that made a society more inventive. However, while demonstrating some awareness of the social context of invention, Edgeworth's focus remained firmly on the individual: her primary concern was to encourage young men to become inventors, rather than to explain why some societies might generate more new knowledge or produce more inventions than others. In this she was far from untypical.

A similar concern, this time intended to inspire the ambitions of working men, informed Brougham's tract in praise of scientific study, written for the SDUK two years later, and the two biographical volumes that George Craik produced, again for the SDUK, in 1830–1.[100] Both authors shared Edgeworth's (Baconian) anxiety to eliminate chance and emphasize research as a source of new inventions. Brougham advised artisans that they were best placed to identify and remedy 'what is wanting, or what is amiss with the old methods' in their trades – especially if they were equipped with a scientific understanding of the processes involved.[101]

---

[97] See above, p. 101.

[98] Edgeworth, *Harry and Lucy*, vol. IV, p. 194. For a similar, contemporary acknowledgement of 'simultaneous' inventions, see Charles Wyatt on the rival claims of his father, John Wyatt, and Richard Arkwright, in *Memoirs of the Literary and Philosophical Society of Manchester*, 2nd ser., 3 (1819), 137.

[99] Edgeworth, *Harry and Lucy*, vol. IV, p. 331.

[100] For Hodgskin's worsening relations with the SDUK between 1827 and 1831, when it published a tract that attacked his theory of property, and the hostility to the SDUK from other radicals, see Stack, *Nature and artifice*, pp. 135–43.

[101] [Henry Brougham], *A discourse of the objects, advantages, and pleasures of science* (London: Baldwin, Cradock & Joy, for the SDUK, 1827), p. 42. For the SDUK and Brougham's pivotal role in it, see R. K. Webb, *The British working class reader, 1790–1848: literacy and social tension* (London: George Allen & Unwin, 1955), pp. 66–73, 85–90, 114–20; Richard D. Altick, *The English common reader: a social history of the mass reading public, 1800–1900* (Chicago: University of Chicago Press, 1957), pp. 269–73, 333–5; Berg, *Machinery question*, pp. 292–3; Gray, 'Charles Knight', 24–8.

Thus, Watt's steam engine was the product of 'the most learned investigation of mathematical, mechanical, and chemical truths'; similarly, Arkwright's spinning jenny [sic], Davy's safety lamp, and Howard's sugar-refining process all stemmed from a long and well-prepared concentration on their respective problems.[102] Craik likewise rejected those 'fables' of 'lucky discoveries ... which strike an uneducated fancy', and stressed instead the importance of methodical but alert inquiry, driven by an ardent thirst for knowledge.[103] He was emphatic that knowledge must be sought for its own sake, not for any social advancement that education might bring. His title, *The pursuit of knowledge under difficulties*, was deliberately chosen to reflect his concern with men 'who, whether in humble or in high life, have pursued knowledge with ardour'; indeed, his preferred title had been 'Anecdotes of the love of knowledge'.[104] His examples came from a broad range of fields ('philosophy, literature, and art'), unrestricted by time or place, but included an unusually large number of 'men of science'. Watt, Arkwright, Brindley and Cartwright were accorded a chapter each, and Benjamin Franklin, three. The road builder John Metcalfe exemplified 'Difficulties occasioned by blindness', while the astronomer Kepler helped to illustrate 'Devotion to knowledge in extreme poverty'. In pride of place, however, Sir Isaac Newton 'of all men that ever lived, is the one who has most extended the territory of human knowledge' – shared an introductory chapter with Galileo, Torricelli, Pascal, Prince Rupert and the Montgolfier brothers.[105]

Craik introduced Watt by remarking that all other modern inventions 'sink into insignificance ... [by comparison] with the extraordinary results which have followed the employment of steam as a mechanical agent'; the credit for which was 'pre-eminently due' to Watt alone.[106] His account of the separate condenser's invention presents it as the very model of methodical investigation: in pursuit of a defined goal (that is, the more efficient use of steam), and 'prepared by a complete knowledge of the properties' of steam, thanks to the 'extensive course of experiments' which he had undertaken, Watt proceeded to reflect on how to correct the defects that he had identified in Newcomen's engine. Only after this lengthy and careful preparation had the 'fortunate idea' of the separate

---

[102] [Brougham], *Discourse*, p. 41.

[103] [George L. Craik], *The pursuit of knowledge under difficulties; illustrated by anecdotes*, 2 vols. (London: Charles Knight, 1830–1), vol. I, p. 3. See also [Cooper], *Triumphs of perseverance*, pp. 80–1, 93–5.

[104] Charles Knight, *Passages of a working life*, 3 vols. (London, 1864–5), vol. II, pp. 133–4, quoted in T. H. E. Travers, *Samuel Smiles and the Victorian work ethic* (London and New York: Garland, 1987), p. 357.

[105] [Craik], *Pursuit of knowledge*, vol. I, p. 1.   [106] Ibid., vol. II, p. 295.

condenser 'presented itself to his thoughts'; shortly afterwards, 'his ingenuity also suggested to him the means of realizing it'.[107] Naturally, in executing his idea, Watt had to overcome 'many difficulties' – in his case, the sheer technical challenge, which arose 'principally from the impossibility of realizing theoretical perfection of structure with such materials as human art is obliged to work with'.[108] Craik accentuated Watt's 'ingenuity and perseverance' as the two great virtues that brought him success in meeting it.

However, although any workman might resolve to emulate Watt, as 'he continued ... to persevere with unwearied diligence', it was improbable he could match Watt's 'unrivalled mechanical ingenuity'.[109] Herein lay the unresolved, but not uncommon, tension in Craik's presentation of Watt as the epitome of good practice – between the methodical, scientific approach to invention, which Watt exemplified, and the unexplained (and possibly inexplicable) 'ingenuity' that supposedly set him above the crowd. Even if one insisted that fortune favours the well prepared and avoided describing the inventor as a mysteriously inspired 'genius', any explanatory dependence on innate capacities risked undermining the attempt to keep invention within everyone's reach. Only a strictly anti-heroic stance, such as Hodgskin's, could achieve that: it was impossible to combine the hero and everyman in a single Watt. It was more fundamental to Craik's purpose, however, to combat both the Romantic concept of the inspired genius and the popular notion of the lucky accident, since neither recognized the importance of effort and preparation as the necessary prerequisites for achievement in any field. Indeed, he had begun by addressing this issue head-on, applying his theory to the test case of Sir Isaac Newton, who, he believed, had expanded the boundaries of knowledge further than any other individual. What might appear superficially to be the product of divine inspiration or serendipity was nothing more, said Craik, than the result of applying a well-prepared and open mind to 'such common occurrences as, from their very commonness, had escaped the attention of all less active and original minds'.[110] This, he suggested, was the proper conclusion to draw from the legend of Newton and the apple.

Craik recognized that accounts of discovery and invention that were couched in terms of 'slow and successive efforts' had less dramatic impact than tales of 'a sudden inspiration' – including, by implication, the sort that Carlyle elaborated. Astutely, Craik accused discoverers themselves of some responsibility for such fictions, 'preferring ... the credit of being the chosen transmitter of supernatural communications to his fellow-mortals,

---

[107] Ibid., pp. 309–12.   [108] Ibid., p. 313.   [109] Ibid., pp. 313, 317, 319.
[110] Ibid., p. 3.

to that of excelling those around him in such mere human and unvalued attributes as philosophic sagacity and patience.'[111] Moreover, in conservative societies, which were in the thrall of superstition, what better recommendation could an innovation enjoy than divine inspiration? Modern, rational man would, of course, Craik flattered his readers, identify such legends as fallacious.[112]

Despite the paradox that Watt's elevated status presented, he was included in many subsequent collective biographies of inventors, engineers, 'men of science' or 'self-made men', which underscored the more mundane virtues necessary for 'getting on' in any sphere of life. Rarely did the paradox seem to trouble these authors. One apparent exception was Samuel Smiles. Despite his firm identification today with the ideology of 'self help', Smiles' intellectual roots tapped into early nineteenth-century radical thought; he brought to his biographical writing a number of assumptions that did not sit easily with a heroic approach to invention. We may even detect the influence of Hodgskin.[113] At the beginning of *Self-help* (1859), Smiles stresses the inter-generational nature of progress: 'All nations have been made what they are by the thinking and the working of many generations of men.'[114] When, in the second chapter, he turns specifically to examine 'the leaders of industry – inventors and producers', his gaze remains incremental and inclusive: contemporary material comforts were 'the result of the labour and ingenuity of many men and many minds'; the steam engine was 'effected step by step'.[115] Echoes of Hodgskin are even more distinct when Smiles assesses the role played by the famous few:

Arkwright probably stood in the same relation to the spinning machine that Watt did to the steam-engine and Stephenson to the locomotive. He *gathered together the scattered threads of ingenuity which already existed*, and wove them, after his own design, into a new and original fabric.[116]

The needs of industry prompted similar ideas in many minds, said Smiles, but it took 'the master mind, the strong practical man' to deliver the solution.[117]

---

[111] Ibid., vol. I, p. 3.   [112] Ibid., p. 4.

[113] Smiles commented that the title was often misunderstood: it was not 'a eulogy of selfishness' but the opposite – 'the duty of helping one's self in the highest sense involves the helping of one's neighbours': *Self-help: with illustrations of conduct and perseverance* (new edn, London: John Murray, 1875), pp. iii–iv. See Travers, *Samuel Smiles*, esp. p. 371; Asa Briggs, *Victorian people: a re-assessment of persons and themes, 1851–67* (rev. edn, Harmondsworth: Penguin, 1971), p. 118.

[114] Smiles, *Self-help*, p. 5.   [115] Ibid., p. 29.

[116] Ibid., p. 32; my emphasis. Note that Arkwright's role in invention is unquestioned.

[117] Ibid., p. 32. See also Samuel Smiles, *Industrial biography* (1863), p. 209, quoted in Travis, *Samuel Smiles*, p. 269; Samuel Smiles, *Lives of the engineers: the locomotive, George and Robert Stephenson* (London: John Murray, 1877), p. 374.

Despite Smiles' recognition of both the social context and the wider inventive community, he should not be aligned too closely with Hodgskin. In particular, Smiles rejected any notion of either a providential scheme of invention or of the shaping of individual character by the society into which one was born. The essential message of 'self-help' was that a man's character was of his own making.[118] Likewise, whatever inventions a society enjoyed were produced through the effort and skill of a succession of self-directing individuals, responding to the needs and opportunities they perceived. As Jarvis points out, none of Smiles' subjects are said 'to have owed anything to the help of God' – nor, we might add, to Hodgskin's beneficent 'Nature'.[119] Smiles was also prepared to allow that not all inventors were equal: Watt, for example, was more than simply the last in a long line of skilled workers. But how much more?

The publication of Muirhead's biography made Smiles abandon the idea of writing his own, until access to the archive of Matthew Boulton, at Soho, prompted the notion of a double biography – which remained, nonetheless, primarily focused on Watt and the steam engine ('the greatest invention of modern times').[120] For at least the first hundred pages, one feels more in the presence of Hodgskin than of Smiles (as commonly conceived), as he charts the early development of the engine, and contends: 'Thus, step by step, Newcomen's engine grew in power and efficiency ... [L]ike all other inventions it was not the product of one man's ingenuity, but of many. One contributed one improvement, one another.'[121] It was also consistent with Hodgskin's insistence on the skills of working men as the source of technological change that Smiles repeatedly stressed the importance of mechanical experience in developing the engine. While unusually complimentary, for a British author, to Denis Papin, Smiles considered that 'he laboured under the greatest possible disadvantage of not being a mechanic. The eyes and hands of others are not to be relied on in the execution of new and untried machines.' In this, Papin suffered by comparison with several British inventors, 'above all, James Watt'.[122] Smiles was dismissive of the famous incident with the tea kettle, emphasizing instead the experience Watt gained in his father's

---

[118] MacKay (ed.), *Autobiography of Samuel Smiles*, p. 106. For the prominence of 'the ideal of character' in Victorian thought, see Stefan Collini, *Public moralists: political thought and intellectual life in Britain, 1850–1930* (Oxford: Clarendon Press, 1991), pp. 94–116. For a perceptive discussion of Smiles' construction of a 'working-class scientific hero', see Secord, '"Be what you would seem to be"', 147–73.

[119] Jarvis, *Samuel Smiles*, p. 6. See also Travis, *Samuel Smiles*, pp. 260, 263.

[120] Smiles, *Lives of Boulton and Watt*, preface. Smiles was also granted access to Watt's garret workshop at Heathfield: ibid., pp. 512–14.

[121] Ibid., p. 67; see also, p. 38.   [122] Ibid., p. 34.

workshop, where he learned 'to use his hands dextrously ... training himself in the habits of application, industry, and invention ... [and] there he constructed many ingenious little objects'. Indeed, Smiles suggests that '[t]he mechanical dexterity which he thus cultivated even as a child was probably in a great measure the foundation on which he built the speculations to which he owes his glory'.[123]

As this reference to 'his glory' suggests, when Smiles' focus shifts from the history of the steam engine in general to Watt's particular contribution, he starts to eulogize Watt in ways that border on the heroic. From this point, his approach is similar to Craik's: Watt's invention is the result of 'an independent course of experiments', to which he devoted hard thought and great effort, before the idea of the separate condenser 'suddenly flashed upon his mind'.[124] Like Craik, Brougham and Edgeworth, Smiles insists that the invention was not accidental, but 'the result of close and continuous study'; furthermore, although Watt had the complete idea of the condenser in his mind, 'it took him many long and laborious years to work out the details of the engine'.[125] Similarly, Smiles wrestles with the contradictions inherent in admiring Watt's intellect – which he perceives as extraordinary in its facility for invention – while maintaining his gospel of effort and perseverance. 'Although,' he concedes, 'the true inventor, like the true poet, is born, not made ... yet [Watt's] greatest achievements were accomplished by unremitting application and industry. He was a keen observer and incessant experimenter ... His patience was inexhaustible.'[126] Yet, even more than all these strengths (note that mechanical skill has dropped out of this summation), 'it was probably because Watt was a great theorist, that he was a great inventor. His invention of the separate condenser was itself the result of a theory, the soundness of which he proved by experiment.'[127] Eventually, but only by quoting a French author (who compared Watt's creativity with that of Newton and Shakespeare), Smiles describes Watt as drawing 'brilliant inventions' from 'his fertile imagination'. Watt's 'immense superiority' as a 'mechanician' is demonstrated by contrast with Smeaton (again second to him in achievement), who 'worked long and patiently, but in an entirely technical spirit ... In a word, Smeaton knew how to improve, but Watt knew how to create.'[128] Having journeyed far from his initial, democratic emphasis on collective effort and skill, Smiles ultimately

---

[123] Ibid., pp. 91, 88. There are parallels here with other accounts of inventors' and engineers' boyhoods: see, in particular, Cooper, 'Myth, rumor and history', 83–7, 95.
[124] Smiles, *Lives of Boulton and Watt*, pp. 122–7.   [125] Ibid., pp. 129–30.
[126] Ibid., p. 510.   [127] Ibid.
[128] Ibid., p. 511. Smiles appears to have plagiarized John Bourne in his 'improve/create' distinction: see above, p. 149.

allows that Watt was incomparable: even impeccable habits of work and a scientific approach were insufficient to explain his outstanding achievement. Smiles lifts Watt beyond his readers' emulative reach, salvaging only the message that even Watt could not succeed by brilliance alone – his innate 'inventive faculty' was necessary but not sufficient. Without those good habits and his application to scientific research (and, let us not forget, Boulton's financial and moral support), Watt's natural abilities would have produced nothing.[129] Through a tortuous route – that permits even a nod of obeisance to Hodgskin's ideas – Smiles manages to celebrate Watt as an extraordinary product of the working class, while keeping his workaday prescription for achievement essentially intact.

Nevertheless, whatever concessions Smiles made to Watt's extraordinary abilities, they were intended to explain Watt, not to explain invention. In his *Autobiography* Smiles allowed that, '[w]e might, it is true, have had the steam engine without James Watt, the locomotive without George Stephenson'.[130] Although he devoted whole books to such major figures, he filled others with the achievements of many more obscure men and intimated that any invention was the sum of the intergenerational contributions of thousands more. Indeed, Smiles' true hero was no single individual but the entire band of working men who were responsible for Britain's mid-nineteenth-century predominance.

England was nothing, compared with continental nations, until she had become commercial. She fought wonderfully ... but she was gradually becoming less powerful as a state, until about the middle of last century, when a number of ingenious and inventive men, without apparent relation to each other, arose in various parts of the kingdom, and succeeded in giving an immense impulse to all the branches of the national industry; the result of which has been a harvest of wealth and prosperity.[131]

Where Jeffrey had promoted Watt as the civilian saviour of his country – albeit as representative of the enlightened men of science and commerce who surrounded him – Smiles picked up the radical baton, insisting that the true source of Britain's greatness was its working people. He envisaged a 'meritocracy of labour' not only inventing new machines and processes but also energizing a population which, under an idle and self-serving aristocracy, was equally passive and dissolute. The road and canal builders, such as Telford and the duke of Bridgewater, had been the first to induce good work-habits; Arkwright's factory system and Boulton and Watt's workshops

---

[129] For a similar interpretation, see Travis, *Samuel Smiles*, pp. 270–1. For Smiles' tribute to Boulton's role, see *Lives of Boulton and Watt*, pp. 477–8, 485.
[130] MacKay (ed.), *Autobiography of Samuel Smiles*, p. 275.
[131] Smiles, *Lives of the engineers*, vol. II, pp. 54, 66, 220; the quotation is from ibid., vol. I, p. xvii, quoted in Travis, *Samuel Smiles*, p. 264.

had similarly overcome 'the irregular habits of the work people' and exerted 'an important moral influence'.[132]

Hodgskin's answer to the political economists' pessimism had been to locate the source of technological progress in the very population growth that they blamed for stasis: the people, said Hodgskin, were not feckless but fruitful and inventive. According to Smiles, the people had once been feckless (under equally feckless governors), but had been converted from a burden into an invaluable resource by the efforts of an 'aristocracy of labour'. By implication, if there had ever been a 'Malthusian threat', it was continually neutralized by the technical ingenuity which was widespread among Britain's working people. Although Smiles' publications belong overwhelmingly to the second half of the nineteenth century, his work has been discussed here because of his roots in the radical thought of the 1820s–40s. Like the radicals' model of invention, Smiles himself was not a stand-alone hero but part of an incremental authorial development, and a bridge between the two halves of the century. As we shall see in subsequent chapters, many of the issues that were raised in the celebration of Watt and his 'brother projectors' continued to resonate after the mid-century – not least the claims, first, that Britain's greatness lay in her invention and technology, not her military prowess, and secondly that it was the achievement of her skilled working men. It would remain important to fight for the inclusion of inventors in the national pantheon – and to contest their precise identity.

[132] Travis, *Samuel Smiles*, pp. 266–8.

The technological pantheon

Until the 1850s, it was as though James Watt had obtained a patent on glory. Just as his extended patent of 1769 had obstructed further improvements to the steam engine until its expiry in 1800, for three decades after his death no other inventor was celebrated as a national hero. Yet, he was one among many thousands who contributed to the technological transformation of the British economy. For most of them, even simple fame was elusive. Only Watt and Jenner found a place in *The worthies of the United Kingdom* (1828), which eulogized approximately eighty of 'the original geniuses of the country'.[1] As late as 1854, it was still Watt and Brindley in whose inventive footprints boys were urged to follow.[2] Inventors were completely absent from many other biographical volumes. When Charles Knight included the textile-machinery inventor, Edmund Cartwright, in the *Gallery of portraits* in 1833, he commented that, although Cartwright ranked second only to Arkwright among national benefactors, his name was 'far less well known to the world at large'.[3] Similarly, George Crompton, the son of the inventor of the spinning mule, commended a projected volume of 'Worthies and early inventors of Lancashire', since it would 'tend to rescue their memories from oblivion (for how little of them is known, even by those who are reaping the fruits of their genius)'.[4] Edward Baines complained in 1835 of such neglect as a national disgrace, and Sir David Brewster contrasted it sharply with the honours conferred by continental countries, especially France.[5] During this time, however, a number of individuals – railway engineers, in

---

[1] *The worthies of the United Kingdom; or biographical accounts of the lives of the most illustrious men, in arts, arms, literature, and science, connected with Great Britain* (London: Knight & Lacey, 1828).

[2] Edgar, *Footprints of famous men*, pp. 335–51.

[3] *Gallery of portraits*, vol. VI, pp. 102–3; for Arkwright, see ibid., vol. V, pp. 181–8. Cf. F. Espinasse, 'Lancashire industrialism: James Brindley and his duke of Bridgewater and Richard Arkwright', *The Roscoe Magazine, and Lancashire and Cheshire Literary Reporter* 1 (1849), 202.

[4] George Crompton to Col. Sutcliffe [1845], Crompton MSS, ZCR 66/2, Bolton District Archives. See also MacLeod, 'Concepts of invention', p. 139.

[5] Edward Baines, Junior, *History of the cotton manufacture in Great Britain* [1835], ed. W. H. Chaloner (London: Frank Cass & Co., 1966), p. 53; [David Brewster], 'The decline of

7.1 The commemorative shield of the Great Exhibition, with which the London bookbinders, J. & J. Leighton, ornamented their display of blotting books. The names around the rim include nine British inventors: Arkwright, Caxton, Cartwright, Crompton, Davy, Hargreaves, Stanhope, Watt and Wedgwood (photograph by Ann Pethers).

particular – were emerging to challenge Watt's throne, and collectively the status of inventors continued to rise, thanks in large part to the public's growing appreciation of Watt's and others' achievements. In 1851, the commemorative shield of the Great Exhibition, with which the London bookbinders, J. & J. Leighton, ornamented their display of blotting books, named nine British inventors among the twenty-one artists and men of science, whose names surround the rim: the pantheon was expanding (figure 7.1).

science in England', *Quarterly Review* 43 (1830), 306–7, 314–16, 320–1. Edward Baines listed six pioneers of canals and the cotton industry in his ninety-strong 'Lancashire Temple of Fame', *Baines's Lancashire*, vol. I, pp. 142–3.

Patents, pensions and publicity

While the collective reputation of inventors had been improving since the late eighteenth century, there were now explicit calls for them to receive better treatment, as a matter of both private justice and public benefit.[6] In 1825, an article in the *Quarterly Review* advised against prejudiced and hasty judgements, since an invention, 'which at first blush may appear frivolous, and even ludicrous, turns out in the end to be extremely useful ... every invention should have fair play'.[7] Shortly afterwards, the *Saturday Magazine* declared that 'the prosperity of nations depends on nothing more than the encouragement of the inventive power of individuals'.[8] The *Mechanic's Magazine* began to agitate for cheaper patents, invoking the image of inventors as benefactors of society and the importance of invention to national wealth creation.[9] More surprisingly, *The Times*, endorsing this campaign, described inventors as 'the elect of the human race'.[10] In response to such pleas, the Attorney General affirmed it was Parliament's duty to facilitate the work of inventors, for it was 'likely to become useful to their country', and 'beneficial to mankind'.[11] Four years later, Parliament held its first ever investigation into the operation of the patent system: a select committee listened sympathetically to evidence of the difficulties faced by inventors in both affording and enforcing a patent. Although this produced no immediate reform, lobbying continued and several abortive bills were introduced. In 1835, Lord Brougham secured a minor legislative change, which benefited patentees by allowing them to disclaim a part of their specification without resort to a new patent.[12]

In a devastating critique of the patent system, David Brewster argued that its high charges should be abolished because they either penalized worthy inventors, who benefited the country and humanity as a whole, or they fined the 'inexperienced and sanguine projector' (the victim of his own folly). Successful inventors and failed projectors were equally victims

---

[6] See above, pp. 59–81, 136–43.

[7] [Barrow], 'Canals and railroads', 355. See also, for example, the appreciative comments about J. L. McAdam's road-building techniques: 'McAdam, John Loudon (1756–1836)', by [Anon.], 1893, *ODNB, Archive*, www.oxforddnb.com/view/article/17325, accessed 18 October 2006.

[8] Anon., 'Encouragement of inventions', *Saturday Magazine* (18 June 1825), 172, quoted in Pettitt, *Patent inventions*, p. 45.

[9] *Mechanic's Magazine*, 3 (1825), 171–3; ibid., 7 (1827), 149–50, 187–8, 315–16, 324–6, 350–1, 362–4, 371–3; ibid., 8 (1827), 74–8, 140–1; ibid., 11 (1829), 152–4; Dutton, *Patent system*, p. 43.

[10] *The Times*, 22 April 1826, 3a.   [11] Hansard, *P.D.*, 2nd ser., XV (1825), 72–3.

[12] *Report from the select committee ... patents for invention*, BPP 1829, III; Dutton, *Patent system*, pp. 43–4, 48–50.

of the patent system; the only villain was the government in its blind cupidity.[13] Jeffrey's rhetorical portrait of Watt as the saviour of his country provided critics of the government, in general, and of the inadequacies of the patent system, in particular, with an invaluable image.[14] In a glowing account of the cotton industry and its inventors, J. R. McCulloch condemned the paltriness of Parliament's award of £5,000 to Samuel Crompton. McCulloch described it as shamefully typical of official attitudes to 'individuals whose genius and inventions have alone enabled Parliament to meet the immense expenses the country has had to sustain'.[15] John Farey also drew on this whiggish axiom, when lobbying Brougham in 1833 to take up the cause of patent reform. Farey could expect a friendly hearing, when he contrasted the great national benefits of invention with the poor rewards earned by all but a few inventors, adding in justification that, '[t]he great increase in wealth which has taken place in Britain during the last fifty years can be traced direct from the practice of new inventions, as its chief source'.[16] Arago's extended diatribe against those who either opposed or infringed Watt's patent played on the same contrast and implicitly supported the cause of patent reform.[17] As a Frenchman, attuned to the idea that an inventor possessed a natural right in his intellectual property, Arago lambasted the niggardly attitude that he found in Britain, where, he said, it was common to take refuge in a deterministic argument that ideas 'cost no time and no trouble' and soon would have 'occurred to all the world'. He commented sardonically:

Men of genius, and the manufacturers of ideas, it seemed, ought to remain strangers to any thing like material enjoyments; and their histories, forsooth, should continue to resemble the legends of the martyrs.[18]

When Charles Dickens published 'A poor man's tale of a patent' in 1850, he was satirizing the labyrinthine ways of government bureaucracy

---

[13] [Brewster], 'Decline of science', 334. See also below, p. 357; Woolrich, 'John Farey Jr', 117; Richard Noakes, 'Representing "A Century of Inventions": nineteenth-century technology and Victorian *Punch*', in L. Henson *et al.* (eds.), *Culture and science in the nineteenth-century media* (Aldershot: Ashgate, 2004), p. 158. In a clever play on words, Brewster's daughter described him as, 'himself an inventor of no ordinary success in the higher sense, and of no ordinary want of success in the lower and commercial meaning of the word', Gordon, *Home life of Sir David Brewster*, p. 349.

[14] See above, pp. 94–7. For Watt's own complaints against the patent system, see Dutton, *Patent system*, pp. 36–41; Robinson, 'James Watt and the law of patents', 115–39.

[15] [McCulloch], 'British cotton manufacture', 16.

[16] John Farey to Lord Henry Brougham, 21 August 1833, Brougham MSS 45,493, University College London.

[17] Arago, *Life of James Watt*, pp. 86–95. See above, pp. 122–3.

[18] Ibid., p. 94. See Machlup and Penrose, 'Patent controversy', 11–13, and above, pp. 45–6.

generally, and, more particularly, the pointless expense and trouble required of inventors by the unreformed patent system, as they danced attendance on thirty-five different officials, starting with 'the Queen upon the Throne' and ending with 'the Deputy Chaff-Wax'.[19] Crucial to the acceptance of Dickens' satire is the credibility and upright character of his 'poor man', for there had to be no excuse for the stream of petty officials who preyed on him. These parasites were not providing a useful service, protecting the public from the unscrupulous or the self-deceiving 'inventor'; they only stamped bits of paper. Dickens' inventor, 'Old John', tells his story in the vernacular of the decent skilled worker. He is 'a smith by trade', hard-working, 'a good workman', not a Teetotaller but never drunk, a responsible family man, married for thirty-five years and father to six children, all now making their own way in the world; 'I am not a Chartist, and I never was.' To secure his patent he spent a small inheritance, long kept safe in case of misfortune and old age, and then only after a discussion with his wife: he is independent, self-sufficient, reliable, not a man to go into debt or to ruin his family and friends by ill-judged scheming.

Moreover, Old John is a competent and successful inventor. He has always been 'of an ingenious turn', and once got £20 by inventing a screw – 'it's in use now'. The patented invention has taken him twenty years 'off and on' to perfect, and his quiet pride in it is such that he can remember the exact moment when he finally completed it and, with tears of joy, brought his wife to see it. The patent (for England alone) cost him 'ninety-six pound, seven [shillings], and eight pence', which, with six weeks' lost work and lodgings in London (while he navigated the maze of officialdom), must have used up the entire inheritance of £128. But this is a tale of exploitation, not ruin: 'my invention is took up now, I am thankful to say, and doing well'. Old John had been unusually fortunate in his inheritance, which afforded him an English patent, but protection for the entire United Kingdom – at over £300 – still eluded him. Dickens thought the cost should be only 'half-a-crown' (12.5 pence). Britain's tortuous system was 'a Patent way of making Chartists', men resentful of the obstacles thrown across their route to fame and fortune. 'Old John' is no Watt or Stephenson, transforming the country with his inventions, but, nevertheless, an ingenious man whose ideas would profit his family and benefit the public in a modest way. 'Is it reasonable', he asks, 'to make a man feel as if, in inventing an ingenious improvement meant to do good, he had done something wrong?'

---

[19] [Charles Dickens], 'A poor man's tale of a patent', *Household Words* 2 (1850), 73–5.

It is a measure of the shift in the inventor's reputation that Dickens clearly expected this injured protest to be met with a sympathetic shake of the head, not a sceptical laugh. Evidence that his judgement proved correct appears in Old John's reincarnation, six years later, in the character of Daniel Doyce in *Little Dorrit*. Menaced by scheming speculators and failed by the patent system, Doyce is 'a man of great modesty and good sense', a talented engineer, whose ingenuity is matched by his integrity. Doyce's invention would benefit the country, if only the country's ridiculous bureaucracy did not persist in treating him as 'a public offender'. By contrast, the real threat to the country's wellbeing (and ultimately to Doyce's too) is the socially ambitious and amoral financial speculator, Merdle, the epitome of the modern projector.[20] In the meantime, however, pressure for patent reform had continued to mount, reaching its goal in the Patent Law Amendment Act of 1852, which finally established the system on a positive statutory basis, with a dedicated Patent Office. A single patent for the whole United Kingdom was now available for an initial cost of £25 – less than a twelfth of the amount that 'Old John' would have had to pay.[21]

Litigation was the next hurdle for the inventor to jump, if he were to prevent infringements and reap large profits from his patent. It was lowered during the second quarter of the nineteenth century, as judges and juries became more sympathetic towards patentees. One of Brewster's principal allegations had been that 'the law contrives, on the most frivolous grounds, to rob him [i.e. the patentee] of his privilege'; thirty of forty-nine recent trials of a patent's validity had resulted in revocation.[22] Modern research supports this observation. In the thirty years to 1829, patentees successfully prosecuted an infringement in only 30.9 per cent of cases at common law and in 45.5 per cent of cases heard in the equity courts. During the 1830s, however, their success rate rose to 76 per cent and 60 per cent respectively, and was maintained during the 1840s at 76.2 per cent and 55.5 per cent.[23] We may infer that this turn-around in outcomes resulted, at least in part, from changing attitudes towards inventors, as patentees came to be regarded less as grasping

---

[20] Charles Dickens, *Little Dorrit* (Harmondsworth: Penguin Books, 1967), pp. 159–65, 310–13, 568–72, 804–5; James M. Brown, *Dickens: novelist of the market place* (London and Basingstoke: Macmillan Press, 1982), pp. 45–51, 107–11. *Little Dorrit* was set in the 1820s; Doyce was dealing with the unreformed patent system.

[21] Dutton, *Patent system*, pp. 57–68; Pettitt, *Patent inventions*, pp. 122–32. For continuing causes for complaint against the new act, see below, p. 191.

[22] [Brewster], 'Decline of science', 338.

[23] Dutton, *Patent system*, pp. 77–9. Lubar notes a similar phenomenon in the United States, then at an earlier stage of industrialization: Lubar, 'Transformation of antebellum patent law', pp. 938–40. It would require further research to discover whether this was anything more than a coincidence.

monopolists and 'projectors', and more as ingenious national benefactors. Another innovative factor may have been the publication of treatises on patent litigation, which presumably helped to improve the drafting of specifications and to deter inadvisable prosecutions.[24] Nonetheless, the barrister, Matthew Davenport Hill, told the 1851 select committee on patents that, 'there is a strong bias in favour of inventors among jurors'.[25] Watt would have been both delighted and astonished to hear it.

There was also a revival of rewards outside the patent system, in which both private charity and public patronage were called on to relieve the poverty, and simultaneously recognize the achievement, of struggling inventors.[26] The pioneers of steam navigation were the earliest individual beneficiaries of Watt's reflected glory. It was an opportune moment, in the mid-1820s, to address the financial difficulties of Henry Bell, whose *Comet*, launched on the River Clyde in 1812, had provided Britain's first commercial steam-boat service. Edward Morris, distressed by Bell's poverty, campaigned to improve his situation. As a result, Bell received £500 from a public subscription in Glasgow, which was sponsored by the Lord Provost, several local MPs, engineers and others, and the Clyde Trustees were persuaded to double the annual pension they allowed him to £100. Morris found the national and provincial press very supportive, especially the *Liverpool Mercury* and the *Manchester Times*. Although the English public's financial response was generally poor, Liverpool Corporation contributed £20, the London Mechanics' Society collected £11 at its lectures, and several engineers, including Marc Isambard Brunel and William Fawcett, made generous donations.[27] Morris' tone, however, is one of reproach – that more was not done for Bell, especially by the British government and the city of Liverpool – but the usual difficulties of securing a reward were compounded by the fierce dispute among several contenders for the credit of inventing steam navigation.

William Symington had already presented his case to the Lords of the Treasury, securing a payment of £100 (increased on appeal to £150).[28] James Taylor, another pioneer of steam navigation, had extracted an annual pension of £50 from Lord Liverpool's government.[29] Morris

---

[24] John Davies, *A collection of the most important cases respecting patents of invention and the rights of patentees* (London: W. Reed, 1816); Edward Holroyd, *A practical treatise of the law of patents for inventions* (London, 1830).

[25] *Report from the select committee of the House of Lords*, BPP 1851, XVIII, p. 516; see also ibid., p. 384, and Andrew Carnegie, *James Watt* (Edinburgh, 1905), p. 52.

[26] See above, p. 82.   [27] Morris, *Life of Henry Bell*, passim.

[28] W. S. Harvey and G. Downs-Rose, *William Symington, inventor and engine builder* (London: Northgate Publishing Co. Ltd, 1980), p. 152.

[29] This was still being enjoyed by his widow in 1848: Bennet Woodcroft, *A sketch of the origin and progress of steam navigation* (London: Taylor, Walton, & Maberly, 1848), p. 41.

mobilized thirty-five Scottish towns and counties to petition the government on Bell's behalf, which prompted the prime minister, George Canning, to authorize a grant of £200: Morris evidently considered this 'too little, too late'.[30] However, the various sums raised for Bell indicate a growing appreciation of inventors, especially in the localities most immediately benefiting by his activities.[31] Neither was Bell forgotten after his death. A freestone obelisk was erected beside the Clyde at Dunglass in 1839, probably thanks either to Morris or the Clyde Trustees. A second monument, a seated statue of Bell, installed in Rhu churchyard, near Helensburgh, in 1853, was indubitably the gift of the marine engineer, Robert Napier, as a personal testimony of respect and gratitude. Napier was also responsible for the erection of a red granite obelisk, inscribed to Bell, on the esplanade at Helensburgh in 1872; he and Sir James Colquhoun bore most of its £800 cost.[32]

From the 1830s, government patronage was extended retrospectively to inventors and their indigent relations. Initially, this was thanks largely to one minister, Robert Peel. Peel had been closely involved with Watt's commemoration in 1824; he enjoyed friendships with leading men of science and maintained a keen interest in their research, particularly its practical implications.[33] Through his tapping of royal patronage, the early 1830s witnessed a small crop of scientific knighthoods and baronetcies, and Civil List pensions awarded to the astronomers, James South and George Airy, and the chemists, Michael Faraday and John Dalton.[34]

Since the market was generally deemed to be the fairest judge of inventions, no place in this embryonic system of patronage was reserved for inventors. Nonetheless, where market mechanisms had clearly failed to reward a deserving individual, this restriction might be relaxed. William Radcliffe, for example, petitioned Peel for a small grant, as recompense for his invention, many years earlier, of the dressing machine (an important auxiliary to weaving by power). Radcliffe's success, in turn,

---

[30] Morris, *Life of Henry Bell*, pp. 8–9, 94–6. In 1829, the Navy Board rejected Morris' application for a subscription for Bell, on the grounds that it was 'not at liberty to make any grant of money': ADM106/2168b/76/29, National Archives.

[31] Compare the subscription for a memorial to Jenner, above, p. 88.

[32] Brian D. Osborne, *The ingenious Mr Bell: a life of Henry Bell (1767–1830), pioneer of steam navigation* (Glendaruel: Argyll Publishing, 1995), pp. 236, 247–8; Donald MacLeod, *A nonagenarian's reminiscences of Garelochside and Helensburgh* (Helensburgh: Macneur & Bryden, 1883), p. 156.

[33] Roy MacLeod, 'Of models and men: a reward system in Victorian science, 1826–1914', *Notes and Records of the Royal Society of London* 26 (1971), 82.

[34] Roy MacLeod, 'Science and the Civil List, 1824–1914', *Technology and Society* 6 (1970), 50–1.

prompted a request from George Crompton.[35] In 1842, at the age of sixty-one and made redundant during the economic depression, Crompton sought government assistance. His petition, supported by testimonials from leading Lancashire manufacturers, rested on the gross disparity between the spinning mule's supreme importance in Britain's cotton industry and its inventor's limited reward. He repeated the story of his father's bad luck: having never sought a patent, in 1812 Samuel Crompton secured a parliamentary reward of £20,000, only to see it reduced to £5,000 by the ill-timed assassination of the prime minister, Spencer Percival. Thirty years later, several wretched days of lobbying MPs 'in this labrinth [sic] of hope and fear and expenses' paid off: on Peel's recommendation, George received £200 from the Royal Bounty Fund, to be shared equally with his surviving brother and sister.[36] Another exception was made for Henry Fourdrinier's family. His daughter, Harriet, complained that the £7,000 awarded him by Parliament in 1837 had scarcely reduced the debts he had incurred in introducing the paper-making machine to Britain, three decades earlier; poignantly, she asked Lord Brougham for a loan of £10 to tide her over Christmas.[37] Following Brougham's intervention with Palmerston's government, she and her sister received a Civil List pension of £100 per annum.[38] Brougham also helped the daughter of Richard Roberts to secure a royal pension of £200 per annum.[39] A public campaign in the 1850s to relieve the poverty of Henry Cort's now elderly and infirm offspring achieved, however, only a modicum of success.[40]

Hard-luck stories, such as these, which were recounted in the pursuit of grants, pensions, subscriptions and indeed patent reform, helped to create the hero's antithesis – the inventor as victim or martyr, who was reduced to poverty by his unworldly pursuit of novelties or was robbed of his ideas by wealthier or more cunning men.[41] 'Mr Arkwright was a happy mechanic', said one cotton spinner to another in 1787, 'in his lifetime he

---

[35] [Alfred Mallalieu], 'The cotton manufacture', *Blackwood's Edinburgh Magazine* 39 (1836), 411–13.

[36] Crompton MSS, ZCR 63/6–9, 63/11, 63/16, 64/3.

[37] *Report from the select committee on Fourdrinier's patent*, BPP 1837, XX; Harriet Elizabeth Fourdrinier to Lord Brougham [15 December 1856], Brougham MSS, 36,913.

[38] Harriet Elizabeth Fourdrinier to Lord Brougham, 18 July 1859, 3 June 1862, Brougham MSS 5064, 32,968.

[39] *The Builder* 24 (1866), 91.

[40] H. W. Dickinson, 'Henry Cort's bicentenary', *TNS* 21 (1940–1), 45; *JSA* 4 (4 July 1856), 583.

[41] These dual 'obstacle[s] to the beneficial exercise of ... genius' are clearly described in [Anon.], 'On the necessity and means of protecting needy genius', *London Journal of Arts and Sciences* 9 (1825), 317–19.

has received the reward of his ingenuity – it does not happen so in general.'[42] Clare Pettitt cites a long list of sorry descriptions, 'taken from cheap texts and periodicals' that were published between 1827 and the end of the century: the inventor was poor, solitary, persecuted, in need of protection from himself and others, a visionary and a lunatic.[43] (Henry Broadhurst, MP, told the annual dinner of the Inventors' Institute, in 1880, that, if they were too radical in their proposal for reform of the patent system, they would be dismissed as 'mad inventors'.)[44] Such sympathy as these sad tales were designed to elicit was, ironically, a further effect of the growing respect for inventors, which was consequent, in part, upon the celebration of Watt. For, as long as inventors had been seen as 'projectors' or charlatans, it was unlikely that they would ever be viewed in this light. During most of the previous two centuries, they had been regarded as the perpetrators of fraud and deception, not its victims.[45]

Moreover, the dissonance between the new rhetoric, which portrayed the inventor as a major national benefactor, and the frequently heard accusation that he was badly served by a dysfunctional patent system, gave critics of the latter ample scope for outraged condemnation. During the mid-century 'patent controversy', which succeeded the 1852 act, a similar tactic would be adopted in defence of the patent system – as providing the poor inventor's only refuge.[46] It was an easy (and not inaccurate) strategy to portray the inventor as the victim of the state's ingratitude and the capitalist's ruthlessness. In particular, those who were demanding a reduction in the cost of patent protection had good reason to present the inventor in this light: if he were a working man, not only was such expensive protection normally far beyond his means, but he was evidently distinct from the wily capitalist intending to monopolize the trade through cheap patents. Simultaneously, the identification of the inventor with the skilled worker was being promoted in other literatures: by radicals, such as Thomas Hodgskin, who were challenging orthodox political economy; and by liberals, such as Brougham, whose blandishments to workers to follow their educational programmes included the prospect of fame and fortune through invention.[47]

There could be no doubt that the term 'projector' had lost its pejorative force when we find James Watt being described as 'the greatest of our

[42] S. Salte to S. Oldknow, 5 November 1787, quoted in Richard L. Hills, *Power in the industrial revolution* (Manchester: Manchester University Press, 1970), p. 217.
[43] Pettitt, *Patent inventions*, p. 41.
[44] *The Times*, 26 November 1880, 5f.   [45] See above, pp. 33–8.
[46] See below, pp. 253–6.
[47] See above, pp. 161–9, 173–4.

engineers, the projector of a machine'.[48] Nonetheless, the fear of visionary schemers – whether or not they were called 'projectors' – long continued to impair the treatment of inventors; the 'Watt effect' had
limitations. Campaigners urging a reduction in the cost of patents consistently met the objection that cheap patents would lead to a flood of
useless ideas and the mercenary harassment of manufacturers by men
who were either promoting some minor improvement or demanding
satisfaction for the infringement of their patent.[49] While the 1852 act
reduced the initial cost of a patent, it also introduced high renewal fees
(payable to keep it in force), specifically in order to weed out vexatious
patents. The same argument – between access for poor inventors and the
nuisance of 'frivolous' patents – was continually rehearsed in the ensuing
'patent controversy'. At its close, the 1883 Patents, Designs and
Trademarks Act (46 & 47 Vic. c. 57) again dramatically cut the initial
cost of a patent, while retaining the high renewal charges.[50] Without
patent examination, the system was open to abuse by fools and deceivers,
which, throughout the century, Parliament tried to check by the market
mechanism of high fees. Its concern that this sieve, while filtering the gold
from the dross, should not exclude the real-life Old Johns and Daniel
Doyces was expressed in the diminishing initial cost of patent protection.

Indicative of the rising esteem of inventors is their more frequent
appearance in the obituary columns of national newspapers and journals,
in particular *The Times*.[51] Before the mid century, *The Times* noticed the
deaths of only those inventors who were also wealthy industrialists or
distinguished engineers – Smeaton, Arkwright, Wedgwood, Watt,
Rennie, Davy, Telford. Thereafter, even relatively obscure men attracted
the attention of this loftiest of newspapers, simply because they had been
inventors. In July 1851, it published an obituary of Thomas Edmondson
of Manchester, 'the inventor and the patentee of the railway ticket'.
This recounted how Edmondson, in 1839 a station clerk earning
£60 per annum with the Lancashire and Yorkshire Railway Company,
had devised not only the machine to print and number tickets but also an
efficient system of keeping track of railway traffic (the genesis of the
railway clearing house): during the next twelve years, both inventions
were adopted by every railway company in the country. Edmondson rose
to become chief of the audit department – an achievement by itself

---

[48] Fairbairn, 'Rise and progress', p. iv.
[49] [Brewster], 'Decline of science', 335. See also below, p. 265.
[50] MacLeod *et al.*, 'Evaluating inventive activity', 544–7, 560–1.
[51] The *Mechanic's Magazine* published brief obituaries of inventors, as did local newspapers: Pettitt, *Patent inventions*, p. 9n.

normally insufficient to lay claim to an obituary in *The Times*.[52] Edmondson's story captured the imagination of Harriet Martineau, who expanded it for *Household Words*, and forty years later it secured him an entry in the *Dictionary of National Biography*.[53] Many such obituaries were signalled with the by-line 'The Inventor of ...' (electro-plate, or the Bude light, for instance), or simply 'An Inventor' or 'An American Inventor'.[54] When *The Times* failed to print an obituary of Samuel Baldwyn Rogers in 1863, a correspondent corrected the omission. His letter, headed 'The Fate of the Inventor', recounted how this elderly and impoverished Welsh inventor had introduced iron bottoms for puddling furnaces: at first treated with derision, Rogers' valuable invention was 'now universally adopted'.[55]

Moreover, the content of obituaries changed, to take much greater account of their subject's inventive achievements. An article on Patrick Miller, written by his grandson, quoted his obituary from 1815: it praised his great mental powers and 'moral character', but made no direct reference to his many inventions and his experiments with steam navigation during the 1780s and 90s.[56] By contrast, when John Heathcoat died in 1861, his obituary devoted one sentence to his thirty years' uninterrupted service in the House of Commons and the remaining half-column of text to his invention, fifty years earlier, of lace-making machinery and his consequent manufacturing success. It heralded him as

one of those men of remarkable constructive genius who, towards the end of the last and in the early part of the present century, by their inventive powers so improved our machinery and increased its productiveness as to lay the foundation, deep and strong, of our present manufacturing greatness.[57]

Similarly, the obituary of H. D. P. Cunningham dealt only briefly with his distinguished career in the Royal Navy, as a prelude to carefully detailing

---

[52] *The Times*, 19 July 1851, 5f.

[53] Harriet Martineau, 'The English passport system', *Household Words* 6 (1852), 31–4; J. Holyoake, 'Edmondson, Thomas (1792–1851)', rev. Philip S. Bagwell, *ODNB*, online edn, May 2006, www.oxforddnb.com/view/article/8492, accessed 18 October 2006; MacLeod and Nuvolari, 'Pitfalls of prosopography', 757–76.

[54] *The Times*, 5 December 1865, 9c; 8 March 1875, 6b; 4 February 1876, 5f; 3 May 1877, 11a; 25 May 1877, 4e.

[55] *The Times*, 16 September 1863, 7d.

[56] [W. H. Miller], 'Patrick Miller', in William Anderson (ed.), *The Scottish nation: or, the surnames, families, literature, honours, and biographical history of the people of Scotland* (Edinburgh: Fullarton, 1862), quoting *The Caledonian Mercury*, 14 December 1815, Woodcroft MSS, Z27B, fo. 497, Science Museum Library.

[57] *The Times*, 26 January 1861, 12d.

his numerous inventions: he was best known as 'the inventor of the "self-reefing topsail"', which had reduced the hazards of life at sea.[58]

Richard Arkwright, the Napoleon of the factory system

In the first half of the nineteenth century, Arkwright's was the name most commonly coupled with Watt's – apart, of course, from that of his business partner, Matthew Boulton's – and in the second, it was George Stephenson's.[59] Although the stories of both Arkwright and Stephenson remain familiar today, the history of their respective reputations differs a great deal. In the remainder of this chapter, we shall explore why it was Stephenson, not Arkwright, who came to share Watt's laurels and thus reinforce both the early Victorians' image of the inventor as an engineer and the steam engine's position at the heart of their technological narrative.

In 1820, Lord Liverpool told Parliament that 'England was indebted for its present greatness' to men such as Watt, Boulton and Arkwright.[60] Similarly, the novelist John Galt, defending mechanized industry against the charge of creating unemployment, referred to 'the boon that mankind received from the genius of Arkwright and Watt'.[61] George Philips' grandiloquent speech in Manchester, in July 1824, linked Watt's names with Arkwright's and Crompton's, as the progenitors of Manchester's success. To Dr Robert Vaughan, a conservative critic, Arkwright and Watt typified modern utilitarian science, as Plato and Aristotle symbolized the ancient tradition.[62] And Thomas Carlyle paired, as the dreadful personifications of modern industry, 'Watt of the Steam engine ... this man with blackened fingers, with grim brow ... searching out, in his workshop, the Fire-secret' with Arkwright, the 'bag-cheeked, potbellied, much-enduring, much-inventing barber' who gave England 'the power of cotton'.[63] It was also Watt, Arkwright and Crompton, whom a very

---

[58] *The Times*, 23 January 1875, 5e. See also 'The inventor of the heliograph', *The Times*, 9 January 1883, 4d.

[59] The British executive of the commission for the Paris Exhibition of 1867 had window blinds designed for the machinery gallery that showed the inventions of Watt, Stephenson, Arkwright and William Hedley: Leone Levi, *History of British commerce and of the economic progress of the British nation, 1763–1870* (London, 1872), p. 444.

[60] Hansard, *P.D.*, 2nd ser., I (1820), 421.

[61] 'Bandana' [John Galt], 'Hints to the country gentleman', *Blackwood's Edinburgh Magazine* 12 (1822), 489. I am grateful to Will Hardy for this reference.

[62] Robert Vaughan, D. D., *The age of great cities: or, modern society viewed in its relation to intelligence, morals, and religion* (London: Jackson & Walford, 1843), p. 112. For Philips, see above, pp. 116–17.

[63] Carlyle, *Chartism*, pp. 181–5.

different section of society, the Amalgamated Society of Engineers, Machinists, Millwrights, Smiths and Pattern Makers (formed in 1851), chose to represent in its intricately designed membership certificate.[64] Of course, Arkwright was also praised singly and in the company of other textile inventors.

Given the cotton industry's rise to prominence since the late eighteenth century, Arkwright might have been expected to enjoy an even greater celebrity.[65] At his death in 1792, there had been a proposal for Manchester to erect a statue, which was revived by the engineer, William Fairbairn, in 1836, but nothing was done.[66] Neither was he publicly commemorated anywhere in Britain during the 1850s and 60s, when the erection of monuments to Watt and other inventors proceeded apace.[67] Why was Arkwright impeded at the threshold of the national pantheon?

Just as Watt lacked admirers among his immediate rivals in business, so Arkwright's reputation suffered from the politics of patents and perhaps professional jealousy.[68] Indeed, it may have suited some Mancunians in 1824 to submerge Arkwright's claims on their gratitude beneath a show of admiration for Watt and to establish 'this man with blackened fingers' as the city's true benefactor. A charge of hypocrisy was always likely to greet any monument to Arkwright there, for it was Manchester cotton spinners, under the leadership of Sir Robert Peel (father of the politician), who combined to defeat Arkwright's patents in the 1780s.[69] Never generous in their remuneration of inventors, they found Arkwright's high licence fees intolerable and determined to break his hold over the industry. In a successful legal challenge, they maintained that Arkwright was not the inventor of his cotton-spinning machinery but the plagiarist of other men's ideas.[70] By contrast, Arkwright's claim was supported by a succession of Scots, who argued that he had been deprived unjustly of his patents. North of the border, where Arkwright's process had helped the younger Lanarkshire cotton industry to compete against Lancashire's, he was even rewarded with the freedom of the cities of Glasgow and Perth.[71]

---

[64] See below, pp. 286–7.   [65] See above, pp. 64–5.
[66] *The Times*, 8 August, 1792, 3b; Fairbairn, *Observations*, p. 17.
[67] See below, pp. 230–8, 290–314.   [68] See above, p. 107.
[69] Arthur Redford, *Manchester merchants and foreign trade, 1794–1858* (Manchester: Manchester University Press, 1934), p. 5; Hewish, 'From Cromford to Chancery Lane', pp. 85–6. Cf. James Butterworth, *The antiquities of the town and a complete history of the trade of Manchester* (Manchester, 1822), p. 46.
[70] Hewish, 'From Cromford to Chancery Lane', pp. 80–6.
[71] David J. Jeremy, 'British and American entrepreneurial values in the early nineteenth century: a parting of the ways', in R. A. Burchell (ed.), *The end of Anglo-America: historical essays in the study of cultural divergence* (Manchester: Manchester University Press, 1991), pp. 34, 39.

The controversy was re-ignited in 1823, when Richard Guest resurrected the case that Thomas Highs had invented the water-frame (the spinning machine patented by Arkwright), and a fierce battle between the two major centres of the cotton industry ensued: Lancastrians renewed their accusations; Scots protested Arkwright's innocence and his genius.[72] Even among Arkwright's few supporters in Lancashire, émigré Scots were prominent: John Kennedy, an inventive and influential cotton spinner and machine maker, resident in Lancashire since the 1790s, was especially concerned for the reputation of his fellow inventors (Watt and Crompton as well as Arkwright).[73] Crompton's grandson believed that 'though Mr Kennedy was a great friend of my grandfather's, he was intimate with the Arkwrights', and that it was Kennedy who persuaded the political economist, J. R. McCulloch, to damn Guest's attack on Arkwright, in the *Edinburgh Review*.[74] It was also Kennedy's paper in defence of Arkwright that prompted Fairbairn (another Scot) to propose that Manchester erect a statue to him in 1836.[75] But Arkwright's Scottish apologists were unable to clear his name: although popular accounts continued (and continue still) to credit him with the invention of the water-frame, in more specialist literatures the doubts lingered. An article published by the Inventors' Institute referred scornfully to 'the Arkwright class of pseudo-inventors, the men of business'.[76]

Despite this ambiguity, Arkwright's fame persisted. His was too good a story to lose: it offered the quintessential tale of upward social mobility, from impoverished barber to fabulously wealthy knight of the shire. It was Arkwright's portrait that R. A. Davenport chose as the frontispiece to his *Lives of individuals who raised themselves from poverty to eminence or fortune* (1841). Davenport paid little attention to Arkwright's technical achievements, more to his entrepreneurial and managerial talents.[77] (Except for James Brindley, Davenport's other seventeen cases of 'self-exaltation' were mostly literary or military figures.) Many authors similarly rested their case on Arkwright's entrepreneurial and innovatory talents, and recommended his methods as a sure route to social advancement. At

---

[72] Ibid., pp. 35–9; Guest, *Compendious history of the cotton manufacture*, pp. 3–4.
[73] See below, p. 298.
[74] Samuel Crompton to Gilbert French [1859], Crompton MSS, ZCR 74/4.
[75] Fairbairn, *Observations*, p. 17.
[76] Thomas Richardson, 'A review of the arguments for and against the patent laws', *The Scientific Review, and Journal of the Inventors' Institute* 2 (1 April 1867), 224. See also the lecture by Frederic Warren to the Society of Arts, reported in *The Spectator* (19 February 1853), which attracted a letter in Arkwright's defence from 'Z. Z.' in the *Manchester Guardian* [1853]: Crompton MSS, ZCR 69/6; Tann, 'Richard Arkwright and technology', 29–44.
[77] Davenport, *Lives of individuals*, p. 434.

the time, this was not an exceptional way to consider inventors. From the late 1820s, the SDUK, under Brougham's leadership, pioneered biographies of inventors and engineers, but its prospectus shows it did not yet conceive of a separate 'technological' category. It announced a series of 'History of individuals' that was to comprise patriots, warriors, discoverers, self-exalted men, moral philosophers, navigators and statesmen. The twelve discoverers were chemists, such as Lavoisier and Black, or physicists, such as Galileo and Newton, with the addition of Bacon and Harvey. The inventors and engineers provided the chief exemplars of a different category, 'self-exalted' or socially mobile men, defined not by their profession or achievement but by the fact of their socio-economic ascent: Sir Richard Arkwright, Benjamin Franklin, John Rennie, John Smeaton, James Watt and Sir Christopher Wren.[78] This was evidently Brougham's perception of the principal value of these biographies: 'men who have greatly altered their situation by force of merit ... making the ground of division or classification *self-exaltation* rather than self-education, though they often will coincide'.[79]

Maria Edgeworth ignored the accusations of plagiarism completely, to offer her young readers an uncomplicated picture of a man whose 'inventions and improvements' – but, above all, his perseverance – had secured him an 'immense fortune' and (she wrongly implied) a knighthood.[80] Other authors contended that, even if there were substance to the charge of plagiarism, it could not diminish Arkwright's merit as the innovator, as the man who saw the project through to successful completion. According to Craik, for example, without Arkwright the invention would probably have come to nothing, for nobody else 'had the determination and courage to face the multiple fatigues and dangers' of setting it to work; his portrait formed the frontispiece to Craik's second volume.[81] Andrew Ure, who admired Arkwright's strategic grasp and managerial skills, notoriously saw him as the Napoleon of the factory system.[82] And J. R. McCulloch, despite his initial defence of Arkwright's claim to authorship of the inventions, retreated to a similar position in 1835, in

---

[78] *Society for the Diffusion of Useful Knowledge*, appended to [Brougham], *Discourse of objects*.
[79] Knight, *Passages of a working life*, vol. II, p. 134, quoted in Travers, *Smiles*, p. 358; original emphasis.
[80] See above, p. 65 n. 26.
[81] [Craik], *Pursuit of knowledge*, vol. II, p. 338. See also, Edgeworth, *Harry and Lucy*, vol. I, pp. 229–30; Davenport, *Lives of individuals*, pp. 433–4; *Gallery of portraits*, vol. V, pp. 181–8.
[82] Andrew Ure, *Philosophy of manufactures: or, an exposition of the scientific, moral, and commercial economy of the factory system of Great Britain* (London, 1835), p. 16. For Napoleon's reputation in nineteenth-century Britain, see Pears, 'The gentleman and the hero', pp. 216–36.

the face of Edward Baines' case that John Wyatt had been the first to invent the process of spinning by rollers.[83] Another commentator even made a virtue out of Arkwright's lack of inventive talent:

He was largely endowed with those powers of enterprise ... and that unquenchable ardour for action, so rarely found [with] the accompanying attributes of inventive talent, which, musing in its studio or brooding over mechanical combinations in its workshop, becomes unfitted for the jostle of the world beyond.[84]

Similarly, Francis Espinasse told his audience, at Manchester's Mechanics Institute in 1849, that Arkwright was 'an uneducated genius', who rose to fame and fortune 'as a manager, not a contriver'; it was true that he took other men's inventions, but what of it? Crassly denying any notion of intellectual property, Espinasse suggested that invention was but a minor talent compared with the 'genius' required to 'manage men'.[85] Lancashire, he proposed, should act quickly to preserve Arkwright's heritage: it should buy his Cromford mill (no matter that it was in Derbyshire?), and appoint one of its poets or novelists to collect biographical material and write 'an Arkwrightiad – a serio-comic epic'. It would probably be a light-hearted affair for, although without Arkwright and his cotton 'Napoleon could not have been put down', there were few epics whose heroes had started life 'shaving chins in the town of Preston'.[86]

Less disposed to consider Arkwright so benignly, Karl Marx distinguished sharply between the two men whom his contemporaries usually credited with the rise of manufactures. While Marx admired 'the greatness of Watt's genius', he took advantage of the charge of plagiarism to vilify Arkwright: 'Of all the great inventors of the eighteenth century, he was unquestionably the greatest thief of other people's inventions and the meanest character.'[87] It was as the creator of the factory system that Marx ultimately condemned him: the cotton-spinning machinery, which Arkwright introduced, epitomized the goal of deskilling that was inherent in new technology; it showed the way to the emasculation and

---

[83] [J. R. McCulloch], 'Philosophy of manufactures', *Edinburgh Review* 61 (1835), 471. Baines himself accorded Arkwright considerable credit for his mechanical improvements and adaptations and his great entrepreneurial talents: *Gallery of portraits*, vol. V p. 187.

[84] [Mallalieu], 'Cotton manufacture', 407.

[85] Espinasse, 'Lancashire industrialism', pp. 204, 207. See also Gilbert J. French, *The life and times of Samuel Crompton, inventor of the spinning machine called the mule* (London: Simpkin, Marshall & Co., 1859), pp. 96–7.

[86] Espinasse, 'Lancashire industrialism', p. 205.

[87] Karl Marx, *Capital: a critique of political economy*, intro. Ernest Mandel, trans. Ben Fowkes (Harmondsworth: Penguin and New Left Review, 1976), pp. 499, 549n.

impoverishment of the working class.[88] Possibly Marx exculpated Watt because his connection with the factory system was less direct. Although the steam engine was becoming an increasingly important source of power in textile factories, in supplying them Watt profited only indirectly from the factory system. As an engine-maker and employer, he provided new opportunities for male skilled workers; as an inventor, he could be applauded for his combination of intellectual and manual abilities (a worker by both hand and brain) – with never, of course, a hint of plagiarism.[89]

The romance of the railways

It was not the cotton lords but the civil engineers who first took up Watt's heroic mantle and helped to reinforce the identification of invention with mechanics and engineering. The railway builders, in particular, generated technological excitement – and terror. Whether they provoked anxious ribaldry or optimistic awe, they were rarely out of the public gaze. Unlike the stationary steam engine, which, being confined to the mill and the mine, was known to most only by its reputed effects, the locomotive engine and its tracks were eminently visible. They affected the mass of the population far more immediately.[90] Railways remodelled the landscape – the rural and remote as much as the urban and metropolitan. They offered everyone the thrill and convenience of rapid travel, the prospect of new experiences, and access to fresh produce and fresh news. They attracted artists, who celebrated the latest developments in railway architecture and locomotives, and cartoonists, who envisaged death and destruction in the headlong pursuit of progress.[91] Other cartoons predicted crumbling coaching inns and, more fancifully, redundant horses busking or begging for their living, while equine skeletons littered the countryside (figure 7.2). A pictorial handkerchief from the early 1830s, entitled 'The Century of Inventions anno domini 2000, Or the March of Aerostation, Steam, and Perpetual Motion', illustrated (not too inaccurately) a townscape choked by steam carriages, its skies thronging with steam-propelled balloons and wing-powered men; even its buildings were

---

[88] See above, p. 41, for machinery-breaking attacks on Arkwright's factories.
[89] Torrens, 'Jonathan Hornblower', pp. 28–34.
[90] Wolfgang Schivelbusch, *The railway journey: the industrialization of time and space in the 19th century* (Leamington Spa, Hamburg, New York: Berg, 1986), pp. 52–69, and passim. For a similar case of 'unapologetic' romanticizing, see Iwan Rhys Morus, '"The nervous system of Britain": space, time and the electric telegraph in the Victorian age', *BJHS* 33 (2000), 463.
[91] Freeman, *Railways and the Victorian imagination*, pp. 215–39, and passim.

7.2 *Effects of the Railroad on the Brute Creation*, 1831, a cartoon predicting that Britain's equine population would be obliterated by the railways. On the contrary, there was a massive rise in the horse population to transport goods and passengers to and from railway stations.

on wheels, progressing over a viaduct.[92] *Punch* appeared in 1841, in time to track the railway 'mania' of the 1840s. While directing its satire at the twin dangers of investing in and travelling on the railways, its underlying faith in them as the epitome of progress often made it the cheerleader for the railway engineers, especially Robert Stephenson.[93]

The two father-and-son partnerships, Marc and Isambard Kingdom Brunel, and George and Robert Stephenson, became celebrities during the second quarter of the nineteenth century.[94] Both had a talent for

[92] *Not to be sneezed at: images of London on pocket handkerchiefs*, Exhibition at the Guildhall Library, London, 1995. See also M. Dorothy George, *Hogarth to Cruikshank: social change in graphic satire* (London: Allen Lane, 1967), pp. 177–84; Julie Wosk, *Breaking frame: technology and the visual arts in the nineteenth century* (New Brunswick, NJ: Rutgers University Press, 1992), pp. 30–66.

[93] Noakes, 'Representing "A Century of Inventions"', pp. 155, 161.

[94] Celebrity status was itself a novel phenomenon in the early nineteenth century, promoted by the industrialization of printing: Tom Mole, 'Are celebrities a thing of the past?', www.bris.ac.uk/researchreview/2005/1115994436, accessed 13 May 2005.

self-publicity.[95] With Marc's name already well known for his Portsmouth block-making machinery, the two Brunels caught the public's imagination with their ambitious scheme for a tunnel beneath the Thames (using the tunnelling shield patented by Marc), which they regularly 'puffed' in print and, in 1827, by an elaborate banquet inside the tunnel workings.[96] Despite fatal inundations and other costly accidents, which helped to fuel the public's curiosity, the tunnel was finally opened in 1843 and secured a knighthood for Marc Brunel. The Tunnel Company issued a commemorative medallion, displaying Marc's heroic profile (figure 7.3). For nearly a decade, the tunnel's brightly lit roadways, crowded with stalls, anticipated the Crystal Palace as London's major tourist attraction and supplied a souvenir trade, which depicted the Brunels' stupendous achievement on everything from plates to lithographed peepshows.[97] By then, Isambard's acclaimed Great Western Railway was on the verge of completion and his powerful steamship, the ss *Great Western*, had confounded the sceptics and demonstrated the commercial viability of transatlantic steam shipping.[98]

Meanwhile, the Manchester and Liverpool Railway, opened in 1830, made the name of George and Robert Stephenson. The construction of this and subsequent schemes provoked incessant coverage in the press and an enormous demand for souvenirs, prints, games and toys.[99] George Stephenson's portrait by John Lucas celebrates his conquest of Chat

[95] Jack Simmons (ed.), *The men who built railways: a reprint of F. R. Conder's Personal Recollections of English Engineers* (London: Thomas Telford, Ltd, 1983), preface, p. 1; *The Times*, 1 August 1844, 6a.

[96] M. M. Chrimes, J. Elton, J. May, T. Millett (eds.), *The triumphant bore: a celebration of Marc Brunel's Thames Tunnel* (London: Science Museum, 1993), pp. 25–9; Andrew Nahum, 'Marc Isambard Brunel', in Andrew Kelly and Melanie Kelly (eds.), *Brunel, in love with the impossible: A celebration of the life, work and legacy of Isambard Kingdom Brunel* (Bristol: Bristol Cultural Development Partnership, 2006), pp. 40–56; Christine MacLeod, 'The nineteenth-century engineer as cultural hero', in ibid., pp. 62–5; Iwan Rhys Morus, 'Manufacturing nature: science, technology and Victorian consumer culture', *BJHS* 29 (1996), 423–4.

[97] Richard Trench and Ellis Hillman, *London under London: a subterranean guide*, (2nd edn, London: John Murray, 1993), pp. 104–15; Chrimes *et al.*, *The triumphant bore*, pp. 21–3; Michael Chrimes, 'The engineering of the Thames Tunnel', in Eric Kentley, Angie Hudson and James Peto (eds.), *Isambard Kingdom Brunel: recent works*, (London: Design Museum, 2000), pp. 26–33. For a critique in verse, see James Smith, 'The Thames Tunnel', in *Comic Miscellanies* (1840), *Literature on line*: http://lion.chadwick.co.uk/.

[98] Steven Brindle, 'The Great Western Railway', in Kelly and Kelly (eds.), *Brunel, in love with the impossible*, pp. 133–55; Andrew Lambert, 'ss *Great Britain*', ibid., pp. 165–6.

[99] Freeman, *Railways and the Victorian imagination*, pp. 73, 203–13. Souvenirs, etc., are on display, for example, in the Greater Manchester Museum of Science and Industry, the National Railway Museum, York, and in the 'Making of the Modern World' gallery of the Science Museum, London.

7.3 The Thames Tunnel Company's medallion of Sir Marc Isambard Brunel, issued to commemorate the Tunnel's opening, is supported in this engraving from *The Illustrated London News* by one of the Tunnel excavators (photograph by Ann Pethers).

Moss – the severest technical challenge he faced in the line's construction. When he died in 1848, subscribers were offered 'whole-length' engravings of it, by T. L. Atkinson, at prices from two to six guineas (figure 7.4).[100] His death was timely. Coincident with the development of a national rail network (the product of the 'railway mania' of the mid 1840s), it provided the occasion finally to construct a figure of heroic stature to rival Watt. Stephenson was widely perceived as the pioneer of Britain's railway system, the period's most acclaimed technical innovation, an engineer whose firm's steam locomotives put him in the direct line of succession from Watt, and whose reputation was burnished for a further decade by his son, Robert's achievements. In 1847, Stephenson had been the natural choice of the Institution of Mechanical Engineers for its first president; in 1849, Robert was elected to succeed him.[101] His renown was already a major asset to the nascent engineering profession as

---

[100] *George Stephenson*, line engraving by T. L. Atkinson (1849), after John Lucas (1847): printed advertisement by Messrs Henry Graves & Co., with obituaries and order form [1849], Institution of Mechanical Engineers, London; *The Times*, 5 June 1849, 5f.
[101] Buchanan, *The engineers*, pp. 80–2.

7.4 Portrait of George Stephenson at Chat Moss, on the Manchester and
Liverpool Railway; mezzotint engraving by Thomas Lewis Atkinson, after
an oil painting by John Lucas, c. 1830.

well as to the railway companies. Following his death, both groups were
reluctant to relinquish this advantage.

Two commemorative projects were soon initiated by Stephenson's
former patrons and colleagues. The directors of the London and North
Western Railway negotiated a site, in the recently completed St George's
Hall in Liverpool, for a statue of 'heroic size' by John Gibson, which they
had commissioned 'some years since' (prior to Stephenson's death),

apparently from company funds.[102] They chose to celebrate Stephenson as a classical intellectual, not as a great railway engineer, for his seated figure is clad in a Roman toga and holds a tablet in one hand, a pair of dividers in the other, but its style was in keeping with the Hall's neo-classical architecture (figure 7.5).[103] Meanwhile, the Institution of Mechanical Engineers launched a subscription to celebrate its first president with a marble statue in the grand hall of Euston station. With the £3,000 it quickly raised among its members and Stephenson's other friends and admirers (including 3,150 working men), it commissioned a ten-foot high statue, from Edward Baily, of the engineer in modern dress and holding plans or drawings in his right hand (figure 7.6).[104] Of particular interest is *The Times'* complaint, when this statue was inaugurated in April 1854, that the event understated the significance of its subject. 'Without much ceremonial observance,' the statue had been unveiled 'in the presence only of the more active members of the committee'. Yet Stephenson, *The Times* acknowledged, was 'a man who stands more nearly and intimately associated with the spirit of the 19th century than we are yet willing to recognize'; his 'life possesses an interest of the highest order'; his rise from 'a "hurrier" in a coal-pit shed, by the force of native genius ... may well be regarded as proof that the days of romance are not yet over'. In effect, with this modest ceremony, the engineering profession had failed to proclaim its own rising status, leaving *The Times* to conclude (with undue pessimism): 'Perhaps it is to be viewed as a characteristic of the age that the fame of such a man is so quietly left to the good keeping of the works which he had achieved.'[105]

In the construction of his reputation, however, George Stephenson was doubly fortunate. The engineers' grand gesture in marble, which kept him in the eye of the travelling public, was to be arrayed with human

---

[102] *The Times*, 27 March 1851, 8b; Smiles, *Lives of the engineers*, p. 354; Martin Greenwood, 'Gibson, John (1790–1866)', *ODNB*, www.oxforddnb.com/view/article/10625, accessed 18 October 2006.

[103] Sir Nikolaus Pevsner, *Lancashire: I, The industrial and commercial south* (Harmondsworth: Penguin, 1969), pp. 156–7; my thanks to Gillian Clarke for this observation on the classical references. Stephenson's statue in St George's Hall was joined, in 1874, by one to Henry Booth (1788–1869), the chief promoter of the Liverpool and Manchester Railway, who was also an inventor (it is his pedestal that bears a drawing of the *Rocket*): Cavanagh, *Public sculpture of Liverpool*, pp. 292–4.

[104] *The Times*, 17 December 1851, 7f ; 3 January 1853, 5f; 11 April 1854, 10a; Katharine Eustace, 'Baily, Edward Hodges (1788–1867)', *ODNB*, online edn, October 2005, www.oxforddnb.com/view/article/1076, accessed 18 October 2006; the statue may now be seen in the National Railway Museum, York. For the workers' contributions, see Chapter 10 below.

[105] *The Times*, 11 April 1854, 10a. For another early paean to civil engineering, see *Edinburgh Review* 141 (October 1839), 47.

7.5 Marble statue of George Stephenson, as a classical intellectual or engineer, by John Gibson, in St George's Hall, Liverpool, 1851.

interest through the biographical talent of Samuel Smiles. It was Smiles, sharing *The Times'* faith in the intrinsic interest of Stephenson's life and work, who revealed to the engineering profession that it had a large audience, eager for more information about the men who were recasting its social world. Having often heard Stephenson talk at 'soirees' in the Leeds Mechanics Institute, where he was 'a great favourite', Smiles wrote a brief obituary for *Eliza Cook's Journal*.[106] Its republication in a number of newspapers prompted him to consider writing a full-length biography.

---

[106] MacKay (ed.), *Autobiography of Samuel Smiles*, p. 135. For 'the sentimental *Eliza Cook's Journal* (1849–54)', see Peter Roger Mountjoy, 'The working-class press and working-class conservatism', in George Boyce, James Curran and Pauline Wingate (eds.), *Newspaper history from the seventeenth century to the present day* (London: Constable, and Beverly Hills: Sage Publications, 1978), pp. 267, 273–4.

7.6 Marble statue of George Stephenson by Edward Baily, 1854; photographed in the grand hall of Euston Station, London, 1890.

At first, he had difficulty in persuading Robert Stephenson to support the project: "'If people get a railroad,' said Stephenson, "it is all that they want: they do not care how or by whom it is made. Look at the *Life of Telford*, a very interesting man: it has ... fallen stillborn from the press.'"[107] Convinced that Telford's biography had failed because of its dry, technical approach, Smiles determined that his life of Stephenson 'would endeavour to treat of his character as a man as well as an engineer'.[108] Despite his reservations, Robert supplied Smiles with many of the anecdotes and details that made this possible. *The life of George Stephenson* was published in 1857 to widespread acclaim, with the result that five editions (7,500 copies) were printed in little over a year.[109]

---

[107] MacKay (ed.), *Autobiography of Samuel Smiles*, p. 162. The reference was to J. Rickman (ed.), *Life of Thomas Telford, civil engineer, written by himself* (London: Payne & Foss, 1838), reviewed in *Edinburgh Review* 141 (1839), 5.

[108] MacKay (ed.), *Autobiography of Samuel Smiles*, p. 163. For Smiles' research and writing of *The Life*, see ibid., p. 216.

[109] By 1900, Smiles estimated 60,000 copies had been sold in Britain alone: ibid., pp. 221, 223. Cf. Oswald Dodd Hedley, *Who invented the locomotive engine? With a review of*

The biography's publication was opportune, for, in 1857, *The Builder* denounced the proposal by Newcastle upon Tyne's corporation to demolish George Stephenson's cottage (Robert Stephenson's birthplace), to make way for a new school. Just as it would now be deemed 'a sort of sacrilege to destroy' the birthplaces of Shakespeare and Newton, it protested, Newcastle should assume that, 'as the years roll on, the fame of George Stephenson will increase' and, in its turn, attract thousands of visitors to the city.[110] By the time that the Stephenson Memorial School at Willington Quay was opened with great fanfare, in 1860, it had become a memorial to both Stephensons; Robert, a major benefactor, had died in October 1859.[111] Although the cottage had been demolished, George Stephenson's birthplace, at Wylam, was explicitly preserved.[112]

Indeed, the Stephensons' reputation was firmly rooted on Tyneside: both George and Robert were born and lived most of their lives there, and their locomotive workshops (Robert Stephenson & Co.) provided an important source of employment. Long before his railway exploits brought him to national attention, George had been fêted locally for the invention of a miners' safety lamp. Humphry Davy's simultaneous invention won the contest for historical celebrity but it was much disputed at the time. The north east's mine owners showed their support for Stephenson, in 1818, by subscribing £1,000 to hold a banquet and present him with an expensive piece of plate, 'for the valuable service he has rendered to science and humanity, by the invention of his safety-lamp'.[113]

Newcastle's principal memorial to George Stephenson resulted from a public meeting, called in October 1858. According to Thomas Oliver, a local architect, this gathering 'largely represented the wealthy and scientific classes of the northern counties': chaired by Lord Ravensworth, its timing (at 2 p.m.) precluded the attendance of those who had to work for their living. Oliver detected considerable enthusiasm for a memorial in the city, but also disagreement over the form it should take, which, he

Smiles's Life of Stephenson (London: Ward & Lock, 1858), in which William Hedley's son advanced his father's (and others') claims to the invention, detailing what he considered to be Smiles' many errors.

[110] *The Builder* 15 (1857), 581. See also ibid., 598, and the engraving of the cottage and disapproving text in *ILN* 33 (9 October 1858), 323–4.

[111] *The Times*, 14 February 1860, 12f.

[112] *The Times*, 10 June 1881, 7e. George Stephenson's birthplace is now in the keeping of the National Trust, which is testimony to his standing today.

[113] *The Times*, 20 January 1818, 3c–d, repr. from the *Newcastle Chronicle*; 'Account of resolutions made by the committee for remuneration of George Stephenson for the safety lamp, including list of subscribers', Institution of Mechanical Engineers, IMS129/fo.7. A silver tankard, in the Institution's keeping, is inscribed as having been purchased out of the £1,000 subscribed for George Stephenson. See also above, p. 79.

believed, might have been diffused by proper public consultation.[114] Robert Stephenson reportedly favoured 'a terrestrial globe as the pedestal, by way of typifying the world-wide extension of the railway system'.[115] Oliver himself had strong views: it should be a grand monument, preferably in the Gothic style, which would 'adorn' one of the city's open spaces, not a small statue perched on one end of the High Level Bridge. Nor did he think it should be an arch, since arches were associated with military victors, while Stephenson's 'conquests were peaceful' and his 'victories ... beneficent [and] ... bloodless'. Instead, Oliver proposed 'an architectural canopy ... within which, on a sculptured pedestal dated by his inventions, artistically, and perhaps somewhat emblematically arranged, would stand the man himself as he appeared in the midst of us'.[116]

Nearly £5,000 was subscribed in six months.[117] The monument, designed by John G. Lough, avoided some of the worst solecisms that Oliver had feared, but was essentially neoclassical in style.[118] Stephenson's bronze figure does not wear a toga, though his loose-fitting clothes with a Northumberland plaid over one shoulder certainly hint at such classical attire; standing thirty-feet high on a stone pedestal, from the ground his features become indistinct. At its base, four reclining figures, with indisputably classical heads, bear emblems of his inventive and engineering achievements: a miner carrying a safety ('Geordie') lamp, an engine-driver leaning on a locomotive, a plate-layer holding a 'fish-bellied' rail, and a blacksmith with hammer and anvil (figure 7.7).[119] The monument was erected in Neville Street, close to the railway station: according to Smiles, it was 'a very thoroughfare of working-men, thousands of whom see it daily as they pass to and fro from their work'. He thought it 'unquestionably the finest and most appropriate statue' to Stephenson's memory; *The Builder* commended its realism and reported that it found

---

[114] Thomas Oliver, Architect, *The Stephenson monument: what should it be? A question and answer addressed to the subscribers* (3rd edn, Newcastle upon Tyne: M. & M. W. Lambert, 1858), pp. 5–6. See also *The Times*, 29 October 1858, 8e. For Oliver, see Robert Colls, 'Remembering George Stephenson: genius and modern memory', in Robert Colls and Bill Lancaster (eds.), *Newcastle upon Tyne: a modern history* (Chichester: Phillimore, 2001), p. 276. For Ravensworth, see W. A. J. Archbold, 'Liddell, Henry Thomas, first earl of Ravensworth (1797–1878)', rev. H. C. G. Matthew, *ODNB*, www.oxforddnb.com/view/article/16641, accessed 18 October 2006.

[115] *The Builder* 17 (1859), 599.

[116] Oliver, *Stephenson monument*, pp. 6, 8–9, 12–13, 16.

[117] *The Builder* 17 (1859), 240, 317; Colls, 'Remembering George Stephenson', p. 275.

[118] Colls, 'Remembering George Stephenson', pp. 278–83; P. Usherwood, J. Beach, and C. Morris, *Public sculpture of north-east England* (Liverpool: Liverpool University Press, 2000), pp. 149–52.

[119] *ILN* 41 (1 November 1862), p. 456; see also *ILN* 91 (16 July 1887), 79, 81.

7.7 Monument to George Stephenson, by John Graham Lough, 1862, in Neville Street, Newcastle upon Tyne; engraving from *The Illustrated London News* (photograph by Ann Pethers). Unfortunately, it is now overshadowed by a modern office block.

widespread approval.[120] The celebrations that marked its unveiling, in 1862, contrasted sharply with Euston's simple ceremony eight years

[120] Smiles, *Lives of the engineers*, pp. 355–6; *The Builder* 18 (1860), 204; ibid., 19 (1861), 468; see also *The Times*, 15 September 1862, 10b, and below, pp. 293–6. Cf. Colls, 'Remembering George Stephenson', pp. 283, 287.

earlier. With a general holiday declared on Tyneside, an estimated 70,000 people attended the festivities, including 'almost every person of eminence connected with the trade of the north'. A procession of 10,000, containing many employees of Robert Stephenson & Co. and members of the region's trade unions and friendly societies, took half an hour to file through the city centre.[121]

The north east's pride in George Stephenson is evinced by other contemporary memorials, both private and public. He appears in the decorative scheme for the newly converted courtyard at Wallington House (Northumberland), home of the staunchly Liberal Trevelyan family. On its walls, the young Pre-Raphaelite painter, William Bell Scott of Newcastle, depicted the Whig idea of progress, through the region's history from the Roman Wall to the industrious present day – illustrated in 'Iron and Coal' (1856–61). In this final scene, 'Charles Edward Trevelyan himself, the heir to Wallington, raises a sledgehammer as an equal alongside the brawny ironworkers of Stephenson's and Hawk's and Crawshaw's.'[122] The many industrial references in 'Iron and Coal' include a 'Geordie' lamp and Robert Stephenson's High Level Bridge, in Newcastle, with a locomotive puffing across it. Above, the portrait medallions in the roof spandrels depict associated historical figures, from the emperor Hadrian to George Stephenson – by implication, at the acme of progress.[123] In 1858, the sculptor Edward W. Wyon, of London, presented copies of his busts of both Stephensons, to be displayed in Newcastle's town hall. George's had been paid for by his nephew, G. R. Stephenson; Robert's by his friend, G. P. Bidder. The *Newcastle Chronicle* trumpeted its approval, while regretting Stephenson's omission from the works of Emerson and Carlyle, for here truly was a hero: 'the hero as the self-made man ... as the worker, the inventor, the creator of new motive power, and, indirectly, of a new age'.[124]

When Sir Joseph Paxton proposed, at the time of Robert Stephenson's funeral in 1859, that his father's body should be brought from Chesterfield (Derbys.) and re-interred beside his in Westminster Abbey,

---

[121] *The Times*, 3 October 1862, 10b; *The Builder* 20 (1862), 736.

[122] Clare A. P. Willsdon, *Mural painting in Britain, 1840–1940: image and meaning* (Oxford: Oxford University Press, 2001), p. 309; plate 173. Ironically, both Stephensons were extreme Tories, Robert being described as 'protectionist to the marrow': J. C. Jeaffreson, *The life of Robert Stephenson, FRS*, 2 vols. (London: Longman, Green, Longman, Roberts & Green, 1864), vol. II, p. 145.

[123] Nikolaus Pevsner, *Northumberland* (Harmondsworth: Penguin, 1957), pp. 307–8.

[124] *Newcastle Chronicle*, 5 November 1858, reprinted in *ILN* 33 (11 December 1858), 555. George Robert Stephenson and George Parker Bidder, both civil engineers, were subsequently Robert Stephenson's executors, in company with his solicitor, Charles Parker: Jeaffreson, *Life of Robert Stephenson*, vol. II, p. 253.

the editor of *The Times* demurred: 'there is no reason why we should rob Chesterfield of its object of interest and permanent lesson. The worth of George Stephenson needs no enforcement.'[125] Further testimony to Stephenson's eminence at a national level is his inclusion among a distinguished band of men, whose statues were donated to adorn the great hall of the new University Museum at Oxford. Joining those luminaries of the scientific disciplines that the museum was intended to promote, such as Newton, Copernicus and Lavoisier, were others selected 'on special but very different grounds as benefactors to the human race, Bacon, Volta, Oersted, Watt, and Stephenson'.[126] He also became the subject of genre paintings, which depicted him in domestic settings.[127]

Although both Isambard Kingdom Brunel and Robert Stephenson were much mourned at the time of their deaths, in 1859, it was the elder Stephenson who (until recently) remained the quintessential representative of innovative civil engineering.[128] It was his name that was usually coupled with Watt's, whenever a speech-maker, journalist, or second-rate poet wished to praise Britain's technological achievements in general or the power of steam in particular.[129] And it was most often Stephenson whose deeds were integrated into the grand narrative of the Industrial Revolution, in history books and school texts. That Richard Trevithick did not receive the fame due to him as the first inventor of a steam locomotive is not hard to explain: he died impoverished in 1833, a quarter of a century after his pioneering experiments, and too early for his name to have become identified with any railway company or engineering institution. Trevithick might have been entirely forgotten had not the engineering profession and his native Cornwall belatedly begun to commemorate him in the 1880s.[130] The reputation of Robert Stephenson was

[125] *The Builder* 17 (1859), 709. As much as Smiles admired Robert, he considered George to have been the greater engineer: Mackay (ed.), *Autobiography of Samuel Smiles*, p. 255.

[126] *The Builder* 17 (1859), 401. Thomas Woolner was announced as the putative sculptor for Stephenson's statue: *The Builder* 18 (1 December 1860), but recent scholarship attributes it to Joseph Durham: Jennifer Sherwood and Nikolaus Pevsner, *Oxfordshire* (Harmondsworth: Penguin, 1974), p. 282; Frederick O'Dwyer, *The architecture of Deane and Woodward* (Cork: Cork University Press, 1997), p. 253. See also Henry W. Acland and John Ruskin, *The Oxford Museum* (3rd edn, London and Orpington: George Allen, 1893), pp. 25–7, 102–3. I am grateful to Ms Stella Brecknell, Librarian of the Oxford University Museum, for her help in identifying the sculptors and sponsors of the statues.

[127] *ILN* 40 (4 January 1862), 25–6; Sally Dugan, *Men of iron: Brunel, Stephenson and the inventions that shaped the world* (London: Macmillan, 2003), p. 29.

[128] See below, pp. 320–2.

[129] For poetry that hymns the deeds of Stephenson and Watt, see *Literature on line*: http://lion.chadwyck.co.uk/. Also see their portraits on the late nineteenth-century ASLEF membership certificate, repr. in MacLeod, 'Nineteenth-century engineer', p. 77.

[130] See below, pp. 322–5.

kept alive largely by association with his father's; apart from the magnificent tributes immediately after their deaths, neither he nor Isambard Kingdom Brunel attracted the attention of biographers, sculptors or other commemorations for nearly another century.[131] Marc Brunel, no less a brilliant engineer (and the only one of them to receive a knighthood), in later life was overshadowed by his son and has since suffered even worse neglect.

As we shall see in the next chapter, the final decade of I. K. Brunel's and Robert Stephenson's lives saw the start of a brief period when inventors joined the railway engineers at the forefront of British public life. The outburst of grief that surrounded their deaths was indicative of the celebrity which they and their profession more generally had attained. The public and private commemorations of the great railway engineers, as an almost routine part of the mourning ritual, constituted a new phenomenon, one which represented a bid for social status and recognition of a set of values that esteemed technical achievement and utility as worthy of high regard. These men belonged to an increasingly prominent and wealthy profession, and enjoyed the patronage of some of the most powerful members of society, including aristocratic colliery owners and directors of railway companies. To a considerable degree, the spectacle of their achievements as pioneers of railways, bridges and steamships had itself been responsible for that celebrity. It was boosted further by the excitement generated by the Great Exhibition of 1851, which showcased Britain's technological superiority on a scale never before attempted, and by the contrast that was shortly afterwards forced on public opinion between the triumphs of peace and the renewed horrors and destruction of war, in the Crimea and India.

---

[131] The reasons for this and for Brunel's dramatic resurgence at the end of the twentieth century are considered in MacLeod, 'Nineteenth-century engineer', pp. 77–9.

In 1851, inventors were suddenly thrust into the limelight, thanks initially to the Great Exhibition, held in London's Hyde Park. While celebrating the United Kingdom's predominance in the global economy, the Exhibition focused attention on the wealth of goods that was increasingly available to Victorian consumers and, by association, on the men responsible for their invention. Simultaneously, it helped to revive two controversial issues in which inventors were closely involved. First, because it espoused an ideology of progress through peaceful international competition, the Exhibition led to the inventor's rediscovery as an alternative hero to the warrior. It was not long, however, before both the ideology and its embodiment in the inventor were put to the test. The outbreak of war in the Crimea and India provided the opportunity for inventors of improved armaments to serve the state, leading both to a new level of public recognition and to bitter controversy. Secondly, the Exhibition accelerated the long-mooted reform of the patent system. Not only did its celebration of British manufacturing throw into sharp relief the inadequacy of many inventors' rewards, but the exposure of innovative products and machinery to public view accentuated the difficulty of adequately protecting their intellectual property; clearly, something needed to be done.

The Great Exhibition

From the moment that work began on the Crystal Palace, in November 1850, the country's attention was gripped by the building's size, novel design and speed of construction. With the fervour of expectation this generated in the press, no further publicity was needed to alert the public to the imminent opening of the Exhibition on 1 May 1851. During the next six months, six million visitors passed through the Crystal Palace. Although, once repeat visits and foreigners had been accounted for, the number of British adults that attended the Exhibition may not have exceeded two and a quarter million, this still equated to a tenth of the population.[1] Extensive coverage in the press kept the remainder well informed. In particular, *The Illustrated London News* published a weekly supplement devoted entirely to the Exhibition; with a circulation of over 130,000, its drawings and descriptions played a major role in disseminating awareness of events in Hyde Park around the country.[2] Other journals were launched specifically to cover the Exhibition: for example, *The Illustrated Exhibitor* was published weekly by John Cassell, from June 1851 until December 1852, at a price and with a content that was intended to attract (and perhaps also to empower) artisans.[3] The profusion of guidebooks, catalogues, and articles that the Exhibition generated made it 'by far the best documented event of the nineteenth century'.[4]

Although the Great Exhibition has been much criticized for promoting 'commodity fetishism and rampant imperialism', by its very size and variety of exhibits (not to mention its visitors' independence of mind), it could not avoid being much else besides.[5] Many visitors may have been dazzled by the scale and luminosity of the Crystal Palace and awed by the opulence of exotic commodities, but numerous others were fascinated by the processes of manufacture, in particular by the working of heavy machinery. 'The collection of machinery excites far deeper interest than anything else exhibited', wrote Robert Askrill, while another journalist advised that various machines could be located by 'the large number of persons congregated around such attractions from morning until evening'.[6] Each of these machines was identified by its inventor's or its manufacturer's name (often the two were synonymous): there was reference, for example, to Cox's aerated water apparatus, Applegath's vertical printing machine, Crabtree's card-setting machine, and (of particular fascination in its intricate movements) De La Rue's envelope machine. The crowd's curiosity may have been sparked initially by a report or illustration in the press, which simultaneously alerted them to the

---

[1] Peter Gurney, 'An appropriated space: the Great Exhibition, the Crystal Palace and the working class', in Purbrick (ed.), *Great Exhibition of 1851*, p. 120. See also Su Barton, '"Why should working men visit the Exhibition?" workers and the Great Exhibition and the ethos of industrialism', in Ian Inkster, Colin Griffin, Jeff Hill and Judith Rowbotham (eds.), *The golden age: essays in British social and economic history, 1850–1870* (Aldershot: Ashgate, 2000), pp. 146–63.

[2] Christopher Hibbert, *The Illustrated London News: social history of Victorian Britain* (London: Angus & Robertson, 1975), p. 13.

[3] Maidment, 'Entrepreneurship and the artisans', p. 86.

[4] Klingender, *Art and the industrial revolution*, p. 144.

[5] Maidment, 'Entrepreneurship and the artisans', p. 80; see, for example, Tony Bennett, 'The exhibitionary complex', *New Formations* 4 (1988), 73–102.

[6] Robert Askrill, *The Yorkshire visitor's guide to the Great Exhibition* (1851), quoted in Jeffrey A. Auerbach, *The Great Exhibition of 1851: a nation on display* (New Haven and London: Yale University Press, 1999), p. 104; 'Delarue's envelope machine', *ILN* 18 (21 June 1851), 603.

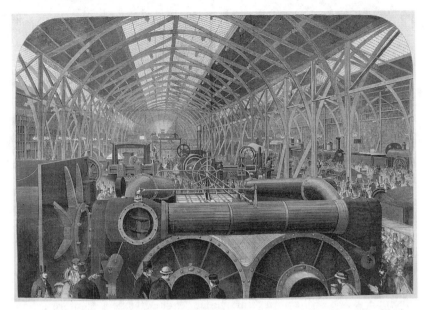

8.1 *The International Exhibition, Department of Machinery in Motion.*
This view of the Machinery Hall, from a double-page engraving in *The
Illustrated London News*, 18 October 1862, emphasizes both the grand
scale of these popular exhibits and the earnest conversations they excited
(photograph by Ann Pethers).

achievements of named inventors.[7] Such a fascination with machinery in
motion was by no means unique to the Great Exhibition, though there
had never been anything before on such a grand scale. Scientific and
mechanical exhibits had been attracting a large public to London and
Manchester galleries, and since 1838 a series of provincial cities hosted
temporary exhibitions of manufactures and inventions under the aegis of
the British Association for the Advancement of Science.[8] At London's
next Great Exhibition, in 1862, the popularity of the machinery hall
and the knowledgeable conversations taking place among its 'shilling'
(working-class) visitors were again to attract *The Illustrated London News'*
attention and prompt it to publish a double-page view (figure 8.1).[9]

[7] *ILN* 18 (31 May 1851), 502; ibid. (21 June 1851), 603.
[8] Morus, 'Manufacturing nature', 417–26; K. G. Beauchamp, *Exhibiting electricity*
    (London: Institution of Electrical Engineers, 1997), pp. 40–7, 61–9; Jack Morrell and
    Arnold Thackray, *Gentlemen of science: early years of the British Association for the
    Advancement of Science* (Oxford: Clarendon Press, 1981), pp. 213, 218–19, 264.
[9] *ILN* 41 (18 October 1862), 420–1, 427. See also *Report of the select committee on the Patent
    Office Library and Museum*, BPP 1864, XII, pp. 67–8.

When the question arose – as it quickly did – concerning what should be done with the Crystal Palace when the Exhibition closed, *The Illustrated London News* advocated that its educational role should continue. 'Why', it asked, 'should we not have a permanent home for the reception and display of the industrial products, the mechanical inventions, the new discoveries and improvements?'[10] Undoubtedly, some visitors may have shared the ambivalence, even dismay, of critics such as John Ruskin and William Morris, at the aesthetic shortcomings of many exhibits and the harmful socio-economic implications of industrialized production.[11] For many others, the Exhibition provided an awe-inspiring introduction to the cornucopia of material comforts, newly available to a widening section of British society, a sanitized view of the industrial technology with which much of it was produced, and a once-in-a-lifetime's glimpse of exotic cultures marvellously transported from across the globe to their doorstep.

The Great Exhibition was much more, however, than a festival of vicarious consumption. It was also intended as a lesson in the advantages of free trade and international competition, infused with the belief that mutual commercial interest was making war between nations obsolete. This had been audible in 1824, in speeches that praised Watt's steam engine as the agent of peaceful progress. During the next three decades, many commentators came to believe that swords had been permanently beaten into ploughshares.[12] This relatively pacific period in Europe also allowed the liberalization of British fiscal policy, culminating in the repeal of the corn laws in 1846.[13] While the Great Exhibition was suffused with the ideology of international peace and goodwill – naturally, under Britain's benign superintendence – it was driven by the anxiety that free trade would entail Britain's loss of industrial pre-eminence unless its manufacturers learned the lessons in design and good taste that their foreign competitors brought to the Crystal Palace.[14]

---

[10] *ILN* 18 (7 June 1851), 569.

[11] Auerbach, *Great Exhibition of 1851*, pp. 107, 113, 118; Richard Pearson, 'Thackeray and *Punch* at the Great Exhibition: authority and ambivalence in verbal and visual caricatures', in Purbrick (ed.), *Great Exhibition of 1851*, pp. 179–205.

[12] See, for example, Henry Bell, 'Steam navigation', in *The Scotsman*, 1824, 503; Baines, *History of the cotton manufacture*, p. 53; Ure, *Philosophy of manufactures*, p. vii; and above, pp. 103–4.

[13] Margot C. Finn, *After Chartism: class and nation in English radical politics, 1848–1874* (Cambridge: Cambridge University Press, 1993), pp. 59, 80–1.

[14] Auerbach, *Great Exhibition of 1851*, pp. 108–10, 113–18; Adrian Forty, *Objects of desire: design and society since 1750* (London: Thames & Hudson, 1986), pp. 42–3, 58; *ILN* 18 (31 May 1851), 477–8, 496–7. Cf. the tensions within the British Association's espousal of internationalism: Morrell and Thackray, *Gentlemen of science*, pp. 372–86, esp. p. 385.

The call to peace was uppermost, however, for a more idealistic minority also meeting in London that summer. Since 1848, the international peace congress had convened annually, in the confident expectation that it was on the verge of persuading national governments to introduce measures, such as arbitration, which would reduce and eventually eliminate their resort to war.[15] Originating in Britain and the USA during the final years of the Napoleonic Wars, the nineteenth-century peace movement had been dominated by men motivated by their religion, primarily Quakers. They were joined in the 1840s by a small but influential group of British middle-class radicals, led by Richard Cobden and John Bright.[16] Although not a thoroughgoing pacifist, Cobden was wholly dedicated to the cause of peace, his commitment to free trade stemming primarily from the belief that it would 'alter the relations of the world for the better, in a moral point of view'.[17] Cobden enthusiastically involved himself in the Great Exhibition's organization; other delegates praised it as 'the world's great protest against war' and its venue as 'the first Temple of Peace'. They heard their millennial sentiments echoed by Prince Albert and their aspirations taken seriously by the mainstream press.[18] The heady atmosphere of a new age dawning is captured in the memoirs of John McKie, a retired engineer, written in 1905:

At the present date ... it is hardly possible to comprehend the universal belief in the amelioration of mankind the inauguration of this exhibition was held to portend: it was to begin a reign of peace and goodwill among all nations, their only rivalry would be in trying who could do most good for their fellow men. A field gun of a peculiar construction had been sent from Prussia ... which led to discussions whether it should be admitted as implements of war were the products of a barbarous age, but under the high moral tone and knowledge the exhibition was bound to impart, these would soon merge into ploughshares and pruning hooks. The gun was eventually admitted.[19]

Whether from a religious or a political perspective, the development of steam transport and the construction of international telegraph

---

[15] David Nicholls, 'Richard Cobden and the International Peace Congress Movement, 1848–1853', *Journal of British Studies* 30 (1991), 351–4, 366–9; Alexander Tyrrell, 'Making the millennium: the mid-nineteenth century peace movement', *HJ* 20 (1978), 93–4; Gavin B. Henderson, 'The pacifists of the fifties', *Journal of Modern History* 9 (1937), 316–25.

[16] For its membership, see Nicholls, 'Richard Cobden', 373–5.

[17] Quoted in ibid., 363; see also ibid., 354–64; Tyrrell, 'Making the millennium', 90–1.

[18] Nicholls, 'Richard Cobden', 366–7; Tyrrell, 'Making the millennium', 93.

[19] 'Memoirs of John McKie (c. 1820–1915)', 5 vols., vol. III, p. 59, MSS Acc 3420, National Library of Scotland, Edinburgh. For Mr Punch's satirical comment on this episode, in which a crowd of little Quaker girls stand around the gun, bemused or dismayed, see *Punch* 21 (1851), 22; see also the title page to ibid., 20 (1851).

networks seemed to promise a more peaceful future. They might be interpreted as the fulfilment of biblical prophecy – the providential means of bringing the nations together in harmony – or, more pragmatically, as the conduits for trade and instantaneous communication to allow the swift and peaceful resolution of conflict.[20] There still ran a current of thought, especially in radical circles, which sought to elevate the man of science into a hero of peace and constructive social progress to rival the military, destructive idols of Britain's governing classes. Voiced during the French Wars of 1792–1815 and surfacing during the commemoration of Watt in 1824, it remained a useful stick with which to beat a government still apparently indifferent to the claims of men of science on its gratitude and support.[21] *Punch*, in particular, directed its wit against this paucity of reward. Probably to Robert Stephenson's embarrassment, it cheered his refusal of a knighthood in 1850: this was too lowly an honour to award the highest ranking engineer in Britain ('perhaps in the world'), who had embellished the country with 'gifts of genius', while generals who returned victorious from India were ennobled and made 'marquesses'.[22] When the Iron Duke himself visited Stephenson's Britannia Bridge, *Punch* mocked his seemingly meditative mood: 'The iron soldier was contemplating another sort of iron conquest which – in the sure progress of time – will make guns and cannonballs iron of the very oldest sort. The engineer will supersede the general'.[23] By 1851, it seemed that Britain could perhaps look forward to the day when Watt, in the company of Shakespeare, Bacon and Newton, might indeed evict even Nelson and Wellington from the national pantheon. It was these four iconic figures with which the firm of Elkington, Mason & Co. of London and Birmingham chose to illustrate the theme of 'the triumph of the science and the industrial arts' (with Prince Albert presiding atop), on the mock Elizabethan vase that crowned its exhibit of electroplated items; allegorical figures, around the base, represented war, rebellion, hatred and revenge, which had been 'overthrown and chained' (figure 8.2).

---

[20] Tyrrell, 'Making the millennium', 82, 89; Paul Greenhalgh, *Ephemeral vistas: the Expositions Universelles, Great Exhibitions and World's Fairs, 1851–1939* (Manchester: Manchester University Press, 1988), pp. 23–4.

[21] F. R. S., *Thoughts on the degradation of science in England* (London: John Rodwell, 1847), p. 3, quoted in George A. Foote, 'The place of science in the British reform movement, 1830–50', *Isis* 42 (1951), 206–7.

[22] *Punch* 19 (1850), 113; see also ibid. 17 (1849), 235, and above, pp. 92–5, 123–4, 200–11.

[23] *Punch* 21 (1851), 113.

8.2 Newton, Bacon, Shakespeare and Watt are presented as heroes of modern civilization on this four-foot high, electroplated vase, modelled by W. Beattie for Elkington, Mason & Co.'s display at the Great Exhibition (photograph by Ann Pethers).

Heroes of peace?

Scarcely had the Exhibition closed than realpolitik deflated the pacifists' euphoria. Louis Napoleon's coup d'état, in December 1851, triggered an invasion scare, leading to the passing of the Militia Act and a reversal of the recent decline in military spending.[24] British anxieties mounted

---

[24] Nicholls, 'Richard Cobden', 367–8.

further when the death of Wellington, in September 1852, was followed by the collapse of the French republic and Louis Napoleon's seizure of the imperial crown. 'The sword of Wellington', mourned *The Illustrated London News*, 'was never drawn to enslave, but to liberate'.[25] Who now would meet the Bonapartist threat? Napoleon III, however, proved to be an ally and it was not against France but Russia that Britain went to war in 1854. Cobden and his fellow peace campaigners worked in vain to moderate the war-fever; their reward was a storm of patriotic abuse, even from their erstwhile allies.[26] 'Free trade logic', as Miles Taylor remarks, 'proved to no avail in the midst of war.'[27] Cobden and Bright both lost their seats at the 1857 election. As Palmerston's government lurched from inglorious victory in the Crimea to the bombardment of Canton and the suppression of rebellion in India, the Congress Movement fizzled out. It was only in the late 1860s that a new, international peace movement began slowly to emerge.[28]

Faced with these serious setbacks, a beleaguered minority held onto its vision of a peace-loving society, which would recognize that its true benefactors were the creators, not the destroyers.[29] *Punch* continued to snipe in the cause of peace. In the middle of the Crimean War, it published a rousing satire, entitled 'They manage these things better in France'. One of the many things the French allegedly did better than 'John Bull' was to reward its inventors and scientists at least as well as its warriors:

> John Bull's every town is a centre
> Of inventions most useful to man;
> But alas! for John's greatest inventor,
> Unless he can patent his plan!
> John's titles, and ribands, and garters
> Are for rank, or for wealth, or for war,
> His great ones of science are martyrs,
> Who have still worn the cross, not the star –
> At John's court art and science are zeroes,
> Or if courted, 'tis favour or chance;

[25] *ILN* 21 (18 September 1852), 225. The *ILN*'s coverage of the duke's life and career and associated topics, including commemoration, continued throughout the autumn of 1852.

[26] Miles Taylor, *The decline of English radicalism, 1847–1860* (Oxford: Clarendon Press, 1995), pp. 231–58; Finn, *After Chartism*, pp. 172–5, 200–1.

[27] Taylor, *Decline of English radicalism*, pp. 244–5.

[28] Henderson, 'Pacifists of the fifties', 326–41; Nicholls, 'Richard Cobden', 369; Tyrrell, 'Making the millennium', 94–5; Peter Brock, *Pacifism in Europe to 1914* (Princeton, NJ: Princeton University Press, 1972), pp. 390–1.

[29] Taylor, *Decline of English radicalism*, pp. 255–7; W. H. van der Linden, *The international peace movement, 1815–1874* (Amsterdam: Tilleul Publications, 1987), pp. 467–71.

>   As for homage to peace and its heroes,
>   They manage things better in France.[30]

Punch's reaction to the news that Charles Wheatstone, a leading inventor of the electric telegraph, was finally to be knighted echoed its ironic response to Robert Stephenson's refusal of the same honour two decades before: it was too little, too late.[31] Others, however, might perceive both Wheatstone's and Stephenson's inventions in a more martial light.[32]

The case for creating humanitarian heroes out of inventors was vulnerable to an unresolved dilemma: they were at risk of co-option by the military state. Jenner had been applauded for vaccination's part in defeating the French (by safeguarding British troops from smallpox), and Watt for his steam engine's underpinning of the military effort (by strengthening the British economy). Few thought fit to examine this tension.[33] A rare exception to such complacency found expression in Edward Morris' biography of Henry Bell, the pioneer of steam shipping on the Clyde, published in 1844. Morris struggled to reconcile the government's current, belligerent employment of steam-powered vessels in China and the Middle East with his Christian faith and his trust in the benevolence of providentially inspired invention and commerce.

> The [inhabitants] ... will never forget their dreadful power to destroy forts, and lay cities in ashes; but we firmly trust a nobler work is theirs – to diffuse civilisation, truth, and peace, industry, commerce, and prosperity through the nations. This is Heaven's design in kindling the genius of men to invent them – and let not man madly fight against his gracious Creator, to turn a blessing into a curse.[34]

Morris' quandary intensified when the 1850s witnessed a large-scale return to arms that shook, where it did not completely undermine, the assumption that free trade would forestall warfare. In this unexpectedly bellicose new climate, those who had venerated inventors as heroes of peace were confronted with the inescapable fact that some of Britain's most famous inventors and engineers were designing and manufacturing weapons of war. If Jenner's, Watt's and Bell's contributions had been indirect and unintended, now inventors, such as William Armstrong and

---

[30] *Punch* 29 (1855), 221. See also ibid. 33 (1857), 136; 37 (1859), 169; 41 (1861), 182; *ILN* 21 (2 October 1852), 295.

[31] *Punch* 54 (1868), 44.   [32] See below, pp. 229–30 and 245.

[33] See above, pp. 82, 94–5.

[34] Morris, *Life of Henry Bell*, p. 83. For the military background to Morris' anxieties, see Headrick, *Tools of empire* pp. 17–57. For an unambiguous opposing of pacific inventors ('the true nobles of the land') to Nelson and Wellington, see *Mechanic's Magazine*, 3 December 1836, 170, quoted in Pettitt, *Patent inventions*, p. 40.

Joseph Whitworth, were integral to the war effort, supplying Britain and her allies with armaments and battleships.

When war prompted a close scrutiny of the facile description of inventors as national benefactors, a great divergence in values emerged. While pacifists and other opponents of war deplored the involvement of inventors in arms production, many non-pacifists regarded their contribution to the war effort as further proof of modern society's dependence on the inventor. Endorsing the campaign to commemorate Henry Cort, *The Times* lauded his inventions in the iron-refining industry, which had released Britain from 'commercial servitude to Russia and Sweden'; in particular, the Royal Navy's iron ships demonstrated the nation's indebtedness to one 'who endowed his country with such an amount of wealth and power'.[35] An article in *The Builder*, which called for more public statues to be erected to men in 'literature and science', included the inventors of weaponry:

When we reflect how powerless the efforts of the wisest general, or the bravest soldier, would be against those modern cannon and rifled muskets and other means which science has brought into use ... it would seem the time has arrived when equal honour should be shown to peaceful benefactors of the state, with that which has been shown to the mighty men of the sword.[36]

Neither author nor editor seems to have intended any irony in applying the adjective 'peaceful' to inventors of lethal weapons.

Such a contradiction was likely to have jarred with the *Mechanic's Magazine*, which idealistically (and inaccurately) contrasted the current situation with the early decades of the century, when 'the construction of weapons of war was not ... within the province of the engineer' and his skills were devoted to 'the advancement and the peaceful prosperity of the human race'. It fervently hoped, 'that our engineers may, ere long, be permitted to return to their legitimate occupations, and learn the arts of war no more'.[37] Samuel Crompton's biographer, Gilbert French, concurred: Crompton had 'fought the battle of *Invention* and of *Industry* which, more than any or all the

---

[35] *The Times*, 29 July 1856, 8a, 8e–f. For the failure of this campaign, see below, p. 340.

[36] *The Builder* 18 (22 December 1860), 823. See also Henry Lonsdale, *The worthies of Cumberland*, 6 vols. (London: George Routledge & Sons, 1867–75), vol. III, pp. 310–11. In 1865, at the end of the end of the American Civil War, Bennet Woodcroft wrote to John Ericsson that he believed 'the Monitors [warships] saved the Union, and that you created the Monitors; if this be so then you have individually done more for the Union than any other Patriot': Woodcroft MSS, Z27A, fos. 212–13.

[37] *Mechanic's Magazine*, 27 September 1861, 203. See also ibid., 3 May 1861, 299–300; the testimony of the Manchester machine makers to the 1841 select committee, quoted in Maxine Berg (ed.), *Technology and toil in nineteenth-century Britain* (London: CSE Press, 1979), p. 39; the poem, 'England's Heroes', by Matthias Barr, in *The Working Man* 1 (5 May 1866), 277; and above, p. 133. For the inaccuracy of this statement, see below, p. 228.

boasted sanguinary conflicts of military science or brute force, has contributed to the supremacy of Great Britain'.[38] The Chartist, Thomas Cooper's
choice of men to personify *The triumphs of perseverance and enterprise* (1856)
were entirely civilian, ranging from artists and linguists to men of business
and civil engineers. 'Scientific discoverers' comprised his largest category,
with Davy, Arkwright, Cartwright and Watt joining Columbus, Newton,
William Herschel, Réamur and Boyle.

[These] toiling intelligences who have taught us to subdue the physical world . . .
[are] the pioneers of civilisation, who make the world worth living in . . . the grand
revealers of the physical security, health, plenty and means of locomotion, which
give the mind vantage ground for its reach after higher refinement and purer
pleasures.[39]

Cooper justified his omission of military exemplars, the results of whose
actions contrasted sharply with the benefits that flowed from those of the
scientific discoverers:

Gradually, the truth dawns upon the world that war is an evil immeasurable; that
military glory is a false and destructive light; and that the grandest enterprises are
those which serve to increase the comfort, happiness, and knowledge of the race.[40]

The shock engendered by the outbreak of war among people who had
imagined it to be extinct and by the patriotic brouhaha surrounding the
new military heroes it produced – not least, Sir Henry Havelock, the
'Hero of Lucknow' – seems to have prompted many authors to restate
the rhetoric of 'peaceful conquest'.[41] It may even have been responsible
for inspiring them to write about those other heroes whom they believed
the country ought to venerate instead. Perhaps we should add the wars of
the 1850s to the causes of the ascendant hero-worship of inventors in the
third quarter of the nineteenth century.

The controversy was revivified by London's second Great Exhibition,
held at South Kensington in 1862.[42] John McKie remarked the change in
ethos since 1851, when the admission of a Prussian artillery piece had
provoked much heart-searching: 'In the intervening space, the war with
Prussia [i.e. Russia] and the Indian Mutiny had taken place, warlike

---

[38] French, *Samuel Crompton*, p. 34; original emphasis. See also the cutting from *The
Dewsbury Reporter*, 4 February 1860, in ZCR80/12, Crompton MSS.

[39] [Cooper], *Triumphs of perseverance and enterprise*, p. 80.

[40] Ibid., p. 280. Cooper was at odds here with many radicals, who supported national wars
in Europe: Finn, *After Chartism*, pp. 172–5, 200–1.

[41] For Havelock as hero, see Dawson, *Soldier heroes*, pp. 79–121. Smiles thought him a 'man
of truly heroic mould': *Self-help*, p. 235. For Smiles' views on military heroes more
generally, see ibid., pp. 229–42.

[42] Greenhalgh, *Ephemeral vistas*, pp. 31–3.

PEACE.

MR. PUNCH'S DESIGN FOR A COLOSSAL STATUE, WHICH OUGHT TO HAVE BEEN PLACED IN THE
INTERNATIONAL EXHIBITION.

8.3 *Peace*. In *Punch's* sardonic comment on the enormous quantity of
military hardware in the International Exhibition of 1862, a disconsolate
angel of peace perches on a cannon (photograph by Ann Pethers).

implements of every description were in it a leading feature.'[43] *Punch*
published its own wry comment, a full-page drawing entitled 'Peace', in
which a sorrowful angel sits on a cannon: it is 'Mr Punch's design for a
colossal statue, which ought to have been placed in the International
Exhibition' (figure 8.3). It commended the inclusion of weapons at 'the
Brick Palace', because 'they remind us how very much lower we are than
the angels' and how close we are to 'some foreigners who are very little
above the fiends'.[44] For those with long memories, *Punch's* 'Peace' drew a
stark contrast with Armitage's painting of the same name, exhibited in
1851, in which the Goddess of Peace (supported by the British lion)
triumphs over war, its tangled instruments lying rusting at her feet,

---

[43] Memoirs of John McKie, vol. III, p. 60, MS Acc 3420. Cf. this comment on the Paris
Exhibition of 1867 that, 'The number of military toys has very much decreased of late
years; the present nations being in favour of giving children toys more suggestive of the
arts of peace': *Reports on the Paris Universal Exhibition*, BPP 1867–8, XXX, p. 136.

[44] *Punch* 42 (1862), 177, 184; also ibid., 209–10.

8.4 *Peace*, by Edward Armitage. This painting, on display in the Fine Arts Court of the Great Exhibition and engraved for *The Illustrated London News*, 31 May 1851, expressed the common faith that international trade and the 'Pax Britannica' had made weaponry obsolete (photograph by Ann Pethers).

while 'her brow is wreathed with corn, indicative of her companion, Plenty' (figure 8.4).[45]

Mr Punch had kept William Armstrong and his armaments in its sights ever since he was knighted in 1859.[46] A favourite theme was the futile arms race 'between gun-makers and shipbuilders', with the escalating expense borne by long-suffering taxpayers. It imagined a chronology, in which Armstrong's gunnery inventions would be pitted against the Admiralty's attempts to find a resistant material: in 1862, his gun

---

[45] *ILN* 18 (31 May 1851), 477, 478; Robyn Asleson, 'Armitage, Edward (1817–1896)', *ODNB*, online edn, May 2006, www.oxforddnb.com/view/article/650, accessed 6 December 2006. See also the critical comparison in the *British Workman* 90 (June 1862), 358.
[46] *Punch* 36 (1859), 108; see also ibid., 97.

'smashes the iron ships into blacksmithereens'; by 1868, the Admiralty has invented 'a stone fleet, with cork keels', but Armstrong counteracts it with 'the Hannibal, or Alp-Shell, which contains the strongest vinegar, and melts the stone ships'. Having now destroyed the British fleet for the third time, Armstrong is 'raised to the peerage as Lord Bomb', the Admiralty invents an 'aerial fleet' to soar 'out of shot range', and Gladstone doubles the income tax for the fourth time in ten years. The contest ends only when the French emperor proclaims the millennium.[47]

Two contemporary group portraits, indicative of the eminence attained by leading inventors and engineers, may throw further light on this ideological dilemma. One makes explicit their contribution to Britain's military might; the other is more open to interpretation. The latter is William Walker and George Zobel's engraving of *The Distinguished Men of Science of Great Britain Living in A.D. 1807/8, Assembled in the Library of the Royal Institution*, published in 1862 (figure 8.5).[48] An imaginary scene, it is set half a century earlier, in the newly furbished upper library of the Royal Institution in London. At its centre sits James Watt; behind him is Count Rumford, who had founded the Institution in 1799.[49] It portrays fifty-one men, arranged in three clusters. Around Watt (with a diagram of his greatest inventions on his knee) is a central grouping of inventive engineers and chemists. His associates at Soho, Matthew Boulton, William Murdoch and John Rennie, and his close friend, Joseph Huddart, are joined by fellow engineers, Thomas Telford, Sir Marc Isambard Brunel, Henry Maudslay and Sir Samuel Bentham. Across the table sits a pensive John Dalton, the doyen of Manchester science, surrounded by a knot of other chemists, including Sir Humphry Davy, Henry Cavendish, William Henry and E. C. Howard (the sugar-pan patentee). The cluster on the right of the

---

[47] *Punch* 42 (1862), 160; see also ibid., 195; 44 (1863), 164–5; 45 (1863), 111; 45 (1868), 257.

[48] For the composition of the group and its publishing history, see Archibald Clow, 'A re-examination of William Walker's "Distinguished Men of Science"', *Annals of Science* 11 (1956), 183–93; Ludmilla Jordanova, 'Science and nationhood: cultures of imagined communities', in Geoffrey Cubitt (ed.), *Imagining nations* (Manchester: Manchester University Press, 1998), pp. 192–3; Mary Pettman (ed.), K. K. Yung (comp.), *National Portrait Gallery, complete illustrated catalogue, 1856–1979* (London: National Portrait Gallery, 1981), pp. 648–9. It is exactly contemporary with Christian Schussele's *Men of Progress*. This American group portrait, which was equally fictitious and male, differed in featuring only inventors and innovators, all nineteen of them alive at the time of its painting: Henry Petroski, *Reshaping the world: adventures in engineering* (New York: Alfred A. Knopf, 1997), pp. 88–94. My thanks to Alessandro Nuvolari for this reference.

[49] David Knight, 'Thompson, Sir Benjamin, Count Rumford in the nobility of the Holy Roman empire (1753–1814)', *ODNB*, www.oxforddnb.com/view/article/27255, accessed 18 October 2006.

8.5 *The Distinguished Men of Science of Great Britain Living in A.D. 1807/8, Assembled in the Library of the Royal Institution*, engraved by William Walker and George Zobel, 1862, after a pencil-and-wash drawing (1855–8), designed by Sir John Gilbert, R. A., the figures drawn by John F. Skill and finished by William and Elizabeth Walker.

picture comprises other inventors, most of whom are captivated by the stereotype printing plate held by Charles, Earl Stanhope; meanwhile, Joseph Bramah, his back turned to the painter (no likeness of him was available) engages Richard Trevithick in conversation. The coterie on the left consists of astronomers, botanists and geologists: prominent among them are Sir Joseph Banks, president of the Royal Society, William Smith (the founder of stratigraphical geology) and Edward Jenner. It is striking that two-thirds (thirty-three) of these 'men of science' were inventors (including men better known for their scientific research, such as W. H. Wollaston and Sir Francis Ronalds), seven were civil engineers and only eleven were natural philosophers who are not known to have made an invention. Inventors and engineers are portrayed on equal terms with the elite of British science, as represented by successive presidents and numerous fellows of the Royal Societies of London and of Edinburgh. No contemporary reviewer seems to have quibbled or thought this merited remark: they were all 'distinguished men of science'.[50]

The engraving reportedly took Walker six years and an investment of £6,000 to produce. It was published by private subscription, at prices ranging from two to ten guineas, according to size and the inclusion of autographs; each impression was supplied with a key and a volume of memoirs.[51] It received an enthusiastic reception in the press and the volume sold so well, independently of the engraving, that a second edition was published in 1864.[52] Walker intended that his print, begun during the Crimean War, should remind his countrymen that the inventions and discoveries of 'these gifted men ... are the grand Main-Springs of our National Wealth and Enterprise'.[53] He depicted them as cultivated men of the Enlightenment, socializing in a library, yet contemporaries would have been aware that, in 1807–8, not only was Britain entering 'the era of manufactories' but it was also at war with Napoleon.[54] A high proportion

---

[50] See below, pp. 352–5. For the mid-nineteenth-century origin of the word 'scientist' and the continuing currency of 'man of science', see Sydney Ross, 'Scientist: the story of a word', *Annals of Science* 18 (1962), 65–86; also Raymond Williams, *Keywords: a vocabulary of culture and society* (rev. edn, London: Fontana, 1983), pp. 276–80.

[51] *The Times*, 10 September 1867, 9d; proof sheets, Crompton MSS, ZCR 73/3, 75/17; William Walker, Junior (ed.), *Memoirs of the distinguished men of science of Great Britain living in the years 1807–8*, intro. Robert Hunt (London: Walker, 1862).

[52] For press notices, see Walker (ed.), *Memoirs* (2nd edn, London: E. and F. N. Spon, 1864), pp. 164–7.

[53] Proof sheets of advertisement, Crompton MSS, ZCR 73/3, 75/17.

[54] A library (or a desk with books) was a common setting for portraits of early nineteenth-century men of science, especially engineers, signifying their claim to professional status: Ben Marsden, 'Imprinting engineers: reading, writing, and technological identities in nineteenth-century Britain', British Society for the History of Science Conference, Liverpool Hope University, June 2004.

of Walker's subjects had been involved in that earlier war effort. Watt's steam engine and Jenner's discovery of vaccination had long been credited with major roles in Napoleon's defeat. At Watt's side, in the centre of the composition, were Bentham, Brunel and Maudslay, who had introduced the highly innovative block-making machinery into the Royal Dockyard at Portsmouth, while Huddart had invented steam-driven machinery that improved the quality of the ropes running through those blocks on board sailing ships.[55] To their right were two pioneers of steam shipping, William Symington and Patrick Miller; Watt's and Maudslay's firms had become major suppliers of steam ships to the Navy. Civil engineers, such as Rennie and Telford, had designed docks, as well as bridges and roads, which had both military and civilian uses. Trevithick was a pioneer of steam railways and Ronalds, of the electric telegraph, two inventions of escalating importance for commerce and imperial control alike. In addition to manufacturing paper-making machinery, Bryan Donkin devised methods of preserving food, which extended the time that ships could remain at sea. Walker included several cartographers and instrument-makers, responsible for improved tele-scopes, chronometers and other navigational devices; astronomers, such as Nevil Maskelyne and Francis Baily, had established and reformed the *Nautical Almanac*. The geologists' researches were reinforcing Britain's coal and metallurgical industries; those of the botanists (with Banks at their head) were introducing new crops from around the globe. Crucial to Britain's manufacturing supremacy were such textile machines as those invented by Crompton and Cartwright, and such chemical inventions as Howard's and Charles Tennant's. By contrast, munitions had a single explicit representative in Sir William Congreve, famous for his epony-mous rockets – a small presence but a no less significant one.[56] Walker and Zobel's print celebrated not only the intellectual achievements of British men of science, but also their enormous contribution to the country's international predominance, where military and commercial advances were inextricably linked.[57] In Shapin's terminology, these men

---

[55] Cooper, 'Portsmouth system of manufacture', 182–225; Coad, *Portsmouth block mills*, pp. 39–103; Walker, *Memoirs* (2nd edn), pp. 64–6.

[56] Congreve obtained at least eighteen patents, in various fields: Roger T. Stearn, 'Congreve, Sir William, second baronet (1772–1828)', *ODNB*, www.oxforddnb.com/view/article/6070, accessed 3 November 2006.

[57] Economic historians have recently started to attach much greater significance to Britain's military state, especially the role of the Royal Navy: P. K. O'Brien, 'The political eco-nomy of British taxation, 1660–1815', *EHR* 41 (1998), 1–32; Brewer, *Sinews of power*, pp. 27–46, and passim.

8.6 *The Intellect and Valour of Great Britain*, engraved key plate by
Charles G. Lewis, of the oil painting by T. J. Barker, 1863.

were 'civic experts', whose 'numbers ... were increasing along with the
expansion of trade, war, and imperialism'.[58]

There shortly followed another composite portrait, Thomas Jones
Barker's painting, *The Intellect and Valour of Great Britain*, which was
dominated by military, imperial and political heroes, all either alive or
only recently deceased (figure 8.6).[59] At its heart are Richard Cobden
and three other architects of the 1860 treaty of free trade with France:
Palmerston, Russell and Gladstone. Among Barker's thirty-six subjects, there were only seven men of science. Two of these, however,
were accorded positions of prominence. Sir David Brewster explains
his invention of the lenticular stereoscope to a centrally positioned
group that comprises three other natural philosophers (Michael
Faraday, Sir Roderick Murchison and Sir Richard Owen), Dickens,

---

[58] Shapin, 'Image of the man of science', p. 182, and the references given there; also Larry
Stewart, 'Global pillage: science, commerce, and empire', in Porter (ed.), *Cambridge
History of Science*, vol. IV, pp. 825–44.

[59] Freeman O'Donohue and Henry M. Hake (eds.), *Catalogue of engraved British portraits
preserved in the Department of Prints and Drawings in the British Museum* (London,
1922), vol. V, p. 87; Roger T. Stearn, 'Barker, Thomas Jones (1813–1882)', *ODNB*,
www.oxforddnb.com/view/article/1416, accessed 6 December 2006.

Tennyson, and the artist Daniel Maclise. Are these perhaps the luminaries of contemporary British society, whose material and cultural benefits free trade, protected by military power, will bring to the rest of the world? Equally prominent, the largest group is dominated by heroes of Britain's recent wars in India and China. They surround Sir William Armstrong as he explains 'the peculiar construction of his famous cannon', and include Robert Stephenson, the personification of railways (soon to be a major tool of imperial governance and military strategy).[60] This positioning of Armstrong and Stephenson makes a more explicit assertion than Walker and Zobel's, that the work of inventors and engineers underpinned the British empire's military and commercial might.

Such choices of subject were never made lightly. The opening of Bradford's new Exchange, in 1865, allowed the Yorkshire town's leading businessmen to celebrate British trade and manufacturing and express symbolically their commitment to political and economic liberalism. They selected nine portrait heads to adorn the exterior of the building: the inventors, Arkwright, Watt and Stephenson accompanied the Elizabethan navigators Ralegh and Drake, the high-priest of free trade Cobden, the liberal politicians Gladstone and Palmerston, and the local manufacturer and philanthropist, Sir Titus Salt.[61] It is further evidence of both the self-consciousness of such choices and the balance of cultural power that the authors of a history and survey of signboards regretted the disparity between the many inns named after military figures and the few that paid tribute to men famous for peaceful pursuits: 'We find hundreds of admirals and generals on the signboard, but we are not aware that there is one Watt, or one Sir Walter Scott; yet, what glory and pleasure has the nation not derived from their genius.'[62]

---

[60] O'Donohue and Hake (eds.), *Catalogue*, vol. V, p. 87. The other civilian members of this group are Sir Benjamin Brodie (president of the Royal Society, 1858–61), David Livingstone, Sir Charles Barry and W. M. Thackeray.

[61] Michael W. Brooks, *John Ruskin and Victorian architecture* (London: Thames and Hudson, 1989), pp. 223–4; Nikolaus Pevsner, *Yorkshire, the West Riding* (Harmondsworth: Penguin Books, 1959), p. 124; Dellheim, *Face of the past*, pp. 153–4. It is unclear from these works which Stephenson was intended; one also wonders whether the belligerent Palmerston was a mistake for Peel, the repealer of the corn laws.

[62] Jacob Larwood and John Camden Hotten, *The history of signboards, from the earliest times to the present day* (London: Chatto and Windus [1866]), pp. 55–6; my thanks for this reference to Mark Goldie. There remain very few inns named after inventors, scientists or authors: Leslie Dunkling and Gordon Wright (eds.), *The Wordsworth dictionary of pub names* (Ware: Wordsworth Reference, 1994).

The battle of Trafalgar Square

This contest between the parties of peace and war adds another dimension to the controversial situation of Edward Jenner's statue in London's Trafalgar Square. Unveiled in 1858, the statue was already a cause for dispute between supporters and opponents of vaccination. It was the product of an international subscription, launched in 1853, after William Calder Marshall's model for such a statue caught the eye of senior members of the medical profession at the Great Exhibition.[63] The centenary of Jenner's birth had gone unremarked in 1849, but 1853 witnessed the passage of the highly contentious Compulsory Vaccination Act.[64] The statue marked this triumph for the vaccinationist cause. The committee proudly announced it had received donations from every country in Europe and the United States; the Philadelphia committee contributed £340 (nearly half the total), and Prince Albert was said to have 'subscribed liberally'.[65] By implication, the British contribution had been slight. With royal support, however, the statue was inaugurated at the south west corner of Trafalgar Square, on 17 May 1858, the 109th anniversary of Jenner's birth.[66]

Predictably, there was a hostile reaction from the anti-vaccinationists to this prominent elevation of Jenner, but theirs was not an influential objection. What ultimately led to the statue's removal to the relative backwater of Kensington Gardens was an outraged belief that Jenner was the wrong kind of hero for Trafalgar Square. Supporters of the military refused to relax their hold on this prestigious site and dilute its patriotic, not to say bellicose, atmosphere by admitting a humanitarian hero, beloved of the pacifists. Vaccination's heroic role in protecting British armed forces from the ravages of smallpox seems to have been overlooked. Jenner's presence there 'insult[ed] the commonest feelings of taste and propriety'.[67] The issue was raised by *The Times* – no supporter of the anti-vaccinationist cause. It first berated the quality of all London's public statues, before turning to castigate the inappropriateness of placing Jenner's in Trafalgar Square, next to that of General Sir Charles Napier, who had conquered swathes of northern India. Napier's proper companion, it argued, was General Havelock, the hero of the relief of Lucknow during the Indian

---

[63] *The Times*, 1 August 1853, 5c; Timbs, *Stories*, pp. 130–1; WORK20/33, National Archives; Roy Porter, 'Where the statue stood: the reputation of Edward Jenner', in Ken Arnold (ed.), *Needles in medical history: an exhibition at the Wellcome Trust History of Medicine Gallery, April 1998* (London: Wellcome Trust, 1998), p. 11. I am grateful to the late Roy Porter for allowing me to read an earlier draft of this chapter.

[64] See above, pp. 82–8. Jenner was hanged in effigy by a Leicestershire crowd in 1885: Durbach, '"They might as well brand us"', 57.

[65] Empson, 'Little honoured in his own country', 516–8; *The Times*, 1 August 1853, 5c.

[66] Porter, 'Where the statue stood', pp. 11–12.   [67] *The Times*, 3 May 1858, 8e.

rebellion (whose statue would indeed soon join it there): 'The two great soldiers, with the greater Admiral between them'. *The Times* professed no disrespect to Jenner: the great men of medicine – Harvey, Hunter and Jenner – were 'quite as worthy to be held in public honour as any warrior who ever lived', but not 'in ridiculous juxtaposition with men whose careers and merits were entirely different from their own'.[68] This line was echoed by the MP for Durham, Lord Adolphus Vane-Tempest, in asking the Chief Commissioner of Works, Lord John Manners, to 'show good taste' by changing the site. The intervention three days later by the anti-vaccinationist member, Thomas Duncombe, who called for 'the removal of the statue of this promulgator of cow-pock nonsense', appears, by contrast, to have been an opportunist leap onto the militarist bandwagon.[69] Contemporary sensitivity to the protocol of place is demonstrated by an earlier letter to *The Times*, which was inspired by inter-service rivalries. The writer objected to the erection of Napier's monument in Trafalgar Square: it would be wrong to site a soldier, whatever his merits, in the place which should be reserved exclusively for *naval* heroes.[70]

Jenner kept his 'incongruous' site for nearly four years, probably thanks to royal protection.[71] Apparently, his fate was sealed by another disease, the typhoid that carried off Prince Albert in December 1861. Within two months, the statue was demoted to a new plinth beside the Serpentine. *The Builder* protested 'as a matter of principle' at this ostensible slur 'to this benefactor to the human race ... [at a time] when the value of science is more generally appreciated than formerly'.[72] *Punch* quipped, 'Some journals complain of his being moved about. But surely the inventor of vaccination has the best possible right to make experiments on various spots.'[73]

If it was a pyrrhic victory for the anti-vaccination cause, it was also an implicit snub to the rhetorical case that inventors were Britain's true heroes. A similar rebuff was meted out to the three great engineers who

---

[68] Ibid. For leading articles strongly in favour of compulsory vaccination, see *The Times*, 8 December 1859, 6c; 19 June 1867, 9c. For Napier and Havelock, see Ainslie T. Embree, 'Napier, Sir Charles James (1782–1853)', *ODNB* online edn, October 2005, www.oxforddnb.com/view/article/19748, accessed 18 October 2006; James Lunt, 'Havelock, Sir Henry (1795–1857)', *ODNB*, online edn, May 2006, www.oxforddnb.com/view/article/12626, accessed 18 October 2006.

[69] Hansard, *P.D.*, 3rd ser., CL (1858), 274, 354.

[70] *The Times*, 30 October 1856, 5d.   [71] WORK20/33, National Archives.

[72] *The Builder* 20 (1862), 273. For a recent argument for restoring Jenner to Trafalgar Square, see Gabriel Scally and Isabel Oliver, 'Putting Jenner back in his place', *The Lancet* 362 (4 October 2003), 1092.

[73] Quoted in *The Times*, 13 February 1862, 9b. *Punch* had earlier offered this more sympathetic verse, 'England's ingratitude still blots/The escutcheon of the brave and free;/I saved you many million spots,/And now you grudge one spot for me': quoted in Empson, 'Little honoured in his own country', p. 517.

died within a year of one another in 1859–60. Although Robert Stephenson was accorded the signal honour of interment in Westminster Abbey (where he had been preceded by Thomas Telford), this still represented a sufficient break with tradition to merit remark. *The Times* commented guardedly on the Dean and Chapter's decision to permit the burial there of 'the body of one who was neither warrior nor statesman, but who was not the less, if, indeed, not the more, a public benefactor in his generation'.[74] Finding a public site in London for his monument proved more problematic. The commemoration of his colleagues, Isambard Kingdom Brunel and Joseph Locke, faced similar difficulties. Their admirers were frustrated in their preference for a common site for all three monuments in Parliament Square, Westminster, which would have combined a socially prestigious location with proximity to Great George Street, where the Institution of Civil Engineers had installed its headquarters.[75]

If, as they were informed by officials, Trafalgar Square was reserved for 'warriors and kings', and Parliament Square for 'statesmen', where were the heroes of science, technology and medicine to be celebrated? The government offered no alternative. In 1871, Baron Carlo Marochetti's nine-foot bronze statue of Stephenson was finally installed at the entrance to Euston railway station.[76] Less appropriately, six years later the Metropolitan Board of Works conceded a site on the Victoria Embankment for Brunel's; strangely, Paddington station seems not to have been considered.[77] Meanwhile, Marochetti's third statue, of Locke, had found refuge in his native Barnsley (Yorks.).[78] The outcome must have proved a serious disappointment to the subscribers and the engineering profession as a whole. Instead of one central, prestigious site, the monuments had been dispersed to separate, relatively obscure places. Despite the aesthetic justifications offered, the implication remained that, in the eyes of Britain's rulers, engineers and physicians, however creative

---

[74] *The Times*, 22 October 1859, 7b.
[75] MacLeod, 'Nineteenth-century engineer', pp. 70–1; Burch, 'Shaping symbolic space', pp. 223–36.
[76] C. Manby to Office of Works, 8 May 1871; Memo dated 20 June 1871, WORK20/253, nos. 6, 14, 17–19; Philip Ward-Jackson, 'Carlo Marochetti, sculptor of Robert Stephenson at Euston station: a romantic sculptor in the railway age', unpublished typescript, pp. 1–2, 7–8; I am grateful to the author for kindly allowing me to read this paper. The statue now stands incongruously on the concourse outside Euston station, against a backdrop of 1960s office buildings.
[77] Memos dated 15 June 1871, 5 April 1877, WORK20/253; C. Davenport to Office of Works, 3 April 1877, WORK20/25; *The Times*, 3 July 1871, 11a; 18 November 1871, 6d; 3 May 1877, 11a; 5 July 1877, 7b; 30 July 1877, 11b. *The Builder* was far from complimentary about the new masonry into which the statue was inserted: 13 October 1877, 1035.
[78] MacLeod, 'Nineteenth-century engineer', p. 72; for a photograph of the statue, see ibid., p. 71.

or virtuous they might be, still ranked second to the traditional heroes of the battlefield and politics. There may also have been a reluctance to concede official recognition to men whom the pacifists and radicals insisted on promoting as alternatives to the warriors and statesmen, symbols of the British state's commitment to an increasingly militaristic and imperialistic ideology.

One of the period's strongest statements in the cause of humanity and international co-operation was made in France, where the Société des Sciences Industrielles, Arts, et Belles Lettres de Paris took the most unusual step of commemorating a foreign inventor, Edward Jenner. The municipality of Boulogne-sur-Mer, where vaccination had been introduced into France in 1800, offered a site for a monument, and the French government provided the requisite permission; the sculptor, M. E. Paul, of Paris, gave his services without charge 'in admiration of Jenner'. The statue was inaugurated in 1865 with full civil honours and festivities. Ten-feet high, made of iron electroplated in bronze, it stood on a twelve-foot granite pedestal, inscribed 'À Edward Jenner, la France recognaisante, 11 septembre 1865'. Jenner was depicted in the costume of 1810, holding a lancet in one hand, his other hand resting on a pile of books, from which there descended a sketch of a cow (figure 8.7). On both sides of the Channel, it was regarded as a gesture of enlightened internationalism, of the common interests of humanity rising above national rivalries. Accordingly, 'The right foot is placed firmly over the word "Angleterre", while the left is advanced over the word "France".'[79]

Proponents of the view that inventors should be elevated above the traditional 'sanguinary' heroes were soon to be engaged, however, in a rearguard action that lasted for the remainder of the period, as, after 1870, most of Europe retreated from free trade, competed for imperial advantage, and engaged in an arms race that eventually led to war in 1914. Yet, although they never ousted the warriors from the pantheon, works about inventors played an important role in reminding a jingoistic populace both of those warriors' dependence upon their ingenuity and technical skills, and that there might be different, infinitely preferable ways to make one's mark.[80] One finds, for example, a history of the

---

[79] *The Times*, 13 September 1865, 11a; Empson, 'Little honoured in his own country', 515–16. Photographs of Jenner's statues in Gloucester, London, Boulogne, Genoa (1873) and Tokyo (1904) may be found in ibid., pp. 514–18, and in *The Jenner Museum, Berkeley, Gloucestershire* (East Grinstead: The Merlin Press [1986]), p. 11.

[80] See below, pp. 377–80. Valerie E. Chancellor detects a shift in history textbooks, at the end of the nineteenth century, towards the increasingly favourable presentation of war heroes and 'less insistence on the moral evils attendant on fighting': *History for their masters: opinion in the English history textbook, 1800–1914* (Bath: Adams & Dart, 1970), pp. 70–7.

8.7 Monument to Edward Jenner, by M. E. Paul, 1865, Boulogne. This engraving from *The Illustrated London News*, 30 September 1865, recognized that, since commemorative statuary rarely ventures beyond national boundaries, this French tribute to Jenner was an exceptional gesture of enlightened humanitarianism (photograph by Ann Pethers).

nineteenth century that followed a chapter on 'Our wars' with two on 'The victories of peace', which covered a range of inventions, and industrial and medical improvements. While inserting, in one of the latter chapters, an anomalous paragraph on 'improved weapons', its author, Robert Mackenzie, chose his words carefully: a new rifle would slaughter 'twenty *human beings* per minute', and British naval artillery could 'destroy the hundreds of *brave* men' in enemy ships. He concluded wistfully:

Mechanically these inventions are very admirable. It is not, however, beyond hope that civilized man approaches the close of his fighting era, and that the perfecting of the implements of slaughter may be coincident, or nearly so, with their disuse.[81]

---

[81] Robert Mackenzie, *The 19th century: a history* (London, 1880), pp. 196–7; my emphasis.

In contrast, Mackenzie wrote with enthusiasm about 'the great outbreak of inventiveness by which our century is distinguished', and which was at the root of Britain's 'industrial eminence' and the improving conditions of daily life: it had been achieved while 'our neighbours were engrossed by the work of invading other people's territories or resisting the invasion of their own'.[82] A contemporary volume, Edwin Hodder's *Heroes of Britain in peace and war*, similarly strove to broaden the concept of heroism: it encompassed courageous action in any worthwhile cause, including the unsung heroism of everyday self-denial – caring for others. These compendious volumes defined a hero as 'a man of distinguished valour, intrepidity, or enterprise in danger'; heroism as 'the qualities of a hero – bravery, gallantry, intrepidity, daring, courage, boldness, magnanimity, self-sacrifice'.[83] Hodder's frontispiece immediately demonstrates his order of values: it carries the portraits of five 'heroes of slave trade abolition', the cause which occupies his first three chapters. He found a place for military heroes, especially those whose bravery had gained them the Victoria Cross, but they were outnumbered by civilian heroes, including 'Great Inventors', 'Great Engineers' and 'Heroic Men of Science'.[84]

An admiration for inventors, however, should not be equated necessarily with the intention of counteracting incipient militarism or imperialism. In particular, it was all too easy for an author, excited at the novelty and technical skills displayed in new weaponry, to overlook the destruction they could wreak. Robert Cochrane, for example, seemed to think that a preliminary reference to the 'sad and salutary lesson' of the 4,470,000 people calculated to have been killed in wars between 1793 and 1877 cleared the way for everyone to 'readily unite in admiring the wonderful mechanism which makes the Maxim Machine Gun an engine of terrible destructiveness'.[85]

Honours from the state

In the later nineteenth century, when the British state regularly began to reward inventors and engineers, it bestowed its honours principally on those whose work served its immediate interests in the fields of weaponry

---

[82] Ibid., pp. 199, 206 and passim.

[83] Edwin Hodder, *Heroes of Britain in peace and war*, 2 vols. (London, Paris, and New York [1878–80]), vol. I, p. 2. Hodder's 'men' included a number of women.

[84] Ibid., vol. I, frontispiece; vol. II, table of contents. Unfortunately, the image of Hodder's 'great inventors' suffered by comparison with the other two: see below, pp. 377–8.

[85] Robert Cochrane, *The romance of industry and invention* (London and Edinburgh: W. & R. Chambers [1896]), p. 177.

or telegraphic and postal communications.[86] Honours from the universities, scientific societies and the City of London tended to accrue to the same men. It is ironic, but not surprising, that it was such servants of the state who reaped the official rewards of the brief period in British history when inventors and engineers were perceived as heroic figures. Instead of providing an alternative set of heroes for those sections of the public who wished to oppose the bellicosity and imperial ambitions of the state, these men of science were co-opted by the official culture. By contrast, the refusal of honours seems to have been a response common to several of the most famous engineers and inventors of the first half of the century. Such indifference to convention may have helped endear them to their public and burnished their fame – if only perhaps by allowing misinformed critics of the state to grumble about its ingratitude.[87]

Naturally, 'Lord Bomb' reaped both national and local honours. William Armstrong was knighted in 1859, for his invention of the riflebore breech-loading gun; he had declined to patent his ordnance inventions, and established a plant at Elswick, on Tyneside, to produce the guns under government contract. A public banquet was held at Newcastle upon Tyne to celebrate his knighthood.[88] In 1887 (rather later than *Punch* had predicted) he was elevated to the peerage as Baron Armstrong of Cragside – one of the earliest industrialists to receive this rare honour.[89] By this time, he was a wealthy arms manufacturer and warship builder. He had received several honorary degrees and engineering medals and, in 1886, the freedom of the city of Newcastle, where he was valued at least as much for the employment created by his firm and his philanthropic largesse as for his 'scientific attainments'.[90] Following his death in 1900, the city raised a monument on Barras Bridge to his memory: his statue, by

---

[86] From a survey of the obituaries of engineers who died before 1900, Buchanan identified ninety-seven who received an honour from the state – approximately one of every thirty-six members of the professional institutions, which was 'not excessively generous' in comparison with other professions: *The engineers*, pp. 20–1.

[87] Several engineers – Telford, Watt, Macadam, Rennie, George and Robert Stephenson – had declined knighthoods or baronetcies: ibid., pp. 192–3. George Stephenson said he 'objected to those empty additions to my name': George Stephenson to J. T. W. Bell, 27 February 1847, IMS157, Institution of Mechanical Engineers.

[88] *The Times*, 12 May, 1859, 12f; 14 May 1859, 6 e–f. See also *ILN* 91 (16 July 1887), 79.

[89] Ralph E. Pumphrey, 'The introduction of industrialists into the British peerage: a study in adaptation of a social institution', *American Historical Review* 45 (1959), 10–12; David Cannadine, *The decline and fall of the British aristocracy* (London and New Haven: Yale University Press, 1990), pp. 406–20; F. M. L. Thompson, *English landed society in the nineteenth century* (London: Routledge & Kegan Paul, 1963), pp. 296, 306–7.

[90] Stafford M. Linsley, 'Armstrong, William George, Baron Armstrong (1810–1900)', *ODNB*, online edn, October 2006, www.oxforddnb.com/view/article/669, accessed 18 October 2006; *The Times*, 9 November 1886, 5f. See also his obituary, *The Times*, 28 December 1900, 8d–f.

8.8 Monument to William Armstrong, Baron Armstrong of Cragside, by Sir William Hamo Thornycroft, 1906, Barras Bridge, Newcastle upon Tyne (photograph by the author).

W. H. Thornycroft, stands proudly between two bas-reliefs that display the guns, battleships, hydraulic cranes and bridges, which made his fortune and his fame (figures 8.8 and 8.9).[91] Armstrong's fellow inventor and rival, Joseph Whitworth, is now best known for his machine tools and his drive to standardize measurements throughout the engineering trades, but in 1869 he was chiefly famous 'through his inventions in improved rifles and ordnance'.[92] He had also played an important part in increasing marine-engine production at the start of the Crimean War. Napoleon III awarded him the Légion d'Honneur for his artillery inventions in 1868, a year before he was created a baronet by Queen Victoria. Whitworth was elected to a fellowship of the Royal Society and received honorary doctorates from Trinity College, Dublin and the University of Oxford. In 1868, he promised a bequest of £100,000 to endow the scholarships at Owen's College,

[91] Usherwood, Beach and Morris, *Public sculpture of north-east England*, pp. 92–3.
[92] *The Times*, 11 October 1869, 10f.

8.9 Bas-relief on the monument to Baron Armstrong of Cragside, Newcastle upon Tyne, showing a cannon of his design being winched onto a battleship. Armstrong's shipyards and armaments factory at Elswick, on Tyneside, were major local employers (photograph by the author).

Manchester, that bore his name; some of the beneficiaries erected a large brass plaque as a memorial to him in Crewe Mechanics' Institute in 1900.[93]

Four of the other nine new baronets created in October 1869 were industrialists. They included another distinguished and innovative mechanical engineer, William Fairbairn, FRS. Fairbairn, also 'a self-made man' at the head of a large machine-making firm in Manchester, had many patents to his name for steam boilers, wrought-iron girders, cranes and so forth. He had been president of both the Institution of Mechanical Engineers and the British Association, and held honorary doctorates from the Universities of Edinburgh and Cambridge.[94] On his death in 1874 a public subscription raised £2,700 for a marble statue in

[93] *The Times*, 24 January 1887, 8b; *Mechanical Engineer* 6 (7 July 1900), 22; Thomas Seccombe, 'Whitworth, Sir Joseph, baronet (1803–1887)', rev. R. Angus Buchanan, *ODNB*, www.oxforddnb.com/view/article/29339, accessed 18 October 2006.

[94] *The Times*, 9 October 1869, 4d; 11 October 1869, 10f; James Burnley, 'Fairbairn, Sir William, first baronet (1789–1874)', rev. Robert Brown, *ODNB*, www.oxforddnb.com/view/article/9067, accessed 18 October 2006; Fairbairn had declined the offer of a knighthood for his 'eminent services ... to science' in 1861, when he was president of the British Association: *The Times*, 25 October 1861, 6e.

Manchester Town Hall and the endowment of scholarships at Owen's College, Manchester.[95] When Charles Parsons was knighted in 1911, he was not merely the inventor of the steam turbine, but the head of several major engineering and manufacturing firms, one of which supplied turbines to the Royal Navy.[96] In 1927, he became the first mechanical engineer to receive the Order of Merit.

Recognition came more slowly to Francis Pettit Smith, who was largely responsible for introducing the screw propeller into the Royal Navy in the 1840s – a feat of dogged persistence. Without a manufacturing base, 'Smith's screw' had not joined the 'Armstrong gun' in the list of eponymous inventions, nor had Smith reaped comparable financial gains. He was awarded a state pension of £200 per annum in 1855. The same year, a number of leading engineers and shipbuilders launched a subscription that led to his being presented with a service of plate and £2,678 at a public banquet in 1857.[97] The knighthood was eventually conferred in 1871. By this time, approximately 600 Royal Navy vessels and 2,000 merchant ships had been fitted with screw propellers, but Smith was still earning his living as Curator of the Patent Office Museum.[98] Robert Whitehead, the inventor of the 'locomotive torpedo', fared worse. Described as 'a mechanical genius of great originality and exceptional skill', who won 'fame and fortune' by his invention and its manufacture, Whitehead received many awards from foreign governments. Yet, no British honours were forthcoming: to the country with the world's largest fleet, the bulwark of its imperial defence and global trade, an effective torpedo was apparently regarded as an unpatriotic use of his inventive abilities.[99]

Henry Bessemer's invention of cheap bulk steel had obvious military and naval advantages.[100] It was but the most successful and lucrative of

---

[95] Fairbairn, *Life*, p. 446; *The Times*, 20 October 1874, 8c; 16 November 1874, 6c.

[96] Claude Gibb, 'Parsons, Sir Charles Algernon (1854–1931)', rev. Anita McConnell, *ODNB*, online edn, May 2005, www.oxforddnb.com/view/article/35396, accessed 18 October 2006.

[97] *The Builder* 13 (1855), 202; *The Times*, 12 April 1855, 6c–d; 17 February 1874, 7b; Smiles, *Men of invention and industry* (London: John Murray, 1884), pp. 71–2; David K. Brown, 'Smith, Sir Francis Pettit (1808–1874)', *ODNB*, www.oxforddnb.com/view/article/25798, accessed 18 October 2006.

[98] *The Times*, 7 August 1871, 5e.

[99] *The Times*, 15 November 1905, 3a–b; Alan Cowpe, 'The Royal Navy and the Whitehead torpedo', in Bryan Ranft (ed.), *Technical change and British naval policy, 1860–1939* (London: Hodder & Stoughton, 1977), pp. 23–5; *ILN* 93 (18 August 1888), 305; S. E. Fryer, 'Whitehead, Robert (1823–1905)', rev. David K. Brown, *ODNB*, www.oxforddnb.com/view/article/36868, accessed 18 October 2006.

[100] 'It is a remarkable circumstance that we owe the perhaps most important discovery of the age – Bessemer steel – to the exertions made by Mr Bessemer to procure a good metal for guns': *The Builder* 22 (1864), 111.

a long series of inventions in numerous fields: not all of them were patented, yet between 1838 and 1894 he secured 114 patents.[101] British honours began to rain down in 1879 – twenty years after Bessemer had demonstrated his faith in the then controversial process, by establishing a steelworks in Sheffield. By 1879, he was extremely rich, having received over £1 million from royalties on the steel-making process alone; he had been offered the Légion d'Honneur by Napoleon III, which, he complained, the British government had not allowed him to accept.[102] Perhaps it was this jibe that finally stung it into knighting him. *The Times* thought the occasion worthy of a leading article, which presented Bessemer as virtually the single-handed creator of the modern steel industry. It was, of course, to invite correction to proclaim that, 'It may safely be said that there is no other instance in history of an analogous impetus to manufacture, or an analogous economy, being the result of the brainwork of a single individual'; a letter demanding that David Mushet be given due credit for his contribution was published two days later.[103]

The same year saw Bessemer made a fellow of the Royal Society. In 1880, as one of 'the very front rank of the inventors of the age', he was awarded the freedom of the City of London and presented with a gold casket containing a document illustrating his greatest invention, followed by a mayoral banquet for over 300 people.[104] 'The annals of human progress in the arts', the City Chamberlain told Sir Henry, 'furnish few parallels to the revolution which has been effected by the invention with which your name will ever be associated.' Bessemer himself, more modestly, paid tribute to his predecessors who had advanced the technology of the iron and steel industry, contrasting his own lavish rewards with the fate of 'the hundreds of intelligent and persevering men ... [who had] shared ... the misfortune of being an inventor'; he was fortunate, he said, to live in an era 'when the intelligent sympathies of every citizen are with, and not against, those who devote their lives to scientific studies and the advancement of ... manufactures'.[105] *The Times* ran another leading article in praise of Sir Henry, and chided the City of London for having conferred its freedom

---

[101] Geoffrey Tweedale, 'Bessemer, Sir Henry (1813–1898)', *ODNB*, online edn, May 2006, www.oxforddnb.com/view/article/2287, accessed 18 October 2006; Sir Henry Bessemer, *Sir Henry Bessemer, FRS, an autobiography* (London, 1905).

[102] *The Times*, 21 October 1878, 9f; 1 November 1878, 6b–c; 5 June 1879, 9d–e.

[103] *The Times*, 4 June, 1879, 11f; 5 June 1879, 9d–e; 7 June 1879, 13f.

[104] *The Times*, 14 May 1880, 6e.

[105] *The Times*, 7 October 1880, 4e–f. In this speech Bessemer gave the credit for first smelting iron with mineral fuel to Dud Dudley in 1640.

on so few like him, whose work 'enhanced ... the commercial operations on which the greatness of the City depends'.[106] Bessemer and
Sir Rowland Hill were indeed the only two 'great discoverer[s]' since
Jenner to have received this honour.[107] The City, however, continued
to concentrate its gratitude on Bessemer: between 1880 and 1885, three
City Companies made him an honorary freeman, fêting him with ban-
quets, speeches and presentations.[108] The Master of the Armourers'
Company professed there to be only two other events in the century of
comparable importance with Bessemer's steel: 'the invention of the
steam engine by James Watt and the introduction of the Penny Post
system by Sir Rowland Hill'.[109] The inclusion of Bessemer's portrait
photograph in the *Men of mark* series and a caricature in *Vanity Fair*
were indicative of the high regard in which he was more generally held
(figure 8.10).[110] North American tributes were of an entirely different
nature. 'It was a source of constant pride and gratification to my father,'
wrote Henry Bessemer Jnr, 'that several towns in the United States were
named after him.' The 1900 US Census revealed thirteen 'Bessemers',
concentrated, unsurprisingly, in steel-making districts.[111]

Bessemer's death in 1898 was marked by fulsome obituaries but, at his
own request, he was buried quietly, beside his wife, in a south London
cemetery.[112] Inevitably, there were posthumous honours but, consistent
with a growing trend for utilitarian projects, there was no statue.[113] The
Iron and Steel Institute founded an annual Bessemer Gold Medal.[114] In
1903, the Lord Mayor of London united with the duke of Norfolk, the
principal of London University, leading engineers, and others to launch a
memorial fund for two ambitious educational projects – the establishment
of metallurgical testing and research centres in London, Birmingham and
Sheffield, and international scholarships for postgraduates in practical

---

[106] *The Times*, 7 October 1880, 7d–e.
[107] *The Times*, 7 October 1880, 4e. For Hill, see below, pp. 244, 312–14.
[108] *The Times*, 16 April 1880, 11c; 17 February 1881, 6f; 16 January 1885, 6d.
[109] *The Times*, 16 January 1885, 6d. In a double irony, the past Master of the Armourers,
E. A. Pontifex, conveniently overlooking Bessemer's gun-making activities, congratulated him on having 'conquered nature' for purely peaceful ends.
[110] Thompson Cooper (ed.), *Men of mark: a gallery of contemporary portraits of men distinguished in the senate, the church, in science, literature and art, the army, navy, law, medicine,
etc.*, photo. by Lock and Whitfield, 7 vols. in 4 (London: Sampson Low, Marston, Searle
& Rivington, 1876–83), vol. V, p. 29; caricature by Sir Leslie Ward, *Vanity Fair*, 6
November 1880.
[111] Bessemer, *Autobiography*, pp. 367–8.
[112] *The Times*, 16 March 1898, 8a–b; 21 March 1898, 8c. Lady Bessemer, who died in June
1896, was responsible for at least one of her husband's inventions: *The Times*,
1 November 1878, 6b–c.
[113] See below, pp. 296–7.   [114] *The Times*, 28 February 1901, 12e.

8.10 Photograph of Sir Henry Bessemer, by Lock and Whitfield, in *Men of mark*, 1881. Bessemer's inclusion in this select gallery of photographs is indicative of his contemporary celebrity (photograph by Ann Pethers).

metallurgy courses.[115] Bessemer's celebration was evidently a popular measure, but while the state saw his chief invention primarily through military eyes, to most British people cheap steel probably meant stronger rails and more dramatic bridges (such as that over the Firth of Forth), while Bessemer's ingenuity was a source of wonder and national pride.

William Siemens was well qualified for a knighthood by all apparent criteria, though he only received it immediately before his sudden death, in 1883, at the age of sixty-one. Holder of 113 patents, a successful manufacturer, engineer and experimental scientist, Siemens invented (jointly with his brother) the regenerative-furnace method of steel-making, which rivalled the Bessemer process, and also helped to lay the second Atlantic telegraph cable in 1874. Academic and professional honours recognized his achievements: in the words of *Engineering*, 'he died with honours thick upon him'.[116] Although burial in Westminster Abbey was refused, ostensibly on grounds

[115] *The Times*, 1 May 1903, 3f; 30 June 1903, 8c–d; 23 July 1903, 15d.
[116] *The Times*, 17 April 1883, 8e; 28 April 1883, 7e; 21 November 1883, 6a–b; H. T. Wood, 'Siemens, Sir (Charles) William (1823–1883)', rev. Brian Bowers, *ODNB*, www.oxforddnb.com/view/article/25528, accessed 18 October 2006. *Engineering's* obituary was reprinted in William Pole, *The life of Sir William Siemens* (London: John Murray, 1888), p. 387.

of space, the Institution of Civil Engineers was successful (with the Prince of Wales' support) in securing permission for the funeral service there.[117]

Communications provided the other field in which the state regularly honoured inventors. As with Bessemer's steel, there were military implications but these were probably not foremost in the public's mind. Sir Rowland Hill, who introduced the national penny-postage system in 1840, was genuinely popular. He may not have fitted the Victorian stereotype of an inventor, which was restricted quite narrowly to the mechanical sphere; the term '*originator* of the penny postal system' was preferred for his memorial in Westminster Abbey.[118] He was identified by *The Times*, however, as belonging 'to that class of self-made men which, perhaps more than any other, has raised England to her present height', which included George Stephenson (and Lord Clive).[119] Moreover, Hill's burial in Westminster Abbey, beneath Chantrey's statue of Watt, was regarded as particularly appropriate: Canon Duckworth's memorial sermon referred to Watt as 'a kindred benefactor, the genius of whose discoveries paved the way for [Hill's] work, and blend inseparably with it'.[120] Hill's material rewards included a parliamentary grant of £20,000 and a pension of £2,000 per annum (the equivalent of his full salary as Postmaster-General). He was knighted in 1860. Whether Whitehall thought it was honouring an inventor or a public servant is impossible to say. Hill was elected to a fellowship of the Royal Society in 1857, and made an honorary Doctor of Laws by the University of Oxford in 1864. In 1879, he received the much rarer honours of the freedom of the City of London (which he was too frail to accept in public) and, shortly afterwards, of burial in Westminster Abbey.[121] According to *The Times*, Hill had 'done almost more than any other single man to bind the nations together and to make the whole world kin'.[122]

---

[117] *The Times*, 23 November 1883, 5f; 24 November 1883, 7a; 27 November 1883, 10a; Pole, *Sir William Siemens*, pp. 367–8.

[118] *The Times*, 5 May 1881, 9f. The same committee preferred the inscription, 'Sir Rowland Hill. He *founded* uniform Penny Postage, 1840', for his monument at the Royal Exchange: *The Times*, 28 November 1881, 11f; 29 March 1882, 8b; 22 April 1882, 12d; my emphasis in both instances. The memorial tablet placed on Hill's Hampstead house in 1893 by the Society of Arts again used the term 'originator': *The Times*, 30 June 1983, 10d. Hill had several mechanical as well as other organizational inventions to his credit: C. R. Perry, 'Hill, Sir Rowland (1795–1879)', *ODNB*, www.oxforddnb.com/view/article/13299, accessed 18 October 2006.

[119] *The Times*, 28 August 1879, 4c–f.

[120] *The Times*, 8 September 1879, 7f; see also ibid., 5 September 1879, 8a–b. See also below, p. 313.

[121] *The Times*, 31 January 1879, 12a; 7 June 1879, 12e; 28 August 1879, 4f.

[122] *The Times*, 28 August 1879, 4f.

Rewards also flowed to those responsible for giving the state immediate communication with its vast empire through the electric telegraph. Honours came most quickly to William Thomson, knighted in 1866 for succeeding, where others had failed, in laying the Atlantic cable. A brilliant career as both an academic scientist and a practical inventor was recognized by numerous professional honours, and again by the state, with his elevation to the peerage as Baron Kelvin of Largs in 1892 (he was science's first peer). The Order of Merit followed, at its inception in 1902, when Kelvin was also made a Privy Councillor. As the 'foremost physicist' of his day there was no difficulty in securing his burial in Westminster Abbey in 1907; posthumous memorials from his profession, his university and his birthplace were legion.[123] The transatlantic telegraph link prompted the belated recognition of two earlier pioneers, Charles Wheatstone and Francis Ronalds, knighted in 1868 and 1871 respectively. *The Times* had protested loudly in 1866 when Wheatstone was passed over: without mentioning Thomson, it judged that, 'To Wheatstone we really owe the fact that the whole civilized world is now brought within an instant of time', and bewailed the 'tragic' fate of inventors.[124]

By 1900, prominent civil engineers were knighted almost routinely on the successful completion of an ambitious project; others, in recognition of a long and distinguished career, particularly one involving work for the state or a local authority.[125] Benjamin Baker received his knighthood (KCMG) in 1890, the year that saw his rail bridge over the Forth opened, followed by promotion to the more prestigious rank of KCB in 1902, for the Aswan Dam in Egypt.[126] Similarly, John Wolfe-Barry was knighted for Tower Bridge in 1894, and raised to KCB in 1897.[127]

---

[123] *The Times*, 18 December 1907, 8a–d; 19 December 1907, 7f; 20 December 1907, 14d; 24 December 1907, 4b; Crosbie Smith, 'Thomson, William, Baron Kelvin (1824–1907)', *ODNB*, online edn, May 2006, www.oxforddnb.com/view/article/36507, accessed 18 October 2006; see also below, pp. 326, 365–7.

[124] *The Times*, 10 October 1866, 8e; S. P. Thompson, 'Wheatstone, Sir Charles (1802–1875)', rev. Brian Bowers, *ODNB*, www.oxforddnb.com/view/article/29184, accessed 18 October 2006; Eleanor Putnam Symons, 'Ronalds, Sir Francis (1788–1873)', *ODNB*, www.oxforddnb.com/view/article/24057, accessed 18 October 2006. For the intense interest in who invented the telegraph, see *Invention of the telegraph: the charge against Sir Charles Wheatstone, of "tampering with the press", as evidenced by a letter of the editor of the "Quarterly Review" in 1855. Reprinted from the "Scientific Review"* (London: Simpkin, Marshall & Co.; Bath: R. E. Peach, 1869), pp. 27–31.

[125] See, for example, the list in *The Engineer* 2 (5 August 1881), 91.

[126] W. F. Spear, 'Baker, Sir Benjamin (1840–1907)', rev. Mike Chrimes, *ODNB*, www.oxforddnb.com/view/article/30545, accessed 18 October 2006; *The Times*, 20 May 1907, 7f.

[127] Robert C. McWilliam, 'Barry, Sir John Wolfe Wolfe- (1836–1918)', *ODNB*, www.oxforddnb.com/view/article/36989, accessed 18 October 2006; *The Times*, 24 January 1918, 9d.

Eventually, the state began to honour creative men who were distinguished in their own professions or who had proved themselves as industrialists. Consequently, a small number of inventors in fields of less immediate interest to the state received official recognition. None were 'mere' inventors. Samuel Cunliffe Lister, with over 150 patents to his name (mostly for textile inventions), was created Baron Masham in 1891; he was both a leading industrialist and a philanthropist.[128] The chemist, William Perkin, was finally knighted on the fiftieth anniversary of his discovery of the first aniline dye in 1856, presumably at the suggestion of the committee established by the Chemical Society, the Royal Society and the chemical industry to organize the jubilee celebrations. Since selling his synthetic dye company in 1873, Perkin had resumed laboratory research, published over sixty scientific papers, taken leading roles in national scientific societies, and received many honours from fellow scientists.[129] His name was scarcely known, however, to the general public. Perkin needed some persuasion to accept the knighthood. His elder son convinced him it was more than a personal honour.

[It was] also an honour done to science and especially to industry ... As you know, there has long been a feeling in scientific circles that research work has never been adequately recognised by our past Governments, as it is in Germany, and this is therefore a welcome step.[130]

Would the official recognition of Perkin's achievements have been so tardy if the British dye industry had not succumbed to foreign competition? The loudest acclaim came indeed from overseas. In a lengthy ceremony at the Royal Institution, Perkin received the Hofmann medal from the German Chemical Society, the Lavoisier medal from the Chemical Society of Paris, and a clutch of other medals and congratulatory addresses from scientific and industrial societies across Europe. By no means, were these Perkin's first marks of recognition in either Germany or France, where the synthetic dye industry had flourished. The speeches stressed the international character of the chemical

---

[128] S. E. Fryer, 'Lister, Samuel Cunliffe-, first Baron Masham (1815–1906)', rev. D. T. Jenkins, *ODNB*, online edn, October 2006, www.oxforddnb.com/view/article/34554, accessed 18 October 2006; *The Times*, 3 February 1906, 9d–f. See also below, p. 361.

[129] Anthony S. Travis, 'Perkin, Sir William Henry (1838–1907)', *ODNB*, www.oxforddnb.com/view/article/35477, accessed 18 October 2006; Simon Garfield, *Mauve: how one man invented a colour that changed the world* (London: Faber & Faber, 2000), pp. 124–7; *The Times*, 27 February 1906, 4e.

[130] W. H. Perkin Jnr to W. H. Perkin, February 1906, quoted in Garfield, *Mauve*, p. 128.

industry and the contribution of men, such as Perkin, 'to the wealth and learning and talent of the world at large'.[131] Less euphemistically, *The Times* again pondered why the dye industry had vanished from Britain: it blamed the universities in particular and British attitudes in general.[132] A few weeks later, Sir William crossed the Atlantic to be received by President Roosevelt, greeted by a fanfare in the press, and fêted by a distinguished committee of 150 'leading scientific and public men'.[133]

Baronetcies (hereditary knighthoods) were conferred on the respective pioneers of anaesthetics and antiseptic surgery, James Young Simpson in 1866, and Joseph Lister in 1883; both were well established in the medical profession. Simpson was also honoured with the freedom of the city of Edinburgh and, following his death in 1870, with memorials, organized by members of the medical profession, both in Edinburgh and Westminster Abbey.[134] Lister lived long enough to amass many honours, including in 1897 a peerage, 'the first ever conferred upon a surgeon, and only the second ever conferred for scientific distinction', and the Order of Merit in 1902. A funeral service in Westminster Abbey and numerous monuments were to mark the culmination of a glorious career.[135]

The Victorian bourgeoisie's hopes had been fulfilled – that the contribution of inventors and engineers to Britain's prosperity and international standing would be officially recognized – but not in the way that many had intended. An elite few had been fully accepted into the national pantheon, but on the governing class's own terms. Hesitant in honouring inventors and engineers, the state initially preferred those who had served it directly, through the improvement of its military or communications capabilities. The men of science did not displace the warriors and the statesmen whose statues continued to monopolize London's most prestigious sites, but were ceded places only in the more obscure squares and

---

[131] *The Times*, 27 July 1906, 12c–e; Garfield, *Mauve*, pp. 128–36 and pl. 6.

[132] *The Times*, 24 February 1906, 14a; 27 July 1906, 9e. See also the comments in the *Daily Telegraph* quoted in Garfield, *Mauve*, pp. 134–5.

[133] *The Times*, 6 September 1906, 10c; 15 July 1907, 6d; Garfield, *Mauve*, pp. 3–13.

[134] *The Times*, 7 May 1870, 9f; 9 November 1870, 7e; 28 May 1877, 9f; *British Medical Journal* 2 (1874), 378–9, 718; I am grateful to Barbara Mortimer for this reference. Malcolm Nicolson, 'Simpson, Sir James Young, first baronet (1811–1870)', *ODNB*, www.oxforddnb.com/view/article/25584, accessed 18 October 2006.

[135] *The Times*, 31 December 1883, 7d; 12 February 1912, 9f–10c; 17 February 1912, 6e; Christopher Lawrence, 'Lister, Joseph, Baron Lister (1827–1912)', *ODNB*, www. oxforddnb.com/view/article/34553, accessed 18 October 2006. Burial in the Abbey (subject to cremation) was offered by the Dean, but refused, since Lister had expressly requested he be buried, next to his wife, in Hampstead churchyard.

gardens of the capital.[136] Yet, if in the eyes of Britain's conventional social elite, inventors, engineers and other men of science remained only second-class heroes, we should not lose sight of the social distance they had travelled during the nineteenth century. Nor were national honours and symbolic sites in the capital their only measure of achievement. In the following two chapters, we shall see how the heroic inventor was recruited both to defend the patent system from the threat of abolition and to justify again the widening of the parliamentary franchise.

[136] In W. T. Pike (ed.), *Northumberland, at the opening of the twentieth century by James Jameson* (Brighton: Pike, 1905), 'aristocrats continued to lead the rankings [of Northumberland worthies]; engineers came ninth': Colls, 'Remembering George Stephenson', p. 287.

9 Debating the patent system

Contemporary with the Great Exhibition, the Patent Law Amendment Act of 1852 introduced a single patent system for the entire United Kingdom. It established a dedicated Patent Office and massively reduced the initial cost. It also sparked a controversy that threatened to abolish the patent system, until it was secured by further legislation in 1883.[1] This type of debate was heard throughout Europe during the mid-nineteenth century, usually initiated by a proposed reform that would strengthen patent protection. First, the formation of the Zollverein raised questions about patent protection in individual German states: despite an agreement in 1842, calls to adopt uniform patent legislation throughout the customs union prompted ever louder demands for abolition of all patents.[2] It was the Netherlands, however, that took this unprecedented step in 1869, restoring its patent system only in 1912, under strong moral pressure from the International Union for the Protection of Industrial Property (founded in 1884).[3] Switzerland, which had previously never had a patent system, succumbed to the same pressure in 1907.[4]

It was not by chance that this pan-European questioning of the legitimacy of patents for invention coincided with the rise in free-trade thought among economists and policy makers. The same liberalizing impulse, which had helped to found the Zollverein and, in Britain, to repeal the corn laws, queried the justice and the benefits – to both the individual inventor and society – of granting even this temporary monopoly over an

---

[1] Moureen Coulter, *Property in ideas: the patent question in mid-Victorian Britain* (Kirksville, MO: Thomas Jefferson Press, 1992); Victor M. Batzel, 'Legal monopoly in Liberal England: the patent controversy in the mid-nineteenth century', *Business History* 22 (1980), 189–202.
[2] Edith Tilton Penrose, *The economics of the international patent system* (Baltimore: Johns Hopkins Press, 1951), p. 14; Machlup and Penrose, 'Patent controversy', 4.
[3] Penrose, *Economics*, p. 15; Eric Schiff, *Industrialization without national patents: the Netherlands, 1869–1912, Switzerland, 1850–1907* (Princeton, NJ: Princeton University Press, 1971), pp. 19–24, 39–41, 124–5.
[4] Penrose, *Economics*, pp. 15–16; Schiff, *Industrialization*, pp. 85–95.

invention.[5] Even in France, where uniquely the patent law of 1791 enshrined the concept of the inventor's natural right to own his intellectual property, economists could be heard condemning in one breath both patents and protective tariffs.[6] In Britain, the pressure for abolition mounted to the point where, in 1869, with the Netherlands showing the way and Parliament debating yet another abolitionist bill, *The Economist* predicted that 'it is probable enough that the patent laws will be abolished ere long'.[7]

Abolition of the patent system had been advocated by eight of the thirty-three witnesses before the parliamentary select committee, established in 1851 to scrutinize its operation and consider its reform. Although a minority, they included such influential and innovative figures as Isambard Kingdom Brunel, William Armstrong and William Cubitt, the president of the Institution of Civil Engineers.[8] Their largely pragmatic arguments were endorsed by the committee's chairman, Lord Granville, who dissented from the reformist recommendations of the report he presented to Parliament. Granville declared that 'the whole system was unadvisable to the public, disadvantageous to inventors, and wrong in principle'.[9] Nonetheless, reforming legislation was enacted in 1852, and the abolitionists' case would probably have subsided, had it not been for a clause in the new act that stung British sugar manufacturers into action. By restricting the exercise of UK patents to the British Isles, the act effectively granted exemption to colonial sugar refiners from the payment of any patent royalties (to which British-based refiners would be liable). Led by Robert Andrew Macfie, a member of a large sugar-refining dynasty based in Liverpool and Leith, the sugar manufacturers and their allies demanded the abolition not merely of this one clause but of the entire patent system. Their vociferous campaign kept the patent question alive, both within Parliament and beyond, for the next three decades.[10]

---

[5] Penrose, *Economics*, pp. 20–39; Machlup and Penrose, 'Patent controversy', 3–5, 7–9, 23–8.

[6] Machlup and Penrose, 'Patent controversy', 8–9, 11–13, 16–17.

[7] Batzel, 'Legal monopoly', 190.

[8] Brunel obtained no patents; Cubitt obtained one in 1807, but had been closely involved, as a workman, with the intensive patenting strategy of Messrs Ransome of Ipswich: *Report from the select committee of the House of Lords*, BPP 1851, XVIII, pp. 450, 455, 482. For Armstrong, see above, pp. 237–8.

[9] Hansard, *P. D.*, 3rd ser., CXVIII (1851), col. 16.

[10] Christine MacLeod, 'Macfie, Robert Andrew (1811–1893)', *ODNB*, www.oxforddnb. com/view/article/17499, accessed 19 October 2006. Macfie had testified before the 1851 select committee, as had another sugar refiner, John Fairrie: *Report from the select committee of the House of Lords*, BPP 1851, XVIII, pp. 381–5, 390–1.

Ranged against them, determined not merely to preserve but further to improve the system, were thousands of patentees, would-be patentees and manufacturers to whom patents had been sold or licensed; their spokesmen were primarily patent agents and barristers who specialized in patent litigation. At the centre of this defensive network, tirelessly providing information and encouragement, was Bennet Woodcroft, the first Superintendent of Specifications at the newly established Patent Office. A stalwart champion of inventors and patentees, Woodcroft undertook the first systematic attempt to preserve the history of British invention. He strove to record and to bring to public attention the achievements of inventive men, both living and dead. Whether he would have been quite so energetic in this pursuit (which transcended his already heavy duties), without the serious threat to the patent system that persisted throughout his period of office is cause for speculation.[11]

The heroic defence of the patent system

Already before 1852, Woodcroft was an ardent campaigner for reform on behalf of his fellow patentees and a fount of historical and technical knowledge (figure 9.1).[12] When appointed to the new Patent Office, he continued to lobby for improved facilities and still cheaper patents. The son of a Lancashire dyer, he had 'worked at the loom', before turning his hand to invention and patent agency; briefly Professor of Machinery at University College London, he published *A sketch of the origin and progress of steam navigation* (1848) – in which his own invention of a screw propeller played a part.[13] Like other patent agents, Woodcroft had compiled his own indexes of patents and specifications to compensate for the lack of any official series.[14] Now, interpreting expansively a clause in the act that required this lack be remedied, he oversaw the institution of a system of printed indexes, lists and specifications, which was designed to provide intending patentees with as much information as possible. These

[11] Christine MacLeod, 'Concepts of invention and the patent controversy in Victorian Britain', in Robert Fox (ed.), *Technological change: methods and themes in the history of technology* (Amsterdam: Harwood Academic Publishers, 1996), pp. 137–54.

[12] *Report from the select committee of the House of Lords*, BPP 1851, XVIII, pp. 461–81.

[13] John Hewish, *The indefatigable Mr Woodcroft: the legacy of invention* (London: Science Reference Library, 1982); John Hewish, *Rooms near Chancery Lane: the Patent Office under the Commissioners, 1852–1883* (London: British Library, 2000), pp. 18–19; Anita McConnell, 'Woodcroft, Bennet (1803–1879)', *ODNB*, www.oxforddnb.com/view/article/29908, accessed 19 October 2006.

[14] Hewish, *Indefatigable Mr Woodcroft*, pp. 17, 23; Woolrich, 'John Farey Jr: engineer and polymath', 117–18; *Report from the select committee of the House of Lords*, BPP 1851, XVIII, pp. 460–1.

9.1 Portrait of Bennet Woodcroft, by Sibley, c. 1840s.

publications were donated – on condition of their free availability – to institutions across the country; where public libraries did not exist, they sometimes prompted their establishment. Favourable comment in the national and local press helped to bring the Patent Office and its clients to public attention. Such volumes also formed the currency of exchanges, agreed with the US and various European patent offices, which boosted the range of information available at London's.[15]

Woodcroft did not neglect the historical dimension: his small army of clerks extended the printed series back to 1617 – a laborious, not to say filthy, task, as anyone who has ever unrolled a patent roll will testify. In the peak year of 1856, over three million words and 1,500 drawings were copied from the rolls, preparatory to their printing.[16] By the time of this task's completion in 1858, Woodcroft had inaugurated a series of abridgements of specifications, 'in classes and chronologically arranged', from 1617 onwards: he intended these short abstracts 'to enable the humblest of inventors to examine for himself whether his discovery has been previously patented or not'.[17] Some of these volumes even predate the official series of specifications, and contain historical introductions to

---

[15] Hewish, *Rooms near Chancery Lane*, pp. 33–5, 45–53; Ian Inkster, 'Patents as indicators of technological change and innovation – an historical analysis of the patent data, 1830–1914', *TNS* 73 (2003), 198–201.
[16] Hewish, *Rooms near Chancery Lane*, pp. 37–41.   [17] Ibid., pp. 41–2.

their subject. He also published a brief series of 'scarce pamphlets descriptive of early patented inventions', which included the marquis of Worcester's account of his steam engine.[18] Some of these pamphlets were among Woodcroft's own collection of books that accompanied him to the Patent Office in 1852, and formed the kernel of the Patent Office Library, at Southampton Buildings. By 1860, it was reputedly 'the greatest technical library in the country, and probably in Europe'.[19]

Woodcroft's perspective on invention was entirely biographical: he sought to preserve the historical records, the physical objects, and the memory of the men responsible for them. He pursued information and portraits of eighteenth- and nineteenth-century textile inventors for a collective biography, which appeared in 1863. His introduction to this volume situated it in the tradition of 'the inventor as victim' literature: society, he claimed, superstitiously reverencing tradition, derided and exaggerated every failed invention, while withholding praise from the successful. Most of Woodcroft's ten subjects died in poverty, but, had they lived in ancient times, 'altars would have been erected in their honour, and they would have been worshipped as demigods'.[20] His primary concern, however, was less with honour than with material reward – to defend the patent system against its critics, who advocated parliamentary grants or public subscriptions as a viable alternative.[21] Samuel Crompton, said Woodcroft, had been cruelly deceived by the cotton spinners who promised a subscription to deter him from patenting the mule; his parliamentary grant of £5,000 was 'a mockery of a reward'. The £10,000 that Parliament awarded Edmund Cartwright in 1808 might appear generous, but the power loom had cost him £30,000 to develop. William Radcliffe was bankrupted by his experiments and spent the last twenty-seven years of his life 'in very straitened circumstances'. By contrast, although Joseph Jacquard undoubtedly suffered the hostility of unemployed weavers, this French inventor was honoured by Napoleon in his lifetime and with a host of posthumous memorials.[22] (As *Punch* quipped, 'they do things better in France'.)[23]

Woodcroft was in contact with a number of like spirits, such as John Timbs and Samuel Smiles. Individual biographies of inventors and other

---

[18] Ibid., pp. 43–4; Edward Somerset, second marquis of Worcester, *An exact and true definition of the most stupendious water-commanding engine* (London, 1663).

[19] Hewish, *Rooms near Chancery Lane*, pp. 44, 147–59; Hewish, *Indefatigable Mr Woodcroft*, p. 7.

[20] Bennet Woodcroft, FRS, *Brief biographies of inventors of machines for the manufacture of textile fabrics* (London: Longman, 1863), pp. vii–viii, xii–xiii, xv.

[21] Ibid., p. 46; see below, p. 272.   [22] Ibid., pp. 15–19, 29–31, 35.

[23] See above, pp. 219–20.

men of science were still rare, but 1859–60 saw the publication of four collective volumes.[24] Timbs' *Stories of inventors and discoverers in science and the useful arts* contained sixty chapters, over half of them dealing with inventions made during recent decades, the remainder dating back to Archimedes. All but a few chapters were titled with a name and an invention; others bore headings indicative of Timbs' concern for correct attribution and reward, such as 'Who invented printing, and where?' and 'Who invented gunpowder?' A professional author, Timbs recalled having been prompted by the portraits of inventors and models of their inventions in the Patent Office Museum at South Kensington to reflect on Britain's indebtedness to such men. 'Conservative as are my opinions generally,' he admitted, 'I must own that, to such men as Watt and Crompton – to the inventors and discoverers – and not to what are vulgarly termed "the great men" we owe our supremacy as a nation.'[25] Like Woodcroft, Timbs showed a particular concern for the honours paid, or due, to his inventors: a lack of recognition from the state or tardiness of commemoration by private individuals prompted his frequent censure, while he evinced great pride in the grandeur of Robert Stephenson's funeral.[26] One dissenting reviewer tartly commented that 'for every persecuted benefactor of society, we will find at least two who met their reward'.[27]

Readers of Lucy Brightwell's volume, *Heroes of the laboratory and the workshop*, might have concurred. Brightwell rarely omitted to mention the honours her heroes received, whether from the hands of Napoleon, the Royal Society, or their own workmen (contributing to a posthumous monument or bust). No doubt, she wished to encourage the working men for whom she wrote with the prospect of ultimate glory and renown, although she also emphasized that many had 'toiled and striven' and contributed their efforts anonymously to the ultimate success of 'the fortunate few'.[28] A talented etcher, Brightwell inherited her nonconformist

[24] Smiles himself, reviewing Muirhead's biography of Watt, commented on the dearth of biographies of 'distinguished inventors': 'James Watt', 411. An American precedent was Henry Howe, *Memoirs of the most eminent American mechanics: also, lives of distinguished European mechanics* (New York, 1841); it contained biographical sketches of eleven Americans and eighteen Europeans (sixteen of them British).

[25] John Timbs to Gilbert French, 5 October 1859, Crompton MSS, ZCR82/16; John Timbs [to Bennet Woodcroft], 29 August 1859, Woodcroft MSS, Z27/B, fo. 246; John Timbs, *Stories of inventors and discoverers in science and the useful arts* (London: Kent & Co., 1860), p. viii.

[26] Timbs, *Stories of inventors*, pp. viii, 130, 153, 270, 299, 307.

[27] 'Inventors and inventions', *All the Year Round* 2 (4 February 1860), 353.

[28] C[elia] L[ucy] Brightwell, *Heroes of the laboratory and the workshop* (London: Routledge & Co., 1859), pp. vi–vii, 60, 65, 96, 104, and passim.

father's passion for natural history and microscopy; her previous ventures into print had been chiefly biographies of religious figures.[29] Her heroes included an unusually high proportion of non-British inventors, several of them Huguenots who had been persecuted for their faith – which perhaps, for her, put the 'persecution' experienced by other inventors into perspective – but they were all workingmen.[30] Even the few who were 'devoted to science', she insisted, fell into this category; like the rest, 'they all rose to eminence solely by the force of their own talent and energy'.[31] Brightwell cited as her inspiration both sympathy for the artisan – the 'hardships of his lot' – and envy for his 'feelings of honest independence'.[32]

No such religious or romantic sympathies inspired Frederick Collier Bakewell to compile his *Great facts*. Bakewell was a physicist and inventor of a 'fax' machine. His approach was unusual at this period, though it became common later in the century: he organized his material primarily by invention, rather than inventor, which provided scope to mention the work of more men, even such neglected figures (in Britain) as Denis Papin and De Jouffroy.[33] Neither Brightwell nor Bakewell demonstrated any concern with the patent system, but their books helped to show inventors in a positive light and, in Brightwell's case, to brand them unambiguously as heroes.

All three volumes were outshone and outsold by the fourth, which, while not mentioning inventors or inventions in its title, focused almost exclusively on them. Samuel Smiles' *Self-help* sold 20,000 copies in its first year, and more than a quarter of a million by 1905 – far exceeding the sales of the great nineteenth-century novels.[34] Smiles was concerned not with the patent question but with the lessons of conduct that these men's lives could teach, 'as illustrations of what each might ... do for himself'.[35] Nonetheless, such an influential text could scarcely avoid affecting the current debate. Not only did his focus on inventors bring their life and work to prominence, but his treatment of them as shining exemplars of virtue was likely to win his readers' sympathy. Arkwright, for instance, was 'a man of great force of character [and] indomitable courage'. John

[29] Norma Watt, 'Brightwell, (Cecilia) Lucy (1811–1875)', *ODNB*, www.oxforddnb.com/view/article/3426, accessed 19 October 2006.

[30] Brightwell, *Heroes*, pp. viii, 69, 86–7.   [31] Ibid., p. vi.   [32] Ibid., p. v.

[33] Frederick Collier Bakewell, *Great facts: a popular history and description of the most remarkable inventions during the present century* (London: Houlston & Wright, 1859). See also below, pp. 375–6. For Bakewell's invention, see chem.ch.huji.ac.il/~eugenik/history/bakewell.html, accessed 12 August 2005.

[34] Briggs, *Victorian people*, p. 118. See also above, pp. 176–7.

[35] Smiles, *Self-help*, preface [1859], p. ix. Judith Rowbotham offers some valuable insights into the genre in '"All our past proclaims our future": popular biography and masculine identity during the golden age, 1850–1870', in Inkster *et al.* (eds.), *Golden age*, pp. 272–5.

Heathcoat was 'undaunted by failures and mistakes', a man of 'upright-ness, honesty, and integrity – qualities which are the true glory of human character', a model employer, and well-read too. As for the steam engine, 'what a noble story of patient, laborious investigation, of difficulties encountered and overcome by heroic industry, does not that marvellous machine tell of'. Such men were all 'the Industrial Heroes of the civilized world'.[36]

Smiles' biographies were implicitly supportive of the patent system in two, more specific ways: they stressed the effort, labour and perseverance required to bring any invention to completion, and they instanced cases where a patent gave a deserving inventor insufficient protection from grasping 'pirates'. Without exception, Smiles' inventors achieve their goals through sheer hard work: Watt had been 'the most indus-trious of men', none 'laboured so assiduously'; Wedgwood 'overcame his difficulties ... by repeated experiments and unfaltering perseverance'; Arkwright's 'success was only secured by long and patient labour'.[37] Invention and discovery, by implication, were not easily achieved; they were not mere 'accidents' waiting to happen; those who accomplished them truly merited whatever reward resulted.[38] Yet inventive success, in Smiles' biographies, tended to be crowned not with gold and glory but with acrimony and theft – the inventor's struggles were not yet over. Lancashire manufacturers 'fell upon Arkwright's patent' and pulled it 'in pieces' (it was voided 'to the disgust of right-minded people'), just as Cornish miners had turned on Boulton and Watt 'to rob' them of their profits. Heathcoat, like Arkwright, had to fend off both Luddite 'rioters' and interlopers who infringed his patents. Unlike Arkwright, he was finally successful in the courts and levied 'a large sum' in royalties. Lest anyone should think to carp at such wealth, Smiles reminded them that the consumer had benefited from a massive reduction in the price of lace, and the lace trade gave 'remunerative employment' to 150,000 people.[39] Many other inventors in Smiles' volumes had been less fortunate: they had had to flee from the 'mob', had been denounced, ridiculed and ostracized, or had died in poverty.[40] By implication, they all needed stronger protection.

---

[36] Smiles, *Self-help*, pp. 30, 36, 48, 54, 93.
[37] Ibid., pp. 30, 90, 95. See also Smiles, *Men of industry and invention*, pp. 57–8, 71–2, 77, and above, pp. 177–80.
[38] Smiles, *Self-help*, pp. 118–24.
[39] Ibid., pp. 356, 50–4. See also pp. 212–14, and Smiles, *Men of industry and invention*, p. 160.
[40] Smiles, *Self-help*, pp. 35, 44, 60, 66, 136, 148.

In January 1863, Woodcroft told a descendent of Patrick Miller that 'Smiles the historian called on me a week ago and said, "Who introduced steam navigation, was it Symington, Miller, or Taylor?" I told him Miller and gave him a copy of your letter.'[41] Smiles' confidence that there existed a market for 'the lives of departed engineers' had again been vindicated in 1861, when the first edition of *The lives of the engineers* (in four volumes) scarcely touched the booksellers' shelves: although priced at four guineas per set, approximately 6,000 copies were quickly sold.[42] 'The *Saturday Review* expressed surprise "that the idea of handling the subject of engineering in this manner should not sooner have been seized."'[43] Spurred on by critical acclaim and the attention of public figures, such as Gladstone and Sir Stafford Northcote, Smiles turned to write the biographies of 'the leading Mechanical Inventors', in particular machine-tool makers from Bramah to Nasmyth. With the co-operation of leading 'mechanics', including Penn, Field, Nasmyth and Sir William Fairbairn, the resultant *Industrial biography* appeared in 1863. It was in the preface of this workshop-based book, rather than when recounting the lives of the socially superior civil engineers, that Smiles defended himself from 'critics, who might think I had treated of a vulgar and commonplace subject'. Forty years later, he explained:

History, no doubt, deals with the affairs of courts, the deeds of statesmen, and the exploits of warriors, and takes but little heed of inventors or mechanics, on whose industrial labours *civilisation and history of the best sort* mainly depends, but without exaggerating the importance of this class of biography, I insisted that it had not yet received its due share of attention ... Without derogating from the biographical claims of those who minister to intellect and taste, those who minister to utility need not be overlooked.[44]

The response of reviewers suggested that such defensiveness was unnecessary. 'Mr Smiles rescues no name, but many histories, from oblivion', said one. 'His heroes are known and gratefully remembered for the benefits they have conferred on mankind, but our knowledge of our benefactors has hitherto been mostly confined to our knowledge of the benefit.'[45]

---

[41] Woodcroft to W. H. Miller, 9 January 1863, Woodcroft MSS, Z27, fo. 197.

[42] MacKay (ed.), *Autobiography of Samuel Smiles*, pp. 248–51.   [43] Ibid., pp. 255–6.

[44] Ibid., p. 257. See also Smiles, *Men of invention and industry*, pp. 77–8; and above, p. 205. For the disparity in social status between the Civils and the Mechanicals, see Reader, '"At the head of all the new professions"', pp. 178–9.

[45] *Edinburgh Daily Review*, reprinted in an advertisement for *Industrial biography: iron workers and tool makers* (London: John Murray, 1863), in the endpapers of Smiles, *Lives of the engineers: the locomotive*. See also 'The philosophy of invention and patent laws', *Fraser's Magazine* 66 (1863), 505. This anonymous author cited 'Young's paraffin oil and Bessemer's steel' as being 'on every lip', while Young and Bessemer themselves were 'little more than myths'.

Over the next half century, there followed a stream of popular works on invention and engineering, for both adults and children.[46] Technical details rarely hang heavy on them. Initially, the principal approach was biographical, with emphasis on the personal qualities of the inventors and the scale of the changes wrought by their efforts. One is left in no doubt about their significance. In *Great inventors: the sources of their usefulness and the results of their efforts*, a wide-ranging volume, published anonymously (but apparently from a radical pen) in 1864, the heroic tone is set by the first chapter, on printing. This ends with the rhetorical questions,

And what shall be said of the result of Caxton's labours – the invention of Printing? What has Printing done for the world – what has it not done? Printing sows the seeds of knowledge broadcast, and all mankind reap the harvest.

Just as Tom Paine's books had 'freed the American colonies', so newspapers and 'placard journals' had instigated the French Revolution.[47] The impact of Watt's steam engine was treated with the customary hyperbole (including the claim that, without it, there would have been no victory at Trafalgar) and the chapter on 'George Stephenson and Railways' concluded 'O Geordie, Geordie, what a revolution hast thou brought into the world!'[48] What nobler ambition could one have than to be an inventor? Despite the 'derision' with which most modern inventors were initially greeted, the honour that was the inventor's due is encapsulated in an imaginary scene, where the young Stephenson returns home from Scotland with £28 in his pocket, his reward for resolving a technical conundrum. Better even than the money – three to six months' wages for a skilled man – is his consciousness 'that he was, in a very humble way – *an inventor*'.[49]

Equally flattering to the inventive ego was *The inventor's almanac*, published annually from 1859 to 1873 by Michael Henry, a London patent agent.[50] The *Almanac* was covered with the names of inventors,

[46] For example, [Robert Cochrane], *Heroes of invention and discovery: lives of eminent inventors and pioneers in science* (Edinburgh: William P. Nimmo & Co., 1879); John Timbs, *Wonderful inventions: from the mariner's compass to the electric telegraph cable* (London: G. Routledge & Sons, 1868), 2nd edn, London 1881; James Burnley, *The romance of invention: vignettes from the annals of industry and science* (London, Paris, New York and Melbourne: Cassell & Co., 1886); Edward E. Hale, *Stories of inventors, told by inventors and their friends* (London, Edinburgh and New York: T. Nelson & Sons, 1887).

[47] *Great inventors: the sources of their usefulness and the results of their efforts* [1864], p. 34.

[48] Ibid., pp. 34, 50–3, 133.

[49] Ibid., p. 114. See also pp. vi–viii for the customary contrast between ancient deification and modern derision.

[50] *The inventor's almanac* (London: Michael Henry, 1859–73).

ancient and modern, British and foreign (like all patent agents, Henry could not afford to be insular). Some names were entwined around six engravings of inventions, which decorated the four corners and the centre of the page: textile inventors, for example, around a knitting frame; steam-engine inventors around a locomotive. Most names were prominently inscribed on oak leaves around the margins; an elite few were repeated in a list of the vital dates of sixteen men of science, and again in a chronology of major inventions and discoveries. In the first issue, the calendar was a conventional compilation of holy days, royal birthdays, and dates of the legal terms, but it also noted the anniversaries of the birth and death of Franklin, Watt, Arkwright and George Stephenson; by 1861, the anniversaries of inventors and scientists overwhelmed the other categories. A neo-Gothic redesign in 1864 made the names of inventors even more prominent, and replaced the pictures of inventions with high-flown quotations (many of them of the 'swords into ploughshares' variety).

The collections of portraits and models in the Patent Office Museum, to which John Timbs attributed his inspiration, were largely the product of Bennet Woodcroft's dedication to the history of technology. Woodcroft maintained an extensive correspondence, combing the country for extant likenesses of inventors to be displayed in a projected National Gallery of Inventors, and urging contemporary inventors to have their portraits painted for inclusion in it (and their biographies written).[51] His collection began in 1853, with a drawing in chalk of the Rev. John Harmar, the late eighteenth-century patentee of cloth-shearing machinery, presented by his family.[52] In 1855, Woodcroft announced his first catalogue, which contained sixty portraits of inventors 'from Arkwright to the Marquis of Worcester', and appealed for further donations. He gave his enthusiastic support to earl Stanhope's proposal in 1856 that led to the establishment of the National Portrait Gallery, but he continued to collect independently.[53] By 1859, he had amassed 190 items, including some duplicates: they were mostly engravings, but there were also a few original portraits in oil, daguerreotypes, medallions and busts. Their subjects were overwhelmingly eighteenth- or nineteenth-century, and

---

[51] Woodcroft MSS, Z27A, fos. 53, 79, 93, 151; Z27B, fos. 46, 48, 329, 511.
[52] *Catalogue of the gallery of portraits of inventors, discoverers, and introducers of useful arts* (5th edn, London, 1859). For successive catalogues of the collection, published 1857–9, see Woodcroft MSS, Z27B, fos. 98, 110, 200. Registers and lists of portraits compiled in the 1870s may be found in Woodcroft MSS, Z28–Z31. At his retirement in 1876, Woodcroft claimed to own approximately 440 of the portraits in the Patent Office Museum's collection: Woodcroft MSS, Z30–Z31.
[53] Hewish, *Rooms near Chancery Lane*, pp. 118–19.

British.[54] Occasionally, they extended beyond inventors. In 1864, for example, John Hick, of the Bolton steam-engineering firm, informed Woodcroft that he was 'trying to induce William Gowland who drove the Engine [i.e. the *Sans Pareil*] at the [Rainhill] trial in 1829 to sit for his photograph'; Woodcroft was delighted with this 'excellent' portrait, as 'an interesting adjunct to the old engine'.[55] Without this collection of portraits, it seems unlikely that Zobel and Walker's engraving of the *Distinguished Men of Science* could have been produced; it was begun in the year that Woodcroft announced his collection in the *Patent Journal*. Walker acknowledged the assistance of private individuals in locating portraits and information, but especially thanked Woodcroft, 'by whom every facility has been offered for making copies from many unique originals in that Gallery formed by him'.[56]

The interest taken by Prince Albert in continuing the work started by the Great Exhibition provided Woodcroft with the opportunity to establish a museum of inventions in connection with the Patent Office. The 'Commissioners of Patents' Museum' opened in June 1857, in a hastily erected iron building, adjacent to the South Kensington Museum (the future Victoria & Albert Museum). Woodcroft added its superintendence to his other duties.[57] He insisted that the Museum should display not only current or patented inventions but also be 'an archaeological collection referring to the lives of eminent mechanists ... to illustrate, historically, their lives and recollections ... and to illustrate also the progress of mechanical inventions'.[58] Initially, the collection was largely comprised of mechanical models once belonging to the Swiss engineer, J. G. Bodmer, and 'supernumerary' ones acquired by Woodcroft from the Society of Arts; in 1859, there were 300 (somewhat miscellaneous) exhibits.[59] Despite the lack of an acquisitions budget, the new Superintendent and his small staff rescued machinery and models that marked 'the great steps in every invention'.[60] When Woodcroft received a

[54] *Catalogue of the gallery* (5th edn).
[55] John Hick to Bennet Woodcroft, 26 November 1864, Woodcroft MSS, Z24/D, fo. 1020; Bennet Woodcroft to John Hick, 8 December 1864, ibid., fo. 1034.
[56] Proof sheets, Crompton MSS, ZCR 73/3, 75/17. Eliza Meteyard also acknowledged Woodcroft's help: *The life of Josiah Wedgwood* [1865], repr. with introduction by R. W. Lightbourn (London: Cornmarket Press, 1970), p. xxii.
[57] Hewish, *Rooms near Chancery Lane*, pp. 115–21.
[58] *Report ... Patent Office Library*, BPP 1864, XII, p. 26.
[59] Hewish, *Rooms near Chancery Lane*, p. 11.
[60] Ibid., p. 122; *Report ... Patent Office Library*, BPP 1864, XII, p. 19. See also Woodcroft MSS, Z27A, fo. 213. For the contemporary efforts of George Wilson in Edinburgh, see R. G. W. Anderson, '"What is technology?" education through museums in the mid-nineteenth century', *BJHS* 25 (1992), 179–80.

cutting from the *Glasgow Citizen*, mentioning that the engine of Henry Bell's *Comet* was lying neglected in the premises of a recently deceased Glaswegian machine maker, he immediately wrote to secure its preservation.[61] To the widow of the Rev. Patrick Bell he offered the choice of a new reaper from the catalogue of Samuelson & Co., if she would donate the original one invented by her late husband, which she was still using. 'She cannily asked for a state-of-the-art two-horse machine which Woodcroft paid for himself.'[62] By 1863, the collection had trebled in size. Increasingly, impressed and enthused by Woodcroft's efforts to preserve their history, engineering firms started to present the Museum with both historical and current products.[63]

Not all Woodcroft's quests were successful. In 1864, on hearing that Watt's workshop at Heathfield Hall would be opened for the first time since 1819, Woodcroft secured an invitation to attend. He and Francis Pettit Smith spent an excited seven hours inspecting the contents, with a view to procuring them for the Museum, but were unable to persuade the trustees to allow their removal to London.[64] Woodcroft's enthusiasm took him, after protracted negotiations, as far as the excavation of lead coffins in the Somerset family vault beneath the church at Raglan (Monmouthshire). He was in pursuit of a model of the steam engine that its inventor, the second marquis of Worcester, had intimated would be buried with him; sadly, neither model nor drawing was exhumed in this grizzly quest.[65]

Stephenson's *Rocket* posed problems of a different nature. Having rescued this rusting and neglected 'national trophy', the Museum found that its iconic status put it at risk from souvenir hunters. In 1877, Archibald Stuart Wortley, Pettit Smith's successor as Curator, wrote in alarm that *Rocket* was 'suffering much from the public picking off scaling pieces of rust' and 'carrying them away as memorials'. When the locomotive was removed for conservation, 'every second visitor at least asked

---

[61] Woodcroft MSS, Z24D, fos. 844, 857; Hewish, *Rooms near Chancery Lane*, p. 129. The engine had been a prime attractions of the exhibition sponsored by the BAAS meeting in Glasgow in 1840: Morrell and Thackray, *Gentlemen of science*, p. 218.

[62] Hewish, *Rooms near Chancery Lane*, p. 131; Z24E, fos. 1222, 1224, 1236; Z24F, fo. 1328, Woodcroft MSS.

[63] Hewish, *Rooms near Chancery Lane*, p. 123; *Report ... Patent Office Library*, BPP 1864, XII, p. 19; Woodcroft MSS, Z24D, fos. 833, 834, 845, 854; Z24G, fos. 1502, 1526.

[64] Woodcroft MSS, Z24D, fos. 930, 978, 980; Z24G, fo. 1536, Hewish, *Rooms near Chancery Lane*, pp. 127–8. Woodcroft's goal was achieved in 1924, when Watt's workshop was removed to the Science Museum, after Heathfield Hall had failed to find a buyer and was demolished.

[65] John Hewish, 'The raid on Raglan: sacred ground and profane curiosity', *British Library Journal* 8 (1982), 182–98; Hewish, *Rooms near Chancery Lane*, p. 128.

where "Rocket" was and when she was coming back'; on that Easter Monday, the Museum had received nearly 6,000 visitors.[66] In May 1876, it lent the cream of its collection to the important 'Loan Exhibition of Scientific Apparatus' at the South Kensington Museum, which was organized by an international committee with strictly peda-gogical aims in mind.[67] *Engineering* was pleased to find many 'old friends' displayed to better effect there than in their normally 'crowded' and 'dingy haunts in the Patent Museum':

Familiar as they are to us, the feeling is still almost irresistible that one should lift one's hat in passing them in token of respect both to their designers, the men who laid the very foundations of our profession, and to the queer old constructions themselves, which in picture or reality have been the friends of all our generation of engineers since their boyhood.[68]

Woodcroft's retirement, that year, was marred by prolonged disputes over the ownership of many items in the Museum, Gallery and Library, which he had contributed and which he wished to withdraw from the collection.[69] *Engineering* had recently criticized his 'policy of "masterly inactivity"'.[70] It is possible that advancing years had finally brought this patent whirlwind of energy to a halt; more likely, the Museum's deficient accommodation and shortage of staff – themselves the product of ongoing niggardliness at the Treasury – bore the prime responsibility for 'the disgraceful condition of the collection', of which the journal com-plained.[71] In its first twenty years the Museum had attracted four and a half million visitors, and in 1880 was featured on the front page of *The Graphic* (figure 9.2).[72] It was largely thanks to Woodcroft's passionate commitment that these 'valuable relics' – not to mention the portraits, archives and patent records of numerous inventors – had been preserved. In addition to his own efforts, he had inspired, bullied and cajoled many others to support his projects and undertake parallel ones of their own. Some continued it after his death. R. B. Prosser, for example, a close colleague at the Patent Office, brought to light a host of previously

---

[66] Woodcroft MSS, Z24D, fos. 833, 834, 854; Z24I, fos. 1847, 1850, 1871; Science Museum MSS, T/1862–5, Science Museum, London. See also *The Engineer*, 30 June 1876, p. 481, 28 July 1876, p. 65 on the poor condition of the locomotives. I am grateful to John Liffen, Curator of Communications at the Science Museum, for his kind help in locating these archives and allowing me to use his transcripts from engineering journals.

[67] Hewish, *Rooms near Chancery Lane*, p. 137.

[68] *Engineering*, 2 June 1876, 465; 16 June 1876, 445.

[69] Hewish, *Rooms near Chancery Lane*, pp. 137–40.   [70] *Engineering*, 3 April 1874, 244.

[71] Ibid., 22 October 1874, 275.

[72] Inkster, 'Patents as indicators', 199; *The Graphic: an illustrated weekly magazine*, 3 January 1880, 1.

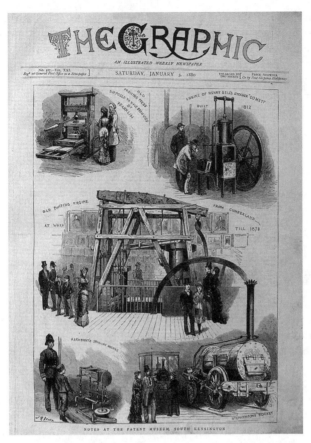

9.2 The Patent Office Museum, South Kensington, featured on the front page of *The Graphic*, 3 January 1880. Iconic objects evidently attracted a keen interest from both male and female visitors; portraits of inventors were exhibited behind the early beam engine (photograph by Ann Pethers).

unnoticed inventors in the west Midlands, with the help primarily of early patent specifications; where reliable information was available he included unpatented inventions.[73]

The scale of their collective achievement may be calibrated by the prominence of inventors among the entries of the *Dictionary of National Biography*, published in sixty-three volumes between 1885 and 1900.

---

[73] Prosser, *Birmingham inventors*, preface. For Prosser ('Woodcroft's Boswell'), see Hewish, *Rooms near Chancery Lane*, pp. 59, 92–3, 108–9, 149–50.

There were 383 inventors born between 1650 and 1850 in this first attempt to provide 'full, accurate, and concise biographies of all note-worthy inhabitants of the British Islands and the colonies (exclusive of living persons) from the earliest historical period to the present time'.[74] Among over 29,000 entries this may seem a small total, but the very comprehensiveness of the *DNB* made it difficult for any occupational category to dominate the entries. For a group that had emerged from anonymity only a century before and which often complained of neglect, it was not a poor tally.[75] Not only did the *DNB's* compilers owe their awareness of many inventors to Woodcroft and others whom he had inspired to record their achievements, but they were probably also indebted to the records that he had had collected and conserved. Prosser was a major contributor of entries, as was his colleague at the Patent Office, Henry Trueman Wood.[76] Less tangible but no less signifi-cant was their role in the preservation of the UK's patent system.

The patent controversy and the nature of invention

The threat to the patent system prompted a group of inventors and patent agents, in 1862, to establish the Inventors' Institute; by 1869, its mem-bership numbered 700, including such major figures as Bessemer, Brewster, Siemens, William Fairbairn and Samuel Courtauld.[77] Its con-ferences and publications critically examined the existing system and various proposals for its reform (or replacement).[78] Concern was such that when Sir Frederick Bramwell, the president of the Institution of Mechanical Engineers, gave an anti-abolition paper to the Society of Arts in 1874, the resulting discussion ran for a further three meetings, with only a slight decline in attendance. Having dismissed rewards from the public purse as productive of insoluble problems of equity, Bramwell turned to 'honorary distinctions'. Cheers greeted his assertion that 'stat-ues, even if good, and public addresses, though eloquent, would not pay taxes nor find clothes'.[79] In the subsequent discussion, an opponent of patents, who disagreed with Bramwell's estimation of the satisfaction to

[74] Sidney Lee's memoir of George Smith, cited in Colin Matthew, 'The New DNB', *History Today* 43 (September 1993), 10.

[75] MacLeod and Nuvolari, 'Pitfalls of prosopography', 758–9. The criteria by which inven-tors were selected for inclusion in the *DNB* are discussed in ibid., 764–74.

[76] Ibid., 766.

[77] *The Scientific Review, and Journal of the Inventors' Institute* 1 (March, 1865), v.

[78] Ibid., 2 (1 January 1866), 173; 2 (2 September 1866), 308–9; *The Times*, 25 June 1869, 8b; 30 November 1877, 10d.

[79] *The Times*, 3 December 1874, 7e.

be had from honour and fame – he referred to the Stephensons' statues at Euston station 'as likely to inspire an inventor with patriotic ambition' – was ridiculed by several inventors; they 'declared that their object was to make money and benefit others by benefiting themselves'.[80] Doubtless they would not refuse honour and fame, provided these were *additional* to financial rewards.

Most of the debate was conducted in purely pragmatic terms and within the ideological framework of free trade. Abolitionists contended that patents were a restraint on trade, limiting the free competition that was the prime stimulus to economic growth: while imposing a 'tax' on manufacturers, they also hobbled inventiveness.[81] Isambard Kingdom Brunel, for example, condemned the patent system because it 'impedes everything it means to encourage, and ruins the class it professes to protect, and ... it is productive of immense mischief to the public'.[82] To its defenders, however, such arguments smacked of special pleading: it was from powerful employers that the individual inventor – typically a working man – needed the protection afforded by a patent. Their armoury was well stocked with the double-edged literary weapon of the inventor as victim and as hero, and everyone had an anecdote to tell of a working man who had made his fortune through a patented invention.[83] John Stuart Mill protested that abolition 'would enthrone free stealing under the prostituted name of free trade, and make the brains of men, still more than at present, the needy retainers and dependents of the men of money bags'.[84]

As Mill's reference to 'the prostituted name of free trade' implied, supporters of patents could appeal to the authority of Adam Smith, who

---

[80] *The Times*, 11 December 1874, 10f; 17 December 1874, 10f; also 19 December 1874, 7e–f.

[81] Robert Andrew Macfie (ed.), *The patent question in 1875: the Lord Chancellor's bill and the exigencies of foreign competition* (London: Longmans, Green & Co., 1875), pp. 12–13; Moureen Coulter, 'Property in ideas: the patent question in mid-Victorian Britain', unpublished Ph.D., Indiana University (1986), pp. 149–53.

[82] 'Memorandum for evidence before the select committee of the House of Lords on the patent laws, 1851', in Isambard Brunel, *Life of Isambard Kingdom Brunel, civil engineer* (London: Longmans, Green, 1870) pp. 491, 496. See MacLeod, 'Concepts of invention', pp. 145–50. For the increasing currency of such views, see Hansard, *P. D.*, 3rd ser., CLXVII (27 May 1862), 49.

[83] See, for example, Hansard, *P. D.*, 3rd ser., CXVIII (1851), 1544–5, 1546, 1548. Some inventors did not appreciate being represented as 'lachrymose and much-to-be-pitied people', which they thought might be turned against patentees, who 'should be saved from their own insanity': Capt. Selwyn, RN, in *The Scientific Review* 2 (1 January 1866), 173; Christine MacLeod, 'Negotiating the rewards of invention: the shop-floor inventor in Victorian Britain', *Business History* 41 (1999), 17–36.

[84] John Stuart Mill, *Principles of political economy* (5th edn, London: Parker, Son & Bourn, 1862), quoted in Machlup and Penrose, 'Patent controversy', 9 n.32.

had exempted this particular temporary monopoly from his influential attack on restraints on trade. Both Mill and Bentham had endorsed Smith's view. In the mid-century heyday of free trade, however, economists began to query whether the great theorist of laissez-faire should have allowed any exception to his case.[85] Machlup and Penrose identify four types of argument that were developed to justify the retention of patent rights and were often deployed in its defence, together or singly, 'without regard to consistency'. Two were of an ethical nature – concerning the just treatment of inventors by society – and two rested on political and economic expediency, involving the benefits that society derived from technological progress. To every argument the abolitionists posed a counter-argument, and, since neither side was able to support its case with anything stronger than anecdotal evidence, the debate rumbled on for over two decades.[86]

Despite the debate's essential pragmatism, participants were challenged to consider the nature of invention. Was it the case, for example, that, without incentives (such as a patent), the rate of invention would grind to a halt, or was there a profound urge to invention rooted in society as a whole that would impel it ever onwards? Similarly, was a particular invention contingent upon the birth of one individual, or would it have materialized (sooner or later) without him? These discussions were no more conclusive than the ethical and economic ones, but they offer an insight into how the Victorians conceived of invention. A quarter century after Farey's and Hodgskin's contrasting statements about the role of Watt's 'genius' in the steam engine's development, similar types of argument were counter-posed. This time, however, in the context of a hard-fought and crucial debate, supporters of both positions were forced to develop and refine their views.

The heroic account of invention was inflated by the self-interested justifications offered by patentees, patent agents and their supporters, and shaped by their need to establish a conceptual understanding of invention that would legitimize the granting of patents. In particular, this encouraged the idea that inventions arose through hard work and perseverance – perspiration needed incentives and merited reward, inspiration (being unlooked for and effortless) arguably did not. By contrast, it was incumbent on opponents of the patent system to develop a coherent explanation of invention that minimized the role of the individual inventor. There had been no such requirement since Hodgskin had elaborated an account of invention consistent with his theory of the working man's

---

[85] Machlup and Penrose, 'Patent controversy', 7–10.   [86] Ibid., 10–28.

'capital' in his skills, by reducing Watt from an exceptional genius to a model worker in a collaborative venture; it had been an argument holding ambiguous implications for the patent system.[87] Opponents would find it hard to dislodge the heroic image, implanted in the national psyche through the glorification of Watt and currently reinforced by the Great Exhibition and the efforts of Woodcroft, Smiles and their ilk.

Isambard Kingdom Brunel was one of the patent system's most cogent critics. In addition to his pragmatic objections, he offered an account of invention redolent of Hodgskin's: in response to the particular needs of the time, he argued, astute tradesmen improve on the knowledge and techniques accumulated over the generations.

I believe that the most useful and novel inventions and improvements of the present day are mere progressive steps in a highly wrought and highly advanced system, suggested by, and dependent on, other previous steps, their whole value and the means of their application probably dependent on the success of some or many other inventions, some old, some new . . . [I]n most cases they result from a demand which circumstances happen to create. The consequence is that most good things are being thought of by many persons at the same time.[88]

This notion of the incremental, systemic nature of invention was encapsulated in the epigram quoted by the abolitionist barrister, John Coryton, that 'it is society that invents'; or, in the more colourful words of a French opponent of patents, '"Who discovered the motive force of steam? Is it Rapin [sic]? Is it Watt? Is it Fulton? No; rather it is the eighteenth century; just as the nineteenth has discovered railroads and the electric telegraph!"'[89] But Brunel's down-to-earth formulation does not sound like a philosophical abstraction: rather, it has the tenor of a reflection on his personal experiences. He is not enunciating an impersonal determinism, but explaining how he perceives those around him dealing with the technical challenges that daily arise on-site and in the workshop.

Sir William Armstrong (*Punch's* 'Lord Bomb') was equally keen to dispense with the patent system. Less subtle in his reasoning than Brunel, Armstrong depended more heavily on the phenomenon of

---

[87] See above, pp. 165–7.   [88] Brunel, *Life of Isambard Kingdom Brunel*, p. 492.

[89] John Coryton, 'The policy of granting letters patent for invention, with observations on the working of the English law', *Sessional Proceedings of the National Association for the Promotion of Social Science* 7 (1873–4), 168; Arthur Legrand, in *Revue Contemporaine* (31 January 1862), quoted in Robert Andrew Macfie, *The patent question: a solution of difficulties by abolishing or shortening the inventor's monopoly, and instituting national recompenses* (London: W. J. Johnson, 1863), p. 72. See also J. Stirling, 'Patent right', in [R. A. Macfie (ed.)], *Recent discussions on the abolition of patents for inventions in the United Kingdom, France, Germany, and the Netherlands* (London: Longmans, Green, Reader and Dyer, 1869), p. 119; and *The Economist*, 26 July 1851, 182, quoted in Penrose, *Economics*, p. 33 n. 17.

simultaneous inventions to argue that patents were both unnecessary and unjust.[90] His evidence to the Royal Commission in 1863 portrayed invention as absurdly easy and therefore unworthy of reward. 'As soon as a demand arises for any machine or implement or process,' he claimed, 'the means of satisfying that demand present themselves to very many persons at the same time.' Almost eliminating the inventor entirely, he continued: 'the great majority of inventions are the result of mere accident – if you let them alone they will turn up of themselves.'[91] Elsewhere, Armstrong had expressed these views less glibly, making it apparent that he believed the real merit in invention to lie seldom 'in the fundamental conception, but . . . in the subsequent elaboration, and in the struggle with difficulties . . . which often require years of labour, blended with disappointment, for their removal'.[92] Again, he seems to have been reflecting on his personal experiences as an inventor, who had expended great effort in bringing his ideas into commercial use – and who was no stranger to disappointment, especially at the hands of the War Office.[93] The patent system, Armstrong argued, offered no reward at all to the scientists whose fundamental research many patentees exploited, and probably no more to the 'practical men', like Watt and Stephenson, who devoted their whole lives to perfecting inventions, than would have accrued without a patent. Rather, it tended to bring 'disproportionate wealth' to mere opportunists and 'schemers'.[94]

There may seem to be a paradox here, as professional engineers, eager to be rid of 'pestiferous' patentees, undermined the heroic status of inventors, while contemporaneously their professional bodies were raising memorials to their illustrious colleagues, such as the Stephensons, Locke – and Brunel himself.[95] It was a paradox that John Hawkshaw

---

[90] For a useful discussion and (twentieth-century) historiography of this phenomenon, see David Lamb and S. M. Easton, *Multiple discovery: the pattern of scientific discovery* (Amersham: Avebury Press, 1984), and, for a valuable critique, Schaffer, 'Making up discovery', pp. 33–6.

[91] *Report of the commissioners appointed to inquire into the working of the law relating to letters patent for inventions*, BPP 1864, XXIX, pp. 414, 415. See also Hansard, *P. D.*, 3rd ser., CXCVI (1869), 895.

[92] William G. Armstrong, 'Address of the president', *Proceedings of the Institution of Mechanical Engineers* (1861), 119. Smiles largely endorsed this view of invention in 1884, without drawing any implications for the patent system: *Men of invention and industry*, p. 60.

[93] Stafford M. Linsley, 'Armstrong, William George, Baron Armstrong (1810–1900)', *ODNB*, online edn, October 2006, www.oxforddnb.com/view/article/669, accessed 18 October 2006.

[94] Indeed, Armstrong had opened his speech by referring to the great mechanical inventors of the past century: 'Address of the president', 110–12.

[95] See above, p. 265.

implicitly explored in his presidential address to the Institution of Civil Engineers in 1862. Hawkshaw's views tended more to the democratic model of Brunel (or Hodgskin) than to the facile dismissal of inventions as the spontaneous results of chance, represented by Armstrong's later testimony. The Institution's new president urged his members to observe an ethos of co-operation, drawing freely on one another's experience: 'let no inventive genius suppose,' he admonished, 'that his own tendencies or capabilities relieve him of this necessity.' There was, Hawkshaw continued, 'no such thing as discovery and invention, in the sense which is sometimes attached to the words'. Nobody invented new machines *de novo*; some might be more adept at it than others, but all depended on 'a chain of previous research and inquiry', to which many had contributed their mite.[96] It was in this collective spirit that Hawkshaw concluded his speech with a triumphant flourish of pride in the profession:

no man can look back on the last twenty or thirty years without feeling that it has been the age of Engineers and Mechanicians. The profession to which we belong has in that period of time done much to change the aspect of human affairs … aiding a great moral and social work.[97]

By implication, the engineers they celebrated were to be seen, not as exceptional figures towering above their peers, but as their representatives, singled out only to receive the public's gratitude on behalf of the whole profession. Indeed, there appears to have existed a 'guild' ethos among professional engineers, which frowned upon patenting and the exclusive use of what should be freely available to all practitioners as 'tools of the trade'.[98] Patents not only restricted the sharing of information but risked causing dissension among members of the 'guild'.[99] It was as though they had taken a collective decision to prefer glory to wealth – subsequently, determining to erect a shrine to engineering in Westminster Abbey, where the profession's luminaries would be celebrated in perpetuity.[100] Individual glory reflected on all; intellectual property was exclusive.

---

[96] John Hawkshaw, 'Inaugural address', *Proceedings and Minutes of the Institution of Civil Engineers* 21 (1861–2), 174. For a 'down-to-earth' account of collaborative invention by mechanics, see the letter from 'Inventor' [a patent agent], in *The Engineer*, 2 March 1883, 165.

[97] Hawkshaw, 'Inaugural address', 186.

[98] MacLeod, *Inventing the industrial revolution*, pp. 104–5.

[99] As the dissension caused (earlier in the century) by Watt's enforcement of his patent had demonstrated. Despite this unfortunate implication, Watt, as ever, was allowed an exceptional status: Hawkshaw commended 'the sagacity, industry, and untiring perseverance of that great man', and compared his 'patient concentration of will on his great object' with 'Newton's similar labours', 'Inaugural address', 184.

[100] See below, pp. 318–19, 322–7.

Armstrong's emphasis on the ease of invention was common among opponents of the patent system. Some leading critics argued that invention was the nearly automatic product of necessity – attested by the argument from simultaneity – while others professed that individual inventors could not help but invent – it was 'almost a madness with some people'.[101] Certainly, it required no artificial stimulus or reward – no patent. Their choice of vocabulary was telling: for example, opponents often used the expression 'to hit upon' an invention, as though it were nothing more than a lucky thought. '[I]t commonly happened,' claimed Lord Stanley dismissively, 'that half a dozen men ... were on the track of the same discovery. Each of these ... would probably have *hit upon* the invention which was wanted, independently', but the first 'who *hit upon* it' took out a patent and excluded all the rest, though they too 'would probably have *hit upon* it within a few weeks'.[102] For some abolitionists the competitiveness inherent in commerce provided a 'natural' stimulus to invention: they took the creative response to it for granted. As Mr J. Stirling told the Glasgow Chamber of Commerce in 1869, 'Nature has amply provided all needful and wholesome encouragement, in the additional profit afforded by improved methods of production ... The whole history of industrial progress is an unceasing striving after improvement with a view to profit.'[103]

The argument from simultaneity, deployed by abolitionists, tended to carry a positivist assumption about the nature of technology. It implied there was a single right solution to every technical problem, which would be reached by any sufficiently intelligent man who put his mind to it. According to the economic historian Professor Thorold Rogers it constituted 'a piece of insolent vanity' for an inventor to imagine that he might be alone in his achievement. Consequently, it was unjust that, 'A man who *discovers* a mechanical contrivance which a hundred men could as well have invented as himself, and which many frequently do invent, either simultaneously or speedily, is protected against them and the public'.[104] Rogers' use of the word 'discovers' is significant in its implication that there was only one mechanical prototype available, one

---

[101] Hansard, *P. D.*, 3rd ser., CXVIII, 14–16; 'Our patent laws', *The North British Daily Mail*, 2 February 1875, repr. in Macfie (ed.), *Patent question in 1875*; Stirling, 'Patent right', pp. 119–20; see also Eugene Schneider's testimony, *Report from the select committee on letters patent*, BPP 1871, X, p. 742.

[102] Quoted in Macfie (ed.), *Recent discussions*, p. 113, and in Machlup and Penrose, 'Patent controversy', 24 n. 93; emphasis added.

[103] Stirling, 'Patent right', p. 119.

[104] J. E. Thorold Rogers, 'On the rationale and working of the patent laws', *Journal of the Statistical Society of London* 26 (1863), 125–6; emphasis added. W. A. S. Hewins, 'Rogers, James Edwin Thorold (1823–1890)', rev. Alon Kadish, *ODNB*, online edn,

obvious next step in the march of progress; it was the counterpart of a positivist conception of science, and it denied any scope for individual creativity. Neither, obviously, was there any call for 'genius' or exceptional qualities of mind: ordinary intelligence, combined with perseverance, would be sufficient.

To proponents of this view, the notion that the inventor's property in his invention was akin to that of an author in his or her text was necessarily absurd: they were two distinct activities, one requiring imagination and creativity, the other not. Contrary, therefore, to the analogy frequently made by the patent system's supporters, the copyright protection available to the author provided no ideal standard to which the inventor could reasonably assimilate his case. Robert Macfie eagerly seized upon the explicit contrast between authors and inventors, drawn by Arthur Legrand in the *Revue Contemporaine*:

There is, in what flows from the pen of a writer, evident originality. Artists really create something; they produce work which no other would have produced. In the domain of industry, on the contrary, the inventor is not, properly speaking, any more the creator than he could be the exclusive possessor. *He finds, he discovers, but he does not create.* He only makes use of things already existing in the material world.[105]

In similar terms, Sir Roundell Palmer, MP, contended that inventions were not analogous to literary works, because they were 'discoveries of something which is not the creation of the discoverer's mind; they are the result of the pursuit of common knowledge, for an end to which the laws of nature are simultaneously directing a number of minds'.[106]

Faced with such arguments, which threatened to undermine the ideology of unique creativity on which the patent system rested, its supporters were pressured into more detailed rebuttals. It was necessary to establish that inventions, in the words of Henry Cole, were 'not things which rise up like mushrooms', but were difficult and time-consuming to produce, with success far from guaranteed.[107] The frequent emphasis on 'perseverance' and 'persistence' in invention narratives may have served a purpose beyond their character-building aspect. It was not merely an encouragement to adopt the protestant work ethic and practise good

May 2006, www.oxforddnb.com/view/article/23979, accessed 19 October 2006. Rogers was a friend of Richard Cobden and adamant in his faith in an unrestricted market economy.

[105] Macfie, *Patent question*, p. 18; original emphasis.

[106] *Report from the select committee on letters patent*, BPP 1871, X, p. 690; see also ibid., p. 694, and Palmer's speech to the Commons, reported in Hansard, *P. D.*, 3rd ser., CXCVI (28 May 1869), 893.

[107] *Report from the select committee of the House of Lords*, BPP 1851, XVIII, p. 499.

habits in daily life, but an argument for the laboriousness of invention, which merited reward – preferably with a patent.[108] Furthermore, the positivist model of invention as 'discovery' had to be refuted by a demonstration of the specificity of individual ingenuity – the unique creativity of a particular mind – in the absence of which, the invention (if it had been made at all) would have been quite different. In effect, supporters of the patent system were required to move beyond the idea of invention as mere problem-solving to introduce an imaginative element of design into their argument.

Bennet Woodcroft intended his biographical compilation of textile inventors to show the long struggles against prejudice and poverty that they endured and the inadequacy of 'parliamentary or popular grants ... in lieu of patents'.[109] On a more theoretical level, he used the case of John Kay's invention of the flying shuttle to subvert the recently elaborated 'challenge and response' account – here, of the stimulus given by faster weaving to the mechanization of spinning. He turned it into an anti-determinist argument through an emphasis on the long hiatus between the two inventions:

A yarn famine followed [from Kay's invention of the flying shuttle]. A powerful stimulus was thus given to the inventive talents of the whole community to devise a more mechanical and expeditious mode of spinning. But it was soon found that there was no royal road to invention. That faculty is a gift bestowed on few minds. Notwithstanding the urgent necessity for spinning machinery and notwithstanding the number of minds employed on the subject, nearly forty years elapsed before the hand-spinning gave place to machine-spinning.[110]

For Woodcroft, an inventor himself, the awareness that technical solutions were far from obvious led to this unusually emphatic denial of the existence of an automatic or straightforward inventive solution to every 'need' or 'want'; the sufficiency of the dedicated inventor's mental capacities should not be taken for granted. Smiles deployed a less subtle argument against simultaneity: the great inventors, he explained, were those who were able to resolve the 'demands of industry', which had inevitably set 'many ingenious minds' to work in the same area. Although many had laboured long 'in the throes of invention', finally it was 'the master mind, the strong practical man', who 'straightway' provides the

---

[108] For the frequent denial of mere 'accident' in invention, see above, pp. 151–2, 172–4, 256.

[109] Woodcroft, *Brief biographies*, p. 46. See above, p. 253.

[110] Ibid., p. 3. For the early history of the model and its critical evaluation, see Trevor Griffiths, Philip Hunt and Patrick O'Brien, 'The curious history and the imminent demise of the challenge and response model', in Berg and Bruland (eds.), *Technological revolutions in Europe*, pp. 119–37, esp. p. 123.

solution; '[t]hen there is a loud outcry among all the small contrivers, who see themselves distanced in the race'. Smiles' strategy, however, of dismissing simultaneous invention as the sour grapes of 'small contrivers' appears to undermine his usual insistence on the perseverance required of every successful inventor – no matter how brilliant his mind, he was not meant to succeed 'straightway'.[111]

An ingenious argument, which conceded more to the abolitionist case, accepted that a certain invention was, in Harriet Martineau's words, 'sure to come because it is so much wanted', but contended that the precise manner of its coming was moulded by the character and capacity of the particular inventor. This was a sophisticated attempt to reintegrate human agency into accounts that privileged the determination of invention by culture: accepting that the inventor responded to the challenges of a particular time and place did not require the denial of his individuality or his exceptional abilities. Hence, according to Martineau, it was fortunate that it was Thomas Edmondson, and not another, who invented railway-ticket machinery, for he 'conceived a vast idea with the true sagacity of genius, and worked it out with industry and patience, and enjoyed its honours with modesty, and dispensed its fruits with honour and generosity'.[112] Similarly, the anonymous author of *Great inventors* (1864) accepted that, in the absence of James Brindley, Britain would still have had a canal network, 'for the time was ripe for its introduction', but it would not have been the *same* network. Without Brindley's 'adventurous genius', progress would have been relatively 'timid and slow', with canal construction long restricted to but 'a few small ones, cut in the more level parts of the country'; Brindley's bold refusal to recognize any topographical obstacle was decisive. 'It is in the conception and accomplishment of such grand and fortunate deviations from ordinary practice that we discern the power and confess the value of original genius.'[113]

Extending such insights on the basis of their own experience, 'practical men' responded to the abolitionists' denial of any analogy between literary and technical invention by emphasizing the uniqueness of design inherent in any mechanical construct.[114] James Howard turned the literary case back on the abolitionist camp, in 1869, with an incisive redefinition of the nature of authorship:

no two men ever wrote the same book at the same time … but he had frequently found that two authors writing almost simultaneously conveyed precisely the

---

[111] Smiles, *Self-help*, pp. 32–3. For Smiles' insistence on perseverance, see above, p. 256.
[112] Martineau, 'English passport system', 34.   [113] *Great inventors*, pp. 294–5.
[114] This seems to be an anticipation of some of the ideas developed by Edwin T. Layton and Eugene S. Ferguson in the 1970s, discussed in McGee, 'Making up mind', 799.

same ideas, though not in the same language. Exactly so, if two men invented similar machines simultaneously, it was never found they carried out their ideas precisely in the same mechanical way ... The inventor made use of the laws of nature just as the author of a book used the common language of mankind.[115]

If authors were as much products of the *zeitgeist* as inventors, Howard contended, inventors were equally the individual creators of novelty: their materials were drawn from a common stock of knowledge but arranged according to a unique design. Or, in the words of the engineer, James Nasmyth, 'every machinist has a distinct individuality in his contrivances, just as every man has his own handwriting'.[116]

From the pen of another engineer (and inventor of the theatrical illusion known as 'Pepper's ghost'), Henry Dircks, came the period's most sustained defence of the heroic account of invention and a hard-hitting critique of the abolitionists' case. Dircks' *Inventors and inventions* (1867), dedicated to his friend Henry Bessemer, developed many of the points used in defence of the patent system. He dismissed out-of-hand the notions that inventions resulted purely from accidental observation, were parented by 'necessity', or occurred simultaneously – indeed, claimed Dircks, an invention might 'anticipate the age'.[117] He attacked the opponents of patents (unfairly) as men who underrated the difficulty of invention because, being incapable of it themselves, they were unable to recognize that 'invention *precedes* ... progress'.[118] In company with Woodcroft, Dircks stressed the non-automatic character of invention, by reference both to its failures and its unpredictable successes; with typical Victorian arrogance, he pointed to the existence of primitive peoples whose technologies appeared rudimentary as evidence that technical progress was 'not inherent in man'.[119] Like Howard and Nasmyth, he stressed the individuality of inventors, calling design 'the Poetry of Invention', and identifying truly great inventors as those who possessed 'a natural gift'.[120] Invention was 'a faculty of the mind more strongly developed in some men than in others, and ... possessed by comparatively few

---

[115] Hansard, *P. D.*, 3rd ser., CXCVI (1869), 912. See also ibid., 920–1. Gordon Goodwin, 'Howard, James (1821–1889)', rev. Jonathan Brown, *ODNB*, www.oxforddnb.com/view/article/13920, accessed 19 October 2006.

[116] *Report from the select committee on letters patent*, BPP 1871, X, p. 792.

[117] Henry Dircks, *Inventors and inventions* (London: E. and F. N. Spon, 1867), pp. 10, 11, 44, 47. Roger Hutchins, 'Dircks, Henry (1806–1873)', *ODNB*, www.oxforddnb.com/view/article/7681, accessed 19 October 2006.

[118] Dircks, *Inventors and inventions*, p. 85; emphasis added.

[119] Ibid., pp. 7–9. For similar arguments, see McGee, 'Making up mind', 789–96; Michael Adas, *Machines as the measure of men: science, technology, and ideologies of western dominance* (Ithaca: Cornell University Press, 1989), pp. 143–53, and passim.

[120] Dircks, *Inventors and inventions*, pp. 46, 56.

in any great degree'.[121] Such rare abilities should be encouraged, said Dircks, not taken for granted. Dircks' treatise added little, if anything, to the understanding of invention. It was a compendium of baldly stated views, rather than a work of reasoned argument, but it stands as a tract for its time, a tribute to the promptings to popular theorizing that were occasioned by the Victorian patent controversy.

What was scarcely questioned throughout this long debate was the entitlement of inventors to adequate reward in some form. Fully paid-up cultural determinists, confident of 'society's' capacity to invent unaided, were scarce.[122] There was a fear of disrupting the status quo, which appeared to have delivered the industrial revolution into Britain's lap.[123] *The Times*, which promoted abolition, in the 1860s, with a view to eradicating vexatious 'petty monopolies', advocated that inventors of 'really great inventions', who were not remunerated by the market, should receive *ad hominem* payments from the state.[124] Ultimately, the abolitionists' inability to devise a fair alternative system weakened their case before a public that believed that history was made by 'great men' and inventors were among Britain's greatest. The patent system's supporters had all the best tunes. When most of Europe – under pressure from cheap imports of US grain – started retreating behind protective tariffs in the 1870s, abolition had had its day. *The Times* retreated to calling for reform, not abolition.[125]

It was the Patents, Designs and Trademarks Act of 1883 that finally rendered abolition 'defunct'.[126] The act's reforms were much to the patentee's advantage, in particular, a massive reduction in the initial cost of a patent, which made it accessible to a far wider pool of people. This concession symbolized a new confidence in the rationality of the inventor, expressed by Joseph Chamberlain, president of the Board of Trade, as he steered the bill through the Commons:

The Bill proceeded on the assumption that an inventor was a person to be encouraged, and not repressed, for he was a creator of trade ... There was no article which we used, there was nothing connected with the necessities of our life,

---

[121] Ibid., p. 39.

[122] For the unacceptability of determinist views in general among Victorian academics, see Philippa Levine, *The amateur and the professional; antiquarians, historians and archaeologists in Victorian England, 1838–1886* (Cambridge: Cambridge University Press, 1986), p. 76.

[123] See, for example, Levi, *History of British commerce*, p. 340: Levi's profound faith in free trade did not prevent him advocating the retention of the patent system for fear of damaging industry, 'were the rights of the inventor ignored or insufficiently recognised'.

[124] *The Times*, 7 February 1863, 9a–b. [125] *The Times*, 9 December 1874, 9c.

[126] Hansard, *P. D.*, 3rd ser., CCLXXVIII (1883), 369.

or that contributed to the health or happiness, or security of the population, which had not, at some time or other, been the subject of a patentable invention.[127]

Eliminating the hero: the economics of invention

Beyond the patent controversy, there continued to be little theoretical discussion of invention. It included, however, some work of exceptionally high quality – probably the most insightful analyses of technology published since Babbage's treatise in 1832.[128] As we have seen, the psychologist, Alexander Bain, was drawn to analyse the mental characteristics of great inventors and discoverers.[129] While Bain's discipline dictated an individualist approach to invention, those working in other fields had greater freedom to explore the question from other angles. Three works, all written by university professors between 1855 and 1865, demonstrate an unusual concern to examine the stimuli to invention in socio-economic and historical contexts. While the first, George Wilson, assumed that it was a heroic elite which had responded to those stimuli, both the others, W. E. Hearn and W. S. Jevons, looked beyond individual inventors to offer a complex and sophisticated analysis of technological change; simultaneously, they each demonstrated a profound understanding of the course of British industrialization.[130] A fourth such analysis was soon available – at least, to those who could read German or French. Ultimately, Karl Marx's *Das Kapital* (1867) completely overshadowed these three contemporary works, principally, of course, through its contributions to disciplines other than technology and its profound impact on politics.[131] Re-inserted into this context, however, Marx's analysis, in chapter 15 of the first volume of *Das*

---

[127] Ibid., 361. See also MacLeod *et al.*, 'Evaluating inventive activity', 544–6.
[128] Charles Babbage, *On the economy of machinery and manufactures* (London: Charles Knight, 1832).
[129] See above, pp. 150–2.
[130] George Wilson, MD, FRSE, Regius Professor of Technology in the University, and Director of the Industrial Museum of Scotland, *What is technology? An inaugural lecture delivered in the University of Edinburgh on November 7, 1855* (Edinburgh: Sutherland & Knox, and London: Simpkin, Marshall & Co., 1855); William Stanley Jevons, *The coal question: an inquiry concerning the progress of the nation, and the probable exhaustion of our coal-mines* (London and Cambridge: Macmillan & Co., 1865); William Edward Hearn, LL D, *Plutology: or the theory of the efforts to satisfy human wants* (London: Macmillan & Co.; Melbourne: George Robertson, 1864).
[131] An English edition of the first volume of *Das Kapital* appeared only in 1887: Coleman, *Myth, history and the industrial revolution*, pp. 17–18; Kirk Willis, 'The introduction and critical reception of Marxist thought in Britain, 1850–1900', *HJ* 20 (1977), 423–44.

Kapital, can be seen as not only symptomatic of a novel concern in mid-Victorian Britain to understand technology's place in society but also as its supreme achievement.[132]

For Marx, as Rosenberg observes, '[t]he history of invention is, most emphatically, not the history of inventors.'[133] Perhaps uniquely among contemporary commentators, Marx was unperturbed by Watt and the steam engine. While he could appreciate 'the greatness of Watt's genius', his account of British industrialization was unusual in not privileging the steam engine: steam was merely the most recent form of motive power, its development prompted by the expansion of manufacturing (not vice versa). The crucial innovation, for Marx, was the substitution of the machine for the tool in the worker's hand: remorselessly, the skill with which the man had manipulated that tool was being built into the machine, depriving him of his economic power (or, in Hodgskin's terms, of his capital).[134] It was this long-term social process that concerned Marx. How those machines were invented scarcely interested him any more than the identity of their inventors; his analysis concentrated instead on the innovation of machinery (its introduction into commercial use) and its impact on working people. From this perspective, Marx remarked the stimulus provided to invention by capital's strategy of using mechanization to break the power of skilled workers (especially during strikes) – a strategy commended by Andrew Ure. It would be possible, said Marx, 'to write a whole history of the inventions made since 1830 for the sole purpose of providing capital with weapons against working-class revolt'.[135] Although he might have been expected to condemn inventors for their collusion with capital, such criticism was far below his concerns.[136] In his determinist philosophy, technological change took little account of individuals: it was an inexorable historical process, driven by man's interaction with his natural environment and with other men, under conditions that were largely not of their choosing.[137] Marx was too good a historian to eliminate human agency – there

---

[132] Nathan Rosenberg, *Inside the black box: technology and economics* (Cambridge: Cambridge University Press, 1982), p. 34.

[133] Ibid., p. 48; see also ibid., p. 35.   [134] Marx, *Capital*, I, pp. 497–9, 504–7, 545.

[135] Ibid., pp. 563–4; Ure, *Philosophy of manufactures*, p. 370. For a critical review of the historical literature on this question, see MacKenzie, 'Marx and the machine', 488–98; Bruland, 'Industrial conflict', 92–121.

[136] For Marx's views on Arkwright and Watt, see above, pp. 197–8.

[137] Marx did not espouse technological determinism: Mackenzie, 'Marx and the machine', 473–80; Rosenberg, *Inside the black box*, pp. 36–9. Technological determinism at this period was more commonly found among those who proposed a heroic model of invention: see above, pp. 134–6.

were always men behind the machines – but his insistence on class struggle, as the primary motor in his dialectical analysis, left little causal scope for the actions of 'great men'. Indeed, his model of invention was of the cumulative type, preferred by Hodgskin and most opponents of the patent system. 'A critical history of technology', said Marx, 'would show how little any of the inventions of the eighteenth century are the work of a single individual.'[138] Not least, it generally took more than one individual to break free of the assumptions designed into a technology.

It is only after considerable development of the science of mechanics, and accumulated practical experience, that the form of a machine becomes settled entirely in accordance with mechanical principles, and emancipated from the traditional form of the tool that gave rise to it.[139]

As this and other acute observations make clear, Marx was no less aware than Woodcroft that invention was far from a straightforward operation which could be taken for granted. Given, however, his particular concerns, it was not an aspect of technological change that he needed to investigate as closely.

The careful and profound analyses of invention and technological change, pioneered by mid-nineteenth-century social scientists, remained outside the mainstream of contemporary debate. Their complexity did not translate well into the theatres of practice or politics, where the nature of invention had suddenly become a hotly contested issue and arguments polarized between two warring camps. Although both sides generally espoused relatively crude and superficial concepts of invention, as we have seen, they were sometimes provoked into more sophisticated insights. The failure of the abolitionists' campaign removed the pressure to develop such insights further. Its ideology of the cultural determination of invention disappeared from view in Victorian Britain, until its re-emergence in the English edition of *Capital* (1887), where it was subsumed into Marx's politically charged analysis of technological change. Nor was an academic debate ignited. Economists persisted in treating invention as an exogenous 'black box', of no significance unless it made a perceptibly major impact on the economy. Economic historians similarly ignored it, as they built their new discipline around an exposure of the damaging social consequences of industrialization; social investigators, such as Booth and Rowntree, shared their concerns.

[138] Quoted in Rosenberg, *Inside the black box*, pp. 34–5.
[139] Quoted in ibid., p. 48.

Consequently, if early twentieth-century American sociologists and historians of technology, such as Ogborn, Usher, Gilfillan and, later, Merton were unaware that their deterministic attacks on the heroic ideology of invention had been anticipated in mid-Victorian Britain, it is hardly surprising.[140]

---

[140] McGee, 'Making up mind', 773–89. Jevons' and Hearn's work was briefly cited in Plant, 'Economic theory', 34–5.

10   The workers' heroes

While the 1850s and 60s saw the inventor constructed as a hero of peace and defender of patents, he had another constituency, among the 'labour aristocracy'.[1] For skilled working men, in trades that rose with industrialization, the inventor was someone to admire and emulate. This high regard was demonstrated, in particular, by the generosity with which they contributed to inventors' memorials; sometimes, it was their initiative that launched such tributes. The 1860s also witnessed artisans campaigning for the extension of the parliamentary franchise; their efforts culminated in the Reform Act for England and Wales of 1867 (and 1868, for Scotland).[2] The inflated reputations of great inventors were assets available for their cause: they personified the skilled workers' claim to economic worth and respectability. Few artisans would have read Thomas Hodgskin's books, but they believed, nonetheless, that their skills and ingenuity were the bedrock of Britain's prosperity and power.[3] Nobody represented that claim more visibly than inventors, such as Watt, Stephenson and Davy, all of them once artisans.

To make a clear public statement of the national significance of inventors consequently acquired a political resonance. With Britain engaged in 'monument mania', it was a short step to appreciate the pertinence of public monuments.[4] It had, after all, been done before: whatever claims to political participation were made for the middle classes by Watt's monument in Westminster Abbey were still available to working-class campaigners in the 1860s. It would be hard to repeat that glorious masterstroke, but the

---

[1] For the continuing descriptive (if not explanatory) validity of this term, see Royden Harrison, *Before the socialists: studies in labour and politics, 1861–1881* (2nd edn, Aldershot: Gregg Revivals, 1994), pp. xvii–xxvii; Finn, *After Chartism*, pp. 2–4.

[2] See the essays in Catherine Hall, Keith McClelland and Jane Rendall (eds.), *Defining the Victorian nation: class, race, gender and the Reform Act of 1867* (Cambridge: Cambridge University Press, 2000); Harrison, *Before the socialists*, pp. 27–39, 78–136; Finn, *After Chartism*, pp. 226–61; and more generally, Fentress and Wickham, *Social memory*, pp. 115–26.

[3] See above, pp. 164–5, 169.   [4] *The Spectator*, repr. *The Times*, 12 August 1850, 3e.

mid-nineteenth-century vogue for commemorative statuary provided a series of opportunities for working men to make their point, be it at a less august level. At the very least, overt celebrations of inventors whom they considered to be 'one of their own' boosted the self-confidence of skilled workers, as they actively resumed their campaign for the franchise.

The indifference to monuments, which many radicals professed in the 1820s, had been overtaken by a more combative perspective.[5] When the Chartist leader, Feargus O'Connor, died in August 1855, a monument was soon proposed. Ernest Jones left the readers of the *People's Paper* in no doubt of its political significance: 'It will be a disgrace if Democracy cannot raise a statue to its hero, when the Peels, and Pitts and Wellingtons of the aristocracy have their effigies all around us.'[6] Sufficient funds were collected to erect a Gothic spire in Kensal Green cemetery and a life-size statue in Nottingham.[7] The resulting disapproval of a Nottingham councillor provided an unintended tribute to Jones' rallying call. 'If statues are raised to the Feargus O'Connors of England,' he protested, 'what "honour" does a similar tribute confer on a Pitt, a Wellington, or a Newton?'[8] Leading Chartists and reformers were not the only heroes who carried the political ambitions of skilled working men. Monuments to inventors made more subtle, political statements.

The inventive artisan

The working-class origin of most inventors was a truism in mid-nineteenth-century Britain. It informed both popular writing and debates on economic policy.[9] In 1824, William Huskisson argued that, if legislation prohibiting the emigration of artisans were repealed, 'as the machinery was in general of their invention', it would be logical also to lift the ban on its export.[10] Thirty years later, the marine engineer, John Bourne, disapproved of formal technical education for engineers, because 'it is from the race of artizans that genius is chiefly recruited': their imaginations had not been stifled by books.[11] The same shibboleth was current on both sides of the patent controversy: abolitionists and reformers both

---

[5] Some radicals still preferred more utilitarian memorials: see below, pp. 296–7, 299–300.

[6] *People's Paper*, 27 October 1855, quoted in Paul A. Pickering, 'The Chartist rites of passage: commemorating Feargus O'Connor', in Pickering and Tyrrell (eds.), *Contested sites*, p. 105.

[7] Pickering, 'Chartist rites of passage', pp. 106–15. See also Paul Salveson, *The people's monuments: a guide to sites and memorials in north west England* (Manchester: WEA, 1987), pp. 6, 31–3.

[8] Pickering, 'Chartist rites of passage', p. 117.   [9] Bowden, *Industrial society*, p. 19.

[10] Hansard, *P. D.*, 2nd ser., X (12 February 1824), 149.

[11] Bourne, *Treatise on the steam engine* (1853), p. 21.

identified inventors as working men and claimed to be acting in their interest.[12] Sir Frederick Bramwell, FRS, told the Society of Arts, in 1883, that, while the scientific principle behind an invention was probably the discovery of a more 'philosophical' mind, the role of the 'ingenious' man, who typically 'sees a means of improving some process of manufacture about which he is habitually concerned', was crucial. 'Between the discovery and its application', said Bramwell, 'there is a gap over which none but the workman can throw a bridge.'[13]

This identification of the inventor with the artisan underwrote an assertion of the skilled worker's role in the creation of British prosperity and predominance, which at mid-century assumed a new political importance. In 1851, a petition from the provost and bailies of Kirkcaldy (Fife) attributed 'the high position of this country among civilized nations ... to the inventive discoveries of such men as Watt, Hargreaves, Crompton, Arkwright, Stephenson, and others'. Another, from Manchester, ascribed Britain's 'high position' to 'the inventive genius of artizans in humble life'.[14] Samuel Smiles systematically emphasized the lowly origins of his paragons of self-improvement.[15] His apparently conservative message of individual 'getting on' has recently been subjected to re-interpretation. Smiles was a leading exponent of the 'ideal of character', which constituted a new conceptual element in Victorian political thought. It took on major significance because a man's character 'was, notoriously, the favoured explanatory element in the analysis of different human fates'; more controversially, the formation of character was largely within his own control.[16] For Smiles, among others, the proving ground of character was the workplace: it was here that a man displayed his true worth. Smiles' insistence on 'the elevation of character' was part of a wider reaction against aristocratic mores, which stressed that personal worth was unrelated to social position; nobility of character, attainable by anyone, was superior to noble birth.[17] By 1867, the language of character

---

[12] MacLeod, 'Negotiating the rewards', 18–19.

[13] *The Times*, 15 February 1883, 9c–d; B. P. Cronin, 'Bramwell, Sir Frederick Joseph, baronet (1818–1903)', *ODNB*, www.oxforddnb.com/view/article/32040, accessed 20 October 2006.

[14] House of Lords Record Office, 200, Appendix to reports, public petitions, 1851 (app. 472, 20–21 March 1851), pp. 210–11; also (app. 709, 14 April 1851), p. 319. See also *Manchester Guardian*, 18 December 1850, 6f; *The Times*, 6 December 1850, 4e; *ILN* 18 (31 May 1851), 487, 490; *The Builder* 22 (1864), 427; Woodcroft, *Brief biographies*, p. vii; Ince and Gilbert, *Outlines of English history*, p. 134

[15] See above, pp. 255–6.   [16] Collini, *Public moralists*, pp. 94–116, esp. p. 100.

[17] Ibid., p. 106; quotation from Smiles, *Self-help*, preface to 1866 edn, p. v. The discourse of 'the industrious versus the idle, the common people versus the upper ten thousand' reappeared: Taylor, *Decline of British radicalism*, p. 334.

was central to the franchise debate, Smiles affirming that the moral qualities of the artisan qualified him to vote. It is significant, comments Stefan Collini, 'that so much of the discussion in 1867 was not about the respectable workman's rights but about his habits'.[18]

This is a point developed by Keith McClelland: demarcating the 'respectable working man' was crucial to the extension of the franchise. Apart from the evident discrimination by gender, precise boundaries between adult males had to be drawn. A debate about working-class culture, in particular about masculinity, resulted. The Chartists' demand for universal manhood suffrage narrowed, in the hands of the Reform League and the trade unions, into a campaign to enfranchise the 'intelligent artisan' – economically independent and of good character, able to maintain and control a household – the epitome of working-class 'manliness'.[19] As McClelland demonstrates, there was a new emphasis on skilled employment. The notion that all working men held property in their labour – the basis of the Chartists' claim for universal manhood suffrage – was overridden by a distinction between the respectable independence of the skilled worker and the inadequacy of the 'rough' unskilled or casual labourer, who lacked a trade, steady habits and 'a family wage' (sufficient to maintain a wife and children).[20] The expansion of employment in heavy industry, especially during the mid-Victorian boom of 1848–73, accentuated this division and strengthened the position of trade unions, which represented the most highly skilled and best-paid workers.[21] The entitlement to participate in national politics would recognize their contribution to the nation's strength and prosperity. 'England's Greatness, the Working Man' proclaimed the banner carried by the Boilermakers' Society (Tyne and Wear district) in a public demonstration on Tyneside in 1865.[22]

An important facet of the 'intelligent artisan's' demand for the franchise was the insistence not only on his skill but also on his ingenuity – his inventiveness. Although Smiles made no explicit intervention in the franchise debate, this was a major thrust of *Self-help* and his other

---

[18] Collini, *Public moralists*, pp. 111–12.

[19] Keith McClelland, '"England's greatness, the working man"', in Hall, McClelland and Rendall (eds.), *Defining the Victorian nation*, pp. 71–2, 89–116. See also above, pp. 161–9.

[20] The frontispiece to the second edition of Brightwell's volume showed George Stephenson not only as an artisan, with the tools of his trade on the workshop bench beside him, but as a husband and father, demonstrating them to his wife and baby Robert: *Heroes* (new edn, 1865), frontispiece.

[21] McClelland, '"England's greatness"', pp. 102–14; Harrison, *Before the socialists*, pp. 33, 113–19.

[22] McClelland, '"England's greatness"', p. 106.

biographies of inventors and engineers. Early in the first chapter, Smiles announces this credo:

All nations have been made what they are by the thinking and the working of many generations of men. Patient and persevering labourers in all ranks and conditions of life, cultivators of the soil and explorers of the mine, *inventors and discoverers, manufacturers, mechanics, and artisans*, poets, philosophers, and politicians, all have contributed toward the grand result, one generation building upon another's labours, and carrying them forward to still higher stages.[23]

His insistence on the classlessness of virtue and success is reinforced at the start of the next chapter ('Leaders of industry – inventors and producers'):

It is this spirit [of industry], displayed by the commons of England, which has laid the foundations and built up the industrial greatness of the empire ... [I]t has also been its saving and remedial [principle], counteracting from time to time the effects of errors in our laws and imperfections in our constitution.[24]

Smiles becomes more specific, as he introduces his case-studies of inventors, which will occupy the next hundred pages:

As respects the great contrivances and inventions which have conferred so much power and wealth upon the nation, it is unquestionable that for the greater part of them we have been indebted to men of the humblest rank.[25]

Here, in his most influential work, Smiles completes the syllogism: Britain is great, thanks to 'men of the humblest rank'.

'Humblest', however, will turn out not to mean the very lowest 'rank', but a succession of men in skilled trades. The steam engine, as usual, takes pride of place. 'It is indeed, in itself,' says Smiles, 'a monument of the power of self-help in man' – one created by artisans and engineers:

Grouped around it we find Savary [sic], the military engineer; Newcomen, the Dartmouth blacksmith; Cawley, the glazier; Potter, the engine-boy; Smeaton, the civil engineer; and towering above all, the laborious, patient, never-tiring James Watt, the mathematical-instrument maker.[26]

Heroes of the labour aristocracy

By the 1850s, Smiles' was far from a lone voice. Neither was his perspective an original one: working people were not simply passive recipients of

---

[23] Smiles, *Self-help*, p. 5; my emphasis. Note that all the occupations he mentions are civilian ones.
[24] Ibid., p. 27.   [25] Ibid., p. 29.   [26] Ibid., p. 30.

a published message. There is much evidence that for skilled working men, especially in the engineering and metalworking trades, leading inventors and engineers were indeed heroic figures – starting with Watt in the 1820s. They were celebrated on trade union membership certificates and possibly banners (many of which have not survived); they were referred to admiringly in daily conversations; their memorials attracted subscriptions from hundreds (sometimes thousands) of working men. The pride their achievements generated is encapsulated in the response of the engineer, J. P. B. Westhead, MP, to the 1851 select committee on the patent law. Asked whether patents provided an incentive to invention, Westhead replied:

Yes; I remember when I was a young man, and much interested in mechanics, that I thought it as great a distinction to be a patentee or an inventor, as I should now to be promoted to the peerage. That sort of feeling exists, I think, on the part of a great many persons who are brought up in connection with machinists and in manufacturing districts.[27]

Westhead did not reveal how he had encountered patentees and inventors. He was of the right age to have read about them in the *Mechanic's Magazine* or similar publications, to have heard about them from an itinerant lecturer or a talk at a mechanics' institute, or to have visited an exhibition of machinery and manufactures.[28] Three decades later, *The Working Man* evidently expected its working-class audience to be interested in the information that Mr Woodcroft's collection, at the Patent Office Museum, 'contains about 250 portraits, busts, and medallions of celebrated inventors and discoverers'.[29] Alternatively, Westhead might have learned about inventors as an apprentice being inducted into the lore of the trade. The names of a select few appear to have been in everyday, totemic use among members of the labour aristocracy. Thomas Wright, the 'Journeyman Engineer' who wrote about the mores and customs of mid-nineteenth-century skilled workers, recounted how a boy new to the workshop would be interrogated by his peers, 'about himself and relatives, and more especially as to his designs about becoming the Stephenson or Watt of his day: in a word to "taking his measure"'.[30] At

[27] *Report from the select committee of the House of Lords*, BPP 1851, XVIII, p. 585. See also ibid., p. 583.
[28] See above, pp. 213–14.
[29] *The Working Man: a weekly record of social and industrial progress* 1 (2 June 1866), 341.
[30] [Thomas Wright], *Some habits and customs of the working classes by a Journeyman Engineer* [London, 1867], p. 88. See Alastair Reid, 'Intelligent artisans and aristocrats of labour: the essays of Thomas Wright', in J. M. Winter (ed.), *The working class in modern British history: essays in honour of Henry Pelling* (Cambridge: Cambridge University Press, 1983), pp. 171–86.

a dinner organized by the Crewe branch of the Journeymen Steam-Engine and Machine Makers' Friendly Society in 1846, the members toasted 'the immortal memory of James Watt, Henry Bell and Arkwright'.[31] The persistence of Watt's fame among mechanics is illustrated by an incident recounted in Robert Roberts' autobiography. As an engineering apprentice in Salford in the 1920s, Roberts, having dared to venture an opinion concerning a mechanical problem that was baffling his seniors, met with the sarcastic riposte: '"When we want your fuckin' advice, James Watt ... we'll ask for it!"'[32]

Another route was through the iconography of his trade union membership certificate or banner. Nineteenth-century trade unionists sometimes portrayed their heroes – men whose achievements had brought credit to the trade or who had played a major role in establishing or defending the union – on such ceremonial tableaux.[33] Particularly striking is the membership certificate of the Amalgamated Society of Engineers, Machinists, Millwrights, Smiths and Pattern Makers, formed in 1851 (figure 10.1). It was designed by James Sharples, an artistically gifted blacksmith (later engine-smith) from Bury, the heart of the Lancashire textile and engineering industries.[34] At its centre is a manufactory built in classical style and cut away to show a steam engine and five scenes of engineering workers plying their trades. It is surmounted by a plinth containing a central portrait of Watt in a toga (indicative of his status as a 'philosopher') and, either side of him, Crompton and Arkwright recognizable in their contemporary dress: the heroic inventors of Lancashire's steam-driven cotton mills. The plinth supports two mechanics, one wearing a smith's leather apron, the other standing beside a vice. Together they represent the liberal faith that the arts of peace have driven out the barbarism of war: the first man refuses to mend Mars' broken sword; the second accepts a scroll from Minerva, goddess of wisdom. They are blessed by 'a winged genius on a cornucopia' (symbolizing prosperity and fecundity), while above her hovers 'a pentecostal dove' bearing the olive branch of peace. In the background are depicted

---

[31] Keith Burgess, *The origins of British industrial relations: the nineteenth-century experience* (London: Croom Helm, 1975), p. 8.

[32] Robert Roberts, *A ragged schooling: growing up in the classic slum* (Manchester: Manchester University Press, 1976), pp. 198–9; Andrew Davies, 'Roberts, Robert (1905–1974)', *ODNB*, www.oxforddnb.com/view/article/61606, accessed 20 October 2006. Watt's name was reasonably familiar to working people in Sheffield in 1918 – though possibly less so than Edison's: Jonathan Rose, *The intellectual life of the British working classes* (New Haven and London: Yale University Press, 2001), pp. 190–5.

[33] John Gorman, *Banner bright: an illustrated history of the banners of the British trade union movement* (London: Allen Lane, 1973), pp. 103–16.

[34] Smiles, *Self-help*, pp. 190–6, esp. p. 195.

10.1 Membership certificate of the Amalgamated Society of Engineers, Machinists, Millwrights, Smiths and Pattern Makers, designed by James Sharples, 1851. Watt, Arkwright and Crompton are celebrated as heroes of peace and prosperity in the upper part of the neo-classical pedestal; in the lower, a Watt engine and the skilled work of the union's members are positioned at the heart of Britain's steam-powered prowess.

some of the triumphs of modern mechanical engineering: textile mills, a locomotive passing beneath a railway arch, a paddle steamer in the bay, and, on shore, a steam crane piling up its cargo of timber. As Klingender comments, 'the workers of mid-Victorian England still used the old mixture of allegory and engineering detail to express their deep and genuine emotions in a true folk art that decorated the walls of countless workers' homes.'[35] A turn-of-the-century certificate for the Associated Society of Locomotive Engineers and Firemen paid tribute to Watt and George Stephenson; their portraits adorn its top two corners; symbols of industry and peace its lower corners. In the centre, we find the *Rocket*, two more recent locomotives, an electric train, an ocean liner and agricultural machinery harvesting the crops beside a textile mill.[36]

A campaign to perpetuate a particular inventor's memory might also have played an educational role. Subscription lists for the Glasgow and Edinburgh appeals for Watt's memorials in 1824–5 record several workplaces collecting substantial sums, mostly in the engineering and metalworking trades or the cotton industry, but also contributions among printers, bricklayers, brewery workers and furniture makers.[37] The 'mechanics and other workers' at the Catrine and Deanston cotton mills of James Finlay & Co. gave nearly £33; both mills were managed by inventors of spinning machinery – Archibald Buchanan and James Smith respectively.[38] Robert Napier, then starting out as a marine engineer on Clydeside, donated five guineas, while his foundry workers added a further ten; the engineer, John Neilson and his mechanics gave similar sums. Well-attended public lectures on the steam engine, given by Andrew Ure, at Anderson's Institution, Glasgow, and by George Longstaff, at the Glasgow Mechanics' Institute, raised approximately £80 for the city's monument; Longstaff's audience was estimated to be 655, though we cannot assume that all were working men.[39] In Birmingham, 257 men employed by the Soho Foundry of Boulton, Watt & Co. subscribed a total of £54 8s (£54.40) towards the Westminster Abbey monument, principally in sums of one to five shillings (5 to 25p); thirty-one men (probably foremen and managers) gave more, up to £3 10s

---

[35] Klingender, *Art and the industrial revolution*, p. 153. The portraits of Crompton and Arkwright also appeared in a membership certificate issued by the National Cotton Mule Spinners Association of America, in the late nineteenth century: Collection of Lowell National Historical Park.
[36] MacLeod, 'Nineteenth-century engineer', p. 77.
[37] *Glasgow Chronicle*, 25 November 1824, 3b; 11 December 1824, 3a; 30 December 1824, 3b; 5 February 1825, 3d; 2 April 1825, 3c; *Glasgow Mechanics' Magazine* 2 (27 November 1824), 303–4; *The Scotsman*, 24 July 1824, 559; 14 August 1824, 606.
[38] James Finlay & Co. donated 200 guineas to the Glasgow appeal in February 1825: *James Finlay & Company Limited: manufacturers and East India merchants, 1750–1950* (Glasgow: Jackson, Son & Company, 1951), pp. 6–7. The firm's principal, Kirkman Finlay, who was on both the Glasgow and London committees, donated 100 guineas; James Smith of Deanston gave a more typical 5 guineas: *Glasgow Chronicle*, 25 November 1824, 3b; 11 December 1824, 3a.
[39] *Glasgow Chronicle*, 20 December 1824, 2d, 3b.

(£3.50) each.[40] These were generous amounts at a time when their wages approximated £2–3 per week.[41]

Apparently workers tended to follow the lead of employers who subscribed (and sometimes sat on the memorial committee). It is impossible to know how freely such donations were given. While an element of coercion in workplace collections cannot be ruled out, evidently for some working men a donation was both a sacred duty and an opportunity to profess the artisans' contribution to the nation's wellbeing. When Glasgow launched its campaign to commemorate Watt, the *Glasgow Mechanics' Magazine* printed a letter from 'W. G.' that left no doubt about the great significance which, in his opinion, the city's artisans should invest in this monument. Surely it was impossible to refrain, he cajoled, 'from expressing our admiration and our esteem for such a distinguished brother Mechanic ... who by his superior talents, has shed a lustre over our employments and our pursuits'.[42] 'W. G.' identified himself as a member of Anderson's Institution, 'the parent of all the numerous [mechanics'] institutes in the Kingdom', but it is unclear whether he was himself a mechanic or perhaps a middle-class supporter. His enthusiasm for the project, however, was reflected in the article that followed his letter. This reported the resolutions passed – 'with loud cheering' – in the mechanics' class at the Institution, to support the monument both morally and financially. The chairman, Mr Archibald Burns, urged that 'no body of men were more imperatively called on to express their feelings than the members of this class'. Not only did Burns assume their full acquaintance with Watt's fine character and the details of his discoveries, but he concluded with a telling observation:

That it was not long since the term Mechanic, even in this very country, enlightened as it now pretended to be, was used as a term of reproach, and, he believed, they could recollect passages in Shakespeare, which would bear him out in his assertion. To Mr Watt, however, we were indebted for rescuing that name from opprobrium, and for rendering it as honourable a title as a man could possess.[43]

---

[40] Boulton & Watt (Muirhead) MSS, MI/5/9; see above, p. 106.

[41] Eric Roll, *An early experiment in industrial organisation: being a history of the firm of Boulton & Watt, 1775–1805* (repr. New York: Augustus M. Kelley, 1930), pp. 189–91. Roll's figures for the 1790s need to be read in the context of wage rises during the next two decades: Charles M. Feinstein, 'Pessimism perpetuated: real wages and the standard of living in Britain during and after the industrial revolution', *Journal of Economic History* 58 (1998), 625–58.

[42] *Glasgow Mechanics' Magazine* 1 (November 1824), 317. The journal's masthead declared that it was 'conducted by A Committee of Civil Engineers and Practical Mechanics'.

[43] Ibid., 318–19.

In 1854, when the Institution of Mechanical Engineers erected George Stephenson's statue at Euston station, 3,150 subscriptions – the overwhelming majority – comprised small sums averaging two shillings (10p) each. 'A very gratifying feature of the subscription', it remarked, 'was the large number of working mechanics who had joined in promoting the object.'[44] Five years later, during Tyneside's campaign to commemorate Stephenson, *The Times* printed a letter from five former employees of Robert Stephenson and Co., now in Hong Kong and engaged in good positions, such as chief engineer of a steam-ship. Together they subscribed £25 (perhaps a week's wages each), 'as members of that class of mechanics who have been most benefited by his discoveries and improvements', and in gratitude for their long employment in the Stephensons' firm. Gratitude shaded into pride, as these men – themselves pursuing an upwardly mobile trajectory – expressed their 'admiration for one of our own class, who, by his successful application of such discoveries and improvements, had raised himself to the companionship of the highest of the nobility, and left behind a name more durable than any potentate of the last century'.[45] Similarly, Robert Stephenson's pupils were said to regard him 'with a sort of worship'. At his death in 1859, his workers requested their parish church to hold a special service, while the official funeral took place in Westminster Abbey; a thousand people attended.[46] They also turned out in force, a month later, for the meeting to organize a monument for him.[47]

Isambard Kingdom Brunel's monument, on the Victoria Embankment, was largely funded by men connected with the railways, in particular those companies with which he had been personally involved: they accounted for nearly half of the 860 named subscribers. Collections were made in the engineering departments of the Great Western Railway and other railway workshops across southern and south-western England.[48] When the engineering profession was raising money to commemorate Richard Trevithick in 1883, employers were specifically requested 'to allow penny subscriptions from their workmen'. *The Engineer* considered that Trevithick would have been

[44] *Proceedings of the Institution of Mechanical Engineers* (1852), 34; see above, p. 203.
[45] *The Times*, 25 April 1859, 9e. Stephenson, however, might have been happier with the latter description rather than the notion that he was 'one of us': Colls, 'Remembering George Stephenson', p. 274.
[46] *The Times*, 13 October 1859, 7c–d; 20 October 1859, 7f; 22 October 1859, 7b. For a similar devotion to John Elder, see below, p. 335.
[47] *The Times*, 21 November 1859, 7b.
[48] *Brunel Memorial* [printed subscription list, n.d.], WORK20/253, no. 1, National Archives; MacLeod, 'Nineteenth-century engineer', p. 67.

especially pleased with the ten shillings (50p) subscribed, in pennies, by the workers of Peter Brotherhood, a railway contractor.[49] Nearly one-seventh of the total £272 10s 2d (£272.51), was donated by railway employees through workplace collections, including more than £45 from the Great Western Railway's Swindon locomotive works and just over £42 from the London and North Western Railway's Crewe works.[50]

Similar evidence attests that working men in the west Midlands continued to cherish the memory of Watt, independently of the firm he helped to found. Whenever the opportunity arose, they contributed in greater numbers (and perhaps more generously relative to their incomes) than did local employers. In 1868, under the aegis of a group of local historians and engineers, Birmingham commissioned a statue of Watt, from Alexander Munro, to stand in front of the town hall: dressed in everyday clothes, Watt rests one hand on a steam-engine cylinder. The unveiling ceremony attracted both a large audience and complimentary coverage in the press.[51] *The Times* commented that 'no small share of [the public subscription] was contributed by the working-men of Birmingham'.[52] Half a century later, in 1919, when Birmingham commemorated the centenary of Watt's death, by far the largest category of donors to its appeal (primarily to establish a chair in mechanical engineering at the University of Birmingham) comprised workers in engineering and metalworking firms throughout the area. Workplace sales of commemorative 'flags' or 'bannerettes', at 2d (1p) each, raised over £218: this translates into more than 26,000 individual purchases.[53] Nor was 2d an insignificant sum, at a time when engineering workers were earning £4–5 per week and their family's food budget took approximately half of

---

[49] Dickinson and Titley, *Richard Trevithick*, p. 264; *The Engineer*, 21 September 1883, 229. The scheme for a working men's memorial to Robert Peel attracted 400,000 penny subscriptions: *The Builder* 24 (1866), 240.

[50] *The Richard Trevithick memorial* [London, 1888], Institution of Civil Engineers Archives, London. See also below, pp. 322–5.

[51] *The Times*, 5 October 1868, 7b; *The Builder* 26 (1868), 757; *ILN* 53 (7 November 1868), 440; G. Noszlopy, *Public sculpture of Birmingham*, ed. Jeremy Beach (Liverpool: Liverpool University Press, 1998), p. 20.

[52] *The Times*, 5 October 1868, 7b; Noszlopy, *Public sculpture of Birmingham*, p. 32. See also Pemberton, *James Watt of Soho and Heathfield*, pp. 166–7. Similarly, in Scotland, 'Seeing that the often talked of monument to James Watt, in Greenock ... is making no progress, the workmen connected with the engineering and boiler-making trades, etc. of the town, have now taken the matter in hand': *Engineering*, 26 August 1881. I am grateful to Jim Andrew for this reference.

[53] MacLeod and Tann, 'From engineer to scientist', 397.

that.[54] Large numbers processed with their trade-union banners behind a model Watt engine; they displayed their machinery, tools, and products, together with 'tableaux ... depicting the processes of manufacture' and the impact of machinery on industry.[55] For men of both generations, these tributes to Watt simultaneously constituted a claim for recognition of their own contribution to the country's prosperity: as much as the Tyneside Boilermakers' banner in 1865, they proclaimed that it was the skills and ingenuity of working men that were responsible for 'England's greatness', in peace as well as war.[56]

Only a few indications remain of how workers responded to their heroes' monuments. *The Illustrated London News* was enthusiastic about Munro's statue of Watt but more profoundly impressed by the response of Birmingham's working men.

[They] stand grouped around it in the early morning as they are going to work, or at the time of the noonday meal, or when the day's labour is at an end ... hundreds of men looking up at this statue with silent awe and admiration, their feelings best expressed by their rapt gaze and their whispering remarks to each other as they learn and discover what James Watt did to lighten human labour and to advance the manufactures of their country. Who, then, may calculate the moral and intellectual influences of such a statue?[57]

While the workmen's thoughts were attributed to them by the journalist, their interest in the statue and, by implication, in Watt, appears spontaneous and authentic. This report is reminiscent of Brightwell's statement that watchmakers used to make 'frequent pilgrimages' to the graves of Thomas Tompion and George Graham in Westminster Abbey: until 1838, these were marked with a slab that bore a laudatory inscription to their incumbents' 'curious inventions' and 'accurate performances'.[58] It also recalls a contemporary painting, by William Stewart, of the interior of the first Hunterian Museum, in Glasgow. Stewart's canvas shows two artisans, one gazing intently at Chantrey's statue of Watt, the other

[54] Arthur Lyon Bowley, *Prices and wages in the United Kingdom, 1914–1920* (Oxford: Clarendon Press, 1921), cited in J. M. Winter, *Sites of memory, sites of mourning: the Great War in European cultural history* (Cambridge: Cambridge University Press, 1995), pp. 233–4.

[55] *James Watt Centenary 1919, Programme,* Watt Centenary MSS; MacLeod and Tann, 'From engineer to scientist', 396–7. For a detailed description of a comparable procession, see W. Duncan (ed.), *The Stephenson centenary, 1881* (Newcastle upon Tyne: Graham, 1975), pp. 11–19, 38–50.

[56] See above, p. 283.   [57] *ILN* 63 (7 November 1868), 440.

[58] Brightwell, *Heroes,* p. 68, citing Adam Thomson, *Time and timekeepers* (London, 1842). According to Brightwell, the slab had been replaced by 'a small lozenge-shaped bit of marble bearing their names and dates of their death': ibid., p. 69. The slab with its inscription has now been restored.

10.2 *The Interior of the first Hunterian Museum with the statue of James Watt*, by William Stewart. The unusual subject matter of this mid-nineteenth-century oil painting is indicative of the persistent admiration for Watt among artisans.

peering into the showcase containing his most famous invention – an atmospheric (Newcomen) engine modified with Watt's separate condenser (figure 10.2). Watt had been an instrument-maker; it was while repairing the University of Glasgow's model Newcomen engine that he invented the separate condenser.[59] Stewart may have painted an imaginary scene, proposing Watt as an exemplar for artisans to emulate; or, possibly, he captured a real occurrence – even a regular one.

Similar problems of interpretation surround the statue of George Stephenson in Newcastle, which was said to inspire pride among coal

[59] *The Interior of the first Hunterian Museum with the statue of James Watt* (oil painting), by William Stewart (1823–1906): Hunterian Art Gallery Collections, GLAHA 44095. The statue had been donated to the Gallery by James Watt Jnr: McKenzie, *Public sculpture of Glasgow*, pp. 393–4.

miners. *The Working Man*, an Evangelical weekly founded in 1866, selected Stephenson as an early subject for its series of 'Men who have risen from the ranks'.

It is a matter of pride in every coal mine in Britain that a pitman has a statue standing firm and proudly on the upper earth. As the traveller enters Newcastle, there meets him ... the statue of George Stephenson, supported at the base by four bronze massive pitmen – a noble and appropriate statue.[60]

It also quoted the rousing speech of Mr Galpin (of the publishers, Cassell, Petter and Galpin), at the inauguration, which can hardly have pleased the memorial committee.

Every working man has within himself the elements of power. He has skill, which is his capital; and if working men will only unite their varied powers, they can bear down everything opposed to their real interests. (Cheers.) If the working bees unite, they will drive out the drones, who misappropriate the results of honest industry.[61]

At a period before the features of famous people were widely known through a host of visual media, we should not underrate the capacity of a statue to attract the public's attention or inspire interest and emotion. From the 1840s, photography had started to make the appearance of public figures more familiar (Howlett's iconic portrait of Brunel in front of the launching chains of the *Great Eastern* is a striking example), and the contemporary craze for *cartes de visite* helped to disseminate their image.[62] Watt and Stephenson, however, having died in 1819 and 1848 respectively, were only to be known through paintings, busts and statues (and their reproduction in illustrated magazines and journals, as, for example, in figures 7.7 and 10.3). It seems probable that simple curiosity about a famous person's features and demeanour would be sufficient to excite an interest in a statue.[63] Nor would it be surprising if monuments to Watt and Stephenson stirred feelings of pride in working men. When Stephenson's imposing statue was unveiled in Newcastle, it had only one predecessor in the entire city, that of the second earl Grey, who

[60] *The Working Man: a weekly record of social and industrial progress* 1 (13 January 1866), 26.
[61] Ibid. For the statue and its controversial origins, see above, pp. 206–9.
[62] Peter Hamilton and Roger Hargreaves, *The beautiful and the damned: the creation of identity in nineteenth-century photography* (Aldershot: Lund Humphries, 2001), passim; John Tagg, *The burden of representation: essays on photographies and histories* (Basingstoke: Macmillan, 1988), pp. 34–59. For the Howlett photograph, see Kelly and Kelly (eds.), *Brunel, in love with the impossible*, pp. 36–7.
[63] See, for example, the 'ecstatic' description of Watt's statue in the Hunterian Museum by the travel writer, T. F. Dibdin, in 1838: McKenzie, *Public sculpture of Glasgow*, p. 394. Cf. James Vernon, *Politics and the people: a study in English political culture, c. 1815–1867* (Cambridge: Cambridge University Press, 1993), pp. 58–62.

10.3 The front cover of the *British Workman*, January 1859, presents George Stephenson as a model for its working-class readership. The caption beneath his birthplace remarks that 'out of the humblest homes, in the lowest depths of social life, God has sometimes caused a man to arise, who has attained to the summit of human greatness' (photograph by Ann Pethers).

since 1838 had presided over the new city centre from his column at the top of Grey Street.[64] For a 'pitman' to share the honour of a civic statue with this reforming prime minister was indeed cause for celebration. Similarly, the statue that Glasgow erected to Watt, in 1832, was only the second to grace George Square; the first, to the British general, Sir John Moore (a native of the city, killed during the Napoleonic Wars), had occupied the square in isolated – and controversial – splendour since 1819.[65] Moore's had been 'the first public monument in Glasgow for nearly a century'.[66]

We should be careful of not reading back into an earlier period the statue-weariness often expressed at the turn of the century. By then, there were plenty of images, including moving ones, available to the public, and statues (themselves no longer scarce in major towns and cities) probably appeared old-fashioned. Familiarity and time would have tended to dull whatever excitement and awe those first generations might have felt. It was reported in 1881, for example, that in Newcastle, 'at 12.30 every day Stephenson's own "greasy and grimy" toilers would break for dinner and stroll in the vicinity of his monument', but also that their 'leading heroes' were the local rowing champions, Chambers and Renforth.[67] Nor is it too surprising, by 1912, to find a cynical commentary on public memorials in general, which concludes that, 'when the statue is erected nobody looks at it'.[68] In Glasgow, by 1916, thirty free-standing statues had been erected, and a leading article in the *Glasgow Herald* had recently carped that, 'it is scarcely an open question whether the open space of George Square is best put to the best aesthetic use in being clothed with images of the dead'.[69] Glaswegians regularly proposed either imposing a moratorium on new statues or even removing existing ones to other sites.[70] In smaller, more remote places, however, a statue might still have been a novelty, with the power to enthral local inhabitants.[71]

Where there is some objection recorded to a commemorative campaign, it concerns the nature of the memorial. Radicals, in particular, questioned the wisdom of monuments and advocated more utilitarian projects. James Clephan, the radical editor of the *Gateshead Observer*, was

---

[64] Colls, 'Remembering George Stephenson', p. 275; Usherwood *et al.*, *Public sculpture of north-east England*, pp. 96–8.

[65] McKenzie, *Public sculpture of Glasgow*, pp. 114–23. For the distinction accorded Watt by a statue in Westminster Abbey, see above, p. 98.

[66] Ibid., p. xii.

[67] Colls, 'Remembering George Stephenson', p. 288, quoting *The Graphic*, 4 June 1881.

[68] *The Times*, 2 October 1912. Cf. Agulhon, 'Politics, images, and symbols', pp. 192–3.

[69] McKenzie, *Public sculpture of Glasgow*, pp. xiii, 116.

[70] Ibid., pp. 116–18.   [71] See below, pp. 338–43.

a great admirer of George Stephenson and paid him the rare tribute of allocating the entire front page to his obituary.[72] Clephan was among the first to propose a memorial to Stephenson, in 1851, but had no wish for a statue: he revived an older scheme for a Stephenson Institute, 'a sort of cross between a mechanics' institute and a working-class university'.[73] In 1859, an educational institution was also proposed by a group of radicals for Robert Stephenson's memorial. This group included the workers' delegate from Stephensons' locomotive workshops, Mr Rapier, T. E. Harrison, of the North Eastern Railway, and William Newton, a radical surgeon and councillor for Newcastle's poorest ward. Newton subsequently published a penny pamphlet, which called for named schol-arships (after great Novocastrians, not only the Stephensons) at the new grammar school, and described statues as ' "a huge mistake" ... cold and lifeless and backward looking'.[74] The radicals' and workers' preferences were ignored in Newcastle, but, in 1863, the committee of the United Kingdom Railway Officers and Servants Association proposed that a 'George Stephenson Fund' be set up, to assist disabled and elderly railway-men, as a more suitable commemoration than a statue.[75] Moreover, Stephenson's centenaries, in 1879–81, provided opportunities to raise funds for several educational projects, a railway union's orphanage, and Chesterfield's community hall.[76] Such preferences were also heard among Samuel Crompton's admirers in Bolton (Lancs.).

'Our' Samuel Crompton

In one unusually well-documented case, in 1860, a group of Bolton's workers revealed the strength of their feelings, both in their determination that Samuel Crompton should be properly commemorated and in their explanations of why it was important. It is evident that they identified closely with Crompton, as one of their own, a working man who was primarily responsible for the prosperity of the region.[77]

It was over thirty years since Crompton, the inventor of the spinning mule, had died in poverty. Having neglected to patent his invention, he

---

[72] Colls, 'Remembering George Stephenson', p. 277.   [73] Ibid., pp. 275, 277.
[74] W. Newton, *A letter on the Stephenson monument, and the education of the district, addressed to the Right Hon. Lord Ravensworth* (Newcastle upon Tyne: Robert Fisher, 1859), cited in ibid., p. 278.
[75] *The Builder* 21 (1863), 285.   [76] See below, pp. 320–2.
[77] There were precedents among Bolton's workers for taking such communal initiatives: Barton, ' "Why should working men visit the Exhibition?" ', pp. 154–5; Patrick Joyce, *Work, society and politics: the culture of the factory in later Victorian England* (Brighton: Harvester Press, 1980), p. 181.

could only regret the huge royalties he might have enjoyed, as British textile-spinning mills equipped themselves overwhelmingly with mules.[78] In 1812, he secured a parliamentary reward of £5,000 – a small sum in comparison with what astute patent management might have produced – but further demonstrated his lack of business competence by sinking it in a bleaching enterprise that soon failed.[79] By 1824, concerns over Crompton's poverty initiated a subscription among local cotton-mill owners; the resulting annuity produced a modest income of £63 per annum. At his death in 1827, the sale of his meagre household goods barely covered his debts and his family could afford only a plain slab to mark his grave in Bolton churchyard.[80] This was partially rectified, in 1839, by his old friend, John Kennedy, the Manchester cotton spinner, and James Hardcastle, a local gentleman, who paid for it to be inscribed with Crompton's name and the words 'Inventor of the Spinning Machine called the Mule'.[81] Kennedy also compiled a biographical memoir, for publication by the Manchester 'Lit and Phil'.[82] Yet, Crompton's descendents had continuing cause to bewail his lack of recognition and their persistent poverty.[83] The former, if not the latter, changed dramatically during the 1860s, thanks initially to the efforts of one man.

Gilbert French was a Scot, a fabrics merchant with a business in Bolton, and a keen antiquarian.[84] He contacted Crompton's family in 1853 (the centenary of Samuel's birth), announcing his intention 'to do just honour to him *after death* which was unjustly withheld from him

---

[78] *Bolton Chronicle*, 30 June 1827, quoted in *Samuel Crompton, the inventor of the spinning mule: a brief survey of his life and work, with which is incorporated a short history of Messrs Dobson & Barlow, Limited* (Bolton, 1927), pp. 43–4.

[79] Michael E. Rose, 'Samuel Crompton (1753–1827): inventor of the spinning mule: a reconsideration', *Trans. Lancashire and Cheshire Antiquarian Society* 75 (1965), 21–7.

[80] Ibid., 27–8; John Kennedy, 'A brief memoir of Samuel Crompton; with a description of his machine called the mule, and of the subsequent improvement of the machine by others', *Memoirs of the Literary and Philosophical Society of Manchester*, 2nd ser., 5 (1831), 321–4. 'Valuation of the furniture of the late Samuel Crompton', 1827, Crompton MSS, ZCR 45/17; Samuel Crompton, last will and testament, ZCR 45/18; J. Horton to Mr Crompton, [1827]', ZCR 46/9; Invoice, Hargreaves & Hutchinson to George Crompton, 1 February 1828, ZCR 47/3; William Crompton to George Crompton, 2 April 1828, ZCR 47/8.

[81] Epitaphs for Samuel Crompton's gravestone [1839], Crompton MSS, ZCR 45/4; James Hardcastle to George Crompton, 18 January 1839, ZCR 58/1; George Crompton to James Hardcastle, 19 January 1839, ZCR 59/2. By 1859 'the neglected state of the grave', its flat stone 'trodden by hundreds', was causing comment: 'The Crompton Memorial', *Bolton Chronicle*, 11 April 1859, cutting in ZCR74/14; report of visit by Lancashire and Cheshire Historical Society, *Bolton Chronicle*, 9 July 1859, ZCR 75/20.

[82] Kennedy, 'Brief memoir'. For Kennedy, see above, p. 195.

[83] See above, pp. 188–9.

[84] Emma Plaskitt, 'French, Gilbert James (1804–1866)', *ODNB*, www.oxforddnb.com/view/article/10163, accessed 20 October 2006.

during life', in the belief that Bolton was 'indebted [to him] for its great prosperity'. He had had a portrait painted from 'the bust which was taken post mortem', which he planned to have engraved, and the same artist was painting him a view of Crompton's home at Hall i' th' Wood.[85] Over five years later, the rapturous response to his two lectures on Crompton, for the Bolton Mechanics' Institute, inspired him to greater efforts.[86] The *Bolton Chronicle* proposed 'a double monument'. First, the people of Bolton should purchase Hall i' th' Wood to convert it into a museum of spinning. Secondly, they should launch a national, even an international, appeal to erect a statue in Bolton, for Crompton's invention was 'not only one of the landmarks of English history', but it was 'affecting the destinies and modifying the future of every nation under Heaven'.[87]

French was encouraged to publish the lectures, but the meeting that he and others of Bolton's 'leading men' called to discuss a public memorial proved 'a miserable failure': 200 printed invitations to Bolton cotton spinners elicited an attendance of fourteen.[88] French sardonically suggested casting a statue 'out of material from old mules'; someone else reckoned that 'at least a good obelisk' might be obtained for £1,000. The town's radical MP, Mr Crook, challenged the whole idea. In his opinion, 'Crompton was sufficiently immortalised in the history of the cotton trade without sticking him against a wall.' When somebody responded that, since 'statues were raised to warriors and statesmen ... why not to the actual benefactors of the human race?' Crook was dismissive of Crompton's achievement: the mule was nothing but a combination of the spinning jenny and the throstle (i.e. Arkwright's water-frame). True to his radical colours, however, Crook's principal objection was to wasting money on a useless object, when valuable institutions, such as the Infirmary, were in desperate need of funds; if Crompton's memorial were to be an educational institution, he would subscribe. Several others expressed a similar preference, but the meeting disbanded inconclusively.[89] French, thoroughly dispirited, was ready to drop the whole idea. His hopes were revived by a visit from Robert Heywood, 'one of our oldest manufacturers, a JP,

---

[85] G. French to G. Crompton, 29 November 1853, Crompton MSS, ZCR 69/4; same to same, 2 December 1853, ZCR 69/5; original emphasis.

[86] G. French to S. Crompton, 20 November 1858, Crompton MSS, ZCR 70/12.

[87] *Bolton Chronicle*, 29 January 1859, 5 February 1859, Crompton MSS, ZCR 71/2, 71/4.

[88] G. French to S. Crompton, 18 March 1859, Crompton MSS, ZCR 71/16; same to same, 18 May 1859, ZCR 73/6; printed invitation to public meeting, 23 May 1859, ZCR 73/10; G. French to S. Crompton, 27 May 1859, ZCR 74/1.

[89] *Bolton Chronicle*, 4 June 1859, Crompton MSS, ZCR 74/13.

Unitarian and almost a Radical', who deplored the behaviour of Crook, 'his co-religionist'. To demonstrate his support, Heywood promised a contribution of £5 if they decided on a memorial over Crompton's grave; £50, for a public statue; £500, for an educational institution. While condemning Crook's outspokenness, Heywood clearly shared his utilitarian values. Two similar offers, together with the backing (and increasingly ambitious proposals) of the *Chronicle*, proved insufficient to persuade French to risk the humiliation of another meeting.[90] Yet, the *Life and times of Samuel Crompton* found a ready market; by January 1860, French was preparing a second edition.[91] Unilaterally, he ordered 'a substantial block of granite' for Crompton's grave; unsolicited contributions more than defrayed his expense, allowing the granite to be raised on a free-stone pedestal.[92]

At this point, with his campaign for a statue in abeyance, French received a letter from William Slater, a manager at the large machine-making firm of Dobson & Barlow, who had prepared drawings of mules for French's biography. Slater explained that, 'a number of our foremen together with a few of the managers and over-lookers of cotton mills in the town', had met and unanimously determined 'to erect a monument to Samuel Crompton and not wait longer for other people to do it for them'. They favoured a statue and were confident that, with the right publicity, 'working men would subscribe liberally to accomplish this object'. He enclosed a list of donations pledged at their meeting, which totalled nearly £30, including twenty-one gifts of £1 and one of £5.[93] These forty or so men were demonstrating the seriousness of their intent, with pledges that represented generous proportions of weekly wages of probably £2 to £3.

Eight months later, a second public meeting convened by the mayor 'in compliance with a most influentially-signed requisition', attracted over 500 people.[94] While attendance on the platform was again embarrassingly

[90] G. French to S. Crompton, 9 June 1859, Crompton MSS, ZCR 74/12; *Bolton Chronicle*, 11 June 1859, ZCR 74/14; G. French to S. Crompton, 11 June 1859, ZCR 74/16; same to same, 12 June 1859, ZCR 75/1; *Bolton Chronicle*, 18 June 1859, ZCR 75/2.
[91] Printed advertisement for French's lectures, 'Life and times of Samuel Crompton' [1859], Crompton MSS, ZCR 75/11; G. French to S. Crompton, 24 January 1860, ZCR 80/7; *Dewsbury Reporter*, 28 January 1860, ZCR 80/9; *Dewsbury Reporter*, 4 February 1860, ZCR 80/12; G. French to S. Crompton, 7 May 1860, ZCR 82/9.
[92] *Bolton Chronicle*, 1 September 1860, Crompton MSS, ZCR 82/12.
[93] W. Slater to G. French, 6 January 1860, Crompton MSS, ZCR 80/1. This sum was probably used for the new memorial over Crompton's grave: *Bolton Chronicle*, 1 September 1860, ZCR 82/12; *Bolton Guardian, Crompton Supplement*, 24 September 1862, ZCR 84/3.
[94] The next two paragraphs are based on the report in *Bolton Chronicle*, 1 September 1860, Crompton MSS, ZCR 82/12.

'meagre', the body of the hall teemed with working men and women. The first two speakers, Alderman [Robert?] Heywood and Councillor Barlow (of Dobson & Barlow), emphatically welcomed the participation of the working classes as well as the wealthy. This theme was echoed from the floor by the appropriately named William Thirlwind, whose lively speech drew a good-humoured response. Although his preference was for a technical school, Thirlwind offered to support anything that was worthy of its subject, 'so that the people might point and say, "That's the founder of all this wealth!" "That's the image of the man!"' Thirlwind appealed to his fellow workers to take possession of Crompton's memory. Let it never be forgotten that it was a working man who had 'made Manchester twice Manchester ... Bolton twice Bolton; and Lancashire twice Lancashire'. The chief beneficiaries of Crompton's invention, he declared, might be 'these cotton lords – these chaps at the back (pointing over his shoulder to the platform, amidst loud laughter and cheers) ... [and] the lords of the soil', but it was for working men to celebrate Crompton as one of their own; 'if they could only afford a penny, it was equal to "these lad's [sic] pound" (laughter)'.

Next, William Slater reiterated the call for 'a public subscription ... both male and female, high and low, rich and poor'. He urged every working man to 'give his mite', so that the wealthy would see they were 'in earnest' and co-operate to secure their goal. Slater also used Crompton's example to remind the employers that their wealth rested on the skill and ingenuity of their workers. Especially striking is these men's personal pride in the inventor's ingenuity and a fierce sense of possession. The mule, said Slater, had marked a breakthrough in cotton spinning: 'It was not a number of inventions patched together, but a distinct and separate invention. It was not the work of a number of individuals, but the invention of one man, and that man Samuel Crompton (hear, hear).' Whatever its subsequent improvements, the machine was still basically his. Slater's own technical knowledge enabled him to recognize Crompton's achievement; one highly skilled man was appreciating the work of another – and refuting Crook's earlier put-down. With enthusiasm mounting, the platform could scarcely keep control of the meeting; Heywood conceded the committee should include 'a number of operatives'.

Despite the threat to trade from the American Civil War, the appeal was widely supported. Immediate pledges totalling £763 were received from fifty-five firms and individuals, including nineteen cotton spinners and manufacturers and eight engineers or machine makers. Workplace collections in Bolton's machine-making shops and cotton mills, which raised several pounds each, helped to double that sum within two months. By February 1861, £1,700 had been raised, and a central site in Nelson Square donated by the earl of Bradford; only £300

10.4 *Samuel Crompton* by William Calder Marshall, 1862, in Nelson
Square, Bolton. The bas-relief illustrates Hall i' th' Wood, Bolton,
Crompton's boyhood home (photograph by the author).

was still needed.[95] William Calder Marshall was commissioned to
design alternative models for the committee's consideration. It preferred
the representation of Crompton in a relaxed seated pose (figure 10.4),
and accepted the sculptor's proposal for two bas-reliefs on the pedestal,

[95] Subscription list, 1 September 1860, *Bolton Chronicle* [September 1860], Crompton
MSS, ZCR 82/15; *Bolton Chronicle*, 19 September 1860, ZCR 83/5; *Bolton Chronicle*,
20 October 1860, ZCR 83/6; *Bolton Chronicle*, 27 October 1860, ZCR 83/7; *Bolton
Guardian, Crompton Supplement*, 24 September 1862, ZCR 84/3.

10.5 Bas-relief on the monument to Samuel Crompton, in Bolton, showing Crompton inventing the spinning mule, his inspirational violin at his side (photograph by the author).

one illustrating Hall i' th' Wood, the other showing Crompton with the mule – and his violin (figure 10.5).[96]

Bolton celebrated the statue's inauguration, in September 1862, with a general holiday. *The Illustrated London News* showed Nelson Square thronged with people, listening to the speeches in praise of Crompton, cotton and Bolton (figure 10.6). The day continued with a promenade concert at the Temperance Hall, a balloon ascent, free food ('a distribution of 2,000 loaves and one or more fat bullocks'), a ball, a performance of Hayden's 'Creation', and a firework display – its finale, 'a grand illuminated piece commemorative of Crompton with a transparency of Crompton and over it the word "Crompton" in all the colours of the rainbow'.[97] *The Bolton Guardian* ran a special supplement, which congratulated French on saving Crompton 'from oblivion' and announced a new 'people's edition' of his biography, price one shilling (5p).[98]

The only sour note was the alleged neglect of the Crompton family, which prompted some jaundiced reflections on the inventor's lot. According to the *Manchester Guardian*, none of Crompton's descendants was invited to the social events; his one surviving son was so impoverished that he had to borrow a friend's suit to attend the statue's inauguration.

---

[96] *Bolton Chronicle*, 27 October 1860, Crompton MSS, ZCR 83/7; *Bolton Guardian, Crompton Supplement*, 24 September 1862, ZCR 84/3.
[97] *Inauguration of the Crompton Statue* [printed programme], Crompton MSS, ZCR 84/2; *ILN* 41(4 October 1862), 361.
[98] *Bolton Guardian, Crompton Supplement*, 24 September 1862, Crompton MSS, ZCR 84/3.

10.6 Nelson Square, Bolton, is thronged with people (including many women) for the inauguration of Samuel Crompton's monument, in this engraving from *The Illustrated London News*, 4 October 1862 (photograph by Ann Pethers).

The statue was a 'tardy recognition ... of a national benefactor who was permitted to die in indigence'; even now, 'while mayors and wealthy cotton spinners ride in procession and talk of honouring themselves by honouring Crompton', his family was allowed to live in poverty, 'neglected, if not despised'.[99] *Punch* was equally critical: 'All Cottonia owes its pounds and its mites to the same cause'; the statue was a monument to the shame of the 'cotton counties'.[100] The *Journal of the Society of Arts*, with an eye to the patent controversy, contrasted the misfortune of Crompton with the wealth and high position achieved by Arkwright and Watt. While Crompton had suffered for lack of a patent, neither the manufacturers nor the nation had 'prospered the less' because Arkwright and Watt had patented their inventions.[101]

Even less noticed than Crompton's descendents, was another inventor and handloom weaver, John Osbaldeston, who died that same year

[99] *Manchester Guardian*, quoted in *JSA* 10 (17 October 1862), 714.
[100] *Punch* 43 (1862), 154.
[101] *JSA* 10 (1862), 713–14. Woodcroft made a similar point: see above, p. 253.

in a nearby workhouse. His grave in Tockholes churchyard, near Blackburn (Lancs.), is marked by a stone monument, which resembles a cop (the piece onto which the spun cotton was wound on a mule). Osbaldeston had invented the weft fork, a device that improved the efficiency of looms, and was embittered by his lack of recognition and reward. He left instructions that his headstone should be inscribed: 'Here lies John Osbaldeston, a humble inventor, who raised many to wealth and fortune, but himself lived in poverty and died in obscurity, the dupe of false friends and the victim of misplaced confidence.'[102] Osbaldeston's request in 1862 could easily have been Crompton's in 1827. It was a fine line between hero and victim – the twin fates of the nineteenth-century inventor. But for French and his allies in Bolton's machinery workshops and cotton mills, we might know as little today of Crompton as we do of Osbaldeston.

Whose heroes?

The class tensions that surfaced in Bolton were also illuminated in the Staffordshire Potteries by proposals to commemorate Josiah Wedgwood, over sixty years after his death. There were, however, important differences, which allowed less opportunity for the workers' views to be voiced so explicitly in the Potteries. Unlike Crompton, who by the 1850s had almost disappeared from Bolton's memory, Wedgwood's name and reputation lived on in the pottery industry, thanks to the famous firm that still bore his name and attracted royal and aristocratic patronage. With the firm's reputation at stake, the pottery workers would scarcely be allowed to claim Wedgwood as one of their own – except in the most deferential way.

In February 1859, *The Builder* announced two commemorative proposals, 'so that a rather unfortunate competition for Wedgwood honours has been got up'. The 'official' campaign, endorsed by the Wedgwood family and firm, was launched at a 'crowded meeting of the inhabitants of the Potteries' at Burslem. The earl of Carlisle took the chair, and the cream of local society announced its support, either in person or by letter. Their intention was to construct a memorial building: its use should reflect Josiah's character as 'a benefactor of the neighbourhood, his country, and his race', who 'had led the way in useful inventions, or fostered the arts of progress'. Over £800 had already been subscribed. Meanwhile, the 'unofficial' meeting at nearby Stoke-on-Trent (where

---

[102] Salveson, *The people's monuments*, p. 56; for a photograph of the grave, see p. 57. There are three patents for weaving equipment in Osbaldeston's name, between 1824 and 1842.

Wedgwood is buried) had resolved to erect a statue, but only thanks to the chairman's casting vote; the district's working people were also said to prefer a meeting hall.[103]

A yet more radical tone was sounded in an anonymous letter to *The Times*, which proposed two, more appropriate monuments to Wedgwood's 'philanthropy': either smoke-consuming measures, to encourage the wealthy to return to live in the Potteries and improve the district, or almshouses for disabled potters, whose health had been ruined by foul working conditions (described in graphic detail). The writer reserved his scorn for the proposed statue and for a rumoured monument in Westminster Abbey, which was 'simply inadmissible'. Wedgwood had invented the pyrometer and made valuable experiments, enjoying the material rewards they entailed: he was 'innocent of so ambitious a claim' as others were now making on his behalf. Sardonically but presciently, the writer protested:

If every manufacturer who pursued his craft with perseverance, ability, and success is to be distinguished by a statue to his memory; if the patent office is to issue henceforth our English patents of nobility; if our national character is to be wholly and solely commercial, proclaim by all means, this new truth, and let the commercial element predominate in our public monuments.[104]

It was indicative of the Wedgwoods' economic predominance and social standing in the region that, despite the 'unfortunate competition', neither campaign experienced any apparent difficulty in raising funds. Within three weeks, over £1,900 had been subscribed for the institute at Burslem and approximately £2,000 for the statue at Stoke ('raised chiefly by local subscription') (figure 10.7).[105] In January 1862, the casting of the eight-foot bronze statue at Mr Rogers' foundry in Southwark provided an afternoon's entertainment for 'a number of persons, including ladies'. Designed by Edward Davis and first displayed at the International Exhibition in London, in 1862 it was inaugurated in front of Stoke railway station, before 'an immense concourse of spectators'. It represents Wedgwood in the costume of his own time, holding the Portland vase; his features were modelled on the portrait by Sir Joshua Reynolds.[106] Later that year, Gladstone, then Lord Palmerston's Chancellor of the Exchequer, laid the foundation stone of the Wedgwood Institute at Burslem, witnessed by members of the local elite and a holiday crowd. The Institute was intended to provide a school of art, a museum and a public library. Another statue of Wedgwood, stands over the main

[103] *The Builder* 17 (1859), 98.   [104] *The Times*, 17 February 1859, 10e.
[105] *The Builder* 17 (1859), 151.
[106] *The Builder* 20 (1862), 31; *ILN* 40 (28 June 1862), 666–7; *ILN* 42 (7 March 1863), 247; Nikolaus Pevsner, *Staffordshire* (Harmondsworth: Penguin, 1974), p. 262.

10.7 *Josiah Wedgwood* by Edward Davis, 1862, in Wilton Square, Stoke-on-Trent. Wedgwood holds the Portland vase, which he imitated in a limited edition to great acclaim (photograph by the author).

doorway, and a terracotta frieze illustrates the pottery workers of the district engaging in a series of skilled tasks.[107]

In an address to Gladstone, a 'representative' of the working class praised free trade and Wedgwood. It was an appropriate moment to celebrate the theme of upward social mobility. This man, whom *The*

[107] *The Times*, 27 October 1863, 5e–6d. Photographs of the statue and the frieze on the Institute's façade may be viewed on: www.artandarchitecture.org.uk/images/ conway/1707f2c9.html, accessed 19 August 2005, and www.thepotteries.org/photos/ burslem_centre/wedgwood_institute.html, accessed 19 August 2005. For the Wedgwood Centenary Exhibition, held at the Institute, see *The Times*, 28 June 1895, 10c.

Times did not dignify with a name, but who was probably a senior employee at the Wedgwood factory, expressed:

our gratification that he to whose memory this institute is being founded commenced in life as a working man, and by his genius, providence and industry obtained a world-wide and honourable fame, and added his influence to that of a host of other worthies who have risen from the humbler ranks, to assist in uplifting in social estimation the great labouring community.[108]

Gladstone's long speech presented Wedgwood as a rare exemplar of artistic taste and talent combined with business acumen:

Wedgwood was not only an active, careful, clear-headed, liberal-minded, enterprising man of business – not only, that is to say, a great manufacturer – but also a great man. He had in him that turn and fashion of true genius which we may frequently recognize in our great engineers, but which the immediate heads of industry, whether in agriculture, manufacture, or commerce, have more rarely exhibited.[109]

Gladstone expressed his surprise that no biography of Wedgwood had been published. Within two years this lacuna was twice remedied; both were dedicated to the Chancellor. The first to appear, by Llewellynn Jewitt, a Derby newspaper editor and antiquary, was a comparatively lightweight work.[110] The second was the authoritative, if idealizing, two-volume biography by Eliza Meteyard, which was based on the Wedgwood papers (many of them rescued, in 1843, by her friend Joseph Mayer of Liverpool, a collector of Wedgwood ware).[111] In 1861, Meteyard, a radical and feminist journalist, wrote in Mayer's visitors' book:

I formed the first idea of writing a life of Wedgwood as long ago as 1850. Being called upon in that year to write a notice of him, I found materials so scanty, and so little seemed to be known of our great ceramic artist, as to lead me to the resolution to write as exhaustive a memoir as possible of him as soon as time permitted.[112]

Her long list of acknowledgements included Bennet Woodcroft and Samuel Smiles; she was also a close friend of Harriet Martineau.[113] The *Life* was well received by the critics. It did not make Meteyard's fortune, but, in 1869, Gladstone granted her a Civil List pension of £60 per annum for services to literature and the Liberal Party, which was increased to £100 in 1874.[114]

[108] *The Times*, 27 October 1863, 5e–6d.   [109] Ibid.
[110] Llewellynn Frederick William Jewitt, *The Wedgwoods: being a life of Josiah Wedgwood* (London: Virtue, 1865).
[111] Meteyard, *Life of Josiah Wedgwood*.
[112] Quoted in R. W. Lightbourn, introduction to Meteyard, *Life of Josiah Wedgwood* (unpaginated).
[113] Ibid., p. xxii, and Lightbourn, introduction.   [114] Ibid., Lightbourn, introduction.

Unlike Bolton or the Potteries, the economy of Penzance (Cornwall) owed nothing to its most famous son, Sir Humphry Davy. Nonetheless, when a scheme was announced in 1862, *The Builder* expressed surprise that Davy's native town had been so slow to commemorate him, considering his eminence and the benefits his work had bestowed on his country.[115] While hardly a fair comment, given that such commemorations had only become fashionable in the 1850s, it is itself symptomatic of that vogue. It took a further ten years before the statue was finally unveiled, on a prominent site outside the old Market House. Then, *The Builder* paid tribute to 'the energy and perseverance of some working men of Penzance' in bringing it to fruition; one in particular, Mr John May, 'for many years has devoted himself to its accomplishment'.[116] It was a tribute re-iterated in several speeches. May explained that the plan to commemorate Davy arose in 1861, in a casual conversation between several members of the 'Young Tradesmen's Society', but he indicated nothing deeper than a sense that a monument to such a famous native of the town ought to exist.[117] It is perhaps surprising that nothing was said to link Davy with the Cornish mining industry, since Penzance was on its edge. Although the problem of explosions that Davy's safety lamp addressed was specific to coal mines, one imagines that the county's tin and copper miners would have empathized with fellow miners.

The men's original scheme envisaged a statue surmounting a tower, itself atop a high cliff north of Mount's Bay. The angles of the parapet were to be decorated with 'emblems characteristic of Davy's discoveries; viz, the Davy lamp, a Leyden jar, a gas receiver, and a galvanic battery'.[118] They would commemorate him as both inventor and experimental chemist. *The Builder* criticized the proposal for committing a stylistic solecism: a column in the style of 'a period anterior to that of the alchemist' would provide an incongruous base for the 'effigy of one of the chiefs of a science exclusively modern'.[119] Whether for stylistic or – more probably – financial

[115] *The Builder* 20 (1862), 714. A statue of Davy by Alexander Munro had recently been presented to the new University Museum at Oxford by the marquis of Lothian: *The Builder* 17 (1859) 401; 18 (1860), 479; see below, p. 000 [ch. 12]. In 1870, Davy featured twice in groups of scientists, artists and writers: a statue by Noble, on the exterior of Burlington House, the new headquarters of the University of London, and on a panel in the gilt-bronze doors at the South Kensington Museum: Nikolaus Pevsner, *The buildings of England: London. vol. I, The cities of London and Westminster* (Harmondsworth: Penguin, 1957), pp. 549–50; *The Builder* 28 (1870), 467, 469. For a photograph of the doors, see: www.victorianweb.org/sculpture/misc/va/1.html, accessed 23 December 2005.

[116] *The Builder* 30 (1872), 823.

[117] *Cornish Telegraph*, 16 October 1872. I am grateful to Annabelle Reid, Librarian of the Morrab Library, Penzance, for this reference and a photocopy of the article.

[118] *The Builder* 20 (1862), 14, 714–15; 30 (1872), 823.   [119] *The Builder* 21 (1863), 6.

10.8 *Sir Humphry Davy* by W. J. and T. Wills, 1872, in front of the Market House, Penzance; Davy's right hand rests on his safety lamp (photograph by Dorothy Livingston).

reasons, this scheme was quietly dropped; its estimated cost was £4,000.[120] By 1864, £1,500 had been pledged, but this included £1,000 offered by 'a lady' on condition that the memorial should take the form of almshouses. Boldly, the committee announced that it would aim for both almshouses and a statue, at a cost of £10,000.[121] This was clearly much too ambitious: over the next seven years, the subscriptions seem scarcely to have advanced. In 1871, however, in expectation of further donations, the committee commissioned a statue from W. J. and T. Wills of London.[122]

The initial scheme to symbolize the broad range of Davy's scientific and inventive achievements narrowed to the invention for which he was most famous (figure 10.8). In the words of *The Times*: 'the right hand rests on a safety lamp, the product and symbol of the beneficent genius of the

---

[120] *Cornish Telegraph*, 16 October 1872. This report said the plan had been for a tower surmounted by an observatory (not a statue).
[121] *The Times*, 17 April 1864, 14e; 14 June 1864, 11e.
[122] *The Times*, 23 September 1870, 6e; 9 August 1871, 9c; 18 October 1872, 3a; *The Builder* 30 (1872), 450, 823; *Cornish Telegraph*, 16 October 1872.

chymist.' According to the *Cornish Telegraph*, it symbolized 'one of the most useful works of Davy's life'.[123] It was also left largely to the safety lamp to identify the subject of the monument. The eight-and-a-half-feet-tall statue represented Davy in his 'favourite' costume of 'over-coat, breeches, and neck-cloth'; the inscription simply read 'Davy', though the massive base and plinth lifted him high above the crowd.[124]

The inauguration was also a simple, but dignified affair; no national politician made the long journey to Cornwall. A half-day holiday allowed a lengthy procession of freemasons' and Oddfellows' lodges to assemble in their regalia; the 'Young Tradesmen's Society' had pride of place, in front of the committee, the band and the Mayor and Corporation. The speakers were mostly local dignitaries, their themes, principally ones of pride in Davy's upward social mobility – Penzance had the honour, it was remarked, of having produced *two* presidents of the Royal Society (the other was Davies Gilbert) – and of praise for the life-saving quality of his greatest invention. Several referred to the town having finally done its duty by Davy, and the role of its working men in accomplishing this.[125] The Royal Society was represented by Warrington Smith, also president of the Royal Cornwall Geological Society. Smith emphasized that Davy was, above all, a highly accomplished scientist who, through a long series of observations, experiments and logical deductions, 'had established chemistry upon a secure basis, and had made of it a large and magnificent science'. Only then turning to Davy's 'wonderful invention', he left his audience in no doubt either of its dependence on Davy's prior scientific understanding of gases, or its importance in the coal-mining industry. The industry employed 350,000 men, said Smith, whose daily safety still relied on Davy's lamp; it allowed the exploitation of otherwise inaccessible tracts of 'this indispensable material'. If there were still accidents, he opined, it was not because the lamp 'led some men into danger', but because they did not use it properly. Smith's speech was, nonetheless, applauded throughout.[126]

In neither local nor national reports is there any sense that the class tensions, expressed explicitly in Bolton and mutedly in the Potteries, were

---

[123] *The Times*, 9 August 1871, 9c; *Cornish Telegraph*, 16 October 1872. A bicentenary plaque beside the statue compensates for Davy's exclusive identification with the safety lamp, by describing his major work as being 'in the field of electro-chemistry': Darke, *Monument guide*, p. 107.

[124] *Cornish Telegraph*, 16 October 1872.

[125] Ibid; David Philip Miller, 'Gilbert [Giddy], Davies (1767–1839)', *ODNB*, www. oxforddnb.com/view/article/10686, accessed 20 October 2006.

[126] *Cornish Telegraph*, 16 October 1872. For the tendency to blame the victims of occupational hazards, see Barbara Harrison, *Not only the 'dangerous trades': women's work and health in Britain, 1880–1914* (London and Bristol: Taylor & Francis, 1996).

current in Penzance. While there was a strange mixture of pride and embarrassment that the performance of the town's duty had been left to its working men, there were no grounds for accusing its middle classes of miserly ingratitude. Unlike in Bolton, they had not benefited directly from their hero's invention, and John May's speech paid tribute to the financial support and advice of 'many kind gentlemen of position in the town and neighbourhood'.[127] In the event (as ultimately in Bolton), Davy offered his fellow townsmen some social cement: not only as a civic figurehead in whom they could all take pride, but his commemoration gave a group of working men the opportunity to make a highly visible contribution to civic life. Within five years it was time for Penzance to celebrate the centenary of Davy's birth, which it did with more general enthusiasm and greater support from local notables. The town held an exhibition of scientific apparatus, mainly on loan from the Science and Art Department of the South Kensington Museum, and a series of lectures on scientific subjects. Sir John St Aubyn and Mr Pendarves Vivian, MP, having both sent their apologies in 1872, now spoke at the opening of the exhibition. They both focused on Davy's invention of the safety lamp: while St Aubyn presented it in the conventional, humanitarian light, Vivian voiced the economic truism that, without it, 'some of the best seams of coal could not have been worked'.[128]

Although Crompton, Davy and Wedgwood enjoyed strong local support among working people, Sir Rowland Hill could lay claim to being the most popular inventor of the period. Neither a working man nor by any means a 'martyr' or 'victim', Hill's name was widely known and the donations that flowed in to commemorate him were numerous and apparently not class-specific.[129] His revolutionary reform of the postal system was widely acknowledged to be of particular benefit to the poorest people. Moreover, as someone of relatively humble birth who had risen through merit, apparently defeating sceptics and vested interests to introduce his reforms, Hill was perceived as the epitome of a self-made man.[130] Birmingham and Kidderminster, disputing his birthplace, each began to raise a subscription during his lifetime. Birmingham's marble statue, by local sculptor Peter Hollins, was unveiled in 1870 (two years after Watt's). Hill was represented standing 'in an easy attitude', holding a roll of postage stamps. The bas-relief, on the pedestal, illustrated 'the

---

[127] *Cornish Telegraph*, 16 October 1872.
[128] *The Times*, 12 February 1879, 7c; 17 February 1879, 11f.   [129] See above, p. 244.
[130] *The Times*, 27 August 1879, 4c–f. Within the Post Office, Hill was far from universally admired: M. J. Daunton, *Royal Mail: the Post Office since 1840* (London and Dover, NH: The Athlone Press, 1985), pp. 5, 34.

value of the penny postage' – a postman delivering a welcome letter to a
sick woman on her couch.[131] It expressed the widespread gratitude felt
toward Hill, by the implicit contrast between this domestic scene and
familiar stories of the anguish suffered through the literally prohibitive
cost of receiving some letters under the previous system.[132]
Kidderminster launched its subscription in December 1876 and, within
fourteen months, had collected over £1,600 from more than 100,000
donors, one of the largest number of contributors ever to a national
memorial. These figures imply an average subscription of just under
four pence (1.5p), suggesting that many working people may have
donated one penny – a particularly appropriate sum. A marble statue
was commissioned from Thomas Brock; by the time of its unveiling, in
June 1881, there were reportedly 200,000 contributors worldwide.[133]
Popular tributes continued to flow posthumously. A committee based
in the City of London, with support promised from 125 places throughout the realm, collected the exceptionally large sum of over £16,000.
Spending no more than £2,000 on a statue in the City and a bust above
Hill's grave, with the remainder it established a benevolent fund for 'aged
and distressed Post Office servants'. The statue, by E. Onslow Ford, was
unveiled by the Prince of Wales in 1882, in front of the Royal Exchange,
in the heart of London's financial district; it now stands (appropriately
flanked by two red pillar boxes) in nearby King Edward Street.[134] *The
Times* report of Hill's funeral provides further testimony to the public's
high esteem. Immediately following the service, Westminster Abbey
thronged with ordinary people. 'Even the youngest and poorest of them
knew what they had come to gaze upon. "To see the grave of Sir Rowland
Hill, who made the first penny postage," said a boy among those pressing
forward.' The reporter was astonished at the boy's knowledge, for he had
expressly selected him as one probably drawn along in the crowd, ignorant of the occasion's true nature.[135]

Since it was working people who usually experienced innovation most
directly, through its impact on their workplace and livelihoods, it is
hardly surprising if they entertained strong views, whether negative or
positive, about it. Those displaced by new machinery could not be
expected to approve of its inventors, yet they might still appreciate the

---

[131] *The Times*, 14 September 1870, 6f.
[132] See, for example, *The Times*, 7 June 1879, 11b; and the cartoon, 'Sir Rowland le Grand',
by Tenniel, repr. in Daunton, *Royal Mail*, p. 4.
[133] *The Times*, 5 December 1876, 5b; 17 December 1877, 7f; 23 January 1878, 10e; 11 July
1878, 6f; 12 May 1880, 13b; 23 June, 1881, 10b.
[134] Ward-Jackson, *Public sculpture of the City of London*, pp. 218–20.
[135] *The Times*, 5 September 1879, 8b.

benefits of Hill's penny post or Stephenson's railways. By contrast, those in the vanguard of the industrial revolution needed no special persuasion from middle-class proselytizers to find their heroes among inventors and engineers. To skilled men in the engineering trades or on the railways, such inventors and engineers were fellow workers of a superior cast, in whom they could take immense pride and to whose success they could aspire. In these and other 'modernized' industries, such as cotton textiles, they could also experience gratitude towards them as the 'creators' of their industry, their jobs and their relative prosperity. In particular, a sense of both pride and indebtedness made them willing to make a financial sacrifice, more readily than many wealthier people, in order to revive the memory of some neglected pioneer of their trade, such as Crompton, or a perceived benefactor of working men, like Davy.

11   Maintaining the industrial spirit

By 1880, three major impulses to the glorification of inventors had run their course: the early Victorians' hero was to be a victim of his own success. First, the patent controversy had abated: the United Kingdom's system was secure, and its reform in 1883 made it more accessible to men of few resources. Second, since 1867 skilled working men had enjoyed the parliamentary franchise and had less cause to prove – with the inventor as their cynosure – that the country was in their debt. Third, the inventor's reputation as a hero of peace was becoming outmoded; free trade was firmly established, but fresher, more glamorous rivals were appearing and ultimately he would look rather dowdy by comparison.

When Sir William Siemens died in 1883, every London newspaper – both morning and evening – carried an obituary. Over fifty notices appeared in the London weeklies and bi-weeklies, at least as many again in the provincial press. In the proud words of Siemens' biographer, 'Every paper in every town had its notice, and Sir William's name seemed familiar to the whole kingdom.'[1] Indeed, his photograph appeared in the most recent volume of *Men of mark* (figure 11.1).[2] Distinguished as a professional engineer and successful industrialist, with many scientific discoveries to his credit, Siemens could have been described in various ways. For *The Times*, however, there was no choice: 'Sir William Siemens was essentially an inventor.'[3] Siemens, the inventor, merited not only an obituary but also a laudatory leading article. Here, perhaps, was the heroic inventor's apogee. Yet, Siemens' multi-faceted identity embodied several advantages to which most inventors – especially the multitude who obtained patents under the new act – could not aspire. The image of the inventor was again changing.

---

[1] Pole, *Sir William Siemens*, p. 383.   [2] Cooper (ed.), *Men of mark*, vol. VII (1883), p. 34.
[3] *The Times*, 21 November 1883, 9e; repr. in Pole, *William Siemens*, p. 384.

11.1 Photograph of Sir William Siemens, by Lock and Whitfield, published in *Men of mark*, 1883, the year in which the recently knighted inventor died (photograph by Ann Pethers).

Two major contenders for his laurels emerged, who would take centre stage in the early twentieth century: the scientist and the entrepreneur.[4] The thirteen 'Victorian men of achievement', whose portraits graced the cover of *The Illustrated London News* to mark the queen's diamond jubilee, in 1897, were, with the exception of Sir Rowland Hill, all scientists or engineers by profession (some were both). They included Siemens, the two Stephensons, I. K. Brunel and Lord Kelvin: all could be described as inventors but none as an independent (or 'mere') inventor; all were successful entrepreneurs (figure 11.2). It was partly a matter of vested interests and financial resources; partly, a shift in the rhetoric of invention, as powerful groups and individuals tried to appropriate the credit for Britain's industrial strength. While the innovative founder of a successful firm could generally rely on it to perpetuate his memory, distinguished members of the engineering and medical professions enjoyed the collective support of their Institutions and Royal Colleges, and professional scientists, that of their universities and learned bodies, such as the Royal Society. By contrast, the inventor who belonged to none of these groups was a solitary creature. The Inventors' Institute apparently having

---

[4] For the scientists' challenge, see Chapter 12, below.

11.2 *The Illustrated London News* marked Queen Victoria's diamond jubilee, in 1897, with this celebration of British science and technology, which depicts three great advances in transport made during her reign. George and Robert Stephenson's portraits occupy the top central medallions; Michael Faraday appears half-way down the left side, opposite Isambard Kingdom Brunel; William Siemens, immediately beneath Brunel, and Lord Kelvin immediately above him; Charles Darwin is at the top-left corner.

disbanded around 1880 – its immediate battles won – was resurrected in 1912, with the goals of protecting 'the rights of inventors and patentees, the reform of the patent laws, and generally to assist inventors'.[5] This revival seems indicative of their awareness of stronger rivals contesting their reputation as the source of national wealth and power. The independent inventor was disappearing from view, except as a museum piece. Soon, his place in popular memory would depend largely on the goodwill and affection of his fellow citizens, especially those with a keen interest in local history or regional pride.

Engineering the establishment

The nascent engineering profession had been quick to appreciate the value of commemoration in enhancing its status, perhaps because the Institution of Civil Engineers' first decade witnessed the veneration of Watt in Westminster Abbey. Although the Institution was not involved in this, its founding president, Thomas Telford, served on the memorial committee.[6] When Telford died in 1834, the Institution (ignoring his wishes) secured permission for his burial in the Abbey.[7] Its subsequent appeal to install a monument there, while by no means as successful as Watt's, raised sufficient funds to commission a statue from Edward Baily – provoking similar complaints that its 'colossal dimensions' and modern style were out of place.[8]

When the 'railway triumvirate' – Robert Stephenson, Isambard Kingdom Brunel and Joseph Locke – died within a year of one another, in 1859–60, the Institution remained on the sidelines. Families, friends and the most closely associated railway companies quickly rallied to organize and to a considerable degree to finance a series of commemorative tributes. While difficulties were to arise in finding suitable sites for their statues,[9] in Westminster Abbey their executors instigated the tradition of commemorating leading engineers in the windows of the north aisle of the nave. The first, in memory of Robert Stephenson, made the boldest statement in celebration of modern engineering. It depicts four of Stephenson's great bridges and associates them with the engineering feats of biblical and ancient times, including the first and second

[5] *The Times*, 16 January 1912, 4f.
[6] Buchanan, *The engineers*, p. 63; MacLeod, 'James Watt', pp. 101, 116.
[7] It respected Telford's request for a private funeral: *The Times*, 12 September 1834, 1a, 3a.
[8] Timbs reported that Baily sculpted the statue for £1,000, one-third of his normal fee, and the Dean reduced the Abbey's charge from £300 to £200: *Stories of inventors*, p. 270; *The Times*, 23 August 1844, 5f; 26 August 1844, 3d.
[9] See above, pp. 233–4.

11.3 Detail of the memorial window to Robert Stephenson, in Westminster Abbey, 1862. The lowest medallion shows Stephenson's tubular Britannia Bridge, between Anglesey and the Welsh mainland.

Temples in Jerusalem, and the Colosseum at Rome. Linking them together are smaller, medallion portraits of engineers and architects, from Noah and Tubal Cain to Sir Christopher Wren (figure 11.3).[10] At the apex, Stephenson's own portrait is surrounded by those of five of his peers: George Stephenson, Thomas Telford, John Smeaton, James Watt and John Rennie. The inscription commemorates both father and son: on the left, 'Robert Stephenson MP DCL FRS 1803–1859, President of the Institution of Civil Engineers'; on the right, 'Son of George Stephenson 1781–1848 Father of Railways'. More modestly, the memorial window to Brunel represents the history of the Temple, each of the upper two lights depicting three subjects from the Old and the New Testaments – topped by his initials, 'IKB'. The lower ones contain four allegorical figures (proposed by the designer, R. Norman Shaw and approved by Brunel's family), to represent his personal qualities: fortitude, justice, faith and charity. A quatrefoil at the top contains, not portraits of great engineers, but 'the Saviour in Glory, surrounded by angels'.[11] The third window, to Locke, has unfortunately not survived.[12]

---

[10] *The Builder* 20 (1862), 537; *The Times*, 29 July 1862, 11f. One critic evidently considered the designer too timid, reproving him for draping the principal portraits in scarves to hide their modern costume: *The Builder* 20 (1862), 557.

[11] Brunel MSS, Henry Marc Brunel Letter Book 8, fos. 50–6, Bristol University Library. For further details and coloured illustrations of both windows, see MacLeod, 'Nineteenth-century engineer', pp. 68–9.

[12] According to the *Westminster Abbey Official Guide* (1966), p. 119, the window was destroyed by bombing during the First World War, but E. C. Smith claimed it was

George Stephenson, however, still reigned supreme. The six years from 1875 to 1881 provided three occasions to embellish his heroic reputation: the golden jubilees of the Stockton and Darlington Railway (1875) and of the *Rocket* (1879), and the centenary of his birth (1881). The fiftieth anniversary of the country's first passenger railway was celebrated at both Stockton and Darlington, as well as along the route, with 'an efflorescence of decoration', illuminations, feasting and excursions. Darlington unveiled a statue to Joseph Pease, its principal promoter; *The Illustrated London News* made it the centrepiece of a full-page illustration, surrounded by portrait busts of four other protagonists, including Stephenson; underneath, were depicted three famous locomotives.[13]

The *Rocket*'s jubilee witnessed the achievement of an ambitious and costly scheme in Chesterfield, where Stephenson had spent his final years. The George Stephenson Memorial Hall was opened by the duke of Devonshire, to provide a free library, a museum, meeting halls, art studios, a laboratory and a theatre to seat 900 people (£8,000 had been raised by public subscription, but nearly £6,000 more remained as a debt on the property).[14] The laying of the foundation stone in 1877 had already occasioned a banquet for 200, a grand procession that brought landed and civic dignitaries together with representatives of working men's institutions, and a speech by the marquis of Hartington, which could scarcely be bettered as an example of the heroic genre. To a crescendo of cheers, he ascribed fifty years of British material and imperial progress to the railways alone, and the railways, even more implausibly, to 'the invention, the industry, and perseverance of one man'. These, said Hartington, were 'things which exceed the dreams of poetry and romance'. No government had rivalled the railways in bringing 'comfort, happiness, prosperity, and plenty' to the people or even in filling its own coffers with the millions produced for the national revenue through one man's invention.[15]

The centenary, on 9 June 1881, of Stephenson's birth was widely celebrated, but nowhere more flamboyantly than Newcastle upon Tyne.

removed and placed in store before 1914: 'Memorials to engineers and men of science', *TNS* 28 (1951–3), 138. The sole, brief description of it I have found says it had a predominantly brilliant blue and red colour scheme: *The Times*, 26 January 1869, 10f.

[13] *ILN* 67 (2 October 1875), 337, 340–3; ibid. (9 October 1875), p. 363.

[14] *The Times*, 16 July 1879, 4f. Although the *Rocket* was primarily the work of Robert Stephenson, this distinction was regularly lost, so that George has received much of the credit due to his son – a mistake perpetuated by the British £5 note issued between 1990 and 2002.

[15] *The Times*, 18 October 1877, 4a–c, 7d–e. For Hartington, see Jonathan Parry, 'Cavendish, Spencer Compton, marquess of Hartington and eighth duke of Devonshire (1833–1908)', *ODNB*, online edn, May 2006, www.oxforddnb.com/view/article/32331, accessed 21 October 2006.

A regional holiday was declared, and special trains brought thousands of people to enjoy the festivities. Shops decorated with Stephenson memorabilia sold centenary souvenirs; there was bunting in profusion, and a grand parade of local dignitaries, trades and friendly societies. More unusually, a procession of sixteen modern locomotives, on loan from the chief railway companies, steamed its way from the central station to Stephenson's birthplace at Wylam and back. Together with some vintage engines they were then put on display, while the Newcastle Literary and Philosophical Society held another exhibition of Stephenson 'relics' and model locomotives. A lecture on the history of early locomotive engineering attracted 'a large and interested audience', and, on the Town Moor, there was a competition in hyperbole, as speakers hymned the wondrous effects 'of the inventions that Stephenson perfected and to a large extent conceived'.[16] A banquet and a firework display closed the celebrations, which had begun more seriously with a public breakfast to launch the Stephenson scholarship fund, its goal to provide at least ten scholarships in secondary and tertiary education. Another recently announced scheme aimed to raise £20,000 to construct new 'Stephenson buildings' for the College of Physical Science, which had been established in cramped conditions ten years before.[17] The Illustrated London News published a special supplement, and an enterprising London artist struck a medallion that showed both Stephenson and Locomotion 1.[18]

The 125th anniversary of Stephenson's birth in 1906 prompted no such celebrations, which elicited a letter of complaint to The Times from Darlington's MP, Henry Pike Pease. He proposed that, in future, 9 June should be known in England as 'Stephenson Day' and, on it, Stephenson's admirers worldwide should make small donations to railway charities – a suggestion immediately adopted by several branches of the Amalgamated Society of Railway Servants.[19] Pease's concern was premature: Stephenson's fame was to survive another century, kept alive by commemorative events, histories of the railways and the industrial

---

[16] The Engineer, 15 April 1881, 278; 10 June 1881, 430; 17 June 1881, 449; The Times, 10 June 1881, 7e–f.

[17] The Times, 30 March 1881, 9f; 6 June 1881, 12c; 10 June 1881, 7f; The Builder 39 (1881), 748.

[18] ILN 78 (4 June 1881), supplement, 553–66; see also ibid. (11 June 1881), 585–92; (18 June 1881), 604–10; The Engineer, 10 June 1881, 425. For other Stephenson centenary celebrations in Britain and abroad, see MacLeod, 'Nineteenth-century engineer', pp. 76–7.

[19] The Times, 26 May 1906; 14e, 2 June 1906, 10c. Stephenson was represented on the Victoria Monument, unveiled in Lancaster's Dalton Square in 1906, at the expense of Lord Ashton, a local plutocrat; standing among other scientific and literary figures, he holds a model locomotive.

revolution, and a range of media. In the 1920s, Italian railwaymen presented a large bronze plaque, 'in honour of George Stephenson' to mark the centenary of the Stockton and Darlington Railway,[20] and the Argentine's ambassador bestowed memorials, given by his country's railways and Society of Inventors, on the Institution of Mechanical Engineers.[21] As the Institution's first president, Stephenson enjoyed a particular status: his image (and the *Rocket*) appears on its bookplate, surrounded by the names of seven contemporaries (figure 11.4); naturally, his portraits grace the walls of its headquarters.[22] The centenary of his death in 1948 was commemorated in both Newcastle and Chesterfield.[23]

After a hiatus of two decades, the engineers resumed the glazing of the north aisle of Westminster Abbey's nave, as though it were their colonizing mission. In February 1883, the profession began to rescue the memory of Richard Trevithick, by marking the fiftieth anniversary of his death. The importance it attached to its commemorative duties was demonstrated by *The Engineer*'s enjoinder to members to support this subscription. The appeal must not fail, it cried, for 'a slur would be cast, not on Trevithick, but on the engineers, who, being asked to help to raise a monument to the memory of one who was an honour to his profession, refused'.[24] Although considered by many to merit the title 'father of the locomotive', Trevithick had allegedly been spared the ignominy of a pauper's grave only through the generosity of his fellow workers at John Hall's Dartford foundry.[25] Although doubt has been cast on this, it remains indicative of Trevithick's misfortune and posthumous neglect, especially by comparison with George Stephenson's wealth and celebrity.[26] Only the *Mechanic's Magazine* seems to have noticed his passing, with a brief obituary.[27] During the next fifty years Trevithick's memory was preserved unassumingly. His portrait (painted in 1816) was

---

[20] *Railway Magazine*, July–December 1925, 130–3. The plaque now embellishes the entrance to the National Railway Museum, York, and is reproduced in MacLeod, 'Nineteenth-century engineer', p. 76; my thanks to John Clarke, of the NRM, for providing this reference.

[21] *Proceedings of the Institution of Mechanical Engineers* 114 (1928), 237, and frontispiece.

[22] Bookplate, engr. by J. R. G. Exley, NPG 37125; Atkinson's engraving of Lucas' portrait of Stephenson at Chat Moss (above, p. 202) was reproduced for the Institution's Jubilee Meeting in 1897 and is bound into the *Proceedings* (1897).

[23] Colls, 'Remembering George Stephenson', p. 289, n. 70.

[24] *The Engineer*, 16 February 1883, 128.

[25] John Dunkin, *History and antiquities of Dartford* (London: John Russell Smith, 1844), p. 406, cited in Dickinson and Titley, *Richard Trevithick*, pp. 255–6n.

[26] Dickinson and Titley, *Richard Trevithick*, p. 256; Anthony Burton, *Richard Trevithick: giant of steam* (London; Aurum Press, 2000), p. 229.

[27] *Mechanic's Magazine* 19 (1833), 80; Dickinson and Titley, *Richard Trevithick*, p. 256.

PARSONS · WATT · WHITWORTH · MAUDSLAY · PENN · FAIRBAIRN · TREVITHICK

GEORGE STEPHENSON
FIRST PRESIDENT · 1847–1848

THE INSTITUTION OF
MECHANICAL ENGINEERS

J·R·G·Exley, fecit.

11.4 Book plate of The Institution of Mechanical Engineers, designed by J. R. G. Exley. George Stephenson and *Rocket* are framed by the names of seven great nineteenth-century mechanical engineers.

presented by his widow, at Woodcroft's insistence, to the Patent Office Museum's gallery and was used to engrave Trevithick among the *Distinguished Men of Science*.[28] Several copies of a bust sculpted for the family by N. N. Burnard, were on private display, including one in the boardroom at Euston station.[29] His inventions were regularly

---

[28] Dickinson and Titley, *Richard Trevithick*, p. 260; see *The Times'* praise for Trevithick's inclusion: Walker (ed.), *Memoirs* (2nd edn, 1864), p. 164.

[29] Dickinson and Titley, *Richard Trevithick*, p. 261; *The Engineer*, 16 February 1883, 128.

described in histories of the steam engine, and several authors (drawing on first-hand information) produced brief memoirs of his life and works. In 1872, Francis Trevithick expanded this material into a two-volume biography of his father, but with a highly technical approach it lacked the 'Smilesean' touch needed to become a bestseller.[30]

Trevithick, however, had another identity, as a Cornishman. A sub-committee, formed in Cornwall, desired that the memorial fund should provide scholarships to educate future mining engineers.[31] Since insufficient was raised to cover both schemes, a compromise was necessary: with £1,000, a triennial Trevithick scholarship was endowed at Owen's College, Manchester; a further £1,066 sufficed to commission a window, if not a statue. The window, installed in 1888, represents Trevithick's dual identity as both an inventive engineer and a Cornishman. Its upper lights contain the figures of nine Cornish saints and the arms of the duchy and see of Cornwall; its lower lights, four angels holding scrolls with diagrams of Trevithick's inventions, which are labelled 'Tramroad Locomotive 1803', 'Cornish Pumping Engine', 'Steam Dredger 1803', 'Railway Locomotive 1808' (figure 11.5).[32] Not only did its saints and heraldry proclaim the county's historic identity, deeply ensconced in the Christian tradition, but the drawings signalled its more recent importance as a centre of mining and steam engineering. It was a clever tribute to Trevithick's two constituencies: not only a pioneer of the British engineering profession as a whole, he was also the foremost representative of a major industrial region.[33]

With the appeal for Trevithick still in progress, the death of Sir William Siemens prompted the Institution of Civil Engineers and four other professional societies to organize an 'engineers' memorial' to him. Subscriptions, although limited to one guinea and confined to members of the five societies, quickly amounted to over £700.[34] The second anniversary of Siemens' funeral, in November 1885, saw the unveiling of a commemorative window, next to Stephenson's, and renewed tributes

[30] Dickinson and Titley, *Richard Trevithick*, pp. 282–3.
[31] *The Engineer*, 13 April 1883, 294. See also the letter from Miss Anna Gurney, *The Times*, 17 January 1878, 6d; G. C. Boase and W. P. Courtney, *Bibliotheca Cornubiensis: a catalogue of the writings of Cornishmen*, 3 vols. (London: Longmans, 1878), vol. II, pp. 799–800; Walter Hawkan Tregallas, 'Trevithick the engineer', in *Cornish worthies: sketches of some eminent Cornish men and families*, 2 vols. (London: E. Stock, 1884), vol. II, pp. 305–44.
[32] Dickinson and Titley, *Richard Trevithick*, p. 265. The final £100 raised was entrusted to the Institution of Civil Engineers, to award the Trevithick Premium biennially from 1900: Edith K. Harper, *A Cornish giant: Richard Trevithick, the father of the locomotive* (London: E. & F. N. Spon, 1913), pp. 58–60.
[33] See below, pp. 344–5.   [34] Pole, *Sir William Siemens*, pp. 372–3.

11.5 Detail of the memorial window to Richard Trevithick, Westminster Abbey, 1888. Two angels hold drawings of Trevithick's inventions, a tramroad locomotive and a Cornish (steam) pumping engine.

to the man and his profession.[35] Siemens' window shared some similarities in conception with its neighbour, making direct reference to the engineer and his work. In the words of its designers, Clayton and Bell:

The design of this window is to set forth the sanctity of Labour, illustrating the maxim 'Laborare est orare' [to work is to pray]. The treatment of the work comprises a series of groups representing, respectively, workers in Science, Art, and Manual Labour ... In the left-hand light appear Ironsmiths, Chemists, and Agriculturalists; in the other, groups in corresponding positions show Astronomers, Artists, and the Professor with his scholars.[36]

Siemens' portrait appeared in the professor's, and the iconography accorded with his distinctive philosophy of invention, which insisted on collaboration between the laboratory and the workshop.[37]

The early twentieth century saw a significant shift in the iconography that the engineering profession sponsored. In 1909, the Institution of Civil Engineers presided over the installation of a sixth window in the north aisle, to Sir Benjamin Baker (1840–1907). It was the first in a scheme of nine to be designed by Sir Ninian Comper, 'a feature of which will be standing figures, a king and an abbot, in each light'. The Dean of Westminster envisaged it as a means of improving the nave by introducing more light; consequently, white glass predominated.[38] Windows to four other engineers followed: to Lord Kelvin in 1913; to Sir John Wolfe-Barry and to Sir Henry Royce during the interwar period; and finally to Sir Charles Parsons in 1950, replacing the Brunel window, which was moved to the south aisle.[39] Only the inscriptions indicate that these windows commemorate engineers; the pictorial elements celebrate medieval kings and abbots, the more traditional heroes of Church and state.

Ultimately, it is impossible to discriminate between the rival influences of aesthetic preference and social prejudice on this stylistic shift. There is no reason to question the architectural case for clear glass, especially at a time when designers were fleeing from Victorian gloom's deep, dark colours. It is the restoration of kings and abbots and the total absence of any reference to technology that are puzzling. Trevithick's window had

---

[35] Ibid., p. 375.
[36] Ibid., p. 378; for a photograph of the window, see the plate facing p. 378. This window suffered the same (uncertain) fate as that to Joseph Locke: see above, n. 12.
[37] See below, p. 363.   [38] *The Times*, 4 December 1909, 8f.
[39] *Westminster Abbey official guide*, p. 118; *The Times*, 10 July 1913, 6c; 16 July 1913, 6d; 8 December 1922, 9e. Smith records that the window to Stephenson was taken down in 1912 to make way for Kelvin's, and restored (in a different place) following protests in the 1930s: 'Memorials to engineers', 138. For interwar memorials to Parsons, see *The Times*, 18 February 1931, 16d; 4 March 1931, 17c; 5 December 1932, 9c.

amalgamated saints and engineering drawings: why was a similarly imaginative merger of symbols not pursued in this later series? It might be argued, by proponents of Britain's declining 'industrial spirit', that the leaders of its engineering profession were now ashamed to make overt references to their 'trade', or perhaps that it was the sacrifice demanded, by the Abbey authorities, for a humbled profession to maintain its near-monopoly of the north aisle's stained glass. Although both interpretations are possible, neither seems probable. I have found no hint in the contemporary press of such a slur on the profession either given or taken. Moreover, the innovative engineers whom the windows commemorated were highly honoured, not least by the state: none had received less than a knighthood; Kelvin was science and engineering's first peer. The engineering profession was on the crest of the wave. What reason could there be for embarrassment or humility? On the contrary, the iconography of Comper's windows reflects the hubris of the profession, revelling not only in these national honours but also in the spectacular achievements that these windows unobtrusively celebrated. From Kelvin's transatlantic telegraph cable to Baker's Forth rail bridge and Aswan dam, it is hard to imagine that any Edwardian engineer could doubt that these were still 'glorious times'.[40] They no longer had any need to boast: the importance of the engineer's national role was so evident and his place in society so well established that their memorials could be discreetly assimilated with those of other members of Britain's social elite.

Models of enterprise

Thanks to James Watt, the nineteenth-century's image of the inventor had always embraced the engineering professions – a link that was strengthened by the celebration of George Stephenson and the railway 'triumvirate'. The relationship between the inventor and the entrepreneur, however, was a more difficult one. Richard Arkwright was often praised for his entrepreneurial abilities in explicit comparison with his more dubious claim to invention: they earned him the plaudits of Ure and the condemnation of Marx. For some commentators, the commercialization of mechanized spinning provided the greater challenge and the superior reason for his celebrity – an ordering of achievements echoed

---

[40] The phrase is taken from a letter of James Nasmyth's, 11 July 1836, quoted in A. E. Musson, 'James Nasmyth and the early growth of mechanical engineering', *EHR* 10 (1957), 124; my thanks to Alessandro Nuvolari for identifying the source. Cf. Rolt, *Victorian engineering*, p. 163, and Reader, '"At the head of all the new professions"', pp. 173–4, 184.

by William Armstrong, whose claim to success in both roles was unquestioned.[41]

The tension occasionally exploded into view, bringing other resentments with it – especially once the patent system's reform made the alliance of inventor and innovator in its defence unnecessary. In 1905, Alexander Siemens, a leading figure in the electrical industry, told the Society of Arts that, 'It was easy to invent ... but it was extremely difficult to introduce a new manufacture, and the people who did introduce new manufactures ought to be the people who were rewarded'.[42] In front of such an audience, Siemens' opinion raised a predictable storm of protest. In a sharp (if hardly original) riposte, the brass-maker, Isaac Smith told him, 'The reward of a valuable and useful invention often goes to the keen, energetic, business people, while the obscure genius "who gave it birth" receives but scant recognition or adequate remuneration.'[43] Less publicly, this issue often festered at the level of the firm, where the working man's ingenuity might be concealed by a patent in his employer's name. Only an enlightened minority anticipated disputes over intellectual property by clauses in employment contracts or schemes designed to elicit and reward their workers' inventiveness.[44] When a Birkenhead newspaper reported that a vessel recently completed in Laird Brothers' shipyard had been 'designed by Mr William Perry', then head of their ship drawing office, the senior partner tersely corrected the report – 'the ship was designed by Laird Brothers'.[45]

Although most of the nineteenth-century's famous inventors were also successful entrepreneurs and employers, it is a feature that was rarely remarked. Watt notoriously had Matthew Boulton to shoulder the burdens of management, but was no less a partner in the engine-making firm that bore both their names. George and Robert Stephenson established a major locomotive-building works and as railway engineers (like Isambard Kingdom Brunel), managed a consultancy business and directed aspects of on-site construction. William Siemens, Joseph Bramah, Henry Maudslay and many other engineers established firms that bore their names – alone or in partnership. Josiah Wedgwood was completely identified with the pottery manufacture that he built into an international enterprise; Ransomes made ploughs and Heathcoats made

[41] See above, pp. 237, 268.
[42] *JSA* 53 (1905), 173. Siemens had been managing director of Siemens Brothers Ltd, 1889–99, and president of the Institution of Electrical Engineers in 1894 and 1904: Brian Bowers, 'Siemens, Alexander (1847–1928)', *ODNB*, www.oxforddnb.com/view/article/48189, accessed 21 October 2006.
[43] *JSA* 53 (1905), 173.   [44] MacLeod, 'Negotiating the rewards', 22–3, 29–31.
[45] J. Foster Petree, 'Some reflections on engineering biography', *TNS* 40 (1967), 155.

lace. On the technological benches of the nineteenth-century pantheon, 'mere' inventors such as Crompton and Trevithick, who did not establish a firm, were the exceptions. It was not by chance that the interval between their death and the commemoration of their achievements – thirty-five and fifty years respectively – was significantly longer than most, nor that it took the efforts of enthusiasts to rescue their histories from oblivion. In both cases, that rescue was a close-run thing, and to this day (outside Cornwall) Trevithick remains unfairly in the shadow of Stephenson. Many others, famous in their own time, failed completely to enjoy a posthumous celebrity, not least because they founded no firm to bear their name and embellish their reputation: who now, for example, has heard of Thomas Edmondson?[46] Arkwright had not been the exception but the rule, distinctive only in the explicit lauding of his entrepreneurship. The more common emphasis on invention to the exclusion of enterprise allowed the Victorians to maintain the ambiguity of the socially mobile, heroic inventor and his *doppelgänger*, the martyr of invention.[47]

By 1900, the displacement of the 'mere' inventor by the innovative (sometimes, the inventive) entrepreneur was becoming more pronounced. The 'Arkwrights' were taking over from the 'Cromptons'. At the head of a large firm, the entrepreneur or his family naturally had the means to impress his reputation more surely on the public (and official) mind. If he entered politics or made generous philanthropic gestures, he had further calls on public recognition. Consequently, it was such men whose image increasingly occupied the public plinths; it was they whose exemplary lives began to attract biographers in the footsteps of Smiles; it was they who received most of the few honours that the state dispensed to non-traditional recipients.[48] And, after half a century's neglect by economists, in 1912 the entrepreneur's star began to rise again, when Joseph Schumpeter acknowledged his crucial role in innovation. It was thanks to 'the will and the action' of the entrepreneurs, 'not to the mere inventors', said Schumpeter, that productivity was raised; as they '"carried out new combinations"', they generated new wealth – their 'entrepreneurial profit'.[49] Over the next thirty years, Schumpeter developed 'an heroic vision of the entrepreneur as someone motivated by the "dream and the

---

[46] See above, pp. 191–2.   [47] See above, pp. 189–90.
[48] For the award of honours, see above, pp. 236–48.
[49] Joseph A. Schumpeter, *The theory of economic development: an inquiry into profits, capital, interest and the business cycle* [1912], trans. R. Opie (Cambridge, MA: Harvard University Press, 1962), p. 132.

will to found a private kingdom"; the "will to conquer: the impulse to fight, to prove oneself superior to others"; and the "joy of creating" '.[50]

Samuel Cunliffe Lister offers a prime example of this reversal in the fortunes of inventor and entrepreneur. Especially revealing is the change, between 1875 and 1906, in the rhetoric praising his achievements. Lister first succeeded through the mechanization of wool combing. As with Arkwright, it is unclear how much he personally contributed to the invention: not only did Lister patent wool-combing machinery in his own name, but he consolidated his position by purchasing every relevant patent possible and by litigating aggressively.[51] From his enormous mill, which still dominates the skyline, he made Bradford (W. Yorks.) the indubitable centre of the worsted industry, before diversifying through similar methods into silk and velvet production.

In 1870, Lister sold his family estate to Bradford Corporation at a price far below its market value, in order to provide the town with a public park and, later, the building for an art gallery and museum (named Cartwright Hall, after the first inventor of wool-combing machinery).[52] In return, the borough paid him the unusual tribute of erecting a statue during his life-time. Sculpted by Matthew Noble, it stands at the park's lower entrance, its bas-reliefs graphically illustrating the transformation of the wool-combing trade brought about by Lister's professed inventions (figure 11.6).[53] At its inauguration in 1875, the speech by Bradford's MP, W. E. Forster was a masterpiece of diplomacy that glossed over the disputed paternity of the machines' invention, the wool-combers' resistance to their introduction, and the controversy provoked by the town's current celebration of Lister. What Forster emphasized was the economic and social benefits to Bradford of the worsted industry, particularly the employment created by Lister's mills. In celebrating Lister's personal qualities, he stressed both his 'inventive faculty' and the strengths of character that had made him a successful businessman – his 'energy ... industry ... determination' and especially 'the pluck which this man has shown'.[54]

---

[50] Mark Casson, 'Entrepreneurship', *The concise encyclopaedia of economics*, www.econlib. org/library/Enc/Entrepreneurship.html, accessed 22 December 2005.

[51] Christine MacLeod, 'Strategies for innovation: the diffusion of new technology in nineteenth-century British industry', *EHR* 45 (1992), 296–7.

[52] *The Times*, 19 April 1870, 9d; 18 May 1870, 11b; Beesley, *Through the mill*, pls. 40–1.

[53] *The Times*, 17 May 1875, 12d–e; Lister was reported to have had one of the bas-reliefs changed, c. 1904, to illustrate a different machine (the square motion comb) 'to emphasise his claims for its invention' over those of his rival, Isaac Holden: J. A. Iredale, *Noble Lister: the enigma of a statue* (Bradford Art Galleries and Museums, n.d.), p. 6. See also Katrina Honeyman, 'Holden, Sir Isaac, first baronet (1807–1897)', *ODNB*, online edn, May 2006, www.oxforddnb.com/view/article/13491, accessed 21 October 2006.

[54] *The Times*, 17 May 1875, 12d–e.

11.6 *Samuel Cunliffe Lister* by Matthew Noble, monument, 1875, in Lister Park, Bradford, W. Yorks. (photograph by the author).

Raised to the peerage as Baron Masham in 1891, Lister died fifteen years later at the age of ninety-one.[55] His obituary in *The Times* drew heavily on his autobiography, but this introductory paragraph, which owed nothing to Lister himself, encapsulates the novel image of the entrepreneurial hero of innovation and its attendant devaluation of the 'mere' inventor.

[55] See above, p. 246; Pumphrey, 'Introduction of industrialists', 10–12.

If Carlyle's gallery of heroes were extended to the nineteenth century, two new portraits would assuredly be added – the man of science and the man of industry; and among the half-dozen or so who might sit for the latter Lord Masham would have a place. Two great faculties have gone to the building of the vast industrial edifice which, even more than science, marks out this age from all others and alone enables the multiplying multitude to live. They are invention and organization ... But there seems generally to be a sort of antagonism or incompatibility between them; inventors are notoriously bad men of business, and great commercial enterprise is very often associated with a total lack of ideas ... But on some rare individuals nature is pleased to bestow both gifts, and then she produces the 'hero' or great man in industry – a Krupp, an Armstrong, a Siemens, or a Lister.[56]

While recognized as an inventor, Lister is applauded as a 'man of industry'; he belongs to a tiny elite, talented in both 'invention and organization'. The typical inventor, however, has been evicted by the scientists and the heroes of industry – those rare individuals whose 'gift' for invention was bolstered by a 'gift' for enterprise.

Scottish engineering workers at this period appeared especially keen to pay tribute to employers whose inventive talents they admired. James Carmichael had been a popular local figure, especially with his workers, and was well known to engineers for his inventions.[57] In 1876, a statue to him was inaugurated in Dundee, twenty-three years after his death; the subscription had been opened 'many years ago'. Carmichael had been in business there with his brother Charles, as iron-founders and engineers, since 1810; they built Scotland's first locomotives and early iron steamships. James invented a reversing gear for marine engines and the fan blast, which was widely used in foundries and to ventilate coal mines. In 1841, Scottish iron manufacturers and engineers presented each brother with a service of plate, engraved with the fan blast, in appreciation of their not having patented it.[58] The bronze statue, by John Hutchinson, stood seventeen feet high on its pedestal. For *The Illustrated London News*, it apparently represented the quintessential inventor, seized by a happy thought, which would ultimately materialize in a new piece of machinery (figure 11.7).

The plain old Scotch mechanician, in his ordinary dress, is supposed to have been taking a turn through his works, when becoming suddenly possessed of an idea, he has sat down to think it out. He sits in a posture slightly stooping ... an intent expression indicative of mental occupation. The left hand hangs over the edge of a

[56] *The Times*, 3 February 1906, 9d–f; [S. C. Lister], *Lord Masham's inventions, written by himself* (Bradford, 1905).
[57] *The Times*, 19 June 1876, 11f.
[58] E. Gauldie (ed.), *The Dundee textile industry, 1790–1885* (Edinburgh: the Scottish Historical Society, 1969), p. 91.

11.7 *James Carmichael* by John Hutchinson, in Dundee; engraving
published in *The Illustrated London News*, 9 September 1876
(photograph by Ann Pethers).

steam cylinder, while the right, grasping a foot-rule, rests on a drawing ... a
representation of a reversing gear for marine engines ... one of Carmichael's
inventions, and ... a model of the fan-blast machinery, which lies near his right
foot.[59]

As this description makes clear, in Dundee's representation of
Carmichael, the inventor still took precedence over the entrepreneur, as
it had in Bradford's contemporary tribute to Lister. Three statues in
Glasgow, erected during the following quarter century, chart the emergence of the heroic entrepreneur. The first was a bronze, by J. E. Boehm, of
John Elder, unveiled in Elder Park, opposite his Govan shipyard, in 1888
(figure 11.8). A contemporary source commented that his 'countenance

[59] *ILN* 69 (9 September 1876), 245.

11.8 *John Elder* by Joseph Edgar Boehm, 1888, in Elder Park, Govan. Elder's left hand rests on a model compound steam engine (photograph by the author).

reflects thought and that contentment which is born of success'.[60] By his bearing and costume, Elder is far removed from 'the plain old Scotch mechanician', sitting in the middle of his works, yet his left hand rests on a model of the compound marine engine, to which he had contributed significant improvements.

---

[60] Archibald Craig, *The Elder Park, Govan: an account of the gift of the Elder Park and the erection and unveiling of the statue of John Elder* (Glasgow, 1891), p. 115, quoted in McKenzie, *Public sculpture of Glasgow*, p. 97.

Had it not been for the intervention of the memorial committee (which included representatives of the shipyard workers), the image of the successful entrepreneur would have prevailed: in Boehm's original design, Elder's hand rested only on a square pillar. Following the Lord Provost's suggestion, the committee requested its replacement by the engine, as a 'memorial of the genius of John Elder'.[61] At the unveiling ceremony – a major public event which attracted enormous crowds, despite dreadful weather – Elder's widow, Isabella, conveyed her profound appreciation that 'the idea of such a memorial originated and had been carried into execution mainly by the efforts of the working men of Govan'.[62] With the local economy severely depressed, the committee had been ingenious as well as determined in its fund-raising strategies, which finally produced just over £2,000.[63] The long inscription evinced the men's pride in working for one who was both a great inventor (who 'effected a revolution in engineering second only to that accomplished by James Watt') and a caring and fair-minded employer.[64]

The second statue, also in Govan, was erected in 1894 to the memory of Sir William Pearce, one of the three men appointed to manage the Fairfield yard after Elder's death.[65] Pearce was credited with dynamic managerial abilities, which helped to make the shipyard the biggest in the world, but not with any particular invention. The statue embodies Pearce's professional vigour and efficiency as, with coat buttoned up and engineering drawing (for one of his famous 'Ocean Greyhounds') between his hands, he strides purposefully forward. No time for creative musings here! Pearce had worked his way up from an apprenticeship in Chatham Naval Dockyard; elected as Govan's first MP, in 1885, and appointed to numerous national and local bodies, he was created a baronet in 1887. Despite his 'consistent anti-labour position' in the Commons, Pearce's effective management of the shipyard, combined with his well-publicized philanthropy (and perhaps even his 'flamboyant lifestyle'), secured him the loyalty of both workforce and local community. According to the *Govan Press*, 'scarcely had the grave closed', in 1888, 'when the working-men of Govan and their more opulent brethren' (fresh from their successful campaign to commemorate Elder) launched a subscription and approached the sculptor, Edward Onslow Ford. The

---

[61] *Minute book of the John Elder statue committee, 1884–1888*, 14 September 1887, H-GOV 27(1), Glasgow City Archive.

[62] *Glasgow Herald*, 30 July 1888, 9, quoted in McKenzie, *Public sculpture of Glasgow*, p. 99.

[63] McKenzie, *Public sculpture of Glasgow*, pp. 98–9.

[64] Ibid., p. 97. For factory workers' idealization of paternalistic employers more generally, see Joyce, *Work, society and politics*, pp. 152–4, 179–86, and passim.

[65] This paragraph is based on McKenzie, *Public sculpture of Glasgow*, pp. 184–6.

inauguration ceremony, performed by Lord Kelvin, was as lavish and crowded as that for Elder, six years earlier.

Like Pearce, John Reid, proprietor of the Hyde Park Locomotive Works in Springburn, also became a Glaswegian 'hero of industry' through his capacity for organization, not invention.[66] Reid was another model of the self-made man, working his way up from blacksmithing, through engineering draughtsmanship, to become manager, then owner, of the Hyde Park Works. His energy and vision took the firm to new heights, so that by the 1890s it was employing 2,500 men and producing 200 locomotives per year. Among his many civic and professional duties, Reid served as president of the Institution of Engineers and Shipbuilders in Scotland (1882), and was a keen patron of the arts. He died in 1894. When his sons – all now partners in Neilson, Reid & Co. – donated £10,000 towards Springburn's new municipal park, the local newspaper proposed a public monument to him. Reid's bronze figure, unveiled in 1903, stands confidently on its plinth, but with less urgency than Pearce's; his knee-length frock-coat is open, and his left hand insouciantly holds a half-unrolled set of plans. The inscription boasts only of his public offices and carries the motto 'Duce deo/merce beati' ('With God as leader, business will be blessed'). This pious tribute to enterprise encapsulates the shift, over the course of these three commemorations, from the upsurge of self-referential pride in their employer's inventiveness, visible among Elder's workforce, to the seamless integration into civic life of the dynamic local entrepreneur, the patriarch of his firm. It mirrored the transition in S. C. Lister's public persona during the same period.

It would be inaccurate to suggest, however, that this was a novel development in the 1890s: nationally, it was already several decades old.[67] An industrialist might be applauded for creating employment, for his civic or political contribution, or his philanthropy, especially where his firm dominated the local economy. The 1870s saw Bradford also erect a statue to Sir Titus Salt, a model of industrial paternalism who served as its second mayor.[68] Across the Pennines, Oldham (Lancs.) similarly

[66] This paragraph is based on McKenzie, *Public sculpture of Glasgow*, pp. 354–5.
[67] The commemorations of Josiah Wedgwood, in the 1860s, might be deemed a precursor: see above, pp. 305–7. Collected volumes of entrepreneurs' biographies began to be published in the 1880s: see, for example, James Hogg (ed.), *Fortunes made in business: a series of original sketches, biographical and anecdotic, from the recent history of industry and commerce, by various authors* (London: Sampson Low, Marston, Searle and Rivington, 1884–7). A new, enlarged edition appeared in 1891.
[68] Darke, *Monument guide*, pp. 221–2; *The Times*, 3 August 1874, 8b–c; David James, 'Salt, Sir Titus, first baronet (1803–1876)', *ODNB*, www.oxforddnb.com/view/article/24565,

honoured John Platt (1817–72). Although Platt held a number of patents, it was not as an inventor that he was celebrated, but as the head of
the largest machine-making firm in the world, as well as Oldham's MP,
three times mayor, and sponsor of municipal development. Under his
inspired management, Platt Brothers expanded twelve-fold in thirty years
and, in 1871, 8,000 working men signed a loyal address in recognition of
his twenty-five years' civic service.[69] Birkenhead paid similar tributes to
John Laird, MP, 'the well-known local shipbuilder': the unveiling of a
bronze statue, in 1877, was attended by a procession of 3,000 members of
trade and friendly societies.[70] Middlesborough (E. Yorks.) commemorated H. W. F. Bolckow, MP, and John Vaughan in 1881 and 1884
respectively: together the two men were pivotal in founding the
Cleveland iron industry, establishing a company that, in 1864, was
worth £2.5 million. Vaughan died in 1868, but Bolckow became the
town's first mayor and first MP: his statue, by D. W. Stevenson, shows
him holding Middlesborough's charter of incorporation. The town's
third statue, unveiled in 1913, was to Sir Samuel Slater (1842–1911), a
coal-tar manufacturer and three times mayor.[71]

While Newcastle upon Tyne showered honours upon Lord Armstrong,
it was slow to recognize his friend, Sir Joseph Swan. Swan died before he
could receive the freedom of the city; in a posthumous ceremony, his son
accepted it. Best known for his invention of the incandescent electric
lamp, Swan had remained a professional inventor rather than become an
industrialist.[72] In Edinburgh, nothing came of the attempt to raise a
statue to John Boyd Dunlop, the inventor of the pneumatic tyre, by a
committee which contained representatives of the Society of Motor
Manufacturers and Traders, the Scottish Cyclists Union and several
Scottish cities.[73] Failure may be explained by Dunlop having had little
connection with Scotland (an Irishman, he had removed his tyre factory
to Coventry, in the English Midlands). Alternatively, despite having his

accessed 21 October 2006. The statue is depicted on its original site, in the centre of
Bradford, in *Great industries of Great Britain*, 3 vols. (London, Paris and New York:
Cassell & Co., [1877–80]), vol. I, p. 84.
[69] *The Times*, 16 September 1878, 6e; D. A. Farnie, 'Platt family (*per. c.*1815–1930)',
ODNB, www.oxforddnb.com/view/article/50762, accessed 21 October 2006; Vernon,
Politics and the people, pp. 58–62.
[70] *ILN* 71 (10 November 1877), 461.
[71] *The Times*, 2 June 1884, 12a; 3 June 1884, 5a, 7c; Darke, *Monument guide*, pp. 226–7 (for
the continuation of the tradition, see ibid., pp. 171–2, 176, 245).
[72] Evan Rowland Jones, *Heroes of industry: biographical sketches* (London: Sampson Low,
Marston, Searle and Rivington, 1886) featured both Armstrong and Swan, the only
inventors among its sixteen enterprising subjects. C. N. Brown, 'Swan, Sir Joseph
Wilson (1828–1914)', *ODNB*, www.oxforddnb.com/view/article/36382, accessed
21 October 2006.
[73] *The Times*, 17 May 1910, 7f.

own factory, Dunlop's obituary in *The Times* remarked that he had taken little part in the tyre's commercial development – an observation reinforced by a leading article, which commented that, 'like many inventors', he was dissatisfied with his own financial reward in comparison with 'the gigantic wealth of the industry based on his device. He underestimated the patient experiment, the inventive skill, the business ability and the huge expenditure of capital required to transform a somewhat crude idea into its modern developments.'[74] This emerging stereotype of the inventor as an incompetent businessman may already have had adverse consequences both for individual inventors and the economy as a whole. Swan, for example, was reportedly frustrated in his business dealings by the assumption that inventors were rarely 'sound guides on questions of manufacturing policy'.[75]

Local heroes of invention

It was thanks primarily to history that the 'mere' inventor was not entirely displaced by more enterprising colleagues. While the latter tended to be commemorated shortly after their deaths (or even before), the late-Victorian and Edwardian periods continued to celebrate inventors whom the mid-nineteenth century had identified as lynchpins of the Industrial Revolution – with a few additions. The exploitation of local connections was especially influential. An industrial town might develop its affinity with an inventor, mimicking older centres that boasted of their links with a particular monarch, aristocratic family, statesman or warrior. The opportunity was often crystallized by an imminent anniversary. In various fields, the Victorians seized upon the French custom of celebrating the centenary of an event or the birth, death or *chef d'oeuvre* of a national or local figure.[76] It became a common form of civic celebration – a vehicle for identification with some major achievement – and an opportunity to introduce new secular ceremonies into urban cultures that lacked traditional and religious rituals. While the centenary of George Stephenson's birth, in 1881, helped to perpetuate the heroic reputation of an already famous man, for other inventors a centenary (or bicentenary, etc.) provided the occasion to revive a largely forgotten name or pay old debts. Alternatively, it might be used as a fund-raising device. It is a mark

---

[74] *The Times*, 25 October 1921, 7d, 11d.
[75] M. E. Swan and K. R. Swan, *Sir Joseph Wilson Swan, FRS: a memoir* (London: Ernest Benn, 1929, repr. 1968), p. 123.
[76] Surveyed in Nora, *Realms of memory*, passim; Quinault, 'Cult of the centenary', 303–23; Eric Hobsbawm, 'Mass-producing traditions: Europe, 1870–1914', in Hobsbawm and Ranger (eds.), *Invention of tradition*, pp. 263–307.

of the high status reached by inventors that fundraisers perceived the perpetuation of their names in village halls, schools and scholarships as a valuable promotional strategy. A virtuous circle was established: such commemorations reinforced popular awareness of a select band of inventors. Their rhetoric also tended to promote a particular history, one driven by technology, in which a certain invention – be it the steam engine, the railways, a cotton-spinning machine or cheap iron – had irrevocably and single-handedly changed the course of Britain's fortunes.

The late 1880s saw two Scottish towns vying to celebrate the achievements of the previously neglected steamboat pioneer, William Symington (1763–1831), a hundred years after he had conducted his first trials. Grangemouth, where Symington's two boats had been built, commissioned a bust from D. W. Stevenson, which, following its display at the 1890 Edinburgh International Exhibition, was presented to the capital's Museum of Science and Art. The following year, Symington's birthplace, the mining village of Leadhills, erected a granite obelisk to him, which bore *bas-relief* panels depicting both the *Charlotte Dundas II* and her creator – apparently at the instigation of his great-nephew, the mine's manager. Symington's rediscovery was such that, in 1903, the Lord Mayor of London marked the centenary of the *Charlotte Dundas II* by placing a plaque to him in St Botolph's church, Aldgate, in whose graveyard he was buried. Apart from his final resting place, Symington's connection with London had been slight.[77]

William Murdoch (1754–1839), another Scottish inventor employed for many years by Boulton and Watt, was rescued from oblivion by the combined forces of his home village and trade associations in the gas industry. The approaching centenary of 'the application of steam to road locomotion', in 1884, provoked a flurry of outrage concerning his neglect. Matthew Macfie, of the Balloon Society of Great Britain, gave several lectures in which he exhibited Murdoch's original locomotive and pressed for a suitable memorial. A committee, chaired by William Siemens, was formed to erect a statue in London and to convert Murdoch's old house in Birmingham into an 'international gas museum'. That Murdoch had not patented gas lighting was specifically mentioned as a reason to ensure he received his due.[78] It was perhaps Siemens' death, shortly afterwards, that stalled the campaign. In 1892 the

[77] Harvey and Downs-Rose, *William Symington*, pp. 165, 167–71; *The Times*, 22 November 1890, 13a; *The Scotsman*, 22 November 1890, 6f. See also above, pp. 187, 228.
[78] *The Times*, 1 September 1883, 8d; 11 September 1883, 4d–e; 15 September 1883, 7f; 5 January 1884, 7b. For the role of the Tangyes of Birmingham in preserving Murdoch's model locomotive and erecting a plaque to his memory in Redruth, see Pemberton, *James Watt of Soho and Heathfield*, pp. 176–7, 179.

Incorporated Gas Institute commemorated Murdoch and a century of gas lighting with a centenary lecture. Eleven years later, a bronze panel with a life-size portrait medallion of him in bold relief was unveiled in his native village, Lugar (Ayrshire), its cost defrayed by the North British Association of Gasmakers.[79] As the gas industry tried to fend off the challenge of electric lighting, it probably appreciated the opportunity to secure some relatively cheap publicity. Against the novelty offered by electricity, it could reassure customers with its accumulation of a century's experience and counter-pose a trusty (and safely dead) inventor to the showmanship of Thomas Edison. In Scotland, this involved association with a new national hero: thanks to these campaigns, by 1900 Murdoch's star had risen to the point where his bust was included in the select Hall of Heroes, in the Wallace Monument at Stirling.[80]

The centenary, in 1876, of the death of John Harrison, the inventor of the marine chronometer, prompted the London Clockmakers' Company to restore his 'dilapidated' tomb in Hampstead churchyard. Its renewed inscription lovingly details Harrison's achievements in a way that those skilled in the trade would have appreciated.[81] After the failure of a sustained campaign led by the Society of Arts, in the 1850s, to commemorate Henry Cort's contribution to Britain's booming iron industry, the centenary of his death was marked thanks to a private benefaction: two bronze plaques, one for Lancaster parish church (his birthplace) and a second for the church in Hampstead, where he was buried, were the gift of Charles H. Morgan, of Worcester, Massachusetts.[82] The Leicester hosiery industry celebrated the tercentenary of William Lee's stocking-knitting frame, in 1889, with a banquet for over 700 'aged stockingers', hosted by its leading employers. Students at Leicester Technical School raised a subscription to commission an oil painting depicting Lee.[83] The Lancashire town of Bury chose the bicentenary of John Kay's birth, in 1904, finally to remedy its previous neglect, for which it had been chided by Bennet Woodcroft half a century earlier. The Weavers' Union was joined by the earl of Derby and other local notables in an appeal for a civic

[79] *The Times*, 17 June 1892, 3e; 28 July 1913, 4e.   [80] See below, p. 346.
[81] *The Times*, 17 January 1880, 4f. The gravestone of John Wyatt (1700–66), the inventor of spinning machinery, was restored 'a few years ago': Prosser, *Birmingham inventors*, p. 11.
[82] *The Times*, 10 May 1905, 15e; 13 May 1905, 12d; Chris Evans, 'Cort, Henry (1741?–1800)', *ODNB*, online edn, October 2006, www.oxforddnb.com/view/article/6359, accessed 21 October 2006.
[83] *The Times*, 29 November 1889, 5c; James Henry Quilter and John Chamberlain, *Framework knitting and hosiery manufacture* (Leicester: Hosiery Trade Journal, 1911), p. 6.

monument, which was inaugurated in 1908.[84] In 1877, Robert Hall and Sons, the large Bury loom-making firm, had anticipated the town's commemoration by installing a statue of Kay on the façade of its foundry offices. It represented him in eighteenth-century costume, holding his flying shuttle in one hand and a scroll (probably his patent) in the other.[85] In nearby Manchester, in 1890, Ford Madox Brown had used the theme of a machine-breaking attack on Kay for one of his twelve murals, in the Town Hall, illustrating the city's history.[86]

A bicentennial memorial to Thomas Newcomen was proposed in his birthplace, Dartmouth (Devon). Newcomen had been absent from all but the fullest histories of steam engineering, his name not even gracing the oak leaves of the *Inventor's almanac*. Two centuries after his invention of the atmospheric engine, in 1712, a letter to *The Times* from a memorial committee in Dartmouth claimed that 'a large section' of the townspeople desired a permanent memorial. In a belated attempt to share in the fame of Watt, Stephenson and now Trevithick, the local MP described Newcomen's engine as 'the rough idea out of which the modern steam engine had been evolved ... of untold value to the country and the world'.[87] The Great War intervened, so that it was 1921 before a memorial stone was unveiled. It carries an engraving of a Newcomen engine of 1712 and a brief memorial text.[88]

The most glittering celebration of all was mounted by Glasgow, in 1912, for the centenary of Bell's *Comet*, the first steamboat in Europe to carry passengers. Glasgow was probably seeking to outdo the 'great pomp and circumstance' with which, in 1909, New York had celebrated the centenary of Robert Fulton's *Clermont*, the first passenger-carrying steam vessel anywhere.[89] Three days of civic festivities culminated in a 'naval pageant' of sixty vessels, at the mouth of the Clyde, to which the Admiralty contributed a squadron of first-class battleships and a division of destroyers. They were 'inspected' by a procession of boats from Glasgow, and 'immense numbers' of workers went to watch. A model of the *Comet* was paraded through the streets; there were fireworks, illuminations and 'patriotic displays of various kinds' in towns along the

[84] Woodcroft, *Brief biographies*, p. 6; *The Times*, 18 July 1904, 6e; John Lord, *Memoir of John Kay of Bury, County of Lancaster, inventor of the fly-shuttle, metal reeds, etc. etc.* (Rochdale: Aldine Press, 1903), pp. 151–8; D. A. Farnie, 'Kay, John (1704–1780/81)', *ODNB*, www.oxforddnb.com/view/article/15194, accessed 27 October 2006.
[85] Illustrated in Lord, *Memoir of John Kay*, p. 117; *The Textile Manufacturer*, June 1933, 229.
[86] Dellheim, *Face of the past*, pp. 163–75; Lord, *Memoir of John Kay*, p. 60.
[87] *The Times*, 5 January 1912, 9b; 11 January 1912, 4a.
[88] 'Accounts of the Society, 1920–1', *TNS* 1 (1920–1), 79; Titley, 'Beginnings of the Society', 38.
[89] *The Times*, 31 August 1912, 5c.

Clyde.[90] At a Corporation luncheon for 450 guests, the Secretary of State for Scotland, McKinnon Wood, sang the praises of Henry Bell, regretted his inadequate reward, and heralded 'the true centenary of the birth of our vast and world-wide modern commerce'.[91] This partial view, typical of centenary rhetoric, was endorsed by *The Times*: 'Bell laid the foundations not merely of the commercial prosperity of Glasgow but of the maritime supremacy of Great Britain.'[92] As Bell was already commemorated by monuments beside the Clyde,[93] the centenary committee concentrated on two ambitious educational projects, including 'the provision and maintenance of a suitable steamship to enable the Royal Technical College, Glasgow to train students in practical steam navigation'.[94] Two local communities unveiled memorials to men involved in building the *Comet*. A large obelisk of grey granite attested to John Robertson's role as 'the designer and erector of the engine of the Comet', in his native village of Neilston, and a plaque at Port Glasgow commemorated the *Comet*'s construction there by John Wood.[95]

There was sometimes a fine balance between a disinterested desire to honour an inventor and a more mercenary urge to exploit his name in furtherance of a fund-raising effort. Lacock Abbey church (Wilts.) associated its restoration appeal, in 1900, with Henry Fox Talbot, 'the inventor of photography', who had inhabited Lacock Abbey and lies buried in the churchyard. It was probably his son and committee secretary, C. H. Talbot, who realized that the centenary of his father's birth was imminent. *The Times* bewailed the lack of a memorial to Fox Talbot, by contrast with the many to J. M. Daguerre, the French inventor of *daguerreotypes*; as a 'successful showman', Daguerre had prevailed, while the public's memory of Fox Talbot, the dignified scholar, had faded. Britons could now right this national wrong by purchasing a limited edition of prints made from Fox Talbot's photo-engravings, in aid of the restoration fund – a memorial the inventor 'would most have desired'.[96]

One previously neglected inventor was disputed by two parishes. In 1890, the vicar of Hythe (Kent) wrote to *The Times*, lamenting the neglect of Lionel Lukin (1742–1834), who was buried in the churchyard. As the inscription on his tombstone helpfully explained,

---

[90] *The Times*, 25 July 1912, 8f; 2 September 1912, 5f.   [91] *The Times*, 31 August 1912, 5e.
[92] *The Times*, 2 September 1912, 5f.   [93] See above, p. 188.
[94] *The Times*, 29 August 1912, 7e.
[95] *The Times*, 27 August 1912, 6f; 2 September 1912, 5f.
[96] *The Times*, 8 February 1900, 12d; 16 February 1900, 13d. For a similar use of Edward Jenner's more famous name by the church restoration fund at Berkeley (Glos.), see *The Times*, 7 December 1871, 4f; 1 February 1872, 12c.

This Lionel Lukin was the first who built a lifeboat, and was the original inventor of that principle of safety, by which many lives and much property have been preserved from shipwreck; and he obtained for it the King's patent in the year 1785.[97]

The vicar invited contributions for a memorial window in the church's recently restored chancel. Immediately, the vicar of Great Dunmow (Essex) challenged Hythe's appropriation of this inventive asset: 'If a memorial to Lionel Lukin is to be erected anywhere it should surely be in this parish church, where he was baptized ... and his first model lifeboat was launched on the doctor's pond in this parish.' He hoped at least one light in his church's new east window would be dedicated to 'the inventor of the lifeboat'.[98] Helped probably by its coastal location, burial trumped baptism: two years later, lifeboat-men and coastguards joined the mayor and corporation to dedicate Hythe's new memorial window.[99] In a neatly symbiotic relationship, the preservation of Lukin's memory helped to beautify and conserve the church. Inventors, the Victorians discovered, could be financial assets as well as heroes.

National heroes

In Cornwall and the central belt of Scotland, pride in the region's industrial heritage was becoming an important aspect of its self-identity.[100] By the late nineteenth century, Cornwall's mining industry was succumbing to international competition, but the memory of its global significance as recently as the 1860s (when 30 per cent of adult Cornishmen were employed in the sector) remained strong.[101] Central Scotland was still an industrial powerhouse, its heavy industry and shipbuilding at the height of its worldwide predominance and fame. Both regions reached

---

[97] *The Times*, 8 November 1890, 6c. See H. M. Chichester, 'Lukin, Lionel (1742–1834)', rev. R. C. Cox, *ODNB*, www.oxforddnb.com/view/article/17170, accessed 21 October 2006.

[98] *The Times*, 13 November 1890, 6d. For Henry Greathead's rival claim to its invention, see above, pp. 82–3.

[99] *The Times*, 4 October 1892, 10b. The four remaining lights in Great Dunmow's east window commemorate the wife of a local JP, as recorded on a brass plaque on the chancel wall: personal visit, 1996.

[100] Philip Payton, 'Industrial Celts? Cornish identity in the age of technological prowess', *Cornish Studies* 10 (2002), 127–30; Bernard Deacon, '"The hollow jarring of distant steam engines": images of Cornwall between West Barbary and Delectable Duchy', in Ella Westland (ed.), *Cornwall: the cultural construction of place* (Penzance: Patten Press, 1997), pp. 12–14, 18–21; Christopher Harvie, 'Larry Doyle and Captain MacWhirr: the engineer and the Celtic Fringe', in Geraint H. Jenkins (ed.), *Cymru a'r Cymry 2000: Wales and the Welsh, 2000* (Aberystwyth: University of Wales Press, 2001), pp. 119–21, 136–9. I am grateful to Alessandro Nuvolari for these references.

[101] Deacon, '"Hollow jarring of distant steam engines"', p. 11.

back to the early industrial revolution to celebrate inventors regarded as responsible for their prosperity and prestige; both possessed connections to its greatest icon, the steam engine. Cornwall, specifically Camborne, restored and cherished the memory of Richard Trevithick; central Scotland, in particular Glasgow, perpetuated its close association with Watt (and Bell). Both took on a larger significance: from the Celtic peripheries of the United Kingdom, Watt carried the claims of Scotland, Trevithick, those of Cornwall, to have been fundamental to the whole country's – even the empire's – international supremacy. Both are indicative of the emergence of new national or regional identities in the late nineteenth century.

Especially striking, in the Cornish case, is the contrast between the commemoration of Davy in 1872 and Trevithick in the 1880s. No speaker at the inauguration of Davy's statue sought to claim him for Cornwall: Davy was 'the most eminent townsman Penzance could boast of', and their rhetoric focused entirely on the town.[102] Only a decade later, when Camborne rediscovered Trevithick, the town shared its native hero with the entire county, identifying him closely with Cornwall's industrial heritage. Trevithick's achievement of national recognition, in 1888, represented a rescue of reputation comparable only to Crompton's, not only in its lateness but also in the fervour that it generated. While the engineering profession shared the responsibility for Trevithick's commemoration, Cornwall – in requiring unambiguous symbolic references to his Cornish roots – made a statement equivalent to that made by Watt's Scottish supporters in the Abbey six decades earlier.[103]

Camborne subsequently reinforced its links with Trevithick, ensuring that his role in the industrial revolution would no longer be overlooked. On Christmas Eve 1901, the town celebrated the centenary of his road locomotive's first trial with a parade of traction engines over the original route, accompanied by local miners and engineers, and the unveiling of a bronze plaque.[104] The celebrations were orchestrated by John Holman, one of the partners in Camborne's leading engine-building firm, and J. J. Beringer, the chairman of Camborne School of Mines, who also edited a memorial volume of papers.[105] Holman and his brother, James Miners

[102] *Cornish Telegraph*, 16 October 1872; see above, pp. 309–12.   [103] See above, pp. 322–5.
[104] *The Times*, 25 December 1901, 9b; Dickinson and Titley, *Richard Trevithick*, p. 266; Harper, *Cornish giant*, p. 29.
[105] Dickinson and Titley, *Richard Trevithick*, p. 284; Clive Carter, *Cornish engineering, 1801–2001: Holman, two centuries of industrial excellence in Camborne* (Camborne: Trevithick Society, 2001), pp. 32–3. Carter states that the bronze tablet was installed in 1919, by the Memorial Committee (which is supported by Harper's failure to mention it), p. 78.

Holman, were proud of their family's links with Trevithick: their grandfather had built boilers to Trevithick's innovative designs. In 1911, James Holman, together with Beringer and other Camborne residents, launched a subscription for a statue: £600 had been collected when the Great War intervened, leaving the project to be completed in 1932.[106] A popular biography, published in 1913, proclaimed Trevithick's Cornish identity, while throwing down the gauntlet to the Stephenson camp. Edith K. Harper skilfully entitled her work *A Cornish giant: Richard Trevithick, the father of the locomotive*. By inference, Trevithick's famously tall and strong physique was matched by his gigantic achievements – as much a part of Cornwall's heritage as any legendary giant from its Celtic past.[107]

In 1897, the Institution of Civil Engineers commissioned a marble bust of Trevithick from C. H. Mabey for its London headquarters.[108] Other places now sought to establish a link with his memory. A bronze commemorative tablet, depicting both Trevithick and his locomotive, was placed in Dartford parish church, the gift of a member of the firm for which he had worked.[109] The centenary of his death prompted the erection of monuments in two places where Trevithick had first demonstrated his locomotives. Merthyr Tydfil, in the heart of the South Wales coalfield, grandly proclaimed itself 'the cradle and birthplace of the locomotive'; its borough seal already incorporated a reference to Trevithick's locomotive tram-engine. In 1934, with much pomp and circumstance in the midst of the great depression, it inaugurated a memorial near the old Penydarren Ironworks, where Trevithick had worked.[110] A few days later, the Minister of Transport unveiled a plaque on the wall of the engineering laboratories of University College, London, to mark the spot where, in 1808, Trevithick demonstrated 'the first steam locomotive to draw passengers'.[111]

Watt's reputation, like Trevithick's, was grounded in two principal constituencies – the engineering profession and his native land.[112] While certainly not ignored in England, in Scotland it was more actively cherished. Throughout the nineteenth century, Watt represented the pinnacle of modern Scottish achievement, the most tangible expression of what Scotland contributed to the United Kingdom. Ironically, it was

[106] Dickinson and Titley, *Richard Trevithick*, p. 262, pl. XVII.
[107] Philip Payton, 'Paralysis and revival: the reconstruction of Celtic-Catholic Cornwall, 1890–1945', in Westland (ed.), *Cornwall*, pp. 25–39.
[108] Dickinson and Titley, *Richard Trevithick*, p. 262.   [109] Ibid., p. 266, pl. XVIII.
[110] *The Times*, 20 April 1934, 11f; Harper, *Cornish giant*, p. 37.
[111] *The Times*, 24 April 1934, 6g.
[112] See above, pp. 93–119; Kidd, *Subverting Scotland's past*, pp. 1–6, 97–9, 250–1, 268–74.

largely thanks to a rising nationalist challenge to the Union settlement, in the second half of the nineteenth century, that Scots actively resumed the promotion of Watt's heroic status.[113] Much of Scotland's 'tradition' was newly minted by publishers and promoters of tourism, who 'made historic Scotland a marketable commodity'.[114] Late in Victoria's reign, an apolitical national pride infused with the century's predilection for heroic history found expression among an elite minority. In this restatement of a separate historical and heroic identity, inventors, engineers and scientists shared the honours with medieval kings and warriors, writers and other intellectuals. Its first manifestation in public art was the National Wallace Monument built at Stirling, in the 1860s, and embellished during the next thirty years with a Caledonian Temple of Fame.[115] By this time, the Enlightenment's ideological distinctions among its heroes had been lost beneath a century of hegemonic political Liberalism.[116] One great Scot was now as good as another for nascent nationalism's purposes: the busts of Watt and Adam Smith rubbed shoulders with those of Robert the Bruce and a dozen other famous men of science (William Murdoch, David Brewster and Hugh Miller), literature, religion and politics.[117] This idea of a Caledonian Temple of Fame was also expressed in the Scottish National Portrait Gallery in Edinburgh. There, Watt, easily identified by the model beam-engine that he holds, stands prominently – between Telford, the engineer, and Adam, the architect – in the procession of famous Scots that winds its way around the entrance hall's frieze.

Simultaneously, biographers of Watt began to emphasize his Scottish origins. There are precedents in Muirhead's and Williamson's biographies, published in the 1850s, but for nostalgic and sentimental Scottishness, none could outdo Andrew Carnegie's (for Oliphants' 'Famous Scots' series).[118] According to the Scottish-American steel

---

[113] R. J. Finlay, *Independent and free: Scottish politics and the origins of the Scottish Nationalist Party, 1918–1945* (Edinburgh: John Donald, 1994), pp. 1–9; M. Fry, *Patronage and principle: a political history of modern Scotland* (Aberdeen: Aberdeen University Press, 1991).

[114] Christopher Harvie, *Scotland and nationalism: Scottish society and politics, 1707–1977* (London: George Allen and Unwin, 1977), p. 134; Anderson, *Imagined communities*, pp. 199–206. See also Hugh Trevor-Roper, 'The invention of tradition: the Highland tradition of Scotland', in Hobsbawm and Ranger (eds.), *Invention of tradition*, pp. 15–42.

[115] Morton, *William Wallace*, pp. 78–9.

[116] Fry, *Patronage and principle*, pp. 69, 73–5.

[117] 'Hall of Heroes, National Wallace Monument': www.scran.ac.uk/ixbin/hixclient, accessed 29 October 2001.

[118] Williamson, *Memorials*; Harvie, *Scotland and nationalism*, pp. 141–2. Ironically, the same year saw the publication of T. E. Pemberton's distinctively 'Birmingham' biography: *James Watt of Soho and Heathfield*.

magnate turned philanthropist, Watt's descent from the Celts and the Covenanters was crucial to his success: 'the heather was on fire within Jamie's breast'. Unmoved by ancient heroes, Watt relished 'the story of his own romantic land', and 'when things looked darkest' during his time in London, found inspiration in William Wallace and Robert the Bruce.[119] In 1913, Dewar's whisky cashed in, recruiting Watt to its own 'famous Scots' series of advertisements (figure 11.9).[120] It was certainly an image far removed from the cosmopolitan 'philosopher' of Enlightenment Edinburgh.

This nationalistic celebration was underpinned by a strong civic pride, especially in Glasgow and his native Greenock.[121] In 1824, the citizens of Glasgow had preferred to erect their own monument to Watt: within ten years, the city could boast three statues – two the result of public subscriptions, one the gift of James Watt Jnr to the University.[122] All Glasgow's subsequent statuary of Watt resulted from private commissions: between 1864 and 1906, five more of the city's major buildings helped to prolong the memory of the man and his most famous invention.[123] Glasgow's engineers held an annual 'James Watt Anniversary Dinner' – a collaborative effort by the Institution of Engineers and Shipbuilders in Scotland and the Philosophical Society of Glasgow, to which they invited distinguished speakers.[124] The University of Glasgow also identified itself very closely with Watt. In the 1860s, his name was freely used by professors who canvassed subscriptions to fund the University's expansion on a new site to the west of the city, and at the opening of the new buildings, in 1870, several speakers 'highlighted the perceived connections between "science" and "wealth", embodied in the mythology of James Watt'.[125] In

---

[119] Andrew Carnegie, *James Watt* (Edinburgh and London [1905]), pp. 11, 13, 15, 22; Geoffrey Tweedale, 'Carnegie, Andrew (1835–1919)', *ODNB*, www.oxforddnb.com/view/article/32296, accessed 21 October 2006.

[120] *ILN* 143 (12 July 1913), 71.

[121] MacLeod and Tann, 'From engineer to scientist', 397–9.

[122] See above, pp. 112–15; McKenzie, *Public sculpture of Glasgow*, pp. 393–4, 404.

[123] Ibid., pp. 107–8, 270–1, 282–3, 305–7, 331–6, 393–4, 417–19. See also the beam-engine erected in Kelvin Grove Park, in *Glasgow of today (Industries of Glasgow)* (London: Historical Publishing Company, 1888): www.scran.ac.uk./ixbin/hixclient, accessed 29 October 2001.

[124] *The Scotsman*, 20 January 1893, 5; 23 January 1895, 4f. The IESS, which was founded in 1857 (as the Institution of Engineers in Scotland), had commemorated its incorporation in 1871 by issuing a silver medal depicting a bust of Watt: National Museums of Scotland (H.1958.1828): www.scran.ac.uk/ixbin/hixclient, accessed 29 October 2001.

[125] Crosbie Smith, ' "Nowhere but in a great town": William Thomson's spiral of classroom credibility', in Crosbie Smith and Jon Agar (eds.), *Making space for science: territorial themes in the shaping of knowledge* (Basingstoke: Macmillan, 1998), pp. 139–42. See also

DEWAR

Joseph Simpson, R.B.A.   *Copyright. John Dewar & Sons, Ltd.*

JAMES WATT

11.9 An advertisement for Dewar's whisky, in *The Illustrated London News*, 12 July 1913, depicts James Watt as a 'famous Scot', drinking his whisky from a thistle-shaped glass (photograph by Ann Pethers).

1919–20, Scottish engineers would commemorate the centenary of Watt's death by raising £30,000 to found two James Watt chairs in engineering at Glasgow University.[126]

The west of Scotland was not alone. In 1850, Baxter Brothers of Dundee surmounted their new five-storey, flax-spinning mill with Watt's statue.[127] Edinburgh finally erected a memorial to him in 1851,

---

Ben Marsden, '"A most important trespass": Lewis Gordon and the Glasgow Chair of Civil Engineering and Mechanics, 1840–55', in ibid., p. 98; MacLeod and Tann, 'From engineer to scientist', 398.

[126] MacLeod and Tann, 'From engineer to scientist', 391; Glasgow University Archives, Minutes of the Meeting of the University Court, 16 December 1920, 11 March 1921.

[127] Gauldie (ed.), *Dundee textile industry*, p. 129.

when the funds, which had slowly accumulated since 1824, purchased a building in Adam Square (now Chambers Street) for the School of Arts. Renamed the Watt Institution and School of Arts, its exterior would soon be embellished by a seated statue of Watt, sculpted by Peter Slater; in 1885 it was again renamed, becoming Heriot-Watt College (following amalgamation with George Heriot Hospital).[128] Shortly afterwards, across Chambers Street, a portrait bust of Watt was carved over the entrance to the Royal Scottish Museum (opened in 1866).[129] His Scottish nationality seems incidental in this setting; more probably he represents achievement in the mechanical arts, joining Michelangelo as representative of the fine arts, and Newton and Darwin, of the physical and biological sciences respectively.

Watt's image was similarly used south of the border, especially in educational contexts. His statue features among the 'great men of science', commissioned for Oxford's University Museum in 1860.[130] He occupies one of the six panels of a gilt-bronze door in the courtyard of the South Kensington (Victoria & Albert) Museum; the others commemorate Davy, Newton, Titian, Bramante and the Great Exhibition of 1851.[131] At University College, Nottingham, his bust accompanied those of Bacon, Newton, Cuvier, Shakespeare and Milton (1881).[132] When the University of Birmingham commissioned nine statues representing the arts and sciences for the entrance to its Great Hall, in 1907, Watt (especially given his links to the city) was the natural choice to represent engineering.[133]

---

[128] W. L. Bride, *James Watt – his inventions and his connections with Heriot-Watt University* (Edinburgh: Heriot-Watt University, 1969), p. 26; *The Scotsman*, 16 December 1840, 3f. Heriot-Watt University received its charter in 1966; the statue now stands in the grounds of its Riccarton Campus.

[129] John Gifford, Colin McWilliam, David Walker, *Edinburgh* (Harmondsworth: Penguin Books, 1984), p. 187.

[130] See below, figure 12.1. Sherwood and Pevsner, *Oxfordshire*, p. 282; *The Builder* 17 (1859), 401. The sponsor of Watt's statue was Matthew Piers Watt Boulton, the grandson of Watt's partner: *Oxford University Museum* (4 June, 1860), printed prospectus in 'History of the Building of the Museum', Oxford University Museum Archives, Box 5, fldr 5. I am grateful to Ms Stella Brecknell for this reference.

[131] For a photograph of the doors, see www.victorianweb.org/sculpture/misc/va/1.html, accessed 23 December 2005.

[132] *The Builder* 40 (1881), 786; 41 (1881), 484.

[133] Noszlopy, *Public sculpture of Birmingham*, pp. 133–4. The other statues were of Beethoven, Virgil, Michelangelo, Plato, Shakespeare, Newton, Faraday and Darwin. A further civic statue of Watt, by H. C. Fehr, was erected in 1898 in City Square, Leeds, one of an incongruous group with the Black Prince as its equestrian centrepiece, which also included Joseph Priestley: Pevsner, *Yorkshire, the West Riding*, p. 319; Julian Orbach, *Victorian architecture in Britain* (London and New York: A. & C. Black, 1987) pp. 474–5. A. P. Woolrich reminds me that, as Kilburn Scott observed, Matthew

It had been Scottish Whigs who initially elevated Watt to the British pantheon, in order to challenge the militaristic heroes espoused by their political foes. In the later nineteenth century, it was a reversion to Scottish nationalist sentiments, in opposition to the Union of 1707, which helped to reconstruct Watt as a distinctively Scottish hero. Posthumously, Watt had served the causes of both unionist and nationalist Scots, but also of liberal English politicians, of several British towns and cities, of educational and scientific reformers, and, not least, the commercial interest of the firm of Boulton, Watt & Co. (and its successor, James Watt & Co.). Not only had this most private of men become Britain's best known engineer and inventor, but his greatest invention had become identified with 'the Industrial Revolution'.

One is forced to wonder, however, whether Watt remained the most suitable champion for the cause of inventors. With the economy poised for a second industrial revolution – based on electricity, the internal combustion engine, cheap steel and organic chemistry – Watt no longer represented the cutting edge of technological change. Indeed, the whole model of invention was changing, and the independent inventor's star was dimming. By the late nineteenth century, the man at the head of a powerful firm – especially if he combined inventive ability with entrepreneurial flair – was thrusting aside the 'mere' inventor. Celebrated locally for their creation of employment and philanthropy, such men as William Armstrong, Samuel Cunliffe Lister and John Platt received the tributes of grateful towns and cities, while playing a minor role in Parliament or local government, sufficient to earn them a knighthood, baronetcy, or even a peerage. Outside the sphere of manufacturing industry, the engineering and medical professions ensured their luminaries received due recognition. A growing cadre of professional scientists was also taking its cue from these bodies, and, as we shall see in the next chapter, some leading scientists advanced an account of discovery and invention that disparaged the 'mere' inventor. Thus, between the empire-building entrepreneur, on one side, and the self-important scientist, on the other, by 1914 there was less and less public space for the independent inventor to occupy – especially in an age that was increasingly taking technological change for granted.

Murray, the Leeds engineer harassed by Boulton, Watt & Co., might have been a better choice. A centenary plaque to Murray, unveiled in 1929, may be seen near the site of his works in Holbeck.

12   Science and the disappearing inventor

There is an impression that the day of heaven-born inventors is nearly over, that the lawyer or the clergyman who revolutionizes some branch of chemical or electrical industry, if he ever existed, is now unknown; and that useful inventions are, with few exceptions, the production of those whose daily business is to study the subject-matter.[1]

The inventor, continued this *Times* leading article in 1898, was 'active in perfecting or improving little devices for the comfort of us all'; it wondered, by contrast, '[with what] the cleverest inventive minds of our time are now wrestling'. Three disparate images of invention collide in this one article: one, the heroic inventor, was obsolescent if not mythical; the other two heralded an unheroic bipolarity that was to prevail in the twentieth century – between the tinkerer in the garden shed and the faceless employee of the industrial R&D laboratory. Whether the latter category was intended to contain 'the cleverest inventive minds' remains unclear; probably they were elsewhere, among the scientific professoriate.

Five years before, the physicist, Oliver Lodge, had reserved the description 'great and heaven-born' for a tiny elite of disinterested 'men of science', which included 'Thales, Archimedes, Hipparchus, Copernicus, pre-eminently Newton' – 'the epoch-making men', of whom there were only one or two per generation. Viewed thus from Lodge's Chair of Physics at Victoria University College, London, the inventor appeared even less glorious than he did from the editorial office of *The Times*. 'Amid the throng of inventions,' asserted Lodge, 'there are a multitude of small men using the name of science but working for their own ends, jostling and scrambling just as they would jostle and scramble in any other trade or profession.'[2] During the century's final two decades, the heroic status of the inventor – already under pressure from the entrepreneur's rising status – was subjected to continuous assault from leading men of science, such as Lodge. If they failed to replace it with

[1] *The Times*, 19 August 1898, 7d.
[2] Oliver Lodge, *Pioneers of science* (London: Macmillan & Co., 1893), p. 7.

351

the *heroic* scientist, they at least succeeded in elevating 'science' (and 'scientist') to a higher status than 'invention' (and 'inventor') or 'technology' (and 'technologist') – a position it held throughout the twentieth century.

Simultaneously, inventors fell victim to their own success. While the 1883 act secured the future of the patent system, by cutting the initial charge for a UK patent from £25 to £4 it also spawned a 'plague' of patentees and an upsurge in litigation. Inventors now seemed anything but an endangered species, as patent applications quickly trebled to approximately 20,000 per annum. It was hardly surprising if people began to take inventions for granted. Perhaps their opinion of the inventor had already been damaged by the negative arguments advanced for three decades by opponents of the patent system.[3] Others grew weary of Smilesean tales that recycled the stories of a famous few.

A further form of success that possibly undermined the popular admiration of inventors was the state's recognition of those whose ingenuity supported its war aims.[4] The widespread disillusionment occasioned by the Crimean War among those who had believed in a new age of peace, sanctioned by international trade and supported by steam technology, was, of course, as nothing in comparison with the collective shock of the First World War. Even before 1914, however, influential voices were questioning the value of technological change: while many still equated it with 'progress', a vociferous minority suggested that material gains were purchased at too high a price – socially, spiritually, environmentally. The 'condition of England' question returned in a new guise in the 1890s, when the surveys of York by Rowntree and of London's East End by Booth revealed unexpected depths of poverty. Meanwhile, the first generation of professional economic historians was casting 'the Industrial Revolution' in a sombre light: it had torn apart communities, stunted the lives of factory children, and choked both town and country with its effluent. It was hardly a promising context for heroic inventors.[5]

Men of science: the mid-nineteenth-century symbiosis

When the British Association met in Glasgow in 1840, the dinner guests raised their glasses to 'The memory of James Watt, and the other eminent men of Great Britain who have contributed to the Advancement of

---

[3] See above, pp. 250–1, 264–71.   [4] See above, pp. 236–40.
[5] David Cannadine, 'The present and the past', 133–42.

Science'.[6] Twenty years later, the statues of great 'men of science', commissioned for the new University Museum at Oxford, placed Watt, George Stephenson and Davy (with his safety lamp) in the company of Galileo, Newton, Priestley and others esteemed for their theoretical insights into the natural world (figure 12.1).[7] To those behind the scheme, they were all 'the great founders and improvers of Natural Knowledge in those departments of Science to which the Museum is devoted'.[8]

By no means, however, were all inventors ever recognized as 'men of science'.[9] The mathematician and inventor, Charles Babbage, while numbering Watt among 'the greatest scientific benefactors' of the country, was emphatic in discriminating between the elite and the swarm.[10]

The power of inventing mechanical contrivances and of combining machinery, does not appear, if we may judge from the frequency of its occurrence, to be a difficult or a rare gift ... yet the more beautiful combinations are exceedingly rare. Those which should command our admiration equally by the perfection of their effects and the simplicity of their means, are found amongst the happiest productions of genius.[11]

Babbage had harsh words for 'mechanical projectors', whose crime was not an intention to deceive but 'ignorance of the scientific principles, and of the history of their own art'.[12] Moreover, an acute awareness of social distinctions between the 'gentlemen of science' and active engineers and manufacturers — not to mention their inventive employees — was evident

[6] *List of Toasts*, repr. in Morrell and Thackray, *Gentlemen of science*, pl. 23; see also p. 218. The toast to Watt was ninth in a series of twenty-two — ahead of 'Noblemen and gentlemen [guests]', and 'The Royal Society, and its Noble Chairman, the Marquis of Northampton'. See also above, pp. 225–9.

[7] Acland and Ruskin, *Oxford Museum*, pp. 25–7, 102–3; O'Dwyer, *Architecture of Deane and Woodward*, pp. 253–7. See also the assorted list of 'very distinguished scientific men' in Robert Peel's letter to Prince Albert, 18 December 1844, quoted in Foote, 'Place of science', 210, n. 47.

[8] See above, pp. 210 and 349; also *The Builder* 39 (1881), 757. The lack of discrimination continues in Francis Galton, *English men of science: their nature and nurture* (London: Macmillan & Co., 1874), pp. 7–8, 51–3, 62–3.

[9] Whewell had strong philosophical and political reasons for restricting the description to a theoretical elite, wishing in particular to deny it (and the title of 'philosopher') to Watt: Miller, *Discovering water*, pp. 137, 145–52, and passim.

[10] Charles Babbage, *Reflections on the decline of science in England and on some of its causes* (London: B. Fellowes & J. Booth, 1830), p. 199. For Babbage's defence of Watt in the 'water controversy', see Miller, *Discovering water*, pp. 136–7.

[11] Babbage, *Economy of machinery*, p. 206. See also [E. L. Bulwer-Lytton], *England and the English* (New York: J. & J. Harper, 1833), pp. 120–1, quoted in Foote, 'Place of science', 203.

[12] Babbage, *Economy of machinery*, p. 213.

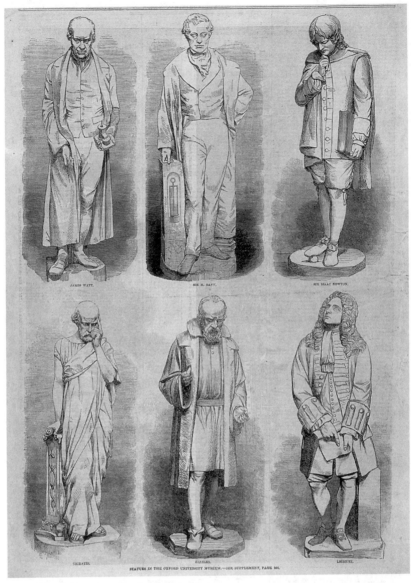

12.1 *The first six statues in the Oxford University Museum*, an engraving published in *The Illustrated London News*, 13 October 1860. By various sculptors, they represent (clockwise from top left): James Watt, Sir Humphry Davy, Sir Isaac Newton, Leibnitz, Galileo, Socrates (photograph by Ann Pethers).

in the tortuous efforts of the early British Association to accommodate the more distinguished practical men. In 1836, it created a new section for them, devoted pointedly to 'mechanical *science*' (not art), but its senior officeholders were usually academics or 'savants', while the practising engineers dominated 'the lowlier secretariat'.[13] It was 1861 before an engineer was elected president of the British Association – William Fairbairn at Manchester, followed by William Armstrong at Newcastle in 1863.[14] Yet, although an influential tranche of its academic members, led by William Whewell, insisted that science should be valued for its intellectual value not its utility, the British Association trumpeted the achievements of its 'practical' members. 'Technology was nurtured not only to embody an ideology about the relation between superior theory and subordinate practice, but also to render visible the Association's attachment to the idea of progress.'[15]

There was a symbiotic relationship between inventors and natural philosophers ('scientists'). They hung together in a society that still valued classical learning above all other, and whose more conservative elements would gladly have hanged the former as charlatans and the latter as dilettantes and infidels. Together they forged a new identity as 'men of science'. By the time of the Great Exhibition in 1851, even Whewell announced very publicly a shift in his position towards utility, celebrating 'such a great spectacle of the works of material art' and conceding that, in chemistry at least, science was now 'the whole foundation, the entire creator of the art'. A few years later, he extended that claim to the modern steam engine and the electric telegraph.[16]

Tensions, however, lurked beneath the surface. The complaint was regularly voiced among early nineteenth-century natural philosophers that their subject had died with Newton, because (variously) neither the Royal Society nor the state offered them any encouragement. Invidious comparisons were made with the continent, particularly France, where the state heaped 'pensions and honours … upon those who devote themselves exclusively to works of science'.[17] Others remarked on the irony that 'Science, on which the wealth and power of Britain depends, is

---

[13] Morrell and Thackray, *Gentlemen of science*, pp. 256–66. There was also an intense struggle for the intellectual ownership of the British Association, which added to the difficulty of accommodating the practical men: Miller, *Discovering water*, pp. 138–42.
[14] Morrell and Thackray, *Gentlemen of science*, p. 265.
[15] Ibid., p. 266; Yeo, *Defining science*, pp. 224–9.
[16] Rev. William Whewell, 'The general bearing of the Great Exhibition on the progress of art and science', in *Lectures on the results of the Great Exhibition of 1851*, 2 vols. (London: David Bogue, 1852–3), vol. I, pp. 4, 28; Yeo, *Defining science*, pp. 228–9.
[17] Review of 'An Elementary Treatise on Astronomy', *Edinburgh Review* 31 (1819), 394, quoted in Foote, 'Place of science', 192.

not honoured in Britain.'[18] The public allegedly considered scientific research to be pointless unless it were visibly applied to some utilitarian purpose – say, by an engineer.[19] One contributor to the 'Decline' debate in 1831 opined that '[natural] philosophers are often regarded as little better than jugglers', while the Savillian Professor of Geometry at Oxford complained they were 'not uncommonly regarded with suspicion, dislike, or ridicule'.[20]

Prominent in the early 'Decline of science' agitation that foreshadowed the establishment of the British Association, in 1832, were three physical scientists whose public recognition rested primarily on an invention: Sir Humphry Davy, Charles Babbage and Sir David Brewster.[21] While none of them can be accused, therefore, of using technological progress cynically to bolster the case for science, they all seized the opportunity it offered. The miners' safety lamp had taken Davy from celebrity as an entertaining lecturer at the Royal Institution to national renown as an inventor and philanthropist, especially because he did not patent it. The president of the Royal Society, Sir Joseph Banks, congratulated him on having 'placed both science in general and the Royal Society in particular on a better public footing by showing how the application of natural philosophy could eradicate a social evil'.[22] Davy, in turn, skilfully used the 1824 memorial meeting to claim Watt's inventions for 'science'.[23]

Charles Babbage's notorious attack, in 1830, on the dilatory leadership of the Royal Society and his summons to the state to support the research of natural philosophers drew unfavourable comparisons with the honours bestowed elsewhere in Europe on 'the improvers of the arts of life, or successful discoverers in science'.[24] Fundamental to his case was the call for *financial* recognition of the theoretical advances that lay behind great inventions. To invent the separate condenser, he argued, Watt had had to

---

[18] 'Present system of education', *Westminster Review* 4 (1825), 175, quoted in Foote, 'Place of science', 193.

[19] 'Scientific education of upper classes', *Westminster Review* 9 (1828), 330, quoted in Foote, 'Place of science', 193. See also the views of Mandeville and Say, quoted in G. N. von Tunzelmann, *Technology and industrial progress: the foundations of economic growth* (Aldershot and Brookfield, VE: Edward Elgar, 1995), pp. 39, 120.

[20] 'Herschel's Treatise on Sound', *Quarterly Review* 44 (1831), 476, quoted in Foote, 'Place of science', 195; A. N. L. Munby, *The history and bibliography of science in England: the first phase, 1837–1845* (Los Angeles: University of California Press, 1968), pp. 5–6.

[21] A. D. Orange, 'The origins of the British Association for the Advancement of Science', *BJHS* 6 (1972), 152–76; Morrell and Thackray, *Gentlemen of science*, pp. 35–94, and passim.

[22] Jonathan Smith, *Fact and feeling: Baconian science and the nineteenth-century literary imagination* (Madison, WI: University of Wisconsin Press, 1994), p. 87.

[23] See above, p. 101.

[24] Babbage, *Decline of science*, pp. 198–9.

draw on the discoveries of Joseph Black concerning latent heat: Watt had been well rewarded by the market, but there was no mechanism to recompense Black.[25] Beyond the question of natural justice, it was essential to maintain the flow of research in natural philosophy that would generate further inventions: it would be prudent, as well as just, for the state to support basic research through pensions and grants.[26]

Brewster's review of Babbage's book endorsed his argument, but went further in demanding government salaries for the 'most distinguished men of science' who, under the Royal Society's aegis, would become 'the scientific advisers of the Crown', on the model of the Académie des Sciences in Paris.[27] Indiscriminately, he listed as worthy of reward '[William] Murdoch and Henry Bell, who first introduced into actual use the two greatest practical inventions of modern times', in company with botanists, chemists and astronomers.[28] Brewster, whose own patent had failed to prevent the pirating of his immensely popular (and potentially profitable) kaleidoscope in 1816, campaigned equally for better treatment of inventors.[29] In the 1860s, he was still writing critically of the patent law and of the superior rewards accorded authors by copyright. Whatever the glories of ancient and modern literature, said Brewster, their disappearance would scarcely affect society, but 'withdraw the gifts with which art [i.e. technology] and science have enriched us – the substantial realities through which we live, and move, and enjoy our being – and society collapses into barbarism'.[30]

The authors of popular collective biographies helped to perpetuate the justification of natural philosophy by its technical inventions. It was easier, for example, to illustrate Newton's invention of the reflecting telescope than to make an explanation of his optics or laws of motion exciting; to hymn the benefit of Davy's safety lamp in terms of the preclusion of gruesome mining accidents, instead of explicating his work on the chemistry of gases.[31] Frederick Bakewell's volume seemed to promise explanation:

The conveniences, the comforts, and luxuries conferred on society by the many important inventions of the present century must naturally excite a desire to know the origin and progress of the application of scientific principles by which such advantages have been gained.

---

[25] Ibid., pp. 16–17.   [26] Ibid., pp. 18–21, 131–2.
[27] 'The decline of science in England', *Quarterly Review* 43 (1830), 330.   [28] Ibid., 320.
[29] Ibid., 332–41; Gordon, *Home life of Sir David Brewster*, pp. 141–8; Morrell and Thackray, *Gentlemen of science*, pp. 256–7.
[30] Gordon, *Home life of Sir David Brewster*, pp. 210–12. See also Miller, *Discovering water*, pp. 152–66.
[31] For example, Timbs, *Stories of inventors*; also see Brightwell, *Heroes*, pp. v–vii.

Yet, continued Bakewell, himself both a physicist and an inventor, 'practically considered, these inventions are of much greater value than the discoveries of science on which most of them depend'.[32] This ranking of the relative value of invention and 'the discoveries of science' is indicative of the problem that scientists continued to face. The public's willingness to fund them was subject to a parsimonious utilitarian calculation, which might perceive the connections *post hoc* but was unable to imagine the future possibilities of current research. A more ruthless attempt was about to be made, however, to forge the link between even 'pure' research and technical innovation to the detriment of the latter.

Scientists and inventors: the new hierarchy

The 'small shower of honours, pensions, and awards' that the 'Declinist' campaign had wrung out of the government was increasingly denounced as insufficient.[33] Professional scientists were not alone in canvassing the importance of research and the dangers of its neglect; the case was being widely made, particularly in the field of education and training, as concern mounted over threats to Britain's industrial competitiveness. Ironically, its proponents believed they had to confront the enormous complacency that sprang from the country's triumphant history of empirical invention, and urged the importance of formal technical training and 'theoretical and mathematical education'.[34] Ranged against them, many industrialists distrusted 'book learning' and preferred to maintain apprenticeships and shop-floor training.[35] Textile manufacturers were advised, in 1875, that, 'the isolated inventor or worker has little chance in the competitive race of the present day; success depends now on scientific knowledge, coupled with an intimate acquaintance with the inventions, the experiments, the successes, and the failures of others'.[36] Ten years later, Swire Smith warned the Ossett Chamber of Commerce that, 'the

---

[32] Bakewell, *Great facts*, p. vii. See also ibid., pp. 1, 5.

[33] Roy M. MacLeod, 'The support of Victorian science: the endowment of research movement in Great Britain, 1868–1900', *Minerva* 9 (1971), 197–8.

[34] J. Anderson, 'Machine Tools', *Reports on the Paris Universal Exhibition*, BPP 1867–8, XXX(2), p. 725. See also *Report of the select committee on scientific instruction*, BPP 1867–8, XV, p. 172; W. Ashworth, *An economic history of England, 1870–1913* (London: Methuen, 1960), p. 195.

[35] D. C. Coleman and Christine MacLeod, 'Attitudes to new techniques: British businessmen, 1800–1950', *EHR* 39 (1986), 601–4. Also see Bourne, above pp. 149–50.

[36] *Textile Manufacturer* 1 (1875), 1.

Stephensons and Arkwrights of the future would be the men who took advantage of scientific training and knowledge'.[37]

The international threat, perceived only dimly in the 1830s, now seemed imminent and stark: in particular, the reputedly dismal performance of British firms at the Paris Exhibition of 1867 caused serious alarm.[38] One of the Exhibition jurors, Lieutenant-Colonel Alexander Strange, an amateur astronomer and retired officer of the Indian Army, urged the British Association to campaign anew 'for state intervention to secure the progress of physical science'.[39] In response, it lobbied the government for a formal inquiry. Although the Samuelson committee on technical instruction had only just reported, in 1870 Gladstone appointed a royal commission, chaired by William Cavendish, seventh duke of Devonshire, to investigate the state of scientific instruction and research.[40] Its nine members included two professional scientists, T. H. Huxley and John Lubbock, who belonged to the tiny but influential 'X Club', which, since its formation in 1864, had been campaigning for increased state and private intervention in support of science; nothing less than a properly funded career structure would satisfy them. For the six years' duration of the Devonshire Commission, *Nature* (to some extent the mouthpiece of the X Club) relayed the evidence it heard of 'the distressed state of scientific men' and the lamentable provision of scientific instruction, which were reducing England to 'a third-rate or fourth-rate power' in science.[41] In 1873, it published a series of leading articles that canvassed the 'endowment of research' and reform of the universities of Oxford and Cambridge, arousing opposition within the

---

[37] *The Textile Recorder* 2 (1885), 280. See also ibid. 2 (1885), 185; *The Builder* 39 (1881), 757; Dircks, *Inventors and inventions*, pp. 31–3; Thomas Brassey, MP, *Lectures on the labour question* (London: Longmans, Green, 1878), p. 14.

[38] For a sceptical investigation of the rhetoric of 'decline', see Graeme Gooday, 'Lies, damned lies and declinism: Lyon Playfair, the Paris 1867 Exhibition and the contested rhetorics of scientific education and industrial performance': in Inkster *et al.* (eds.), *Golden age*, pp. 105–20.

[39] MacLeod, 'Support of Victorian science', 202–3. The following two paragraphs draw heavily on MacLeod's article, which should be read alongside more recent scholarship: Ruth Barton, '"Huxley, Lubbock, and half a dozen others": professionals and gentlemen in the formation of the X Club', *Isis* 89 (1998), 410–44; Ruth Barton, 'Scientific authority and scientific controversy in *Nature*: North Britain against the X Club', in L. Henson *et al.* (eds.), *Culture and science in the nineteenth-century media* (Aldershot: Ashgate, 2004), pp. 223–34; Crosbie Smith, *The science of energy: a cultural history of energy physics in Victorian Britain* (London: Athlone, 1998), esp. ch. 9; Turner, 'Public science', 589–608; David A. Roos, 'The "aims and intentions" of "Nature"', in James Paradis and Thomas Postlewait (eds.), *Victorian science and Victorian values: literary perspectives* (New York: New York Academy of Sciences, 1981), pp. 159–80.

[40] Gooday, 'Lies, damned lies and declinism', pp. 118–20.

[41] MacLeod, 'Support of Victorian science', 205–6.

universities and unsympathetic comment from popular journals, such as *Punch*. Indeed, despite the Commission's endorsement of most of *Nature*'s recommendations, the campaign proved to be a long and arduous one.

The limited gains made in the 1870s stalled in the 1880s: Gladstone's Liberal governments, committed to the ideology of laissez-faire, were unsympathetic to state funding and in tune with a rising tide of public hostility that condemned science as atheistic, immoral and authoritarian. There were doubts among scientists themselves about the wisdom of extending state support from capital expenditure (for buildings and equipment) to salaries and day-to-day expenses – with attendant government interference in the universities. The *English Mechanic* cast doubt on the integrity of its rival, *Nature*, publishing regular allegations against 'the endowment intrigue', which it depicted as the self-seeking clamour of 'pseudo-scientific men, [and] ... quacks'.[42] In more restrained language, establishment figures, such as the Astronomer Royal, Sir George Airy, supported the Society for Opposing the Endowment of Research, founded in 1880. The Royal Society was far from united in opinion and tried to maintain its distance. The uproar gradually subsided, and the 1890s witnessed a piecemeal resumption of private and governmental endowment, but there remained considerable scepticism, both in the universities and in industry, concerning the value of research and research training. In comparison particularly with Germany and the United States, Britain produced few science graduates and employed only a small minority of them in positions where they could use their education to the full.[43] The proponents of endowment could not yet lower their guard.[44]

Throughout the long campaign, the attribution of material benefit to scientific research and discovery was a major tactic. To a much greater degree than formerly, however, the role of the 'mere' inventor who lacked a scientific education was downplayed, even disparaged; the term 'applied science' threatened to overwhelm the use of 'invention'.[45] This rhetoric often chimed with that of the campaign to abolish the patent system, which shared a vested interest in debunking heroic accounts of invention.[46] Scientific witnesses before parliamentary commissions regularly seized the opportunity to link valuable inventions with scientific research, but now

---

[42] Ibid., 224.   [43] Ibid., 228.

[44] Sir Norman Lockyer, 'The influence of brain-power on history', *Nature*, 10 September 1903, 439–46; E. H. Griffiths, University College, Cardiff, letter in ibid., 28 December 1907, 12a.

[45] See below, pp. 365–8, 370. In 1855, George Wilson denounced the term 'applied science' as an otiose misnomer, 'a clumsy circumlocution for art or practice': *What is technology?*, pp. 4–6, 24–5.

[46] See above, pp. 265–71.

with a much greater emphasis on the latter's importance. Edward Frankland, a professor at the Royal College of Chemistry, told the Samuelson committee in 1867 that,

the [only] two great chemical inventions of this country during the last twenty years have been made by men who have been specially trained in chemistry. I mean the invention of the manufacture of paraffin from coal made by Mr Young ... and secondly, the invention of the manufacture of the aniline colours from coal tar ... by Mr Perkin.[47]

The committee's report endorsed the connection with a pithy comment that boded ill for the inventor as the man on the shop-floor: a scientific education would prevent 'costly and unphilosophical attempts at impossible inventions'.[48] This new image of the scientist-inventor was epitomized in the portrait of Sir William Perkin, commissioned by his fellow chemists from Sir Arthur Stockdale Cope to celebrate the golden jubilee of his invention of mauve dye in 1906 (figure 12.2). Cope showed the elderly Perkin standing at his bench, 'with a skein of mauve dyed silk in his hands'. Surrounded by coloured liquids in glass retorts and other accoutrements of the laboratory, the inventor displays the fruits of his scientific researches.[49] Many speakers at the jubilee ceremonies, including Perkin himself, emphasized the role of scientific research in the dyeing industry's 'marvellous growth'; Perkin paid especial tribute to Faraday.[50]

The presidential address to the British Association's annual conference was, to a considerable extent, the 'shop window' for British science. Time and again, eminent scientists used the occasion to proclaim the value of scientific research and education. Despite significant differences among them, particularly concerning the material benefits of 'pure' science, by the late nineteenth century they showed scant regard for independent inventors. When the Association celebrated its golden jubilee in 1881, the president was Sir John Lubbock, one of the luminaries of the X Club and the 'endowment of science' campaign. His exhaustive speech surveyed fifty years of progress in every branch of science.[51] When Lubbock turned

[47] *Report of the select committee on scientific instruction*, BPP 1867–8, XV, pp. 439–40.
[48] Ibid., p. 8. See also *Report of the royal commission on scientific instruction* (Devonshire), BPP 1872, XXV, pp. 625–6.
[49] *The Times*, 27 July 1906, 12c–e. See above, p. 246. Perkin bequeathed the portrait to the nation.
[50] *The Times*, 24 February 1906, 14a; 27 February 1906, 4e; 27 July 1906, 12c–e; see also 6 September 1906, 10c; 5 July 1907, 6d; 18 July 1907, 10c. For Faraday's symbolic role, see below, pp. 367–8.
[51] Sir John Lubbock, 'Presidential address', *BAAS, Report for 1881, York* (1882), p. 42. For Lubbock's views on science as the distinctive feature of 'civilized man', see McGee, 'Making up mind', 791–2.

12.2 *Sir William Henry Perkin* by Sir Arthur Stockdale Cope, 1906.
Commissioned by Perkin's fellow chemists to celebrate the golden
jubilee of his 'discovery' of the aniline dye, 'mauve', the portrait
depicts the elderly Perkin at his laboratory bench, holding a skein of
mauve silk.

to 'mechanical science', he appeared to take a traditional tack, asserting
that, 'to the progress in mechanics, we owe no small part of our advance
in practical civilization, and of the increase in our national prosperity
during the last fifty years'.[52] His list of the principal scientific advances
made since 1831 included the theories of evolution and the conservation
of energy, spectrum analysis, higher algebra and modern geometry; it also
encompassed '*the innumerable applications of science to practical life* – as, for

[52] Lubbock, 'Presidential address', p. 47.

instance, in photography, the locomotive engine, the electric telegraph, the spectroscope, and more recently the electric light and the telephone'.[53] Admission to the lofty heights of scientific progress required mechanics to cover up its dirty working clothes and not complain that too much was being claimed for 'science' to the neglect of practical skills and technical know-how.

Not everyone accepted the bargain. Indeed, the following year, the retreat from this advanced salient of science was sounded by William Siemens. Famed as a manufacturing engineer and prolific inventor, Siemens was dismissive of the contribution to practice of those he sardonically termed 'the high priests of science', who concentrated on research, distracted by no thoughts 'of utilitarianism and of self-interest'; still more, he berated 'the "rule of thumb" practitioner', who was guided more by instinct than by reason. From the workshop of a modern engineering firm, not a university laboratory, Siemens' perspective drew heavily on his own experience and eschewed the one-way process implied by the term 'applied science'.

It is to the man of science who also gives attention to practical questions, and to the practitioner who devotes part of his time to the prosecution of strictly scientific investigations, that we owe the rapid progress of the present day, both merging more and more into one class, that of pioneers in the domain of nature.[54]

This, for Siemens, provided the rationale of the British Association, in bringing together men of science from different disciplines and backgrounds; it was a faith illustrated in his memorial window in Westminster Abbey.[55]

Siemens, however, was in a minority among contemporary presidents of the British Association. Most were professors of science in the universities. Sir Lyon Playfair, in 1885, and Oliver Lodge, in 1891, both gave speeches that returned aggressively to a model that separated scientific research and its practical 'application'; moreover, to one that belittled the latter by presenting it as automatic.[56] Playfair, a long-term campaigner

---

[53] Ibid., pp. 50–1; emphasis added.
[54] C. William Siemens, 'Presidential address', *BAAS, Report for 1882, Southampton* (1883), p. 2. See also Engels' insightful comment, quoted in Lamb and Easton, *Multiple discovery*, p. 191, and Nathan Rosenberg's more recent challenge to the assumption by both scientists and economists of a uni-directional flow from science to technology: *Inside the black box*, pp. 141–59.
[55] See above, p. 326.
[56] In 1891, Lodge was president of the Mathematical and Physical Sciences Section; he was president of the British Association in 1913: Peter Rowlands, 'Lodge, Sir Oliver Joseph (1851–1940)', *ODNB*, online edn, May 2005, www.oxforddnb.com/view/article/34583, accessed 22 October 2006.

for government-funded scientific and technical education, contended
that the middle classes should be taught science, but not technology,
'because, when the seeds of science are sown, technics as its first fruit will
appear at the appointed time'.[57] He reiterated this point in another telling
metaphor: 'Industrial applications are but the overflowings of science
welling over from the fullness of its measure'.[58] Playfair was by no
means hostile to inventors – he spoke in glowing terms of the contribution
of Watt, Stephenson and the inventors of textile machinery to Britain's
wealth and imperial power – but he identified a looming threat to industrial competitiveness through the neglect of fundamental scientific
research. Scientific discovery and technical invention, he argued, had
different goals and required different qualities of mind. While the inventor might succeed in ignorance of science, said Playfair, 'his labours are
infinitely more productive when he understands the causes of the effects
he desires to produce'.[59] Conversely, the scientist should pursue his
research without the distraction of its immediate application, which
indeed was not necessarily the most important outcome of research: the
discoveries of Newton, for example, 'levelled many barriers to human
progress' less through their practical benefits than through 'the expansion
of the human intellect'.[60]

Lodge had even less time for 'practical applications', which he loftily
thought could 'be left to take care of themselves'. These were the mundane,
minor pickings, he said (quoting Huxley), the 'flotsam and jetsam of the tide
of investigation' that kept workers employed, capitalists wealthy and the
population as a whole contented; meanwhile, 'the crest of the wave of
scientific investigation is far away on its course over the illimitable oceans
of the unknown'.[61] Scientific research was an exciting adventure reserved

[57] Sir Lyon Playfair, 'Presidential address', *BAAS, Report for 1885, Aberdeen* (1886), p. 11;
Graeme J. N. Gooday, 'Playfair, Lyon, first Baron Playfair (1818–1898)', *ODNB*,
www.oxforddnb.com/view/article/22368, accessed 22 October 2006. Playfair had foreshadowed these remarks in 'The chemical principles involved in the manufactures of the
Exhibition', in *Lectures on the results of the Great Exhibition of 1851*, vol. I, pp. 190–1.

[58] Playfair, 'Presidential address', p. 23.

[59] Ibid., p. 23. For a similarly sympathetic speech by Frederick Bramwell, which, nonetheless, distinguished between 'the discovery and its application' and between the 'philosophical' mind and the 'ingenious' inventor, see above, p. 264.

[60] Ibid., pp. 26–8.

[61] Oliver Lodge, 'Address to Section A', *BAAS, 1891, Cardiff* (1892), pp. 550–1. This
passage from Huxley was often quoted: it clearly chimed with the self-image of late
nineteenth-century men of science. Lodge may have reflected on these words when he
was subsequently embroiled in patent disputes with Marconi: Sungook Hong, 'Marconi
and the Maxwellians: the origins of wireless telegraphy revisited', *T&C* 335 (1994),
717–49; Sungook Hong, *Wireless: from Marconi's black box to the audion* (Cambridge,
MA, and London: MIT Press, 2000); cf. Hugh G. J. Aitken, *Syntony and spark: the origins
of radio* (2nd edn, Princeton: Princeton University Press, 1985), pp. 25–6.

for an elite: most scientists were best suited to the supporting tasks that freed 'the advance guard ... to explore fresh territory'; inventors were beyond the pale.[62] Lodge's characterization of inventors as 'a multitude of small men ... jostling and scrambling' was particularly unflattering.[63] In 1909, Lodge (now principal of the University of Birmingham) tactfully conceded one exemption from this disdain, when he referred to Watt as not only 'one of the greatest scientific men of the world', but also as 'more than an inventor ... a creator'.[64]

Authors of obituaries in *The Times* were anonymous, but it would not be surprising if Lodge had penned that of fellow physicist, Lord Kelvin – certainly its author shared his prejudices. Kelvin, it said, had excelled both in 'the domains of scientific speculation ... [and, even more, in] applied science', for which he had been an unashamed apologist. Explicitly it disassociated him from the common inventor:

A prolific and successful inventor, [Kelvin] had nothing in common with that frequent class of patentees who are brimming over with ideas, all crude, most worthless, and only in occasional instances capable of being worked up into something valuable by men combining the requisite mechanical skill with an adequate knowledge of scientific first principles. Invention with him was not a mere blind groping in the dark, but a reasoned process leading to a definitely conceived end.[65]

The scientific politics of commemoration

The statue erected to Lord Kelvin by the city and University of Glasgow in 1913 is of a unique design. From the front, Kelvin, in his doctoral robes, his pen poised above a notebook, appears the very model of a university professor; his greatest inventions and technical achievements – the mariner's compass and a navigational sounding machine – are visible only from behind (figure 12.3).[66] This was out-of-step with recent statues to inventors, where their inventions were a prominent feature. Davy was regularly portrayed beside his safety lamp, and George Stephenson with his (or a locomotive); Elder's and Carmichael's statues boast their respective marine engines; Lister even used his monument to bolster his claim to the invention of wool-combing machinery.[67] In Belfast (his birthplace), Kelvin was portrayed in his academic robes, but

---

[62] Lodge, 'Address to Section A', p. 550.
[63] See above, p. 351. Similarly, Sir John Tyndall represented the relationship as one-way and the inventor as a parasite on scientific research: George Iles, *The inventor at work, with chapters on discovery* (London: Doubleday, Page & Co., 1906), p. 273.
[64] Boulton & Watt MSS, Timmins, vol. 2, fos. 59–60. See also Carnegie, *James Watt*, p. 37.
[65] *The Times*, 18 December 1907, 8c.   [66] McKenzie, *Public statues of Glasgow*, p. 229.
[67] See above, pp. 207, 310, 330, 333, 334.

12.3 *William Thomson, Lord Kelvin* by Archibald Macfarlane Shane, 1913, in Kelvingrove Park, Glasgow. Behind Kelvin's seated bronze figure, are represented his most famous inventions, including a mariner's compass and a navigational sounding machine.

with the mariner's compass prominently at his side.[68] None of these statues, however, was sponsored by professional scientists. Glasgow's unique relegation of Kelvin's inventions to the back hints at a compromise between the university scientists and the city fathers who were jointly responsible for his monument – indeed, that a powerful lobby may not have wanted his inventions to be noticed at all.[69] This can be no more than speculation, however, as the monument committee's

[68] *The Times*, 22 January 1908, 14c; 20 June 1913, 11e. Speakers at the inauguration of Belfast's statue seem to have been more concerned with his national and religious identity.

[69] The city's shipping interests evinced great gratitude for Kelvin's inventions, which was reflected in Principal MacAlister's speech, where he elevated Kelvin to a par with Watt, boasting that he 'domesticated electricity by his inventions – his meters, his dynamos, his recorders ... What did not the trade of Glasgow owe to the submarine cable?', in *Glasgow Herald*, 6 May 1908, in 'Minute Book of Lord Kelvin Memorial Fund', Glasgow City Archives, G4/1 (b), fo. 50.

minutes announce only the choice of design, intimating no such dispute.[70]

Certainly, some ambivalence in academic science's attitude to Kelvin's broad accomplishments is audible in A. J. Balfour's speech at the lunch that followed the statue's inauguration. Kelvin, said Balfour (then Gifford Lecturer at the University of Glasgow, during a break from politics), appeared to be 'a unique example of the association in the same mind of those practical instincts which enabled the *inventor on the one side* to make use of the speculation of *the man of science on the other*'. It was surely 'one of those felicitous coincidences which had never occurred before ... and probably was never likely to occur again'.[71] While indicative of the great physicist's intellectual prowess (and notable trophies for the utilitarian case), Kelvin's inventions muddied the argument for 'pure' research. Indeed, Balfour insisted, Kelvin 'never for one instant fell into the heresy of supposing that the business of a man of science is to develop our knowledge of the laws of nature consciously aiming at some practical result', but always impressed on his students that 'the man who pursues that knowledge must pursue it for itself'.[72] Balfour implied that others should not be expected to follow in this 'unique' man's footsteps or similarly to fund their own research by patenting any practical 'spin-offs'.[73] The 'endowment of science' rhetoric of the past three decades had emphasized that leading scientists should be allowed to pursue what is now termed 'blue sky' research – justified, one might say, by faith alone, not by good works.

Much more valuable for the campaign was Michael Faraday's research into electricity. As Sir Norman Lockyer proclaimed in 1903, 'Years ago we had Faraday apparently wasting his energies and time in playing with

---

[70] On 21 February 1910, the committee viewed three plaster cast models prepared by the sculptor, Archibald Macfarlane Shannan, and 'were unanimously of the opinion that the sitting model No 1 was the preferable one and it was accordingly adopted': ibid., G4/1 (b), fo. 70.

[71] *The Times*, 9 October 1913, 4a; emphases added. See Ruddock Mackay and H. C. G. Matthew, 'Balfour, Arthur James, first earl of Balfour (1848–1930)', *ODNB*, online edn, May 2006, www.oxforddnb.com/view/article/30553, accessed 22 October 2006; L. S. Jacyna, 'Science and the social order in the thought of A. J. Balfour', *Isis* 71 (1980), 24–5.

[72] *Glasgow Herald*, 9 October 1913, in 'Minute Book of Lord Kelvin Memorial Fund', Glasgow City Archives, G4/1 (b), fo. 87. The *Herald*'s leader writer echoed this judgement, as did *The Scotsman*'s, 9 October 1913, in ibid., fos. 88, 92.

[73] Cf. the obituary of Sir Charles Wheatstone, which moved easily between his research into electricity and his telegraphic inventions, referring at one point to 'scientific labours which, perhaps, have never been equalled in their extent, their variety, and their fruitfulness': *The Times*, 28 October 1875, 8a–c. Even closer in time, also undercutting Balfour's claim that Kelvin was 'unique', was Sir Joseph Swan, FRS, recipient in 1904 of the Royal Society's Hughes Medal: see below, p. 379.

needles; electricity now fills the world.'[74] Faraday's iconic value for the cause of 'pure' science had first been highlighted in 1874, by the barrister John Coryton. Savaging the patent system, Coryton believed Faraday typified the 'patient and unselfish workers' in scientific occupations responsible for 'discoveries of great principles'. Such men he regarded as the 'true improvers of our manufactures'; it was to them 'that the patentee is indebted for the invention of which he has obtained the exclusive use'. The abolition of the patent system, he contended, was essential to 'marshalling our scientific power' and employment of Faraday's successors where they would be most effective.[75] Six years later, the researcher's resentment against the patentee was voiced by an editorial in *The Times*:

Men of science have, perhaps, most reason to complain. What ingenious chemist has not seen his ideas utilized by others and become the basis of a lucrative patent? ... It is not wonderful that men of science grumble much at the patent law when they see it so often rewards, not the discoverer or the 'true and first inventor', but the copyist, imitator, or plagiarist.[76]

When the Davy-Faraday Research Laboratory, the gift of the innovative alkali manufacturer, Dr Ludwig Mond, was opened at the Royal Institution in 1896, *The Times* again emphasized society's and industry's indebtedness to scientific research. Mond's alkali works were 'a splendid example of applied science'; his generosity should be emulated by other men 'who in like manner have accumulated great wealth by the application of discoveries frequently, indeed we may say generally, made in the course of researches carried out by scientific workers who neither sought nor obtained great material reward'.[77]

   The emergent scientific profession became attuned to the symbolic value of commemorating its own figureheads. When Charles Darwin died in 1882 'a small but influential band' within the Royal Society overturned the family's plans to bury him in the local churchyard.[78] Rapidly pulling progressive clerical and political strings, they secured the Dean of

---

[74] Lockyer, 'Influence of brain power', 445. Similarly, *The Times*, 8 June 1891, 9b; and Ayrton's inaugural lecture as the University of London's first Professor of Technical Physics, in 1879, quoted in Graeme Gooday, 'Faraday reinvented: moral imagery and institutional icons in Victorian electrical engineering', *HT* 15 (1993), 196.

[75] Coryton, 'Policy of granting patents', 172, 183; see above, p. 267; also 'Review of H. Dircks, *Inventors and inventions*', *The Scientific Review, And Journal of the Inventors' Institute* 2 (2 September 1867), 308; W. R. Grove's testimony in *Report from the select committee on letters patent*, BPP 1871, X, p. 619; MacLeod and Tann, 'From engineer to scientist', 408–9.

[76] *The Times*, 19 March 1880, 9d.

[77] *The Times*, 23 December 1896, 7c–d; for the report of the opening, see ibid., 6b.

[78] Moore, 'Charles Darwin', 97–101.

Westminster's permission for his interment in the Abbey.[79] This intrusion of the body of Victorian Britain's most controversial man of science into the nation's most sacred site represented a triumph for 'an emerging hegemony of professional scientists, politicians, and progressive churchmen'.[80] This lobby's leadership overlapped with that of the 'endowment of science' campaign: it included Huxley, Galton, Lubbock and other members of the X Club and the Athenaeum. The same men gathered to establish an international memorial fund: it would commission a statue of Darwin for the great staircase in the Museum of Natural History at South Kensington and place a bronze medallion in Westminster Abbey.[81] Marking the centenary of Darwin's birth in 1909 (and fiftieth anniversary of the publication of *Origin of Species*), *The Times* endorsed the 'campaign's' success: 'he became in a peculiar degree the representative of his time; and it is his name that more than any other serves as a compendious general symbol of the scientific activities of the last century'.[82]

While the engineering profession glazed the north aisle of Westminster Abbey's nave, the scientists colonized its walls and floor with plaques to recently deceased colleagues. ('Like the poets and the statesmen, the men of science have their own place of rest in the Abbey – a corner set apart.')[83] Among them were the botanist, Joseph Hooker (an early supporter of Darwin), the mathematician and astronomer, John Couch Adams and the physicist, James Prescott Joule.[84] Other commemorations demonstrated a concern to resurrect and celebrate the memory of distinguished predecessors, thereby drawing attention to the 'trophies' of scientific research and authenticating a history of science. The transit of Venus in 1874 was marked (with a year's delay) by the unveiling of a plaque, under the aegis of the Royal Astronomical Society, to the memory of Jeremiah Horrocks; as a young Lancashire curate, Horrocks had correctly predicted the transit of 1639.[85]

[79] *The Times*, 27 April 1882, 5f. *The Times* downplayed any notion of a 'coup', remarking that Darwin was no longer a controversial figure and merited his place in the line of 'English deeds and intellect' that the Abbey recorded: *The Times*, 26 April 1882, 11f.
[80] Moore, 'Charles Darwin', 111.
[81] Ibid., 107–8; *The Times*, 3 July 1882, 4f; 16 May 1885, 11e; 10 June 1885, 9d–e, 10d–e.
[82] *The Times*, 12 February 1909, 11f. It was a view that finds support in contemporary surveys: Rose, *Intellectual life of the British working classes*, pp. 192–5. For the Darwin centenary celebrations, see Richmond, 'The 1909 Darwin celebration', 447–84.
[83] *The Times*, 24 December 1907, 4a.
[84] *The Times*, 12 December 1911, 11b; 16 December 1911, 11b; 22 January 1892, 6d; 22 February 1892, 10d; 18 October 1889, 8a; 23 January 1890, 8d.
[85] *The Times*, 4 December 1875, 7f. Bizarrely, the plaque was attached to the pedestal of the monument of John Conduitt, nephew of Sir Isaac Newton, which prompted a letter of protest: *The Times*, 7 December 1875, 11f. See also Wilbur Applebaum, 'Horrocks, Jeremiah (1618–1641)', *ODNB*, www.oxforddnb.com/view/article/13806, accessed 22 October 2006.

The scientists' success in belittling invention and inventors may be detected in the increasing substitution of the term 'applied science' for 'invention'. In 1885, *The Times* justified the International Inventions Exhibition: its function was 'not to bring together a mere collection of models of inventions, but rather to illustrate the progress which has been made in the practical application of science during the past twenty years'.[86] Benjamin Kidd similarly suppressed the inventor as he asserted that, 'Since the beginning of the century applied science has transformed the world.'[87] And 'scientists', according to a popular newspaper in 1897, were 'a race of men who have conquered time, space, air, fire, water, nature's deepest secrets'.[88] By 1941, when the physicist Sir Richard Gregory used the title *British scientists* for his popular biographical volume, which included famous engineers and inventors of the previous two centuries, the Victorians' image of the inventor as a working man had long been subsumed by that of the scientist.[89]

Ironically, the scientist was destined to become increasingly anonymous – just as W. S. Jevons had presciently forecast in 1874.[90] The installation of R&D (research and development) facilities, employing graduate scientists in pursuit of innovation, was already an identifiable trend in late nineteenth-century British industry; the First World War greatly accelerated it.[91] It reduced the visibility of the individual scientist at the same time as it pushed the independent inventor further to the periphery. In 1919, the economist, Alfred Marshall, dismissed the possibility that individuals would be able to provide the new 'methods and appliances' that were needed: 'many of these ... during the last decades,

[86] *The Times*, 13 August 1884, 2d.
[87] Benjamin Kidd, *Social evolution* (London: Macmillan, 1894), p. 6. For Kidd, see D. P. Crook, *Benjamin Kidd: portrait of a Social Darwinist* (Cambridge: Cambridge University Press, 1984); Collini, *Public moralists*, p. 87. See also Ronald Kline, 'Construing "technology" as "applied science": public rhetoric of scientists and engineers in the US, 1880–1945', *Isis* 86 (1995), 194–221.
[88] *The British Workman* (1897), quoted in Peter Broks, *Media science before the Great War* (Basingstoke: Macmillan and New York: St Martin's Press, 1996), p. 105. Interestingly, it flattered its readers by suggesting that the 'king of the coming age' would be the engineer – the shop-floor engineer, not the professional man. See also MacLeod and Tann, 'From engineer to scientist', 404–7.
[89] Richard Gregory, *British scientists* (London: W. Collins, 1941).
[90] W. Stanley Jevons, *The principles of science: a treatise on logic and scientific method*, 2 vols. (London: Macmillan & Co., 1874), vol. II, p. 217.
[91] D. E. H. Edgerton and S. M. Horrocks, 'British industrial research and development before 1945', *EHR* 47 (1994), 213–38; Michael Sanderson, *The universities and British industry, 1850–1970* (London: Routledge & Kegan Paul, 1972), passim.

have been the product of sustained research by large groups'.[92] Working systematically together, said the director of the Eastman-Kodak research laboratory, such researchers succeeded through 'the accumulation of facts and measurements'; they did not need 'the fire of genius'.[93] Independent inventors continued to make important breakthroughs, as a major 1950s study demonstrated, but their achievements (along with that study's conclusions) have tended to be ignored – their activities downgraded to the status of a 'hobby'.[94]

Indifference, anxiety, antipathy

The dawn of the twentieth century saw the profusion of a type of exercise scarcely conceivable a century before – forecasting future inventions. A title such as *Twentieth century inventions: a forecast* (1901) had no antecedents.[95] One of the most striking developments induced by rapid technological change was the expectation that the future would differ radically from the present, and there would be no let-up in that change.[96] 'As the nineteenth century draws to its close', remarked *Popular Science Magazine* in 1898, 'there is no slackening in that onward march of scientific discovery and invention which has been its chief characteristic.'[97] For the naturalist, Alfred Russel Wallace, the nineteenth century had been *The wonderful century* (1898). In his historical balance sheet, its

[92] Alfred Marshall, *Industry and trade* (London: Macmillan, 1919), p. 96. See also Otis T. Mason, *The origins of invention: a study of industry among primitive peoples* (Cambridge, MA, and London: MIT Press, 1895), p. 13; J. Fenwick Allen, *Some founders of the chemical industry: men to be remembered* (London and Manchester, 1906), pp. vii–viii. I am grateful to Thomas Jackson for lending me his copy of this work.

[93] C. E. K. Mees, *The organization of industrial scientific research* (1920), pp. 24–5, quoted in Reese V. Jenkins, *Images and enterprise: technology and the American photographic industry, 1839–1925* (London and Baltimore: Johns Hopkins Press, 1975), p. 309. See also Autumn Stanley, *Mothers and daughters of invention: notes for a revised history of technology* (Metuchen, NJ: Scarecrow Press, 1993), p. 769.

[94] John Jewkes, David Sawers and Richard Stillerman, *The sources of invention* (London: Macmillan, 1958), pp. 91–126; see below, pp. 393–4.

[95] George Sutherland, *Twentieth century inventions: a forecast* (London: Longmans, Green & Co., 1901). Compare I. F. Clarke, *The tale of the future, from the beginning to the present day: a check-list* (London: Library Association, 1961), pp. 20–1 with pp. 34–50.

[96] Asa Briggs, 'The 1890s: past, present and future in the headlines', in Asa Briggs and Daniel Snowman (eds.), *Fins de siècles: how centuries end, 1400–2000* (New Haven and London: Yale University Press, 1996), pp. 159–62. Briggs observes that the nineteenth century was 'the first century to be thought of by most people as possessing a number', and it was common to relate the century to 'the whole of history that had gone before it'.

[97] Quoted in John F. Kasson, *Civilizing the machine: technology and republican values in America, 1776–1900* (Harmondsworth: Penguin, 1977), p. 179. See also 'Britain a hundred years hence: a peep into 1997', *Tit-Bits*, 9 January 1897, 270, quoted in Broks, *Media science*, p. 106, and the works surveyed in Briggs, 'The 1890s', pp. 162–75.

successes outweighed its failures by a ratio of four to one: the successes consisted exclusively of major technological inventions and scientific discoveries. These, he believed, outnumbered all those made between the dawn of humanity and 1800. It was this material and intellectual progress that made the century 'wonderful' – despite its serious social and moral failings – and which indicated that it heralded 'the beginning of a new era of human progress'.[98] Similarly, the pictorial contrasts on the cover of *The Illustrated London News*' diamond jubilee edition – between steamship and sail (buffeted by the winds); locomotive/telegraph and stagecoach (in the snow); bright electric street-lighting and gloomy oil-lamps – defined the reign's achievements in terms of its technological prowess.[99]

A widespread sense of 'the vast and enormous difference between the present and the past' encouraged speculation about the future.[100] The literary genre of science fiction was born in the 1870s: it grew rapidly, from thirty fictional futures in that decade to nearly ninety in the 1890s.[101] Not all commentators were optimistic. Unsurprisingly, at a period which experienced escalating concern about the 'degeneration of the race', the turn of the century saw the publication of at least as many dystopias as utopias. Many books, whether science fiction or non-fiction, issued a dire prognostication of events that would ensue unless some urgent course of action were followed.[102] As Peter Broks has remarked, the scientist of popular fiction fared less well than his non-fiction counter-part; some of this negativity may have rubbed off onto the inventor with whom he was so closely associated. The scientist was often 'portrayed as, at best, unemotional and detached, and at worst, inhuman and insane'.[103] The ambivalence felt by many Victorians towards the pace of change – not to mention the hostility aroused by vivisection and compulsory vaccination – surfaced in dystopian science fiction. The dark underside of the 'benefactor' and the 'martyr' emerged in the

---

[98] Alfred Russel Wallace, *The wonderful century: its successes and failures* (London: Swan Sonnenschein, 1898), p. 2. See also Edward W. Byrn, *The progress of invention in the nineteenth century* (New York, 1900), cited in Kasson, *Civilizing the machine*, pp. 184–5.

[99] See above, figure 11.2. Knight drew similar contrasts (but between medieval and modern) on the cover of his *Popular history* volumes.

[100] [Pieter Harting], Dr Dioscorides [pseud.], *Anno domini 2071*, translated from the Dutch original, by Alex. V. W. Bikkers (London: William Tegg, 1871), p. 2. See also *The Times*' call for the study of history to maintain a proper perspective on the modern tendency – caused by the changes wrought by 'invention' – 'to think of our society as entirely different from all past societies': 8 April 1913, 9e.

[101] Clarke, *Tale of the future*, pp. 23–7, 34–44.

[102] Ibid., pp. 34–50; Briggs, 'The 1890s', pp. 166–8.

[103] Broks, *Media science*, pp. 41–2, 46–9.

monstrous creations of fictional scientists and inventors, from Shelley's Frankenstein to H. G. Wells' Dr Moreau.[104] While their activities were little understood, their power to effect change appeared enormous; it was a power over which the ordinary citizen felt he or she had little control. The socialist newspaper, *The Clarion*, which was sympathetic to both the anti-vivisectionist and anti-vaccination movements, expressed a cry of outraged powerlessness: 'Nothing remains to ordinary mortals than to surrender themselves blindly to the tender care of the scientists, and let them make of us whatever they will'.[105] Similar feelings permeated Frances Power Cobbe's darkly ironic *The age of science, a newspaper of the twentieth century by Merlin Nostrodamus* (1877).[106]

Anxieties concerning the military misappropriation of technology, which proved all too well-founded in 1914–18, were already surfacing in much late nineteenth-century fiction.[107] The inventor, pursuing his fascination for technical novelty without heed for its ultimate use or abuse, could be regarded as a dangerous, clever fool. W. Holt White's dire warning about air power, *The man who stole the earth* (1909), offers a prime example.[108] A 'weird' naive genius who has invented an airship, Joe Langley is the tool of Strong, an ambitious upper-class Englishman, who has the reckless bravery and foresight he lacks. Strong appropriates Langley's invention to defeat the other European powers and establish a benevolent dictatorship over the world; however, its appropriation for evil was equally plausible. On a more immediate, mundane level, there is no mistaking the hostility towards the inventor, as the selfish creator of unemployment, in a newspaper cartoon of 1912.[109] One panel, 'For the inventor fame', shows the inventor holding his mechanism and kneeling to be crowned with laurels, before a cheering crowd; the other, 'For the

---

[104] For *Frankenstein*, see above, pp. 54–8; H. G. Wells, *The island of Dr Moreau*, in *The works of H. G. Wells: Atlantic edition. Vol. 2*, (London: T. Fisher Unwin, 1924).

[105] Broks, *Media science*, p. 51.

[106] [Frances Power Cobbe], *The age of science, a newspaper of the twentieth century, by Merlin Nostrodamus* [1877].

[107] Clarke, *Tale of the future*, pp. 23–44; I. F. Clarke (ed.), *The tale of the next Great War, 1871–1914: fictions of future warfare and of battles still-to-come* (Liverpool: Liverpool University Press, 1995).

[108] William Edward Holt White, *The man who stole the earth* (London, 1909), pp. 23–5, 37–47. Langley had 'a pertinacious affection and blind faith of which only women and inventors are capable', p. 23. Misogyny is indeed a striking characteristic of much early science fiction.

[109] 'The Benefactor?', *Cassell's Saturday Journal*, 1 June 1912, repr. in Broks, *Media science*, p. 122. For the impact of technological change on various skilled trades, see P. L. Robertson and I. J. Alston, 'Technological change and the organization of work in capitalist firms', *EHR* 45 (1992), 330–49, and the essays in Royden Harrison and Jonathan Zeitlin (eds.), *Divisions of labour: skilled workers and technological change in nineteenth-century Britain* (Brighton: Harvester Press, 1985).

worker, poverty' depicts working men leaving their workplace for the last time – a notice on the wall announces that, 'Owing to the improvement of machinery, 1,000 less hands will be needed'.

Developments in science and technology reached the public through the new mass media; at the turn of the century, they occupied approximately ten per cent of the space in popular magazines and newspapers published monthly for a middle-class audience, four per cent in the more down-market weeklies.[110] The former showed a particular interest in technology (and natural history). Reflecting much scepticism concerning the public's capacity to understand theory, it was usually presented either as a series of curious facts or by reference to its material benefits: any unease about science was 'more than offset' by its presumed utility in daily life.[111] Such regular coverage contributed to the sense that technological progress was virtually automatic. As one popular publication commented in 1906, 'We have become so accustomed to hearing of new inventions that nowadays they hardly surprise us.'[112]

Already in 1885, the reporting of the international Inventions Exhibition suggests that the public was less impressed by displays of technology than in the heady days of 1851. *The Illustrated London News*, for example, which both in 1851 and 1862 devoted entire issues to reporting the Exhibition, allowed this event far less space; in August 1885, three months after its opening, readers were finally offered 'a glance round'.[113] Moreover, like the public, whose 'favourite recreation ground of London' 'the Inventories' had become, the magazine concentrated on the delights of the pleasure garden. It almost apologized for reporting the technical side of the exhibition:

it may occur to a serious-minded minority of the visitors ... that an Inventions Exhibition does not consist entirely of pleasure gardens, fountains, illuminations, bands of music, and 'the old London street'. The aims and the plan of the Exhibition are practical, utilitarian, industrial, and scientific.

Although it reported the latter aspects, its overwhelmingly light-hearted illustrations trivialized them. *The Times'* coverage was more serious but again relatively brief and matter-of-fact, except for a sympathetic editorial that expressed pleasure in witnessing 'a triumph of ingenuity'. Its regular report from the Exhibition concerned the number of visitors – an impressive three and three-quarter million in six months.[114]

---

[110] Broks, *Media science*, pp. 26–7.   [111] Ibid., pp. 35–40. See above, p. 357.
[112] *Cottager and Artisan* (1906), 11, quoted in Broks, *Media science*, p. 100.
[113] *ILN* 87 (8 August 1885), 139.
[114] *The Times*, 31 May 1884, 6b; 13 August 1884, 2d; 8 October 1884, 9e–f; 15 October 1884, 4a; 18 May 1885, 13a; 1 June 1885, 7f; 29 June 1885, 7c; 10 November 1885, 9e.

A tendency to take new inventions for granted was exacerbated by the liberalization of the patent laws in 1852 and again in 1883, which reduced a patent's initial cost to a sum affordable by most working men. With no official provision for examination (until 1905), this allowed the number of patents to soar: 'trivial' inventions were said to be overwhelming the system.[115] In this climate of over-production, inventors found it harder to maintain public curiosity and respect. The problem of success is captured by the technical journalist George Sutherland's complaint, in a work that was generally favourable to inventors (many of them were 'the heroes and statesmen of ... Civilization'):

Thousands of men, who imagine that they possess the inventive talent in a highly developed degree, are either crack-brained enthusiasts or else utterly unpractical men whose services would never be worth anything at all in the work of attacking difficult mechanical problems. It is in the task of discriminating between this class and the true inventors that many industrial organizers fail.[116]

Sutherland's complaint is oddly reminiscent of Babbage's and Brewster's, seventy years earlier: perhaps 'the projector' was always destined to dog the inventor's heels.[117]

At the same time, the celebration of inventors in 'Smilesean' literature had run its course (except for children). Through frequent repetition and their heavy moral message, tales of men who achieved fame and fortune through invention became hackneyed. With few exceptions, the subjects chosen were entirely predictable; Watt and Stephenson, in particular, were rarely absent. A reviewer of *Fortunes made in business*, a collective biography of successful businessmen, was pleasantly surprised by its substantially new material. He confessed to having opened it with a heavy heart, and when 'the old familiar names appeared on its pages, the sigh welled up at the thought of the wearisome drudgery involved in plodding through page after page of oft told tales'.[118]

A subtle shift in the publication of books about technology was in progress: the focus moved from inventor to invention, from man to machine. It is exemplified by two works edited by Robert Cochrane.

---

[115] Klaus Boehm and Aubrey Silberston, *The British patent system, 1. Administration* (Cambridge: Cambridge University Press, 1967), pp. 33–4; Khan and Sokoloff, 'Patent institutions', pp. 298–302; MacLeod *et al.*, 'Evaluating inventive activity', 542, 555–60.

[116] Sutherland, *Twentieth century inventions*, pp. viii–ix, 276–7. One sympathizes with a fellow historian's tones of faint despair at the numbers problem: Sydney George Checkland, *The rise of industrial society in England, 1815–1885* (London: Longmans, 1964), p. 95.

[117] See above, p. 353; also Pemberton, *James Watt of Soho and Heathfield*, pp. 14–31.

[118] *Textile Recorder* 1 (1884), 285.

His *Heroes of invention and discovery* (1879) and *The romance of industry and invention* (1896) cover similar ground, but the second abandons the first's biographical approach for a thematic one – by industry.[119] Perhaps, like the reviewer of *Fortunes made in business*, publishers recognized that 'this class of literature has been overdone'; or, maybe they identified a new market in the rising provision of technical education, which would demand a less biographical focus.[120] Another possibility is that more authors espoused a cumulative and co-operative model of invention. In the words of Robert Routledge, whose *Discoveries and inventions of the nineteenth century* offered a thematic, alphabetical compendium, 'great inventions are ever the outcome not of the labours of one but of a hundred minds'.[121] Even the heroically minded Cochrane admitted that 'every fresh labourer in the field adds some link to the chain of progress, and brings it nearer perfection'.[122]

Also symbolic of the conceptual shift away from heroic individuals was the redesign of *The inventor's almanac*. Under the ownership of Michael Henry, between 1859 and 1873, the names of inventors dominated both its overall design and its calendar, from which they ousted the traditional monarchs and saints.[123] When the *Almanac* was revived in 1879 (under new ownership), the design was radically different. The names, in much smaller print, were literally marginalized and, except for the calendar, all the tables of information had been excised. The space thus created was filled by twelve medallions each containing a precise engraving of an 'invention' – large-scale, up-to-date industrial and agricultural machinery, such as a steam plough, a lathe, a tram and – let it be said – a cannon. On the masthead was a dockside scene featuring ships (steam-powered and sailing vessels), cranes, a gasometer, a locomotive, a pithead and lighthouses; at the bottom, telegraphic equipment.[124]

If the publisher of *The inventor's almanac*, which was targeted at inventors, thought the machines more interesting than the men, what of books written for the general public? Despite academic critiques of the 'great man' approach to history, the Victorians' passion for heroic tales was generally

---

[119] See, however, Cochrane's identification of romance 'in the career of the inventor': *Romance of industry and invention*, preface. Neither did the biographical genre entirely disappear: for example, Allen, *Some founders of the chemical industry*.

[120] *Textile Recorder* 1 (1884), 285. See essays in Roy MacLeod (ed.), *Days of judgement* (Driffield: Nafferton, 1982), and in Robert Fox and Anna Guagnini (eds.), *Education, technology and industrial performance in Europe, 1850–1939* (Cambridge: Cambridge University Press, 1993).

[121] Robert Routledge, *Discoveries and inventions of the nineteenth century* [1890] (repr. London: Bracken Books, 1989), p. 445; Lamb and Easton, *Multiple discovery*, p. 26.

[122] Cochrane, *Romance of industry and invention*, preface.   [123] See above, pp. 258–9.

[124] *Inventor's almanac* (1879–80).

undimmed. Their interest was maintained, however, by accounts containing a higher quotient of adventure and suspense than even the most resilient inventor in the Smilesean mould could muster. Not only was the late-Victorian hero expected to face mortal danger, he should also be acting for a higher cause – whether the defence of empire, the rescue of endangered lives, or the saving of souls.[125] By comparison, the story of dogged perseverance that solved a knotty technical problem and culminated in worldly success was soporific. Worse, the stay-at-home 'inventor' paled beside his nearest rival, the 'scientist' constructed as a disinterested searcher after truth often employed on journeys of exploration to the ends of the earth.

So it proved in Hodder's compendious *Heroes of Britain in peace and war* (1878–80).[126] Physical courage alone did not make a hero. Hodder contrasted the thrill-seeking behaviour of acrobats and reckless adventurers with the true heroism of 'the man of science who risks his life in solving a problem that shall benefit all humanity … [and] the scientific explorer who sets before him some great object, having for its result a definite good, and to accomplish this, sacrifices comfort, health, it may be life itself'.[127] Not only did his category of 'scientific heroes' – 'explorers, chemists, electricians, aëronauts, physicians' – omit inventors, but explorers and other risk-takers could expect to steal the show every time.[128] In a chapter entitled 'The perils of scientific discovery', Sir James Simpson risks his life by experimenting with chloroform on himself, while Sir Humphry Davy goes 'into fiery mines fearlessly' to test his safety lamp.[129] Although Hodder noticed both Simpson and Davy for their inventions, he followed contemporary practice in defining them as 'scientists'. The chapter on 'Great engineers' similarly emphasized the physical perils to be overcome: it featured John Smeaton, who willingly faces danger to construct the Eddystone Lighthouse, and John Metcalf who courageously succeeds in spite of his blindness. More sensational still was Isambard Kingdom Brunel's narrow escape from the deluge of the Thames Tunnel: it was 'one of the most daring things in modern engineering'.[130] By contrast, the common-and-garden inventor's distance from such melodramas is epitomized in the bathetic opening to the chapter on 'Great inventors': 'There are phases of Heroism which are apt to be overlooked'. Hodder adopted the familiar trope of the inventor as a hero of peace, superior to even the most virtuous, self-sacrificing warrior in his contribution to national greatness.

---

[125] Broks, *Media science*, pp. 44–5.   [126] See above, p. 236.
[127] Hodder, *Heroes of Britain*, vol. I, p. 2.
[128] Ibid., vol. I, p. 11. See, however, vol. I, p. 13, where Hodder refers to 'the risks run by great inventors'.
[129] Ibid., pp. 84–102, esp. p. 91.   [130] Ibid., vol. II, pp. 34–50.

To follow in the path of duty, persevering in the face of difficulty, opposition, and prejudice, is more prosaic than to follow in the path of glory; and in some of the chapters of this work which, like the present, tell of the struggle and great works of men who only toiled patiently, wrought out ideas perseveringly, and endured opposition and disappointment calmly, if we find less of dramatic incident, we shall find that which is apt to be overlooked, but which is the strength and backbone of our nation – the Heroism of Duty.[131]

It scarcely promised to be the most exciting chapter, especially as it rehearsed the well-worn stories of Wedgwood, Watt, George Stephenson and (with slightly more originality) Rowland Hill.

The everyday dangers of the inventor's workshop or laboratory were unlikely to enhance his reputation – such accidents implied incompetence rather than bravery.[132] In the twentieth century they would become an aspect of the inventor's comic persona. Further evidence of the 'adventurous' model of heroism, which was beyond the inventor's reach, appears in Thomas Escott's contemporary survey of English life. In a romantic flourish, Escott lauded the heroic civil engineer who ventured abroad, after the manner of an explorer: the engineer 'who spans rocky defiles, pierces mountains, unites continents, and ... annihilates space and time' was allegedly the modern world's Hawkins, Raleigh or Drake.[133] Although engineers active after 1860 failed to capture the imagination of contemporary biographers or historians, they did enjoy some imperial limelight.[134]

Neither inventor nor engineer could compete for attention with the explorer – the quintessential hero of late nineteenth-century imperialism. Most celebrated of all was undoubtedly David Livingstone, who was portrayed as a hero of both 'science' and the protestant religion – a powerful combination of 'spiritual and secular hero' and 'the prime subject for an elevated interpretation of empire'.[135] Smiles was fascinated by this combination of values and, subsequent to Livingstone's death in

---

[131] Ibid., p. 143.

[132] The catastrophic but non-fatal explosions of the inventors' workshop are treated lightly, interspersed with the 'joy' and 'pleasurable anticipation' of invention, in Wirt Gerrare, *The warstock: a tale of tomorrow* (London: W. W. Greener, 1898), p. 3.

[133] Thomas Hay Sweet Escott, *England: its people, polity and pursuits* (rev. edn, London: Chapman and Hall, 1890), p. 555; see also Adas, *Machines as the measure of men*, p. 216. See above, pp. 23–4.

[134] Buchanan, *The engineers*, pp. 16–24; R. A. Buchanan, 'The lives of the engineers', *Industrial Archaeology Review* 11 (1988), 5–15. See also above, pp. 326–7.

[135] MacKenzie, 'Iconography of the exemplary life', pp. 94, 100. See also John M. MacKenzie, 'Heroic myths of empire', in John M. MacKenzie (ed.), *Popular imperialism and the military: 1850–1950* (Manchester: Manchester University Press, 1992), pp. 109–37; R. H. MacDonald, *The language of empire: myths and metaphors of popular imperialism, 1880–1918* (Manchester: Manchester University Press, 1994), esp. ch. 3.

1873, made his portrait the frontispiece of every edition of *Self-help*.[136] There could scarcely be a more telling symbol of the displacement of the inventor by the scientist-explorer. On the eve of the First World War, Antarctic exploration added two further national heroes to the pantheon of science: Robert Falcon Scott and Ernest Shackleton. News of the deaths of Scott and his team, cabled to London in February 1913, caused a national (and international) sensation and stimulated the production of numerous memorials.[137] Scott's heroism was claimed by many different, even conflicting, constituencies; in particular, he was made a martyr for science. *Nature* paid tribute: the expedition's members, who had been conducting a broad range of scientific research, had 'laid down their lives' in its pursuit.[138] Scott's 'martyrdom' (and the Great War) tended to overshadow Shackleton's greater feat of bringing all his men back alive, after the *Endurance* was trapped by Antarctic ice, but his heroism was prominently commemorated by a statue installed, in 1932, outside the Royal Geographical Society's headquarters in South Kensington.[139]

When receiving the Royal Society's prestigious Hughes Medal, in 1904, Sir Joseph Swan modestly conceded that, to a greater or lesser extent, 'the inventor uses the work of others'. In a telling simile, he proceeded to 'liken him to the man who essays the conquest of some virgin alp'. For much of the ascent he uses the steps made by his predecessors; 'it is only after the last footprints have died out that he takes ice-axe in hand and cuts the remaining steps, few or many, that lift him to the crowning height which is his goal'.[140] Swan's alpine simile expressed the excitement he felt for invention. Implicitly, it also recognized that the modern hero was not to be found in the workshop (or even the laboratory) but facing extreme physical danger in some distant corner of the earth.

Alternatively, he might be found in the air. The first decade of the twentieth century witnessed huge excitement surrounding the first flights in heavier-than-air machines.[141] Not all aeronauts were inventors, but the

---

[136] MacKenzie, 'Iconography of the exemplary life', p. 92.

[137] Jones, '"Our king upon his knees"', pp. 106–18.   [138] Quoted in ibid., p. 115.

[139] Ann Savours, 'Shackleton, Sir Ernest Henry (1874–1922)', *ODNB*, online edn, May 2006, www.oxforddnb.com/view/article/36034, accessed 22 October 2006.

[140] Swan and Swan, *Sir Joseph Wilson Swan*, p. 139. Swan remarked that seven of the eight Hughes Medals that year had been awarded for 'discovery', his alone was for 'invention': ibid., p. 137. One wonders whether Swan was aware of Tyndall's use of Alpine and mountaineering metaphors for Faraday's scientific achievements: Cantor, 'The scientist as hero', p. 177; Alice Jenkins, 'Spatial imagery in nineteenth-century science: Faraday and Tyndall', in Crosbie Smith and John Agar (eds.), *Making space for science: territorial themes in the shaping of knowledge* (Basingstoke: Macmillan, and New York: St Martin's Press, 1998), pp. 185–7.

[141] Darke, *Monument guide*, pp. 78, 141.

feats of the Wright brothers, in particular, associated displays of bravado with inventiveness. When Wilbur Wright was killed in 1912, *The Times* could scarcely have been more effusive. It praised him as an inventor who had triumphed through 'moral no less than intellectual qualities': he had combined great courage and perseverance with a reflective and intuitive empiricism. Through the 'laborious experiments' of the Wright brothers a viable machine had been created.[142] This respect for their methods chimed with the newspaper's call, the previous year, for a more 'scientific' approach to aviation. Deploring the public's fascination for 'the circus tricks and unnecessarily dangerous competitions', it looked to serious research on both machines and aerial conditions – 'laboratory work, tested by practical experiment' – to effect safer, more reliable flights.[143] However salutary such an approach, the Wright brothers were not the first inventors to discover that spectacle was the necessary precursor to commercial success as well as fame. Among their contemporaries, Thomas Edison notoriously demonstrated the value of transatlantic showmanship, while Guglielmo Marconi's earth-bound stunts, designed primarily to convince the Admiralty, won him the doting attention of the press.[144] Neither Josiah Wedgwood nor Matthew Boulton would have had much to learn from them about the manipulation of public opinion, but in their time this required the provision of nothing more spectacular than a London showroom.

In a final, ironic twist, the grand narrative of British industrialization that had carried forward the heroic reputations of Watt and his contemporaries began to transmute from an epic into a tragedy. At the point, in 1882, that Toynbee famously termed it (in English) 'the Industrial Revolution', negative interpretations were returning to predominance.[145] Toynbee himself depicted it in this vein:

[it was] a period as disastrous and as terrible as any through which a nation ever passed; disastrous and terrible because, side by side with a great increase in wealth was seen an enormous increase in pauperism ... and ... the degradation of a large body of producers.[146]

[142] *The Times*, 31 May 1912, 6c–d, 7c–d.   [143] *The Times*, 3 January 1911, 8a–c.

[144] 'The Hero of the Hour' (1889), in Robert Fox and Anna Guagnini, *Laboratories, work-shops, and sites: concepts and practices of research in industrial Europe, 1800–1914* (Berkeley, CA: Office for History of Science and Technology, University of California, 1999), p. 72; Anna Guagnini, 'Guglielmo Marconi, inventore e imprenditore', in Anna Guagnini and Giuliano Pancaldi (eds.), *Cento anni di radio: le radici dell'invenzione* (Torino: Edizione Seat, 1995) pp. 355–418; Robert Fox, 'Thomas Edison's Parisian campaign: incandescent lighting and the hidden face of technology transfer', *Annals of Science* 53 (1996), 157–93.

[145] See above, pp. 143–4.   [146] Toynbee, *Lectures on the industrial revolution*, p. 84.

Steam – still all-powerful – became again the anti-hero: the old order had been 'suddenly broken in pieces by the mighty blows of the steam engine and the powerloom'.[147] Equally culpable was laissez-faire in having abandoned the defenceless and demoralized worker to the mercy of unrestrained capitalism. Toynbee's perspective was shared not only by fellow radicals and socialists, such as the Hammonds and the Webbs, but also for the next half-century by 'historical economists' of all stripes who were sympathetic to tariff reform and hostile to the ahistorical theorizing of the neoclassicists, led by Alfred Marshall.[148] In a wider social context, their writings reflected the guilt-inducing recognition of the inequitable distribution of industrialization's material benefits that marked the end of Victoria's reign. The surveys of Booth and Rowntree, the findings of various royal commissions and a host of investigative journalists, the wretched condition of the army's rejects, all suggested that for the bulk of the population 'the Industrial Revolution *had not worked.*'[149]

A variety of pressures was thus leading to the disappearance of the heroic inventor at the turn of the twentieth century. It was essentially a problem of recruitment. The established heroes of invention, most of them stemming from the early industrial revolution – despite its perceived failings – retained their hold on the public's imagination, but few of those active since the mid-nineteenth century developed a reputation that was to withstand the test of time. A poll in the popular press, in 1907, to find 'Britain's greatest benefactor' produced a list headed by Darwin and containing four inventors in its 'top ten': Caxton, Watt, George Stephenson and Sir James Simpson (best known for his development of anaesthetics).[150] Simpson, who died in 1870, was the most recent, and probably the one least likely to be recognized today.[151] Almost

---

[147] Ibid., p. 31.

[148] Cannadine, 'The present and the past', 133–9; D. C. Coleman, *History and the economic past: an account of the rise and decline of economic history in Britain* (Oxford: Clarendon Press, 1987), pp. 37–62; Coleman, *Myth, history and the industrial revolution*, pp. 16–30.

[149] Cannadine, 'The present and the past', 134.

[150] Broks, *Media science*, p. 35. See also the Sheffield survey of 1918 in which recognition of Watt's name was outdistanced by Darwin's and Edison's – but not Oliver Lodge's: Rose, *Intellectual life of the British working classes*, pp. 190–6.

[151] Although Lord Kelvin's was a household name at the turn of the century – and 'to perhaps the majority of people he is known as an inventor' – his name is scarcely recognized today outside scientific circles: Professor Andrew Gray, *Good Words* (1900), p. 29, quoted in Broks, *Media science*, p. 43; see also ibid., pp. 43–4, 143 n. 11. Sir James Simpson's statue still looms over the west end of Princes Street, Edinburgh, and his image is to be found on the £100 notes issued by the Clydesdale Bank; previously it featured on the £20 notes.

certainly, if there had been such a poll fifty years earlier, Caxton, Watt and Stephenson would have been similarly placed; in a poll conducted nearly a century later, all three (and Darwin) still feature in the top hundred 'Great Britons'. The Victorians' heroes of invention have indeed been set in stone.

Epilogue: the Victorian legacy

Ancestor worship

The findings of a nationwide poll, conducted in 2002, testify to the British public's perpetual admiration of the Victorians' heroes of invention and engineering. Voted into the top hundred 'Great Britons' were Charles Babbage, Alexander Graham Bell, Isambard Kingdom Brunel, William Caxton, John Harrison, Edward Jenner, George Stephenson and James Watt, all of them active before 1900; their post-1900 successors were Sir Tim Berners-Lee, Sir Alexander Fleming, John Logie Baird, Alan Turing, Sir Barnes Wallis and Sir Frank Whittle. The score is eight to six, and the only one in the top ten is Brunel (notoriously, second to Sir Winston Churchill). This pre-1900 predominance runs counter to the poll's general outcome: fifty-two of the hundred 'Great Britons' belonged to the twentieth century – thirty-nine (including seventeen entertainers and four sportsmen) to its second half. Berners-Lee is contemporary invention's sole representative. Not even Sir James Dyson (despite his eponymous vacuum cleaner) or the 'test-tube baby' pioneers, Patrick Steptoe and Robert Edwards, found a place.[1]

Of the eight 'early' inventors and engineers, six were active between the mid-eighteenth and mid-nineteenth centuries; Bell was slightly later and Caxton much earlier. That result is entirely consistent with my argument. While the nineteenth century was exceptional in glorifying inventors and engineers, we have inherited its heroes, in particular through an account of the industrial revolution populated by an inventive elite. The phenomenon that Hugh Torrens dubs 'idolatry and ancestor worship' now colonizes popular bookshelves, television documentaries and the

---

[1] news.bbc.co.uk/1/hi/entertainment/tv_and_radio/2208671.stm, accessed 8 September 2006. Over 30,000 people responded to the poll in late 2001. An impressive nineteen 'heroes' came from 'the world of science, engineering, and invention', including three – Brunel, Darwin and Newton – in the top ten. Four of the five scientists were also active before 1900. Unsurprisingly, all nineteen were male, as were all but thirteen of the 100 'Great Britons'.

'heritage' trail of industrial museums and restored steam railways.[2] This is hardly surprising (and there is much to be said for it), since it is full of good stories and larger-than-life characters, of men who rose through their inventiveness and enterprise from cottage to castle, of others who failed to prosper because their ideas were stolen or ignored or were too far ahead of their time, of accidental discoveries, and of perseverance rewarded. In a country where much history of technology is written by engineers, who naturally tend to idolize their great predecessors, it has rarely been subjected to the prolonged critical scrutiny that it merits; it has resisted the best efforts of economic historians, on one side, and sociologists of technology, on the other, to cut it down to size.[3] The decline of economic and social history at secondary and tertiary levels is likely to promote this 'heroic' interpretation even further, as most students will encounter the industrial revolution, if at all, in relatively elementary texts and industrial museums, where the accurate recreation of past living conditions is unavoidably constrained by the commercial imperative not to disgust the visitors.[4]

To a large extent, these heroic reputations have been preserved in the same way that they were created, by interested local communities and professional associations. Some have never 'died'; others have been resurrected and refurbished. Locally, they have become part of the urban heritage, a community symbol. While used initially to help engender an identity that was simultaneously both modern (that is, technological) and venerable (that is, historical), more recently they have been promoted by the tourist industry and adopted as a commercial icon by local enterprises. Centenaries provide occasions for refreshing memory and reinforcing identity. In 1927, for example, Bolton commemorated the centenary of Samuel Crompton's death with a week-long series of events that included civic receptions, processions, concerts, exhibitions, conferences, a 'pilgrimage' to Crompton-related sites, a window-dressing competition and a pageant involving 3,500 children, who enacted the story of his invention and its significance, culminating in a specially composed

---

[2] Torrens, 'Some thoughts on the history of technology', 226–9. There is a related condition, identified by John Griffiths as 'Wattolatry', ibid., 226. For its transmission in documentary films of the interwar period, see Boon, 'Industrialisation and catastrophe', pp. 115–17.

[3] Cannadine, 'Engineering history', 167–70; Torrens, 'Some thoughts on the history of technology', 227–9. See also below, p. 388.

[4] Coleman, *History and the economic past*, pp. 1–3, 93–127; Bob West, 'The making of the English working past: a critical view of the Ironbridge Gorge Museum', in Robert Lumley (ed.), *The museum time machine: putting cultures on display* (London: Routledge, 1988), pp. 36–62; Tony Bennett, 'Museums and "the people"', in ibid., pp. 63–85; Torrens, 'Some thoughts on the history of technology', 229–30.

song that enjoined 'Ye men of Crompton's native town ... [to] sound his fame across the earth'.[5] It also involved the restoration of his statue, the naming of a new road after him, and new plaques to both him and Arkwright.[6] Two biographies were published, one by the curator of the local museum, the other under the auspices of Dobson & Barlow, the machine-making firm whose foremen had led the campaign for the statue. The town again paid its respects in 1953, the bicentenary of Crompton's birth.[7] Today, the well-maintained statue presides over a major shopping street, close to a pub called 'The Spinning Mule'; the Museum prominently displays its collection of Crompton artefacts, and Hall i' th' Wood, Crompton's childhood home, is open to the public. When the churchyard was flattened to make a car park, Crompton's grave was among the few preserved – an historical irony and tribute to the efforts of Gilbert French.[8]

The Cornish town of Camborne conserves the memory of Richard Trevithick even more actively. Every Christmas Eve, it celebrates 'Trevithick Day', a tradition invented in 1901 for the centenary of his road engine's eventful first run; for the bicentenary in 2001, a replica engine was built.[9] The Trevithick Society, founded in 1935, promotes the study of industrial history in Cornwall and jealously guards Trevithick's reputation. Presumably, it had a hand in the issue, in 2004, of a commemorative £2 coin and a set of postage stamps to mark the bicentenary of the first journey of a steam locomotive – Trevithick's Penydarren engine – though it ceded the ceremony to Merthyr Tydfil, where that journey began.[10]

The cities of Birmingham and Bristol were relatively slow to associate themselves with their great engineer-inventors but in recent years have made up for lost time.[11] In 1956, Birmingham City Council contributed £7,500 towards the cost of William Bloye's bronze 'Conversazione', which represents Watt, Boulton and William Murdoch discussing an engineering drawing.[12] A more unusual tribute to Watt followed in

<hr>

[5] The second verse echoed a nineteenth-century theme, made all the more poignant by the carnage of 1914–18: 'No hero, he, of glorious fight ... He gained a victory of peace': *Samuel Crompton Centenary, Bolton June 7th–10th 1927* (Bolton, 1927), p. 16; I am very grateful to Thomas Jackson for lending me his copy of this official souvenir booklet.

[6] Ibid., pp. 3–16; Crompton MSS, ZCR 90, and 102.

[7] Rose, 'Samuel Crompton', 12, 29 n.1.   [8] See above, pp. 298, 300.

[9] www.zawn.freeserve.co.uk/press.htm, accessed 23 December 2005. See above, p. 344.

[10] www.trevithick-society.org.uk/coin_stamps.htm, accessed 23 August 2006.

[11] Professional engineers, rather than the city, were responsible for the Watt centenary celebrations in Birmingham: MacLeod and Tann, 'From engineer to scientist', 394–5.

[12] In 1939, Richard Wheatley had bequeathed £8,000 to embellish the city centre: Noszlopy, *Public sculpture in Birmingham*, p. 16; Darke, *Monument guide*, p. 163.

13.1 *Wattilisk* by Vincent Woropay, 1988, at the corners of James Watt Street and Newton Street, Birmingham. Watt's features gradually emerge from the four surmounted blocks of black Indian granite (photograph by Caroline Williams).

1988, when Vincent Woropay's 'Wattilisk' was unveiled on the corner of Newton Street and James Watt Street (figure 13.1). Sculpted from black Indian granite, Watt's features gradually emerge as the four surmounted heads achieve an increasingly precise finish, alluding not to the steam engine but to the copying machines he invented.[13] In 1995, Soho House (once the home of Matthew Boulton) was restored and opened to the public.

It was thanks to private enthusiasts that the wreck of the ss *Great Britain* was towed back to Bristol (from the Falkland Islands) in 1970, 127 years

---

[13] Noszlopy, *Public sculpture in Birmingham*, pp. 94–5; Darke, *Monument guide*, p. 164.

to the day since her launching, and restored over the course of thirty-five years.[14] Now a major tourist attraction and worthy winner of the Gulbenkian prize for Britain's best museum of 2006, her return played an important role in Bristol's rediscovery of Isambard Kingdom Brunel, her architect and engineer. In 1982, the Bristol and West Building Society sponsored the city's first statue of him – and a second at Paddington station, unveiled on the same day.[15] Brunel's image is now so prominent that his name has been adopted by nearly thirty Bristolian organizations and commercial enterprises. The spectacular celebration of 'Brunel's 200th birthday' on 9 April 2006 – plus a year of exhibitions, conferences, concerts, new plays, school projects and a specially commissioned volume of essays – has knocked the relatively low-key events of 1959 (the centenary of his death) into a stove-pipe hat.[16] At a time when Bristol has begun to acknowledge its close historical links with the early transatlantic slave trade, Brunel offers a positive figurehead – by no means an inappropriate one – for a major centre of (aeronautical) engineering.

James Brindley owes his statuary resurrection to the revival of Britain's canal network for leisure purposes. His lack of a contemporary monument was corrected twice at the end of the twentieth century. One statue embellishes the junction of the Caldon and the Trent and Mersey Canals, at Etruria (Staffs.).[17] The second stands in the canal basin at Coventry, where a National Lottery grant of £1 million for the Coventry Canal corridor scheme included its commissioning from Warwickshire sculptor, James Butler.[18] In the 1960s, a discreet stone memorial to Thomas Telford was erected at Westerkirk, in the remote Scottish valley where he was born, both detailing his achievements and providing a resting place for walkers.[19] By contrast, recipient of the exceptional accolade of an eponymous new town, in the 1960s, Telford's name is spelled out in enormous letters in André Wallace's 1987 sculpture – part of the Shropshire town's programme of 'art as landmark'.[20] In a similar initiative ('Art in the Metro'), Newcastle upon Tyne commemorated the centenary of Charles Parsons' steam-turbine patent, in 1984, with 'Parsons' Polygon' by David Hamilton, an abstract design for a pavement

[14] Lambert, 'ss *Great Britain*', pp. 176–80.
[15] 'The Brunel statues', in Kelly and Kelly (eds.), *Brunel, in love with the impossible*, pp. 82–3.
[16] MacLeod, 'Nineteenth-century engineer', pp. 78–9.
[17] www.manchester2002-uk.com/celebs/engineers2.html. I have been unable to establish the name of the sculptor. This website is unusual in continuing the list of local celebrities in science and technology through to the present day.
[18] www.cwn.org.uk/arts/news/9809/980915-brindley-statue.htm, accessed 10 November 2006.
[19] Brian Bracegirdle and Patricia H. Miles, *Thomas Telford* (Newton Abbot: David & Charles, 1973).
[20] Darke, *Monument guide*, p. 146.

ventilator serving the city's metro.[21] Rather more grandly, ten years later, London Underground provided ventilation for its remodelled Bank station through a 4.5 metre-high statue, by James Butler, of a previously unsung Victorian hero of engineering, James Henry Greathead, who had developed the tunnelling shields used in the Underground's construction.[22]

Collectively and individually, the engineering profession has played an important role in preserving the memory of its predecessors. Following in Woodcroft's footsteps, the Birmingham engineer, George Tangye, not only presented his large collection of Watt, Boulton and Murdoch archives and artefacts to the city of Birmingham, in 1915, but conserved Watt's garret workshop at Heathfield Hall (where he lived) as it had been left by Watt in 1819.[23] Engineers attending the Watt centenary celebrations in Birmingham, in 1919, resolved to found a society to conserve the history of their profession. The Newcomen Society – the result of their deliberations – continues to provide a major focus for the history of technology in Britain, especially through its published *Transactions*.[24] Appropriately, one of its first activities was to endorse Dartmouth's commemoration of Thomas Newcomen. In 1934, the Junior Institution of Engineers commemorated its golden jubilee by installing a bronze tablet, at Lambeth North underground station in London, to the mark the site where the great nineteenth-century steam-engineering firm of Maudslay, Sons and Field had had its workshops.[25] Not to be outdone, in 1956 the chemical industry sponsored a lavish jamboree, its events suitably colour-coded, to celebrate the centenary of Perkin's discovery of 'mauve'.[26] And, in 2006, the Worshipful Company of Clockmakers secured a memorial to John Harrison (a familiar name again thanks to Dava Sobel's best-seller, *Longitude*) in Westminster Abbey.[27]

Just as places in search of a civic identity have been glad to burnish or restore their links with an established local hero of invention or engineering, so the emergent engineering and scientific professions of the late nineteenth century enthusiastically promoted iconic figures, who would rally their memberships and symbolize their claims to national

[21] Ibid., p. 231; Usherwood *et al.*, *Public sculpture of north-east England*, pp. 98–9.
[22] Ward-Jackson, *Public sculpture of the City of London*, pp. 84–6.
[23] *The Times*, 2 October 1912, 24f; *James Watt Centenary Commemoration* [programme], Birmingham, 1919. My thanks to Jennifer Tann for bringing this to my attention.
[24] Titley, 'Beginnings of the Society', p. 37; Cannadine, 'Engineering history', 104–7; see above, p. 341.
[25] *The Times*, 13 March 1935, 8f.
[26] Garfield, *Mauve*, pp. 168–76.
[27] Dava Sobel, 'Harrison memorial: Longitude hero's slow road to the abbey', *The Guardian*, 25 March 2006, 8; see above, p. 340.

recognition. As Simon Schaffer remarks, 'to share a cultural hero is a key part of belonging to the same cultural group'.[28] Once chosen, such a cultural hero is hard to dislodge: celebrating 'the founding father' becomes a ritual obeisance; to consider replacing him would be not only to contemplate symbolic patricide but also to risk civil war over the choice of his successor. Indeed, it is almost unthinkable: induction into any profession involves inculcation with its traditions and loyalties – being surrounded by portraits and busts of famous 'ancestors', competing for prizes that bear their names, attending dinners and conferences called to mark their anniversaries.[29] Hence, initial choices tend to be highly influential, and the expansion and professionalization of engineering that occurred in the late nineteenth century (coincident with the high point of Victorian hero-worship) has frozen in time Britain's technical pantheon.

Have inventors become extinct?

'The names of great inventors are less likely to be household words than the names of great scientists and artists. At least that is true for the inventors of this [twentieth] century.'[30] While an eighteenth- and early nineteenth-century elite remains extremely famous, its successors struggle for recognition, even for respect.[31] Nowadays, we take technological progress so much for granted that we no longer marvel at the creative talents behind the 'high-tech' products we use, perhaps we even forget that human ingenuity is the key ingredient. A billboard at London's Heathrow airport, in 2004, proudly proclaimed 'Scotland of Inventions', listing twenty-eight inventions with dates but no names (the most recent, '1997 single cell cloning'). Indeed, another advertising campaign played on the accustomed anonymity of inventors: how incredible, how weird, it implied, that the man or woman sitting next to you on the bus might have invented your

---

[28] Schaffer, 'Making up discovery', p. 48. See also Gooday, 'Faraday reinvented', 201–2; Miller, *Discovering water*, passim; Andrew Warwick, 'Cambridge mathematics and Cavendish physics', *Studies in History and Philosophy of Science* 23 (1992), 631–4.

[29] Schaffer, 'Making up discovery', pp. 18–23.

[30] Robert J. Weber and David N. Perkins (eds.), *Inventive minds: creativity in technology* (New York and Oxford: Oxford University Press, 1992), p. 330.

[31] Awareness of other inventors beyond this elite has been raised thanks, in particular, to the 'Local Heroes' series on BBC television in the 1990s, which is reflected in the beautifully illustrated book produced by its presenter: Hart-Davis, *Chain reactions*. It is noticeable, however, that the vast majority of them lived in the eighteenth and nineteenth centuries; the early twentieth-century additions are scientists, not inventors, seemingly chosen with a view to correcting (slightly) the gender imbalance.

390 Heroes of Invention

latest gadget – a real person![32] The problem is invisibility, not a shortage of scientific and technological achievements. The latter's profusion, ironically, is part of the problem: it is hard to keep track of even the minority reported in the national press, especially when individual names are often submerged beneath those of corporations and universities.[33]

Undoubtedly, the silence is not complete. As we have seen, the names of several twentieth-century British inventors are in common parlance and the profusion of knighthoods among them testifies to a high degree of public regard. Also, if some nineteenth-century forms of tribute – the portrait statue and the memorial window, in particular – are much rarer today, new ones have been introduced. Frank Whittle, for example, finally achieved great distinction, after a long, sometimes bitter struggle to persuade the Air Ministry to adopt his jet engine. Retiring from the RAF with the rank of air commodore in 1948, he had recently been knighted, elected to the Royal Society, and awarded £100,000 by the Royal Commission on Awards to Inventors. A stream of honours culminated in the Order of Merit in 1986.[34] His biography appears in books and on film, and his invention is featured on a set of British postage stamps.[35] Near his birthplace, in Coventry, is to be found the Sir Frank Whittle Jet Heritage Centre, and 2001 saw Coventry University name an engineering building after him.[36] There are many parallels here with the way that Bessemer, Siemens, Perkin or Kelvin were honoured in the quarter century before 1914, but film and commemorative stamps are new media that probably reach wider audiences.

Barnes Wallis, also recognized by the Royal Society and the Royal Commission on Awards to Inventors, finally received his knighthood in 1968 (having twice been denied it for political reasons).[37] Meanwhile, *The dam busters* (1954) enthralled British filmgoers with Wallis' invention of the dam-busting, 'bouncing' bombs, deployed in the RAF's raids designed to cripple Nazi Germany's steel industry. 'The heroic and

[32] Scotland Development International, 2004; Hewlett Packard, 2002.
[33] For an attempt to lift the veil on the latter, see *Eureka UK – 100 discoveries and developments in UK universities that have changed the world* (Universities UK, 2006).
[34] G. B. R. Feilden, 'Whittle, Sir Frank (1907–1996)', *ODNB*, www.oxforddnb.com/view/article/67854, accessed 7 September 2006.
[35] Ibid.; Ken Peters, *Inventors on stamps* (Seaford, E. Sussex: Aptimage Ltd, 1985), pp. 79, 100–3. Another postage stamp was issued on 15 May 1991 to mark the fiftieth anniversary of the Whittle engine's first flight, and a commemorative certificate by Rolls Royce and Esso: Whittle MSS, 205/7–8, Institution of Mechanical Engineers.
[36] www.cwn.org.uk/education/coventry-university/2001, accessed 7 September 2006. Aeronautical engineers have paid similar tributes to F. W. Lanchester: P. W. Kingsford, *F. W. Lanchester: a life of an engineer* (London: Edward Arnold, 1960), p. 236.
[37] Robin Higham, 'Wallis, Sir Barnes Neville (1887–1979), *ODNB*, www.oxforddnb.com/view/article/31795, accessed 7 September 2006.

hagiographic aspects of Brickhill's book were carried over into the film, and Michael Redgrave's representation of Wallis as the much misunderstood genius ... subsequently became ever more part of Wallis's public persona.'[38]

By contrast, it has taken half a century for the achievements of Alan Turing to receive public recognition, but the present-day prominence of computing technologies combined with diminishing homophobia have facilitated his commemoration, primarily in academic circles. Since 2001, statues to Turing have been inaugurated at the Universities of Manchester and Surrey and a mathematical research institute named for him at the former. Many subscribers to the Manchester memorial specifically cited their gratitude to Turing for his wartime role in breaking the German Navy's Enigma codes.[39]

The race for honours and celebrity had been easily won, however, by the bacteriologist and Nobel laureate, Alexander Fleming. Fleming shot to fame in the early 1940s, with the press trumpeting the story of his 'discovery' of penicillin as a piece of patriotic, even providential, good news during the hardships and uncertainties of war. Thereafter, penicillin 'stood as an icon for post-war reconstruction, improving welfare, and modernization' and Fleming 'toured the world as a modern hero ... further prizes were awarded, honorary degrees by the dozen were conferred, statues were unveiled, freedom of cities granted, and streets named in his honour'.[40]

It is not hard to explain why these three twentieth-century inventors have enjoyed exceptional national (and international) honours, popular celebrity and posthumous fame.[41] First, they belonged to professions that nurtured their reputations for invention and innovation: Whittle and Wallis were engineers, Fleming a medical scientist. Although usually portrayed as isolated, heroic 'loners', ultimately they received the support of powerful colleagues and institutions who, from either loyalty or self-interest, groomed their reputations through prestigious awards,

---

[38] Ibid.; Paul Brickhill, *The dam busters* (London: Evans Bros., 1951). For the 'Dambusters' first-day cover, some bearing Wallis' autograph, see Peters, *Inventors on stamps*, p. 73.

[39] Dennis A. Hejhal, 'Turing: a bit off the beaten path', *The Mathematical Intelligencer*, 29 (2007), 27–35.

[40] Michael Warboys, 'Fleming, Sir Alexander (1881–1955)', *ODNB*, www.oxforddnb. com/view/article/33163, accessed 7 September 2006; Warboys lists four bronze busts, all in London institutions, including the National Portrait Gallery, but no full-length statues.

[41] Although Fleming is often described as a 'discoverer', I deem him equally an 'inventor', since the immediate outcome of his observation was a new product, the drug 'penicillin'; initially, indeed, he misunderstood the nature of the mould that had contaminated his petri dish.

hagiographic accounts on paper and celluloid and partisan letters to *The Times*.[42] Secondly, like the inventors of the Industrial Revolution, they belong to a grand narrative in modern British history, the Second World War and Britain's heroic defeat of Nazi Germany. Within that narrative, each can be cast in the familiar romantic and heroic genre of the lone inventor who struggles against all the odds to bring the great, war-winning invention to fruition. If Whittle and Wallis were the twentieth-century's Watt and Armstrong, Fleming was its Jenner, and any obdurate bureaucrat who might frustrate their genius was the reincarnation of Dickens' Circumlocution Office.

The explanation, however, does not stop there. Whittle and Fleming, in particular, play a role in other popular narratives, not least that which Robert Bud has termed 'defiant modernism', a strand of 'declinist' thought that mixes national pride in technical prowess with bitterness over loss of empire and cession of international leadership to the United States: at best, through lack of enterprise Britain squandered its inventive brilliance; at worst, '"we" had been robbed'. In the case of penicillin, while the pioneering work of Fleming and of Howard Florey and Ernst Chain's team, at Oxford, brought them the Nobel prize for medicine in 1945, it was to the American firms, which had solved how to scale up production, that enormous profits were to flow.[43] Bud has perceptively analysed the multiple facets of Fleming's iconic postwar status, demonstrating that it rested on much more than appreciation of a major medical advance:

The story was full of ambiguities and contradictions through which the complex new world could be interpreted. With its complicated scientific origins it served to bring together accounts of the role of the scientist, as individual and team member, of modernization in attitudes to patents, the functions of the state, industry and academe, the needs of a new industry, the ambiguous role of the United States and the running of the proud new Health Service.[44]

Of particular interest here is the issue of the inventor's (or scientist's) identity: was he an individual or a member of a team? Had the nature of invention changed dramatically with the new century? Michael Warboys regrets that 'the Fleming myth', of a lone scientist making a chance discovery that led to the conquest of infectious diseases, was an unhelpful representation of the scientific enterprise in the post-1945 world of 'big

---

[42] Bud, 'Penicillin and the new Elizabethans', 321–33; Feilden, 'Whittle, Sir Frank'; Higham, 'Wallis, Sir Barnes Neville'.

[43] Bud, 'Penicillin and the new Elizabethans', 312–21.

[44] Ibid., 314. Compare the interpretations in 1956 of Perkin's discovery of 'mauve': Garfield, *Mauve*, pp. 168–76.

science'. For, it is a myth that prevails at the expense of the Oxford team, whose methodical research on penicillin had reached the stage of clinical trials, before Fleming claimed priority for his earlier but abandoned 'discovery'.[45] Yet, while reasonable in this instance, from a wider perspective it is hard to see the force of Warboys' complaint. The fame of Fleming, Whittle and the few other recognizable twentieth-century names never seems to impinge on the truism that the independent inventor is an extinct species – now, as in postwar Britain.[46] Already by the 1950s, it was a commonplace that 'science', or the R&D laboratories of large firms, had replaced the lone individual, with the result that modern innovation was more efficient, indeed almost automatic – a view endorsed by such influential authorities as J. K. Galbraith and J. D. Bernal.[47] Neither was this belief apparently dented by the result of Jewkes, Sawers and Stillerman's careful analysis of sixty-one major inventions made since 1900:

More than one-half of the cases can be ranked as individual invention in the sense that much of the pioneering work was carried through by men who were working on their own behalf without the backing of research institutions and usually with limited resources and assistance or, where the inventors were employed in institutions [such as universities] ... the individuals were autonomous, free to follow their own ideas without hindrance.[48]

Jewkes and his team were contesting several decades of weighty sociological opinion, that inventions and discoveries were generally multiple phenomena, occurring simultaneously in a number of places, and new technologies were no more than an accumulation of many small, incremental steps.[49] Such deterministic accounts of technological change left little scope for individuals to play an important – let alone a heroic – role. Neither did such accounts explore in depth the other side of these findings – that most modern innovations are ultimately collaborative. Although individual insights play an important (often instigating) role, modern technologies are usually too complex and the facilities required

---

[45] Warboys, 'Fleming, Sir Alexander'. Warboys refers to 'what Fleming himself called the Fleming myth'. See also Bud, 'Penicillin and the new Elizabethans', 332, for contrasting plaques!

[46] Whether Dyson or Berners-Lee will fare any better in shifting the consensus remains to be seen.

[47] Jewkes, Sawers and Stillerman, *Sources of invention*, pp. 29–32. While they quote other authorities who insisted that the day of the independent inventor 'is not past by any means', most of these explicitly commented that they were contradicting a truism: ibid., pp. 91–3.

[48] Ibid., p. 82. For further definition of the 'individual inventor' and reflections on the complexity of the question, see ibid., pp. 93–115.

[49] McGee, 'Making up mind', 773–801.

too expensive to allow a single inventor to proceed very far unaided by others' knowledge, skills or finance.[50]

Significantly, Jewkes, Sawers and Stillerman's findings were published as dry 'case histories', analysed in an academic monograph, not as romantic tales for a popular audience, which once would have enjoyed hearing biographical accounts of the invention of everything from the helicopter to the zip, from 'Bakelite' to automatic transmissions.[51] While a few 'Smilesean' volumes still found a publisher, the twentieth-century market was limited principally to children's books – targeted, of course, mostly at boys.[52] This is not the place to challenge the common misapprehension that women do not (even cannot) invent: others have already done an excellent job.[53] It is worth remarking, however, that female inventors still face a double hurdle for recognition – as independent inventors and as female ones. Excluded by gender from the Victorians' pantheon (including the *Dictionary of National Biography* (1885–1900), which scarcely found a niche for *any* non-royal woman), they now suffer – to a greater extent – the fate of the male independent inventor, of whose very existence, if not sanity, the public is highly sceptical.[54]

While much interwar inventive activity disappeared into corporate research laboratories, the independent inventor, busy in 'his' quintessential garage or garden shed, acquired a reputation for ineffective eccentricity. It was a development of the Edwardians' lack of faith in the inventor's commercial instincts, from which Swan and others had reportedly suffered.[55] Reinforcing it, from the 1920s, the cartoons of William Heath Robinson portrayed the inventor as a benign, ridiculous obsessive; 'Heath-Robinson' became the by-word for ingenious but complex interweavings of everyday objects to achieve a simple, banal purpose. In 1933, Heath Robinson illustrated *The incredible adventures of Professor Branestawm*, the first of a series of books for children by Norman Hunter, in which the absent-minded professor's weird inventions lead him into bizarre adventures. In similar (but corporate) vein, *The man in the white suit*, a film comedy produced in 1951, starred Alec Guinness as a

[50] Jewkes, Sawers and Stillerman, *Sources of invention*, pp. 108–19, 127–96; James Bessen, 'Where have the great inventors gone?' Research on Innovation Working Paper no. 0402 (2004), www.researchoninnovation.org/GreatInventors.pdf
[51] Jewkes, Sawers and Stillerman, *Sources of invention*, pp. 71–126, 263–410.
[52] For example, J. G. Crowther, *Six great inventors: Watt, Stephenson, Edison, Marconi, Wright Brothers, Whittle* (London: Hamish Hamilton, 1954).
[53] Stanley, *Mothers and daughters of invention*, passim; McGaw, 'Inventors and other great women', 214–31.
[54] MacLeod and Nuvolari, 'Pitfalls of prosopography', 764, 770; McDaniel *et al.*, 'Mothers of invention?', 1–12.
[55] See above, p. 338.

naïve inventor in the R&D laboratory of a textile company, the product of whose ingenuity (an indestructible fabric) threatens his employers with commercial disaster and their equally hostile workers with unemployment.[56]

A case for iconoclasm?

Does it matter that our pantheon of inventors is essentially that bequeathed us by the Victorians? Indeed, isn't it in the nature of all pantheons – if not popular polls – that time is the necessary judge of more recent candidates? Why shouldn't we still celebrate the heroes of the Industrial Revolution, who breached the aristocratic and militaristic citadel? And appreciate their relatively strong representation in the 'Great Britons' poll (2002) as a riposte to the shibboleth that British culture is both profoundly antagonistic to science and technology and historically ill-informed?

More pessimistically, the question always arises whether these Victorian heroes' unshakable hold on our notions of invention – in default of a strong twentieth-century challenge – might be symptomatic of Britain's subsequent decline. We might also wish to consider whether there could be a causal link with the faltering interest of twenty-first-century students in gaining scientific qualifications and careers.[57] Do these outmoded inventors fail to convey the excitement of working at the forefront of today's science and technology? In particular, how far might these alpha males of the noisy, dirty Victorian workshop deter young women from pursuing a career in these fields?

There can be no short and simple answer to such hard-fought and little-researched debates. It has been my purpose to explain why a small band of eighteenth- and nineteenth-century inventors looms so large in our national memory and shapes the way we think about technological change. I hope this book will assist historians in deconstructing some of the myths that surround the heroes of invention and encourage others to approach the history of technology from different angles. I also hope it will contribute to a critical understanding of 'declinism', by exonerating the Victorians from the charge of denigrating or betraying their inventors and engineers. Not only were the Victorians exceptionally active and sincere in their glorification of inventors, but they were responsible for

---

[56] en.wikipedia.org/wiki/Professor_Branestawm, accessed 7 November 2006. See also above, p. 5, n. 9 and p. 373. David Edgerton, *The shock of the old: technology and global history since 1900* (London: Profile Books, 2006).

[57] *Observer*, 5 November 2006, 3.

effecting the long-needed reform of the patent system in 1852 and again in 1883, to the great benefit of inventors. If the British economy did sow the seeds of decline in the late nineteenth century (and much recent research suggests otherwise), it was certainly not because the bourgeoisie failed to appreciate its own industrial achievements.

As for presenting the history of technology, there will always be a dilemma, a choice between the familiar, heroic story full of human interest, which readily captures the attention of students, viewers and museum visitors, and the more accurate representation of invention that, at the risk of forfeiting it, makes a simple story more complex and reintroduces a larger cast of assistants, collaborators and competitors – not to mention consumers, operators and objectors – and an explanatory framework that encompasses wider political and cultural developments. Reducing the 'human interest' would undoubtedly be disastrous, leading to a major loss of interest among the many people drawn to history precisely because it is one of the *humanities*. Fortunately, however, a bland, deterministic account of invention is no longer the real alternative to heroic history, as it threatened to be for much of the twentieth century.[58] The kaleidoscope of research into the history of technology (pursued in British universities and museums in many different disciplinary guises and beyond their walls by independent scholars) offers a much richer diet of topics than the traditional focus on invention and the hardware of the industrial revolution may suggest. It offers new perspectives on the multiplicity of ways that technology affects the lives of ordinary people, both positively and negatively, in the kitchen or bedroom, internet café or night-club, as much as in the workplace, on the road, or under the flight-path. The challenge for historians is to persuade students that it can be an exciting and important subject even if they are not among the more technically adept.[59]

The Victorian age was exceptional in witnessing a brief interlude in British history when the inventor was a popular hero. However sophisticated our theories and however extensive our knowledge of the history of technology might be, it is often hard to escape that formidable legacy with its stereotype of the great inventor. Recognizing its hold on our imaginations is the first step to subverting it.

---

[58] For the demise of the 'Mertonian programme', see Schaffer, 'Making up discovery', pp. 31–6.

[59] Graeme Gooday, 'The flourishing of history of technology in the United Kingdom: a critique of antiquarian complaints of "neglect"', *HT* 22 (2000), 189–201; David Edgerton, 'Reflections on the history of technology in Britain', ibid., 181–7; David Edgerton, 'From innovation to use: ten (eclectic) theses on the history of technology', *History and Technology* 16 (1999), 1–26.

Bibliography

Unpublished manuscripts

Additional MSS, British Library, London
Admiralty MSS, National Archives, Kew
Board of Works MSS, National Archives, Kew
Boulton & Watt MSS, Birmingham City Archives
Brougham MSS, University College London
Brunel MSS, Bristol University Library
Crompton MSS, Bolton District Archives
Glasgow University Archives
Hatherton MSS, Staffordshire County Record Office
H-GOV 27(1), Glasgow City Archives
Institution MSS, Institution of Mechanical Engineers, London
Memoirs of John McKie, MS Acc 3420, National Library of Scotland, Edinburgh
National Portrait Gallery Archives, London
Oxford University Museum Archives
Public petitions, House of Lords Records Office, London
Science Museum MSS, Science Museum, London
James Watt MSS, Birmingham City Archives
Watt Centenary MSS, Birmingham City Archives
Whittle MSS, Institution of Mechanical Engineers, London
Woodcroft MSS, Science Museum Library, London

Official publications

Report from the select committee appointed to inquire into the present state of the law and practice relative to the granting of patents for invention, BPP 1829, III
Report from the select committee on Fourdrinier's patent, BPP 1837, XX
Report from the select committee of the House of Lords to consider the bill intituled 'An act further to amend the law touching letters patent for inventions'; and the bill, intituled, 'An act for the further amendment of the law touching letters patent for invention', BPP 1851, XVIII
Report of the select committee on the Patent Office Library and Museum, BPP 1864, XII

Report of the commissioners appointed to inquire into the working of the law relating to letters patent for inventions, BPP 1864, XXIX

Report of the select committee on scientific instruction (Samuelson), BPP 1867–8, XV

Reports on the Paris Universal Exhibition, BPP 1867–8, XXX

Report from the select committee on letters patent, BPP 1871, X

Report of the royal commission on scientific instruction (Devonshire), BPP 1872, XXV

Hansard, T. C. (ed.), *Parliamentary Debates* (London: T. C. Hansard, 1803–1920)

Newspapers and journals

Birmingham Chronicle
Birmingham Gazette
Bolton Chronicle
Bolton Guardian
British Medical Journal
The Builder
The Chemist
Cobbett's Political Register
Cornish Telegraph
The Economist
Edinburgh Review
The Engineer
Engineering
European Magazine
Gentleman's Magazine
Glasgow Chronicle
Glasgow Herald
Glasgow Mechanics' Magazine
The Graphic
The Illustrated London News
Journal of the Society of Arts
Manchester Guardian
Mechanical Engineer
Mechanic's Magazine
Monthly Magazine, or British Register
Morning Chronicle
Proceedings of the Institution of Mechanical Engineers
Punch
Railway Magazine
Scientific Review, and Journal of the Inventors' Institute
The Scotsman
The Spectator
Sunday Times
The Times
Textile Manufacturer
Textile Recorder
The Working Man: a weekly record of social and industrial progress

Books and articles

Abir-Am, Pnina G., 'Essay review: how scientists view their heroes: some remarks on the mechanism of myth construction', *Journal of the History of Biology* 15 (1982), 281–315

Abir-Am, Pnina G., and Eliot, C. A. (eds.), *Commemorative practices in science*, *Osiris* 14 (2000), 1–14

Abrams, M. H., *The mirror and the lamp: romantic theory and the critical tradition* (New York: Oxford University Press, 1953)

Acland, Henry W., and Ruskin, John, *The Oxford Museum* (3rd edn, London and Orpington: George Allen, 1893)

Adas, Michael, *Machines as the measure of men: science, technology, and ideologies of western dominance* (Ithaca: Cornell University Press, 1989)

Agar, Jon, 'Technology and British cartoonists in the twentieth century', *TNS* 74 (2004), 181–96

Agulhon, Maurice, 'Politics, images, and symbols in post-Revolutionary France', in Sean Wilentz (ed.), *Rites of power: symbolism, ritual and politics since the Middle Ages* (Philadelphia: University of Pennsylvania Press, 1985), pp. 177–205

Aikin, John, *A description of the country from thirty to forty miles around Manchester* (London, 1795, repr. Newton Abbot: David & Charles, 1968)

Aikin, John, and Enfield, Rev. William (eds.), *General biography; or lives, critical and historical, of the most eminent persons of all ages, countries, conditions, and professions* (London: G. G and J. Robinson, and Edinburgh: Bell and Badfute, 1799–1815), vol. I

Aitken, Hugh G. J., *Syntony and spark: the origins of radio* (2nd edn, Princeton: Princeton University Press, 1985)

Alison, Sir Archibald, 1st Bart., *History of Europe during the French Revolution* (Edinburgh: William Blackwood; London: T. Cadell, 1833–42), vol. VIII

[Alison, Sir Archibald], 'Free trade and protection', *Blackwood's* 55 (1844), 385–400

Allan, D. G. C., *William Shipley, founder of the Royal Society of Arts* (London: Hutchinson, 1968)

Allen, J. Fenwick, *Some founders of the chemical industry: men to be remembered* (London and Manchester, 1906)

Allen, Robert C., 'Britain's economic ascendancy in a European context', in Leandro Prados de la Escosura (ed.), *Exceptionalism and industrialisation: Britain and its European rivals, 1688–1815* (Cambridge: Cambridge University Press, 2004), pp. 15–35

Altick, Richard D., *The English common reader: a social history of the mass reading public, 1800–1900* (Chicago: University of Chicago Press, 1957)

Anderson, Adam, *An historical and chronological deduction of the origins of commerce*, 4 vols. (London: J. Walter, 1789), vol. IV, rev. William Combe

Anderson, Benedict, *Imagined communities: reflections on the origin and spread of nationalism* (rev. edn, London: Verso, 1991)

Anderson, Patricia, *The printed image and the transformation of popular culture, 1790–1860* (Oxford: Clarendon Press, 1991)

Anderson, R. G. W., '"What is technology?" education through museums in the mid-nineteenth century', *BJHS* 25 (1992), 169–84

Anon., 'Encouragement of inventions', *Saturday Magazine* (18 June 1825), 171–3

Anon., 'On the necessity and means of protecting needy genius', *London Journal of Arts and Sciences* 9 (1825), 308–19

Anon., *The worthies of the United Kingdom; or biographical accounts of the lives of the most illustrious men, in arts, arms, literature, and science, connected with Great Britain* (London: Knight & Lacey, 1828)

Anon., 'Railroads and locomotive steam carriages', *Quarterly Review* 42 (1830), 377–404

Anon., 'Herschell's *Treatise on Sound*', *Quarterly Review* 44 (1831), 475–511

Anon., 'Inventors and inventions', *All the Year Round* 2 (4 February 1860), 353–6

Anon., 'The philosophy of invention and patent laws', *Fraser's Magazine* 66 (1863), 504–15

Anon., *Great inventors: the sources of their usefulness and the results of their efforts* [1864]

Anon., *Invention of the telegraph: the charge against Sir Charles Wheatstone, of 'tampering with the press', as evidenced by a letter of the editor of the 'Quarterly Review' in 1855. Reprinted from the 'Scientific Review'* (London: Simpkin, Marshall & Co.; Bath: R. E. Peach, 1869)

Anon., *The story of Watt and Stephenson, illustrated* (London and Edinburgh: W. & R. Chambers Ltd, 1892)

Anon., *Samuel Crompton, the inventor of the spinning mule: a brief survey of his life and work, with which is incorporated a short history of Messrs Dobson & Barlow, Limited* (Bolton, 1927)

Anon., 'The Brunel statues', in Andrew Kelly and Melanie Kelly (eds.), *Brunel, in love with the impossible: A celebration of the life, work and legacy of Isambard Kingdom Brunel* (Bristol: Bristol Cultural Development Partnership, 2006), pp. 82–3

Arago, Dominique François Jean, *Life of James Watt* (3rd edn, Edinburgh: A. & C. Black, 1839)

Armstrong, William G., 'Address of the president', *Proceedings of the Institution of Mechanical Engineers*, (1861), 110–20

Ashton, T. S., *The industrial revolution, 1760–1830* (Oxford: Oxford University Press, 1948)

Ashworth, W., *An economic history of England, 1870–1913* (London: Methuen, 1960)

[Athenaeum, The], *An alphabetical list of the members, with the rules and regulations, of the Athenaeum* (London, 1826)

Auerbach, Jeffrey A., *The Great Exhibition of 1851: a nation on display* (New Haven and London: Yale University Press, 1999)

Babbage, Charles, *Reflections on the decline of science in England and on some of its causes* (London: B. Fellowes & J. Booth, 1830)

  On the economy of machinery and manufactures (London: Charles Knight, 1832)

Bacon, Francis, *The advancement of learning and New Atlantis*, ed. Thomas Case (London: Oxford University Press, 1951)

Bain, Alexander, *The senses and the intellect* (London: John W. Parker & Son, 1855)

[Baines, Edward], *Baines's Lancashire: a new printing of the two volumes of history, directory and gazetteer of the County Palatine of Lancaster by Edward Baines [1824]*, ed. Owen Ashmore (Newton Abbot: David & Charles, 1968), vol. II

[Baines, Jnr, Edward], *History of the cotton manufacture in Great Britain* [1835], ed. W. H. Chaloner (London: Frank Cass & Co., 1966)

Bakewell, Frederick Collier, *Great facts: a popular history and description of the most remarkable inventions during the present century* (London: Houlston & Wright, 1859)

'Bandana' [John Galt], 'Hints to the country gentleman', in *Blackwood's Edinburgh Magazine* 12 (October 1822), 482–91

Barbauld, Mrs, and Aikin, Dr, *Evenings at home: or, The juvenile budget opened* (Dublin: H. Colbert, 1794)

Barlow, Paul, 'Facing the past and present: the National Portrait Gallery and the search for "authentic" portraiture', in Joanna Woodall (ed.), *Portraiture: facing the subject* (Manchester: Manchester University Press, 1997), pp. 219–38

Barnes, Barry, *T. S. Kuhn and social science* (London: Macmillan, 1982)

Barnett, Correlli, *The audit of war: the illusion and reality of Britain as a great nation* (London: Macmillan, 1986)

Baron, John, *The life of Edward Jenner, M. D., LL. D., F. R. S., Physician Extraordinary to the King, etc. etc.* (London: Henry Colborn, 1827), vol. II

[Barrow, John], 'Canals and railroads', *Quarterly Review* 31 (March 1825), 349–78

Barton, Ruth, '"Huxley, Lubbock, and half a dozen others": professionals and gentlemen in the formation of the X Club', *Isis* 89 (1998), 410–44

'Scientific authority and scientific controversy in *Nature*: North Britain against the X Club', in L. Henson *et al.* (eds.), *Culture and science in the nineteenth-century media* (Aldershot: Ashgate, 2004), pp. 223–34

Barton, Su, '"Why should working men visit the Exhibition?": workers and the Great Exhibition and the ethos of industrialism', in Ian Inkster, Colin Griffin, Jeff Hill and Judith Rowbotham (eds.), *The golden age: essays in British social and economic history, 1850–1870* (Aldershot: Ashgate, 2000), pp. 146–63

Basalla, George, *The evolution of technology* (Cambridge: Cambridge University Press, 1988)

Bate, Jonathan, *The genius of Shakespeare* (London: Picador, 1997)

Batzel, Victor M., 'Legal monopoly in Liberal England: the patent controversy in the mid-nineteenth century', *Business History* 22 (1980), 189–202

Beauchamp, K. G., *Exhibiting electricity* (London: Institution of Electrical Engineers, 1997)

Beckmann, John, *A history of inventions, discoveries, and origins*, trans. William Johnston, 4th edn, ed. William Francis and J. W. Griffith (London: Henry G. Bohn, 1846), vol. II

Beesley, Ian, *Through the mill: the story of Yorkshire wool in photographs* (Clapham: Dalesman Books and National Museum for Photography, Film and Television, 1987)

Belfanti, Carlo Marco, 'Guilds, patents, and the circulation of technical knowledge: northern Italy during the early modern age', *T&C* 45 (2004), 569–89

Bennett, J., *et al.*, *Science and profit in 18th-century London* (Cambridge: the Whipple Museum, 1985)

Bennett, Tony, 'The exhibitionary complex', *New Formations* 4 (1988), 73–102
'Museums and "the people"', in Robert Lumley (ed.), *The museum time machine: putting cultures on display* (London: Routledge, 1988), pp. 63–85

Bérenger, Agnès, 'Le statut de l'invention dans la Rome impériale: entre méfiance et valorisation', in Marie-Sophy Corcy, Christiane Douyère-Demeulenaere and Liliane Hilaire-Pérez (eds.), *Les Archives de l'invention: Ecrits, objets et images de l'activité inventive, de l'Antiquité à nos jours* (Toulouse: CNRS-Université Toulouse-Le Mirail, Collections Méridiennes, 2007), 513–25

Berg, Maxine (ed.), *Technology and toil in nineteenth-century Britain* (London: CSE Press, 1979)
The machinery question and the making of political economy, 1815–1848 (Cambridge: Cambridge University Press, 1980)
The age of manufactures, 1700–1820: industry, innovation and work in Britain (2nd edn, London and New York: Routledge, 1994)

Bessemer, Sir Henry, *Sir Henry Bessemer, FRS, an autobiography* (London, 1905)

Bewell, Alan, '"Jacobin plants": botany as social theory in the 1790s', *The Wordsworth Circle* 20 (1989), 132–9

Binfield, Kevin (ed.), *Writings of the Luddites* (Baltimore and London: Johns Hopkins University Press, 2004)

Blackner, John, *The history of Nottingham* (Nottingham: Sutton & Son, 1815)

Boase, G. C., and W. P. Courtney, *Bibliotheca Cornubiensis: a catalogue of the writings of Cornishmen* (London: Longmans, 1874–8)

Boehm, Klaus, and Silberston, Aubrey, *The British patent system, 1. Administration* (Cambridge: Cambridge University Press, 1967)

Boon, Timothy, 'Industrialisation and catastrophe: the Victorian economy in British film documentary, 1930–50', in Miles Taylor and Michael Wolff (eds.), *The Victorians since 1901: histories, representations and revisions* (Manchester: Manchester University Press, 2004), pp. 107–20

Botting, Fred, *Making monstrous: Frankenstein, criticism, theory* (Manchester: Manchester University Press, 1991)

Boucher, C. T. G., *James Brindley, engineer, 1716–1772* (Norwich: Goose, 1968)

Bourne, John, *A treatise on the steam engine* (London: Longman, Brown, Green & Longman, 1853)

Bowden, Witt, *Industrial society in England towards the end of the eighteenth century* (2nd edn, London: Frank Cass & Co., 1965)

Bowler, Peter J., *The invention of progress: the Victorians and the past* (Oxford: Basil Blackwell, 1989)

Bowley, Arthur Lyon, *Prices and wages in the United Kingdom, 1914–1920* (Oxford: Clarendon Press, 1921)

Boyson, Rhodes, *The Ashworth cotton enterprise: the rise and fall of a family firm* (Oxford: Clarendon Press, 1970)

Bracegirdle, Brian, and Miles, Patricia H., *Thomas Telford* (Newton Abbot: David & Charles, 1973)

Bramah, Joseph, *A letter to the Rt Hon. Sir James Eyre, Lord Chief Justice of the Common Pleas; on the subject of the cause,* Boulton & Watt *v.* Hornblower & Maberly: *for infringement of Mr Watt's patent for an improvement on the steam engine* (London: John Stockdale, 1797)

Brannigan, Augustine, *The social basis of scientific discoveries* (Cambridge: Cambridge University Press, 1981)

Branwell, Frederick C., *Great facts: a popular history and description of the most remarkable inventions during the present century* (London: Houltson & Wright, 1859)

Brassey, Thomas, *Lectures on the labour question* (London: Longmans, Green, 1878)

Brewer, John, *The sinews of power: war, money and the English state, 1688–1783* (London: Unwin Hyman, 1989)

[Brewster, David], 'The decline of science in England', *Quarterly Review* 43 (1830), 305–42

[Brewster, Sir David], Review of *Éloge Historique de James Watt. Par M. Arago* [etc], *Edinburgh Review* 142 (January 1840), 466–502

Brickhill, Paul, *The dam busters* (London: Evans Bros., 1951)

Bride, W. L., *James Watt – his inventions and his connections with Heriot-Watt University* (Edinburgh: Heriot-Watt University, 1969)

Briggs, Asa, *Victorian people: a re-assessment of persons and themes, 1851–67* (rev. edn, Harmondsworth: Penguin, 1971)

  Iron Bridge to Crystal Palace: impact and images of the industrial revolution (London: Thames & Hudson, 1979)

  'The 1890s: past, present and future in the headlines', in Asa Briggs and Daniel Snowman (eds.), *Fins de siècles: how centuries end, 1400–2000* (New Haven and London: Yale University Press, 1996), pp. 159–62

Briggs, Robin, 'The *Académie royale des sciences* and the pursuit of utility', *Past & Present* 131 (1991), 38–87

Brightwell, C[elia] L[ucy], *Heroes of the laboratory and the workshop* (London: Routledge & Co., 1859)

Brindle, Steven, 'The Great Western Railway', in Andrew Kelly and Melanie Kelly (eds.), *Brunel, in love with the impossible: a celebration of the life, work and legacy of Isambard Kingdom Brunel* (Bristol: Bristol Cultural Development Partnership, 2006), pp. 133–55

Brock, Peter, *Pacifism in Europe to 1914* (Princeton, NJ: Princeton University Press, 1972)

Broks, Peter, *Media science before the Great War* (Basingstoke: Macmillan; New York: St Martin's Press, 1996)

Brooks, Michael W., *John Ruskin and Victorian architecture* (London: Thames and Hudson, 1989)

[Brougham, Henry], *A discourse of the objects, advantages, and pleasures of science* (London: Baldwin, Cradock & Joy, for the SDUK, 1827)

Brougham, Henry, *Lives of men of letters and science who flourished in the time of George III* (London: Charles Knight, 1845–6), vol. I

Brown, James M., *Dickens: novelist of the market place* (London and Basingstoke: Macmillan Press, 1982)

Browne, Janet, 'Botany for gentlemen: Erasmus Darwin and *The Loves of the Plants*', *Isis* 80 (1989), 593–620

  'Presidential address: commemorating Darwin', *BJHS* 38 (2005), 251–74

Bruland, Kristine, 'Industrial conflict as a source of technical innovation: three cases', *Economy and Society* 11 (1982), 92–121

'Industrialisation and technological change', in Roderick Floud and Paul Johnson (eds.), *The Cambridge economic history of modern Britain, Volume 1: 1700–1860* (Cambridge: Cambridge University Press, 2004), pp. 117–46

Brunel, Isambard, *Life of Isambard Kingdom Brunel, civil engineer* (London: Longmans, Green, 1870)

Buchanan, R. A., 'The Rolt Memorial Lecture 1987: the lives of the engineers', *Industrial Archaeology Review* 11 (1988–9), 5–15

The engineers: a history of the engineering profession in Britain, 1750–1914 (London: Jessica Kingsley, 1989)

'Reflections on the decline of the history of technology in Britain', *HT* 22 (2000), 211–21

Brunel: the life and times of Isambard Kingdom Brunel (London: Hambledon and London, 2002)

Buckle, Henry Thomas, *History of civilization in England* [1857–61], The World's Classics, ed. Henry Froude (London: Oxford University Press, 1903–4), vol. III

Bud, Robert, 'Penicillin and the new Elizabethans', *BJHS* 31 (1998), 305–33

[Bulwer-Lytton, E. L.], *England and the English* (New York: J. & J. Harper, 1833)

Burch, Stuart, 'Shaping symbolic space: Parliament Square, London as a sacred site', in Angela Phelps (ed.), *The construction of built heritage* (Aldershot: Ashgate, 2002), pp. 223–36

Burgess, Keith, *The origins of British industrial relations: the nineteenth-century experience* (London: Croom Helm, 1975)

Burke, Peter, 'History as social memory', in Thomas Butler (ed.), *Memory: history, culture and the mind* (Oxford: Basil Blackwell, 1989), pp. 97–114

Burnley, James, *The romance of invention: vignettes from the annals of industry and science* (London, Paris, New York and Melbourne: Cassell & Co., 1886)

The history of wool and wool-combing (London: Low, Marston, Searle & Rivington, 1889)

Burrow, J. W., *A liberal descent: Victorian historians and the English past* (Cambridge: Cambridge University Press, 1981)

Burt, Roger, 'The extractive industries', in Roderick Floud and Paul Johnson (eds.), *The Cambridge economic history of modern Britain, Volume 1: 1700–1860* (Cambridge: Cambridge University Press, 2004), pp. 417–50

Burton, Anthony, *Richard Trevithick: giant of steam* (London; Aurum Press, 2000)

Butterworth, James, *The antiquities of the town and a complete history of the trade of Manchester* (Manchester, 1822)

Cannadine, David, 'The present and the past in the English industrial revolution', *P&P* 103 (1984), 131–72

The decline and fall of the British aristocracy (New Haven and London: Yale University Press, 1990)

'Engineering history, or the history of engineering? Rewriting the technological past', *TNS* 74 (2004), 163–80

Cantor, Geoffrey, 'Anti-Newton', in John Fauvel, Raymond Flood, Michael Shortland and Robin Wilson (eds.), *Let Newton be!* (Oxford: Oxford University Press, 1988), pp. 202–2

'The scientist as hero: public images of Michael Faraday', in Michael Shortland and Richard Yeo (eds.), *Telling lives in science: essays on scientific biography* (Cambridge: Cambridge University Press, 1996), pp. 171–94

Cantor, Paul A., *Creature and creator: myth-making and English Romanticism* (Cambridge: Cambridge University Press, 1984)

Cardwell, D. S. L., *The Fontana history of technology* (London: Fontana, 1994)

Carlyle, Thomas, *Sartor resartus* (1832), in *The works of Thomas Carlyle, centenary edition* (London: Chapman and Hall, 1896–9), vol. I

Chartism (1839), in *The works of Thomas Carlyle, centenary edition* (London: Chapman and Hall, 1896–9), vol. XXIX

On heroes, hero-worship, and the heroic in history, intro. Michael K. Goldberg (Berkeley: University of California Press, 1993)

Carnegie, Andrew, *James Watt* (Edinburgh, 1905)

Carswell, John, *The South Sea Bubble* (rev. edn, Stroud: Alan Sutton, 1993)

Carter, Clive, *Cornish engineering, 1801–2001: Holman, two centuries of industrial excellence in Camborne* (Camborne: Trevithick Society, 2001)

Carter, Ian, *Railways and culture in Britain: the epitome of modernity* (Manchester: Manchester University Press, 2001)

Case, Arthur E., *Four essays on Gulliver's Travels* (Princeton, NJ: Princeton University Press, 1950)

Cavanagh, Terry, *Public sculpture of Liverpool* (Liverpool: Liverpool University Press, 1996)

Chalmers, George, *An estimate of the comparative strength of Great Britain during the present and four preceding reigns* (new edn, London: John Stockdale, 1794)

Chambers, Robert (ed.), *A biographical dictionary of eminent Scotsmen* (Glasgow: Blackie & Son, 1835), vols. I, IV

Chancellor, Valerie E., *History for their masters: opinion in the English history textbook, 1800–1914* (Bath: Adams & Dart, 1970)

Chappell, Metius, *British engineers* (London: William Collins, 1942)

Charlesworth, Andrew, *et al.*, *An atlas of industrial protest in Britain, 1750–1990* (London: Macmillan, 1996)

Checkland, Sydney George, *The rise of industrial society in England, 1815–1885* (London: Longmans, 1964)

Chrimes, Michael, 'The engineering of the Thames Tunnel', in Eric Kentley, Angie Hudson and James Peto (eds.), *Isambard Kingdom Brunel: recent works* (London: Design Museum, 2000), pp. 26–33

Chrimes, M. M., Elton, J., May, J., and Millett, T. (eds.), *The triumphant bore: a celebration of Marc Brunel's Thames Tunnel* (London: Science Museum, 1993)

Christie, John R. R., 'Laputa revisited', in John Christie and Sally Shuttleworth (eds.), *Nature transfigured: science and literature, 1700–1900* (Manchester and New York: Manchester University Press, 1989), pp. 45–60

Clark, G. N., *The idea of the industrial revolution* (Glasgow: Jackson, Son & Co., 1953)

Clark, Jennifer, 'The American image of technology from the Revolution to 1840', *American Quarterly* 39 (1987), 431–49

Clarke, I. F., *The tale of the future, from the beginning to the present day: a check-list* (London: Library Association, 1961)

Clarke, I. F. (ed.), *The tale of the next Great War, 1871–1914: fictions of future warfare and of battles still-to-come* (Liverpool: Liverpool University Press, 1995)

Cleland, James, *Historical account of the steam engine* (Glasgow: Khull, Blackie & Co., 1825)

Clow, Archibald, 'A re-examination of William Walker's "Distinguished Men of Science"', *Annals of Science* 11 (1956), 183–93

Coad, Jonathan, *The Portsmouth block mills: Bentham, Brunel and the start of the Royal Navy's industrial revolution* (Swindon: English Heritage, 2005)

[Cobbe, Frances Power], *The age of science, a newspaper of the twentieth century*, by *Merlin Nostrodamus* [1877]

Cochrane, Rexmond C., 'Francis Bacon and the rise of the mechanical arts in eighteenth-century England', *Annals of Science* 12 (1956), 137–56

[Cochrane, Robert], *Heroes of invention and discovery: lives of eminent inventors and pioneers in science* (Edinburgh: William P. Nimmo & Co., 1879)

Cochrane, Robert, *The romance of industry and invention* (London and Edinburgh: W. & R. Chambers [1896])

Coleman, D. C., *The economy of England, 1450–1750* (Oxford: Oxford University Press, 1977)

    History and the economic past: an account of the rise and decline of economic history in Britain (Oxford: Clarendon Press, 1987)

    'Adam Smith, businessmen, and the mercantile system in England', *History of European Ideas* 9 (1988), 161–70

    Myth, history and the industrial revolution (London and Rio Grande: Hambledon Press, 1992)

Coleman, D. C., and MacLeod, Christine, 'Attitudes to new techniques: British businessmen, 1800–1950', *EHR* 39 (1986), 588–611

Colley, Linda, *Britons: forging the nation, 1707–1837* (New Haven and London: Yale University Press, 1992)

Collini, Stefan, *Public moralists: political thought and intellectual life in Britain, 1850–1930* (Oxford: Clarendon Press, 1991)

    'The literary critic and the village labourer: "culture" in twentieth-century Britain', *Transactions of the Royal Historical Society*, 6th series, 14 (2004), 93–116

Collins, Bruce, and Robbins, Keith (eds.), *British culture and economic decline* (London: Weidenfeld and Nicolson, 1990)

Colls, Robert, 'Remembering George Stephenson: genius and modern memory', in Robert Colls and Bill Lancaster (eds.), *Newcastle upon Tyne: a modern history* (Chichester: Phillimore, 2001), pp. 267–92

[Colquhoun, Patrick], *An important crisis, in the callico and muslin manufactory in Great Britain, explained* (London, 1788)

    A treatise on the wealth, power, and resources, of the British empire (2nd edn, London: Joseph Mawman, 1815)

Connerton, Paul, *How societies remember* (Cambridge: Cambridge University Press, 1989)

Cookson, J. E., 'Political arithmetic and war in Britain, 1793–1815', *War and Society* 1 (1983), 37–60

'The Napoleonic wars, military Scotland, and Tory Highlandism in the early nineteenth century', *Scottish Historical Review* 78 (1999), 60–75

'The Edinburgh and Glasgow Duke of Wellington statues: early nineteenth-century unionist nationalism as a Tory project', *Scottish Historical Review* 83 (2004), 24–40

Cooper, Carolyn C., 'The Portsmouth system of manufacture', *T&C* 25 (1984), 182–225

Shaping invention: Thomas Blanchard's machinery and patent management in nineteenth-century America (New York and Oxford: Columbia University Press, 1991)

'Myth, rumor, and history: the Yankee whittling boy as hero and villain', *T&C* 44 (2003), 82–96

[Cooper, Thomas, the Chartist], *The triumphs of perseverance and enterprise: recorded as examples for the young* (London: Darton & Co., 1856)

The life of Thomas Cooper, written by himself, ed. John Savile (New York: Leicester University Press, 1971)

Cooper, Thompson (ed.), *Men of mark: a gallery of contemporary portraits of men distinguished in the senate, the church, in science, literature and art, the army, navy, law, medicine, etc.*, photo. Lock and Whitfield (London: Sampson Low, Marston, Searle and Rivington, 1876–83), vols. V and VII

Coryton, John, 'The policy of granting letters patent for invention, with observations on the working of the English law', *Sessional Proceedings of the National Association for the Promotion of Social Science* 7 (1873–4), 163–90

Coulter, Moureen, *Property in ideas: the patent question in mid-Victorian Britain* (Kirksville, MO: Thomas Jefferson Press, 1992)

Cowpe, Alan, 'The Royal Navy and the Whitehead torpedo', in Bryan Ranft (ed.), *Technical change and British naval policy, 1860–1939* (London: Hodder & Stoughton, 1977), pp. 23–36

Craig, Archibald, *The Elder Park, Govan: an account of the gift of the Elder Park and the erection and unveiling of the statue of John Elder* (Glasgow, 1891)

[Craik, George L.], *The pursuit of knowledge under difficulties; illustrated by anecdotes* (London: Charles Knight, 1830–1), vols. I and II

Craik, George L., and MacFarlane, Charles, *The pictorial history of England during the reign of George the Third: being a history of the people, as well as a history of the kingdom* (London: Charles Knight & Co., 1841–4), vol. II

Craske, Matthew, 'Westminster Abbey 1720–1770: a public pantheon built upon private interest', in Richard Wrigley and Matthew Craske (eds.), *Pantheons: transformations of a monumental idea* (Aldershot: Ashgate, 2004), pp. 57–80

Cressy, David, 'National memory in early modern England', in John R. Gillis (ed.), *Commemorations: the politics of identity* (Princeton, NJ: Princeton University Press, 1994), pp. 61–73

[Crompton, Samuel], *Samuel Crompton Centenary, Bolton June 7th–10th 1927* (Bolton, 1927)

Crook, D. P., *Benjamin Kidd: portrait of a Social Darwinist* (Cambridge: Cambridge University Press, 1984)

Crouzet, François, *Britain ascendant: comparative studies in Franco-British economic history* (Cambridge: Cambridge University Press, 1985)

Crowther, J. G., *Six great inventors: Watt, Stephenson, Edison, Marconi, Wright Brothers, Whittle* (London: Hamish Hamilton, 1954)

Cubitt, Geoffrey, 'Introduction: heroic reputations and exemplary lives', in Geoffrey Cubitt and Allen Warren (eds.), *Heroic reputations and exemplary lives* (Manchester: Manchester University Press, 2000), pp. 1–27

Cummings, A. J. G., and Stewart, Larry, 'The case of the eighteenth-century projector: entrepreneurs, engineers, and legitimacy at the Hanoverian court in Britain', in Bruce T. Moran (ed.), *Patronage and institutions: science, technology, and medicine at the European court, 1500–1750* (Rochester, NY, and Woodbridge: Boydell, 1991), pp. 235–61

Daniels, Stephen, 'Loutherbourg's chemical theatre: *Coalbrookdale by Night*', in John Barrell (ed.), *Painting and the politics of culture: new essays on British art, 1700–1850* (Oxford: Oxford University Press, 1992), pp. 195–230

Fields of vision: landscape, imagery and national identity in England and the United States (Princeton, NJ: Princeton University Press, 1993)

Darke, Jo, *The monument guide to England and Wales: a national portrait in bronze and stone* (London: Macdonald Illustrated, 1991)

Darwin, Erasmus, *The Botanic Garden* [1791] (4th edn, London: J. Johnson, 1799)

Daumas, Maurice, *Scientific instruments of the seventeenth and eighteenth centuries and their makers*, trans. M. Holbrook (London: B. T. Batsford, 1972)

Daunton, M. J., *Royal Mail: The Post Office since 1840* (London and Dover, NH: The Athlone Press, 1985)

Davenport, R. A., *Lives of individuals who raised themselves from poverty to eminence or fortune* (London: SDUK, 1841)

Davies, John, *A collection of the most important cases respecting patents of invention and the rights of patentees* (London: W. Reed, 1816)

Dawson, Graham, *Soldier heroes: British adventure, empire, and the imagining of masculinities* (London and New York: Routledge, 1994)

Deacon, Bernard, '"The hollow jarring of distant steam engines": images of Cornwall between West Barbary and Delectable Duchy', in Ella Westland (ed.), *Cornwall: the cultural construction of place* (Penzance: Patten Press, 1997), pp. 7–24

Defoe, Daniel, *An essay upon projects*, ed. Joyce D. Kennedy, Michael Siedel and Maximilian E. Novak (New York: AMS Press, c. 1999)

Dellheim, Charles, *The face of the past: the preservation of the medieval inheritance in Victorian England* (Cambridge: Cambridge University Press, 1982)

[Dickens, Charles], 'A poor man's tale of a patent', *Household Words* (19 October 1850), 73–5

Dickens, Charles, *Little Dorrit* (Harmondsworth: Penguin Books, 1967)

Dickinson, H. W., 'Henry Cort's bicentenary', *TNS* 21 (1940–1), 31–48

Dickinson, H. W., and Jenkins, Rhys, *James Watt and the steam engine: the memorial volume prepared for the committee of the Watt centenary commemoration at Birmingham 1919*, intro. Jennifer Tann (Ashbourne: Moorland, 1981)

Dickinson, H. W., and Titley, Arthur, *Richard Trevithick: the engineer and the man* (Cambridge: Cambridge University Press, 1934)

Dircks, Henry, *Inventors and inventions* (London: E. and F. N. Spon, 1867)

Dobson, C. R., *Masters and journeymen: a prehistory of industrial relations, 1717–1800* (London: Croom Helm, 1980)

Dresser, Madge, 'Set in stone? Statues and slavery in London', *History Workshop Journal*, 64 (2007)

Duff, William, *An essay on original genius and its various modes of exertion in philosophy and the fine arts particularly in poetry*, ed. John L. Mahoney (Gainesville, Florida: Scholars' Facsimiles and Reprints, 1964)

Dugan, Sally, *Men of iron: Brunel, Stephenson and the inventions that shaped the world* (London: Macmillan, 2003)

Duncan, W. (ed.), *The Stephenson centenary, 1881* (Newcastle upon Tyne: Graham, 1975)

Dunkin, John, *The history and antiquities of Dartford* (London: John Russell Smith, 1844)

Dunkling, Leslie, and Wright, Gordon (eds.), *The Wordsworth dictionary of pub names* (Ware: Wordsworth Reference, 1994)

Durbach, Nadja, '"They might as well brand us": working-class resistance to compulsory vaccination in Victorian England', *Social History of Medicine* 13 (2000), 45–62

Dutton, H. I., *The patent system and inventive activity during the industrial revolution, 1750–1852* (Manchester: Manchester University Press, 1984)

Eden, Sir Frederick Morton, *The state of the poor* (London: B. & J. White, 1797), vol. I

Edgar, John G., *Footprints of famous men, designed as incitements to intellectual industry* (London: David Bogue, 1854)

Edgerton, David, 'The prophet militant and industrial: the peculiarities of Correlli Barnett', *Twentieth Century British History* 2 (1991), 360–79

Science, technology and the British industrial 'decline', 1870–1970 (Cambridge: Cambridge University Press for the Economic History Society, 1996)

'From innovation to use: ten (eclectic) theses on the history of technology', *HT* 16 (1999), 1–26

'Reflections on the history of technology in Britain', *HT* 22 (2000), 181–7

The shock of the old: technology and global history since 1900 (London: Profile Books, 2006)

Edgerton, D. E. H., and Horrocks, S. M., 'British industrial research and development before 1945', *EHR* 47 (1994), 213–38

Edgeworth, Maria, *Harry and Lucy concluded; being the last part of Early lessons* (London: R. Hunter and Baldwin, Cradock and Joy, 1825)

Elliott, Ebenezer, *The poetical works of Ebenezer Elliott*, new edn, ed. Edwin Elliott (London: Henry S. King, 1876), vol. I

Empson, John, 'Little honoured in his own country: statues in recognition of Edward Jenner MD FRS', *Journal of the Royal Society of Medicine* 89 (1996), 514–18

Engels, Friedrich, *The condition of the working class in England*, ed. David McLellan (Oxford and New York: Oxford University Press, 1993)

Epstein, James A., *Radical expression: political language, ritual, and symbol in England, 1790–1850* (New York and Oxford: Oxford University Press, 1994)

Escott, Thomas Hay Sweet, *England: its people, polity and pursuits* (rev. edn, London: Chapman and Hall, 1890)

Espinasse, F., 'Lancashire industrialism: James Brindley and his Duke of Bridgewater and Richard Arkwright', *The Roscoe Magazine, and Lancashire and Cheshire Literary Reporter* 1 (1849), 201–9

Fairbairn, William, *Observations on improvements of the town of Manchester, particularly as regards the importance of blending in those improvements, the chaste and beautiful, with the ornamental and useful* (Manchester: Robert Robinson, 1836)

'The rise and progress of manufacture and commerce and of civil and mechanical engineering in Lancashire and Cheshire', in Thomas Baines, *Lancashire and Cheshire, past and present* (London: W. Mackenzie, 1868–9), vol. II

The life of Sir William Fairbairn, Bart, partly written by himself, ed. and completed by William Pole [1877], repr. with introduction by A. E. Musson (Newton Abbot: David & Charles, 1970)

Fara, Patricia, *Sympathetic attractions: magnetic practices, beliefs, and symbolism in eighteenth-century England* (Princeton, NJ: Princeton University Press, 1996)

'Faces of genius: images of Isaac Newton in eighteenth-century England', in Geoffrey Cubitt and Allen Warren (eds.), *Heroic reputations and exemplary lives* (Manchester: Manchester University Press, 2000), pp. 57–81

'Isaac Newton lived here: sites of memory and scientific heritage', *BJHS* 33 (2000), 407–26

Newton: The making of genius (Basingstoke: Macmillan, 2002)

Farey, John, *A treatise on the steam engine, historical, practical, and descriptive* (London, 1827; repr. Newton Abbot: David & Charles, 1971), vol. I

Federico, P. J., 'Origin and early history of patents', *Journal of the Patent Office Society* 11 (1929), 292–305

Feinstein, Charles M., 'Pessimism perpetuated: real wages and the standard of living in Britain during and after the industrial revolution', *Journal of Economic History* 58 (1998), 625–58

Fentress, James, and Wickham, Chris, *Social memory* (Oxford: Blackwell, 1992)

Fielden, Kenneth, 'Samuel Smiles and self-help', *Victorian Studies* 12 (1968–9), 155–76

[Finlay, James], *James Finlay & Company Limited: manufacturers and East India merchants, 1750–1950* (Glasgow: Jackson, Son & Company, 1951)

Finlay, R. J., *Independent and free: Scottish politics and the origins of the Scottish Nationalist Party, 1918–1945* (Edinburgh: John Donald, 1994)

Finn, Margot C., *After Chartism: class and nation in English radical politics, 1848–1874* (Cambridge: Cambridge University Press, 1993)

Fitton, R. S., *The Arkwrights, spinners of fortune* (Manchester: Manchester University Press, 1989)

Flinn, Michael W., *The history of the British coal industry, volume 2, 1700–1830: the industrial revolution* (Oxford: Clarendon Press, 1984)

Folkenflik, Robert, 'Johnson's heroes', in Robert Folkenflik (ed.), *The English hero, 1660–1800* (Newark, NJ: University of Delaware Press, 1982), pp. 143–67

Foote, George A., 'The place of science in the British reform movement, 1830–50', *Isis* 42 (1951), 192–208

Forty, Adrian, *Objects of desire: design and society since 1750* (London: Thames & Hudson, 1986)

Fox, Robert, 'Thomas Edison's Parisian campaign: incandescent lighting and the hidden face of technology transfer', *Annals of Science* 53 (1996), 157–93

Fox, Robert, and Guagnini, Anna (eds.), *Education, technology and industrial performance in Europe, 1850–1939* (Cambridge: Cambridge University Press, 1993)

Laboratories, workshops, and sites. Concepts and practices of research in industrial Europe, 1800–1914 (Berkeley, CA: Office for History of Science and Technology, University of California, 1999)

Fraser, David, 'Fields of radiance: the scientific and industrial scenes of Joseph Wright', in Denis Cosgrove and Stephen Daniels (eds.), *The iconography of landscape: essays on the symbolic representation, design and use of past environments* (Cambridge: Cambridge University Press, 1988), pp. 119–41

'Joseph Wright and the Lunar Society: painter of light', in Judy Egerton (ed.), *Wright of Derby* (London: Tate Gallery, c. 1990), pp. 15–24

Freeman, Michael, *Railways and the Victorian imagination* (New Haven and London: Yale University Press, 1999)

French, Gilbert J., *The life and times of Samuel Crompton, inventor of the spinning machine called the mule* (London: Simpkin, Marshall & Co., 1859)

Friedman, Alan J., and Donley, Carol C., *Einstein as myth and muse* (Cambridge: Cambridge University Press, 1985)

F. R. S., *Thoughts on the degradation of science in England* (London: John Rodwell, 1847)

Fry, M., *Patronage and principle: a political history of modern Scotland* (Aberdeen: Aberdeen University Press, 1991)

Fulford, Tim, Lee, Debbie, and Kitson, Peter J., *Literature, science and exploration in the romantic era* (Cambridge: Cambridge University Press, 2004)

Fyfe, J. Hamilton, *The triumphs of invention and discovery* (London: T. Nelson & Co., 1861)

Gadian, D. S., 'Class and class-consciousness in Oldham and other north-western industrial towns, 1830–50', *HJ* 21 (1978), 161–72

The gallery of portraits: with memoirs (London: Charles Knight for SDUK, 1833), vols. V and VI

Galloway, Elijah, *History and progress of the steam engine* (2nd edn, London: Thomas Kelly, 1830)

Galton, Francis, *English men of science: their nature and nurture* (London: Macmillan & Co., 1874)

Garber, Peter M., *Famous first bubbles: the fundamentals of early manias* (London and Cambridge, MA: MIT Press, c. 2000)

Garfield, Simon, *Mauve: how one man invented a colour that changed the world* (London: Faber & Faber, 2000)

Garfinkle, N., 'Science and religion in England, 1790–1800: the critical response to the work of Erasmus Darwin', *JHI* 14 (1955), 376–88

Gascoigne, John, 'The Royal Society and the emergence of science as an instrument of state policy', *BJHS* 32 (1999), 171–84

Gash, Norman, *Lord Liverpool: the life and political career of Robert Banks Jenkinson, second earl of Liverpool, 1770–1828* (London: Weidenfeld & Nicolson, 1984)

'The duke of Wellington and the prime ministership, 1824–30', in Norman Gash (ed.), *Wellington: studies in the military and political career of the first duke of Wellington* (Manchester: Manchester University Press, 1990), pp. 117–38

Gaskell, P., *The manufacturing population of England, its moral, social, and physical conditions, and the changes which have arisen from the use of steam machinery; with an examination of infant labour* (London: Baldwin & Cradock, 1833)

Gatrell, V. A. C., 'Incorporation and the pursuit of Liberal hegemony in Manchester, 1790–1839', in Derek Fraser (ed.), *Municipal reform and the industrial city* (Leicester: Leicester University Press, 1982), pp. 15–60

Gauldie, E. (ed.), *The Dundee textile industry, 1790–1885* (Edinburgh: the Scottish Historical Society, 1969)

George, M. Dorothy, *Hogarth to Cruikshank: social change in graphic satire* (London: Allen Lane, 1967)

Gerard, Alexander, *An essay on genius* (London and Edinburgh: W. Strahan, T. Cadell & W. Creech, 1774)

Geritsen, Willem P., and van Mellen, Anthony G., *A dictionary of medieval heroes* (Woodbridge: Boydell Press, 1998)

Gerrare, Wirt, *The warstock: a tale of tomorrow* (London: W. W. Greener, 1898)

Gieryn, Thomas F., *Cultural boundaries of science: credibility on the line* (Chicago: Chicago University Press, 1999)

Gifford, John, McWilliam, Colin, and Walker, David, *Edinburgh* (Harmondsworth: Penguin Books, 1984)

Gilbert, Sandra M., and Gubar, Susan, 'Horror's twin: Mary Shelley's monstrous Eve', *The madwoman in the attic: the woman writer and the nineteenth-century literary imagination* (New Haven: Yale University Press, 1979)

Gillespie, Richard, 'Ballooning in France and Britain, 1783–1786: aerostation and adventurism', *Isis* 75 (1984), 249–68

Gillis, John R., 'Memory and identity: the history of a relationship', in John R. Gillis (ed.), *Commemorations: the politics of identity* (Princeton, NJ: Princeton University Press, 1994), pp. 3–11

Gjertson, Derek, 'Newton's success', in John Fauvel, Raymond Flood, Michael Shortland and Robin Wilson (eds.), *Let Newton be!* (Oxford: Oxford University Press, 1988), pp. 22–41

Glasgow of today (Industries of Glasgow) (London: Historical Publishing Company, 1888)

Golinski, Jan, *Science as public culture: chemistry and enlightenment in Britain, 1760–1820* (Cambridge: Cambridge University Press, 1992)

Gooday, Graeme, 'Faraday reinvented: moral imagery and institutional icons in Victorian electrical engineering', *HT* 15 (1993), 190–205

'The flourishing of history of technology in the United Kingdom: a critique of antiquarian complaints of "neglect"', *HT* 22 (2000), 189–201

'Lies, damned lies and declinism: Lyon Playfair, the Paris 1867 Exhibition and the contested rhetorics of scientific education and industrial performance', in Ian Inkster, Colin Griffin, Jeff Hill and Judith Rowbotham (eds.), *The golden age: essays in British social and economic history, 1850–1870* (Aldershot: Ashgate, 2000), pp. 105–20

Gordon, Mrs, *The home life of Sir David Brewster, by his daughter* (Edinburgh: Edmonston & Douglas, 1869)

Gordon, Barry, *Economic doctrine and Tory liberalism, 1824–1830* (London and Basingstoke: Macmillan, 1979)

Gorman, John, *Banner bright: an illustrated history of the banners of the British trade union movement* (London: Allen Lane, 1973)

Gray, Valerie, 'Charles Knight and the Society for the Diffusion of Useful Knowledge: a special relationship', *Publishing History* 53 (2003), 23–74

Great industries of Great Britain (London, Paris and New York: Cassell & Co. [1877–80]), vols. I–II

Greenhalgh, Paul, *Ephemeral vistas: the Expositions Universelles, Great Exhibitions and World's Fairs, 1851–1939* (Manchester: Manchester University Press, 1988)

Griffiths, Trevor, Hunt, Philip, and O'Brien, Patrick, 'The curious history and the imminent demise of the challenge and response model', in Maxine Berg and Kristine Bruland (eds.), *Technological revolutions in Europe: historical perspectives* (Cheltenham and Northampton, MA: Edward Elgar, 1998), pp. 119–37

Guagnini, Anna, 'Guglielmo Marconi, inventore e imprenditore', in Anna Guagnini and Giuliano Pancaldi (eds.), *Cento anni di radio: le radici dell'invenzione* (Torino: Edizione Seat, 1995), pp. 355–418

Guest, Richard, *A compendious history of the cotton manufacture* [Manchester, 1823], (facsimile edn, London: Frank Cass & Co. Ltd, 1968)

Gunn, Simon, *The public culture of the Victorian middle class: ritual and authority in the English industrial city, 1840–1914* (Manchester: Manchester University Press, 2000)

Gunnis, R., *Dictionary of British sculptors, 1660–1851* (new edn, London: the Abbey Library, n.d.)

Gurney, Peter, 'An appropriated space: the Great Exhibition, the Crystal Palace and the working class', in Louise Purbrick (ed.), *The Great Exhibition of 1851: new interdisciplinary essays* (Manchester and New York: Manchester University Press, 2001), pp. 114–45

[R. H.], *New Atlantis, begun by the Lord Verulam, Viscount St Albans: and continued by R. H. Esquire* (London, 1660)

Hacking, Ian, *The emergence of probability: a philosophical study of early ideas about probability, induction and statistical inference* (Cambridge: Cambridge University Press, 1975)

Hale, Edward E., *Stories of inventors, told by inventors and their friends* (London, Edinburgh and New York: T. Nelson & Sons, 1887)

Hall, Catherine, McClelland, Keith, and Rendall, Jane (eds.), *Defining the Victorian nation: class, race, gender and the Reform Act of 1867* (Cambridge: Cambridge University Press, 2000)

Hamilton, Peter, and Hargreaves, Roger, *The beautiful and the damned: the creation of identity in nineteenth-century photography* (Aldershot: Lund Humphries, 2001)

Hardy, William, *The Liberal Tories and the growth of manufactures* (Shepperton: Aidan Press, 2001)

The origins of the Industrial Revolution (Oxford: Trafford Publishing, 2006)

Harper, Edith K., *A Cornish giant: Richard Trevithick, the father of the locomotive* (London: E. & F. N. Spon, 1913)

Harris, J. R., 'Skills, coal, and British industry in the eighteenth century', *History* 61 (1976), 167–82

Industrial espionage and technology transfer: Britain and France in the eighteenth century (Aldershot: Ashgate, 1998)

Harrison, Barbara, *Not only the 'dangerous trades': women's work and health in Britain, 1880–1914* (London and Bristol: Taylor & Francis, 1996)

Harrison, Frederic, 'A few words about the nineteenth century', *Fortnightly Review* (April 1882)

Harrison, Frederic, Swinney, S. H., and Marvin, F. S. (eds.), *The new calendar of great men: biographies of the 559 worthies of all ages and nations in the positivist calendar of Auguste Comte* (London: Macmillan & Co., 1920)

Harrison, Royden, *Before the socialists: studies in labour and politics, 1861–1881* (2nd edn, Aldershot: Gregg Revivals, 1994)

Harrison, Royden, and Zeitlin, Jonathan (eds.), *Divisions of labour: skilled workers and technological change in nineteenth-century Britain* (Brighton: Harvester Press, 1985)

Hart-Davis, Adam, *Chain reactions: pioneers of British science and technology and the stories that link them* (London: National Portrait Gallery, 2000)

[Harting, Pieter], Dr Dioscorides [pseud.], *Anno domini 2071*, trans. Alex. V. W. Bikkers (London: William Tegg, 1871)

Harvey, W. S., and Downs-Rose, G., *William Symington, inventor and engine builder* (London: Northgate Publishing Co. Ltd, 1980)

Harvie, Christopher, *Scotland and nationalism: Scottish society and politics, 1707–1977* (London: George Allen and Unwin, 1977)

'Larry Doyle and Captain MacWhirr: the engineer and the Celtic Fringe', in Geraint H. Jenkins (ed.), *Cymru a'r Cymry 2000: Wales and the Welsh, 2000* (Aberystwyth: University of Wales Press, 2001), 119–40

Hawkshaw, John, 'Inaugural address', *Proceedings and Minutes of the Institution of Civil Engineers* 21 (1861–2), 173–86

Hay, William Anthony, *The Whig revival, 1808–1830* (Basingstoke and New York: Palgrave Macmillan, 2005)

Headrick, Daniel R., *The tools of empire: technology and European imperialism in the nineteenth century* (New York and Oxford: Oxford University Press, 1981)

Hearn, William Edward, *Plutology: or the theory of the efforts to satisfy human wants* (London: Macmillan & Co.; Melbourne: George Robertson, 1864)

Hedley, Oswald Dodd, *Who invented the locomotive engine? With a review of Smiles's Life of Stephenson* (London: Ward & Lock, 1858)

Hejhal, Dennis A., 'Turing: a bit off the beaten path', *The Mathematical Intelligencer*, 29 (2007), 27–35

Henderson, Gavin B., 'The pacifists of the fifties', *Journal of Modern History*, 9 (1937), 314–41

[Henry, Michael], *The inventor's almanac* (London, Michael Henry, 1859–73)

Hewish, John, *The indefatigable Mr Woodcroft: the legacy of invention* (London: Science Reference Library, 1982)

'The raid on Raglan: sacred ground and profane curiosity', *British Library Journal* 8 (1982), 182–98

Prejudicial and inconvenient? A study of the Arkwright patent trials, 1781 and 1785 (London: British Library, 1985)

'From Cromford to Chancery Lane: new light on the Arkwright patent trials', *T&C* 28 (1987), 80–6.

Rooms near Chancery Lane: the Patent Office under the Commissioners, 1852–1883 (London: British Library, 2000)

Hibbert, Christopher, *The Illustrated London News: social history of Victorian Britain* (London: Angus & Robertson, 1975)

Hilaire-Pérez, Liliane, *L'Invention technique au siècle des Lumières* (Paris: Albin Michel, 2000)

'Diderot's views on artists' and inventors' rights: invention, imitation, and reputation', *BJHS* 35 (2002), 129–50

Hill, K. 'Thoroughly imbued with the spirit of Ancient Greece: symbolism and space in Victorian civic culture', in Alan Kidd and David Nicholls (eds.), *Gender, civic culture and consumerism: middle-class identity in Britain, 1800–1940* (Manchester: Manchester University Press, 1999)

Hills, Richard L., *Power in the industrial revolution* (Manchester: Manchester University Press, 1970)

Life and inventions of Richard Roberts, 1789–1864 (Ashbourne: Landmark, 2002)

Hilton, Boyd, *Corn, cash, commerce: the economic policies of the Tory government, 1815–1830* (Oxford: Oxford University Press, 1977)

Hobsbawm, Eric, 'Introduction: inventing traditions', in Eric Hobsbawm and Terence Ranger (eds.), *The invention of tradition* (Cambridge: Cambridge University Press, 1983), pp. 1–14

'Mass-producing traditions: Europe, 1870–1914', in Eric Hobsbawm and Terence Ranger (eds.), *The invention of tradition* (Cambridge: Cambridge University Press, 1983), pp. 263–307

Hodder, Edwin, *Heroes of Britain in peace and war* (London, Paris, and New York [1878–80]), vol. I

Hodgskin, Thomas, *Popular political economy: four lectures delivered at the London Mechanics' Institution* (London: Charles Tait, and Edinburgh: William Tait, 1827)

[Hodgskin, Thomas], *Labour defended against the claims of capital* [1825], 3rd edn, ed. G. D. H. Cole (London: Cass, 1963)

Hogg, James (ed.), *Fortunes made in business: a series of original sketches, biographical and anecdotic, from the recent history of industry and commerce, by various authors* (London: Sampson Low, Marston, Searle and Rivington, 1884–7)

Holmes, N. M. McQ., *The Scott Monument: a history and architectural guide* (Edinburgh: Edinburgh Museums and Art Galleries, 1979)

Holroyd, Edward, *A practical treatise of the law of patents for inventions* (London, 1830)

Homans, Margaret, *Bearing the word: language and female experience in nineteenth-century women's writing* (Chicago and London: Chicago University Press, 1986)

Hong, Sungook, 'Marconi and the Maxwellians: the origins of wireless telegraphy revisited', *T&C* 35 (1994), 717–49

Wireless: from Marconi's black box to the audion (Cambridge, MA, and London: MIT Press, 2000)

Hoock, Holger, 'The British military pantheon in St Paul's Cathedral: the state, cultural patriotism, and the politics of national monuments, c. 1790–1820', in Richard Wrigley and Matthew Craske (eds.), *Pantheons: transformations of a monumental idea* (Aldershot: Ashgate, 2004), pp. 81–105

Hope Mason, John, *The value of creativity: the origins and emergence of a modern belief* (Aldershot: Ashgate, 2003)

Hoppit, Julian, 'Financial crises in eighteenth-century England', *EHR* 39 (1986), 39–58

   Risk and failure in English business (Cambridge: Cambridge University Press, 1987)

Hort, Per Bolin, *Work, family and the state: child labour and the organization of production in the British cotton industry, 1780–1920* (Lund: Lund University Press, 1989)

Hotherstall, David, *History of psychology* (3rd edn, New York and London: McGraw-Hill Inc. 1984)

Houghton, Walter E., *The Victorian frame of mind, 1830–1870* (New Haven: Yale University Press, 1957)

Howe, Anthony, *The cotton masters, 1830–1860* (Oxford: Clarendon Press, 1984)

Howe, Henry, *Memoirs of the most eminent American mechanics: also, lives of distinguished European mechanics* (New York, 1841)

[Huddart, Joseph, the younger], *Memoir of the late Captain Joseph Huddart, F. R. S.* (London: W. Phillips, 1821)

Hudson, D. and Luckhurst, K. W., *The Royal Society of Arts, 1754–1954* (London: John Murray, 1956)

Hudson, Pat, *The industrial revolution* (London and New York: Edward Arnold, 1992)
   'Industrial organisation and structure', in Roderick Floud and Paul Johnson (eds.), *The Cambridge economic history of modern Britain, Volume 1: 1700–1860* (Cambridge: Cambridge University Press, 2004), pp. 28–57

Hughes-Hallett, Lucy, *Heroes: saviours, traitors, and supermen* (London: Harper Perennial, 2005)

Hume, David, *A treatise of human nature*, ed. P. Nidditch (Oxford: Clarendon Press, 1978)

Hunter, Michael, *Science and society in Restoration England* (Cambridge: Cambridge University Press, 1981)

Hyman, Isabelle (ed.), *Brunelleschi in perspective* (Englewood Cliffs, NJ: Prentice-Hall, 1974)

Iles, George, *The inventor at work, with chapters on discovery* (London: Doubleday, Page & Co., 1906)

Ince, Henry, and Gilbert, James, *Outlines of English history* (rev. edn, London: W. Kent & Co., 1864)

Inkster, Ian, 'Patents as indicators of technological change and innovation – An historical analysis of the patent data, 1830–1914', *TNS* 73 (2003), 179–208

Iredale, J. A., *Noble Lister: the enigma of a statue* (Bradford Art Galleries and Museums, n.d.)

Jacob, Margaret C., *The Newtonians and the English revolution* (Hassocks: Harvester Press, 1976)
   Scientific culture and the making of the industrial west (New York and Oxford: Oxford University Press, 1997)

Jacyna, L. S., 'Science and the social order in the thought of A. J. Balfour', *Isis* 71 (1980), 11–34

Jarvis, Adrian, *Samuel Smiles and the construction of Victorian values* (Stroud: Sutton Publishing Ltd, 1997)

Jeaffreson, J. C., *The life of Robert Stephenson, FRS*, 2 vols. (London: Longman, Green, Longman, Roberts & Green, 1864), vol. II

Jenkins, Alice, 'Spatial imagery in nineteenth-century science: Faraday and Tyndall', in Crosbie Smith and John Agar (eds.), *Making space for science: territorial themes in the shaping of knowledge* (Basingstoke: Macmillan, and New York: St Martin's Press, 1998), pp. 181–92

Jenkins, Reese V., *Images and enterprise: technology and the American photographic industry, 1839–1925* (London and Baltimore: Johns Hopkins Press, 1975)

[Jenner], *The Jenner Museum, Berkeley, Gloucestershire* (East Grinstead: The Merlin Press [1986])

Jennings, Humphrey, *Pandaemonium: the coming of the machine as seen by contemporary observers* (London: Deutsch, 1985)

Jeremy, David J., 'British and American entrepreneurial values in the early nineteenth century: a parting of the ways', in R. A. Burchell (ed.), *The end of Anglo-America: historical essays in the study of cultural divergence* (Manchester: Manchester University Press, 1991), pp. 24–59

'Damming the flood: British government efforts to check the outflow of technicians and machinery, 1780–1843', in D. J. Jeremy (ed.), *Technology transfer and business enterprise* (Aldershot: Ashgate, 1994), pp. 1–34

Jevons, William Stanley, *The coal question: an inquiry concerning the progress of the nation, and the probable exhaustion of our coal-mines* (London and Cambridge: Macmillan & Co., 1865)

The principles of science: a treatise on logic and scientific method, 2 vols. (London: Macmillan & Co., 1874)

Jewitt, Llewellynn Frederick William, *The Wedgwoods: being a life of Josiah Wedgwood* (London: Virtue, 1865)

Jewkes, John, Sawers, David, and Stillerman, Richard, *The sources of invention* (London: Macmillan, 1958)

Johns, Adrian, *The nature of the book: print and knowledge in the making* (Chicago and London: University of Chicago Press, 1998)

Johnson, James William, 'England, 1660–1800: an age without a hero?', in Robert Folkenflik, (ed.), *The English hero, 1660–1800* (Newark, NJ: University of Delaware Press, 1982), pp. 25–34

Johnson, Samuel, *A dictionary of the English language*, 2 vols. (London, 1755)

Jones, Evan Rowland, *Heroes of industry: biographical sketches* (London: Sampson Low, Marston, Searle and Rivington, 1886)

Jones, Gareth Stedman, 'Rethinking Chartism', in his *Languages of class: studies in English working class history, 1832–1982* (Cambridge: Cambridge University Press, 1983), pp. 90–178

An end to poverty? A historical debate (London: Profile, 2004)

Jones, Max, '"Our king upon his knees": the public commemoration of Captain Scott's last Antarctic expedition', in Geoffrey Cubitt and Allen Warren (eds.), *Heroic reputations and exemplary lives* (Manchester: Manchester University Press, 2000), pp. 105–22

The last great quest: Captain Scott's Antarctic sacrifice (Oxford: Oxford University Press, 2003)

Jones, Peter M., 'Living the enlightenment and the French revolution: James Watt, Matthew Boulton, and their sons', *HJ* 42 (1999), 157–82

Jones, Richard Foster, *Ancients and moderns: a study of the rise of the scientific movement in seventeenth century England* (2nd edn, Berkeley and Los Angeles: University of California Press, 1965)

Jones, William Powell, *The rhetoric of science: a study of scientific ideas and imagery in eighteenth-century English poetry* (London: Routledge & Kegan Paul, 1966)

Jordan, Gerald, and Rogers, Nicholas, 'Admirals as heroes: patriotism and liberty in Hanoverian England', *Journal of British Studies* 28 (1989), 201–24

Jordanova, Ludmilla, 'Melancholy reflection: constructing an identity for unveilers of nature', in Stephen Bann (ed.), *Frankenstein, creation and monstrosity* (London: Reaktion Books, 1994), 60–76

'Science and nationhood: cultures of imagined communities', in Geoffrey Cubitt (ed.), *Imagining nations* (Manchester: Manchester University Press, 1998), pp. 192–211

Defining features: scientific and medical portraits, 1660–2000 (London: Reaktion Books, with the National Portrait Gallery, 2000)

'Presidential address: remembrance of science past', *BJHS* 33 (2000), 387–406

Joyce, Patrick, *Work, society and politics: the culture of the factory in later Victorian England* (Brighton: Harvester Press, 1980)

Kargon, Robert, *Science in Victorian Manchester: enterprise and expertise* (Manchester: Manchester University Press, 1977)

Kasson, John F., *Civilizing the machine: technology and republican values in America, 1776–1900* (Harmondsworth: Penguin, 1977)

Keller, Alex, 'Mathematical technologies and the growth of the idea of technical progress in the sixteenth century', in Allen G. Debus (ed.), *Science, medicine and society in the Renaissance: essays to honor Walter Pagel* (London: Heinemann, 1972), vol. I, pp. 11–27

Kelvin, Rt Hon. Lord, *James Watt: An oration delivered at the University of Glasgow on the commemoration of its ninth jubilee* (Glasgow: James Maclehose & Sons, 1901)

Kennedy, John, 'A brief memoir of Samuel Crompton; with a description of his machine called the mule, and of the subsequent improvement of the machine by others', *Memoirs of the Literary and Philosophical Society of Manchester*, 2nd ser., 5 (1831), 318–45

Kenrick, W., *An address to the artists and manufacturers of Great Britain* (London, 1774)

Kent, Christopher, *Brains and numbers: elitism, Comtism, and democracy in mid-Victorian England* (Toronto: University of Toronto Press, 1978)

Kenworthy, William, *Inventions and hours of labour. A letter to master cotton spinners, manufacturers, and mill-owners in general* (Blackburn, 1842), repr. in *The battle for the ten hour day continues: four pamphlets, 1837–43*, ed. Kenneth E. Carpenter (New York: Arno Press, 1972)

Kessel, Neil, 'Genius and mental disorder: a history of ideas concerning their conjunction', in Penelope Murray (ed.), *Genius: the history of an idea* (Oxford: Basil Blackwell, 1989), pp. 197–212

Khan, B. Zorina, and Sokoloff, Kenneth L., 'Patent institutions, industrial organization and early technological change: Britain and the United States, 1790–1850', in Maxine Berg and Kristine Bruland (eds.), *Technological revolutions in Europe: historical perspectives* (Cheltenham and Northampton, MA: Edward Elgar, 1998), pp. 292–313

Kidd, Benjamin, *Social evolution* (London: Macmillan, 1894)

Kidd, Colin, *Subverting Scotland's past: Scottish Whig historians and the creation of an Anglo-British identity, 1689–c.1830* (Cambridge: Cambridge University Press, 1993)

King-Hele, D. G., *Doctor of revolution: the life and genius of Erasmus Darwin* (London: Faber, 1977)

Kingsford, P. W., *F. W. Lanchester* (London: Edward Arnold, 1960)

Kline, Ronald, 'Construing "technology" as "applied science": public rhetoric of scientists and engineers in the US, 1880–1945', *Isis* 86 (1995), 194–221

Klingender, Francis D., *Art and the industrial revolution*, ed. Arthur Elton (London: Evelyn, Adams & Mackay, 1968)

Kneale, W. C., 'The idea of invention', *Proceedings of the British Academy* 41 (1955), 85–108

Knight, Charles, *The popular history of England* (London: Bradbury & Evans, 1859), vol. V

    Passages of a working life during half a century (London: Bradbury & Evans, 1865), vols. II, III

Korshin, Paul J., 'The intellectual context of Swift's flying island', *Philological Quarterly* 50 (1971), 630–46

Kovacevich, Ivanka, 'The mechanical muse: the impact of technical inventions on eighteenth-century neoclassical poetry', *Huntington Library Quarterly* 28 (1964–5), 263–81

Krauss, Rosalind, 'Sculpture in the expanded field', in Hal Foster (ed.), *Postmodern culture* (London: Pluto Press, 1985), pp. 31–42

Laird, Macgregor, and Oldfield, R. A. K., *Narrative of an expedition into the interior of Africa* (London, 1837), vol. II

Lamb, David, and Easton, S. M., *Multiple discovery: the pattern of scientific progress* (Amersham: Avebury Press, 1984)

Lambert, Andrew, 'ss *Great Britain*', in Andrew Kelly and Melanie Kelly (eds.), *Brunel, in love with the impossible: A celebration of the life, work and legacy of Isambard Kingdom Brunel* (Bristol: Bristol Cultural Development Partnership, 2006), pp. 163–81

Lambert, R. L., 'A Victorian National Health Service: state vaccination, 1855–1871', *HJ* 5 (1962), 1–18

Laqueur, Thomas W., 'Memory and naming in the Great War', in John R. Gillis (ed.), *Commemorations: the politics of national identity* (Princeton, NJ: Princeton University Press, 1994), pp. 150–67

Lardner, Dionysius, *The steam engine familiarly explained and illustrated* (London: Taylor & Walton, 1836)

The steam engine explained and illustrated (7th edn, London: Taylor & Walton, 1840)

Larwood, Jacob, and Hotten, John Camden, *The history of signboards, from the earliest times to the present day* (London: Chatto and Windus [1866])

Lazonick, W. H., 'Industrial relations and technical change: the case of the self-acting mule', *Cambridge Journal of Economics* 3 (1979), 231–62

LeFanu, W. R., *A bio-bibliography of Edward Jenner, 1749–1823* (London: Harvey & Blythe Ltd, 1951)

Levi, Leone, *History of British commerce and of the economic progress of the British nation, 1763–1870* (London, 1872)

Levine, Philippa, *The amateur and the professional; antiquarians, historians and archaeologists in Victorian England, 1838–1886* (Cambridge: Cambridge University Press, 1986)

Library of Congress, *A. L. A. portrait index: index to portraits contained in printed books and periodicals*, ed. W. C. Lane and N. E. Browne (Washington, DC: American Library Association, 1906)

[Lister, S. C.], *Lord Masham's inventions, written by himself* (Bradford, 1905)

Lockyer, Sir Norman, 'The influence of brain-power on history', *Nature*, 10 September 1903, 439–46

Lodge, Oliver, 'Address to Section A', BAAS, *Report for 1891, Cardiff* (1892)
Pioneers of science (London: Macmillan & Co., 1893)

Long, Pamela O., 'Invention, authorship, "intellectual property," and the origins of patents: notes toward a conceptual history', *T&C* 32 (1991), 846–84
'Power, patronage, and the authorship of Ars: from mechanical know-how to mechanical knowledge in the last scribal age', *Isis* 88 (1997), 1–41
Openness, secrecy, authorship: technical arts and the culture of knowledge from antiquity to the renaissance (Baltimore and London: Johns Hopkins University Press, 2001)

Long, Pamela O., and Roland, Alex, 'Military secrecy in antiquity and early medieval Europe: a critical reassessment', *History and Technology* 11 (1994), 259–90

Lonsdale, Henry, *The worthies of Cumberland* (London: George Routledge & Sons, 1867–75), vol. III

Lord, John, *Memoir of John Kay of Bury, County of Lancaster, inventor of the fly-shuttle, metal reeds, etc. etc.* (Rochdale: Aldine Press, 1903)

Lovejoy, Arthur O., *Essays in the history of ideas* (New York: George Braziller, 1955)

Lubar, Steven, 'The transformation of antebellum patent law', *T&C* 32 (1991), 932–59

Lubbock, Sir John, 'Presidential address', *BAAS, Report for 1881, York* (1882), 1–51

Macaulay, Lord, *Literary and historical essays contributed to the Edinburgh Review* (London: Humphrey Milford, Oxford University Press, 1934)
The history of England from the accession of James the Second [new edn 1857], ed. Charles Harding Firth (London: Macmillan & Co., 1913), vol. I

McClelland, Keith, '"England's greatness, the working man"', in Hall, Catherine, McClelland, Keith, and Rendall, Jane (eds.), *Defining the*

Victorian nation: class, race, gender and the Reform Act of 1867 (Cambridge: Cambridge University Press, 2000), pp. 71–118

[McCulloch, J. R.], 'Restrictions on foreign commerce', *Edinburgh Review* XXXIII (May 1820), 331–51

'Rise, progress, present state, and prospects of the British cotton manufacture', *Edinburgh Review* XLVI (June 1827), 1–39

'Philosophy of manufactures', *Edinburgh Review* LXI (July 1835), 453–72

McDaniel, Susan, Cummins, Helene, and Beauchamp, Rachelle Spender, 'Mothers of invention? Meshing the roles of inventor, mother and worker', *Women's Studies International Forum* 11 (1988), 1–12

MacDonald, R. H., *The language of empire: myths and metaphors of popular imperialism, 1880–1918* (Manchester: Manchester University Press, 1994)

Macfie, Robert Andrew, *The patent question: a solution of difficulties by abolishing or shortening the inventor's monopoly, and instituting national recompenses* (London: W. J. Johnson, 1863)

[Macfie, Robert Andrew (ed.)], *Recent discussions on the abolition of patents for inventions in the United Kingdom, France, Germany, and the Netherlands* (London: Longmans, Green, Reader and Dyer, 1869)

Macfie, Robert Andrew (ed.), *The patent question in 1875: the Lord Chancellor's bill and the exigencies of foreign competition* (London: Longmans, Green & Co., 1875)

McGaw, Judith, 'Inventors and other great women: toward a feminist history of technological luminaries', *T&C* 38 (1997), 214–31

McGee, David, 'Making up mind: the early sociology of invention', *T&C* 36 (1995), 773–801

McKendrick, Neil, '"Gentlemen and players revisited": the gentlemanly ideal, the business ideal and the professional ideal in English literary culture', in Neil McKendrick and R. B. Outhwaite (eds.), *Business life and public policy: essays in honour of D. C. Coleman* (Cambridge: Cambridge University Press, 1986), pp. 98–136

MacKenzie, Donald, 'Marx and the machine', *T&C* 25 (1984), 473–502

MacKenzie, John M., 'Heroic myths of empire', in John M. MacKenzie (ed.), *Popular imperialism and the military: 1850–1950* (Manchester: Manchester University Press, 1992), pp. 109–37

'The iconography of the exemplary life: the case of David Livingstone', in Geoffrey Cubitt and Allen Warren (eds.), *Heroic reputations and exemplary lives* (Manchester: Manchester University Press, 2000), pp. 84–104

McKenzie, Ray, *Public sculpture of Glasgow* (Liverpool: Liverpool University Press, 2002)

Mackenzie, Robert, *The 19th century: a history* (London: T. Nelson & Sons, 1880)

MacLeod, Christine, 'The 1690s patents boom: invention or stock-jobbing?', *EHR* 39 (1986), 549–71

Inventing the industrial revolution: the English patent system, 1660–1800 (Cambridge: Cambridge University Press, 1988)

'Strategies for innovation: the diffusion of new technology in nineteenth-century British industry', *EHR* 45 (1992), 285–307

'Concepts of invention and the patent controversy in Victorian Britain', in Robert Fox (ed.), *Technological change: methods and themes in the history of technology* (Amsterdam: Harwood Academic Publishers, 1996), pp. 137–54

'Negotiating the rewards of invention: the shop-floor inventor in Victorian Britain', *Business History* 41 (1999), 17–36

'James Watt, heroic invention, and the idea of the industrial revolution', in Maxine Berg and Kristine Bruland (eds.), *Technological revolutions in Europe: historical perspectives* (Cheltenham and Northampton, MA: Edward Elgar, 1998), pp. 96–118

'The European origins of British technological predominance', in Leandro Prados de la Escosura (ed.), *Exceptionalism and industrialisation: Britain and its European rivals, 1688–1815* (Cambridge: Cambridge University Press, 2004), pp. 111–26

'The nineteenth-century engineer as cultural hero', in Andrew Kelly and Melanie Kelly (eds.), *Brunel, in love with the impossible: A celebration of the life, work and legacy of Isambard Kingdom Brunel* (Bristol: Bristol Cultural Development Partnership, 2006), pp. 61–79

MacLeod, Christine, Tann, Jennifer, Andrew, James, and Stein, Jeremy, 'Evaluating inventive activity: the cost of nineteenth-century UK patents and the fallibility of renewal data', *EHR* 56 (2003), 537–62

MacLeod, Christine and Nuvolari, Alessandro, 'The pitfalls of prosopography: inventors in the *Dictionary of National Biography*', *T&C* 48 (2006), 757–76

MacLeod, Christine, and Tann, Jennifer, 'From engineer to scientist: re-inventing invention in the Watt and Faraday centenaries, 1919–1931', *BJHS* (2007), 389–411

MacLeod, Donald, *A nonagenarian's reminiscences of Garelochside and Helensburgh* (Helensburgh: Macneur & Bryden, 1883)

MacLeod, R. M., 'Law, medicine and public opinion: the resistance to compulsory health legislation, 1870–1907', *Public Law* (1967), 107–28

'Science and the Civil List, 1824–1914', *Technology and Society* 6 (1970), 47–55

'Of models and men: a reward system in Victorian science, 1826–1914', *Notes and Records of the Royal Society of London* 26 (1971)

'The support of Victorian science: the endowment of research movement in Great Britain, 1868–1900', *Minerva* 9 (1971), 196–230

(ed.), *Days of judgement* (Driffield: Nafferton, 1982)

McNeil, Maureen, *Under the banner of science: Erasmus Darwin and his age* (Manchester: Manchester University Press, 1987)

'Newton as national hero', in John Fauvel, Raymond Flood, Michael Shortland and Robin Wilson (eds.), *Let Newton be!* (Oxford: Oxford University Press, 1988), pp. 222–40

Macpherson, David, *Annals of commerce, manufactures, fisheries, and navigation* (London: Nichols, 1805), vol. IV

Machlup, F., and Penrose, Edith, 'The patent controversy in the nineteenth century', *Journal of Economic History* 10 (1950), 1–29

Mah, Harold, 'Phantasies of the public sphere: rethinking the Habermas of the historians', *Journal of Modern History* 72 (2000), 153–82

Maidment, Brian, 'Entrepreneurship and the artisans: John Cassell, the Great Exhibition and the periodical idea', in Louise Purbrick (ed.), *The Great Exhibition of 1851: new interdisciplinary essays* (Manchester and New York: Manchester University Press, 2001), pp. 79–113

Malet, Hugh, *Bridgewater: the canal duke, 1736–1803* (Manchester: Manchester University Press, 1977)

[Mallalieu, Alfred], 'The cotton manufacture', *Blackwood's Edinburgh Magazine* 39 (1836), 407–24

Malthus, T. R., *An essay on the principle of population as it affects the future improvement of society, with remarks on the speculations of Mr Godwin, Mr Condorcet, and other writers* (London: J. Johnson, 1798)

Mandeville, Bernard, *The fable of the bees*, ed. F. B. Kaye (Oxford: Clarendon Press, 1924), vol. II

Marsden, Ben, '"A most important trespass": Lewis Gordon and the Glasgow Chair of Civil Engineering and Mechanics, 1840–55', in Crosbie Smith and Jon Agar (eds.), *Making space for science: territorial themes in the shaping of knowledge* (Basingstoke: Macmillan Press Ltd, 1998), pp. 87–117

Marshall, Alfred, *Industry and trade* (London: Macmillan, 1919)

Martin, Julian, *Francis Bacon, the state and the reform of natural philosophy* (Cambridge: Cambridge University Press, 1992)

Martineau, Harriet, *The history of England during the thirty years' peace: 1816–1846*, (London: Charles Knight, 1849–50), vol. I

'The English passport system', *Household Words* 6 (1852), 31–4

Marx, Karl, *Capital: a critique of political economy*, intro. Ernest Mandel, trans. Ben Fowkes (Harmondsworth: Penguin and New Left Review, 1976)

Mason, Otis T., *The origins of invention: a study of industry among primitive peoples* (Cambridge, MA, and London: MIT Press, 1895)

Mather, F. C., 'Achilles or Nestor? The duke of Wellington in British politics, 1832–1846', in Norman Gash (ed.), *Wellington: studies in the military and political career of the first duke of Wellington* (Manchester: Manchester University Press, 1990), pp. 170–95

Matthew, Colin, 'The New DNB', *History Today* 43 (September 1993), 10–13

May, Christopher, 'Antecedents to intellectual property: the European pre-history of the ownership of knowledge', *HT* 24 (2002), 1–20

Meller, Hugh, *London cemeteries: an illustrated guide and gazetteer* (3rd edn, Aldershot: Ashgate, 1999)

Meteyard, Eliza, *The Life of Josiah Wedgwood*, ed. R. W. Lightbourn (London: Hurst & Blackett, 1865–7; repr. London: Cornmarket Press Ltd, 1970)

Mill, John Stuart, *Principles of political economy* (5th edn, London: Parker, Son & Bourn, 1862)

Autobiography (London: Longman, Green, Reader and Dyer, 1873)

Miller, David Philip, *Discovering water: James Watt, Henry Cavendish and the nineteenth-century 'water controversy'* (Aldershot: Ashgate, 2004)

'True myths: James Watt's kettle, his condenser, and his chemistry', *History of Science* 42 (2004), 333–60

Miller, Hugh, *My school and schoolmasters: or, the story of my education*, ed. W. M. Mackenzie (Edinburgh: George A. Morton; London: Simpkin, Marshall & Co., 1905)

[Miller, W. H.], 'Patrick Miller', in William Anderson (ed.), *The Scottish nation: or the surnames, families, literature, honours, and biographical history of the people of Scotland* (Edinburgh: Fullarton, 1862)

Mingay, G. E., *Arthur Young and his times* (London: Macmillan, 1975)

Mitchell, Austin, *The Whigs in opposition, 1815–1830* (Oxford: Clarendon Press, 1967)

Mitchell, B. R., and Deane, Phyllis, *Abstract of British historical statistics* (Cambridge: Cambridge University Press, 1962)

Mitchell, Rosemary, *Picturing the past: English history in text and image, 1830–1870* (Oxford: Clarendon Press, 2000)

Moir, Esther, 'The industrial revolution: a romantic view', *History Today* 9 (1959), 589–97

Mokyr, Joel, *The gifts of Athena: historical origins of the knowledge economy* (Princeton and Oxford: Princeton University Press, 2002)

Moore, James, 'Charles Darwin lies in Westminster Abbey', *Biological Journal of the Linnean Society* 17 (1982), 97–113

More, Charles, *Skill and the English working class, 1870–1914* (London: Croom Helm, 1980)

Morrell, Jack, and Thackray, Arnold, *Gentlemen of science: early years of the British Association for the Advancement of Science* (Oxford: Clarendon Press, 1981)

Morris, Edward, *The life of Henry Bell, the practical introducer of the steam-boat into Great Britain and Ireland* (Glasgow: Blackie & Son, 1844)

Morris, R. J., 'Voluntary societies and British urban elites, 1780–1870', *HJ* 26 (1983), 95–118

   Class, sect and party: the making of the British middle class, Leeds 1820–1850 (Manchester: Manchester University Press, 1990)

Morton, Graeme, *Unionist nationalism: governing urban Scotland, 1830–1860* (Phantasie, E. Linton: Tuckwell Press, 1999)

   William Wallace: man and myth (Stroud: Sutton Publishing, 2001)

Morus, Iwan Rhys, 'Manufacturing nature: science, technology and Victorian consumer culture', *BJHS* 29 (1996), 403–34

   '"The nervous system of Britain": space, time and the electric telegraph in the Victorian age', *BJHS* 33 (2000), 455–75

Mountjoy, Peter Roger, 'The working-class press and working-class conservatism', in George Boyce, James Curran and Pauline Wingate (eds.), *Newspaper history from the seventeenth century to the present day* (London: Constable, and Beverly Hills: Sage Publications, 1978), pp. 265–80

Muirhead, James Patrick (ed.), *The origin and progress of the mechanical inventions of James Watt, illustrated by his correspondence with his friends and the specifications of his patents* (London: John Murray, 1854), vol. I

   The life of James Watt (2nd edn, London: James Murray, 1859)

Munby, A. N. L., *The history and bibliography of science in England: the first phase, 1837–1845* (Los Angeles: University of California Press, 1968)

Murray, Charles, *Debates in Parliament respecting the Jennerian discovery* (London: W. Phillips, 1808)

Murray, Penelope (ed.), *Genius: the history of an idea* (Oxford: Basil Blackwell, 1989)

Musson, A. E., 'James Nasmyth and the early growth of mechanical engineering', *EHR* 10 (1957), 121–7

'The "Manchester School" and exportation of machinery', *Business History* 14 (1972), 17–50

'Industrial motive power in the United Kingdom, 1800–70', *EHR* 29 (1976), 415–39

Musson, A. E., and Robinson, Eric, *Science and technology in the industrial revolution* (Manchester: Manchester University Press, 1969)

Nahum, Andrew, 'Marc Isambard Brunel', in Andrew Kelly and Melanie Kelly (eds.), *Brunel, in love with the impossible: A celebration of the life, work and legacy of Isambard Kingdom Brunel* (Bristol: Bristol Cultural Development Partnership, 2006), pp. 40–56

Napier, M. (ed.), *Supplement to the Fourth, Fifth, and Sixth Editions of the Encyclopaedia Britannica*, 6 vols. (Edinburgh: A. Constable, 1815–24)

Naudé, Gabriel, *Instructions concerning erecting of a library, interpreted by Jo. Evelyn* (London: G. Bedle and T. Collins; J. Crook, 1661)

New, Chester W., *The life of Henry Brougham* (Oxford: Clarendon Press, 1961)

Newton, W., *A letter on the Stephenson monument, and the education of the district, addressed to the Right Hon Lord Ravensworth* (Newcastle upon Tyne: Robert Fisher, 1859)

Nicholls, David, 'Richard Cobden and the International Peace Congress Movement, 1848–1853', *Journal of British Studies* 30 (1991), 351–76

Nicholson, J., *The commerce of Bradford* (1820)

Nickles, Thomas, 'Discovery', in Robert C. Olby, Geoffrey N. Cantor, J. R. R. Christie and M. J. S. Hodge (eds.), *Companion to the history of modern science* (London: Routledge, 1990), pp. 148–65

Noakes, Richard, 'Representing "A Century of Inventions": nineteenth-century technology and Victorian *Punch*', in L. Henson *et al.* (eds.), *Culture and science in the nineteenth-century media* (Aldershot: Ashgate, 2004), pp. 151–63

Nora, Pierre, *Realms of memory*, ed. Lawrence D. Kritzman; trans. Arthur Goldhammer (New York: Columbia University Press, c. 1996–8)

Noszlopy, G., *Public sculpture of Birmingham*, ed. Jeremy Beach (Liverpool: Liverpool University Press, 1998)

Nuvolari, Alessandro, *The making of steam power technology: a study of technical change during the British industrial revolution* (Eindhoven: Eindhoven University Press, 2004)

O'Brien, Patrick, 'The political economy of British taxation, 1660–1815', *EHR* 41 (1988), 1–32

'The micro foundations of macro invention: the case of the Reverend Edmund Cartwright', *Textile History* 28 (1997), 201–33

O'Donohue, Freeman, and Hake, Henry M. (eds.), *Catalogue of engraved British portraits preserved in the Department of Prints and Drawings in the British Museum* (London: Trustees of the British Museum, 1922), vol. V

O'Dwyer, Frederick, *The architecture of Deane and Woodward* (Cork: Cork University Press, 1997)

Oliver, Thomas, *The Stephenson monument: what should it be? A question and answer addressed to the subscribers* (3rd edn, Newcastle upon Tyne: M. & M. W. Lambert, 1858)

Orange, A. D., 'The origins of the British Association for the Advancement of Science', *BJHS* 6 (1972), 152–76

Orbach, Julian, *Victorian architecture in Britain* (London and New York: A. & C. Black, 1987)

Osborne, Brian D., *The ingenious Mr Bell: a life of Henry Bell (1767–1830), pioneer of steam navigation* (Glendaruel: Argyll Publishing, 1995)

Osborne, John W., *John Cartwright* (Cambridge: Cambridge University Press, 1972)

Osborne, Thomas, 'Against "creativity": a philistine rant', *Economy and Society* 32 (2003), 507–25

Oxford Dictionary of National Biography (Oxford: Oxford University Press, 2004)

Oxford University Museum (1860) [printed prospectus]

Ozouf, Mona, 'The Panthéon: the École Normale of the dead', in Pierre Nora (ed.), *Realms of memory: the construction of the French past*, ed. Lawrence D. Kritzman, trans. Arthur Goldhammer (New York: Columbia University Press, c. 1996–8), vol. III, pp. 324–45

Pannell, J. P. M., 'The Taylors of Southampton: pioneers in mechanical engineering', *Proceedings of the Institution of Mechanical Engineers* 169 (1955), 924–31

Parker, Joanne M., 'The day of a thousand years: Winchester's 1901 commemoration of Alfred the Great', *Studies in Medievalism* 12 (2002), 113–36

The patent, a poem, by the author of The graces (London, 1776)

Payton, Philip, 'Paralysis and revival: the reconstruction of Celtic-Catholic Cornwall, 1890–1945', in Ella Westland (ed.), *Cornwall: the cultural construction of place* (Penzance: Patten Press, 1997), pp. 25–39

'Industrial Celts? Cornish identity in the age of technological prowess', *Cornish Studies* 10 (2002), 116–35

Pears, Iain, 'The gentleman and the hero: Wellington and Napoleon in the nineteenth century', in Roy Porter (ed.), *Myths of the English* (Cambridge: Polity Press, 1992), pp. 216–36

Pearson, Richard, 'Thackeray and *Punch* at the Great Exhibition: authority and ambivalence in verbal and visual caricatures', in Louise Purbrick (ed.), *The Great Exhibition of 1851: new interdisciplinary essays* (Manchester and New York: Manchester University Press, 2001), pp. 179–205

Pemberton, T. Edgar, *James Watt of Soho and Heathfield: annals of industry and genius* (Birmingham: Cornish Brothers Ltd, 1905)

Penfold, Alastair E. (ed.), *Thomas Telford: engineer* (London: Thomas Telford Ltd, 1980)

Pennington, R., *A descriptive catalogue of the etched work of Wenceslaus Hollar, 1607–1677* (Cambridge: Cambridge University Press, 1982)

Penny, John, *Up, up, and away! An account of ballooning in and around Bristol and Bath 1784 to 1999* (Bristol: Bristol Branch of the Historical Association, 1999)

Penny, N. B., 'The Whig cult of Fox in early nineteenth-century sculpture', *Past & Present* 70 (1976), 94–105

Penrose, Edith Tilton, *The economics of the international patent system* (Baltimore: Johns Hopkins Press, 1951)

Peters, Ken, *Inventors on stamps* (Seaford, E. Sussex: Aptimage Ltd, 1985)

Petree, J. Foster, 'Some reflections on engineering biography', *TNS* 40 (1967), 147–58

Petroski, Henry, *Reshaping the world: adventures in engineering* (New York: Alfred A. Knopf, 1997)

Pettitt, Clare, *Patent inventions: intellectual property and the Victorian novel* (Oxford: Oxford University Press, 2004)

Pettman, Mary (ed.), Yung, K. K. (comp.), *National Portrait Gallery, complete illustrated catalogue, 1856–1979* (London: National Portrait Gallery, 1981)

Pevsner, Nikolaus, *The buildings of England: London. Vol. I, The cities of London and Westminster* (Harmondsworth: Penguin, 1957)

Northumberland (Harmondsworth: Penguin, 1957)

Yorkshire, the West Riding (Harmondsworth: Penguin Books, 1959)

Lancashire: I, The industrial and commercial south (Harmondsworth: Penguin, 1969)

Staffordshire (Harmondsworth: Penguin, 1974)

Phillips, John, *A general history of inland navigation, foreign and domestic* (5th edn, London, 1805), repr. Charles Hadfield (ed.), *Phillips' inland navigation* (Newton Abbot: David & Charles, 1970)

[Phillips, Richard], *British public characters of 1798* (London: Richard Phillips, 1798)

British public characters of 1802–1803 (London: Richard Phillips, 1803)

British public characters of 1806 (London: Richard Phillips, 1806)

Pickering, Paul. A., 'A "grand ossification": William Cobbett and the commemoration of Tom Paine', in Paul A. Pickering and Alex Tyrrell (eds.), *Contested sites: commemoration, memorial and popular politics in nineteenth-century Britain* (Aldershot: Ashgate, 2004), pp. 57–80

'The Chartist rites of passage: commemorating Feargus O'Connor', in Paul A. Pickering and Alex Tyrrell (eds.), *Contested sites: commemoration, memorial and popular politics in nineteenth-century Britain* (Aldershot: Ashgate, 2004), pp. 105–15

Pickering, Paul A., and Tyrrell, Alex, *The people's bread: a history of the Anti-Corn Law League* (London and New York: Leicester University Press, 2000)

'The public memorial of reform: commemoration and contestation', in Paul A. Pickering and Alex Tyrrell (eds.), *Contested sites: commemoration, memorial and popular politics in nineteenth-century Britain* (Aldershot: Ashgate, 2004), pp. 1–23

Pike, W. T. (ed.), *Northumberland, at the opening of the twentieth century, by James Jameson* (Brighton: Pike, 1905)

Plant, Arnold, 'The economic theory concerning patents for invention', *Economica* 1 (1934), 30–51

Playfair, Lyon, 'The chemical principles involved in the manufactures of the Exhibition', in *Lectures on the results of the Great Exhibition of 1851* (London: David Bogue, 1852), vol. I, pp. 160–208

'Presidential address', *BAAS, Report for 1885, Aberdeen* (1886), 3–29

Pole, William, *The life of Sir William Siemens* (London: John Murray, 1888)

Ponting, Kenneth G. (ed.), *A memoir of the life, writings, and mechanical inventions, of Edmund Cartwright, D. D., F. R. S., inventor of the power loom* (London: Adams & Dart, 1971)

Poovey, Mary, *The proper lady and the woman writer: ideology as style in the works of Mary Wollstonecraft, Mary Shelley and Jane Austen* (Chicago: Chicago University Press, 1984)

Popplow, Marcus, 'Protection and promotion: privileges for inventions and books of machines in the early modern period', *HT* 20 (1998), 103–24

Porter, Dorothy, and Porter, Roy, 'The politics of prevention: anti-vaccinationism and public health in nineteenth-century England', *Medical History* 32 (1988), 231–52

Porter, G. R., *The progress of the nation, in its various social and economical relations, from the beginning of the nineteenth century* (London: John Murray, 1836–43), vol. I

Porter, Roy, 'Where the statue stood: the reputation of Edward Jenner', in Ken Arnold (ed.), *Needles in medical history: an exhibition at the Wellcome Trust History of Medicine Gallery, April 1998* (London: Wellcome Trust, 1998), pp. 7–12

Poulot, Dominique, 'Pantheons in eighteenth-century France: temple, museum, pyramid', in Richard Wrigley and Matthew Craske (eds.), *Pantheons: transformations of a monumental idea* (Aldershot: Ashgate, 2004), pp. 123–45

Power, Henry, *Experimental philosophy* (London: John Martin and James Allestry, 1664)

Prager, Frank D., 'A manuscript of Taccola, quoting Brunelleschi, on problems of inventors and builder', *Proceedings of the American Philosophical Society* 112 (1968), 131–49

Prager, Frank D., and Scaglia, Gustina, *Mariano Taccola and his book "De Ingeniis"* (Cambridge, MA: MIT Press, 1972)

Prior, M. E., 'Bacon's man of science', *JHI* 15 (1954), 348–55

Prosser, R. B., *Birmingham inventors and inventions* [Birmingham: privately published, 1881], with a new foreword by Asa Briggs (Wakefield: S. R. Publishers, 1970)

Prothero, Iorwerth, *Artisans and politics in early nineteenth-century London: John Gast and his times* (London: Methuen & Co., 1981)

Pugin, A. W. N., *Contrasts: or a parallel between the noble edifices of the Middle Ages, and corresponding buildings of the present day; shewing the present decay of taste* (2nd edn, London: Charles Dolman, 1841; repr. with an introduction by H. R. Hitchcock, Leicester University Press, 1969)

Pumfrey, Stephen, 'Who did the work? Experimental philosophers and public demonstrators in Augustan England', *BJHS* 28 (1995), 131–56

Pumphrey, Ralph E., 'The introduction of industrialists into the British peerage: a study in adaptation of a social institution', *American Historical Review* 45 (1959), 1–16

Quilter, James Henry, and Chamberlain, John, *Frame-work knitting and hosiery manufacture* (Leicester: Hosiery Trade Journal, 1911)

Quinault, Roland, 'The cult of the centenary, c. 1784–1914', *Historical Research* 71 (1998), 303–23

Quinlan, Maurice J., 'Balloons and the awareness of a new age', *Studies in Burke and His Time* 14 (1973), 222–38

Raggio, Olga, 'The myth of Prometheus: its survival and metamorphoses up to the eighteenth century', *Journal of the Warburg and Courtauld Institutes* 21 (1958), 44–62

Randall, Adrian J., 'The philosophy of Luddism: the case of the west of England woollen workers, ca. 1790–1809', *T&C* 27 (1986), 1–17

   Before the Luddites: custom, community and machinery in the English woollen industry, 1776–1809 (Cambridge: Cambridge University Press, 1991)

Randall, Anthony G., 'The timekeeper that won the longitude prize', in William J. H. Andrewes (ed.), *The quest for longitude* (Cambridge, MA: Collection of Scientific Instruments, Harvard University, 1996), pp. 236–54

Raven, James, 'British history and the enterprise culture', *Past & Present* 123 (1989), 178–204

   Judging new wealth: popular publishing and responses to commerce in England, 1750–1800 (Oxford: Clarendon Press, 1992)

Read, Benedict, *Victorian sculpture* (New York and London: Yale University Press, 1982)

Read, Donald, *The English provinces, c. 1760–1960: a study in influence* (London: Edward Arnold, 1964)

Reader, W. J., '"At the head of all the new professions": the engineer in Victorian society', in Neil McKendrick and R. B. Outhwaite (eds.), *Business life and public policy: essays in honour of D. C. Coleman* (Cambridge: Cambridge University Press, 1986), pp. 173–84

Redford, Arthur, *Manchester merchants and foreign trade, 1794–1858* (Manchester: Manchester University Press, 1934)

Rees, Abraham (ed.), *The cyclopaedia; or, universal dictionary of arts, sciences, and literature* (London: Longman, Hurst, Rees, Orme and Brown, 1802–20)

Reid, Alastair, 'Intelligent artisans and aristocrats of labour: the essays of Thomas Wright', in J. M. Winter (ed.), *The working class in modern British History: essays in honour of Henry Pelling* (Cambridge: Cambridge University Press, 1983), pp. 171–86

Reid, Hugo, *The steam engine* (Edinburgh: William Tait, 1838)

Rennie, Sir John, 'Presidential address', *Proceedings of the Institution of Civil Engineers* 7 (1847), 81–2

Richardson, Ruth, *Death, dissection and the destitute* (new edn, London: Phoenix, 2001)

Richardson, Thomas, 'A review of the arguments for and against the patent laws', *The Scientific Review, and Journal of the Inventors' Institute* 2 (1 April 1867), 223–5

Richmond, Marsha L., 'The 1909 Darwin celebration: re-examining evolution in the light of Mendel, mutation, and meiosis', *Isis* 97 (2006), 447–84

Rickman, J. (ed.), *Life of Thomas Telford, civil engineer, written by himself* (London: Payne & Foss, 1838)

Roberts, Robert, *A ragged schooling: growing up in the classic slum* (Manchester: Manchester University Press, 1976)

Robertson, P. L., and Alston, I. J., 'Technological change and the organization of work in capitalist firms', *EHR* 45 (1992), 330–49

Robinson, Eric, 'James Watt and the tea kettle: a myth justified', *History Today* (April 1956), 261–5

'James Watt and the law of patents', *T&C* 13 (1972), 115–39

Rodger, Alexander, 'Verses written upon the opening of the Glasgow and Greenock Railway, 30 March, 1841', *Stray Leaves* (Glasgow: Charles Rattray, 1842)

Rogers, J. E. Thorold, 'On the rationale and working of the patent laws', *Journal of the Statistical Society of London* 26 (1863), 121–42

Rogers, Pat, 'Gulliver and the engineers', *Modern Language Review* 70 (1975), 260–70

Roll, Eric, *An early experiment in industrial organisation: being a history of the firm of Boulton & Watt, 1775–1805* (repr. New York: Augustus M. Kelley, 1930)

Rolt, L. T. C., *Victorian engineering* (Harmondsworth: Penguin Books, 1974)

The aeronauts: a history of ballooning, 1783–1903 (2nd edn, Gloucester: Sutton, 1985)

Roos, David A., 'The "aims and intentions" of "Nature"', in James Paradis and Thomas Postlewait (eds.), *Victorian science and Victorian values: literary perspectives* (New York: New York Academy of Sciences, 1981), pp. 159–80

Rose, Jonathan, *The intellectual life of the British working classes* (New Haven and London: Yale University Press, 2001)

Rose, Mark, *Authors and owners: the invention of copyright* (Cambridge, MA and London: Harvard University Press, 1993)

Rose, Michael E., 'Samuel Crompton (1753–1827): inventor of the spinning mule: a reconsideration', *Trans. Lancashire and Cheshire Antiquarian Society* 75 (1965), 11–32

Rose, R. B., 'The Priestley riots of 1791', *Past & Present* 18 (1960), 68–88

Rosenberg, Nathan, *Inside the black box: technology and economics* (Cambridge: Cambridge University Press, 1982)

Ross, Sydney, '*Scientist*: the story of a word', *Annals of Science* 18 (1962), 65–86

Rossi, Paolo, *Philosophy, technology and the arts in the early modern era*, trans. Salvator Attanasio, ed. Benjamin Nelson (New York and London: Harper & Row, 1970)

Routledge, Robert, *Discoveries and inventions of the nineteenth century* [1890] (repr. London: Bracken Books, 1989)

Rowbotham, Judith, '"All our past proclaims our future": popular biography and masculine identity during the golden age, 1850–1870', in Ian Inkster, Colin Griffin, Jeff Hill and Judith Rowbotham (eds.), *The golden age: essays in British social and economic history, 1850–1870* (Aldershot: Ashgate, 2000), 262–75

Rubinstein, W. D., 'The end of "Old Corruption" in Britain, 1780–1860', *Past & Present* 101 (1983), 55–86

Capitalism, culture, and economic decline in Britain, 1750–1990 (London: Routledge, 1993)

Rule, John, 'The property of skill in the period of manufacture', in Patrick Joyce (ed.), *The historical meanings of work* (Cambridge: Cambridge University Press, 1987), pp. 99–118

Sabel, C., and Zeitlin, J., 'Historical alternatives to mass production', *P&P* 108 (1985), 133–76

Salmon, Philip, *Electoral reform at work: local politics and national parties, 1832–1841* (Woodbridge: Royal Historical Society and Boydell Press, 2002)

Salveson, Paul, *The people's monuments: a guide to sites and memorials in north west England* (Manchester: WEA, 1987)

Samuel, Raphael, 'Workshop of the world: steam power and hand technology in mid Victorian Britain', *History Workshop* 3 (1977), 6–72

Scally, Gabriel, and Oliver, Isabel, 'Putting Jenner back in his place', *The Lancet* 362 (4 October 2003), 1092

Schaffer, Simon, 'Natural philosophy and public spectacle', *History of Science* 21 (1983), 1–43

'Scientific discoveries and the end of natural philosophy', *Social Studies of Science* 16 (1986), 387–420

'Priestley and the politics of spirit', in R. G. W. Anderson and Christopher Lawrence (eds.), *Science, medicine and dissent: Joseph Priestley, 1733–1804* (London: Wellcome Institute, 1987), pp. 38–53

'Defoe's natural philosophy and the worlds of credit', in John Christie and Sally Shuttleworth (eds.), *Nature transfigured: science and literature, 1700–1900* (Manchester and New York: Manchester University Press, 1989), 13–44

'Genius in Romantic natural philosophy', in Andrew Cunningham and Nicholas Jardine (eds.), *Romanticism and the sciences* (Cambridge: Cambridge University Press, 1990), pp. 82–98

'A social history of plausibility: country, city and calculation in Augustan Britain', in Adrian Wilson (ed.), *Rethinking social history: English society 1570–1920 and its interpretation* (Manchester and New York: Manchester University Press, 1993), pp. 128–57

'Making up discovery', in Margaret A. Boden (ed.), *Dimensions of creativity* (Cambridge, MA, and London: MIT Press, 1994), pp. 13–51

'The show that never ends: perpetual motion in the early eighteenth century', *BJHS* 28 (1995), 157–89

Schiebinger, Londa, 'The private life of plants: sexual politics in Carl Linnaeus and Erasmus Darwin', in Marina Benjamin (ed.), *Science and sensibility: gender and scientific enquiry, 1780–1945* (Oxford: Blackwell, 1991), pp. 121–43

Schiff, Eric, *Industrialization without national patents: the Netherlands, 1869–1912, Switzerland, 1850–1907* (Princeton, NJ: Princeton University Press, 1971)

Schivelbusch, Wolfgang, *The railway journey: the industrialization of time and space in the 19th century* (Leamington Spa, Hamburg, New York: Berg, 1986)

Schofield, Robert E., *The Lunar Society of Birmingham: a social history of provincial science and industry in eighteenth-century England* (Oxford: Clarendon Press, 1963)

Schumpeter, Joseph A., *The theory of economic development: an inquiry into profits, capital, interest and the business cycle* [1912], trans. R. Opie (Cambridge, MA: Harvard University Press, 1962)

Scott, W. R., *The constitution and finance of English, Scottish and Irish joint-stock companies to 1720* (Cambridge: Cambridge University Press, 1912), vols. I, III

[Scott, Walter], *The monastery: a romance, by the author of 'Waverley'* (Edinburgh: Constable, 1820)

Secord, Anne, '"Be what you would seem to be": Samuel Smiles, Thomas Edward, and the making of a working-class scientific hero', *Science in Context* 16 (2003), 147–73

Semmel, Bernard, *The rise of free trade imperialism: classical political economy and the empire of free trade and imperialism, 1750–1850* (Cambridge: Cambridge University Press, 1970)

Shapin, Steven, 'The image of the man of science', in Roy Porter (ed.), *The Cambridge history of science, volume 4: eighteenth century science* (Cambridge: Cambridge University Press, 2003), pp. 159–83

Shelley, Mary, *Frankenstein or the modern Prometheus, the 1818 text*, ed. Marilyn Butler (Oxford: Oxford University Press, 1993)

Sherwood, Jennifer, and Pevsner, Nikolaus, *Oxfordshire* (Harmondsworth: Penguin, 1974)

Shortland, Michael, and Yeo, Richard (eds.), *Telling lives in science: essays on scientific biography* (Cambridge: Cambridge University Press, 1996)

Siemens, C. William, 'Presidential address', *BAAS, Report for 1882, Southampton* (1883), 1–33

Simmons, Jack (ed.), *The men who built railways: a reprint of F. R. Conder's Personal Recollections of English Engineers* (London: Thomas Telford, Ltd, 1983)

[Smiles, Samuel], 'James Watt', *Quarterly Review* 104 (October 1858), 410–51

Smiles, Samuel, *Industrial biography: iron workers and tool makers* (London: John Murray, 1863)

  The lives of Boulton and Watt (London: John Murray, 1865)

  Self-help: with illustrations of conduct and perseverance (new edn, London: John Murray, 1875)

  Lives of the engineers: the locomotive, George and Robert Stephenson (London: John Murray, 1877)

  Men of invention and industry (London: John Murray, 1884)

[Smiles, Samuel], *The autobiography of Samuel Smiles*, ed. Thomas Mackay (London: John Murray, 1905)

Smith, Christine, *Architecture in the culture of early humanism: ethics, aesthetics, and eloquence, 1400–1470* (New York: Oxford University Press, 1992)

Smith, Crosbie, 'Frankenstein and natural magic', in Stephen Bann (ed.), *Frankenstein, creation and monstrosity* (London: Reaktion Books, 1994), 39–59

  '"Nowhere but in a great town": William Thomson's spiral of classroom credibility', in Crosbie Smith and Jon Agar (eds.), *Making space for science: territorial themes in the shaping of knowledge* (Basingstoke: Macmillan, 1998), pp. 118–46

  The science of energy: a cultural history of energy physics in Victorian Britain (London: Athlone, 1998)

Smith, E. C., 'The first twenty years of screw propulsion', *TNS* 19 (1938–9), 145–64

'Memorials to engineers and men of science', *TNS* 28 (1951–3), 137–9

Smith, James V., *The Watt Institution Dundee, 1824–49*, The Abertay Historical Society publication, 19 (Dundee, 1978)

Smith, Jonathan, *Fact and feeling: Baconian science and the nineteenth-century literary imagination* (Madison, WI: University of Wisconsin Press, 1994)

Smith, Tori, '"A grand work of noble conception"; the Victoria Memorial and imperial London', in Felix Driver and David Gilbert (eds.), *Imperial cities: landscape, display and identity* (Manchester: Manchester University Press, 1999), pp. 21–39

Snow, C. P., *The two cultures and the scientific revolution* (Cambridge: Cambridge University Press, 1961)

Sobel, Dava, 'Harrison memorial: Longitude hero's slow road to the abbey', *The Guardian*, 25 March 2006

Somerset, Edward, 2nd marquis of Worcester, *An exact and true definition of the most stupendious water-commanding engine* (London, 1663)

Sorrenson, R., 'George Graham, visible technician', *BJHS* 32 (1999), 203–21

Spadafora, David, *The idea of progress in eighteenth-century Britain* (New Haven and London: Yale University Press, 1990)

Sprat, Thomas, *History of the Royal Society of London, for the improving of natural knowledge* (London: F. Martyn and J. Allestry, 1667)

Stack, David, *Nature and artifice: the life and thought of Thomas Hodgskin (1787–1869)* (London: The Boydell Press, for the Royal Historical Society, 1998)

Stanley, Arthur Penrhyn, *Historical memorials of Westminster Abbey* (3rd edn, London: John Murray, 1869)

Stanley, Autumn, 'Once and future power: women as inventors', *Women's Studies International Forum* 15 (1992), 193–202

Mothers and daughters of invention: notes for a revised history of technology (Metuchen, NJ: Scarecrow Press, 1993)

Stansfield, Dorothy A., *Thomas Beddoes M.D. 1760–1808: chemist, physician, democrat* (Dordrecht, Boston, Lancaster: D. Reidel Pub. Co., 1984)

Stewart, Larry R., 'Public lectures and private patronage in Newtonian England', *Isis* 77 (1986), 47–58

The rise of public science: rhetoric, technology, and natural philosophy in Newtonian Britain, 1660–1750 (Cambridge: Cambridge University Press, 1992)

'Global pillage: science, commerce, and empire', in Roy Porter (ed.), *The Cambridge history of science, volume 4: eighteenth century science* (Cambridge: Cambridge University Press, 2003), pp. 825–44

Stirling, J., 'Patent right', in [Robert Andrew Macfie (ed.)], *Recent discussions on the abolition of patents for inventions in the United Kingdom, France, Germany, and the Netherlands* (London: Longmans, Green, Reader and Dyer, 1869)

Stuart, Robert, *Historical and descriptive anecdotes of steam engines, and of their inventors and improvers* (London: Wightman & Co., 1829)

Sussman, Herbert L., *Victorians and the machine* (Cambridge, MA: Harvard University Press, 1968)

Sutherland, George, *Twentieth century inventions: a forecast* (London: Longmans, Green & Co., 1901)

Swan, M. E., and Swan, K. R., *Sir Joseph Wilson Swan, FRS: a memoir* (London: Ernest Benn, 1929, repr. 1968)

[Swift, Jonathan], *The prose works of Jonathan Swift*, ed. Herbert Davis (rev. edn, Oxford: Basil Blackwell, 1959), vol. XI

[T.], *Letters on the utility and policy of employing machines to shorten labour* (London: T. Becket, 1780)

Tagg, John, *The burden of representation: essays on photographies and histories* (Basingstoke: Macmillan, 1988)

Tann, Jennifer, *The development of the factory* (London: Cornmarket Press, 1970)
  'Richard Arkwright and technology', *History* 58 (1973), 29–44
  'Mr Hornblower and his crew: Watt engine pirates at the end of the 18th century', *TNS* 51 (1979–80), 95–105
  'Steam and sugar: the diffusion of the stationary steam engine to the Caribbean sugar industry, 1770–1840', *HT* 19 (1997), 63–84

Taylor, Miles, *The decline of English radicalism, 1847–1860* (Oxford: Clarendon Press, 1995)

Taylor, Nicholas, 'The awful sublimity of the Victorian city', in H. J. Dyos and Michael Wolff (eds.), *The Victorian city: images and reality* (London: Routledge & Kegan Paul, 1973), vol. II, pp. 431–48

Thackray, A., 'Natural knowledge in a cultural context: the Manchester model', *American Historical Review* 79 (1974), 672–709

Thirsk, Joan, *Economic policy and projects: the development of a consumer society in early modern England* (Oxford: Oxford University Press, 1978)

Thirsk, Joan, and Cooper, J. P. (eds.), *17th century economic documents* (Oxford: Clarendon Press, 1972)

Thomas, Keith, *Changing conceptions of national biography: the Oxford DNB in historical perspective* (Cambridge: Cambridge University Press, 2005)

Thompson, F. M. L., *English landed society in the nineteenth century* (London: Routledge & Kegan Paul, 1963)
  Gentrification and the enterprise culture, Britain 1780–1980 (Oxford: Oxford University Press, 2001)

[Thompson, William], *Labor rewarded: the claims of labor and capital conciliated: or, how to secure to labor the whole products of its exertions, by one of the idle classes* (London: Hunt & Clarke, 1827)

Timbs, John, *Stories of inventors and discoverers in science and the useful arts* (London: Kent and Co., 1860)
  Wonderful inventions: from the mariner's compass to the electric telegraph cable (2nd edn, London: G. Routledge and Sons, 1882 [1881])

Timmins, Geoffrey, *The last shift: the decline of hand-loom weaving in nineteenth-century Lancashire* (Manchester: Manchester University Press, 1993)

Titley, A., 'Beginnings of the Society', *TNS* 22 (1942), 37–9

Todd, Dennis, 'Laputa, the Whore of Babylon, and the Idols of Science', *Studies in Philology* 75 (1978), 93–120

Tonelli, Giorgio, 'Genius from the Renaissance to 1770', in Philip P. Wiener (ed.), *Dictionary of the history of ideas* (New York: Charles Scribner's Sons, 1973), vol. II, pp. 292–7

Torrens, Hugh, 'Jonathan Hornblower (1753–1815) and the steam engine: a historiographic analysis', in Denis Smith (ed.), *Perceptions of great engineers, fact and fantasy* (London: Science Museum for the Newcomen Society, National Museums and Galleries on Merseyside, and the University of Liverpool, 1994), pp. 23–34

'Some thoughts on the history of technology and its current condition in Britain', *HT* 22 (2000), 223–32

Toynbee, Arnold, *Lectures on the industrial revolution in England* (London, 1884); repr. as *Toynbee's industrial revolution*, intro. T. S. Ashton (Newton Abbot: David & Charles, 1969)

Travers, T. H. E., *Samuel Smiles and the Victorian work ethic* (London and New York: Garland, 1987)

Tredgold, Thomas, *The steam engine: comprising an account of its invention and progressive improvement* (London: J. Taylor, 1827)

Tregallas, Walter Hawkan, 'Trevithick the engineer', in *Cornish worthies: sketches of some eminent Cornish men and families* (London: E. Stock, 1884), vol. II

Trench, Richard, and Hillman, Ellis, *London under London: a subterranean guide*, (2nd edn, London: John Murray, 1993)

[Trevithick, Richard], *The Richard Trevithick memorial* [London, 1888]

Trevor-Roper, Hugh, 'The invention of tradition: the Highland tradition of Scotland', in Eric Hobsbawm and Terence Ranger (eds.), *The invention of tradition* (Cambridge: Cambridge University Press, 1983), pp. 15–42

Tucker, Josiah, *Instructions for travellers* (Dublin, 1758), repr. in Robert L. Schuyler (ed.), *Josiah Tucker: a selection from his economic and political writings* (New York: Columbia University Press, 1931)

Turner, C. H., *Proceedings of the public meeting held at Freemasons' Hall, on the 18th June, 1824, for erecting a monument to … James Watt* (London: John Murray, 1824)

Turner, Frank, 'Public science in Britain', *Isis* 71 (1980), 360–79

Turner, Katherine, 'Defoe's *Tour*: the changing "face of things"', *British Journal for Eighteenth-Century Studies* 24 (2001), 189–206

Tyas, G. 'Matthew Murray: a centenary appreciation', *TNS* 6 (1925), 111–43

Tyrrell, Alex, with Davis, Michael T., 'Bearding the Tories: the commemoration of the Scottish Political Martyrs of 1793–94', in Paul A. Pickering and Alex Tyrrell (eds.), *Contested sites: commemoration, memorial and popular politics in nineteenth-century Britain* (Aldershot: Ashgate, 2004), pp. 25–56

Tyrrell, Alexander, 'Making the millennium: the mid-nineteenth century peace movement', *HJ* 20 (1978), 75–95

Uglow, Jennifer S., *The lunar men: the friends who made the future, 1730–1810* (London: Faber & Faber, 2002)

Ure, Andrew, *Philosophy of manufactures: or, an exposition of the scientific, moral, and commercial economy of the factory system of Great Britain* (London, 1835)

Usherwood, P., Beach, J., and Morris, C., *Public sculpture of north-east England* (Liverpool: Liverpool University Press, 2000)

van der Linden, W. H., *The international peace movement, 1815–1874* (Amsterdam: Tilleul Publications, 1987)

Vaughan, Robert, *The age of great cities: or, modern society viewed in its relation to intelligence, morals, and religion* (London: Jackson & Walford, 1843)

Vernon, James, *Politics and the people: a study in English political culture, c. 1815–1867* (Cambridge: Cambridge University Press, 1993)

Vincenti, Walter G., *What engineers know and how they know it: analytical studies from aeronautical history* (Baltimore: Johns Hopkins University Press, 1991)

von Tunzelmann, G. N., *Steam power and British industrialization to 1860* (Oxford: Oxford University Press, 1978)

[Wade, John], *History of the middle and working classes; with a popular exposition of the economical and political principles which have influenced the past and present conditions of the industrious orders* (London: Effringham Wilson, 1833)

Wadsworth, A. P., and Mann, Julia de Lacy, *The cotton trade and industrial Lancashire, 1600–1870* (Manchester: Manchester University Press, 1965)

Walker, James, 'Address of the President to the Annual General Meeting', *Proceedings of the Institution of Civil Engineers* (1839), vol. I, pp. 15–18

Walker, Ralph, *A treatise on magnetism, with a description and explanation of a meridional and azimuth compass, for ascertaining the quantity of variation, without any calculation whatever, at any time of the day* (London: G. Adams, 1794)

Walker, Jnr, William (ed.), *Memoirs of the distinguished men of science of Great Britain living in the years 1807–8*, intro. Robert Hunt (London: Walker, 1862)

Wallace, Alfred Russel, *The wonderful century: its successes and failures* (London: Swan Sonnenschein, 1898)

Ward, John Towers, *Chartism* (London: Batsford, 1973)

Ward-Jackson, Philip, *Public sculpture of the City of London* (Liverpool: Liverpool University Press, 2003)

Warwick, Andrew, 'Cambridge mathematics and Cavendish physics', *Studies in History and Philosophy of Science* 23 (1992), 625–56

[Watt, James], *James Watt Centenary Commemoration* (Birmingham, 1919)

[Watt, James, Jnr], *Memoir of James Watt, FRSL & FRSE: from the Supplement to the Encyclopaedia Britannica* (London: Hodgson, 1824)

Webb, R. K., *The British working class reader, 1790–1848: literacy and social tension* (London: George Allen & Unwin, 1955)

Weber, Robert J., and Perkins, David N. (eds.), *Inventive minds: creativity in technology* (New York and Oxford: Oxford University Press, 1992)

Webster, Charles, *The great instauration: science, medicine and reform, 1626–1660* (London: Duckworth, 1975)

Weisinger, Herbert, 'English treatment of the relationship between the rise of science and the Renaissance, 1740–1840', *Annals of Science* 7 (1951), 248–73

West, Bob, 'The making of the English working past: a critical view of the Ironbridge Gorge Museum', in Robert Lumley (ed.), *The museum time machine: putting cultures on display* (London: Routledge, 1988), pp. 36–62

Westminster Abbey Official Guide (London, 1966)

Whelan, Yvonne, *Reinventing modern Dublin: streetscape, iconography and the politics of identity* (Dublin: University College Dublin Press, 2003)

Wells, H. G., *The island of Dr Moreau*, in *The works of H. G. Wells: Atlantic edition.Vol. 2* (London: T. Fisher Unwin, 1924)

Whewell, Rev. William, 'The general bearing of the Great Exhibition on the progress of art and science', in *Lectures on the results of the Great Exhibition of 1851* (London: David Bogue, 1852), vol. I

White, William Edward Holt, *The man who stole the earth* (London, 1909)

Wiener, Martin J., *English culture and the decline of the industrial spirit, 1850–1950* (Cambridge: Cambridge University Press, 1981)

Williams, J. F. Lake, *An historical account of inventions and discoveries in those arts and sciences which are of utility or ornament to man, lend assistance to human comfort, a polish to life, and render the civilized state, beyond comparison, preferable to a state of nature; traced from their origin; with every subsequent improvement* (London: T. & J. Allman, 1820), vol. I

Williams, Raymond, *Culture and society, 1780–1950* (London: Chatto & Windus, 1958)

Keywords: a vocabulary of culture and society (London: Fontana, 1983)

Williamson, George, *Memorials of the lineage, early life, education, and development of the genius of James Watt* (Edinburgh: the Watt Club, 1856)

Willis, Kirk, 'The introduction and critical reception of Marxist thought in Britain, 1850–1900', *HJ* 20 (1977), 423–44

Willsdon, Clare A. P., *Mural painting in Britain, 1840–1940: image and meaning* (Oxford: Oxford University Press, 2001)

Wilson, George, *What is technology? An inaugural lecture delivered in the University of Edinburgh on November 7, 1855* (Edinburgh: Sutherland & Knox, and London: Simpkin, Marshall & Co., 1855)

Wilson, Jaspar, *pseud.* [James Currie], *A letter, commercial and political, addressed to the Rt Honble William Pitt* (3rd edn, London, 1793)

Winner, Langdon, 'Do artifacts have politics?', *Daedalus* 109 (1980), 121–36

Winstanley, Gerrard, *The law of freedom*, ed. Christopher Hill (Harmondsworth: Penguin, 1973)

Winter, J. M., *Sites of memory, sites of mourning: the Great War in European cultural history* (Cambridge: Cambridge University Press, 1995)

Wittkower, Rudolf, 'Genius: individualism in art and artists', in Philip P. Wiener (ed.), *Dictionary of the history of ideas* (New York: Charles Scribner's Sons, 1973), vol. II, pp. 297–312

Wolper, Roy S., 'The rhetoric of gunpowder and the idea of progress', *JHI* 31 (1970), 589–98

Wood, Sir Henry Trueman, *A history of the Royal Society of Arts* (London: John Murray, 1913)

Woodcroft, Bennet, *A sketch of the origin and progress of steam navigation* (London: Taylor, Walton & Maberly, 1848)

[Woodcroft, Bennet], *Catalogue of the gallery of portraits of inventors, discoverers, and introducers of useful arts* (5th edn, London, 1859)

Woodcroft, Bennet, *Brief biographies of inventors of machines for the manufacture of textile fabrics* (London: Longman, 1863)

Woolrich, A. P., 'John Farey Jr (1791–1851): engineer and polymath', *HT* 19 (1997), 111–42

'John Farey, jr, technical author and draughtsman: his contribution to Rees's *Cyclopaedia*', *Industrial Archaeology Review* 20 (1998), 49–67

'John Farey and his *Treatise on the Steam Engine* of 1827', *HT* 22 (2000), 63–106

Wosk, Julie, *Breaking frame: technology and the visual arts in the nineteenth century* (New Brunswick, NJ: Rutgers University Press, 1992)

[Wright, Thomas], *Some habits and customs of the working classes by a Journeyman Engineer* [London, 1867]

Wykes, David L., 'The Leicester riots of 1773 and 1787: a study of the victims of popular protest', *Transactions of the Leicestershire Archaeological and Historical Society* 54 (1978–9)

Yarrington, Alison W., *The commemoration of the hero, 1800–64: monuments to the British victors of the Napoleonic wars* (New York and London: Garland, 1988)

His Achilles' heel? Wellington and public art (Southampton: University of Southampton, 1998)

Yarrington, Alison, Lieberman, Ilene D., Potts, Alex, and Baker, Malcolm (eds.), *An edition of the ledger of Sir Francis Chantrey, R. A., at the Royal Academy, 1809–1841* (London: Walpole Society, 1994)

Yeo, Richard, 'Genius, method, and morality: images of Newton in Britain, 1760–1860', *Science in Context* 2 (1988), 257–84

Defining science: William Whewell, natural knowledge, and public debate in early Victorian Britain (Cambridge: Cambridge University Press, 1993)

'Alphabetical lives: scientific biography in historical dictionaries and encyclopaedias', in Michael Shortland and Richard Yeo (eds.), *Telling lives in science: Essays on scientific biography* (Cambridge: Cambridge University Press, 1996), pp. 139–63

[Young, Edward], *Conjectures on original composition* (London: A. Millar, 1759)

Unpublished works

Coulter, Moureen, 'Property in ideas: the patent question in mid-Victorian Britain', Ph.D. thesis, Indiana University (1986)

Firth, Gary, 'The genesis of the industrial revolution in Bradford, 1760–1830', Ph.D. thesis, University of Bradford (1974)

Hardy, William, 'Conceptions of manufacturing advance in British politics, c. 1800–1847', D.Phil. thesis, University of Oxford (1994)

Marsden, Ben, 'Imprinting engineers: reading, writing, and technological identities in nineteenth-century Britain', British Society for the History of Science Conference, Liverpool Hope University (June 2004)

Pettitt, Clare, 'Representations of creativity, progress and social change in the work of Elizabeth Gaskell, Charles Dickens and George Eliot', D.Phil. thesis, University of Oxford (1997)

Ward-Jackson, Philip, 'Carlo Marochetti, sculptor of Robert Stephenson at Euston station: a romantic sculptor in the railway age', typescript

On-line resources

Bessen, James, 'Where have all the great inventors gone?' Research on Innovation Working Paper no. 402 (2004): www.researchoninnovation.org/GreatInventors.pdf

Concise   encyclopaedia   of   economics: www.econlib.org/library/Enc/
   Entrepreneurship.html, accessed 22 December 2005
CWN, News & Information for Coventry and Warwickshire: www.cwn.org.uk/
   arts/news/9809/980915-brindley-statue.htm, accessed 10 November 2006
www.cwn.org.uk/education/coventry-university/2001/02/010222-frank-whittle.
   htm, accessed 10 November 2006
Great Britons Poll: news.bbc.co.uk/1/hi/entertainment/tv_and_radio/2208671.
   stm, accessed 8 September 2006
'Hall of Heroes, National Wallace Monument': www.scran.ac.uk/ixbin/hixclient,
   accessed 29 October 2001
Institute of Chemistry, The Hebrew University of Jerusalem: http://chem.ch.
   huji.ac.il/~eugenik/history/bakewell.html, accessed 12 August 2005
Literature Online: http://lion.chadwyck.co.uk/
Man in the white suit: www.screenonline.org.uk/film/id/441408/index.html,
   accessed 12 September 2006
Manchester UK, Manchester engineers and inventors (2): www.manchester
   2002-uk.com/celebs/engineers2.html, accessed 10 November 2006
Mole, Tom, 'Are celebrities a thing of the past?' University of Bristol: www.bris.
   ac.uk/researchreview/2005/1115994436, accessed 13 May 2005
Oxford Dictionary of National Biography: www.oxforddnb.com
Trevithick Society: www.trevithick-society.org.uk/coin_stamps.htm, accessed
   23 August 2006
Victoria & Albert Museum: www.victorianweb.org/sculpture/misc/va/1.html,
   accessed 23 December 2005
Wedgwood Institute, Burslem: www.artandarchitecture.org.uk/images/conway/
   1707f2c9.html, accessed 19 August 2005
www.thepotteries.org/photos/burslem_centre/wedgwood_institute.html, accessed
   19 August 2005
Wikipedia: http://en.wikipedia.org/wiki/Professor_Branestawm,   accessed   7
   November 2006

Index

440